THE COMEDY OF ERRORS

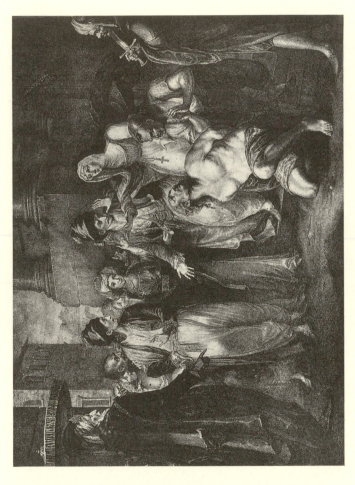

Figure 1. (Frontispiece). The street before the Priory (5.1). From The Boydell Gallery (London: Bickers and Son, 1874), painted by J.F. Rigaud, engraved by C.G. Playter. Used with the permission of the Folger Shakespeare Library.

THE COMEDY OF ERRORS
CRITICAL ESSAYS

EDITED BY

ROBERT S. MIOLA

ROUTLEDGE
NEW YORK AND LONDON

First paperback edition published in 2001 by
Routledge
29 West 35th Street
New York, NY 10001

Published in Great Britain by
Routledge
11 New Fetter Lane
London EC4P 4EE

Routledge is an imprint of the Taylor & Francis Group.

10 9 8 7 6 5 4 3 2 1

Library of Congress Cataloging-in-Publication Data

The comedy of errors : critical essays / edited by Robert S. Miola.
     p. cm.
    ISBN 0-8153-1997-5 (alk. paper)
    ISBN 0-8153-3889-9 (pbk.)
    1. Shakespeare, William, 1564-1616. Comedy of errors. 2. Comedy.
  I. Miola, Robert S. II. Series: Garland reference library of the
  humanities; vol. 1897. III. Series: Garland reference library of the
  humanities. Shakespeare criticism ; v. 18.
PR2804.C66 1997
822.3'3–dc21   97-11299
                                                      CIP

Printed on acid-free, 250-year-life paper
Manufactured in the United States of America

For Steve

mi germane, gemine frater
— Plautus (*Menaechmi*, 1125)

CONTENTS

III. *The Comedy of Errors* in Performance

ILLUSTRATIONS

Figure 1. Frontispiece
The street before the Priory (5.1). From *The Boydell Gallery* (London: Bickers and Son, 1874), painted by J.F. Rigaud, engraved by C.G. Playter. Used with the permission of the Folger Shakespeare Library.

Figure 2. 52
Supple production, 1996, Stratford-upon-Avon, The Other Place. Dromio of Ephesus (Eric Mallett) emphasizing a point to Dromio of Syracuse (Dan Milne) in the closing moments of the play. Used with the permission of the Shakespeare Centre Library.

Figure 3. 226
Scheie production, 1988, Santa Cruz. Antipholus of Ephesus (Bryan Torfeh) looks on from above, Dromio (David Baker), from below, while a demure Abbess (Brad Meyers) meets her shocked husband, Egeon (J. Kenneth Campbell). Used with the permission of D. Scheie.

Figure 4. 392
Williams production, 1962, Stratford-upon-Avon, RSC Theatre. Antipholus of Syracuse (Alec McCowan) wooing Luciana (Susan Maryott). Used with the permission of the Shakespeare Centre Library, Stratford-upon-Avon.

Figure 5. 476
Komisarjevsky production, 1938, Stratford-upon-Avon, RSC Theatre. Dromio of Syracuse (Dennis Roberts) in window; Dr. Pinch (C. Rivers Gadsby) in center with black beard. Used with the permission of the Shakespeare Centre Library, Stratford-upon-Avon.

GENERAL EDITOR'S INTRODUCTION

The continuing goal of the Garland Shakespeare Criticism series is to provide the most influential historical criticism, the most significant contemporary interpretations, and reviews of the most influential productions. Each volume in the series, devoted to a Shakespearean play or poem (e.g., the sonnets, *Venus and Adonis*, *The Rape of Lucrece*), includes the most essential criticism and reviews of Shakespeare's work from the seventeenth century to the present. The series thus provides, through individual volumes, a representative gathering of critical opinion of how a play or poem has been interpreted over the centuries.

A major feature of each volume in the series is the editor's introduction. Each volume editor provides a substantial essay identifying the main critical issues and problems the play (or poem) has raised, charting the critical trends in looking at the work over the centuries, and assessing the critical discourses that have linked the play or poem to various ideological concerns. In addition to examining the critical commentary in light of important historical and theatrical events, each introduction functions as a discursive bibliographic essay that cites and evaluates significant critical works—essays, journal articles, dissertations, books, theatre documents—and gives readers a guide to the research on a particular play or poem.

After the introduction, each volume is organized chronologically, by date of publication of selections, into two sections: critical essays and theatre reviews/documents. The first section includes previously published journal articles and book chapters as well as original essays written for the collection. In selecting essays, editors have chosen works that are representative of a given age and critical approach. Striving for accurate historical representation, editors include earlier as well as contemporary criticism. Their goal is to include the widest possible range of critical approaches to the play or poem, demonstrating the multiplicity and complexity of critical response. In most instances, essays have been reprinted in their entirety, not butchered into snippets. The editors have also commissioned original essays (sometimes as many as five to ten) by leading Shakespearean scholars, thus offering the most contemporary, theoretically attentive analyses. Reflecting some recent critical approaches in Shakespearean studies, these new essays approach the play or poem from many perspectives, including feminist, Marxist, new historical, semiotic, mythic, performance/staging, cultural, and/or a combination of these and other methodologies. Some volumes in the series even include bibliographic analyses that have significant implications for criticism.

The second section of each volume in the series is devoted to the play in performance and, again, is organized chronologically by publication date, beginning with some of the earliest and most significant productions and proceeding to the most recent. This section, which ultimately provides a theatre history of the play, should not be regarded as different from or rigidly isolated from the critical essays in the first section. Shakespearean criticism has often been informed by or has significantly influenced productions. Shakespearean criticism over the last twenty years or so has usefully been labeled the "Age of Performance." Readers will find information in this section on major foreign productions of Shakespeare's plays as well as landmark productions in English. Consisting of more than reviews of specific productions, this section also contains a variety of theatre documents, including interpretations written for the particular volume by notable directors whose comments might be titled "The Director's Choice," histories of seminal productions (e.g., Peter Brook's *Titus Andronicus* in 1955), and even interviews with directors and/or actors. Editors have also included photographs from productions around the world to help readers see and further appreciate the way a Shakespearean play has taken shape in the theatre.

Each volume in the Garland Shakespeare Criticism series strives to give readers a balanced, representative collection of

the best that has been thought and said about a
Shakespearean text. In essence, each volume supplies a
careful survey of essential materials in the history of criticism
for a Shakespearean text. In offering readers complete,
fulfilling, and in some instances very hard to locate materials,
volume editors have made conveniently accessible the
literary and theatrical criticism of Shakespeare's greatest
legacy, his work.

Philip C. Kolin
University of Mississippi

Acknowledgments

I am grateful to Philip C. Kolin for offering me the opportunity to edit this volume, and to Phyllis Korper, Senior Editor at Garland, for assistance throughout; to Yoshiko Kawachi and Gunnar Sorelius, who located items for me in Tokyo and Stockholm respectively; to the journals, presses, newspapers, libraries, photographers, directors, actors, and scholars who granted permission to reprint.

Loyola College has been a loyal benefactor, supplying various kinds of support. The Dean and Humanities Center gave material aid; the English Department secretary, Genevieve Rafferty, researched the highways and byways of various copyrights and ordered the jumble of correspondence with skill and efficiency; Marion Wielgosz put her expertise to the daunting task of providing camera-ready copy; the students kept fresh my encounters with the play, as did the Country Drama players.

I owe a special debt of gratitude to the authors represented here, who have greatly enriched our understanding of *The Comedy of Errors*. Some replied to queries and read proofs; some answered, with generosity and learning, my invitation to write on a specific topic: Peter Milward, S.J., Brennan O'Donnell, Günter Walch, Laurie Maguire, and David Bevington. These last two also favored me with detailed and acute commentary on my critical history review. Other friends in the scholarly world offered timely information, encouragement, or conversation: Gail Paster, Charles Whitworth, Standish Henning, Michael Magoulias, George Walton Williams, and Barbara Freedman.

My children—Rose, Rachel, and especially the twins, Daniel and Christine—taught me to appreciate this play of familial confusion, sorrow, and joy. They well continued my instruction in these mysteries, already begun, of course, by my own parents and fraternal twin, Steve, to whom I dedicate this book: *ego illum scio quam cordi sit carus meo*.

R.S.M.

I THE CRITICAL HISTORY OF
THE COMEDY OF ERRORS

The Play and the Critics

Robert S. Miola

1. PROLOGUE

> I can't understand who planned all of this overnight fame,
> It's a game, it's a game, it's a shame but it must be a game!
> Every step that I take, every move that I make,
> Every place that I've been, every sight that I've seen,
> I've already been there.
> Do I know me?

Pleasantly bewildered, Roger Rees's Antipholus of Syracuse sings and dances the above verse in Trevor Nunn's sprightly musical adaptation (1976). Unlike him, early critics and audiences easily identify the original planner of the game—Plautus, whose *Menaechmi* furnishes Shakespeare with the main confusion of identical twins and the outlines of plot. Witness the first recorded notice, an account of a performance at Gray's Inn in 1594: "a Comedy of Errors (like to Plautus his *Menechmus*) was played by the players" (*Gesta Grayorum* pub. 1688; 1914, 22). Francis Meres does not note the source directly in *Palladis Tamia* (1598), that commonplace book lifted from Erasmus, Ravisius Textor, and many others, but he cites *Errors* among other works by Shakespeare to praise him for being "accounted the best for comedy" among the English, as Plautus was "among the Latins" (ed. Munro, 1: 46). Meres then recalls the tag line about the Muses speaking with Plautus's tongue if they would speak Latin, and declares that they would "speak with Shakespeare's fine filed phrase, if they would speak English." For him, clearly, *Errors* testifies to Shakespeare's Plautine abilities in comic playmaking and rhetoric.

Recording miscellaneous observations, aphorisms, and recollections, John Manningham, a law student in the Middle

Temple, again makes the Plautine association while watching a performance of *Twelfth Night* (2 February 1602), "much like the *Comedy of Errors*, or *Menechmi* in Plautus but most like and near to that in Italian called *Inganni*" (ed. Munro, 1: 98). In passing, Manningham here anticipates two important critical developments: the treatment of *Errors* as a seminal Shakespearean comedy, the tracing of Italian backgrounds and analogues. His casual reference to the play may signal its popularity; certainly the phrase, "comedy of errors," quickly becomes a common expression, appearing with other reminiscences of the play in the works of Dekker (3 times), Middleton, Burton, and other seventeenth-century writers (ed. Munro, 1: 46, 66, 84, 107, 109, 141, 181, 262, 282, 499; 2: 35, 230). Gerard Langbaine (1691, 455), England's first theater-historian, also identifies the source and comments on the play's superiority to William Warner's contemporary English translation: "This play is founded on Plautus his *Menaechmi*: and if it be not a just translation, 'tis at least a paraphrase: and I think far beyond the translation, called *Menechmus*, which was printed 4o. Lond. 1595."

2. SMALL LATIN?

The nature of Shakespeare's debt to Plautus has always occupied editors and critics of *The Comedy of Errors*. Early on, commentators debate Shakespeare's ability to read Latin. Charles Gildon (1710, 300), for example, author of the first extended critical commentary on all of the works of Shakespeare, argues that Shakespeare read Plautus in Latin:

> This comedy is an undeniable proof that Shakespeare was not so ignorant of the Latin tongue as some would fain make him.... Shakespeare did understand Latin enough to read him, and knew so much of him as to be able to form a design out of that of the Roman poet; and which he has improved very much in my opinion.

Many disagree. John Dennis declares that he could "never believe" Shakespeare capable of reading Plautus "without pain and difficulty" and "vehemently" suspects that *Errors* derives from a lost translation or manuscript, or the assistance of a "stranger" or "some learned friend" (1712, 2: 13–14). Charlotte Lennox (1753–4, 2: 219, 239) pronounces Shakespeare "wholly unacquainted with the Latin tongue" and indebted to Warner's translation, opining dourly that "each error is produced by an absurdity." Dr. Johnson thinks it more than coincidence that Shakespeare chose to copy the only play of Plautus then in English (1765, 1: C2^v–C3). So too Richard Farmer (1767), that scornful Cambridge don who highhandedly confounds proponents of Shakespeare's learning by demonstrating his general reliance on translations and intermediaries.

The relation between Warner's translation and Shakespeare's play has always been a matter for controversy. Early on, error about the date of the translation confuses the discussion; Theobald, Gildon, and others think it 1515 instead of 1595, and therefore available to Shakespeare during the composition of *Errors*, usually dated in the early 1590s. Knowledge of the correct date weakens the case for influence. The purported parallels between the translation and play, in any case, have always been inconclusive, both the verbal (e.g., the translation of *spinter*, "bracelet," as "chain" in both texts) and the thematic (e.g., a general emphasis on Fortune). Shakespeare may or may not have seen the translation or its manuscript; the influence, if any there be, could have gone either way; there is simply no proof that Shakespeare used Warner for this play.

Skepticism about Shakespeare's Latin leads some to deny his authorship and to depreciate the play. Joseph Ritson and George Steevens think *Errors* the work of some inferior playwright who had enough Latin to read Plautus in the original (ed. Vickers, 6: 47). Steevens (ed. 1773, 2: 221) delivers this summary verdict, often reprinted:

> In this play we find more intricacy of plot than distinction of character; and our attention is less forcibly engaged, because we can guess in great measure how it will conclude. Yet the poet seems unwilling to part with his subject, even in this last and unnecessary scene, where the same mistakes are continued, till they have lost the power of affording any entertainment at all.

Judgment about Shakespeare's Latinity affects critical appraisal of the play, extending here to depreciation of the ending, generally singled out for praise by later generations.

At stake in this controversy over *Errors* are cherished conceptions about Shakespeare and the nature of art, conceptions central to the larger "small Latin" debate of the eighteenth century. On the one side, advocates of Shakespeare's learning point to his knowledge of Latin in general and of *Menaechmi* in particular to show how Nature and Art conjoined to produce greatness. On the other, the powerful myth of Shakespeare as unlearned genius contradicts the very notion of a lettered bard; this myth begins with Ben Jonson's famous description of Shakespeare's "small Latin and less Greek," and echoes in Leonard Digges' commendatory verses celebrating a poet wholly innocent of art (1640; ed. Vickers, 1: 27), in John Milton's praise of "Fancy's child," warbling "his native wood-notes wild" (*L'Allegro*, 133–4), in John Dryden's revealing assertion, "had he had more learning, perhaps he might have been less a poet" (1696, ed. Vickers, 1: 13).

Responding to Dennis, Farmer, and other skeptics of Shakespeare's learning, T.W. Baldwin (1944) demonstrates the centrality of Latin training to the Elizabethan grammar-school curriculum and to Shakespeare's education. Baldwin (1947, 605–718) goes on to examine the influence of *Menaechmi* and *Amphitruo* on *Errors*, furnishing minute analysis of words, ideas, and scenes. He observes also the presence of other sources including Lambinus' commentary on Plautus (for Shakespeare's conception of "errors" as belief in what is not and failure to believe what is) and the *Aeneid* (for the words and wanderings of Egeon). Baldwin discerns in *Errors* the principles of five-act construction derived from Renaissance commentaries on Terence. Arguing for Shakespeare's originality and sole authorship, Baldwin in 1965 publishes an exhaustive account of sources and influences, political allusions, dramatic and social contexts (including exorcism), the names and geography of the play, the Apollonian frame from Gower, the echoes of phrases from other plays. The conclusion is reprinted below.

Baldwin's monumental labors end a certain phase of the "small Latin" debate by demonstrating that Shakespeare's grammar-school training equipped him to read Latin. Baldwin also demonstrates how diverse texts coalesced in Shakespeare's imagination to form new creations in *Errors*. But many rightly balk at his positivistic, relentlessly verbal approach, Foakes (ed. 1962, xxviii), for example, criticizes him as "determined to find a source for everything in Shakespeare." At times the detailed and minute demonstrations veer into pedantry or self-parody, as, for example, when the mere mention of Menaphon (5.1.369) sets off a run to Marlowe's *1 Tamburlaine*, where the name appears, to Cooper, Stephanus, and Ovid, where it does not, to Greene's *Menaphon*, conjoined, in due course, by Plautus' *Menaechmi*, Gascoigne's *Supposes*, and the New Testament (1947, 670ff.). Such an approach, founded largely on verbal echo, tends finally to undermine itself, as the sheer multiplicity of sources overwhelms the significance of the individual originating instance.

After Baldwin, critics do not concern themselves much with Shakespeare's ability in Latin but rather with the use he makes of sources, here, his transformation of Plautus and other texts. Erma Gill (1925, 1930) previously tried this approach in two detailed analyses of *Errors* and *Menaechmi* and *Amphitruo*—one treating character, the other plot. Scattered throughout her laborious enumeration of comparisons and contrasts is notice of some interesting transferences: Luciana takes over the old man's championing of the husband's liberty; she and Adriana, his chiding of the wife; Antipholus of Syracuse expresses the wonder of the citizen twin at the strange happenings; Antipholus of Ephesus expresses the travelling twin's violence when accused of madness; The Duke plays the slave's role in solving the puzzle. Most modern editions and discussions, including the standard treatments of Bullough (1957) and Muir (1978), likewise focus on the changes: the switch in setting from Epidamnus to Ephesus, the doubling of the twins, the emphasis on the traveller not the citizen, the expansion of the wife into the complex Adriana, the invention of Luciana, Pinch, and others, the elimination of the parasite and the wife's father, the addition of the Egeon-Emilia frame, the lyrical poetry and love plot, the deepening of seriousness in parts, the Christian overtones.

Aside from concentrating on Shakespeare's use of sources, our century reformulates the "small Latin" debate in another way: Plautus is now defined as tradition as well as text. This means that critics view Plautus (together with Terence) generally as a source of New Comedic plots, plot construction (prologue, epitasis [high point of tension], anagnorisis, [discovery or recognition]), stock character types (the tricky slave, doting old man, helpless adolescent, wily courtesan), rhetorical and theatrical conventions. It means also that critics attend to Renaissance understanding of Plautus, as evidenced by commentaries in editions, performances, translations, and adaptations, including especially those in Italy and France.

A pioneer of this approach, Cornelia Coulter (1920), taking as her subject "the Plautine tradition" in Shakespeare, notes in *Errors* Shakespeare's flexible adaptation of the standard classical setting (the street with adjoining house doors), his transformation of the prologue into Egeon's speech, his use of the *servus currens*, or running servant, and the familiar New Comedic restoration of the lost son or daughter, as well as Italian analogues. In a learned study that rewards rereading, Madeleine Doran (1954, 152, 171ff.) suggests the possible influence of Plautine verse variation "on the *motives* of variation from blank verse to riming couplets or to stanza patterns, and from the pentameter line to different meters" in Shakespeare. Using Jonson's *The Case Is Altered*, illustrations in early editions of Terence, De Nores' *Poetica* (1588), and Italian comedy, she also argues that Renaissance readers discerned romance elements in New Comedy, and, therefore, that the marvelous recognition and reunion of Egeon, Emilia, and the family is essentially Plautine. Northrop Frye (1965, 87ff.) remarks the contrast with the usual New Comedic structure, in that the central theme is reunion not of the twins but of their father and mother; he also notes the relevance of the ass and metamorphic motifs of the play, which limn the descent into illusion and emergence into recognition (106–7). Frye (175) perceives the cook as a descendant of the cook in Greek comedy, and (1965, 57) the opening speech as a "sophisticated, if sympathetic, treatment of a structural cliché," the expository prologue.

Shifts in understanding of Shakespeare's relation to Plautus have made for more positive general assessments of *Errors* itself. Instead of classifying the play as the work of an inferior playwright, a bookish exercise, or an apprentice piece, critics now see it as a sophisticated imitation. Leo Salingar (1974, 324) thinks that Shakespeare in this play is the first to realize "fully the potentialities of adapting Plautus for the sake of rapid and coherent action" and for "a continuous dramatic image of changing aspects of personality and the ironies of Fortune." *Errors* is, then, "no less a landmark" than *Henry VI* or *Love's Labor's Lost*. Joel B. Altman (1978, 165–74) argues that *Errors* differs from other Latinate plays like *Supposes* and *Gammer Gurton's Needle* in that it contains no motivating intrigue. Shakespeare here turns the Plautine play into an exercise in defining the self. Not mere mechanical mistakes, the errors in *Errors* reveal the essential egotism of the characters and take on the meaning of moral shortcomings: each twin can't recognize the other's traces; the wife preaches mutuality but shows jealousy; the husband lightly substitutes courtesan for wife; the spinster lectures on marriage.

An ambitious attempt at reevaluation appears in Wolfgang Riehle's book-length study of the play, *Shakespeare, Plautus and the Humanist Tradition* (1990). Riehle helpfully reconstructs the Elizabethan reception of Plautus before attempting a comprehensive discussion of characterization, structure, game-playing, dramatic language, and meter. He contributes good insights throughout, on modern misreadings of Plautus, e.g., on classical word play in Shakespeare, on "error" as possibly meaning "a deficiency in a character's behaviour" (103), on the sharing of lines by several characters in Plautus and Shakespeare (159ff.). Riehle claims *Amphitruo* as a major underappreciated source, attacks Baldwin's analysis of five-act structure, considers context and practical staging effects, and concludes with praise of the play as a "most accomplished achievement" and a document of Shakespeare's "inexhaustible richness" (209, 211). But the book is thesis-ridden in its insistence on Plautus against Terence (it is often not necessary or possible to choose between the two), in its hostility toward non-Plautine sources—classical, medieval, native, and Christian—and in its reliance on generic or thematic generalization (e.g., the chapter on Lucianic traditions).

Reviewing Plautus and Terence in light of their Greek antecedents and Renaissance reception, Robert S. Miola likewise sees *Errors* as a sophisticated recension of classical and Italian elements. Pinch, for example, is a Plautine *senex* and *medicus*, as well as schoolmaster, conjurer, and Italian *pedante*. The lock-out of *Menaechmi* and *Amphitruo* gets replayed in Adriana's lock-out from the Priory, as the Plautine comedy of doors becomes a Shakespearean "comedy of thresholds, of entranceways into new understandings and acceptances" (1994, 38).

3. NON-PLAUTINE ORIGINS

Recognition of non-Plautine sources spurs more debate on the form, meaning, and achievement of *Errors*.

a) The Bible

Since an early editor, Charles Knight (ed. 1842, 1: 161), first glossed Ephesus with reference to Saint Paul, the Bible—particularly the epistle to the Ephesians and Acts—has gained attention as a source or context of the play. Calling Dromio of Syracuse "the principal exponent of Scripture," Richmond Noble (1935, 106–9) furnishes a list of references, including the portrait of an occult Ephesus in Acts 19, and several passages from the Anglican liturgy on matrimony. T.W. Baldwin (1947, 675ff.) notes Pauline presences: the transformed temple of Diana, the portrait of a magical Ephesus, the derivation of Shakespearean geography from Paul's travels as represented by a map illustrating Acts. Naseeb Shaheen (1993, 7–9, 49ff.) lists parallel passages, unpersuasively disputing the assertion that the Ephesian setting and exorcism originally derive from Acts, claiming that the first comes from other sources, the second from the Gospels; he admits, however, that Acts contributes to the play's concern with sorcery and witchcraft, and so, ultimately, makes a distinction without much of a difference. The other echoes, principally from the Geneva and Bishops' Bibles and the Prayer Book, appear to be proverbial or matters of common parlance rather than specific references. We are left with the probable, if intermediated, presence of Genesis and the Pauline materials in the play.

Recognition of Biblical materials as a source of *Errors* complicates response to the play and sometimes encourages moral or explicitly Christian readings. Noting echoes of *Psalm* 8 and *Ephesians* 5 in Adriana's speeches, Peter Milward (1973) argues that Scriptural echoes illuminate a prominent theme—the ideal relations between husband and wife. James L. Sanderson (1975) reviews Paul's exhortation to mercy and forgiveness, patristic traditions, and reformist writings to delineate the theme of patience in *Errors*, which, he argues, joins both plots and unifies the play. R. Chris Hassel (1979, 37ff.) turns attention to the liturgical year, specifically to the dramatic celebrations and Scriptural readings for Holy Innocents' Day; he notes their emphasis on errors and forgiveness, on the dispersal and reunion of families. Patricia Parker (1983) observes an allusion to Jacob and Esau in Egeon's opening speech, Paul's notice in Ephesians of the cross as reconciler between Gentiles and Jews, and other scattered Biblical allusions in the final acts. These appropriately gloss the play's movement from hostile rivalry to reconciliation and to its "New Testamental recognition scene" (327).

Notice of Biblical echoes has produced for these critics a comedy with serious thematic content. Others have noted Biblical influence on form as well. Evoking *Genesis*, the Pauline material, and *Revelations*, Glyn Austen (1987) reads the play as a redemptive comedy which shows the workings of grace, from the fall in the first scene, to the redemption in the last. Less allegorically and more persuasively, Arthur F. Kinney (1988), relates the Biblical background to the staging on Holy Innocents' day (twice), to medieval dramatic traditions, Elizabethan homilies, and the church year: all move the play from a mechanical farce "*toward* a sense of comedy such as that conceived by Dante in his great *Commedia* as providential confusion when wandering and bafflement invite man to contemplate wonder and grace—and achieve, through a kind of rebirth, a baptizing or godparenting" (1988, 33). The essay well argues that this varied background exploits the potential of dramatic form and genre; it is reprinted here.

The moral readings of this century, we should note, variously belong to a long and venerable tradition that flourished in the late eighteenth century. Unlike Milward, Sanderson, or Kinney, who ground themselves in Biblical echo and allusion and exhibit literary sophistication, earlier readers simply interpret character and plot according to broad moral categories of virtue and vice.

Elizabeth Griffith (1775, 141–6), for example, quotes approvingly Luciana's speech on man's pre-eminence; moreover, she continues, Balthazar's plea for Antipholus' forbearance illustrates that "a respect to decency, and the opinion of the world, is an excellent bulwark to our virtues"; another excellent document for wives is the "venom clamours of a jealous woman" speech. Francis Gentleman, well representative of eighteenth-century attitudes, allows that the play does not very obviously illustrate a moral, but he deduces one from it anyway:

> that Providence can happily regulate the most perplexed and unpromising circumstances, and change a temporary apparent evil, into a real and lasting good. Patience and submission are herein justly and properly inculcated. (Bell's edn., 1773–4, 8: 81)

The emphasis on patience here directly anticipates Sanderson's thorough explication of this theme in the play.

In his popular adaptation, *The Twins* (1762), Thomas Hull succinctly points another moral and adorns the tale:

> Joys past the reach of hope!—our lesson this,
> That misery past endears our present bliss;
> Wherein we read with wonder and delight,
> This sacred truth, "Whatever is is right." (1793, 51)

It is hard for moderns to imagine purposes that such vapid didacticism could legitimately serve; but this may be our myopia, as the tradition of such reading is widely pervasive for this and for other comedies where the apologia always seem out of tune with boisterous laughs and knockabout action. W. Woods' adaptation, *The Twins; or, Which Is Which* (1780), likewise has Emilia conclude the play by suggesting that the story might be "worth a serious hearing":

> 'Twill prove, the virtuous never should despair;
> For oft the troubles, which we call amiss,
> Serve to improve the taste of future bliss.

The time for that "serious hearing" seems to have arrived. Recent studies, grounding themselves in Scripture, discern both moral and spiritual aspects to the comedy. But more on this topic remains to be done. A detailed and scholarly examination of Pauline materials, cognizant of the original Greek, early modern translations, exegetic and homiletic traditions, and reformist controversies, is yet a desideratum, especially in view of easy and prevailing assumptions regarding "Catholic" and "Protestant" theologies and views on marriage. One caveat should be entered however: serious hearings ever run the risk of overreading and of wandering far from the theatrical experience of this bright and lively play.

b) Italian and English Drama

John Manningham's reference to "Inganni," surely to the popular Gl'ingannati of the Sienese Accademia degli Intronati, performed in 1531 and printed in 1537, turns out to be prophetic. Another origin for Errors, broadly understood as subtext rather than specific generator, is Italian drama, learned and popular. The search for specific filiations having proven fruitless, critics now recognize family resemblances between Errors and Italian drama, a shared European vocabulary of scene, character, and action. Kathleen M. Lea (1934, 1: 199) notes that Shakespeare's play features the mixing of genres characteristic of the commedia dell'arte, and that L'hospite amorose, for example, has just the same display of farce against a tragi-comic background; she observes that a summary of the play's action bears remarkable resemblances to the scenari in Locatelli's miscellany, both featuring the amplification of action in a doubles play by "denials, beatings, jeerings, defiances, jealousies and apologies" (2: 438), and the typical conclusion in a family reunion. She also notes resemblances to stock Italian episodes and characters: the Dromios, e.g., to the servants, Adriana to the suspicious prima donna, Luciana to the second lady. Richard Hosley (1966), surveying Elizabethan productions and adaptations of Plautus and Terence, notes in passing the Italian intermediaries, specifically the courtesan and the pedante. Leo Salingar (1974, 208) calls attention to Italian traditions in Shakespearean comedy: the Italian principle of the double plot, the zanni of the commedia *dell'arte*, the "bustle of citizen characters and criss-crossing of the action"; the result is a comedy "as much Italian as Roman in spirit." Moving the study of sources into the broader, more capacious realms of intertextuality, Louise George Clubb (1989) establishes Cinquecento theater as a significant context for Elizabethan drama; in an essay reprinted below, she compares *Errors* to the *commedia grave*—plays by Bernardino Pino, Girolamo Bargagli, Giambattista Della Porta, and others, featuring elements of pathos and tragedy, domestic situations with wives, and complicated patterns of errors leading to marvelous reunions.

Contemporary English drama provides another context for the shaping of *Errors*. Early commentators, anachronistically depreciating the play in light of Shakespeare's later development, tend to ignore such drama or dismiss it. They invoke the barbarity of the age and stage to explain perceived flaws in this early neoclassical comedy, just as they do for its companion, that early neoclassical tragedy, *Titus Andronicus*.

Attention to theatrical and dramatic environment, however, reveals other shaping influences on the play. Gascoigne's *Supposes*, from Ariosto's *I suppositi* and acted at Gray's Inn, 1566, later at Oxford and Cambridge and published in 1575, is a source for *Shrew* that might have been in Shakespeare's mind during the composition of *Errors* (Dorsch, ed. 1988, 9). The plot turns on a mistaken series of errors in identification, or "supposes." Shakespeare might well have looked to playwrights like Robert Greene, who exhibits some skill in the art of connecting two intrigues, juxtaposes comic and more serious materials, and also tries the shipwreck device. Or to John Lyly, who presents plots based on improbability, multiple story lines, a character cataloguing his beloved's points, scenes of lyrical courtship, the name Dromio, the new style of wit-cracking clown exemplified in Dromio of Syracuse, and Italianate complications. In an essay written for this volume, David Bevington reexamines the theatrical context, noting Shakespeare's indebtedness to contemporaries for the romantic plotting of the frame, anglicizing moralization, the emphasis on marriage, the conception of character as defined by social role, the rhetoric—particularly Lylyan argumentation and word play—and the fluid staging. Drawing on a wide range of Elizabethan plays and authors,

Bevington shows that Shakespeare, in modifying Plautus, responds creatively to various aspects of his immediate theatrical environment.

Bevington's work and that of the others on Italian context enable us to look forward to *Errors* instead of simply backward on it. Consequently, a new *Errors* begins to emerge. Not simply the first efforts of a classically trained neophyte, or the juvenile exercise that anticipates later, more complex Shakespearean plays, *Errors* now appears as a sophisticated mix of native and neoclassical traditions. It takes its rightful place in the vital community of European theater during a period of creative experimentation; it is culmination as well as commencement.

c) "Apollonius of Tyre"

The Egeon-Emilia story derives from John Gower's "Apollonius of Tyre," a source for *Pericles*. Even before Paul Wislicenus (1879) first identified the source of the frame plot, readers had noted its differences from the Plautine material. The chief critical issue that has emerged, subsequently, is not the nature or extent of Shakespeare's indebtedness to Gower, but the form and function of the Apollonian material, i.e., the frame plot.

A.W. Schlegel (1846, 381), Shakespeare's chief German translator, who postulates a theory of organic as opposed to mechanical form, appreciates the blending of diverse elements in *Errors*; he praises Egeon's opening narration as "masterly" and "affecting" and admires the "greater solemnity" given to the discovery, "from the Prince presiding, and from the reunion of the long separated parents." Similarly Nathan Drake (1817, 2: 288) declares that Egeon's portrait throws "a solemn, dignified, and impressive tone of colouring over this part of the fable." John Boydell, whose collection of Shakespeare illustrations reappears throughout the nineteenth century, commissions a representation of the Priory scene that reflects contemporary appreciation for pathos in the play: bound and barechested, an anguished Egeon waits for deliverance next to a saintly abbess; two turbaned, tasselled, and mustachioed twins express amazement (Frontispiece). C.H. Herford (ed. 1899, 1: 126) judges Egeon to be too pathetic and moving for the rest of the play.

Herford's comment signals the emergence of modern

attitudes and an aesthetic based on unified form rather than on the appreciation of pathos; the new aesthetic generates more pointed analyses of the frame plot and its relation to the errors plot. Allison Gaw (1926, 628–9), for example, notes five related functions: the provision of organic exposition, the promotion of plot unity, the elevation of tone, the increase in happiness at the end, and the element of surprise. The critical imperative to discover structural and thematic unity in drama, dominant throughout this century until just recently, inspires many readings of Egeon's story as coherently relational to that of his sons. In an influential essay Gāmini Salgādo (1972) well contrasts the orderly and sequential sense of time in Egeon's opening speech with the crazy, random clockwork of Ephesian time in the play; the reunion of the family appropriately restores the natural, sequential rhythm of time, reestablishing cause and effect and individual identity. Vincent F. Petronella (1974) notes the structural pattern of separation and union; the images of binding and releasing, manifest in the language as well as in Egeon's bonds and Angelo's chain, produce a clear-sighted comedy that takes "an occasional sojourn into farce" (487). K. Tetzeli von Rosador (1984) finds unity in plot structure, in the repeated threat and evasion of danger, and in the various tightenings and loosenings of tension.

Like her counterpart Lucina in the Apollonius tale, Emilia is a mother lost at sea and found at play's end as a religious figure in Ephesus. Bertrand Evans (1960) notes that *Errors* exploits to the maximum the single gap in awareness between characters and the audience—namely, the knowledge that both sets of twins are present in Ephesus. Shakespeare, however, withholds until the very end a crucial plot element, Emilia's identity; this surprise finds a parallel only in *The Winter's Tale*, again featuring the magical reappearance of a wife and mother. Others remark Emilia's association with the abbey and with Christian symbolism: she says that she has waited 33 years for the birth, not the 23 the play seems to call for, perhaps an echo of the number of years of Christ's life; she invites all to a gossips' feast at the end of the play, i.e., a christening. These lines, spoken by a nun, we imagine, in full habit, encourage those various Christianized readings we have already seen and sort well with her function as a counsellor against nagging and jealousy. A.P. Riemer (1980, 31–3, 113–17) sees other supernatural aspects to Emilia: her role and vocabulary suggest the benevolent, magical medicine of Renaissance Platonism.

Emilia has also figured importantly in feminist revaluations of *Errors* (see below, 26-7). Marilyn French (1981, 76ff.) thinks that the play begins with the feminine as "outlaw, connected with sorcery and rebellion"; later, Luciana and the Abbess symbolize "the superhuman (divine) inlaw feminine principle," connected with voluntary subordination of self and the renunciation of worldly and sexual power. The women, like the men, must find their proper roles. Dorothea Kehler (1991) discusses Shakespearean Emilias, thinking this one a licensed shrew and female patriarch; Emilia renounces sexual power over men and chooses 33 years of celibacy in holy orders; so doing, she assumes the authority of the patriarchal institution that shelters her and takes center stage as the restorer of family and community.

4. GENRE

The Folio title of the play, *The Comedy of Errors*, unique in its use of "comedy," would seem to settle decisively the question of genre. Contemporaries of Shakespeare, following Aristotle, define "comedy" by contrast with tragedy, as an imitation of action that arouses ridicule, performed by common and low characters. The first modern editor of Shakespeare, Nicholas Rowe (1709, xvii), reflects this understanding, praising *Errors*, along with *Wives* and *Shrew*, as "pure" comedy, i.e., comedy unmixed with tragedy. Rowe here appreciates the stageworthy jest and zest of the play; he also expresses a neoclassical preference for integrated plots that have clarity and consistency of purpose. Not coincidentally, *Errors*, along with *Wives* and *The Tempest*, often wins praise in the eighteenth century for observing the unities of time, place, and action.

The traditional reading of this play as simple or pure comedy directly opposes more recent evaluations, particularly those in the modern era which perceive in *Errors* dark and disturbing elements. G.R. Elliott (1939) writes an impressionistic, but nonetheless important, essay on the "weirdness" of the play, which he thinks "penetrated by the comic horror" of its subject; he points to the strangeness of the events and the underlying concern with witchcraft and sorcery. Harold F. Brooks (1961, 60ff.) thinks that the lines about Ephesus seize the audience at the deep level where the ancient dread about losing the self or soul is very much alive; that metamorphosis appears here in hostile aspect also, in confusions, lock-outs, and broken feasts. Brooks also anticipates other developments in the critical history of the play: he notes the artistry in construction, romance possiblities, eclectic mix of sources, and thematic coherences. Gwyn Williams' essay, *"The Comedy of Errors Rescued from Tragedy"* (1964), argues that the play's concern with adultery, jealousy, violence, and loss of identity move it toward tragedy (he compares *Errors* to *Othello* and *Lear*); the presence of the Dromios, however, rescues the play and reclaims it as comedy. Sensitive to the comedic traditions and to the various textures in the play, Harry Levin (1966) deftly explores the darker potentials implicit in the loss of self; invoking *Rashomon*, he discerns in *Errors* a Brechtian sense of alienation and a distinctly modern "shudder of estrangement" (ed. 1965, xxxviii). Gail Kern Paster (1985) thinks that the play reveals the deep ambiguities of personal and civic identity and suggests the fragility of normal social life. The essays of Elliott, Brooks, and Levin are reprinted below.

Nicholas Rowe and Gwyn Williams stand for two extremes in the critical debate on the genre of *Errors*. There is a third generic possibility, one that mediates between comedy and tragedy, variously identified with each—farce. Samuel Taylor Coleridge considers *Errors* remarkable as "the only specimen of poetical farce in our language, that is intentionally such" (ed. Raysor, 1: 213). He writes that farce, like comedy, produces "strange and laughable situations"; farce differs from comedy, however, in "the license allowed, and even required" to these ends. A comedy "would scarcely allow even the two Antipholuses.... But farce dares add the two Dromios." Coleridge's comments, reprinted below, concur with the views of many later writers.

But is *Errors* a farce? Edward Dowden (1903, 650) considers it a farce *manqué*, explaining that Shakespeare tries his hand here at a comedy of incident, but that his imagination can "not rest satisfied with a farce"; he adds lyrical poetry in the love episode and a romantic and pathetic framework; the play opens with grief and impending doom and closes "after a cry of true pathos." Stanley Wells (ed. 1972, 8–9) notes that the play has the characteristics of farce: "absurdities of plot, stylization of action, subordination of character to plot, and a dissociation of response in which violence evokes laughter rather than pity." But, he observes, the play also has "many humanizing episodes" which turn it into something else.

The view of the play as a farce mixed with other elements is prevalent today, *pace* Russ McDonald (1988), who spiritedly defends the play as simple farce. He criticizes those who, suspicious of this genre and eager to justify the bard, read *Errors* as a seedbed for ideas and methods that will flower later, or see in it Shakespeare "transcending" farce and addressing serious issues. McDonald believes that the play merits appreciation as a splendid achievement in an inherently limited mode:

> Certain effects and values are missing from this kind of drama: there is no thorough examination of characters, no great variety of tones, no profound treatment of ideas, no deep emotional engagement. But farce gives us what other dramatic forms may lack: the production of ideas through rowdy action, the pleasures of "non-significant" wordplay, freedom from the limits of credibility, mental exercise induced by the rapid tempo of the action, unrestricted laughter—the satisfactions of various kinds of extravagance. (88)

"And yet," McDonald concedes, "the boisterous action does generate thematic issues" (88).

This concession opens the way for different understandings of farce, its nature and limits. In a series of essays (1980[1], 1980[2], 1991), the last of which is reprinted below, Barbara Freedman undertakes precisely this reevaluation. According to her,

> farce is a type of comedy deriving laughter chiefly from the release and gratification of aggressive impulses, accomplished by the denial of the cause (through absurd

situations) and the effect (through a surrealistic medium) of aggressive action upon an object, and functioning through the plot in a disguised punitive fashion. (1980[2], 238)

"The key to farce," she writes (235), "is that we laugh at violence." It is committed to the discontinuous and the dysfunctional, and shares the qualities of nightmares and the uncanny.

There is also a fourth generic possibility—romance. This is the genre of the marvelous and fantastic, of long loss restored, of sorrow turned to joy, of providential rebirth. In his suggestive mythic taxonomy, Northrop Frye (1957, 166, 184-5) classifies *Errors* as a sea comedy in the company of *Twelfth Night* and the later romances, especially *Pericles* and *The Tempest*. In an essay reprinted below, Charles Whitworth expands this argument, noting the romance elements of form and matter in the play, particularly the narrated adventures of Egeon and his enacted story, the strange atmosphere of Ephesus, the water and sea imagery, the final spectacle of time going backwards and ending in a new beginning. Productions have variously and successfully staged *Errors* as romance. In Japan a translator and producer, Tetsuo Anzai, conveys in the resolution "a sense of deep wonder, almost miraculous" (below, 491); and in Stratford-upon-Avon Tim Supple's 1996 production astonishes audiences with its strange power and moving reunions (below, 34–5).

5. CHARACTERIZATION

Nineteenth-century reverence for characterization, understood as the depiction of figures possessing emotional depth, interiority, and a capacity for change, generates different critical readings of *Errors*. This trend begins in the late eighteenth century with the works of Maurice Morgann, Lord Kames, Thomas Whately, William Richardson, and William Jackson. Critics of *Errors* in this period distinguish between the identical twins. Charles Knight (ed. 1842, 1: 205ff.), for example, praises Shakespeare's "marvelous skill in the delineation of character." Antipholus of Syracuse is a melancholy wanderer, an enthusiast, a lover who beats his slave but is kind. Antipholus of Ephesus, a brave soldier, "decidedly inferior to his brother" in intellect and morals, shows himself to be spiteful, capable of furious passion, and sensual in temperament. Dromio of Ephesus is precise and antithetical, a formal humorist; Dromio of Syracuse, high-spirited, voluble, impulsive. F.J. Furnivall (ed. 1877, xxv) believes the marriage here one of duty not of love; Antipholus is a brave soldier, but consorts with a courtesan; he is resourceful in confinement. His brother, capable of lyrical love, searching for his twin, "has a far higher nature" but also a violent streak; the Syracusan Dromio is better, more humorous—always merry and cool.

The character of Adriana attracts attention all through the nineteenth century. Mary Lamb (1807) notes the curing of her groundless jealousy and the "unlooked-for joy" of the reunion between Egeon and Emilia. William Hazlitt, in a work significantly titled *The Characters of Shakespeare's Plays* (1817), finds only one scene "of a Shakespearean cast" in *Errors*, "the one in which the Abbess, with admirable characteristic artifice, makes Adriana confess her own misconduct in driving her husband mad" (352). H.N. Hudson (1848, 1: 212–17) closely follows Hazlitt's appraisal; so too does Andrew Lang (1891), who expatiates on female jealousy, "too mean for tragedy, too hateful for comedy." These critics subordinate all other dramatic considerations—the creation of comedic scenes, the weaving together of multiple sources, the addition of darker and more serious overtones to a high-energy romp—to character, defined as a type of verisimilar representation, categorized as exclusively Shakespearean. The trend toward moralization that energizes the reactions of adaptors like Hull and Woods, and critics like Griffith and Gentleman, also appears here, but the interest now attaches not to the entire fable but to an individual's reformation or growth.

Not surprisingly, given such critical predispositions and the emphasis on character, nineteenth-century critics also begin to read the play autobiographically: Karl Elze (1901, 331–2), citing an earlier commentator, wonders if the birth of Shakespeare's own twins inspires *Errors*; Frank A. Marshall and Henry Irving (ed. 1888, 1: 77–8) suggest the inattentive Shakespeare and the nagging Anne Hathaway as models for Antipholus of Ephesus and Adriana. Frank Harris (1909, 168ff.) reshapes this autobiography by identifying Antipholus of Syracuse, "refined, melancholy, meditative, book-loving," with the young

Shakespeare, new come to London.

Character criticism treats fictional figures as if they are real people. So likewise its descendant, psychological criticism, which often attributes an extratextual life to characters or treats them as embodiments of human impulses and internal conflicts. The first psychological critic on *Errors*, Otto Rank, thinks that the play presents an Oedipal spectacle at the end—namely, the displaced father and the desired mother. Egeon appears old and debilitated; Adriana, however, becomes young, as though she has just given birth to her sons (Holland, 1964, 157). But this reading distorts the play beyond recognition, neglecting the dramatic fact of Egeon's reprieve from death at the end and portraying the Abbess, a celibate nun for decades, as youthful and fecund. Also perceiving an Oedipal conflict here, A. Bronson Feldman (1955) reads the play as evidence of the author's mental history: *Errors* reveals Shakespeare's attempt to avoid "melancholiac depression," to represent his own errors in matrimony (Luciana being the girl he wooed, Adriana the wife she became), and to express "anal malice" toward his mother as well as his search for her. Such fantasy tells us little about the play.

After these inauspicious beginnings, critics have proposed more plausible psychological readings. W. Thomas MacCary (1978) argues that the pursuit of a twin instead of a mate represents the pursuit of a complete and idealized self. *Errors* is thus a comedy of the pre-Oedipal period of human development, centered on the family and mother and on the person one would like to become. Later (1985) MacCary amplifies these ideas, noting the concentration on water, reflecting pre-Oedipal anxieties of separation, on binding and locking in or out, reflecting fears of sexual incompetence. For MacCary the searching Antipholus of Syracuse is the main character of the play, awakening in us memories of our own psychic development—the trauma of birth separation, the fear of the overwhelming mother, the yearning for individuation and integration. Barbara Freedman (1980[1]), likewise, sees the play as a psychological drama in which disassociated parts of the self become united; thus the Egeon frame is an integral part of the psychodrama which ends in redemption in its multiple senses, primarily financial and theological. Later (1991), rather than apply psychoanalysis to Shakespearean comedy, or offer a single reading of the play, she offers multiple readings which in turn displace each other; she explores the notion of mistaken identity in this play as it illuminates Derridean models of reading and Lacan's notion of subjectivity. Ruth Nevo (1980) says that the characters find themselves *through* the farce; the play allows repressed libidinal material to surface; the confusions reveal latent selves and therapeutically work out "psychic material—the obsessions, compulsions, fantasies which, unresolved, un-remedied, would represent catastrophe" (30). These readings illuminate family dynamics and show the resonant, subliminal power of symbol. The fictional characters here reflect common human aspirations, anxieties, repressions, and struggles. But once again, there is sometimes the unfortunate tendency to reduce action to a template, to read into character, to neglect theatrical tradition and convention, to separate analysis from the affective and performative aspects of the play.

6. LANGUAGE

Eighteenth-century editors and critics of *Errors* often object to its language, particularly the versification. Alexander Pope's first edition (1723) relegates passages deficient in judgment and taste to smaller type at the bottom of the page; these include trivial conceits, like the dialogue about time and hair (2.2.35–108), ribaldries, the "doggerel" verse (14-syllable lines in couplets) of the lock-out scene (3.1), and anything else he doesn't like. Such manifest deficiencies, Pope reasons, indicate a non-Shakespearean origin. Later, Pope (ed. 1728, 1: xxi–xxii) adds *Errors* to the list of those plays that have Shakespeare's hand in only some characters, single scenes, or a few passages. William Warburton (ed. 1747, 1: sigs. [d8ᵛ]–e) thinks *Errors*, along with *Shrew*, the three parts of *Henry VI*, and *Titus Andronicus*, "certainly not of Shakespeare," though the playwright perhaps here and there corrected the dialogue and added a scene. Hugh Blair (ed. 1753, 1: xlviii), the Scottish editor, follows Warburton. In our century J.M. Robertson (1923, 2: 126–57) takes up the disintegrationist arguments again, asserting that Shakespeare's share in the play after the opening scene is very limited, and proposing Marlowe as author on the basis of versification and vocabulary.

Edmond Malone (ed. 1790, 1: Pt. 1, 288–90) delivers a learned account of the play, addressing various aspects including versification. He adduces examples of doggerel verse from early Elizabethan plays (2: 203f.); he finds examples of alternate rhymes and doggerel in other early works of Shakespeare, *Love's Labor's Lost* and *The Two Gentlemen of Verona*; he explains the metrical irregularities as typical of an early Shakespeare play; he makes a strong case for Shakespeare's authorship. Malone considers the verse part of a complicated chain of evidence on date and authorship; he also pioneers the comparative study of verse as a component of style.

Early depreciation of Shakespeare's verse in this play has given way to more positive appraisals. George Lyman Kittredge (ed. 1936, 134) thinks the remarkable metrical variety probably an attempt to imitate the variety of Plautus. Stanley Wells (ed. 1972, 12–13, 21) notices verse variations like the use of couplets in the sisters' disputation and the contrast between the Ephesian Dromio's blank verse with end-stopped lines, monosyllabic diction, rhythmic regularity, staccato sound effects, and the Ephesian Antipholus' blank verse lament, with its melancholy enjambments and long vowels. Kenneth Muir (1979) also observes the variety of verse forms: Egeon's formal style—end-stopped, eloquent, with stock epithets; Antipholus of Syracuse's lyrical style in rhymed quatrains; the absurd conceits; the rhymed stichomythia and doggerel. Discussing 3.2, T.S. Dorsch (ed. 1988, 20) calls the transitions in verse "from quatrains (interspersed with hypermetric rhymes) to couplets in stichomythia, to couplets sustained, to prose, and finally to blank verse...the speaking and theatrical equivalents" of Baroque concertos. In an essay written for this volume, Brennan O'Donnell (1997), contributes a precise description and comprehensive analysis of the metrical variety in this play. Answering the objections of earlier generations, he demonstrates in *Errors* "a virtuoso display of the phonetic resources of the language." That objectionable doggerel in 3.1, for example, O'Donnell argues, transforms "distinct voices to its own tone." "The presentation of homogenous voices creates an acoustic anarchy"; thus, "the gaggle of echoic repulses serves as an aural correlative to the baffling loss of identity" (below, 408).

Shakespeare's use of image and rhetoric in *Errors* has also undergone reevaluation in this century under the microscopes of professional literary critics. G. Wilson Knight (1932, 113ff.) notes the importance of the tempest-music contrast here and in other plays: Egeon's tempest is tragic, effecting separation and loss; the action of the play works toward harmonious reunion and recovery in a magical land of gold and riches. Effusive and emotive, sometimes tending to cut plays to grand preconceived patterns, Knight nonetheless shows acute sensitivity to poetry and uncovers surprising patterns of image. More analytical, but wholly invested in the biographical fallacy (the reconstructing of the author's life and personality from the works), Caroline Spurgeon (1935) discerns in *Errors* typically Shakespearean patterns of association: the greasy kitchen wench recalls Falstaff (in *Wives*) stewed in grease (118–9); the linking of eyes, death, tears, vault, and mouth in the description of Pinch (192) echoes, more seriously, in *King John*, *Romeo and Juliet*, and *King Lear*.

After Knight and Spurgeon, critics have looked harder at images in the play and their significance. John Erskine Hankins (1953, 41ff.), associates Egeon's image of his eyes as "wasting lamps" (5.1.316) with passages from Scripture and the *Zodiacus Vitae*, a prescribed textbook, and also with Macbeth's brief candle, Othello's light, and other references. The image often appears in tragic contexts where death extinguishes the flame of life. R.A. Foakes (ed. 1962, xlv) notes that the Dromios complain of being beaten like asses; "the idea of being made a beast operates more generally in the play, reflecting the process of passion overcoming reason, as an animal rage, fear, or spite seizes on each of the main characters." According to Foakes the characters lie between the poles of Circean transformation and the restoration of order in the gossips' feast. Richard Henze (1971) explores the complex images of chains and the various bindings and loosings in the play: the original binding to the mast, the chain and rope as stage props, the various restraints of marriage and society. The characters attempt to get free but entangle themselves; the play shows that "with freedom comes binding, but with the binding, paradoxically, comes freedom—freedom of trust, of fellowship, of love" (37). These studies collectively expand earlier notions of Shakespearean style to include concatenation of image and theme; they also disclose more serious possibilities in meaning.

Two other studies of language break new boundaries in understanding. Eamon Grennan (1980) explores nature and convention in *Errors*, observing linguistic and poetic elements: Egeon's opening *narratio*, the use of couplets, Luciana's quatrains, the Abbess's sermon, and Shakespeare's frequent use of the pun. The pun is particularly important: "The play is built on a double pun, the two sets of twins being no less than the incarnation of this linguistic phenomena" (158). Grennan goes on to show how the use of puns reflects intensifying chaos in action until the last act, almost devoid of puns, when language and meaning are restored. Reading Elizabethan documents on dining and on huswifery, Joseph Candido (1990) perceives the food and eating imagery and action in its own cultural context. He argues that Shakespeare transforms the Plautine emphasis on food into a metaphor for human longing; Adriana invites the wrong Antipholus to a feast that is symbolic of her marital union with her husband; the play ends in a gossips' feast of reconciliation. The essay is reprinted below.

7. FEMINIST AND NEW HISTORICIST APPROACHES

Charlotte Porter and Helen A. Clarke, precursors of feminist criticism of the play, produce an unfortunately neglected edition (1903) that praises the portrayals of women as evidence of a great genius who would "in the end portray, more fully, greater women"; Adriana and Luciana are "at once human and lovable," the Abbess, "a wise and artful dame" (xxxiii–xxxiv). Agnes Mackenzie (1924, 24–6), the first genuine feminist critic of *Errors*, notes the pairing of two contrasted sisters here and in *Shrew*: Luciana and Bianca, docile and submissive, represent a type "approved of in all ages by the bourgeois mind"; Adriana, a figure of wronged wifehood, becomes almost tragically convincing and thus, "dramatically speaking, the most serious blemish on the play."

Mackenzie's sarcasm regarding the critical response to Luciana and her paradoxical appraisal of Adriana, simultaneously quasi-tragic and a dramatic "blemish," raise issues regarding wifely characters and roles that later feminists explore. Juliet Dusinberre (1975, 77–82), for example, notes Luciana's articulation of the orthodox philosophical view regarding women's subordination, and its conflict with theological views that regard men and women as equal in power and dignity. "Puritanism fostered a concern for the treatment of women which gave respectability to Adriana's discontent" (82). Thomas P. Hennings (1986) follows this line of argument, contrasting Anglican exhortations to marital mutuality with what he terms "Erasmian Catholic advice" and the double standard. Lisa Jardine (1983, 46) sees the play as wittily portraying the "helplessness of the wife in a liberalised marriage which laid strong emphasis on dialogue between partners, but continued…to treat articulateness in women as unseemly and unreliable." These critics have come a long way from Lamb, Hazlitt, and others in the nineteenth century, who simply applaud the curing of Adriana's groundless jealousy; these view her instead in context of gender relations, marital anxieties, and cultural politics.

Feminist criticism has been diverse in its reevaluation of *Errors*. Coppélia Kahn, like some psychological critics, notably MacCary, views the play as concerned with the creation of individual identity, specifically a masculine self. For her, *Errors* recapitulates the adolescent process of mourning the loss of parents and of searching for a mate. The women in the play represent aspects of metamorphosis, both terrible and wonderful to the male seeker. Lorna Hutson (1994) thinks that the play rewrites traditions of Christian Terence by identifying women, rather than men, with the dramatic productivity of error. Adriana and Luciana play at being prodigal daughters and wives and, in so doing, translate the sexually and financially erring men into good husbands. In an essay written for this volume, Laurie Maguire explores the notion of duality as it appears in the portrayal of the Ephesian women and marriage. Reviewing the Ephesian background and recent dramatic productions, she argues that Adriana and Luciana variously embody conflicting types of Ephesian woman (pagan and Christian, independent and submissive, goddess and witch).

Feminist criticism of Shakespeare has principally concerned

itself with patriarchal power, the role of women, the construction of gender, family dynamics, and sexual anxieties. Though often in conflict with what has come to be known as New Historicism, a critical approach that focuses on political self-fashioning and the pervasive dynamic of suppression and subversion, feminist criticism and New Historicism share important similarities. Both see the text as a site for contemporary political, economic, and social struggles; both read literature in terms of social practice and cultural myth; both operate with overt political agendas aimed at exposing and overturning oppressive authorities. At their best these approaches reveal cultural tensions and suggest interesting production possibilities. At other times, ideology substitutes for perception and flattens out character and action.

Duncan Salkeld (1993) takes a New Historicist approach to argue that *Errors* represents madness as arising from endemic social contradictions. Egeon's death sentence opposes societal law and familial concord; the confusions of identity derive from a larger "network of confused economic relations" (69). Under-researched in primary sources and merely teasing in its implications, the essay does not distinguish adequately between social conditions and dramatic actions. More helpfully, Douglas Lanier (1993), in an essay reprinted below, shows that the play sketches the problematic of self-presentation in Elizabethan England; he notes the emphasis on external marks and rituals and on the various readings and misreadings of them. Jonathan Hall (1995) believes that Shakespeare here explores the ancient topos of losing oneself within a newly "monetarized" world where credit, reputation, and the ability to pay are central; the play transforms the quest narrative into metaphors of desire in a mercantile economy and shows how comic drama forms the subject in its generating nation state.

8. THE PLAY IN PERFORMANCE

The *Gesta Grayorum* account, reprinted below, suggests that Shakespeare's bold revision of Plautus particularly suited the Gray's Inn audience during Christmas Revels, 1594. The Inns of Court produced the first English adaptation of a Greek tragedy (*Jocasta*), and the first English prose comedy (*Supposes*), among other firsts. The sophisticated audience of law students could easily recognize a replay of one of the standard, much imitated classical pieces; and they could easily appreciate the gentle havoc Shakespeare wreaks here with Ephesian law and certifying institutions—civic, domestic, medical/theological, ecclesiastical—and with the difficulties of establishing certitude, constructing identity, and finding the truth of perception and event.

In an essay (1984) reprinted below, Margaret Knapp and Michal Kobialka cautiously examine the evidence regarding this first production, reviewing the playscript, the theatrical space of the Inn, and the eyewitness accounts. Their research sets the play more precisely in the original context of the revels and argues for staging on a scaffold erected in front of the dais; they conclude that adaptability and flexibility mark the productions of Elizabethan companies at the Inns of Court. In 1895 William Poel and the Elizabethan Stage Society returned *Errors* to Gray's Inn, much to the delight of William Archer, who describes the play as "a sort of dramatic diagram, an essay in the pure mathematics of situation" (1896, 380). Also in attendance, George Bernard Shaw applauds the boldness of playing on the floor, "without proscenium or fittings of any kind…straight through in less than an hour and a half without any division into acts" (1895; rpt. 1948, 2: 275). His remarks are reprinted below.

During the seventeenth century the play survives only in occasional allusions; during the eighteenth century, largely in adaptations that cut the wordplay while increasing the sentiment and adding music. First there is the farce, *Every Body Mistaken* (1716); then a comedy in two acts taken from Plautus and Shakespeare, *See If You Like It, or, 'Tis All a Mistake* (1734). Harold Child (ed. Wilson, *et al.*, 1922, 116) notes from 1741 on regular performances of *Errors* at Covent Garden and Drury Lane, observing, "It seems to have been a special favourite for benefit nights." Then follow the adaptations already noted above, Thomas Hull, *The Twins* (1762) and W. Woods' three-act farce entitled *The Twins; or, Which Is Which* (1780).

The adaptation that is so signal in this stage history occurs in a specific literary and theatrical context. Those in the neoclassical period, as we have seen, regularly apply prescriptive aesthetic criteria to questions concerning authorship, dating, style, and general evaluation. The resulting conflicts increase rather than diminish the confidence and contentiousness of the disputants, each assuming authority over text and, indeed, author. This assumption of authority may partly account for the phenomenon of adaptation. Shakespeare's Restoration and early eighteenth-century readers do not merely point out obscurities in language, violations of the unities or poetic justice, and breaches in the decorum of action, social position, and genre; nor do they merely conjure up some inferior playwright to take the blame for such lapses. Instead, beginning with John Dryden and William D'Avenant, extending through Colley Cibber, David Garrick, Nahum Tate, and others, they adapt the plays wholesale, cutting, pasting, rewriting, inventing.

In 1819 Frederick Reynolds produces an operatic version of *Errors*, incorporating other Shakespearean songs and lyrics, music from Arne, Mozart, and others, and a climactic scene of drunkenness. The last scene of Act III is a hunting scene with a set of snow-covered mountains; Act IV ends in a Bacchanalian revel in Balthazar's house; Adriana here warbles Desdemona's willow song (Odell, 1920, 2: 132–5).

This tradition of adaptation, especially musical, continues on, well after the neoclassical heyday, into our century. Small wonder. Musical adaptation responds to the play's energetic artificiality, its formal patterning, its repetition with variation, its movement through dissonance to harmony. In 1923 the Ethiopian Art Theatre of Chicago stages a jazz version of *Errors* in New York; black actors, directed by Raymond O'Neil, perform the action in a circus tent, clowns change scenes, a whip-cracking ringmaster presides. There follows the musical comedy *The Boys from Syracuse* (1938); *A New Comedy of Errors, or Too Many Twins* (1940), a mix of Shakespeare, Plautus, and Moliére; the 1954 BBC operetta production with music by Julian Slade; *O Brother* (1981); and the 1985 opera by Stephen Storace, *Komoedie der Irrungen*.

As in the O'Neil production above, circus settings often accompany musical adaptations. Robert Woodruff casts professional circus performers in the 1983 Goodman Theatre production in Chicago (revived 1987, in New York's Vivian Beaumont Theater). (Witness also Gerald Freedman's 2-ring version at Delacorte Theatre, New York, 1967; the 1976 Ashland,

Oregon production, with carnival midway, complete with ferris wheel and roller coaster.) In the Woodruff production, the narrator announces at the outset, "In Syracuse you dress in a tie / In Ephesus you juggle or you die." The play does not go on to exploit that contrast but instead becomes a frenetic display of gags and routines, interspersed with shouted verse lines. We see jugglers, tap-dancers, knife throwers, tumblers, singers, trapeze artists, unicyclists, clowns, baton twirlers, acrobats, a child-firing cannon, pies-in-the-face, and Shakespeare himself, on occasion. Joel G. Fink's review, reprinted below, generously recounts the action and aims of the production. But whatever its value as vaudeville or high-energy entertainment, the Woodruff *Errors* well illustrates the potential problems of circus adaptation: distrust of the script leads to the neglect of language and overall design; the play dwindles into a show, featuring all manner of noise and spectacle.

Theodore Komisarjevsky's bold 1938 Stratford *Errors* contrasts tellingly with such display in its intelligent use of music and spectacle. J.C. Trewin (1964, 179) describes the production as "an operatic, balletic diversion, the men wearing plumed pink bowler hats, the women in farthingales and carrying modern handbags, and the scamper established—to the sound of Handelian glees—in a town square with central grass plot, racing clock, and shuttered windows" (see Figure 5, p. 476). According to the review in *The Sheffield Telegraph*, reprinted below, the minor characters show individuality and verve and the audience always knows which twin is which. The reviewer in *The Birmingham Mail* praises the musical interludes, excellent casting and ensemble work in this, "the most audacious, stimulating, rare and entirely delightful production in Stratford's memory" (below, 474). The fast pace and innovative style—replete with gags, songs, and dances—along with the fluid use of stage space and time period set the prevailing trends for production in this century (ed. Leiter, 1986, 67).

Komisarjevsky recreates *Errors* as a merry, madcap play, a high-energy farce that delights audiences. In 1962 Clifford Williams offers a knockabout *commedia dell'arte* version, which, nevertheless, beautifully accommodates serious moments. Figure 6 (p. 480) illustrates the farcical aspect of the production, evident in the exaggerated gestures of the officious Dr. Pinch and the pursed-lipped Adriana. Figure 4 (p. 392) illustrates the serious aspect, as yearning Antipholus of Syracuse lyrically woos the beautiful and tender Luciana. Williams begins with the actors changing into colorful costumes, thus emphasizing the self-conscious theatricality of the play; he relies on improvisation throughout, but trusts the verse implicitly; he writes that the play's true function is "the celebrating of the sacrament of marriage" (1969, 9). The free-wheeling merriment strikes a rare balance with seriousness of purpose, achieved again only in Tim Supple's 1996 version (see below, 34–5).

Reviewers of Williams' production frequently admire this balance. Robert Speaight writes, for example:

> The merit of the production lay not only in its unflagging invention and verve, but in its refusal to allow the deeper implications of the farce—and nothing is more serious than farce—to become obscured for those who were ready to receive them. Aegeon's long recital of his misfortunes became, in Mr. James Welsh's deeply sincere treatment of it, something much more than a *récit de Théramène*; we were genuinely concerned that he should escape the block. The Shakespearian themes of reconciliation and rediscovered identity announced, already, their later and more famous repetitions. The Abbess was an authentic *dea ex machina*—no mere figure of fun; it was not for nothing that Ephesus and Syracuse would henceforward exist in amity. (1963, 427–8)

Writing on a revival ten years later, Michael Billington discerns those darker elements that contemporary critics like Elliott, Williams, and Brooks also perceive: "but the production's ultimate success lies in its suggestion that behind the mistaken identities and manic confusions of farce there are often genuinely dark and disquieting forces at work" (1972, 8). The Williams production significantly influenced Royal Shakespeare Company style: Kenneth Tynan observes that this style is characterized "by solid Brechtian settings that emphasise wood and metal instead of paint and canvas; and by cogent, deliberate verse-speaking that discards melodic cadenzas in favour of meaning and motivation" (ed. Leiter, 1986, 68).

The Trevor Nunn production (1976), currently available on videotape, is a marvelously fresh musical version that follows Williams' production in its inventive approach, its respect for poetry, and its delineation of character. Starring Roger Rees, Judi Dench, and Michael Gwilym, this production borrows from "the gag-routines of the circus, French farce, and the British music hall" (ed. Leiter, 1986, 78). Ephesus appears as a modern tourist trap, replete with garish shops and colorful minor characters (Figure 8, p. 520). "This disreputable town," writes Sally Emerson, "is very much the domain of the shady Antipholus, played with lean, gum-chewing sleaziness by Mike Gwilym" (1976, 37); and very much a dangerous foreign land to his innocent, youthful twin, played with appropriate comic confusion by Roger Rees. Writing on the play in an essay reprinted below, Rees observes the seriousness of the frame-plot, the potential for fright in farce, and the significance of the theme of searching; these elements, however, are muted in the Nunn production, which succeeds brilliantly as inventive and rollicking fun.

After Nunn, few productions claim serious notice. In 1983 Adrian Noble directs a production at Stratford, which features some brilliant comedy (the Dromios are Emmett Kelly-style clowns, the Antipholuses have bright blue faces) and a moment of pathos with the beaten Dromio of Syracuse. In the same year the BBC releases Cellan-Jones' production for television in the *commedia dell'arte* style, starring rock star Roger Daltrey as both the Dromios, a serious Cyril Cusack as Egeon. Reviewers appreciate the romantic aura and small-scale realism but find the play a bit solemn; students today find it a bore. In 1988 Danny Scheie directs at Santa Cruz a raucously successful version, set in a wooded glen (Figure 3, p. 226); gleefully emphasizing the artificialities and improbabilities of the play, Scheie has one actor play each set of twins. So does Ian Judge in his 1990 version at Stratford, enacted on a pop-art trompe-l'oeil set with a checkerboard floor and nine brightly colored doors to emphasize the instability of perspective (Figure 10, p. 568). Reviewers uniformly criticize this production for elevating style over substance.

Collectively these productions raise an interesting question about the play, one that has been central to its staging from the beginning, namely, the casting. We do not know exactly how Shakespeare's company cast the first production, but we do know that Ben Jonson gave up the idea of making a Plautine doubles play because he could "never find two so like others that he could persuade the spectators they were one" (1: 144). Cellan-Jones, Scheie, and Judge solve Jonson's problem by cleverly using one actor for each set of twins, the BBC version additionally availing itself of the resources of film.

But has this solution merely created new problems? Peter Holland thinks so, incisively discussing Judge's production (in a review reprinted below):

> We know how the play will end, in that moment when the Antipholuses and Dromios will all be on stage together, but along the way we end up nearly as confused as the characters. When both Dromios are played by the same actor the audience's ability to be confused, a confusion that, I am suggesting, the play wants us to undergo, is simply evaded, evaded because the audience comes to follow actor, not rôle, Graham Turner not Dromio.... When, finally, the character has to face his doppelgänger onstage for the last scene, we come to see not two Dromios but two actors, one whom we know and another whom we do not. The history of the characters is replaced by the history of the performance.
>
> (1991, 176)

This is well said; but how seriously we are to take "the history of the characters" in this play remains an open question.

At this writing the Royal Shakespeare Company offers one intriguing answer to the question in Tim Supple's landmark production, The Other Place, 1996 (Figure 2, p. 54). This production breaks with recent theatrical history by taking the history of characters, particularly Egeon and Emilia, very seriously indeed. At the outset we see a glum, shackled old man, who eventually tells his woeful story without gimmickry or distracting stage business, conveying real anguish at his losses and his plight. At the end Emilia appears as a serious woman who has suffered and found strength and peace in the spiritual life, instead of as the usual cartoon in a nun's costume. Their reunion is poetic and moving, though they forgo the customary joyful embrace, that easy solution yielding to the delicate and wary uncertainty of spouses who are now strangers. Uncertainty characterizes that other marital reunion as Adriana, seeing her fears confirmed in the presence of the Courtesan, must work toward acceptance of her (not her husband), under the direction of the Abbess's guiding hand. Husband and wife exit separately to the gossips' feast. Such restraint makes the reunions of brothers, and of children and parents, all the more joyful and affecting. To be sure, there is laughter enough in the production, the shaven-headed Dromios cavorting in high spririts, the brothers Antipholus wandering in amusing frustration and bewilderment, the red-dressed Courtesan making a dramatic entrance in response to the Syracusan Antipholus's plea, "Some blessed power deliver us from hence!" (4.4.44), the bit parts of Angelo (a cowardly Mafioso type) and Pinch (Leo Wringer using his native Jamaican accents and doubling, interestingly, as Duke Solinus), the intelligent and witty Luciana of Thusitha Jayasundera.

This production—so fresh, funny, and moving—disposes of much conventional critical and theatrical wisdom concerning the play: that *Errors* is essentially farce; that the frame is irrelevant to or incompatible with the main action; that the characters are merely caricatures; that the staging requires three doors (the set is an open courtyard with a ramp across the backdrop, which has in it a single door and windows); that Luciana must be a simpering contrast to the more complex Adriana; that the twins need to look alike (the individuals in both pairs are easily distinguishable); that the verse is unremarkable or immature (the rhymes and shifts in rhythm are surprising and delightful). A note of strangeness resounds through the entire production, created in part by the inspired choice of accompanying Turkish chants, sung Latin passages from Ovid and Lucretius, and the music of the *'ud* (progenitor of the fretted lute), the *zarb* and *def* (percussive instruments), and *keman* (Turkish violin). *Errors* here plays as romance, a marvelous tale of loss, laughter, and redemption.

Errors has enjoyed a lively production history outside of England and the United States. In an essay written for this volume, Günter Walch surveys *The Comedy of Errors* in Germany, beginning with G.F.W. Großmann's *Die Irrungen* (1777), an adaptation featuring the Reichard twins, the stammering Mauskopf the tailor, and in place of the courtesan, a nationalistic singer, Madame Hellsang. Hans Rothe's heavily cut and interpolated version, *Komödie der Irrungen*, attains popularity in the first half of this century, playing notably in Berlin at the Schauspielhaus am Gendarmenmarkt in April, 1934, early in the second year of Nazi rule in Germany. Walch notes sinister overtones in the critical response to the play:

> The almost obsessive references to the vivacity and beauty of the young actors, and their young voices, shining faces, and flashing teeth reflect a cult of youth which had been evident in Germany for some time, ready to be exploited by the Third Reich once it had taken over. (below, 459–60)

That a production of Shakespeare's "pure comedy," to echo Rowe, should manifest qualities admired by the Nazi youth cult surely constitutes a bizarre chapter in the history of cultural appropriation. In 1978 Romanian director Sorana Coroama at the National Theater *Weimar* capitalizes on the darker potentialities of the play. According to Eva and Günter Walch, the company makes visible "through the turbulence of the stage-business the underlying insecurity and vulnerability of human existence" (1980, 409–10). A huge handless clock whose pendulum disappears in the beginning suggests temporal confusion; the antics in Ephesus become a desperate search for identity that pushes the twins to the brink of insanity.

In Japan, Peter Milward reports in an essay written for this volume, the Shakespeare Repertory Theatre first produces the play in 1951; Yoshiya Nemoto revives this production in 1969, complete with a prologue and explanatory puppet show. In 1980 Tetsuo Anzai, after having directed *Pericles*, emphasizes in *Errors* "the overall structure as a play showing restoration of harmony through the confusion of mistaken identity" (below, 491). In 1979 and several times thereafter, Norio Deguchi has the characters play in masks until the dénouement. (Figure 7 [p. 484] gives some idea of the charm and magic made possible by the masks.) The moment of unmasking effectively identifies the comedy as indeed a play of recognition. Milward notes that *Errors* has fascinating resonances and points of appeal to the Japanese: the death penalty for a foreign merchant recalls the exclusion of foreigners in Togukawa Japan; the stylization appeals to audiences brought up on Japanese *kyōgen*, a lighter form of Noh play; the weird, supernatural atmosphere accords with the Japanese occult in theater and folklore; the movement from misfortune to a happy end finds parallels in Japanese conceptions of fate, often presented in terms of a turning water-mill (or *meguru mizu-guruma*).

Errors has also undergone wondrous permutations in South Africa where it, according to Rohan Quince's essay reprinted below, frequently embodies the spirit of Bakhtinian carnival in opposition to the ruling ideology and culture. In 1953 the exuberant improvised stage business by the all-black cast alarmed director Colin Romoff just as it delighted the audiences; Quince now reads as "a communal refusal to be bound by the rigid strictures of theatrical norms developed by white culture" (1990–1, 74). In South Africa the arrest of Egeon, for being in the wrong place at the wrong time, reflects the daily realities of apartheid; and the sometimes violent relations between masters and servants allow "an interrogation, albeit fantastic, of class relations in South African society" (75); players and audience delight in the final overturning of harsh Ephesian law. André Brink's Afrikaans adaptation, *Kinkels innie Kabel* (1970), irreverently gibes at police and politicians as well as at liberal anti-apartheid activists. Janice Honeyman's 1985 production features black policemen arresting a white Egeon, a nameless and ignored black worker, whose bucket of paint the confused characters continually upset, without notice or apology.

9. EPILOGUE

The critical and theatrical history of *The Comedy of Errors* requires double vision. Rowe's "pure comedy" is Williams' near tragedy. Coleridge's perfect specimen of laughable farce is Freedman's farcical exploration of the uncanny and dysfunctional. The mechanical action of Plautine puppets, later received as a study in character, now reflects pre-Oedipal processes and anxieties. The frothy confusions disclose primal terrors—the loss of self, the doppelgänger. The sophomoric, apprentice piece of the eighteenth-century commentators, perhaps not Shakespeare's, becomes in this century a sophisticated culmination of classical, native, and continental traditions. The juvenile technique now appears as a skilful display of metrical art, imagery, and rhetoric. The bookish imitation of *Menaechmi* intimates to some Christian mysteries of redemption; to others it reveals contemporary gender politics or economic conflicts. The play speaks to various audiences across unfathomable cultural divides, to the youth movement in Nazi Germany, to patrons of the Japanese *kyōgen*, to oppressed Africans in townships.

This demand of double vision is perhaps the play's greatest gift to us. We can enjoy the laughs—the pratfalls, the slapstick merriment, Dromio's geographical catalogue, the eccentric Dr. Pinch (often a highlight in performance), the wrong Antipholus' response to the aggrieved Adriana, "Plead you to me, fair dame?" And we can also feel discomfort at the errors—the lockout, the misidentifications, the loss of loved ones, the loss of one's very self. Both the laughter and discomfort are inseparable, we finally realize. There's not a long way between Bergsonian risibility and Kafkaesque nightmare, between the pagan Ephesus of witches and sorcerers and the Christian one of the Priory and Abbess. Being lost is not merely prelude to being found but an ongoing condition of being, a condition that enables the daily and mundane findings of self we experience in family and society. The waters of the sea wreck ships and drown voyagers, but they also carry travellers to undreamt shores and reappear in the cleansing initiation of baptism, the gossips' feast. Mundane and marvelous, frothy and serious, comic and tragic, *The Comedy of Errors* awakens our deepest fears and joys.

Works Consulted

Alexander, Peter. *Shakespeare's Life and Art*. London: J. Nisbet, 1939.

Altman, Joel, B. *The Tudor Play of Mind: Rhetorical Inquiry and the Development of Elizabethan Drama*. Berkeley: U of California P, 1978.

Archer, William, *The Theatrical World of 1895*. London, 1896.

Arthos, John. "Shakespeare's Transformation of Plautus." *Comparative Drama* 1 (1967): 239–53.

Austen, Glyn. "Ephesus Restored: Sacramentalism and Redemption in *The Comedy of Errors*." *Literature and Theology* 1 (1987): 54–69.

Baldwin, Thomas Whitfield. *The Organization and Personnel of the Shakespearean Company*. Princeton: Princeton UP, 1927.

———. *William Shakspeare Adapts a Hanging*. Princeton: Princeton UP, 1931.

———. *William Shakspere's Small Latine & Lesse Greeke*. 2 vols. Urbana: U of Illinois P, 1944.

———. *Shakspere's Five-Act Structure*. Urbana: U of Illinois P, 1947.

———. *On the Compositional Genetics of* The Comedy of Errors. Urbana: U of Illinois P, 1965.

Barton, Anne. *The Names of Comedy*. Toronto: U of Toronto P, 1990.

Beiner, G. *Shakespeare's Agonistic Comedy: Poetics, Analysis, Criticism*. Cranbury, NJ: Associated UP, 1993.

Berry, Edward, I. *Shakespeare's Comic Rites*. Cambridge: Cambridge UP, 1984.

Berry, Ralph. *Shakespeare's Comedies: Explorations in Form*. Princeton: Princeton UP, 1972.

———. "Komisarjevsky at Stratford-Upon-Avon." *Shakespeare Survey* 36 (1983): 73–84.

Bevington, David. "*The Comedy of Errors* in Dramatic Context." *The Comedy of Errors: Critical Essays*. Ed. Robert S. Miola. New York: Garland, 1997.

Billington, Michael. "*The Comedy of Errors* at Stratford." *The Guardian*, 21 June 1972, p. 8.

Boydell, John and Josiah. *A Collection of Prints from Pictures Painted for the Purpose of Illustrating the Dramatic Works of Shakespeare*. London, 1803.

Bradbrook, M.C. *The Growth and Structure of Elizabethan Comedy*. Berkeley: U of California P, 1956.

Brandes, Georg. *William Shakespeare: A Critical Study*. Trans. William Archer *et al*. New York: Macmillan, 1899.

Brooks, Charles. "Shakespeare's Romantic Shrews." *Shakespeare Quarterly* 11 (1960): 351–6.

Brooks, Harold F. "Themes and Structure in *The Comedy of Errors*," *Early Shakespeare*. Stratford-upon-Avon Studies, 3. London: Edward Arnold, 1961.

Brown, John Russell. *Shakespeare and His Comedies*. 2nd edn. 1962. Rpt. London: Methuen, 1968.

Bryant, Jr., J.A. *Shakespeare and the Uses of Comedy*. Lexington: UP of Kentucky, 1986.

Bullough, Geoffrey, ed. *Narrative and Dramatic Sources of Shakespeare*. 8 vols. London: Routledge, 1957–75. Vol. 1.

Bulman, James C., and Herbert R. Coursen. *Shakespeare on Television*. Hanover, NH: UP of New England, 1988.

C. Review of Komisarjevsky production, 1938. *The Sheffield Daily Telegraph*, 14 April 1938.

Cacicedo, Alberto. "'A Formal Man Again': Physiological Humours in The Comedy of Errors." *The Upstart-Crow* 11 (1991): 24–38.

Candido, Joseph. "Dining Out in Ephesus: Food in *The Comedy of Errors*." *Studies in English Literature* 30 (1990): 217–41.

Capell, Edward. *Notes and Various Readings to Shakespeare*. 3 vols. London, 1779–83. [1st part 1774].

Chalmers, George. *A Supplemental Apology for the Believers in the Shakespeare-Papers*. 1799. Rpt. New York: A.M. Kelley, 1971.

Chambers, E.K. *William Shakespeare: A Study of Facts and Problems*. 2 vols. Oxford: Clarendon, 1930.

Champion, Larry S. *The Evolution of Shakespeare's Comedy*. Cambridge, Mass.: Harvard UP, 1970.

Charlton, H.B. *Shakespearian Comedy*. New York: Macmillan, 1938.

Charney, Maurice. *All of Shakespeare*. New York: Columbia UP, 1993.

Clubb, Louise George. *Italian Drama in Shakespeare's Time*. New Haven: Yale UP, 1989.

Cody, Richard. *The Landscape of the Mind*. Oxford: Clarendon, 1969.

Coleridge, Samuel Taylor. *Literary Remains*. Ed. Henry Nelson Coleridge. 4 vols. London: William Pickering, 1836–9. Vol. 2.

———. *Samuel Taylor Coleridge: Shakespearean Criticism*. Ed. Thomas Middleton Raysor. 2 vols. 2nd. edn. London: Dent, 1960.

Cotgrave, John. *The English Treasury of Wit and Language*. London, 1655.

Coulter, Cornelia C. "The Plautine Tradition in Shakespeare." *Journal of English and Germanic Philology* 19 (1920): 66–83.

Coursen, H.R. "*The Comedy of Errors* on Television." *The Comedy of Errors: Critical Essays*. Ed. Robert S. Miola. New York: Garland, 1997.

Craig, Hardin. *An Interpretation of Shakespeare.* New York: Citadel P, 1949.

Crewe, Jonathan V. "God or The Good Physician: The Rational Playwright in *The Comedy of Errors.*" *Genre* 15 (1982): 203–223.

Cutts, John P. *The Shattered Glass.* Detroit: Wayne State UP, 1968.

Dennis, John. *Critical Works.* Ed. Edward Niles Hooker. 2 vols. Baltimore: Johns Hopkins UP, 1939–1943.

Doran, Madeleine. *Endeavors of Art: A Study of Form in Elizabethan Drama.* Madison: U of Wisconsin P, 1954.

Dowden, Edward. *Shakspere.* New York: American Book Co., 1890.

———. *Shakspere: A Critical Study of his Mind and Art.* 12th edn. London: Kegan Paul, 1901.

———. "Shakespeare as a Comic Dramatist." *Representative English Comedies.* Ed. Charles Mills Gayley. Vol. 1. 1903. Rpt. New York: AMS, 1969.

———. *Introduction to Shakespeare.* 1907. Rpt. Freeport, NY: Books for Libraries P, 1970.

Drake, Nathan. *Shakspeare and His Times.* 2 vols. London, 1817.

Dusinberre, Juliet. *Shakespeare and the Nature of Women.* New York: Barnes and Noble, 1975.

Dyce, Alexander. *Remarks on Mr. J.P. Collier's and Mr. C. Knight's Editions of Shakespeare.* 1844. Rpt. New York: AMS, 1972.

Edwards, Thomas. *The Canons of Criticism.* 7th edn. 1765. Rpt. New York: A.M. Kelley, 1970.

Elliott, G.R. "Weirdness in *The Comedy of Errors.*" *U of Toronto Quarterly* 9 (1939): 95–106.

Elze, Karl. *William Shakespeare: A Literary Biography.* Tr. L. Dora Schmitz. London: George Bell and Sons, 1901.

Emerson, Sally. Review of Nunn production, 1976. *Plays and Players* 24 (1976): 37.

Evans, Bertrand. *Shakespeare's Comedies.* Oxford: Clarendon, 1960.

F., M.F.K. Review of Komisarjevsky production, 1938. *The Birmingham Mail*, 13 April 1938.

Farmer, Richard. *An Essay on the Learning of Shakespeare.* 2nd edn. Cambridge, 1767.

Feldman, A. Bronson, "Shakespeare's Early Errors," *The International Journal of Psycho-Analysis*, 36 (1955): 114–33.

Fineman, Joel. "Fratricide and Cuckoldry: Shakespeare's Doubles." *Representing Shakespeare: New Psychoanalytic Essays.* Ed. Murray M. Schwartz and Coppélia Kahn. Baltimore: Johns Hopkins UP, 1980. 70–109.

Fink, Joel G. Review of Woodruff Production, 1983. *Theatre Journal* 35 (1983): 415–16.

Fleay, Frederick Gard. *Shakespeare Manual.* London: Macmillan, 1878.

———. *A Chronicle History of the Life and Work of William Shakespeare*. London: J.C. Nimmo, 1886.

Freedman, Barbara. "Egeon's Debt: Self-Division and Self-Redemption in *The Comedy of Errors*." *English Literary Renaissance* 10 (1980): 360–83. [1980¹ in text]

———. "Errors in Comedy: A Psychoanalytic Theory of Farce." *Shakespearean Comedy*. Ed. Maurice Charney. New York: New York Literary Forum, 1980. 233–43. [1980² in text]

———. *Staging the Gaze: Postmodernism, Psychoanalysis, and Shakespearean Comedy*. Ithaca: Cornell UP, 1991.

French, Marilyn. *Shakespeare's Division of Experience*. New York: Summit Books, 1981.

Frye, Northrop. *Anatomy of Criticism: Four Essays*. Princeton: Princeton UP, 1957.

———. *A Natural Perspective*. New York: Columbia UP, 1965.

Gardner, Edmund. Review of Williams' production, 1962. *The Stratford-upon-Avon Herald*, 14 September 1962.

Garton, Charles. "Centaurs, The Sea, and *The Comedy of Errors*." *Arethusa* 12 (1979): 233–54.

Gaw, Allison. "The Evolution of *The Comedy of Errors*." *Publications of the Modern Language Association* 41 (1926): 620–66.

Gentili, Vanna. "*Gli equivoci* di Lorenzo Da Ponte e la *Comedy of Errors* di W. Shakespeare." *Bologna: la cultura italiana e le letterature straniere moderne*. Ravenna: Longo, 1992. 413–9.

Gervinus, G.G. *Shakespeare Commentaries*. Tr. F.E. Bunnètt. London: Smith, Elder, and Co., 1883.

Gesner, Carol. *Shakespeare & the Greek Romance*. Lexington: UP of Kentucky, 1970.

Gesta Grayorum. Ed. W.W. Greg. Oxford: Oxford UP, 1914.

Gildon, Charles. *Remarks on the Plays of Shakespear: and Essay on the Art, Rise, and Progress of the Stage*. London, 1710.

Gill, Erma. "A Comparison of the Characters in *The Comedy of Errors* with Those in the *Menaechmi*." *Texas U Studies in English* 5 (1925): 79–95.

———. "The Plot-Structure of *The Comedy of Errors* in Relation to Its Sources." *Texas U Studies in English* 10 (1930): 13–65.

Girard, René. "Comedies of Errors: Plautus-Shakespeare-Molière." *American Criticism in the Poststructuralist Age*. Ed. Ira Konigsberg. Ann Arbor: U of Michigan P, 1981. 66–86.

Goddard, Harold C. *The Meaning of Shakespeare*. Chicago: U of Chicago P, 1951.

Grady, Hugh. *The Modernist Shakespeare: Critical Texts in a Material World*. Oxford: Clarendon, 1991.

Green, A. Wigfall. *The Inns of Court and Early English Drama*. New Haven: Yale UP, 1931.

Greg, W.W. *The Shakespeare First Folio*. Oxford: Clarendon, 1955.

Grennan, Eamon. "Arm and Sleeve: Nature and Custom in *The Comedy of Errors*." *Philological Quarterly* 59 (1980): 150–64.

Griffith, Elizabeth. *The Morality of Shakespeare's Drama Illustrated*. London, 1775.

Hall, Jonathan. *Anxious Pleasures: Shakespearean Comedy and the Nation-State*. Cranbury, NJ: Associated UP, 1995.

Hamilton, A.C. *The Early Shakespeare*, San Marino, Calif.: Huntington Library, 1967.

Hankins, John Erskine. *Shakespeare's Derived Imagery*. 1953. Rpt. New York: Octagon, 1967.

Harris, Frank. *The Man Shakespeare and His Tragic Life-Story*. New York: Mitchell Kennerly, 1909.

Hassel, R. Chris, Jr. *Renaissance Drama & the English Church Year*. Lincoln: U of Nebraska P, 1979.

Hazlitt, William. *Collected Works*. Ed. P.P. Howe. 21 vols. London: Dent, 1930–4. Vol. 4.

Hennings, Thomas, P. "The Anglican Doctrine of the Affectionate Marriage in *The Comedy of Errors*." *Modern Language Quarterly* 47 (1986): 91–107.

Henze, Richard. "*The Comedy of Errors*: A Freely Binding Chain." *Shakespeare Quarterly* 22 (1971): 35–41.

Hill, Errol. *Shakespeare in Sable: A History of Black Shakespearean Actors*. Amherst: U of Massachusetts P, 1984.

Hinman, Charlton. *The Printing and Proof-Reading of the First Folio of Shakespeare*. 2 vols. Oxford: Clarendon, 1963

Hogan, Charles Beecher. *Shakespeare in the Theatre 1701–1800*. 2 vols. Oxford: Clarendon, 1952–1957.

Holland, Norman. *Psychoanalysis and Shakespeare*. 1966. Rpt. New York: Octagon, 1976.

Holland, Peter. "Shakespeare Performances in England, 1989–90." *Shakespeare Survey* 44 (1991): 157–90.

Holt, John. *An Attempte to Rescue that Aunciente, English Poet, and Play-wrighte, Maister Willaume Shakespere*. London, 1749.

Hosley, Richard. "The Formal Influence of Plautus and Terence." *Elizabethan Theatre*. Stratford-upon-Avon Studies, 9. London: Edward Arnold, 1966. 130–45.

Hudson, H.N. *Lectures on Shakespeare*. 2 vols. New York: Baker and Scribner, 1848.

———. *Shakespeare: His Life, Art, and Characters*. 4th edn. 2 vols. 1872. Rpt. New York: Haskell House, 1970.

Hurdis, James. *Cursory Remarks upon the Arrangement of the Plays of Shakespear*. London, 1792.

Huston, J. Dennis. *Shakespeare's Comedies of Play*. New York: Columbia UP, 1981.

Hutson, Lorna. *The Usurer's Daughter*. London: Routledge, 1994.

Jardine, Lisa. *Still Harping on Daughters*. Sussex: Harvester P, 1983.

Jones, Emrys. *Scenic Form in Shakespeare*. Oxford: Clarendon, 1971.

Jonson, Ben. *Works*. Ed. C.H. Herford, Percy and Evelyn Simpson. 11 vols. Oxford: Clarendon, 1925–52.

F., M.F.K. Review of Komisarjevsky production, 1938. *The Birmingham Mail*, 13 April 1938.

Kahn, Coppélia. *Man's Estate: Masculine Identity in Shakespeare*. Berkeley: U of California P, 1981.

Kehler, Dorothea. "*The Comedy of Errors* as Problem Comedy." *Rocky Mountain Review* 41 (1987): 229–40.

———. "Shakespeare's Emilias and the Politics of Celibacy." *In Another Country: Feminist Perspectives on Renaissance Drama*. Ed. Dorothea Kehler, Susan Baker. Metuchen, NJ: Scarecrow P, 1991. 157–78.

Kinney, Arthur F. "Shakespeare's *Comedy of Errors* and the Nature of Kinds." *Studies in Philology* 85 (1988): 29–52.

Knapp, Margaret, and Michal Kobialka. "Shakespeare and the Prince of Purpoole: The 1594 production of *The Comedy of Errors* at Gray's Inn Hall." *Theatre History Studies* 4 (1984): 71–81.

Knutson, Roslyn Lander. *The Repertory of Shakespeare's Company 1594–1613*. Fayetteville: U of Arkansas P, 1991.

Knight, G. Wilson. *The Shakespearian Tempest*. London: Oxford UP, 1932.

Knight, W. Nicholas. "Comic Twins at the Inns of Court." *Publications of the Missouri Philological Association* 4 (1979): 74–82.

Kolin, Philip, C. *Shakespeare in the South*. Jackson: UP of Mississippi, 1983.

Lamb, Charles and Mary. *Tales from Shakspeare*. 1807. Rpt. London: Constable and Co., 1921.

Lang, Andrew. "The Comedies of Shakespeare. IV. Comedy of Errors." *Harper's New Monthly Magazine* 82 (1891): 550–63.

Langbaine, Gerard. *An Account of the English Dramatick Poets*. 1691. Rpt. New York: Burt Franklin, 1965.

Lanier, Douglas. "'Stigmatical in Making': The Material Character of *The Comedy of Errors*." *English Literary Renaissance* 23 (1993): 81–112.

Lea, Kathleen M. *Italian Popular Comedy*. 2 vols. Oxford: Clarendon, 1934.

Lee, Sidney. *A Life of William Shakespeare*. 2nd. edn. 1916. Rpt. New York: Macmillan, 1923.

Leggatt, Alexander. *Shakespeare's Comedy of Love*. London: Methuen, 1974.

Leiter, Samuel L., ed. *Shakespeare Around the Globe: A Guide to Notable Postwar Revivals*. Westport, Conn.: Greenwood P, 1986.

Lennox, Charlotte. *Shakespear Illustrated*. 3 vols. London, 1753–4.

Levin, Harry. "Two Comedies of Errors." *Refractions: Essays in Comparative Literature*. New York: Oxford UP, 1966. 128–50.

——. *Playboys and Killjoys: An Essay on the Theory and Practice of Comedy*. New York: Oxford UP, 1987.

Levith, Murray J. *What's in Shakespeare's Names*, Hamden, Conn., Archon, 1978.

Lindblad, Ishrat. "Shakespeare in Sweden." *Shakespeare Quarterly*, 35 (1984): 329–34.

MacCary, W. Thomas. "*The Comedy of Errors*: A Different Kind of Comedy." *New Literary History*, 9 (1978): 525–36.

——. *Friends and Lovers: The Phenomenology of Desire in Shakespearean Comedy*. New York: Columbia UP, 1985.

Mackenzie, Agnes Mure. *The Women in Shakespeare's Plays*. London: William Heinemann, 1924.

McDonald, Russ. "Fear of Farce." *"Bad" Shakespeare: Revaluations of the Shakespeare Canon*. Ed. Maurice Charney. Cranbury, NJ: Associated UP, 1988. 77–90.

Magoulias, Michael, ed. *Shakespearean Criticism*. Vol. 26. Detroit: Gale Research Co., 1995.

Maguire, Laurie. "The Girls from Ephesus." *The Comedy of Errors: Critical Essays*. Ed. Robert S. Miola. New York: Garland, 1997.

Mahood, M.M. *Bit Parts in Shakespeare's Plays*. Cambridge: Cambridge UP, 1992.

Marcotte, Paul J. "Luciana's Prothalamion: Comedy, Error, Domestic Tragedy." *College Literature* 7 (1982), 147–9.

Matthews, Brander. *Shakspere as a Playwright*. New York: Charles Scribner's Sons, 1913.

Mercer, John M. "Twin Relationships in Shakespeare." *The Upstart-Crow* 9 (1989): 24–39.

Milward, Peter. *Shakespeare's Religious Background*. Bloomington, Indiana UP, 1973.

——. "*The Comedy of Errors* in Japan." *The Comedy of Errors: Critical Essays*. Ed. Robert S. Miola. New York: Garland, 1997.

Miola, Robert S. *Shakespeare and Classical Comedy*. Oxford: Clarendon, 1994.

Moulton, Richard G. *Shakespeare as a Dramatic Artist*. 2nd edn. Oxford: Clarendon, 1888.

——. *Shakespeare as a Dramatic Thinker*. 1907. Rpt. New York: Macmillan, 1912.

Muir, Kenneth, *The Sources of Shakespeare's Plays*. New Haven: Yale UP, 1978.

———. *Shakespeare's Comic Sequence*. New York: Barnes and Noble, 1979.

Munro, John, ed. *The Shakspere Allusion Book*. 2 vols. London: Humphrey Milford, 1932.

Nevo, Ruth. *Comic Transformations in Shakespeare*. London: Methuen, 1980.

Newman, Karen. *Shakespeare's Rhetoric of Comic Character*. New York: Methuen, 1985.

Noble, Richmond. *Shakespeare's Biblical Knowledge and Use of the Book of Common Prayer*. 1935. Rpt. New York: Octagon, 1970.

Odell, George C. D. *Shakespeare from Betterton to Irving*. 2 vols. New York: Scribner's, 1920.

O'Donnell, Brennan. "The Errors of the Verse: Metrical Reading and Performance in *The Comedy of Errors*." *The Comedy of Errors: Critical Essays*. Ed. Robert S. Miola. New York: Garland, 1997.

Ornstein, Robert. *Shakespeare's Comedies: From Roman Farce to Romantic Mystery*. Newark: U of Delaware P, 1986.

Parker, Patricia. "Elder and Younger: The Opening Scene of *The Comedy of Errors*." *Shakespeare Quarterly* 34 (1983): 325–7.

Parks, George B. "Shakespeare's Map for *The Comedy of Errors*." *Journal of English and Germanic Philology* 39 (1940): 93–7.

Parrott, Thomas Marc. *Shakespearean Comedy* 1949. Rpt. New York: Russell & Russell, 1962.

Paster, Gail Kern. *The Idea of the City in the Age of Shakespeare*. Athens: U of Georgia P, 1985.

Petronella, Vincent F. "Structure and Theme through Separation and Union in Shakespeare's *The Comedy of Errors*." *Modern Language Review* 69 (1974): 481–8.

Phialas, Peter G.. *Shakespeare's Romantic Comedies*. Chapel Hill: U of North Carolina P, 1966.

Quiller-Couch, Arthur. *Notes on Shakespeare's Workmanship*. New York: Henry Holt, 1917.

Quince, Rohan. "Crinkles in the Carnival: Ideology in South African Productions of *The Comedy of Errors* to 1985." *Shakespeare in Southern Africa* 4 (1990–1): 73–81.

Rees, Roger. "*The Comedy of Errors*." *Shakespeare in Perspective*. Ed. Roger Sales. 2 vols. London: British Broadcasting Corporation, 1982–5. 2: 224–31.

Reinhardstoettner, Karl von. *Plautus. Spätere Bearbeitungen plautinischer Lustspiele*. Leipzig: Verlag von Wilhelm Friedrich, 1886.

Richmond, Hugh M. *Shakespeare's Sexual Comedy*. Indianapolis: Bobbs-Merrill, 1971.

Riehle, Wolfgang. *Shakespeare, Plautus and the Humanist Tradition.* Cambridge: D. S. Brewer, 1990.

Riemer, A.P. *Antic Fables: Patterns of Evasion in Shakespeare's Comedies.* Manchester: Manchester UP, 1980.

Ritson, Joseph. *Remarks Critical and Illustrative on the Text and Notes of the Last Edition of Shakespeare* London, 1783.

———. *Cursory Criticisms on the Edition of Shakspeare Published by Edmond Malone.* 1792. Rpt. New York: A.M. Kelley, 1970.

Robertson, J.M. *The Shakespeare Canon.* 6 vols. London: Routledge, 1922–32.

Rudd, Niall. *The Classical Tradition in Operation.* Toronto: U of Toronto P, 1994.

Salgādo, Gāmini. "'Time's Deformed Hand': Sequence, Consequence, and Inconsequence in *The Comedy of Errors.*" *Shakespeare Survey* 25 (1972): 81–91.

———. *Eyewitnesses of Shakespeare: First Hand Accounts of Performances 1590–1890.* New York: Barnes and Noble, 1975.

Salingar, Leo. *Shakespeare and the Traditions of Comedy.* Cambridge: Cambridge UP, 1974.

Salkeld, Duncan. *Madness and Drama in the Age of Shakespeare.* Manchester: Manchester UP, 1993.

Sanderson, James L. "Patience in *The Comedy of Errors.*" *Texas Studies in Literature and Language* 16 (1974–75): 603–18.

Schlegel, Augustus William. *A Course of Lectures on Dramatic Art and Literature.* Tr. John Black. London: Bohn, 1846.

Segal, Erich. *Roman Laughter.* 2nd edn. New York: Oxford UP, 1987.

Seymour, E.H. *Remarks, Critical, Conjectural, and Explanatory, upon the Plays of Shakespeare.* 2 vols. 1805. Rpt. New York: AMS, 1976.

Shaheen, Naseeb. *Biblical References in Shakespeare's Comedies.* Newark: U of Delaware P, 1993.

Shakespeare, William.

    Works. Ed. Nicholas Rowe. 6 vols. London, 1709. 1.

    Works. Ed. Alexander Pope. 6 vols. London, 1723–5. 1; 2nd edn. 8 vols. 1728. 1, 2.

    Works. Ed. Lewis Theobald. 7 vols. London, 1733. 1, 3. [MS notes of Styan Thirlby in Copy 2, Folger Shakespeare Library]

    Works. Ed. William Warburton. 8 vols. London, 1747. 1, 3.

    Works. Ed. Hugh Blair. 8 vols. Edinburgh, 1753. 1, 3.

    Plays. Ed. Samuel Johnson. 8 vols. London, 1765. 1, 3.

    Comedies, Histories, & Tragedies. Ed. Edward Capell. 10 vols. London, 1767–8. 1, 2.

    The Comedy of Errors. London, 1770.

Plays. Ed. Samuel Johnson and George Steevens. 10 vols. London, 1773. 1, 2.

Plays. 9 vols. London, 1773–4. 8. [Bell's edition]

The Twins; or, Which is Which?. Adapted, W. Woods. Edinburgh, 1780.

Plays & Poems. Ed. Edmond Malone. 10 vols. London, 1790. 1, 2 parts.

The Comedy of Errors. Adapted, Thomas Hull. London, 1793.

Plays & Poems. Ed. James Boswell. 21 vols. 1821. 1, 4.

Dramatic Works. Ed. Samuel W. Singer. 10 vols. London, 1826. 1, 4; 2nd ed. 10 vols. London, 1856. 1, 2.

Works. Ed. John Payne Collier. 8 vols. London, 1842–4. 1, 2.

The Comedies, Histories, Tragedies, and Poems. Ed. Charles Knight. 2nd ed. 12 vols. London, 1842–4. 1.

The Family Shakespeare. Ed. Thomas Bowdler. 6 vols. London, 1853–5. 2. [first edn. 1807]

Works. Ed. James O Halliwell. 16 vols. London, 1853–65. 1, 3.

Works. Ed. Richard Grant White. 12 vols. London, 1857–66. 1, 3.

The Complete Illustrated Shakespeare. Ed. Howard Staunton. 1858–61. Rpt. 3 vols. New York, 1979.

Works. Ed. William George Clark, William Aldis Wright. Cambridge, 1864.

Works. Ed. Charles and Mary Cowden Clark. 4 vols. London, 1874. 1.

Works. Ed. F.J. Furnivall. London, 1877.

Works. Ed. Frank A. Marshall and Henry Irving. 8 vols. London, 1888–90. 1.

Plays. Ed. Henry Morley. 17 vols. London, 1897.

Works. Ed. C.H. Herford. 10 vols. London, 1899. 1.

The Comedie of Errors. Ed. Charlotte Porter and Helen A. Clarke. New York, 1903.

The Comedy of Errors. Ed. Henry Cuningham. London, 1907.

The Comedy of Errors. Ed. Arthur Quiller-Couch, John Dover Wilson, Harold Child. Cambridge, 1922; 2nd edn. 1962; rpt. 1968.

The Comedy of Errors. Ed. Robert Dudley French. New Haven, 1926.

The Comedy of Errors. Ed. T.W. Baldwin. Boston, 1928.

Complete Works. Ed. George Lyman Kittredge. Boston, 1936.

The Comedy of Errors. Ed. R.A. Foakes. London, 1962.

The Comedy of Errors. Ed. Harry Levin. New York, 1965.

Complete Works. Ed. Alfred Harbage. Baltimore, 1969.

The Comedy of Errors. Ed. Stanley Wells. Harmondsworth, 1972.

The Riverside Shakespeare. Ed. G. Blakemore Evans. Boston, 1974.

The Comedy of Errors. Ed. David Bevington. New York, 1988.

The Comedy of Errors. Ed. T.S. Dorsch. Cambridge, 1988.

Shattuck, Charles H. *The Shakespeare Promptbooks.* Urbana: U of Illinois P, 1965.

Shaw, G. Bernard. *Our Theatres in the Nineties.* 3 vols. 1932. Rpt. London: Constable and Co., 1948. 2.

Sisson, C.J. *New Readings in Shakespeare.* 2 vols. Cambridge: Cambridge UP, 1956.

Smith, Bruce, R. *Ancient Scripts & Modern Experience on the English Stage 1500–1700.* Princeton: Princeton UP, 1988.

Snider, Denton J. *System of Shakespeare's Dramas.* 2 vols. St. Louis: G.T. Jones, 1877.

Sommers, Pamela. Review of Shenandoah Shakespeare Express production, 1992. *The Washington Post,* 13 July 1992, B1, B5.

Sorelius, Gunnar. *Shakespeare's Early Comedies: Myth, Metamorphosis, Mannerism.* Uppsala: Acta Universitas Upsaliensis, 1993.

Speaight, Robert. *William Poel and the Elizabethan Revival.* London: W. Heinemann, 1954.

——. "Shakespeare in Britain." *Shakespeare Quarterly* 14 (1963): 419–32.

Sprague, Arthur Colby. *Shakespeare and the Actors: The Stage Business in His Plays (1660–1905).* Cambridge, Mass.: Harvard UP, 1944.

Spurgeon, Caroline F.E. *Shakespeare's Imagery and What It Tells Us.* New York: Macmillan, 1935.

Stapfer, Paul. *Shakespeare and Classical Antiquity.* Tr. Emily J. Carey. London: C.K. Paul, 1880.

Stevenson, David Lloyd. *The Love-Game Comedy.* New York: Columbia University Press, 1946.

Stoll, Elmer Edgar. *Shakespeare Studies: Historical and Comparative in Method.* New York: Macmillan, 1927.

Swinburne, Algernon Charles. *A Study of Shakespeare* (1880). *Complete Works.* Ed. Sir Edmund Gosse, Thomas James Wise. 20 vols. London: W. Heinemann, 1925–7. [*Prose Works,* 1926, vol. 1]

Swinden, Patrick. *An Introduction to Shakespeare's Comedies.* London: Macmillan, 1973.

Tannenbaum, Samuel A. "Notes on *The Comedy of Errors.*" *Shakespeare Jahrbuch* 68 (1932): 103–24.

Taylor, Gary. "Textual and Sexual Criticism: A Crux in *The Comedy of Errors.*" *Renaissance Drama* 19 (1988): 195–225.

——, and John Jowett. *Shakespeare Reshaped, 1606–1623.* Oxford: Clarendon, 1993.

Thomas, Sidney. "The Date of *The Comedy of Errors.*" *Shakespeare Quarterly* 7 (1956): 377–84.

Tillyard, E.M.W. *Shakespeare's Early Comedies.* London: Chatto and Windus, 1965.

Trewin, J.C. *Shakespeare on the English Stage 1900–1964*. London: Barrie and Rockliff, 1964.

———. *Going to Shakespeare*. London: George Allen & Unwin, 1978.

Turner, Robert Y. *Shakespeare's Apprenticeship*. Chicago: U of Chicago P, 1974.

Ulrici, Hermann. *Shakespeare's Dramatic Art: History and Character of Shakespeare's Plays*. Trans. Dora L. Schmitz. 2 vols. London: George Bell and Sons, 1876.

Van Doren, Mark. *Shakespeare*. New York: H. Holt, 1939.

Vaughn, Jack A. *Shakespeare's Comedies*. New York: Frederick Ungar, 1980.

Vickers, Brian, ed. *Shakespeare: The Critical Heritage*. 6 vols. London: Routledge and Kegan Paul, 1974–81.

Von Rosador, K. Tetzeli. "Plotting the Early Comedies: *The Comedy of Errors, Love's Labour's Lost, The Two Gentlemen of Verona*." *Shakespeare Survey* 37 (1984): 13–22.

Walch, Günter. "Die Irrungen: *The Comedy of Errors* in Germany." *The Comedy of Errors: Critical Essays*. Ed. Robert S. Miola. New York: Garland, 1997.

———, and Eva Walch. "Shakespeare in the German Democratic Republic." *Shakespeare Quarterly* 31 (1980), 408–410.

Warren, Roger. "Theory and Practice: Stratford 1976." *Shakespeare Survey* 30 (1977): 169–79.

Weiss, Theodore. *The Breath of Clowns and Kings: Shakespeare's Early Comedies and Histories*. London: Chatto and Windus, 1971.

Wells, Stanley. "Shakespeare and Romance." *Later Shakespeare*. Stratford-upon-Avon Studies, 8. London: Edward Arnold, 1966. 48–79.

———. Review of Noble production, 1983. *Times Literary Supplement*, 19 August 1983, 881.

———, Gary Taylor, *et al*. *William Shakespeare: A Textual Companion*. Oxford: Oxford UP, 1987.

Werstine, Paul. "'Foul Papers' and 'Prompt-books': Printers Copy for Shakespeare's *Comedy of Errors*." *Studies in Bibliography* 41 (1988): 232–46.

West, Gilian. "Lost Humour in *The Comedy of Errors* and *Twelfth Night*." *English Studies* 71 (1990): 6–15.

Westfall, Alfred Van Rensselaer. *American Shakespearean Criticism, 1607–1865*. New York: H.W. Wilson Co., 1939.

Whately, Thomas, ed. *Remarks on Some of the Characters of Shakespere*. 3rd edn. 1839. Rpt. New York: A.M. Kelley, 1970.

Whitaker, Virgil K. *Shakespeare's Use of Learning*. San Marino, CA: Huntington Library, 1953.

Whiter, Walter. *A Specimen of a Commentary on Shakespeare*. Ed. Alan Over and Mary Bell. 1794. Rpt. London: Methuen, 1967.

Whitworth, Charles. Review of the Noble production, 1983. *Cahiers Elisabéthains* 24 (1983): 116–18.

————. "Rectifying Shakespeare's *Errors*: Romance and Farce in Bardeditry." *The Theory and Practice of Text-Editing*. Ed. Ian Small, Marcus Walsh. Cambridge: Cambridge UP, 1991. 107–41.

Williams, Clifford. "Introduction," *The Comedy of Errors*. London: Folio Society, 1969.

Williams, Gwyn. "*The Comedy of Errors* Rescued from Tragedy." *Review of English Literature* 5 (1964): 63–71.

Williams, Simon. *Shakespeare on the German Stage Volume 1: 156–1914*. Cambridge: Cambridge UP, 1990.

Willis, Susan. *The BBC Shakespeare Plays: Making the Televised Canon*. Chapel Hill: U of North Carolina P, 1991.

Wislicenus, Paul. "Zwei neuentdeckte Shakespearequellen." *Jahrbuch der Deutschen Shakespeare-Gessellschaft* 14 (1879): 87–96.

Wood, Robert E. "Cooling the Comedy: Television as a Medium for Shakespeare's *The Comedy of Errors*." *Literature/Film Quarterly* 14 (1986): 195–202.

For citations to Shakespeare I have used *The Riverside Shakespeare*, ed. G. Blakemore Evans, *et al.*, 2nd ed. (Boston: Houghton Mifflin, 1997).

Figure 2. Supple production, 1996, Stratford-upon-Avon, The Other Place. Dromio of Ephesus (Eric Mallett) emphasizing a point to Dromio of Syracuse (Dan Milne) in the closing moments of the play. Used with the permission of the Shakespeare Centre Library.

II THE COMEDY OF ERRORS: DIFFERENT VOICES

A Poetical Farce

Samuel Taylor Coleridge

The myriad-minded man, our, and all men's, Shakespeare, has in this piece presented us with a legitimate farce in exactest consonance with the philosophical principles and character of farce, as distinguished from comedy and from other entertainments. A proper farce is mainly distinguished from comedy by the license allowed, and even required, in the fable, in order to produce strange and laughable situations. The story need not be probable, it is enough that it is possible. A comedy would scarcely allow even the two Antipholuses; because, although there have been instances of almost indistinguishable likeness in two persons, yet these are mere individual accidents, *casus ludentis naturae*, and the *verum* will not excuse the *inverisimile*. But farce dares add the two Dromios, and is justified in so doing by the laws of its end and constitution. In a word, farces commence in a postulate which must be granted.

From Samuel Taylor Coleridge, *Literary Remains*, ed. Henry Nelson Coleridge. 4 vols. (London: William Pickering, 1836–9), 2: 114–115.

Weirdness in *The Comedy of Errors*

G.R. Elliott

The "The" in the title of this play may be taken in a generic sense—that is, as the author's characteristically modest intimation that he has provided merely one more species of a well recognized genus. "Here," says he, "are the Twins of Plautus again; here is the age-old comedy of resemblances." But time has made the "The" distinctive: here is indeed *the* comedy of errors. It is hard to see how the hoary sport of mistaken identities could be better worked up as the central theme of a drama.

I think the underlying reason for its success is the fact that Shakespeare was thoroughly penetrated by the comic horror, so to call it, implicit in the subject. Real horror attaches to the notion of the *complete* identity of two human beings; as in Poe's ghastly tale of a girl who turned out to be the re-embodiment of the mother who died in giving birth to her; and as in certain ancient legends of various lands, notably China. All normal persons (and especially Shakespeare) set so much store by human individuality that they shrink from the thought of its being submerged. And since the amusing, when intense, is nigh to the serious, there is something shuddery in the close resemblance of persons just when this appears to us intensely entertaining. I recall a school-teacher many years ago who found in her class at the beginning of the term two little girls who were remarkably, even weirdly, "identical" twins; the very freckles on their noses seemed to correspond; and of course their proud mother attired them precisely alike. At the end of the first week the teacher exclaimed to us all with comic horror: "These two are the same—how can I tell them apart?" After a moment of dead silence a small boy (not I) piped out, "Mary's temper's better'n Martha's." The general laughter which ensued had in it a note of relief that was not exclusively comic. And *The Comedy of Errors* has a note of real weirdness just when its mirth is keenest.

Another and related feature of this play that has also, I think, not been sufficiently appreciated is its structural excellence. Critics have regarded the piece as uninspired because of its comparatively conventional style. But whole form, no less than style, may be the vehicle of inspiration. And the intensity with which Shakespeare gave himself here to the limited but uncanny fun of twinship impelled him to weave his strands into a very close and telling pattern; which, moreover, is often subserved, as I shall point out in a striking instance below, by the very conventionality of the style. I think that in sheer composition this drama surpasses most of his early works and some of his mature ones. It testifies that this poet, who was later to achieve the most expressive of styles, set his heart at the outset upon achieving wholeness of form. How much he was *directly* influenced in this matter by the Latin classics (not to speak of the Greek) cannot be known and is not very important. His friend to be, Ben Jonson, who was notoriously more intimate with those classics than he, was capable in maturity of producing such a work as *Bartholomew Fair*, rich in humour and humanity but hopelessly flimsy in architecture; no doubt it made Plautus turn in his grave. Compared with it *The Comedy of Errors*, by a young and "non-classical" writer, is a beautifully carved gem.

Perhaps it was written, as Professor Adams supposes, during or just after a schoolmastering interval before Shakespeare's migration to London.[1] But in this case how did he attain the warm grasp of theatric art that appears in the play? Maybe his histrionic activity began in early years in the country; a discovery of new but dubious evidence pointing in this direction has recently been announced. Maybe, as Professor Adams and others maintain, he rewrote the play after he had attained a mastery of theatric art in London. In any case it is clear that the budding dramatist, more or less influenced by the ancient classical sense of form, was reacting from the slipshod construction of contemporary romantic comedy. And indeed if he had not early been sharply critical of that mode at its lowest—that "most lamentable comedy," in Quince's phrase—he could not have learned how to carry it to its height, as in *Twelfth Night* and *As You Like It*. In this later period he vented through the mouth of Polonius a feeling which must have been at work in him all along, a kindly but critical sense of the amazing variety and confusion of forms in contemporary drama.[2] He desired for his own work the variety without the confusion. From the first he aimed at the sort of drama so tellingly described by Hamlet soon after Polonius's outburst: "an excellent play, well digested in the scenes, set down with as much modesty as cunning." Accordingly in his first play (as I take the one under discussion to be) he preferred the "scene individable," the unity of place, to the "poem unlimited"; he followed the "law of writ" rather than "the liberty."

> Why, headstrong liberty is lashed with woe.
> There's nothing situate under heaven's eye
> But hath his bound, in earth, in sea, in sky....[3]

This thought, uttered by the gentle Luciana, is reiterated in Shakespeare's subsequent works. Of course it expresses the ancient doctrine of temperance which the writers of the Renaissance so much admired—often only verbally, but deeply at their best. Hamlet's praise of temperance to the Players and then to Horatio (III, ii, 1–74), voices Shakespeare's very real love of it in art and in personality. For him well-temperedness, as it may better be termed, was a quality both moral and artistic. His writings and the records of his character, taken together, show this quality preponderant in him as man and as author. Often enough his work is poorly tempered, ill shaped. But one sees him continually striving for excellence of form even more than for variety of form. Thus it was natural for him in his earliest comedy to have recourse to the aid of unity of time and place.

Obviously he was free from the pedantic notion that this device is an essential principle of drama. But he saw that the outward sort of unity, observed strictly or approximately, could be an aid to inward form. And he saw that a strict observance of it was demanded by the material and mood of *The Comedy of Errors*. Therefore he confined the action to a single day in a single city, Ephesus, summarizing the antecedent events in Aegeon's narrative in the first scene. No doubt a skipping series of scenes displaying some of those adventures on the stage would have pleased the stage audience of the time. But that display would not have fitted the whole emotional pattern at which the author, consciously or not, was aiming and which may be described as follows. An initial mood of swift and strange, almost weird, romance is saturated, as the play proceeds, with fun that is swift, strange, weird. Thus the romance and the fun are congruent. And they are humanized by pathos at the first and last, and, in the central phase of the action, by touches of high comedy (comedy of character) involving pathos.

Such is the ideal mood-and-mode, so to speak, of this drama. It was fulfilled to a remarkable extent by the dramatist but, of course, not perfectly. The opening scene is too heavy—especially when its long speeches are not rendered by the actors "trippingly on the tongue." Aegeon's sorrowfulness is immense. The dramatist hints, unconvincingly, that it is not merely the fruit of circumstance: it is constitutional. The old man tells us that he "would gladly have embraced" death (line 69) on a certain occasion when he was still young, rich, and blessed with a happy household! We don't see why; but we see that this stroke is intended to intensify his air of sadness. To be sure that air is convincing and satisfying in such verses as the following (lines 132 ff.):

> Five summers have I spent in furthest Greece,
> Roaming clean through the bounds of Asia,
> And, coasting homeward, came to Ephesus,
> Hopeless to find—yet loath to leave unsought;
> Or that or any place that harbours men.[4]

This has the very rhythm and movement of seeking, yearning love; in contrast with the "hopeless and helpless" rhetoric of the closing lines of the scene:

> Hopeless and helpless doth Aegeon wend,
> But to procrastinate his lifeless end.

On the whole, his story takes hold of us. His emotion helps to float the strange episode of the mast that served as a "helpful ship" (line 103) to save the lives of six, and then to divide them nicely into the two triads required by the plot. But the author fails to bring out unmistakably the sole aspect of the tale that could render it fully plausible, namely its weirdness or uncanniness. Certainly this note is present, but not explicitly enough. In other words, the opening scene, from the standpoint of the play's whole mood, is not well tempered. Relatively too much stress is placed on the pathos of the romance, and too little on its weirdness. This error is not made in the final scene of the play. There the pathetic joy of the recognition and reunion of the members of Aegeon's household is skilfully intermixed with the characteristic comedy of this drama. But though the last scene of a play is important, the first scene is more so. And it is clear that in the present instance, as not in any later comedy, Shakespeare yielded to the temptation of capturing his audience at the outset by means of a heavy dose of heart-appeal.

The second scene, however, is finely turned: it provides exactly the right transition from the initial scene to the main body of the piece. The old despairing Aegeon is immediately succeeded by a young man who demeans himself very gravely. We are artfully informed at once that he too hails from Syracuse. His name, Antipholus, is here withheld from mention on the stage; but in good time we learn that he is in search of "a mother and a brother" (line 39) and we recall his father's reference to him towards the end of the preceding scene (lines 124 ff.). The fine point, however, is that his very air is felt to be *fathered* by Aegeon's, though quite different. The old man's voluble gloom gives place to the son's sober sadness. And this "humour" (mood) is susceptible of lightening. Antipholus, smiling slightly (not laughing, I think), at his Dromio's joke, remarks that the latter is

A trusty villain, sir, that very oft,
When I am dull with care and melancholy,
Lightens my humour with his merry jests.   [1.2.19–21]

Thus the mood of the play is modulated in the direction of mirth; and the way is actively opened by Antipholus's determination to relieve his lonely sorrow by wandering up and down in this foreign city, viewing its sights. Note the comic irony of his "I will go lose myself" (line 30), repeated (line 40) just as Dromio of

Ephesus enters to take him for his brother. Superb is the sudden but carefully prepared plunge, here, into the comedy of errors. The fact that Antipholus is "not in a sportive mood" is, of course, the soul of the sport. Incidentally the new Dromio is seen by the audience to be brother in soul, even more than in body, to his jestful twin. The closing speech of the scene and act is notable. Antipholus soliloquizes:

> Upon my life, by some device or other
> The villain is o'er-raught of all my money.
> They say this town is full of cozenage;
> As, nimble jugglers that deceive the eye,
> Dark-working sorcerers that change the mind,
> Soul-killing witches that deform the body,
> Disguised cheaters, prating mountebanks,
> And many such-like liberties of sin....   [1.2.95–102]

This sounds the note of weirdness; which, however, is not fully brought out till the close of the second act.

Meanwhile (II, i) high comedy, centered in Adriana, comes upon the scene. From now on, it gleams through the pattern of the play like a thin gold thread, appearing and disappearing. It is closely intertwined with the dominant comedy of action. We cannot imagine Rosalind or Beatrice exclaiming to a servant, "Back, slave, or I will break thy pate across." But it is quite natural for their forerunner, Adriana, to speak thus to Dromio of Ephesus (line 78). Her sister Luciana's rebuke of her—"Fie, how impatience loureth in your face!" [2.1.86]—is histrionically revealing; such was the look that Shakespeare intended the boy-actor who "created" this part to employ continually. That look goes along with conduct, potentially at least, violent. And certainly the heroine of this drama has her full share in its mad doings. Yet louring impatience is merely on the surface of her; deep beneath is a devoted, yearning love for her husband. And the conflict of those two emotions in her is high-comic.

There is pathos, too, in her case, but the dramatist carefully subordinates it. When her sister urges her to be patient with her careless husband, Adriana exclaims (II, i, 34 ff.):

A wretched soul, bruised with adversity,
We bid be silent when we hear it cry;
But were we burdened with like weight of pain,
As much, or more, we would ourselves complain....

True enough. But our sympathy with the speaker is overtopped
by amusement at her mood of angry exaggeration. She is far
from being a "wretched soul bruised with adversity." Her only
real woe, here, is that her husband is very late for dinner. To be
sure, she hints that he may be with another woman (line 30). But
this suspicion, entirely unfounded so far as the audience knows,
is very faint and transient. All the more comical, therefore, is her
great blaze of jealousy (lines 87 ff.) when the strange demeanour
of Antipholus of Syracuse, mistaken for her husband, has been
reported to her. At this juncture the device of mistaken identity
is superbly used for comedy of character. Antipholus of Syracuse,
unlike his jaunty brother, is gravely moral. When finally he
enters Adriana's presence and she regards him as Antipholus of
Ephesus, he is exactly the man to "look strange and frown" (II,
ii, 119). No wonder his bearing turns Adriana's suspicion into a
settled conviction. But now comes the finest stroke of all.
Confronted with real trouble, with a real evil, as she believes, in
her husband's life, her better nature comes to the fore. She drops
her initial notion (II, i, 10) that her own way of life should, by
rights, be as free as her husband's. She maintains indeed that
there should be (in modern parlance) a single standard for both
sexes but she urges passionately that it should be pure and high
(II, ii, 133):

Ah! do not tear thyself away from me,
For know, my love, as easy mayst thou fall[5]
A drop of water in the breaking gulf
And take unmingled thence that drop again,
Without addition or diminishing,
As take from me thyself and not me too.
How dearly would it touch thee to the quick
Shouldst thou but hear I were licentious
And that this body, consecrate to thee,
By ruffian lust should be contaminate!...

I *am* possessed with an adulterate blot;[6]
My blood is mingled with the crime of lust:
For if we two be one and thou play false
I do digest the poison of thy flesh,
Being strumpeted by thy contagion....

How direct and powerful is the style here over against the neat, conventional rhetoric of the preceding quotation! This is one of many instances in the course of the play where Shakespeare's good luck or good revision, or both, enables him to sharpen the style in accordance with the emotion. Here the pathos, by itself, would be too keen for comedy. But it is checked for us, even as Adriana speaks, by the amazed looks of her two Syracusan listeners, wondering what it is all about; and it is submerged by the mirth, madder than ever, that ensues; to which I shall return presently.

In the next scene (III, i) the audience is kept outdoors with Antipholus of Ephesus to watch his obtrusive cheeriness give place to rage, which in turn yields to merry vengefulness; while his double dines with his wife inside. Thus the love and pathos of Adriana are literally kept *within door* at the crucial stage of the plot. Instead we are allowed to witness (III, ii) the slighter episode, couched in conventional rhymed verse, of the Syracusan Antipholus' love for Luciana. And just when that highly moral man has attempted to seize the hand of the gentle girl who believes him to be her sister's husband, Dromio of Syracuse dashes in, escaping the embraces of the spherical Nell: "Marry, sir, she's the kitchen-wench and all grease; and I know not what use to put her to but to make a lamp of her and run from her by her own light." This sudden explosion of fun from below stairs is a superb burlesque of the goings-on of the principal personages. Nell's mistaking the foreign Dromio for his brother at the end of the third act is the sequel of her mistress Adriana's similar error at the end of the second act. But the parallelism is not forced and obvious, as it so often is in Shakespeare's early work. The two episodes are at once vitally related and vitally different: they are at opposite poles in method and tone. Hence they beautifully complement each other.

More significantly, in each case the hyperbolical tone rises to eeriness. In the close of Act II, Dromio of Syracuse, dazed by the staid Luciana's seconding of her tense sister in taking him and his master for two other persons, cries out (II, ii, 197 ff.):

> Oh for my beads! I cross me for a sinner.
> This is the fairy land; oh, spite of spites,
> We talk with goblins, owls, and elvish sprites!
> If we obey them not, this will ensue,
> They'll suck our breath or pinch us black and blue.

He and his Antipholus are overcome by a dreamlike sense of transformation, romantic in the master, grotesque ("'Tis so, I am an ass...") in the man. This "complex" occurs again in the finale of Act III, but with overwhelming emphasis on the weird grotesquerie of the situation. Here the mounting hyperbole of Dromio's account of Nell renders dramatically plausible even the premise that both he and his twin had a similar mark on the shoulder, a mole in the neck, and a great wart on the left arm! These twins are so "identical" that they approach identity. And the vast wench's vast powers of divination cause Dromio, astounded, to run from her "as a witch," in fear of being transformed by her into a bobtail dog at work in the treadmill of her turnspit (III, ii, 151 ff.). Significantly Shakespeare refrains from bringing Nell onto the stage in person. The temptation to do so must have been great; the scene would have rejoiced the hearts of ninety per cent of his audience. But he sacrificed the physical fun of that scene to what we may call the metaphysical fun of Dromio's inspired narrative, culminating in his bizarre picture of the globular wench as a witch. Moreover, Nell's absence from the scene enables the audience to concentrate upon the all-important effect that the tale has on Dromio's master.

"There's none but witches do inhabit here," Antipholus concludes (III, ii, 168). The artfully general and vague premonition that Shakespeare made him utter in the final speech of Act I, quoted earlier, wherein he mentioned "sorcerers" and "witches" among other kinds of cozeners, has been fulfilled with a vengeance. Dromio's story of Nell is the last straw for Antipholus. The fun of the thing impresses this earnest gentleman far less than its weirdness. If the wench who claims his man for her betrothed is a sorceress, all the more so is "She that doth call me husband" [3.2.158]; and he abhors Adriana "for a wife" as utterly as Dromio does Nell, though on higher grounds. These comparisons between his own and Dromio's case are not stated explicitly; Shakespeare's art is here too fine for that; but they are clearly implied in his speech. And the climactic implication is that even the sensible and normal Luciana is infected by the prevalent atmosphere of sorcery in which she lives. She,

> Possessed with such a sovereign gentle grace,
> Of such *enchanting* presence and discourse,
> Hath almost made me traitor to myself.... [3.2.160–2]

The last line recalls the comic irony of his desire to lose himself, at the first, in this strange city (I, ii, 30, 40). And the word that I have italicized in the second line is deliciously ambiguous. By way of developing the equivoque we may say that the *bewitching* Luciana, as Antipholus now sees the matter in retrospect, put him almost *beside himself*. The more he made love to her, the more she insisted he was not himself; he was another man, well known to her, her brother-in-law unfortunately, making immoral advances to her. And he, so the implication runs, had been almost ready to lose his own identity if only thus he could win her interest. But now, "lest myself be guilty of self-wrong," he is determined to fly from the girl who a little while ago feared and fled from him; she is doubly an enchantress: "I'll stop my ears against the mermaid's song."

He must speedily get away from this city, which he had felt at the first to be "full of cozenage" when it seemed that some "cheater" had made away with "all my money" (I, ii, 97 ff.). But now an event of exactly opposite nature occurs as he is hastily moving off. A cheerful and trustful citizen enters, hands him a fine gold chain, refuses present payment, and terms him, what he least is, "a merry man, sir." It takes a good actor to represent Antipholus's state of mind in this masterly finale of the third act. He is so stunned that at first he can only ask weakly, "What is your will that I shall do with this?" [3.2.169]. In the upshot, despite his scrupulous nature, he retains the chain. Why? Because one feature of this illusive city is, apparently, the giving of "such golden gifts" to strangers in the streets. Because, in short, Antipholus's mood, together with the mood of the play, has now become thoroughly fey.

That mood may be traced by the reader in many passages that cannot be treated here. It is worked up more and more during the course of the first three acts and dominates the remainder of the piece. In Act IV the arrest of Antipholus of Ephesus, prominent and wealthy citizen, for the supposed theft of the gold chain brings this personage fully into the atmosphere of enchantment. Hitherto he had moved only in the outskirts of it; his healthy gaiety kept him aloof. At the end of III, i, he had determined to meet his domestic complexities with level head and mirthful heart. But now the increasing complications are too much for him. Soon he is wearing "pale and deadly looks" (IV, iv, 94), or at least something approximating thereto sufficiently for Pinch and others to imagine him insane. A similar look, we may assume, is on the face of Antipholus of Syracuse when he comes on at the close of this act with drawn sword, resolved finally to escape those whom he calls "these witches." Thus the two male principals co-operate, now, to intensify the note of bewitchment.

This note might easily have been overdone by Shakespeare. Of course he offsets the serious desperation of the two masters by the humorous desperation of the two servants, especially Dromio of Syracuse with his persistent nightmare of Nell: "but for the mountain of mad flesh that claims marriage of me, I could find it in my heart to stay here still, and turn witch" (IV, iv, 155 ff.). A further offset to the two Antipholuses is needed, however, and it is provided by Pinch, the conjuring schoolmaster of "saffron face" (IV, iv, 62). Later his complete appearance is given retrospectively by Antipholus of Ephesus (V, i, 238 ff.):

> a hungry lean-faced villain,
> A mere anatomy, a mountebank,
> A threadbare juggler, and a fortune-teller,
> A needy, hollow-eyed, sharp-looking wretch,
> A living dead man....

In passing, notice that these words echo the tone-setting speech of Antipholus of Syracuse, at the end of the first act, upon jugglers, sorcerers, and so forth. Pinch is a tonal masterpiece. His pedantic gravity parodies and relieves the increasing angry seriousness of the two Antipholuses. But, above all, he bodies forth concretely the play's spirit of weird fun.

Adriana, again, contributes to that mood. Convinced that her husband has tried to make love to her sister, she vents her rage in a monstrous picturization of him (IV, ii, 19 ff.):

> He is deformed, crooked, old and sere,
> Ill-faced, worse bodied, shapeless everywhere;
> Vicious, ungentle, foolish, blunt, unkind,
> Stigmatical in making, worse in mind.

Her wrathful, hyperbolic fancy is a better conjurer than Pinch. But the pathos and high comedy of her, though kept subordinate, come out in frequent touches. She closes the present episode with this simple cry: "My heart prays for him, though my tongue do curse." (The subjunctive "do" is nicely suggestive.) Thus we are prepared for the effective dialogue of Adriana and the Abbess early in the last act. Religiously beguiled by the older woman into confessing her fault, Adriana hugely exaggerates her scoldings of her husband (V, i, 62 ff.) and is rebuked by the Abbess, with proportional severity, as the sole cause of his supposed madness. She makes no reply—to the utter astonishment of her sister, who, reversing her customary role as critic of Adriana's impatience, has now to exclaim, "Why bear you these rebukes and answer not?" The other says simply, "She did betray me to my own reproof." Her difficult silence is Adriana's self-imposed penance. Recalling her earlier line, quoted above, we may say that her heart is now praying so entirely for her husband that her tongue, so far from cursing, has no word even of proper self-defence.

That serious touch, together with the ensuing speech of the Second Merchant concerning "the melancholy vale" (V, i, 120), leads up to the re-entrance of the hapless and gloomy Aegeon. But, as remarked earlier, his pathos is not allowed anything like free rein here. He stands in the background during the long climax of the story of Antipholus of Ephesus. This episode opens with Adriana's line, "A most outrageous fit of madness took him" (line 139), and terminates with the Duke's "I think you are *all* mated or stark mad" (line 282, italics mine).[7] The note of witchery is explicitly given by Adriana's fear that her husband "is borne about invisible" (line 187) and the Duke's fancy that "you all have drunk in Circe's cup" (line 271). Upon the close of this episode Aegeon is allowed the centre of the stage for fifty lines. The pathos of his appeal to him whom he takes to be "my only son" is very moving, but, of course, it is checked by his mistaking Antipholus of Ephesus for him of Syracuse. Thus Aegeon is drawn into the atmosphere of illusion; so is even the stiff-backed Duke a little later (line 366). The tearful joys of the reunion of the old man's family are finely interwoven with enchanting mistakes (lines 332–416), and parodied at the close by the conference of the two Dromios. When Dromio of Syracuse declares to his newfound brother (italics mine),

> There is a fat *friend* at your master's house
> That kitchened me for you today at dinner:
> She now shall be my *sister*, *not* my wife....

the speaker's sense of relief is as vast as the girth of Nell. This speech brings us back towards everyday reality. Yet it reminds us, surely, of this Dromio's dread of Nell as a "diviner" and a "witch" (III, ii, 150 ff.). Thus at the close there is a faint, last flicker of the ray of weird light, romantic and comic, that plays upon *The* Comedy of Errors.

Originally published by G.R. Elliott, "Weirdness in *The Comedy of Errors*," *University of Toronto Quarterly* 9 (1939): 95–106. Reprinted with the permission of the University of Toronto Press.

NOTES

1 J.Q. Adams, *Life of Shakespeare*, Boston, 1923, pp. 90–6, 132–3.

2 *Hamlet*, II, ii, 401–7. In this article line-numbers are those of the Oxford Edition, but the text of that edition is not always adhered to.

3 *C. of E.*, II, i, 15ff. Hereafter references to this and other plays are given in brackets in the text.

4 The dash in the fourth line is my insertion; the Folio has a comma there.

5 Fall: let fall.

6 Italics mine.

7 Mated: stupefied and confused.

Themes and Structure in
The Comedy of Errors

Harold F. Brooks

Four of Shakespeare's comedies, there is little doubt, are earlier than the rest: *The Comedy of Errors, The Taming of the Shrew, Two Gentlemen of Verona, Love's Labour's Lost*. Their chronological sequence is uncertain. I incline to think them all subsequent to *Richard III* (*c.* 1591) and conjecture *c.* 1592 for *The Comedy of Errors*. The neo-classical features in *Errors* and *The Shrew* may associate them with the Ovidian narrative poems, *Venus and Adonis* (1593) and *Lucrece* (1594); though I should like to think also that behind them lie youthful experiments in school drama. For if, as Beeston related, Shakespeare was formerly a schoolmaster in the country, and if he had worked in Latin and neo-classical drama with the boys, this would admirably account for the command he shows, from the very outset of his career as a playwright, of the elements of dramatic construction.

No extant play of his, however early, lacks evidence of this command. It operates on the large scale and the small. *The Comedy of Errors* has its large dramatic design, but is no less remarkable for its controlled detail, unparalleled at this date, except in *The Spanish Tragedy*, outside Shakespeare's other plays. His handling of the lesser units of structure, from the scene downwards, is already sure, and indeed within its conventions brilliant. These units include the scene, a new one beginning whenever the stage is clear; the sub-scene, or *scène* as understood in French drama, a new one beginning whenever the group on stage is altered by anyone leaving or joining it; the passage of dialogue or the set speech, more than one, sometimes, going to make up the *scène*; besides every physical action, whether procession, brawl, or bit of minor business. Fully to appreciate the close bonding of such units in the structure one has to ask what is contributed by every passage as it occurs, and how it is interrelated with others throughout the play. Some illustration is possible, however, by taking a single scene. Act 1 scene 2 will serve, the better as it is not exceptionally highly wrought. Yet even a scene so expository (being the first of the main action) is not allowed to lack the immediate interest that holds an audience. Shakespeare has already the art of fulfilling, and with the economy that secures dramatic compression, three principal requirements of dramatic structure: retrospect, preparation, and immediate interest. By retrospect and preparation the playwright keeps his action moving—the great virtue of dynamic or progressive structure—with the strongest continuity. Further, while he concerns himself with the matter of the present scene, he can add force and meaning to what has gone before, and pile them up for what is to come after, so that, in effect, he is building up several (perhaps widely separated) parts of his play at once. This can be of great value in what I will call the harmonic structure: the structure which by parallel, contrast, or cross-reference, independent perhaps of the cause-and-effect connections of the progressive action, makes us compare one passage or person of the play with another, and so find an enriched significance in both. As for immediate interest, that is indispensable: "What one requires in the theatre," wrote William Archer to Gilbert Murray, "is, so to speak, a certain pressure of pleasurable sensation to the square inch, or rather to the minute"; and "pleasurable" being taken in the right sense, this puts it admirably.

With the first entry and speech of our illustrative scene, there is interest in the appearance of three fresh persons, and some tension: Antipholus the alien is warned that he is in danger of the fate which overtook Egeon in the scene before; a fate summarized in the natural course of the warning. This retrospect, and parallel of situation, link the opening of the main action and that of the Egeon action within which it is to be framed. The link is strengthened by reference to three themes already started in the Egeon episode: risk (and in particular the hazards of Ephesus), wealth, and time. Egeon, Antipholus is told:

> ...not being able to buy out his life
> According to the statute of the town
> Dies ere the weary sun set in the west.

Since these themes will now be developed throughout the main action, the references to them are preparatory no less than retrospective. The theme of moneyed wealth is emphasized by stage-"business": the merchant hands back to Antipholus

...your money that I had to keep,

and Antipholus passes it on to his Dromio. The bag of money is to furnish one of the two subjects of the first comic misunderstanding, due to occur later in the scene, and therefore is implanted visually on the audience's mind beforehand; moreover, it will form a parallel with the gold chain and the purse, other concrete visible properties which carry on the theme and become foci of similar cross-purposes in subsequent acts. The second subject of the imminent misunderstanding, the summons to dinner by the Ephesian Dromio, is also prepared, and the time-theme touched, in Antipholus' observation:

Within this hour it will be dinner-time.

Another chief theme of the play is introduced when he is warned to conceal his Syracusan origin; for this concerns his identity. Again, when he bids Dromio depart with the money, Dromio's exit lines:

Many a man would take you at your word,
And go indeed, having so good a mean,

foreshadow the suspicion that his master will shortly entertain, while preparing us to recognize it as groundless, a comic error. The rendezvous arranged, at the Centaur, leads to the reunion of master and servant in II. ii.

Dromio's jesting exit ends the first *scène*. It is Shakespeare's cue for underlining the promise of comedy: the note of tension at the start has now passed into the background. It is the cue also for Antipholus' direct comment upon Dromio's character, which adds to what has been gathered of his own and of the relations between the two of them. The audience's present curiosity about them is gratified, and its appetite whetted, both together; for the promise of comedy is contained in the informative comment itself:

> A trusty villain, sir, that very oft,
> When I am dull with care and melancholy,
> Lightens my humour with his merry jests,

jests, it is clear, which are very timely. Antipholus' experience of Dromio as a jester is needed to explain his coming assumption that the invitation to dinner is his servant's joke, and his slowly mounting surprise and anger when it is persisted in out of season. The rendezvous with the merchant, "at five-o-clock," like that arranged in *scène* 1 with Dromio, helps to establish the theme of timing, and the motifs of timely or untimely meetings or failures to meet. It points forward, moreover, to the hour (cp. V. i. 118) so fateful for Egeon, the hour (though we do not yet know this) of the *dénouement*; somewhat as the mention of dinnertime in *scène* 1 began to make ready for the dinner episode (III. i), the play's central pivot.

The *scènes* of three, then two persons, are succeeded by Antipholus' first soliloquy. Here and in the two remaining *scènes*, the immediate interest for the audience strengthens. From the point of view of comedy and the intrigue, *scène* 4, the encounter with the wrong Dromio, is the climax of the whole scene. It is flanked, in the ABA form so frequent in Shakespeare, by Antipholus' soliloquies, which are the imaginative climaxes, and, together with the moment when he strikes (the Ephesian) Dromio, the emotional climaxes too, though there is contrast between his emotion as an exasperated and as a "melancholy" imaginative man. From the imaginative, introspective man he is, soliloquies (his brother has none) come naturally; his allusion to his "care and melancholy" has prepared the way for them.

The first of them explains both his special occasion of "care," and his arrival, contributing by a single stroke to the logic at once of the character and of the plot. He has an aim, fruitlessly pursued: "to find a mother and a brother." It is a dull member of the audience who does not refer this back to Egeon's retrospect (narrating much of the dramatist's "fable," prior to the part enacted), and so conjecture who Antipholus must be. The audience is held, too, by the revelation of feeling. Antipholus' emotional reflections spring from the farewells just exchanged at the end of *scène* 2: "I will go lose myself," he said, and was commended by the Merchant to his "own content." This is the phrase which prompts his soliloquy, where he laments that what would content him is precisely what he cannot get. The idea of his "losing himself" is taken up in a profound sense, and couched in a fine image commensurate with its thematic importance. The theme of identity is here linked with those of relationship (dislocated or re-established), and of risk. To seek reunion with the lost members of the family, Antipholus is risking his identity; yet he must do so, for only if the full relationship is restored can he find content. And then, hints the image of one water-drop seeking another, the present individual identity will be lost, or transformed, in another way. It is to claim a sinking of identity in the marriage-relation, with the emergence of a new identity, where each is also the other, that Adriana uses the closely similar image in II. ii. In the play's harmonic structure, while this soliloquy is thus recalled at that point, in its own place it recalls the situation of Egeon, who on virtually the same quest as Antipholus, has so risked his mortal identity that it is forfeit to the executioner. Antipholus' fear that he is losing himself is full of comic irony. No sooner has he expressed it, than, with the entry of his brother's Dromio, he begins to be the victim of the successive mistakes of identity to which his words are designed by Shakespeare as a prelude, and in the course of which he will come to wonder whether he is beside himself, and has lost himself indeed. The often uproarious comedy arising from these and the other errors is not my immediate subject; and as regards the *scène* of cross-purposes, I shall make only a few observations, concerned with themes and structure. In the progressive structure of the play, it has two main functions. First, it interests us in Adriana, ready for her entrance in the next scene (II. i), and leads to her personal summoning of the alien Antipholus to dinner (II. ii). Second, it produces the comic dislocation of relationship between him and his own Dromio when they meet in II. ii and Dromio denies the offenses he is supposed to have committed here. The present failure of communication and relationship between Antipholus and the other Dromio, resulting from the mistake of identities, is made visible, audible, and tangible by "business": the blow. Like the theme of relationship, the mistiming theme is brought into close connection with that of mistaken identity. Dromio's impatient mistress, when by strike of clock it was twelve, has "made it one" upon his cheek; and for him Antipholus is her husband, his master, late for dinner, while for Antipholus Dromio is his servant, returned too soon, and obstinate in ill-timed jest. By Dromio's entrance are initiated the enigmas that beset the characters, and Antipholus is given an aptly enigmatic comment upon it:

Here comes the almanack of my true date.

The new arrival has the appearance of his Dromio, who constitutes a record of his span from the time of their simultaneous nativities; but by a comic irony, so does the Dromio who has really entered: the comment fits both the false inference from appearance, and the reality itself. Its enigmatic nature conceals, so one finds from the final speech of the Abbess after the *dénouement* (V. i. 401–7) a further meaning: what approaches with this Dromio is the occasion which will secure Antipholus his true identity through a new date of birth—his true birth into the restored family relationship. That is the metaphor the Abbess employs.

It is by mistaking appearance for reality that Antipholus and his brother's Dromio misidentify one another. The threat to the very self involved in the confusion of appearance and reality is the thought most vividly conveyed in Antipholus' second soliloquy. The soliloquy rounds off the scene, not without certain resemblances to the beginning. Then, the theme of moneyed wealth was given prominence; and there was tension because the Ephesian law spelled danger to Antipholus' goods or life. Now, he is keenly anxious about his money; indeed, that is the motive for his final exit to seek Dromio at the Centaur. And tension rises again with his anxiety; but still more with the profoundly disturbing fears into which it merges, of worse perils than the law's in Ephesus, suggested by its repute as a place of illusions and shape-shifting, of jugglers that deceive the eye, of mountebanks and disguised cheaters, of

Dark-working sorcerers that change the mind:
Soul-killing witches that deform the body.

The lines seize the imagination of the audience at the deep level where the ancient dread of losing the self or soul is very much alive. They are highly characteristic of the imaginative Antipholus, develop the idea in his first soliloquy that his self is at hazard, and set the pattern for his interpretations of the strange experiences that befall him henceforward. At present his sense of those reputed perils of Ephesus, awakened by what seems the extraordinary behaviour of Dromio, produces the provisional resolve:

If it prove so, I will be gone the sooner;

the first sign of the recurrent danger that he will depart before recognition and family reunion, with the consequent saving of Egeon's life, can come about. His fears are not cowardice; such a view of them has been guarded against in *scènes* 1 and 2, where despite the warning of Egeon's fate, he was determined to explore the town. The spirit he showed there prepares us for his acceptance of what will seem to him the mysterious adventure offered him by Adriana and Luciana: in spite of his forebodings now, for a time he will be ready to believe that the mystifications and transmutations of Ephesus may not be all malevolent.

Every passage in our illustrative scene has thus its functions both in the scene itself, and in the wider dynamic, harmonic, thematic, comic structure of the play. Besides this close, economical texture, there are of course other proofs of Shakespeare's early command of construction in the dramatic medium. He constructs in terms of theatre: he knows, for instance, the value of business and of devices and episodes which belong peculiarly to the stage. A famous example is the serenade scene in *Two Gentlemen*, with its music, its distancing of Sylvia at her window, and its eavesdroppers—the Host appreciative or drowsing to sleep, Julia (in male costume) painfully intent. In *The Comedy of Errors*, the gold chain seen, the blows seen and heard, make double the effect they would in narrative. The asides or semi-asides of the alien Antipholus and Dromio in II. ii, by a sound use of dramatic convention, mark the dichotomy between their mental worlds and that of Adriana and Luciana with whom they are in converse. The hilarious and crucial episode of the rightful husband and his party shut out from dinner depends for its full impact upon the stage-arrangement: the parties in altercation are both plainly visible to the audience though not to each other. But the supreme power manifest in Shakespeare's art of dramatic construction is the combinative power well indicated by Hardin Craig, who writes of "his unequalled [skill] in fitting parts together so that they [reinforce] one another," and notes that in working upon materials which often gave him much of his fable ready-made, his "originality seems to have consisted in the selection of great significant patterns." Of such patterns and such combining of parts, *The Shrew*, among the first four comedies, offers in the manifold relationships between its Induction and the main play perhaps the finest illustration.

In *The Comedy of Errors*, the combinative power is exercised in drawing upon diverse sources to compose a play of diverse yet co-operating strands and tones, a play which ranges from the averted-tragical, in prologue and *dénouement*, to low comedy, as in the drubbings and the account of Luce; while the middle comedy of the Antipholi provides its central substance. The adventures of the alien Antipholus, particularly his falling in love with Luciana, have emotional chords that relate them to the tone of the Egeon story; the marital conflict of Antipholus the husband and his Adriana is bourgeois comedy, informed by intellectual and emotional discussion. Both Antipholi, through the association of master and man, take part with the Dromios in the lower comedy, which besides knockabout farce includes burlesque of academical logic and rhetoric, a comic parallel to the more serious concern with ideas at other levels of the action.

The play appealed at once to the taste for neo-Plautine intrigue comedy, and to what may be regarded as the four great interests traditionally supplied by romance. It is based on Plautus' *Menaechmi*. There Shakespeare found twin brothers, the traveller in search of the denizen, lost since childhood. The traveller is mistaken for his brother by all the important characters in turn, except the doctor, and his own servant, who once mistakes the brother for him. The second great source of complications is likewise the same as in Shakespeare: when characters have met the twin they do not know, and taken him for the one they do, they then meet the one they really do know, and debit or credit him with what in fact took place between them and the other. Such a misunderstanding occurs once between the traveller and his servant; and it is through errors of this kind that the denizen is brought into trouble. From his parasite (incensed at the traveller) his wife learns that he has given her cloak to a courtesan he frequents; she turns him out of doors to recover it. The courtesan has entrusted the cloak and her own gold chain to his twin, whom by mistake for him she has had to dinner; and shuts him out when he denies having received them. At the climax just before the final recognition, the traveller, accused of marital injustice by the wife and her father, replies, as they think, like a madman: a doctor is summoned, and catechizes the real husband, who is shortly seized at his orders. Here are the originals of the Antipholi, Adriana, the Courtesan, Dr. Pinch, and the alien Dromio. The other Dromio, as the servant who begins the train of errors by bringing to the wrong twin the summons to dinner afterwards seconded by his mistress, to that extent plays the same part as the courtesan's cook in Plautus. The courtesan has a maid as well as a cook; Adriana has Luce as well as a Dromio. There are minor hints in the dialogue for the personage of the goldsmith, the rope's end, and the alien twin's anxiety about the money handed for safe keeping to his servant. The father reproves the supposed husband for his treatment of the wife, as Luciana does in Shakespeare; but he first reproved the wife, like Luciana again (and like the Abbess later). Shakespeare has gone far to exonerate the husband. For the cloak, the wife's property, the gold chain is substituted as a gift only promised her (its place in the courtesan's plaints is supplied by her ring); and he does not propose to bestow it upon the courtesan until provoked by his wife's barring him out, and that in the face of the guests he had invited. Moreover, he has not frequented the courtesan; and his visit now is suggested by his wife's baseless jealousy of her. Had the wife barred out *this* husband because of her sense of grievance, it would have been hard to believe in her love of him, which is vital to Shakespeare's play; but she does not—she acts under a delusion, without recognizing him.

Even within the ambit of intrigue comedy, the *Menaechmi* did not furnish enough for Shakespeare. He shared the Renaissance and English desire for "copy" or copiousness, and he required an action long enough for the Elizabethan stage. Accordingly, he crossed what he took from the *Menaechmi* with the celebrated situation from Plautus' *Amphitruo*. There, the husband is shut out while Jupiter in his likeness seduces his wife within; the husband's slave, too, Sosia, is impersonated and excluded by Jupiter's henchman, Mercury. The consequences of the cross have been analysed closely by T.W. Baldwin. We may note that it gives Shakespeare one of his far-reaching changes from the plot of the *Menaechmi*, the matching of the twin masters by twin servants; goes with a second, the transfer of the dinner from the courtesan's to the wife's, and helps to prompt a third, the invention of Luciana. With love and marriage conceived in the human terms they are in Shakespeare's comedy, a seduced Adriana would be tragic not comic; chaste, like Lucrece, in mind but not in body. The supposed husband therefore must be in no serious danger of succumbing to her importunities, and partly for this reason, partly for the sake of love-interest and comic effect, Luciana is introduced to be the object of his devout and legitimate passion, that will seem to her and her sister doubly illegitimate. Naturally Shakespeare's changes interlock: thus, as opposite number to the alien servant, the second servant now belongs to the husband and wife not to the courtesan, and so it is from the wife he brings his summons. Since there is no seduction, the summons from the wife is requisite to bring the supposed husband to her house. Above all, the shutting-out of the real husband by the wife in *Menaechmi* is transformed into the much stronger situation derived from *Amphitruo*, and the shutting-out by the courtesan is dropped: hence yet again it is at the wife's, as part of the strong situation there, that the dinner needs to be located. The shift contributes, in keeping with Shakespeare's treatment of the marital conflict and of love, to lay emphasis on the wife, the husband, and the true lover at the centre, and to make the courtesan's part no less subordinate than the goldsmith's, which Shakespeare invents. The shift also obviates the necessity for the husband to order the dinner beforehand, as he does in Act I of *Menaechmi*, where the errors do not begin till Act II. Except for a hint of provocation offered by the wife, and her desire to oversee the husband's comings and goings, Shakespeare jettisons this first act, getting the errors started in the first scene of his main action with Dromio of Ephesus' mistake, which likewise ensures that Dromio's master will be involved more quickly than the denizen in Plautus. Finally, to have two pairs of twins instead of one multiplies and makes more complex the errors available for plot and comedy.

Among the more important neo-Plautine or neo-Terentian features of the play is its observance of the unity of time: Shakespeare advertises the limit of a few hours within which his action is to be, and is, compressed. Other such features are the unity of place, and the setting, with its three houses—and (as Peter Alexander points out) the Harbour imagined "off" on the one side, the Mart or Town on the other: a conception originally from Athens, where it corresponded with fact. The first scene performs the function of a classical prologue: there is Seneca as well as Plautus in its ancestry. The Terentian five-act structure expounded by T.W. Baldwin we shall notice shortly. The contrasts of prose and various sorts of verse, including rhyme, to suit the changing character of the episodes, is compared by Cornelia Coulter to the similar use of lyric measures and the lower-toned senarii in Latin comedy. For other similarities, her article should be consulted; but one has to bear in mind that one and the same feature commonly has antecedents in more than one tradition. Shakespeare's comic servants inherit from Cain's Garcio and the rest in the Miracle Cycles, and from the native Vice, as well as from the Latin Servus, and Lyly's pert lads like the Dromio in *Mother Bombie*. The love of balance seen in the doubling of the twins and the invention of a sister and confidante for Adriana, a prospective wife for the bachelor Antipholus—if we are to seek the sources of it further than in Shakespeare's own artistic sense—is not to be traced only to Terence, Plautus, and Lyly: balanced grouping of personages is characteristic of Moralities and Tudor interludes. Men of the Renaissance read Latin comedy in the light of their own predilections, formed to a considerable extent by the tradition that had come down from medieval romances and had branched into the novelle. Consequently, as Madeleine Doran has shown, they gave to the motifs of recognition, shipwreck, long-lost children, and the like, when they met them in Terence and Plautus, far more than the value they had originally had there as romance. To a lesser degree, what love-interest Terence in particular afforded was similarly magnified.

Hence, when through his neo-Plautine warp Shakespeare ran a weft dyed in colours of romance, he was making no extreme change from the Latin genre as then frequently understood. Rather, he was overgoing Plautus, and Terence, on their supposed romantic side, as well as on that of comic intrigue. For this purpose, and for "copiousness," he drew on additional sources. The leading interests of romance—as one might exemplify from Arthurian romances, from *The Squire's Tale*, or, coming to the period of our play, from the romance aspects of *Arcadia* and *The Faerie Queene*—were adventure; marvel, especially enchantment; the high sentiment of love; and *sens*, the implications brought out in the *matière*, the meaning the reader takes away with him, as a result of the author's treatment. Shakespeare develops into an adventure-story, that of Egeon, the successful quest for the long-lost child which in *Menaechmi* is hardly more than a presupposition of the plot. For the initial peril demanded by a plot of this kind, he provides by translating from hoax into fact the situation of the Sienese merchant in Gascoigne's *Supposes*, where it was already part of a drama of mistaken identities; and by heightening it from a potential threat to goods into a provisional sentence of death. The shipwreck and intervention of piratical fishermen, whereby, Egeon narrates, the family was first divided, have a probable source in Greene's *Menaphon*, and form a link with the source of the happy ending, the adventures of Apollonius of Tyre, related by Gower and Twine. After vicissitudes including shipwreck, succour from a fisherman, loss of his wife at sea, and the kidnapping of his daughter by pirates, Apollonius' reunion with his family is completed at Ephesus. There he discovers his wife in the Priestess of Diana's Temple, as the Abbess is discovered to be Egeon's. The interest of adventure is not confined to the *dénouement* and the opening scene; through the alien Antipholus it is carried into the main action. To him it seems that he has a series of adventures with the supernatural. His thoughts and feelings about them, like the providential coincidences that have brought all the members of the family to Ephesus, speak to our sense of marvel. His illusion of supernatural menace in these experiences is set against the real peril of Egeon, and against the truth of his love, even though his love-adventure, which brings the loftiest of love-sentiment into the comedy, seems to him supernatural and at least equivocally perilous too. In the idea of the town as a home of supernatural delusion, Shakespeare is again combining sources. The Epidamnum of *Menaechmi* (II. i) is notorious for cheats. The denizen's house there is associated by Shakespeare with Amphitruo's, a scene of supernatural shape-shifting. Epidamnum itself he has changed to Ephesus, no doubt as the site of Diana's Temple in the Apollonius story, which becomes his Abbey. Diana of the Ephesians inevitably recalls Acts XIX, whence Shakespeare would remember, besides the uproar on her account, the references to curious (that is, black) arts practised in Ephesus, and to the exorcists, with whom Dr. Pinch (founded on the Medicus in *Menaechmi)* has something in common. The Ephesians are warned against supernatural foes in St. Paul's Epistle, which also exhorts them, Geoffrey Bullough reminds us, to domestic unity, dwelling on the right relationships of husbands and wives, parents and children, masters and servants. With the father's rebuke to the wife in *Menaechmi*, and the long tradition of marital debate in mediaeval and Tudor literature, it thus contributed, no doubt, to the *sens* of the play.

To consider the *sens* is to consider the themes. However they are deepened and interconnected by Shakespeare's treatment, they are not recondite: for the audience, they are the general ideas arising most naturally from the motives and development of the plot, and the response of the characters. The play begins and ends with relationship: a family torn asunder and reunited. Relationship is the motive that has brought Egeon, and the alien Antipholus and Dromio, to the hazards of Ephesus; relationship is threatened by the tensions in the marriage of Antipholus the denizen. The chief entanglements spring from mistaken identity and mistiming:

> I see we still did meet each other's man,
> And I was ta'en for him, and he for me,
> And thereupon these ERRORS are arose.

The twins appear the same, but in reality are different; those who meet them are led by appearance into illusion. Repeatedly one of the persons assumes that he shared an experience with another, when in reality he shared it with a different one. In consequence, the persons cease to be able to follow each other's assumptions, and become isolated in more or less private worlds. Mistakes of identity all but destroy relationship, and loss of relationship calls true identity yet more in question; the chief persons suspect themselves or are suspected of insanity, or of being possessed, surrounded, or assailed by supernatural powers—madness or demoniac possession would be the eclipse of the true self, and sorcery might overwhelm it. The alien Antipholus and Dromio fear Circean metamorphosis; Egeon, that he has been deformed out of recognition by time. Yet the hazard of metamorphosis and of the loss of present identity is also the way to fresh or restored relationship. Antipholus the bachelor desires that Luciana will transform him and create him new; and Adriana's belief, that in marriage the former identities coalesce and emerge identified with each other, is true if rightly interpreted. How the possessive interpretation, not relinquished by Adriana till almost the end, is at odds with the free giving and hazarding in which the wealth and debts of love differ from those of commerce, is another central theme, well traced by J.R. Brown. Adriana's envy of a husband's status contravenes principles of order that for Shakespeare and orthodox Elizabethans extended through the whole cosmos. The status of husband, and of wife, Kate's lines in *The Shrew* imply, are related to their places in this hierarchical order:

> Such duty as the subject owes the prince
> Even such a woman oweth to her husband.

Adriana comes to style her husband lord, and they each lay their case, as each has come to see it, before the Duke, reminding themselves and him that the match was first made by his authority. By this point, disorder from the various disruptions of relationship has gone so far in the community, that only the appeals for justice addressed to the Abbess and to him, God's viceroys spiritual and temporal, are capable, the time now being ripe, of leading to a solution.

Not only are the themes organically developed in the action; they are organically connected in themselves. At the centre is relationship: relationship between human beings, depending on their right relationship to truth and universal law: to the cosmic reality behind appearance, and the cosmic order. Trust in mere appearance results in illusion and mistakes of identity, thus dislocating relationship, and so disrupting order: blind conflict and disorder are inevitable when men misconceive true identity and become isolated in private worlds. Besides illusion, there are other factors of disorder: revolt against a wife's place in the cosmic hierarchy is the original source of discord in Adriana's marriage: order is broken, too, by everything untimely. As Ovid's *Tempus edax rerum*, time opposes mutability to the creative cosmic order. By that mutability, identity itself may be threatened: "*Nec species sua cuique manet...*" —the link of time-theme and appearance-theme is present in Ovid, and particularly clear in the apostrophe to Time wrung from Egeon when he finds himself unrecognized. Here, and in the dread of Circean transformation into beasts, metamorphosis is seen in its hostile aspect; but, as we have observed, it can also transform for the better: time, too, when it is ripe, brings a new order. Till then, patience would mitigate disorder, which cannot be ended till the claims for justice, distorted by the claimants' assumption that their private worlds are real, are laid before those who in the hierarchy of order are founts of justice upon earth. More than justice is needed: without mercy, the godly prince is not himself; and amid the demonstrations of love's wealth, lacking which there would be little of the genial warmth that glows in the conclusion, Solinus is inspired to what he had declared impossible, and freely remits the debt Egeon owes the law. In this organic structure, of the two themes which next to relationship are the most inclusive, the first, cosmic order, presides in Shakespeare's early Histories; its importance in his drama is well recognized, and the importance of the second, appearance and reality, is becoming so. The first is a familiar part of "the Elizabethan world-picture"; the second, presumably, has affiliations with Renaissance neo-Platonism.

The themes are given prominence in several ways. They are voiced by the speakers, who often relate one theme to another:

the examples in our analysis of I. ii are characteristic. The dominant imagery, of man as beast, reflects the ideas of illusory appearance and malign metamorphosis; above all, it mirrors the threats to identity and to status in the cosmic order. Appropriately, it stops on the brink of the *dénouement*, with the Duke's explicit formulation:

I think you all have drunk of Circe's cup.

Thematic, likewise, are the two images of the water-drop, its identity lost for relationship's sake. The whole harmonic structure, of which the correspondence of images forms part, is a vehicle of the themes. How generosity and two degrees of possessiveness in love are defined by juxtaposition of *scènes* in III. ii, with reference back to Adriana's attitude in Act II, has been shown by J.R. Brown. The supreme instance is the parallel between the "gossips' feast" to which everyone is going at the end, and the dinner from which the husband and his guests were shut out. The gossips' or baptismal feast affirms relationship and identity: the kin are united, the Duke is patron, all are friends and godparents, witnesses to the identities now truly established and christened into the family and the community; long travail is rewarded, and increase (the progressive aspect of cosmic order) which, despite the double birth of twins, was mocked by the intervention of mutable fortune, is now truly realized. It is not only as a sensational error of identity that the exclusion from dinner contrasts with this: balked or broken feasts (G. Wilson Knight has made us aware) are recurrent symbols in Shakespeare of the breakdown of human fellowship and its pieties. Both this motif, and the extravagant comedy of the barring-out, are worked up by the burlesque Lylyan or Erasmian colloquy on whether good cheer or welcome makes the feast. The burlesque "turns" for the clowns belong to the harmonic structure in much the same way. The theme of time's depredations, for instance, is the text of the mock disputation on Time and Hair. In IV. ii and iii, the clown's interlocutors are bamboozled by the spate of mock rhetorical similitudes in which he drowns the identity of his subject, the Sergeant, who is verbally transmogrified into devil, wolf, perverse hound, evil angel, and so forth; and whose function, arrest for debt (to be compared with the love-claims of Adriana), is the pith of the jests. To these themes, thus linked, of debt, identity, metamorphosis, and supernatural malice, the further comic fancy of debtor Time, turning back an hour when he meets with a Sergeant, links those of untimeliness and reversal of cosmic order.

The *Comedy* appeals first and foremost to laughter, as is obvious at any performance. I have dwelt on its serious themes and strands of romance, because it is these that student and producer are prone to discount. In his famous Stratford production (1939), Komisarjevsky guyed Egeon, Emilia, and the wooing scene: he could not present them "straight" and still keep them in key with the rest, which he was evidently determined to exploit for all it was worth as farce, thereby turning Shakespeare's comedy with its several finely-balanced tones into his own scintillating single-toned vaudeville. Among dramas of recognition, the *Comedy* is not a superior *Supposes*, without much in it (that signifies) beyond lively intrigue and farcical situations. On the contrary, it resembles the *Ion* and *The Confidential Clerk* in matching a mystification about identity, at the level of intrigue, with an exploration of serious issues appropriate to such a plot. Less than half the total number of lines (some 750, I estimate, out of some 1750) are mainly devoted to the essentials of the intrigue comedy. About 300 are elaborations of comic rhetoric; the remainder develop the romance interests, and, with the comic rhetoric, point the themes. Even so rough a criterion confirms that the play is not to be regarded as a farcical intrigue-comedy and little more.

To recognize this is not to undervalue the intrigue, so brilliantly contrived to make the most of all the opportunities for comic error. The progressive action, in which the intrigue is one factor, develops the comedy and themes of the play along with the fortunes of its persons; and is organized no less firmly on the large scale than the single scenes are on the small. So far as the plot is concerned, this organization corresponds, T.W. Baldwin has shown, to the five-act structure Renaissance and earlier critics found in Terence; particularly the form found in the *Andria*. How far it depends upon neoclassical theory is perhaps a question: among the features Baldwin indicates, those of most consequence for dramatic effect can be paralleled in a mediaeval drama like *The Castle of Perseverance*, and to a playwright well endowed with structural sense might seem natural, theory or no theory, in plays with a central crisis and a final solution. However this may be, the comedy begins *in medias res*, with the partial exposition of what has happened already, and the immediate occasions of the subsidiary and main actions: the suspended sentence on Egeon and the summons to the wrong Antipholus. Act II completes the exposition and *protasis* by introducing the sisters and their motivation, especially Adriana's; and ends, when the same Antipholus accedes to her summons, with the beginning of the *epitasis* or entanglement proper. This leads to the central crisis in III. i: locked out, the husband is brought into the entanglement, and narrowly fails to meet his twin: despite the Dromios' scolding-match, recognition is missed. By the last words of Act IV, with the firm resolve of the alien to depart, there is imminent danger it will be missed for ever; and there follows, in the supposed madness of the twins and the expiration of Egeon's respite, the climax of distresses that precipitates the *dénouement*. There, meeting and recognition are combined with the completion and correction of Egeon's retrospect:

Why here begins his morning story right.

The development of the action is supported by the use made of the stage-set. Acts II and III are focused upon the Phoenix, scene of the central crisis. Act IV brings into play the second *domus*, the Porpentine, and in accord with the fast-extending complications has no one focal point: the action is related by turns to the Phoenix, the Porpentine, and neither. The third *domus*, the Abbey, is kept in reserve as the appropriate focus for the *dénouement*. Dynamic progress is strongly felt in the mounting violence, from the first mere thwack to the drawing of swords, thrashing with a rope's end, overpowering of "madmen," and elaborate (narrated) vengeance upon Pinch; in the spreading of error beyond the family to courtesan, goldsmith, and merchant, until the whole town, at least in Adriana's fevered fancy, seems involved; and in the darkening conviction of the imaginative Antipholus that his supernatural experiences are from the devil.

With this explanation, natural to his melancholy temperament, he has positively encased himself in error, for it is as coherent as it is fallacious. In like fashion his choleric brother comes to attribute all his sufferings to a conspiracy instigated by his wife: both the Antipholi reach the verge of persecution-mania. Since Adriana also is given her point of view, which alters before the end, one can say of the three main persons that although they do not develop in the sense of being felt to change in character as a result of the action, their attitudes of mind develop, so that each is felt to have an inner self. That is, they are not wholly flat characters, such as might be fitting protagonists of pure farce. They are simple, but have just enough depth for the play, which Shakespeare, as we have seen, has deepened considerably beyond the expected limitations of neo-classical comedy.

Even so, in depth and scope he was, of course, far to surpass it. Nonetheless, it is in its own kind an extraordinarily finished work. The kind being one that not even Shakespeare could extend beyond some narrow limits; a less tight form, exemplified in *Two Gentlemen*, held more promise of *Twelfth Night*. Yet in recognizing this, one ought also recognize how much, in the *Comedy*, he has in fact found room for. Like the other early plays, it will always be judged by two standards. One quite properly, is the standard set later by Shakespeare himself. But the play should also be appreciated for what it is in its own right: still actable as a hilarious yet balanced comedy, more pregnant than has perhaps been supposed with Shakespearian ideas.

Originally published by Harold F. Brooks, "Themes and Structure in *The Comedy of Errors*," *Early Shakespeare*, Stratford-upon-Avon Studies, 3, ed. John Russell Brown and Bernard Harris (London: Edward Arnold, 1961): 54–71. Reprinted with the permission of Hodder & Stoughton Ltd.

Notes

First Edition. The original text of *The Comedy of Errors* is that of the First Folio, 1623 (facsimiles by S. Lee [1902] and, less satisfactory, by H. Kokeritz and C.T. Prouty [1955]; Booth's type-facsimile appeared in 1862–4). No other text affords evidence of what Shakespeare wrote.

Modern Editions. Pending up-to-date annotated editions (the new Arden, edited by R.A. Foakes, is near publication), those in the old Arden, Yale, and New Cambridge (1922) are useful. Among plain texts preference may be given to P. Alexander's in his *Complete Works...*(1951). On textual matters consult W.W. Greg, *The Shakespeare First Folio* (1955).

Date. It seems certain that the play was performed at Gray's Inn, 28 December 1594, when S. Thomas, *Shakespeare Quarterly* (1956) believes it was new; P. Alexander, *Shakespeare's Life and Art* (1939) dates it before August 1589, and T.W. Baldwin, *Shakespeare's Five-Act Structure* (1947) in winter 1589–90. H. Brooks finds the vengeance on Pinch indebted to the forcible shaving of Edward II in Marlowe, suggesting a date *c.*1592–4; 1592 suits other supposed echoes and allusions, that to Henry of Navarre having most force between 1589–1593.

Sources. A principal intrigue from Plautus' *Menaechmi*, with elaborations from his *Amphitruo*, is set within the Egeon story, for which suggestions came from Gascoigne's *Supposes* (1566, published 1575), and/or its originals in Ariosto, and the tale of Apollonius of Tyre, retold in Gower's *Confessio Amantis*, VIII, and Twine's *Patterne of Painefull Adventures* (1576, n.d., and 1607). The probable sources are more numerous and more closely combined than this statement indicates, as this chapter shows. G. Bullough's *Narrative and Dramatic Sources of Shakespeare*, Vol. I (1957) reprints *Supposes*, Warner's translation of *Menaechmi* (1595), extracts from *Amphitruo* (trans. Sugden) and from Gower: Twine is reprinted in *Shakespeare's Library* (ed. W.C. Hazlitt, Pt. I. iv). See further T.W. Baldwin; and K. Muir, *Shakespeare's Sources*, Vol. I (1957).

Scholarship and Criticism. Among general studies may be cited H.B. Charlton's *Shakespearian Comedy* (1938), M.C. Bradbrook's *Growth and Structure of Elizabethan Comedy* (1955), J.R. Brown's *Shakespeare and His Comedies* (1957) and M. Doran's *Endeavors of Art* (1954); further relevant studies are H.T. Price's *Construction in Shakespeare* (1951), W.H. Clemen's *Development of Shakespeare's Imagery* (1951) and J.W. Lever's *Elizabethan Love Sonnet* (1956). Among articles may be mentioned N. Coghill's "The Basis of Shakespeare's Comedy," *Essays and Studies* (1950), Cornelia Coulter's "The Plautine Tradition in Shakespeare," *JEGP* (1912), and H. Craig's "Motivation in Shakespeare's Choice of Materials," *Shakespeare Survey* (1951); J.R. Brown has analysed "The Interpretation of Shakespeare's Comedies, 1900–1953," *Shakespeare Survey* (1955).

Brave New World

T.W. Baldwin

Though we have been examining the compositional methods of
Shakspere the rhetorician, we have also caught some fascinating
glimpses of what Shakspere the man saw in the world around
him. As he looked out on the international situation, he was
vividly aware of the Spanish octopus, with tentacles spread out
to strangle not only England, Ireland, and Scotland, but also
France, the Netherlands, the Indies, and America, even with one
grasper left over for Portugal and the rest of the world. But
Spain's Armada had failed, and could be treated jocularly as
"whole Armadoes of Carrects" in the treasure fleet, where also
the octopus was proving to be vulnerable. The Spanish Armada
had been reflected even more jocularly in Armado of *Love's
Labor's Lost*, and Armado finds himself in the court of Navarre,
which had come to be the symbol of opposition to Rome, which
was the ally of Spain. In *Errors*, Romish France is armed and
reverted against her heir, the Protestant King of Navarre, now
rightful King of France, whom the faction of Guise as champions
of Rome is attempting to supplant. Peele's *Farewell*, the manifesto
of the counter-Armada, an expedition which was also to
demonstrate to England and the world the vulnerability of Spain,
has given Shakspere a phrase—again used in the same jocular
setting with Spain—which is eventually to become one of his
most memorable expressions. Shakspere is here a cocky young
Englishman, strutting with the best.

Many places in and around London had strong associations
with this religious-political war. One of these was Holywell
Priory, where, across the ditch from the Theater, two priests had
received the full rites for treason in the wake of the Spanish
Armada in 1588.[1] If Shakspere went to the Theater for any
reason, whether as visitor merely or in some official capacity, he
would proceed to such a priory gate as had Aegeon in *Errors*,

and would look across the ditch to such a "melancholy vale" as that to which Aegeon was being escorted for official attentions. And we are not to forget that Aubrey records from William Beeston that Shakspere "lived in Shoreditch." Shakspere would certainly have been very familiar with the topography and happenings of Shoreditch. Heminges and Cundall in 1623 published Shakspere's plays. The company to which these men belonged had at times performed at the Theater in these early days. *Errors* uses exactly the topography of Holywell Priory which was not duplicated in any other such building in London.[2] To this extent, at least, *Errors* reflects the events of 1588, when Holywell Priory became for the nonce—or twice—a place of execution. Whether Shakspere was himself present, and whether he also reflects to any extent the persons and actions of the occasion, has no bearing on this objective fact. We repeat, the fact is that the topography of *Errors* is the same as that of Holywell Priory, but not the same as that of any other such building in London. And Holywell Priory was used as a place of execution only in 1588. Further, an abbey wall is one of the landmarks in the setting of *Two Gentlemen* and *Romeo*.[3] The structural relationships show that the three plays were written in that order and in close succession, presumably consecutively. The evidence is now conclusive that *Errors* is later than the Spanish Armada, while *Two Gentlemen* was not later than 1590, and *Two Gentlemen* and *Romeo* overlap in construction.[4] These plays belonged, at least eventually, to the company of which Heminges and Cundall had become "residual legatees"; the plays were constructed in 1589–91, thus at a period when that company was playing, at least occasionally, at the Theater. Shakspere would surely have had occasion in these years to proceed to the priory gate and wall, and in doing so to behold across the ditch the "melancholy vale." So would his audience. They should have had no difficulty in recognizing and appreciating Aegeon's plight. It was no improbable fiction; it was a grim possibility for all, and at least a probability for a few, if not even a relative certainty for some. We have now been pretty well brainwashed of these old sad events. Even where we should forgive history, it is unwise to forget it, since through it the present has come, out of which no sound future may be made which does not take into account the past. To forget is to assure recurrence. But these events and associations were as vivid to Shakspere and his contemporaries as were the horrors of bombing in the last (?) world war. Witches and war were probably much more vividly imagined by them.

Shakspere's interest in the current consequences of past history was both natural and induced. That he was interested is shown by other plays than *Errors*. Like Englishmen in general at this period, he was particularly concerned with developments in France, even as we have our dominant concerns with a paralleling threat. *Love's Labor's Lost* is set in France, with titles currently and traditionally prominent in French affairs, but linked as they had been or could have been traditionally before the complete split which had eventuated by 1589, and is reflected in *Errors*. If it should prove that *All's Well* represents *Love's Labor's Won*, then we are to remember that France is used for the setting of that play, much as in *Love's Labor's Lost*. Italy then intervened as the setting of *Two Gentlemen*, though the play does not specifically reflect Italy, and of *Romeo*, which is no more specifically Italianate than its source, Brooke's *Romeus*, which entangles *Two Gentlemen* and *Romeo*. Then French affairs induced the moral of *1 Henry VI* and its sequent consequences. And here we come to the root of these matters.

In the sixteenth-century view, man had significance only as part of God's plan. And this plan is expounded in the Bible, and exemplified in history, as it is working itself out around us in continuation of the past, that past for England being explained in such works as those of Hall and Holinshed, whose essence is extracted in such political sermons as those of Baldwin's *Mirrour*, not to mention the official homilies of the church, etc. All education was subservient to teaching the fundamental plan behind the universe, which was so constructed that the diligent observer

Finds tongues in trees, books in the running brooks,
Sermons in stones and good in every thing.[5]

One was to examine everything for the primary purpose of learning the "good" of God's way.

From the beginning of his career, Shakspere was interested in the meaning, the moral if you will, of "history," and that interest in the meaning was to manifest itself in the history plays, to develop that idea of man in his universe which was to eventuate in Shakspere's great tragedies and his mature comedies. The interest was induced by inculcation, but it also grew because of Shakspere's fundamental and progressively maturing interest in man. This fundamental view of the significance of the universe had been thrust on him from every angle, till eventually he became aware of it not as theology, not as philosophy, etc., but as fact. Man does exist within a limiting universe of interacting causes and effects, by whatever theories we explain them. Shakspere became aware of and presented that fact. He was not exemplifying theology, philosophy, psychology, whatnot, but depicting man as an integral part of God's universe. As a consequence, he has continued to transcend all isms and to be recognized simply as a portrayer of fundamental truth—even by those who profess no God.

Thus this young man from Stratford has also bright eyes and keen ears, not only for the world at large, but particularly for the London which is around him. Fripp has grasped and presented the contrasting reflections, though perhaps weighting the balance somewhat in favor of Stratford.

> London supplies a few features—the port, with its barks and hoys, the mart, (Royal Exchange), the *Porpentine* near the Pike-garden on the Bankside, merchants and goldsmiths, cozenage, harlots, "Hell," and "Counter;" but from Stratford are the stocks (in the Corn Market), *ship* and *sheep* (Sheep Street pronounced "Ship Street"), "luce" and "pike" (here a staff), the score upon a post in a shop, the "gossips' feast" or christening-party (an important family function), the kitchen wench ("greasy Joan" hereafter), the Sergeant-at-the-Mace, the hound that runs counter and draws dry-foot, and the fairy lore, with an idea developed later in *A Midsummer Night's Dream*.[6]

Stratford sheep became London ships. The Stratford yokels, the twin Dromios, find themselves much confused in the witchery of Ephesus-London, as no doubt did their creator. Here is an alert young man of twenty-five, still fresh to all the happenings at the center of the universe, London. So the traveler, Dromio of Syracuse, reflects the position of Spain in the political world, and the abbess of Ephesus gets localized to Holywell Priory, the scene of recent executions in retaliation to Spain after the Great Armada. In the literary world, Shakspere had read Peele's *Farewell*, to be impressed by at least one line, and was also at least well enough aware of Greene's *Menaphon* to use the name for one of his dukes, along with probably some general impressions from the story. No doubt he had read also Nashe's preface to *Menaphon*, with its evaluation of the literary world of the day, especially its caustic devaluation of the learned grammarians, among whom three years later Greene was to place Shakspere as chief. Shakspere had in some way faced closely enough the *Looking Glasse* of Greene and Lodge to have one of Lodge's Virgilian lines stick firmly in his head, as one of Peele's had stuck. He had used two of Lyly's plays for basic ideas in *Love's Labor's Lost*. And the name Dromio indicates[7] that the Italianate complications of *Mother Bombie* had given at least part of the suggestion for out-complicating Lyly on the basis of *Menaechmi* to produce *Errors*. Young Shakspere was thus well aware of most of the literary playwrights of 1589, who, except Peele, were or were to become also "novelists"—Peele, Lyly, Greene, Lodge, and presumably Nashe— but, significantly, he does not reflect Marlowe apparently, who was the rebel, in opposition to established literary "Art," especially in the person of its self-appointed high priest, Robert Greene.[8] Shakspere was aping the good angels—too effectively, the archangel was in 1592 to complain. Aesop's crow is already in 1589 diligently collecting fine feathers, as Greene in 1592 was to accuse Shakescene of having done. The basic charge was true. Shakspere was merely applying to the moderns the methods which all rhetorical art inculcated from the ancients. And for that past Shakspere reflects in *Errors* almost entirely grammar school literature, the notable exception being the Apollonius story, deriving through moral Gower, who was to appear as Chorus to the story in *Pericles*. How had Shakspere come in contact, and was the contact confined to the one story?[9] At least the author of *Pericles* was aware of Gower as source. All in all, it is clear that Shakspere was keenly aware of this superstitiously bewitched world around him, and was doing his best to understand and present it.

As we turn from the man to his work, *The Comedy of Errors* exhibits with the greatest clarity the constructing processes of its author. The basic idea of the play he had from *Menaechmi*; even if we should agree with Rapp that he has inserted the *vis comica* of twinned servants from *Amphitruo*, for even they are substituted in the place of the untwinned parasite and servant in *Menaechmi*, and at most help to furnish the occasion rather than the cause of the proliferated confusions. Into the resultant scheme of errors arising from doubled twins, Shakspere has woven adapted situations, from *Menaechmi* principally, but with supplementary ideas from any source that appealed to him as forwarding his scheme.

Shakspere nowhere translates *Menaechmi*, though he clearly transcribes a few lines into English; he does not imitate *Menaechmi*; he does not even attempt to adapt the play as play, though he adapts everything he finds adaptable from it. Instead, by analysis and synthesis of *Menaechmi*, probably *Amphitruo*, etc., he strives to create something of his own. So *Menaechmi*, as such, goes no further than *Errors*. But the framework that Shakspere derived from *Menaechmi*, with perhaps some assistance from *Amphitruo*, serves as a mould in which to cast the material of *Two Gentlemen*.[10] Plautus was merely part of the meat on which this Caesar fed that he became so great; the power of assimilation and growth was in Shakspere himself. As for Plautus and his *Menaechmi*, it is clear that Shakspere stood in no more awe of them than did the rest of his contemporaries. Terence was the "awesome" literary figure. Plautus was just good fun, and so was pillaged unconscionably by everybody (see Reinhardtstoettner).

Shakspere has thus proceeded to turn *Menaechmi* by analysis and synthesis, not to imitate it by slavishly cutting over its pattern, or any pattern. He has first grasped, and then adapted completely. The reader will have seen the brilliance of both grasp and adaptation. The grasp of the principles is as free of their embodiment in *Menaechmi* as in the truest sense the adaptation is itself original. This is the kind of constructive originality for which the theorists hoped as the eventual result of their system. As Kempe phrases it, "All knowledge is taught generally both by precepts of arte, and also by practise of the same precepts. They are practised partly by obseruing examples of them in other mens workes, and partly by making somewhat of our owne; and that first by imitation, and at length without imitation.... Wherefore first the scholler shall learne the preceptes: secondly, he shall learne to note the examples of the precepts in vnfoulding other mens workes: thirdly, to imitate the examples in some worke of his owne: fourthly and lastly, to make somewhat alone without an example."[11] But Kempe's is the Ramistic system of exact imitation, which was to be systematized further into cutting over a pattern. In his turning of *Menaechmi* into *Errors*, Shakspere has followed the old emulative system of turning commonplaces by analysis and synthesis, for which Erasmus systematized directions in *Copia*, and supplied grist for the resultant mill in *Adagia*, etc.; not the directly imitative method which the English Ramists, notably Brinsley, under continental leading, were to foist into the system.

The man who composed *Errors* had a competent grasp upon the principles and practice of the Erasmian rhetorical system as promulgated in the grammar schools of Shakspere's day. By its fundamental device of procuring copy of words and things through varying, he has composed *Errors* on the principles of *Menaechmi*, using some of the materials also, but supplementing at will from such other sources as were known to him—many of which, no doubt, are not now known to us. But the resultant play is not an exercise in rhetoric, even though in the play Shakspere exercised his rhetoric. Rhetoric was only a means to an end, and Shakspere did not expect his audience to find its chief interest, if direct interest at all, in the rhetorical composition as such. The play was the thing, not the rhetoric. This we also must remember, especially in a work such as the present one, which purposely centers its attention upon the rhetorical construction in *Errors*. It is no part of its purpose to give a balanced account of the artistic merits and demerits of the play.

The what and the how, and to that extent the why, of the construction of *The Comedy of Errors* are now reasonably clear. The external basic source and model was the *Menaechmi* of Plautus as it was known and interpreted in sixteenth-century England. The plan of *Menaechmi* has been adapted to become the plan of *Errors*, and this plan of *Menaechmi* has been much more important in the construction of *Errors* than the materials. *Menaechmi*, as then interpreted, furnished the principle of "errors," which gave the title and theme to *Errors*. The two simple sets of "errors" in *Menaechmi* caused by the substitution of one twin for another, first in the household of the *meretrix* and then in that of the wife, have been magnified manyfold in *Errors*, partly by doubling the twins, but mostly by the erroneous substitution wherever possible of Antipholus of Syracuse for Antipholus of Ephesus.

The mere doubling was already incipient in *Menaechmi* in the parasite of Menaechmus of Epidamnus and the servant of Menaechmus of Syracuse. The usual parody of master by man could then easily have suggested that these servants should also become twins. An analogous relationship was prominent in *Amphitruo*, where Jupiter and Mercury substituted as Amphitruo and Sosia in the one household, that of the husband Amphitruo, throughout. It is thus likely that *Amphitruo* helped to propagate and to crystallize the idea of substituting throughout in the husband's household; but it did not furnish the idea fully embodied, nor did it contribute any as yet located detail to the embodiment in *Errors*. *Amphitruo* was simply a part of the genetic background for the idea, and it was at least this, whether Shakspere in any way or to any extent knew *Amphitruo* directly. As for the idea of parodying, and the idea of doubling, they had become indigenous in the literature of sixteenth-century England.[12] They were not matters of erudition, and they did not require one specific source.

And certainly, the man who constructed *Errors* already knew these principles at that time. He could not have arrived at a sufficient stage in his career to construct such a play without having become acquainted with these principles. The man who constructed *Errors* manifestly already knew a great deal about plays, even though as manifestly he was learning and had yet a great deal to learn. That we know—only because he learned and taught us. The idea upon which *Errors* is constructed is not that of *Menaechmi*, *Amphitruo*, or any other known source; but is an original idea, born from a knowledge of the ideas embodied in those plays, and doubtless also in various other places of which we know nothing. The idea of *Errors* is not an imitation; it is as original as if those analogous ideas had never existed; that is, as original as anything can be on this earth.

The motivations of the errors in *Menaechmi* also beget the motivations of *Errors*. As Menaechmus Sosicles and Messenio entered Epidamnus in fear of the sharpers, and accounted for the mistakings in terms of cozening, so Antipholus of Syracuse and his Dromio entered Ephesus in fear of the witches, and accounted for their mishaps in terms of witchcraft. Here again a basic idea of *Menaechmi* has been varied, transposed, translated into an original idea for *Errors*. The same process continues throughout the composition of *Errors*. The ideas are the important genetic agents, not the materials in which they are embodied.

As he prepared to compose, the dramatist would need at least the sketch of a plot on paper or in his head. In *Menaechmi*, everything is very near the minimum possible. The family there in the play itself consists of the twins only. Father and grandfather are part of the explanation in *argumentum* and *prologus*, but play no part in the actual plot. Mother is only an incidental allusion. Such an attenuated and desiccated plot would not do for Shakspere's day. Any modern story, and it had to be a story, would be on a very much larger scale. Whether Shakspere himself knew few or many current stories, that fundamental fact would remain the same. So he enlarges to a complete family, with both father and mother in the play; but he does not resurrect grandfather from the explanations, though some think grandfather should have been retained, or a substitute for him, to tell us how the twins came to bear the same name. Then Shakspere doubled the twins, by adding twin servants to the twin masters. No such precedent plot with doubled twins is known. The nearest to it is *Amphitruo*, where Jupiter and Mercury play the doubles of Amphitruo and Sosia. But in *Menaechmi* itself, one twin master has a servant, the other a parasite. The idea of parodying the masters by their servants could easily have arisen in this way without knowledge specifically of *Amphitruo*, even though it seems reasonably clear that there are touches from that play. One twin master in *Menaechmi* is already married. So Shakspere lets him stay married, and provides conventionally a sister of the wife for the other twin. In the parody, he provides one servant with a wife, whose attentions were not appreciated by the other, not with a wife apiece. The resultant family, with attendants, is not taken from or modeled upon any known precedent plot. Shakspere has constructed it to his own plan, using current procedures. This part of the plot is not imitated from any single source. It has been synthesized from Shakspere's total experience of such things, using ideas from some recognizable materials, and no doubt from others of which we do not know. This is genesis by analysis and synthesis.

Shakspere must plot to break his family in the beginning and reunite it at the end of his play. The universal device for the large-scale fractionating of a family was shipwreck. Here Shakspere shows some details from the story of Aeneas, others from the wreck of St. Paul, and doubtless still others from still other literary storms, known and unknown to us. But Shakspere's storm and wreck were not directly imitated from any of these. Again, this is genesis by analysis and synthesis from the total background of his knowledge. But the result is his own "original" plan.

According to that master plan, each twin must retain his servant twin, so that the family must be broken into four units. This is done by first separating father and mother, each with a set of twins, by shipwreck. Then father and mother must be separated from the twins. For father, the device in *Menaechmi* was retained. When father's twin reaches adolescence, he sets out with his servant twin to find their fellow twins, as the home twin had done in *Menaechmi*. To separate mother from her set, piratical fishermen are called in. This device of pirates appears, of course, everywhere, and had been used in some of the surviving stories from which Shakspere appears to have borrowed other materials.

After the family has been tragically scattered, it must be happily assembled again. The device chosen for this was that of Apollonius, with everyone assembled before the abbess-mother for recognitions all around. This story also had the separation of the parents at sea, though not directly by shipwreck, and a pirate separation of the daughter, as well as a good wreck or so besides. Greene's *Menaphon* probably furnished the name Menaphon for the character of that name in *Errors*. In the story, husband and wife with small son were separated by shipwreck, and then later mother and son were separated by pirates. In *Menaechmi* also one twin had been stolen. Whether these instances had any specific influence on Shakspere's plot it is impossible to say; but they belonged to the large available assortment from which he shaped his own devices.

For the geography, the story now begins at Syracuse and ends at Ephesus; and alongside of Ephesus, as he supposed, was Epidamnus, which became Epidamium. Corinth was thus a good center through which to reshuffle the family, so that part of it could go on to Ephesus and vicinity, and the rest return to Syracuse. Since Tarentum of *Menaechmi* was no longer needed, it was discarded. At no place in the plot has Shakspere borrowed any feature as such. The plan is always his. Throughout, his genesis is through analysis and synthesis. The starting point is each time *Menaechmi*, but the end product is an "original" creation.

The plot determined, it had to be ordered according to the obligatory five-act system for a play, whether or not these rhetorical divisions were actually to be observed on the stage. Again, *Menaechmi* is the point of departure. *Menaechmi* had centered its errors first around the *meretrix* and then around the wife. Shakspere substitutes the wife in this function of the *meretrix*. Thus the wife is brought immediately "front stage," and kept there throughout the play, almost submerging the *meretrix*. So the machinery that had surrounded the *meretrix* now functions around the wife. In *Menaechmi*, first the servant and then the *meretrix* mistakes the visiting twin, and invites him in, and he finally accepts the invitation of the *meretrix*. In *Errors*, first the servant and then the wife invites the visiting twin, who accepts the invitation of the wife and goes in. The two invitations serve for the endings of the first two acts, the protasis; the acceptance prepares for the third act as the protatic decision at the end of the second act should do. Thus in *Menaechmi* the visiting twin gets the meal which the *meretrix* had prepared for the resident one. Similarly in the third act of *Errors* the visiting twin gets the meal—we hope well before the racket started—which the wife had prepared for her husband. In *Menaechmi*, the parasite of the resident twin arrived to make a scene at the end of the meal. In *Errors*, it is the husband who arrived to make the scene. Here the shut-out husband in *Amphitruo* may have given some suggestion for the device, but did not either originate it or furnish detail. So the machinery of the first three acts has been adapted from *Menaechmi*.

In *Menaechmi*, the visiting twin is taken for mad, thus involving his brother, till accidental confrontation of the two brings recognition. In *Errors*, the visiting twin is also taken for mad, involving his brother, so that at the end of the fourth act he and his servant are, attempting to leave Ephesus but are shunted into an abbey, where in the fifth act general confrontation and recognition take place. In *Menaechmi*, a cloak and *spinter* are used to produce the complications which arouse the wife and lead to the suggestion that her husband is mad. In *Errors*, a chain (with some assistance from a ring) has been used to serve the same function, as more suited to the stage. Again, the machinery of *Menaechmi* has been adapted into a new structure. To give motive force to this machinery, Shakspere has changed the sharping of Epidamnus in *Menaechmi* into the witchery of Ephesus for *Errors*, and has brought it forward at the end of each act in rising sequence of intensity to the final explosion. Yet again, the machinery and motivation of the five-act structure have been adapted from *Menaechmi*; but the structure, as such, of *Menaechmi* has played no vital part. The plan was Shakspere's. Genesis has come from analysis and synthesis into an "original" structure. Some of the actual instances which influenced Shakspere may well have been in the numerous treatments which have perished. But we evidently have the chief sources from which the structure of *Errors* was evolved.

It will be apparent that the structure of *Errors* is adapted completely from that of *Menaechmi*, with only the recognition device from Apollonius. The adaptation is so complete that there can be no doubt that the present is the original structure of *Errors*, without possibility of another play between. The adaptation implies a thorough grasp of the plot of *Menaechmi*, though such a grasp does not of itself imply direct use of the Latin original. Such a grasp of the plot could have come from any form of the play in any language, if that form gave the complete plot.

But while Shakspere could have had his knowledge of the plot of *Menaechmi* without knowing the Latin text, yet the evidence is clear as to how he in fact did acquire his fundamental analysis of *Menaechmi*. It was Lambinus who first analyzed the play in terms of its errors, thus bringing out its fundamental structure.[13] It was because of this analysis that Shakspere called his play *The Comedy of Errors*. Various connections indicate that the explanatory notes of Lambinus also underlie *Errors*. One would acquire such information only in connection with reading and trying to understand the text. Thus these connections precede the actual construction of *Errors* and belong to the original plotting of the play.

Further, when we turn to details, *Errors* has used only the *argumentum* and two patches from the original Latin, the three forming the backbone of the play. Again, Shakspere has not attempted to translate or in any way to reproduce *Menaechmi*, but to adapt its materials to his own purposes. He may have had as good a grasp of the whole text of *Menaechmi* as he certainly did on these patches. That would account completely for his detailed grasp on the structure. That is also the simplest and most probable explanation. For the play as a whole, not merely these details, should have been drilled into him in grammar school, usually to the extent of memorization. At any rate, Shakspere evidently used these patches because predominantly they contributed to the structure, not because they were the only parts of the play he knew.

The systematic adaptation of *Menaechmi*, following the lead of the *argumentum* and the two patches which give the backbone of the play, shows that one person constructed *Errors* as it now stands. We have followed the process in detail and need not repeat it here. It is certain that there has been no haphazard reconstruction. The loose ends have their origins from the source, and are the result of insufficiently skilled, if not merely inattentive, workmanship in some details of adaptation, for in general there are conclusive indications of a careful thinking through of the very intricate structure. We are to remember that the original manuscript of *Errors* would not necessarily nor probably be edited for detail, but was supposed only to present the play in sufficient form to be shaped to the stage. Not even the most careful of surviving play manuscripts—not even those of Massinger—show the care that any modern editor would demand for print. And some are fearful indeed. *Errors* gives the impression of having been more carefully thought through than most. If any loose ends showed up in rehearsal of the stage version, they could be attended to at that stage, without carrying them back to the original manuscript. I do not recall any manuscripts where such back editing shows. The editing for the stage is always forward, and is always aimed at supplying only the minimum essential.

Shakspere, however, has not only turned materials from others, he has then continued to turn and re-turn the already turned materials in myriad ways. Within *Errors* itself, the three connected homilies of Luciana and Adriana, together with the intertwined waterdrop figure, tie a long sequence together as the work of one author, Shakspere. And of these homilies that of Luciana on the "preheminence" of man and the reasons for it gives a significant base of comparison with Hamlet's meditation on the same gloriously sorry "preheminence" of man, based on exactly the same authorities. The positions are the same, but the difference in presentation gives the measure of Shakspere's artistic growth. The relationships of these various passages guarantee that they came from the brain of Shakspere, even though at different levels of maturity.

Then there is the interlocked sequence of figures from Virgil's storm and Ovid's *scopulus*—ragged rock—which ends only in the *Tempest* of Shakspere's last play. Surely no figure was ever so fittingly turned to suit each occasion as it emerged—certainly not the inciting *scopulus* of Ovid.

These sequences of figures, within *Errors*, and particularly with other plays, have peculiar significance as reflecting the workings of Shakspere's mind. *Errors* foreshadows some of the greatest of Shakspere's works in years to come, and is of a piece with the body of those works. To take Aegeon's narration of his woes at the Duke's request, the opening lines (I, 1, 36–37) are patterned upon the opening of the similar narration of Aeneas, just as the immediately preceding lines (I, 1, 33–35) echo the request of Dido. The famous storm of Aeneas is also reflected in situation, and echoed in phraseology in this narration, as elsewhere in *Errors*. The Latin phraseology then continued to be echoed in a progressive series of figures through 2 and 3 *Henry*

VI, and as late as *Othello*. Shakspere had evidently memorized the Latin phraseology of this storm—as any grammar school was supposed to force him to do, if it got the chance—and upon emergent occasion gave it characteristic and progressive phrasing of his own. It was the literary model of all storms, and Shakspere models his literary storms upon it. Taken together, so interwoven, no one can doubt that these progressive adaptations are the work of one person, Shakspere. However it happened, this he knew, and here is his mind and hand, not those of his model Virgil. From the example and materials of Virgil, he created something typically his own.

This storm of Virgil involved a mighty rock, which serves in *Errors* its impressive function of breaking the mast in twain, and then in conjunction with Ovid's *scopulus* functions even to *The Tempest*—from almost the first to the last. This rock and appurtenances belong to Shakspere's rhetorical "properties" (any stage properties by which they may have been represented are quite a different matter), their combination being adapted to each occasion of use. These rhetorical "properties" in their clustered combinations are the physical facts which underlie "groups of images" insofar as there are groups actually, whatever Shakspere's personal prejudices may have been toward those "groups," and however he may have acquired those prejudices. They are at least a part of his "mental furniture." In this particular sequence are some of Shakspere's most famous speeches, as in *Hamlet*, *Lear*, and *Tempest*. This rock was only a rhetorical "property," but it was magnificently adorned as occasion arose; and while we may be amused to irreverence by its recurrent metamorphoses, yet we would not willingly spare any of its appearances.

We have followed the genesis and the evolving synthesis of a complex of figures in Shakspere's work. The rhetorical machinery of composition here has been variation, sometimes evidently conscious, always habitual. Erasmus never had a more brilliant practitioner of variation for *Copia Rerum et Verborum*. Here we have examined one instance of the principle as applied to one complex of figures.

The rhetorical technicalities used so persistently in Shakspere's work are only those expounded in every grammar school in Europe. It could not have been otherwise. Only an erudite person could have transcended the universal system of the time. Others would necessarily conform more or less to the only generally available system; there was nothing else to do. The fundamental question is thus the degree of conformity. The secondary is of the channels through which the contacts with the system came. Here Shakspere shows mastery of the system. But it is an "inspired" mastery, which is the result of his own genius in using the system, not of anything the system as such did to him. Ultimately, the only important thing is learning. Teaching is only one very feeble instrument toward that end. Unless the ability and the will are there, all teaching is vain. If they are, teaching is secondary. If one wants to learn, the best teachers in the world can not prevent him—the worst offer no particular problem. That is the world's hope.

Not only structure and figures, but even the very bases of human existence receive the same turning to serve the purposes of the play. In the tradition of St. Augustine, Sir Thomas Elyot in 1538 had defined *Fatum* as "the ordinance and disposition of almyghty god. Desteny, goddis prouidence." Instead of the old motivation in *Menaechmi*, etc., this fate, God's providence, is specifically used and correspondingly emphasized in *Errors* (1589?), as it is again in Shakspere's last play, *The Tempest* (1611?). This providence became beneficent by "special grace," as was emphasized in *Love's Labor's Lost*, his first play, and was thus "speciall Prouidence," as was emphasized by Hamlet. From Shakspere's first play to his last, God's providence, as the way of God to man, is upon occasion specifically invoked. It had not ceased to function in the other plays, even where it had not been specifically cited.[14] If the reader cares to examine closely, he will find that all of the serious plays have definite allusions which would warn the contemporary audience, and should, therefore, warn us of that fact. To leave out this background is to leave the contemporary Hamlet out of *Hamlet*, So, as we have seen, Shakspere uses and assumes without question the great ordered sequence of God's providence for man from dust to dust. Whether Shakspere refers directly to the doctrine of God's providence or not, it was a fundamental, if not the fundamental, doctrine of the universe—always to be assumed, but to be emphasized only when there was special need for emphasis. This was not primarily a matter of theory, or "ology." Neither was it the specific result of any "ism" (Catholicism, Protestantism, Anglicanism, Lutheranism, Calvinism, what have you). It was almost universally accepted fact; God's way to man.

This view of God's "speciall Prouidence," however, had become for the extreme Calvinist "immutable predestination." Hamlet insists unequivocally on "speciall Prouidence," and its falling sparrow, not "predestinate prouidence" as Q1 substitutes. Edmund derides those who plead "necessity" from their predestined stars as excuse for their actions. Curiously, Shakspere's congenital drunks—Cassio, Falstaff, etc.—appeal to this same doctrine of predestination for being and continuing by "necessity" in their "vocation." Certainly, the fundamental substitution of "immutable predestination" for God's "speciall Prouidence" is not presented favorably in Shakspere.

The true doctrine, promulgated inescapably in the *Catechism* of Alexander Nowell, was (and is?),

> We also assuredly believe, that the whole order of nature and changes of things, which are falsely reputed the alterations of fortune, do hang all upon God: that God guideth the course of the heaven, upholdeth the earth, tempereth the seas, and ruleth this whole world, and that all things obey his divine power, and by his divine power all things are governed: that he is the author of fair weather and of tempest, of rain and of drought, of fruitfulness and of barrenness, of health and of sickness: that of all things that belong to the sustentation and preserving of our life, and which are desired either for necessary use or honest pleasure; finally, of all things that nature needeth, he hath ever given, and yet most largely giveth abundance and plenty with most liberal hand; to this end, verily, that we should so use them as becometh mindful and kind children.
>
> M. To what end dost thou think that Almighty God hath created all these things?
>
> S. The world itself was made for man, and all things that are therein were provided for the use and profit of men.

And as God made all other things for man, so made he man himself for his own glory.[15]

In all his specific statements, Shakspere is in agreement with official Anglican doctrine (the "true Catholic" doctrine, it was claimed), not with any particular aberration of Roman Catholic or Calvinist. Even so, one feels that for these details of disagreement, Shakspere would cheerfully have said, "A plague o' all your houses!"

While all this is true, it cannot nevertheless be too strongly emphasized that always Shakspere was presenting a story, not a thesis of any kind—not even a literary thesis of any sort. For instance, Shakspere's composition shows no special theory of tragedy, beyond the fundamentals felt and held by the masses of his time. The difference is not in the theory of tragedy, or in the materials used; but in the art with which he presents conventionally accepted materials. That art uses anything usable for the purpose at hand. But how did his art know? It certainly was not taught by the aridities of Aristotle, Castelvetro, *et al.*, as such. Ideas of various sorts might serve the machinery of construction, or for various reasons might upon occasion be alluded to; but no play was ever an exemplum of any idea, not even *Love's Labor's Lost*.[16] *Errors* and *Tempest* use "goddis prouidence" heavily, but the plays are not presented to illustrate God's providence. A play may use ideas from theology, philosophy, psychology, etc. But the ideas are never anywhere woven together into a consistent system of theology, philosophy, psychology, etc., even though they may individually fit into one such consistent system. At our peril, we gather the fragments and attempt to fit them into a mosaic. We know a great deal about what Shakspere knew. Any knowledge shown in any work of Shakspere is necessarily Shakspere's knowledge—though presumably only some part of his total knowledge. He has also upon occasion used that knowledge to indicate to us what his characters thought about it. Shakspere knew all this certainly, but what he himself thought about his knowledge is a much more difficult problem to solve.

In the ordered sequence of "the ordinance and disposition of almyghty god. Desteny, goddis prouidence," man was the *naturae nexus, & vinculum.* In the order of God's providence, all nature was created for man, and in this divine plan man must obediently fulfill his assigned role. With the homily on obedience as background, Luciana delivers her homily on the "preheminence" of man in creation. Luciana's lecture on man's "preheminence" is exactly turned for Hamlet's "What a piece of worke is a man." The basic biblical texts are the same, but what a difference in the resultant sermons! In these instances, Shakspere had the same materials and the same mechanical tools for *Errors* as he had for *Hamlet, Lear, Tempest,* etc. He even had the same thoughts. But in *Errors* his "genius" had not ripened. It is not a matter of materials, of tools, even of mere mental furniture. There is that further something which we can sense but cannot define. Something materializes. As the boys learned in illustration of the rule for the colon in Lily's Latin grammar, "Quemadmodum horologij vmbram progessam sentimus, progredientem non cernimus: & fruticem aut herbam creuisse apparet, crescere autem nulli videtur: ita & ingeniorum profectus, quoniam minutis constat auctibus, ex interuallo sentitur."[17] Like the creeping of the dial's shadow, or the growing processes of nature, the development of abilities is apparent only in the process of time. But at least these materializations enable us to become aware of the progression.

From all this interlocking, it is clear that *The Comedy of Errors* is as Shaksperean as *The Tempest.* Through this Joseph's coat of turned patches from would-be Latin, Greek, and Italian, we catch glimpses of the splendor that is to be, in *Hamlet, Lear,* etc. The young man develops into the old, but is the same man still. We can see dimly, and can feebly describe, but we cannot explain even ourselves, much less a person of such myriad potentialities—"how infinite in faculty"—as Shakspere.

Originally published by T.W. Baldwin, *On the Compositional Genetics of "The Comedy of Errors"* (Urbana: University of Illinois Press, 1965): 352–70. Reprinted with the permission of the University of Illinois Press.

NOTES

1 Baldwin, *William Shakespeare Adapts a Hanging.*

2 Baldwin, *Hanging.*

3 Baldwin, *Five-Act*, pp. 763–764.

4 Baldwin, *Five-Act*, pp. 749 ff.; *Genetics 1592–1594*, pp. 238 ff.

5 *As You Like It*, II, 1, 16–17.

6 Fripp, *Shakespeare*, I, 315.

7 Baldwin, ed. *Errors* (1928), pp. x–xi.

8 Baldwin, *Genetics 1593–1594*, Chapter 1.

9 I have suffered through Gower's *Confessio* entire again, but hear no echoing agonies in Shakspere.

10 Baldwin, *Five-Act*, p. 721.

11 W. Kempe, *Education of Children*, F2r.

12 O. Winslow, *Low Comedy.*

13 See pp. 77 ff. [original publication].

14 *Romeo* inherits the stars from the source in Brooke; but even they work within God's providence, though that providence does not specially intervene for the lovers.

15 Corrie, *Catechism*, p. 147.

16 See Baldwin, *Five-Act*, pp. 579 ff.

17 *Brevissima Institutio* (1567, facs.), A4v.

Two Comedies of Errors

Harry Levin

To err is human; and if to forgive be divine, then at least it can be the temporary prerogative of the gallery gods; for it has also been repeatedly said that to understand everything is to forgive everything, and comedy may be described as an exercise in understanding. To put the matter more precisely, it is a planned confusion, created in order to be clarified: a series of misunderstandings, brought about, under the guise of chance or contrivance, by the playwright himself—who is usually at pains to keep the audience alerted at every step, so that it will end by congratulating itself on having foreseen the hazards, seen through the wiles and ruses, shared in the solution of the dilemmas, and taken a thoroughly enlightened view of the whole benighted proceeding. Comedy was defined for Shakespeare's age by Sir Philip Sidney as "an imitation of the common errors of our life, which [the poet] representeth in the most ridiculous and scornful sort that may be, so as it is impossible that any beholder can be content to be such a one." Sidney was propounding—and possibly straining—a moral argument, since he was engaged in the defense of poetry. Yet his definition suggests the relation between the spectators and the comic actor: there, but for the grace of God, go we!

We are invited to look down upon the buffoonery, to survey the scene from the sidelines in intellectual detachment, whereas we look up in an emotional identification with the tragic protagonist, tending as we do to identify ourselves with those whose qualities we most admire. Morally speaking, they are object-lessons, where the comic figures are awful examples. Not that our heroes cannot fall into error: as man strives, he strays, like Goethe's Faust. The ebullient Mayor of New York, Fiorello La Guardia, used to say, "I don't often make a mistake, but when I do, it's a beaut." This reservation could serve as a dividing line between comedy, with its many trivial mistakes, and tragedy, with its monstrously grand one. Think of *Macbeth*, of *Othello*, of *King Lear*; and if *Hamlet* seems to stand apart in this respect as in so many others, it is because the Prince tried so hard—albeit so ineffectually—to avoid making a big mistake. Your hero, for all his virtues, has his tragic flaw; and a single misstep, for him, has fatal consequences. Your buffoon is constantly waylaid by pitfalls, familiar and not terribly consequential, or else upset by pratfalls, from which he scrambles to his feet not very badly harmed, so that he may come closer to us—to the stuff of our experience— after all.

> For never was a story of more woe
> Than this of Juliet and her Romeo,

tragedy thus properly concludes, while Titus Andronicus is regarded as nothing less than "The woefull'st man that ever liv'd in Rome." Tragedy is by nature extraordinary; it envisages men and women as singular and superlative, as the most perfect paragons of woe. Comedy, having to deal with the ordinary and the realistic, is given to generalization. All this has happened before, and may happen again; take the long view; statistics never lie; and patterns of behaviour are predictable. Orlando believes that he is in a most woeful plight; but Rosalind coolly surveys the lovers of classical myth—Troilus, Leander, and so on—and generalizes, "Men have died from time to time, and worms have eaten them, but not for love." Here we are dealing not with extremes but with norms, not with unique individuals but with typical cases. When a young lover says farewell to his lady because he must go off to the wars, the crisis may well enlist our sympathetic concern. But if, while that poignant scene is taking place, an identically similar scene is taking place on the other side of the stage, and both pairs of lovers are going through the same motions at the same time, and all four are singing a quartet to music by Mozart—why, then we cannot but shrug our shoulders and comment, "*Così fan tutte*, thus all women do, it's the way of the world."

Hence it is comedy which typifies, where it is tragedy which individualizes; where tragedy observes the nice distinctions between man and man, comedy stresses those broad resemblances which make it so difficult to tell people apart. The closer the similarity between them, the easier it becomes for us to confuse them. Blunders are most easily committed when two differing alternatives closely resemble one another, though the resemblance be no more than skin-deep. "Two faces that are alike," Pascal observed, "though neither of them excites laughter in itself, make me laugh when together on account of the likeness." It was this sentence of Pascal's that Bergson amplified into his cogent theory of laughter, which found its formula in the repetition, the duplication, and the mechanization of the humane and the natural: *in fine*, a vindication of reality as against artificiality. Now there is an inherent lack of dignity—I am almost tempted to call it a loss of face—in being indistinguishable from, in always being mistaken for, someone else. If that were your problem, you might well prefer to go on living in Ephesus or Epidamnum rather than to return to Syracuse, where you could scarcely hope not to be confounded with your twin; and the moral of the two comedies before us might simply be to let well enough alone.

Those two plays, spanning a distance of some 1800 years, belong to what is perhaps the oldest continuous tradition in drama or literature, and is therefore somewhat ironically known as New Comedy. It was already established when Menander crystallized its usages; by way of the *commedia dell'arte* it furnished prototypes for both Molière and Marivaux; and it is not yet dead so long as Zero Mostel finds his way down Broadway to the Forum.

> Whilst slaves be false, fathers hard, and bawds be whorish
> Whilst harlots flatter, shall Menander flourish.

Such was Ovid's testimonial, as translated by Ben Jonson, another robust upholder of the tradition. This does not betoken the most elevated pinnacle of fame or the most elevating conception of human nature. Yet it does convey some notion of the stock types that keep reappearing in varied combinations throughout the repertory, motivated by a hard-boiled ethic—or, if you prefer, a single-minded psychology: "a niggardly Demea...a crafty Davus...a flattering Gnatho,... a vainglorious Thraso," each summed up by Sidney in a single trait. For, in that constricting geometrical world, motivation is mechanized, and human beings react like automata. The young are animated mainly by sexual appetites, as the old are by monetary considerations; while the perennial conflict between them is abetted by parasites, whose only object is feasting, and by slaves—so much cleverer than their masters—who expend the utmost resources of their cleverness to wriggle out of another beating.

Because of political pressures, New Comedy did not address itself to public issues as Aristophanes had done with his Old Comedy. Dramatists had turned from matters of state to private affairs, to the middle-class sphere of business. If the family was now the dramatic center, it was being decentralized and disrupted; and the dramatic action, so packed with previous events and offstage adventures, so limited in what actually happened on the stage, moved toward domestic reunion and enlargement. The surviving Roman comedies seem to have been adapted from Greek originals, subsequently lost. Their *dramatis personae* still have Greek names; they wear the pallium and not the toga. The background of their escapades is not Rome; and if it is not Athens, still it Hellenizes—or, as the prologue to our play from Plautus announces, it Sicilianizes (*"non atticissat, verum sicilicissitat"*). In any case, the locale was some Hellenistic city—some Mediterranean seaport where fortune veered with the winds of trade, and where piracy, shipwreck, and naval warfare were items of daily report. Though the town changes from play to play, New Comedy is invariably an urban phenomenon. The architectural proscenium of the Roman theater, with its practical doors and upper windows and niches and statues, was a stylization of a street or a square, leading to a harbor on one side (the Piraeus) and to a marketplace on the other (the Agora).

Though that mode of presentation had been drastically transformed during the Renaissance, the Italian designers preserved these associations in the perspective vistas they devised. Pastoral called for woodland scenery, tragedy for temples and palaces, and comedy for shops and domiciles. Something of the tradition has persisted on the stages for vaudeville and burlesque, where a drop-curtain close to the footlights surrounds the fast-talking comedians with an atmosphere of downtown. It was theater in the flat, not in the round, accommodating a drama which was linear rather than plastic. The result may seem too thin for performance without music, as if Hart's libretto for *The Boys from Syracuse* were performed without Rodgers' score. Roman comedy, true to its emphasis on externals and appearances, seldom permitted more than the merest glimpse of what went on behind those inviting façades. The distinctive feature of its setting were the doorways, which represented conveniently neighboring houses. Between them flowed the continual traffic of characters, and most of their interchanges took place at the thresholds—whence other characters would emerge periodically, slapping their thighs and holding their sides, to bring us up-to-date by divulging the goings-on within.

Such a theatrical genre, depending so much upon monologue and narration, must sound rather static to modern tastes; yet the Romans looked on Plautus as the master not of the *modus statarius* but of what they termed the *modus motorius*, the method of movement. He was the most popular of their playwrights, partly because of his racy language and frisky verse, but chiefly because of his sustained animation, which offered their comedians opportunities for slapstick, pantomime, and gags *ad libitum*. In short, he seemed to have that comic energy, that proverbial *vis comica*, which was to be so regrettably deficient in the later and smoother Terence. Terence, never the audience's favorite, was to achieve his greatest success as a text for schools, providing many centuries with a model of elegant style and a mine of sententious quotations. Shakespeare, in his day, was compared to both Plautus and Terence by his earliest critic, Francis Meres. Shakespeare may have had small Latin, by Ben Jonson's standards of erudition; but we cannot afford to be so exacting with him; and the internal evidence from his plays argues a fair acquaintance with certain standard Latin authors. There is even an accredited rumor that, before entering the theater, he had taught in a country school, where the curriculum would have consisted of very little else.

It was not surprising then that Shakespeare, as a journeyman playwright hitherto occupied with a cycle of unclassical English histories, should want to test the range of his medium by experimenting with a Latinate comedy, along with his early experiment in pseudo-Roman tragedy. "Seneca cannot be too heavy," Polonius would boast when announcing the Players, "nor

Plautus too light." If *Titus Andronicus* is indeed a heavy-handed attempt at Senecan melodrama, *The Comedy of Errors* is surely a light-fingered rehandling of a Plautine original. It is not appreciably an improvement, according to Hazlitt. Yet A.W. Schlegel declared that Shakespeare's play was "perhaps the best of all written or possible *Menaechmi.*" (And there were countless others, such as Trissino's *Simillimi.*) Without begging the question, let us consider those conflicting possibilities. We know that *The Comedy of Errors* was accorded a gala production, by the legal gentlemen of Gray's Inn during the Christmas season of 1594, probably two or three years after it was first publicly produced. A contemporary record, which dutifully notes Shakespeare's debt to Plautus, tells us that the festive occasion prompted such crowds and confusions that "it was ever afterwards called *The Night of Errors.*"

The generic title of Shakespeare's play sorts with any comedy or revel, and it has a lost precedent in a *History of Error*, recorded as played in 1577. Indeed the key-word would almost seem to have had the force of a technical term. As a schoolboy, if not as a schoolmaster, Shakespeare could have read Plautus in the edition of Lambinus; so T.W. Baldwin has shown in his massive studies of Shakespeare's modest Latinity. It is noteworthy that the commentary of Lambinus on the *Menaechmi* marks each successive twist and turn of the plot with the Latin verb *errare* or the noun *error*. Moreover, there is another term which ought to be considered in this connection, and which was introduced by the Elizabethan fugleman, George Gascoigne, as the title of his play, *The Supposes*. By a coincidence worthy of two such comedies, *The Supposes* had likewise been acted at Gray's Inn in 1566. This was a free translation of the prose version of Ariosto's comedy, *Gli Suppositi*, and it was to furnish Shakespeare—who takes cognizance of "counterfeit supposes" in *The Two Gentlemen of Verona*—with the underplot for his *Taming of the Shrew*. Ariosto's title literally means "the supposed" in the masculine plural or, more colloquially, "the substitutes."

In the Italian literary comedy, the *commedia erudita*, which is another branch of New Comedy, there is always someone who is deceived and someone else who does the deceiving. One of the most famous is entitled *Gl' Ingannati*, or "The Deceived," and its twin brother and sister were borrowed by Shakespeare for *Twelfth Night*. Still another, more objectively, is entitled *Gl' Inganni*, or "The Deceits," putting its stress upon the process and not the persons involved. Gascoigne's supposes are the substitutions or deceptions of Ariosto's deceivers. Though Gascoigne does not invoke Plautus or Terence in his prologue, as Ariosto did, he formulates the device. These are not to be the suppositions, the premises or hypotheses, of scholastic disputation:

> But, understand, this our Suppose is nothing else but a mistaking or imagination of one thing for another. For you shall see the master supposed for the servant, the servant for the master; the freeman for a slave, and the bondslave for a freeman; the stranger for a well-known friend, and the familiar for a stranger. But, what? [the explanation concludes, not very flatteringly,] I suppose that even already you suppose me very fond that have so simply disclosed unto you the subtleties of these our Supposes, where otherwise, indeed, I suppose you should have heard almost the last of our Supposes before you could have supposed any of them aright.

A prologue is hardly needed to start the game or give away the show. The respective poses of the supposed master and the supposed servant, et cetera, are spelled out by the exposition. If that is not explicit enough for the reader, the printed text (the quarto collection known as *The Posies of George Gascoigne*, with further wordplay on the metaphorical flowers of poesy) has twenty-five marginalia pointing out each suppose as it occurs in the play.

Thus, when the heroine confides to her nurse that her father's putative servant is the hero in disguise, the speech is overtly tagged "The first suppose, and ground of all the supposes." As they proceed, and the changes are rung upon the situations, the marginal epithets are varied. "A crafty suppose," "A knavish suppose," "A shameless suppose"—the adjectives serve more or less synonymously for the disguises, the intrigues, and the lies. When somebody is duly befuddled by them, it is "A doltish suppose." And it is paradoxically marked as "A right suppose" or "A true suppose" when anyone speaks more truly than he realizes, with the ensuing effect of dramatic irony. Among the many Italianate supposes, there is only one which can be classified as an error in the Shakespearean sense: a misconception brought about by accident rather than by deliberate manipulation. This is the circumstance whereby the servant pretending to be the master really turns out to be the long-lost son of the rival suitor; and it is highly significant that the quondam master, who is the *ci-devant* servant, curses the cruel and capricious goddess Fortuna for having revealed what he calls in his naïve pride "our subtle supposes."

In this regard, the comedy of *The Supposes* does not quite live up to the observation of Francesco De Sanctis on Machiavelli's *Mandragola* (or *Mandrake*): that chance plays no part there, that all the mischief is attributable to the malign contrivance of human will. "In the reproof of chance," Nestor will observe in *Troilus and Cressida*, "Lies the true proof of men." *La Mandragola* may well be one of the toughest plays ever written, just as Machiavelli's *Prince* may well be one of the toughest guides to politics; but, as such, it is no more than an extreme application of the tough-minded code that prevails throughout New Comedy. This, in turn, helps to explain why, when a certain W.W. (probably the minor Elizabethan poet William Warner) published a slightly abridged translation of the *Menaechmi* in 1595, it was characterized on the title page as "A pleasant and fine conceited comedy taken out of the most excellent witty poet Plautus: chosen purposely from out the rest, as least harmful and yet most delightful." W.W.'s choice may throw some light on why Shakespeare chose the *Menaechmi* as the one object of his direct imitation within the sphere of Roman comedy; for it is altogether untypical in its all but complete reliance on chance and not on contrivance, not mischief but sheer luck. As the translator promises, it contains, "much pleasant error."

True, it has its professional embodiments of greed and lust in the parasite and the prostitute; but even they intend no harm until their respective claims have been balked; and then the harmful truths, the tales they tell out of school, make clear that they too are victims of the general imbroglio. We are at the roulette table, not the chessboard, here. There is no plotting or counterplotting, in a Machiavellian sense. The sole plotter is the playwright, and whatever that ingenious trickster hatches is fobbed off on us as a trick of fate, a practical joke on the part of providence. For here, with these *gemini*, the mistaken identity is not deliberately cultivated through impersonation or disguise; it is not a pose, a suppose, or an imposture; it is a freak of nature, *lusus naturae*, which Coleridge advises us to accept as a postulate. And Coleridge philosophizes—as is his wont—about farce, distinguishing between it and proper comedy as the basis for a distinction between the possible and the probable. A set of identical twins, leading different lives, constitutes an improbable possibility. The distinction is sometimes drawn in terms of character and plot: farce tends to subordinate the former to the latter. Two characters sufficiently alike, so that each may fit interchangeably into the other's situation, cannot afford to possess distinguishing characteristics.

The *donnée* of Plautus, the initial improbability, was complicated to the very limits of the possible when Shakespeare dared to redouble his twins by providing his pair of protagonists with a brace of retainers and thereby to quadruple his *duplex* plot. If that was a reduction to absurdity, absurdity is man's lot as the Existentialists have redefined it, and what should a farce be if not wholly absurd? Shakespeare again used Plautus to outdo Plautus, drawing upon a play so frequently readapted that Jean Giraudoux could call his version of it *Amphitryon 38*—and that must have been a conservative reckoning. There, however, the double identities are not natural but supernatural. Jupiter, whose powers of metamorphosis endowed him with so many advantages in his amorous exploits, deliberately assumes the person of Amphitryon, in order to lie with Alcmena, the absent general's wife. Jupiter's equerry Mercury makes his appearance in the person of Sosia, Amphitryon's slave; and the opening scene, with those two opposite numbers confronting each other, heralds the scene of the homecoming general, where the false Sosia manages to keep the true Amphitryon out of his own house. These are among the most effective doorway scenes in Roman comedy.

But the play is not a comedy, strictly speaking; it is—and Mercury's prologue coins the term for criticism—a tragicomedy, because it commingles human beings and gods. Nothing short of a *deus ex machina* can resolve the husband's jealousy. The *tragicomoedia* is rounded out with the miraculous announcement that Alcmena has been delivered of two sons at once, Iphicles and Hercules, respectively the scions of Amphitryon and Jupiter, siblings who are far from identical. Unlike the anxious and suspicious Amphitryon, who has the best grounds for his anxieties and suspicions, the two Menaechmuses are bland and blithe. In fact, the first, a local citizen, begins by telling off his wife, in what appears to be a Punch-and-Judy relationship. He is a solid man of affairs, who later favors us with a monologue about his many clients; but for the nonce he is resolved to put aside business for pleasure, the working-day world for a holiday, a day off, a night out. The hanger-on, Peniculus, smells it in the air: *"Furtum, scortum, prandium"* ("Pinching, wenching, lunching"). Whether we name it a lark or a bird of another feather—a bat, in Johann Strauss's slang, *Die Fledermaus*—it presupposes a release from the rules, a dispensation from the routine duties of existence: in short, that carnival spirit which is the first condition of comedy.

By way of contrast, the other Menaechmus—Sosicles, the stay-at-home from Syracuse, who has turned traveler in search of his twin—makes a serious entrance, bent on his objective. With his presence, the errors begin to operate, through the congenial modes of feasting and love-making; and, since he is their beneficiary, he gaily falls in with them. All work and no play would make Jack a dull boy. Consequently the responsible John Worthing, J.P., invents a younger brother, as a playboy role in which to indulge his irresponsible whims, and christens him—with one of Wilde's verbal paradoxes—Ernest. He is soon rivaled in this masquerade by his frivolous friend, Algernon Moncrieff. So might every man wish to have a surrogate self, whose actions would be freed from inhibitions. Now Jack and Algy, in their act of the pseudo-Ernest, are conspirators. There is no conspiracy whatsoever in Epidamnum, despite the punning warnings of the visitor's slave Messenio that no one ever escapes *"sine damno,"* without damage. The visiting Menaechmus Sosicles, like Gogol's government clerk mistaken for an inspector general, is wined and dined and bribed and courted by the corrupt villagers. The larks drop, already roasted, into his mouth.

Like the Russian Hlestakov, the Syracusan Sosicles accepts his windfalls with insouciance; and, as he catches on a bit, he plays up to his benefactors with more and more impudence. When he leaves the prostitute's house, and her maid runs after him with a chain to be left at the goldsmith's shop for repair, he quickly recovers from his surprise and inquires if there be not some bracelets to go along with it. The Epidamnian Menaechmus, who is like his brother psychologically as well as physically (environment seeming to count for less than heredity in their temperaments), has an analogous reaction when he is offered an unsolicited purse. When the stranger is taken for a madman through what he takes to be madness on the part of the wife and her father, he joins in the fun and feigns a mad scene to fend them off. All the knots are bound to be disentangled as soon as both of the Menaechmi encounter; but that fraternal reunion is suspensefully delayed; and when the brothers finally meet, the built-up impact produces on both sides—so to speak—a double take. It is Messenio who puts one and one together, explaining to his Menaechmus that the other Menaechmus is his mirror: "*speculum tuum.*"

And it is Messenio who, on gaining his freedom, pronounces the last words: since his master's brother will be returning to their native Syracuse, there will be an auction of his goods and chattels—including, if there are any bidders, his wife. The *Menaechmi*, for all its climactic pacing, shows its age with Messenio's farewell speech, not so much in his conventional bid for the plaudits of the spectators as in its incidental revelations of ancient mores, the manumission of the slave and the callous treatment of the wife. *The Comedy of Errors*, omitting the Roman feature of the parasite, doubles Messenio into the two Dromios, who are presumably bondservants. It does not alleviate the number of beatings they receive; but these are matters of farcical convention rather than social custom; and besides, like the marginal glosses in Gascoigne's *Supposes*, they register the cross-purposes of the play. (Even Ariel, in *The Tempest*, observes the conventions of Plautine slavery.) As for the Roman matron, Plautus wastes no sympathy on her; her own father judges her from a one-sidedly masculine point of view; and she should be easily forgotten, since she is namelessly designated as *Uxor* or *matrona*, whereas even the *meretrix* has a tradename, Erotium.

Shakespeare, in amplifying the wife's role, reduced the Courtesan's. The pivotal banquet is served not at her hang-out, the Porpentine, but at the home of Antipholus, the Phoenix; while he, a normally faithful husband, seeks out her company only after he has reason to suspect his wife. The latter, Adriana, inherits the Uxor's misunderstanding with her husband; but Shakespeare sublimates it to a plane of genuine, if too possessive, conjugal love. Moreover, he endows her with a sister, to be courted by the bachelor Antipholus; and Luciana proves to be a *raisonneuse*, a mouthpiece of moderation, so that the twins take their place in the great Shakespearean debate on marriage, along with Kate and Petruchio or Rosaline and Beroune or Beatrice and Benedick. Shakespeare's characters move, as usual, in a Christian ethos. The perplexed traveler swears, "as I am a Christian," and— approached by the Courtesan—echoes Christ bidding Satan avaunt. The change in the ethical climate may be noted by the shift from Epidamnum, which is nonetheless mentioned along the way, to Ephesus. Plautus' Syracusans fear Epidamnum because it is an emporium of sharp practice, peopled by rogues and harlots and standard comic types. Shakespeare's Syracusans are cautious too. "They say this town is full of cozenage," the traveling Antipholus warns himself.

Notwithstanding, the Ephesians he meets are not "disguised cheaters." They are, as the traveling Dromio puts it, "a gentle nation," who "speak us fair, give us gold." Shakespeare is more in his milieu where the setting is a room in the palace—or, better still, another part of the forest—than in the mercantile zones of New Comedy. It is not coney-catching but witchcraft and sorcery that envelop Ephesus in its mysterious aura. This is a place of strangers and sojourners, to echo the patron saint of travelers *in partibus infidelium*, the Apostle Paul. Not without pertinence, it has been suggested that Paul's Epistle to the Ephesians, with its injunctions for husbands and wives, and for servants and masters, may have been in the background of Shakespeare's mind. His far-flung romance of *Pericles* reaches its resolution in the famous Temple of Diana at Ephesus. Some of the elements of the late play are present in the early one, notably the vicissitudes of a family progressing through misadventure to recognition. Shakespeare as yet had no need of Gower's folktale; the story was latent nearer at hand in the *Captivi* of Plautus, where the old father, Hegio, seeks and recovers two sons captured and brought up elsewhere under the circumstances of two cities at war.

The framing figure of Egeon contributes an emotional tension, at the very outset, to what would otherwise have remained a two-dimensional drama. His protracted expository narrative—a specimen of the rhetoricians' *narratio*—is enlivened by the awareness that it is a plea, and probably a vain one, for his life. Rightly he blames his misfortunes on hap; for nowhere else in Shakespeare can a whole pattern of incidents be so directly traceable to sheer unmitigated contingency. Egeon is hopeless and helpless because he is hapless. But this is not to be a novel by Thomas Hardy; it is a knockabout farce, where bad fortune will change soon enough into good. The next scene not only offers a hint that the new arrival is one of Egeon's sons—through the mix-up of the Dromios—and that the other son is just around the corner, but virtually guarantees the ransom, since the sum mentioned in both scenes is exactly a thousand marks. Coincidence has already done its best, as well as its worst, and a happy ending was implicit from the beginning. Meanwhile, the sequence of farcical episodes has been framed by the tragicomic overplot; and Shakespeare, by enlisting our sympathies for the fate of Egeon, has charged the air with a suspense which cannot be resolved until the appointed hour of execution, five o'clock in the afternoon.

Both of the Antipholuses have appointments at that hour, one with the Merchant and the other with the Goldsmith; and since it is noon when the Syracusan arrives, and since the Ephesian Dromio gets into his troubles over the question of dinner-time, the time-scheme is firmly fixed within the course of the afternoon. There are frequent reminders of its passing, to reinforce the structure of occurrences. Adhering to the classical unities, as he does just once again in *The Tempest*, Shakespeare takes the traditional city street as his horizon, moving his characters back and forth from port to mart and in and out of the various doorways between. The play would seem to lend itself very conveniently to the simultaneous stage of a great hall, such as that of Gray's Inn, where there or four free-standing or so-called mansions would have corresponded to the labeled locations of the play: the Phoenix, the Porpentine, the other inn, the Centaur, and the ultimate abbey near the place of execution. On the other hand, the production at Stratford, Ontario, demonstrated how well the play could adapt to the multi-level mobility of an Elizabethan playhouse.

The problem of staging ought not to be unduly strained by the presupposition of identical twins. To be sure, the difficulty raised by the twins of two sexes in *Twelfth Night*, which would have been solved when both parts were acted by young men, is virtually insoluble in the modern theater. But, granted an approximate equivalence of stature, plus the same costuming and make-up, the Antipholuses and the Dromios ought to look enough alike to confuse the other characters without confusing the audience. After all, it is our premise that we are brighter than the people on the stage. In the Roman theater, where the employment of masks eliminated the facial disparities, Plautus had to give a tassel to Mercury and a feather to Jupiter so that they would not be confused with Sosia and Amphitryon. The festival at Stratford, Connecticut, I am told, has been casting the same actor as both twins, thereby combining histrionic virtuosity with artistic economy. This directorial tactic must create a bigger dilemma than the one it endeavors to solve, since the audience can never know the moment of catharsis, the visual illumination of seeing the two confusing elements discriminated from one another and exhibited side by side.

That way schizophrenia lies—which does not mean that it would be unproduceable in the Theater of the Absurd. It might turn out to be something in the vein of Pirandello, if not a dramatization of *Dr. Jekyll and Mr. Hyde*. But the actual predicament is that of two personalities forced into the same role, rather than that of one personality playing two roles, since the resident twin has the contacts and continuities, and the roving twin intercepts them, as it were. Their twinship is a sort of human pun. Tweedledum has got to match Tweedledee, more or less, in order to be taken for him; and yet, the less he feels like him, the more the dramatic irony. Plautus did not discriminate between his two very sharply; the discrepancies that emerged largely took the concrete form of objects which fell into the wrong hands; otherwise the interconnecting characters did not seem to notice much difference. The married Menaechmus was angry from the first, so that each new chagrin could be rationalized to his mood. The interloping Menaechmus, though considerably bewildered, had no cause for being dissatisfied with his reception. Neither of them was above the temptation to profit from the *contretemps*; and the interloper finally engaged in a stratagem of his own, when he pretended to be a lunatic.

That sort of conduct is what we have agreed to label a suppose, a deception which is cultivated rather than casual. The most notable fact about Shakespeare's comedy is that it has no supposes, only errors: only mischances, no contrivances by anybody except Shakespeare himself. There is no parallel scene of pretended madness; Shakespeare must have been saving the theme for *Hamlet*. Here the suspected madman, like Malvolio, protests his sanity. He does not act; he is acted upon; and Shakespeare, ever the psychologist, makes a good deal more out of the attempted diagnosis of demonic possession. He makes the exorcism so very painful, and goes so far out of his way to substitute the grim-visaged schoolmaster, Dr. Pinch, for the Plautine Medicus that we sense a virtual obsession possibly connected with Holofernes, the pedant of *Love's Labour's Lost*, or with some other reminiscence from Shakespeare's own teaching days. It is as if the nightmare came so close that the misunderstood hero dare not pretend to be hallucinated. The customary rhetorical questions of comedy, in these mouths, become questions of existential bewilderment or expressions of cosmic vertigo: Do I dream or wake? Do we see double? Is he drunk or sober? Is she a liar or a fool? Who is crazy? Who is sane?

Contrasted with this constant inner questioning, the caricature of Dr. Pinch seems externalized. He is the sole humorous personage of the play, in the Jonsonian usage, a man of obvious quirks and eccentric appearance; if the others are funny, it is because of the plights they find themselves in. No, there is one other exception, though she is peripheral and appears but once on the stage. Nevertheless New Comedy was capable of casting offstage characters in title roles, as with the *Casina* of Plautus. This heroine, invoked indifferently as Luce or Nell, is generically a Dowsabell or, for that matter, a Dulcinea—a kitchenmaid whose formidable proportions are vividly verbalized by the wrong Dromio, her brother-in-law, who is still quaking from the shock of having been claimed by her as a husband. This is the vulgar parallel to Adriana's claim upon her brother-in-law. Dromio's description of his brother's Nell, elicited by his master's queries as straight man, is a set-piece in the manner of Launce or Lancelot Gobbo, and may well have been assigned to the same comedian. With its geographical conceits, comparing the parts of her person to foreign countries, it might almost be a ribald reversal of Othello's traveler's tales when wooing Desdemona.

But it is by no means a farfetched gag, since it embodies—on a more than miniature scale—the principal contrast of the play: on the one hand, extensive voyaging; on the other, intensive domesticity. In using an underplot which burlesques the main plot, Shakespeare employs a device as old as Medwall's interlude of *Fulgens and Lucres*, where the rival suitors have servants who court the mistress's maid under the diagrammatic designations of A and B. With Nell, as with the demanding Adriana, the normal approaches of courtship are reversed. The closest we come to romantic love is the sketchy relationship between her brother-in-law and her husband's sister-in-law. Yet that is a good deal closer than Plautus brings us; and though both masters are suitably mated in the end, the concluding dialogue of the servants emphasizes the pairing of twins, not spouses. Parents and children are reunited, family ties are reasserted; but Dromio of Syracuse remains a free agent. His greatest moment has been the midpoint of the play, when he acted as doorkeeper and kept out his fellow Dromio, as well as that Dromio's master, the master of the house. This is the one point before the dénouement where Shakespeare permits his twins to meet and talk, and the door between them seems to keep the mutual visibility fairly obscure.

It is interesting that their brief colloquy reverts to the doggerel style of *Ralph Roister Doister*, the oldest English imitation of Plautus, in its stichomythic interchanges of rhyming fourteeners. This is the main scene (the first of Act III) that Shakespeare borrowed from the *Amphitryon* (the first of Act I), eking out the comedy of the *Menaechmi* with the underplot of the two Sosias to complete—with a vengeance—the Elizabethan requirements for a double plot. He develops it to the very pitch of the dramatic subversion that he has been exploiting, with the outsider inside and the insider excluded, the stranger in possession of the house and the householder cast into outer darkness. Both parties are translated, as Quince will affirm of

Bottom, and they could not have been so completely translated, had they not been facsimiles to begin with. The most fundamental alteration that Shakespeare made in his Plautine material was to shift the focus from the homekeeping twin to his errant brother, whose sobriquet, Antipholus Erotes, may be a garbling of Erratus or Errans. The *Menaechmi* starts out with the other twin, and with the reassurance of familiar surroundings, into which the disturbing factor will be injected. *The Comedy of Errors* starts with the newcomer, and his impressions of strangeness: the witchery of Ephesus, not the bustle of Epidamnum.

Having a head start, and having to alternate scenes with Antipholus of Ephesus who does not appear until the third act, Antipholus of Syracuse has a much larger part: roughly 272 lines to the other's 207. The disproportion is even clearer between the parts of the two Dromios: there the score is Syracuse 233, Ephesus 162. The *Menaechmi*, though it is the shorter play, has fewer characters, and longer speeches; accordingly, its Syracusan twin has 251 lines, whereas the Epidamnian twin has 300. We therefore tend to visualize what goes on in the Latin play from the denizen's standpoint, and what goes on in the English play from the alien's. Epidamnum could be any old town, where everything should be in its place, *in situ*; where everyone expects his fellow citizen, Menaechmus, to go through the round of his habitual day. No one could suspect that there was another Menaechmus, whose chance encounters would lead to incongruities and discontinuities, except for his one follower, who shares and compounds his perplexities. Ephesus is another story, however. We are put off at once by the hostile reception of Egeon; and when the two other foreigners enter, Antipholus and Dromio, they are the first of those names whom we have met.

We share their misgivings all the more readily because they too have been risking their lives, and because the object of their travels has so far eluded them. When this Antipholus gets caught up in his brother's existence, it is as new to us as it is to him. We participate in an adventure; what might be matter-of-fact to an Ephesian is, for him and ourselves, a fantasy out of the *Arabian Nights*. "What error drives our eyes and ears amiss?" he wonders, after Adriana accosts him, reprimands him, and invites him to dinner. And tentatively he resolves,

> Until I know this sure uncertainty,
> I'll entertain the offer'd fallacy.

Then, after dinner, smitten with Luciana, he asks her to unfold the mystery:

> Teach me, dear creature, how to think and speak.
> Lay open to my earthy gross conceit,
> Smother'd in errors, feeble, shallow, weak,
> The folded meaning of your words' deceit.

But the undeception does not come about until all the participants in this "sympathized one day's error"—for so the Abbess sums it up—have sought the illumination of sanctuary within her Priory. In that cloistered serenity, far from urban corruption, the deferred recognition scenes can coincide at long last. The confessions and counteraccusations piece together a step-by-step recapitulation of how "these errors are arose." The maternal figure of the Abbess is something of a surprise, as Bertrand Evans points out in his recent study, *Shakespeare's Comedies*. Running through all of them, Mr. Evans finds their common structural principle in what he calls a "discrepant awareness." Characteristically, the humor springs from "the exploitable gulf spread between the participants' understanding and ours."

In Shakespeare's development of this resource, *The Comedy of Errors* is primordial, since it is his single comedy where the audience knows all, and all the characters are in the dark. Mr. Evans' suggestive analysis can be perfectly fitted to the *Menaechmi*. Plautus is always saying, "I told you so." But Shakespeare is always asking, "Can such things be?" The exceptional position of the Abbess not only rounds out the recognitions; it lays the spell of wonderment again upon the concluding scene; and it reminds us, as other touches do, of Shakespeare's romances. Even within the venal and angular precincts of New Comedy, he can make us aware of unpathed waters, undreamed shores, and things in heaven and earth that philosophy has not fathomed. Yet philosophers can tell us much, particularly about the processes of learning; and Bergson tells us much about *The Comedy of Errors* when, in his essay on laughter, he borrows a concept from optics and writes of "the reciprocal interference of series." At length we can put our supposes or errors down in scientific terminology. "A situation is invariably comic," Bergson explains, "when it belongs simultaneously to two independent series of events, and is capable of being interpreted in two entirely different meanings at the same time."

It would be hard to conceive of a better illustration than the two different series of events in the respective days of the two Antipholuses, and the ways in which they are imperceptibly crisscrossed. Antipholus of Syracuse has no particular expectations or plans. He derives a gratuitous enjoyment from the inexplicable services rendered and favors due his brother. This interference or substitution induces a certain amnesia on the brother's part, when the bills come in and the witnesses testify; naturally, he cannot remember the items attested. As one error engenders another suspicion is bound to mount and disgruntlement spread, rising to their climax in hot pursuit toward the madhouse or the jail, and ending at the Priory. Now the brunt of these displacements is borne by Antipholus of Ephesus. Of all those discomfited, he comes nearest to being a victim of the situation, since it is his situation, in the last analysis. It is his routine which is broken up, his standing in the community undermined, his normal expectations interfered with; and—to add insult to injury—he is expected to pay for what he has been deprived of. In short, the rug has been pulled out from under the very preconditions of his existence.

Other people's bafflement can be fun, and Plautus makes the most of it. From our spectatorial overview, we need not worry too much about what befalls whom. We are not playing blind man's buff, we are watching the game. But Shakespeare, himself the father of twins, makes us feel what it is like to be this or that Antipholus—all the difference in the world, if we started by being the other one—and the interplay of more or less exact counterparts ends by demonstrating *a fortiori* the uniqueness of the individual. When Adriana and her husband appeal to the Duke, the stories they tell of their day's experience are mutually contradictory; but the discrepancies would disappear if the shadow of the interfering Antipholus were retraced through their reciprocal patterns. (Latter-day readers or viewers may be reminded of the Japanese story or film, *Rashomon*.) It has been a lesson for Adriana, brought home by the gentle rebuke of the Abbess. For Antipholus of Ephesus, it has been an eye-opening misadventure. Apparently, he has never felt the impetus that has incited his brother and his father to sally forth in search of him. Unconcerned with his foundling origin, he rejoices in the good graces of the Duke and takes for granted the solid comforts of his Ephesian citizenship.

What greater shock for him, then, than to bring a party of fellow citizens home to his well-established household for lunch and to discover that household pre-empted by roistering strangers, to be shut out in the street, to have one's own door slammed in one's own face? Or is it one's own? The sense of alienation, that *Verfremdungseffekt* so characteristic of Brecht and of the twentieth-century theater, is all the greater when our image of ourselves depends for its corroboration upon a settled context, and when we come to realize—what tragedy teaches us—that it is our destiny to be displaced. When Messenio saw the two Menaechmuses together, he declared that water was not more like water. After Shakespeare has adapted the metaphor, it stands not for an easy correspondence but for an unending quest.

> I to the world am like a drop of water
> That in the ocean seeks another drop,

Antipholus of Syracuse confesses sadly, realizing that he is less likely to find a mother and a brother than to be irretrievably lost himself. Later Adriana, addressing him as if he were Antipholus of Ephesus, likens their imperiled love to a drop of water falling into the sea; and he has a similar exchange with Luciana. The Syracusan twin is conscious that he must lose his identity in order to find it; the Ephesian twin is not; but he must, and he does. And Dromio too—both Dromios, whichever is which—must undergo their crises of identity: "Am I Dromio? Am I your man? Am I myself?"

The essence of the predicament is embodied in a comic turn which must be as old as Plautus, which I once saw enacted at the Cirque Médrano, and which has been immortalized by the Marx Brothers in one of their films. It involves both an error and a suppose, a mistaken identification and a willful imposture. Two comedians happen somehow to be dressed alike; one of them, seeking concealment and meeting the other, takes refuge in pretending to be a mirror image; whereupon the other proceeds to test his authenticity by going through a series of gestures and grimaces which he is pretty clever at matching and mimicking; but sooner or later he betrays his autonomy by making the wrong response; and the jig is up; again the chase is on. Under the circumstances, it would be a relief to be quite sure that there were two men, not one—or, for that matter, that there was one man, not two, if we could only be sure. But, given the subjective mirrors of our introspection, can we ever be absolutely certain who we are? And, given the reduplicating devices that multiply the sameness of our lives, where, if anywhere, is there any room left for the otherness of unquestionable individuality?

Modern psychological fiction is haunted by doubles, sometimes as overtly as in the tales of Hoffmann, Poe, and Dostoevsky, or in "The Jolly Corner" of Henry James, where the Black Stranger turns out to be the self that might have been. The other self—best friend, worst enemy—stares back at the poets from Heine's pallid ghost ("*Du! Doppelgänger, du bleicher Geselle!*") or Baudelaire's hypocritical reader ("*mon semblable! mon frère!*"). That *alter ego* may be daemon or devil, good angel or evil genius. It may be the retribution of conscience: Philip Drunk reprehended by Philip Sober—or, at the other extreme, the vicarious pleasure the artist enjoys in the playboy, the envy of Shem for Shaun. All this may well be a far cry from Plautine or even Shakespearean farce, to which we should be glad that we can escape. There all aberrations come home to roost and are sorted out by the happy ending; we acknowledge the error of our ways, and false suppositions are replaced by truths. No one really gets damaged in Epidamnum, and everyone enjoys a new lease of life when Egeon is ransomed and reprieved. Yet, as the philosopher Etienne Souriau concludes in his book, *Les 200,000 Situations Dramatiques*: "A comedy of errors—or of ignorances—is inherent in the condition of men, who are perpetually groping through moral shadows and playing a game of blind man's buff with their souls."

From Harry Levin, *Refractions: Essays in Comparative Literature* (New York: Oxford University Press, 1966): 128–50. Copyright © 1966 by Harry Levin. Reprinted by the permission of Oxford University Press, Inc.

Shakespeare's Comedy of Love:
The Comedy of Errors

Alexander Leggatt

In the second scene of *The Comedy of Errors*, Dromio of Ephesus meets Antipholus of Syracuse for the first time, and rebukes him for not coming home to dinner. Antipholus ignores the rebuke (which means nothing to him) and turns to a more urgent matter:

ANTIPHOLUS: Stop in your wind, sir; tell me this, I pray:
Where have you left the money that I gave you?

DROMIO E: O—sixpence that I had a Wednesday last
To pay the saddler for my mistress' crupper?
The saddler had it, sir; I kept it not.

(I. ii. 53–7)

We settle ourselves for a couple of hours of farce. The confusion seems to be on a purely material level—mistaken persons and mislaid goods. Shakespeare is keeping to the spirit of his source, the *Menaechmi* of Plautus, where the action takes place in a hard southern daylight and the issues are all practical ones.

But at the end of this first scene of confusion, Shakespeare introduces a new note. In Plautus, Epidamnum is seen as a place of danger, but danger of a prosaic and familiar kind:

> For assure your selfe, this towne *Epidamnum*, is a place of outragious expenses, exceeding in all ryot and lasciviousness: and (I heare) as full of Ribaulds, Parasites, Drunkards, Catchpoles, Cony-catchers, and Sycophants, as it can hold: then for Curtizans, why here's the currantest stamp of them in the world. Ye may not thinke here to scape with as light cost as in other places.

(II. i. p. 17)[1]

Antipholus of Syracuse sees Ephesus in quite a different way:

> They say this town is full of cozenage;
> As, nimble jugglers that deceive the eye,
> Dark-working sorcerers that change the mind,
> Soul-killing witches that deform the body,
> Disguised cheaters, prating mountebanks,
> And many such-like liberties of sin.
>
> (I. ii. 97–102)

The sleight of hand that deceives the eye, the cunning of the confidence trick, shades into something deeper and more sinister, deception and shape-shifting that attack not merely the purse but the body and soul. There are no such overtones in Plautus. Nor is there much sense of wonder in the characters; only a temporary bewilderment that is easily explained away. Shakespeare's Antipholus of Syracuse, addressed by name by a woman he has never seen before, asks, "How can she thus, then, call us by our names, / Unless it be by inspiration?" (II. ii. 165–6). In the parallel incident in *Menaechmi*, the courtesan's cook addresses Menaechmus by name, and an explanation (wrong, but reasonable) is immediately forthcoming:

> These Courtizans as soone as anie straunge shippe arrive at the Haven, they send a boye or a wench to enquire what they be, what their names be, whence they come, wherefore they come, &c. If they can by any meanes strike acquaintance with him, or allure him to their houses, he is their owne.
>
> (II. i. p. 19)

No such reassuring explanations are offered to Shakespeare's characters. At times even the audience is left in the dark, for Shakespeare takes fewer pains than Plautus to give a logical underpropping to his comic fantasy. There is nothing improbable in identical twins, but identical twins with the same name take some explaining, and Plautus is ready with the answer: "When it was tolde us that you and our father were both dead, our Graundsire (in memorie of my fathers name) chaunged mine to

Menechmus" (v.i.p. 38). Shakespeare provides *two* sets of twins with the same name, and not a word of explanation.

The Roman comedy of confusion takes place in a practical world, where nothing is inexplicable, and where the issues at stake are largely the material ones of who owns what and where the next meal is coming from. The play has a single vision and a uniform texture. But Shakespeare gives us a play in a more mixed dramatic idiom. The market-place atmosphere of Plautus is still present, but it no longer monopolizes the play; it is varied by suggestions of fantasy and mystery, and the result is a mixture of styles that goes much deeper than changes from prose to verse, or the varying of metres. It is a mixture of different ways of viewing the world, of which different dramatic styles are ultimately a reflection. Nor is the decision to mix idioms in this way artificially imposed; it springs from Shakespeare's own fresh and imaginative meditation on the central idea of Plautus, the idea of confusion. *The Comedy of Errors* is unusual in that mistaken identity is itself the primary motif, not (as in *As You Like It* or *Twelfth Night*) a technical device to aid the presentation of some other issue. Perhaps Shakespeare, before he could use mistaken identity as an instrument, had to give it a thorough examination. And in exploiting the situations arising from it, Shakespeare demonstrates that confusion, the gap of understanding between one mind and another, can exist at a deeper level than who's-got-the-chain or which-twin-is-it-*this*-time. These questions are important to the action, and much of the play's immediate comic life depends on them; but they are also signals of a deeper breakdown of understanding; the characters seem at times to inhabit different worlds, different orders of experience.

Some of this effect is created by the mingling—and, at times, the collision—of dramatic styles. In II. ii Adriana, meeting the man she thinks is her husband, attacks him passionately for straying from her, urging him to recognize that as husband and wife they are bound together in a single being, and that consequently she shares in his corruption. Taken out of context, the speech is passionate and earnest, idealistic in its view of marriage and urgent in its emotional response to the breaking of that ideal. But the context is all-important. Adriana's speech follows immediately— with no transition whatever—a racy comic turn between Dromio and Antipholus on time, falling hair and syphilis; she breaks in on two characters who are operating in quite a different dramatic world. And any chance we might have of making the transition from one mode to another and taking Adriana's speech seriously is killed by the fact that all her high talk about the closeness of the marriage bond is directed at the wrong Antipholus, who—after listening to about forty lines on how closely he and Adriana are bound together—asks innocently, "Plead you to me, fair dame?" (II. ii. 146). Or consider the following passage:

ANTIPHOLUS S: The fellow is distract, and so am I;
                And here we wander in illusions.
                Some blessed power deliver us from hence!
                                    [Enter a Courtezan.
COURTEZAN: Well met, well met, Master Antipholus.
                I see, sir, you have found the goldsmith now.
                Is that the chain you promis'd me to-day?
ANTIPHOLUS S: Satan, avoid! I charge thee, tempt me not.
DROMIO S: Master, is this Mistress Satan?
ANTIPHOLUS S: It is the devil.

                                    (IV. iii. 37–45)

Here, the attitude of each character is comically dislocated. The courtesan is simply living her casual, material life, while Antipholus is struggling between heaven and hell, in a metaphysical nightmare where even a call for "some blessed power" is met by (for him) a fresh appearance of evil, and (for the audience) a comic anticlimax. The contrast is driven home, once again, by the different styles of speech—the casual chatter of the courtesan, the explosive horror of Antipholus and, on the side, Dromio's more familiar recognition of the powers of evil. This introduces us to a device we will see Shakespeare using throughout his comedies: a speech is comically dislocated by being placed in the wrong context, usually through being addressed to an unsympathetic or uncomprehending listener. The comic value of this device is obvious, and is exploited throughout the play. Yet, as with many such devices, it requires only a twist of emphasis, or a new situation, to make the effect pathetic or disturbing. The gaps of understanding between us are not always amusing. While we laugh easily enough when Adriana fires a long, emotional speech at the wrong Antipholus, it is not so funny when, later in the play, Aegeon pleads with his son to save his life, and his son refuses to acknowledge him.

The effect is to show how frail and vulnerable our attitudes and assumptions are, to bring into sharp focus the incompleteness of anything we may say or do, the fact that, however serious or important it may seem to us, there is always another viewpoint from which it is wrong, or trivial, or incomprehensible. The collisions of different minds that take place throughout *The Comedy of Errors* help to suggest this. When, for example, Adriana strikes a posture of languishing grief, Luciana's sharp comment deflates it immediately:

ADRIANA: Since that my beauty cannot please his eye,
                 I'll weep what's left away, and weeping die.
LUCIANA: How many fond fools serve mad jealousy!
                               (II. i. 114–16)

The triple rhyme clinches the point: Adriana is not even allowed the neat finality of a concluding couplet. But one might say that Luciana is getting her revenge, for earlier in the same scene she had delivered a lecture to Adriana on the necessity of order in marriage, urging that a wife should submit patiently to her husband, only to receive this reply:

A wretched soul, bruis'd with adversity,
We bid be patient when we hear it cry;
But were we burd'ned with like weight of pain,
As much, or more, we should ourselves complain.
So thou, that hast no unkind mate to grieve thee,
With urging helpless patience would relieve me;
But if thou live to see like right bereft;
This fool-begg'd patience in thee will be left.
                               (II. i. 34–41)

One of the most persistent comic points in Shakespeare is the disparity between theory and reality, the breakdown of philosophy in the face of experience—particularly when the experience is yours and the philosophy is someone else's. Throughout the play, Antipholus of Ephesus is (like his wife) the recipient of much good advice about the necessity of patience—from his friends (III. i. 85–106), from the officer who arrests him (IV. iv. 18)—in short, from people who do not really share his problems. He obviously hears this good advice once too often, and retaliates by giving Pinch an object lesson in the difficulties of philosophy: "My master preaches patience to him, and the while / His man with scissors nicks him like a fool" (V. i. 174–5).

The gap between different understandings of the world is centred on the two Antipholus brothers. In *Menaechmi* the twin brothers inhabit the same prosaic, domestic world and undergo basically the same kind of experience; in *The Comedy of Errors* not only are their characters more sharply distinguished,[2] but the difference between their experiences is more emphasized. In the words of A.C. Hamilton, Antipholus of Ephesus "endures a nightmare" while his brother "enjoys a delightful dream."[3] One is showered with gifts, money and women; the other is locked out of his house, arrested for debt and tied up as a lunatic. The difference in their experiences is signalled by a difference in style. The scene in which Antipholus of Ephesus is locked out of his house (III. i) is noisy, raucous and farcical, full of spluttering threats and bawdy insults; it is immediately followed (III. ii) by his brother's courtship of Luciana, a quiet scene of romantic feeling shot through with more subtle comic irony, a scene in which the focus is on emotional rather than on physical problems. The contrast is not rigid throughout, for Antipholus of Syracuse is involved in a good deal of knockabout farce, but it is significant that as soon as his brother appears (III. i is the latter's first scene) we are made aware of this disparity between them.

They seem to inhabit two different towns. For Antipholus of Ephesus, as for the rest of the native population (and initially for the audience), Ephesus is the familiar seaport town of Plautine comedy, a small world of commerce and domesticity, where, as E.M.W. Tillyard puts it, "everyone knows everyone else's business, where merchants predominate, and where dinner is a serious matter."[4] Shakespeare even sharpens the commercial interests of the town, giving them a distinctly unflattering emphasis. A dispute over the Duke of Syracuse's treatment of Ephesian merchants has led to "mortal and intestine jars" (I. i. 11), and to a sentence of death on any merchant from one town who visits the other. This is the predicament in which Aegeon stands in the first scene. According to the Duke, he is condemned

> Unless a thousand marks be levied,
> To quit the penalty and to ransom him.
> Thy substance, valued at the highest rate,
> Cannot amount unto a hundred marks;
> Therefore by law thou art condemn'd to die.
>
> (I. i. 22–6)

Though the point is not much developed, this crude measuring of human life in financial terms anticipates the inhuman legalism of Shylock;[5] and throughout the play there are several small touches conveying the Ephesians' narrow concern with money. The merchant who talks with Antipholus of Syracuse in the second scene is kind enough to warn him against the law; but he refuses an invitation to keep him company and join him for dinner, on the grounds that he is already engaged "to certain merchants, / Of whom I hope to make much benefit" (I. ii. 24–5). The officer who arrests Antipholus of Ephesus refuses to release him, even when told he is mad and needs treatment:

> ADRIANA: What wilt thou do, thou peevish officer?
> Hast thou delight to see a wretched man
> Do outrage and displeasure to himself?
> OFFICER: He is my prisoner; if I let him go,
> The debt he owes will be requir'd of me.
>
> (IV. iv. 111–115)

In this commercial world, Antipholus of Ephesus appears to have occupied, when the action begins, a solid and respectable place. Angelo the goldsmith describes him as "Of very reverent reputation.../ Of credit infinite, highly belov'd" (V. i. 5–6). His marriage, whatever its internal difficulties, is eminently respectable, having been arranged by the Duke himself (V. i. 137–8, 198). In the commercial and domestic spheres he inhabits, disruption may be fun for the audience, but it is unsettling and unpleasant for the victim. As we see throughout Shakespeare's comedies, love seems to thrive on irrationality and confusion, and emerges from it strengthened, renewed and satisfied: the experience of Antipholus of Syracuse is roughly parallel to that of Demetrius, Orlando and Sebastian. But the world of commerce simply goes crazy when an irrational factor is introduced, and the only satisfaction is for chains and ducats to be restored to their original owners, as though the confusion had never taken place. Nothing is gained in the process, for the transactions of business are barren and limited, incapable of the sudden, spontaneous enrichment that we see in the transactions of love. What is enchantment and enrichment for one brother is simply confusion for the other, a confusion that must be put right. The only party to gain something is the audience: since commercial life has been depicted in such unflattering terms, we are bound to take a special, mischievous delight in seeing it disrupted.

One may even question whether the disruption of Antipholus's marriage leads to any good result for the characters. The disorder produced by mistaken identity is linked to a more familiar disorder, a longstanding unhappiness between husband and wife. Adriana tells the Abbess that her husband has not been himself all week, though his rage has only broken out that afternoon (V. i. 45–8). And when she confesses that her nagging has disrupted the normal rhythms of his life, the Abbess lectures her:

> In food, in sport, and life-preserving rest,
> To be disturb'd would mad or man or beast.
> The consequence is, then, thy jealous fits
> Hath scar'd thy husband from the use of wits.
>
> (V. i. 83–6)

We know, of course, that his "madness" depends more on the mistaken-identity confusion than anything else (we have seen him cheated of a meal for reasons other than his wife's scolding tongue). But the Abbess's speech reminds us there are other, more familiar ways a man's life can be disrupted, and with similar results. It is clear enough that not all of Antipholus's problems stem from the fact that his brother is in town, and we may wonder if these problems can all be cured by the discovery of his brother. One curious feature of the ending is that, while the problems of the marriage have been thoroughly aired, there is no explicit reconciliation between husband and wife. The director may contrive a forgiving embrace, but nothing in the text requires it. At the end of *Menaechmi*, the wife is curtly dismissed as one more piece of household goods to be auctioned off as her husband leaves town to live with his brother (V. i. p. 39). Shakespeare does not give us that, either; he leaves us, instead, with a silence that the performers have to fill by some decision of their own.[6] For the critic, with only the text before him, the final state of this marriage must remain an open question. But we may suggest that in the domestic, commercial world of Ephesus there are no miracles.

No miracles, at least, for the native population. For the outsider, Antipholus of Syracuse, Ephesus is a different kind of town altogether, a place of magic and enchantment. His wonder and bewilderment remind us of the town's reputation as a centre of magic,[7] a reputation to which none of the native population ever refers. And while—if we shake ourselves— we may remember that nothing supernatural actually takes place, we see the town to a great extent through the eyes of the outsiders, for they are given more dramatic prominence than the natives, and treated, on the whole, more sympathetically. Viewed from the special angle of the outsider, even the normal intercourse of life becomes bizarre and unsettling:

> There's not a man I meet but doth salute me
> As if I were their well-acquainted friend;
> And every one doth call me by my name.
> Some tender money to me, some invite me,
> Some other give me thanks for kindnesses,
> Some offer me commodities to buy;
> Even now a tailor call'd me in his shop,
> And show'd me silks that he had bought for me,
> And therewithal took measure of my body.
> Sure these are but imaginary wiles,
> And Lapland sorcerers inhabit here.
>
> (IV. iii. 1–11)

The prosaic, day-to-day business of a commercial town becomes something strange and dreamlike, because it is all happening to the wrong man.

Each brother's experience of the confusion of mistaken identity is matched by the more familiar experience of being unsettled by a woman. Antipholus of Ephesus has his domestic routine disrupted by an unseen brother and a nagging wife; Antipholus of Syracuse is enchanted by a strange town, and suddenly bewitched by love (the curious name given him in the Folio, "Antipholus Erotes," suggests both wandering and love). Even when addressed by Adriana, he sees himself as in a dream, a dream to which he is willing to surrender:

> Am I in earth, in heaven, or in hell?
> Sleeping or waking, mad or well-advis'd?
> Known unto these, and to myself disguis'd!
> I'll say as they say, and persever so,
> And in this mist at all adventures go.
>
> (II. ii. 211–15)

But this surrender is still somewhat tentative; he offers himself to Luciana more recklessly: "Are you a god? Would you create me new? / Transform me, then, and to your pow'r I'll yield" (III. ii. 39–40). Earlier in the play, there was discontent in his words, "So I, to find a mother and a brother, / In quest of them, unhappy, lose myself" (I. ii. 39–40). But now he is eager to lose himself in a more profound way, transformed by love.[8]

There is certainly a transformation in his understanding. As the market-place and the tailor's shop acquire an aura of mystery for him, so too does Luciana. Here the special perspective of the outsider fuses with the special perspective of the lover, whose view of his lady is a transforming vision, comically at odds with reality. In their scene together, we note the practical, worldly manner of Luciana's advice:

> If you did wed my sister for her wealth,
> Then for her wealth's sake use her with more kindness;
> Or, if you like elsewhere, do it by stealth;
> Muffle your false love with some show of blindness...

Then, gentle brother, get you in again;
Comfort my sister, cheer her, call her wife.
'Tis holy sport to be a little vain
When the sweet breath of flattery conquers strife.

(III. ii. 5–8, 25–8)

Her words appear cynical; but there is an undercurrent of sadness in them, as she tries to make the best of a difficult situation. Above all, she is realistic: there are no appeals to higher feelings, and she does not attempt to revive a dead love. But for Antipholus this rueful, worldly, but perfectly clear advice is transformed into a divine, oracular pronouncement, veiled in mystery:

Sweet mistress—what your name is else, I know not,
Nor by what wonder you do hit of mine—
Less in your knowledge and your grace you show not
Than our earth's wonder—more than earth, divine.
Teach me, dear creature, how to think and speak;
Lay open to my earthy-gross conceit,
Smother'd in errors, feeble, shallow, weak,
The folded meaning of your words' deceit.

(III. ii. 29–36)

But the comic disparity between Luciana as we see her and the lover's special vision, though clear enough, is less drastic than it might have been. The alternate rhyme they both use gives a heightened, formal quality to her speech. Despite its worldly content there *is* something oracular in its manner, and the result is a subtler comic effect than we might have expected. The double vision of Luciana is not just a matter of contrasting our reactions with the lover's; it is built into the presentation of Luciana herself—so that, while laughing at the lover, we can see his point of view. Though romantic love is a secondary motif in this play, the balance between mockery and sympathy, characteristic of later comedies, has already been struck.

This surrender to a special vision is placed ironically against Adriana's very different view of the transformations of love as they occur in marriage. Here the woman surrenders to the man (in courtship it is the other way round) and the surrender can be not life-enhancing but ruinous:

> Do their gay vestments his affections bait?
> That's not my fault; he's master of my state.
> What ruins are in me that can be found
> Not by him ruin'd ? Then is he the ground
> Of my defeatures. My decayed fair
> A sunny look of his would soon repair.

> (II. i. 94–9)

And she later insists that her husband's corruption will spread inevitably to her (II. ii. 118–45). In the speeches of the lover, the idea of surrender is still innocent and uncomplicated, unbruised by reality. In the speeches of the wife, it has become tinged with self-pity and resentment, as we move from the idealism of courtship to the tensions of the sex war.[9]

The idea of enchantment and transformation—including surrender in love—is seen from a third angle, that of Dromio of Syracuse, and there is a contrast between master and servant, as there is between brother and brother. What is normal life for the Ephesians and a dream for Antipholus of Syracuse is a folktale horror story come true for Dromio: "This is the fairy land. O spite of spites! / We talk with goblins, owls, and sprites!" (II. ii. 188–9). In place of his master's exotic "Lapland sorcerers," Dromio imagines Ephesus as a town full of more familiar bugbears—fairies and devils. When his master (as he thinks) is arrested for debt, he spins elaborate fantasies about the sergeant as a devil (IV. ii. 31–46; IV. iii. 12–18). (His brother, characteristically, spins smaller fantasies out of the more prosaic business of being beaten—II. i. 82–5; IV. iv. 26–37.) And while Antipholus is eager to surrender himself to a woman and be transformed by her, Dromio's view of this surrender is (like the woman) radically different, and expressed in a comically contrasting style. A few lines after Antipholus has addressed Luciana as "mine own self's better part; / Mine eye's clear eye, my dear heart's dearer heart" (III. ii. 61–2), Dromio enters, fleeing in panic from the fat kitchen wench, and exclaiming, "Do you know me, sir? Am I Dromio? Am I your man? Am I myself?...I am an ass, I am a woman's man, and besides myself" (III. ii. 73–8). He fears that she would have "transform'd me to a curtal dog, and made me turn i'th'wheel" (III. ii. 144). The transformations of love can be comically humiliating as well as exalting.

One of the touching minor effects in the play is the way Antipholus and Dromio of Syracuse listen to each other, and sympathize, with each other's point of view. When he hears what his servant has endured in the kitchen, Antipholus concludes, "There's none but witches do inhabit here" (III. ii. 154) and decides, despite his love for Luciana, to "stop mine ears against the mermaid's song" (III. ii. 162). (He had addressed her, earlier in the scene, as "sweet mermaid"—III. ii. 45.) He yields to Dromio's pleas, and decides to leave town that night. But Dromio can also sink his own fears and recognize how his master is profiting from Ephesus:

> Faith, stay here this night; they will surely do us no
> harm; you saw they speak us fair, give us gold; methinks
> they are such a gentle nation that, but for the mountain
> of mad flesh that claims marriage of me, I could find in
> my heart to stay here still and turn witch.
>
> (IV. iv. 149–53)

To be cast adrift in a town of magic is both exhilarating and frightening; and the interplay between Dromio and Antipholus on this point conveys this dual quality subtly and even movingly. The interest of the play goes deeper than the farcical one of wondering what will happen next; we do wonder that, of course, but we also watch to see how the characters will *react* to what happens.

At the centre of the play, then, is a farcical comedy of situations that gives rise to a more subtle comedy based on contrasting the characters' responses to their situations. The interest springs from a series of immediate, *ad hoc* effects—collisions of style, confrontations of character—and we live from moment to moment, unconcerned, for the most part, with the larger sweep of the story. But there *is* a larger story in the background, and a very different kind of story from the farcical tale of confusion that occupies our attention for most of the play. The story of Aegeon is a tale of wandering, shipwreck and separation, more in the tradition of romance than the tradition of drama.[10]

Aegeon represents yet another area of experience, isolated from the other characters—an isolation signalled dramatically by the fact that after his long opening scene he is virtually forgotten until the end of the play. Even in that first scene, we seem curiously detached from him. His long account of his misfortunes is literary, clever and rhetorical in a way that prevents a full emotional engagement:[11]

> In Syracusa was I born, and wed
> Unto a woman, happy but for me,
> And by me, had not our hap been bad.
>
> (I. i. 36–8)
>
> So that, in this unjust divorce of us,
> Fortune had left to both of us alike
> What to delight in, what to sorrow for.
> Her part, poor soul, seeming as burdened
> With lesser weight, though not with lesser woe,
> Was carried with speed before the wind.... (I. i. 105–10)

Shakespeare restrains our interest in Aegeon's problems in order to focus more sharply on the problems of his children, thereby reversing what might be the natural response—to feel greater concern for loss and suffering than for the confusion of mistaken identity. He keeps the story of wandering very much at a distance as something faintly literary, related rather than experienced; and concentrates instead on the more obviously dramatic material of immediate confrontations between characters. Later, in *Pericles*, *Cymbeline* and *The Winter's Tale*, stories like Aegeon's will be made fully dramatic; but in *The Tempest* Shakespeare returns to the method of *The Comedy of Errors*.

At the end of the play, however, Aegeon returns—as it were, bringing his story with him—and as the characters come together for the traditional comic denouement the barriers between them dissolve and the different worlds they inhabit begin to fuse. A stage image and a joke connect the sufferings of Aegeon, condemned by the laws of Ephesus, to the more comic sufferings of his son:

AEGEON: I am sure you both of you remember me.
DROMIO E: Ourselves we do remember, sir, by you;

For lately we were bound as you are now.
You are not Pinch's patient, are you, sir?

(V. i. 291–4)

And as the knots are (figuratively and literally) untied, some of the wonder experienced by Antipholus of Syracuse begins to touch the more practical Ephesians. When the Duke sees the twins together he exclaims:

And so of these. Which is the natural man,
And which the spirit? Who deciphers them?

(V. i. 331–3)

To some extent the denouement is a practical, Plautine unravelling of the knots: the right people finally come together in the same place, and the various Ephesians who have lost money and property have it restored to them. But there are also strong suggestions that the denouement is an act of destiny (picking up Aegeon's concern with Fortune) and a miracle (recalling Antipholus of Syracuse's view that Ephesus is a town of magic). Certainly it cannot be brought about by institutional authority: the cry of "justice" with which the Ephesians appeal to their Duke is a confused babble that produces no result, since everyone's idea of "justice" is different and the Duke has no idea what the problem is.[12] In the last scene the Abbess, not the Duke, is the real figure of authority, remaining calm and clear-headed while he struggles to make sense of the matter. She alone registers no surprise, accepting the strange events as easily as if she had expected them to happen all along. And she presides over the final feast, suggesting in her invitation that what has taken place is a new birth—thus linking the miracle of the ending with the normal processes of life:

Thirty-three years have I but gone in travail
Of you, my sons; and till this present hour
My heavy burden ne'er delivered.
The Duke, my husband, and my children both,
And you, the calendars of their nativity,
Go to a gossip's feast, and joy with me;

After so long grief, such nativity! (V. i. 399–405)[13]

As the Abbess takes centre stage away from the Duke, so the fussy legalism he has represented is swept away by a deeper authority, the spontaneous force of life. The Duke himself brushes aside the Ephesian law, on being offered the ransom for Aegeon: "It shall not need; thy father hath his life" (V. i. 389). And at the end the Dromios, after debating the question of precedence, conclude that the question is irrelevant: "We came into the world like brother and brother, / And now let's go hand in hand, not one before another" (V. i. 423–4).

The emphasis, at the end, is not on the creation of a "new social unit" (as in Northrop Frye's theory of comedy)[14] but on the renewal of an old family unit. Shakespeare is silent about the marriage of Adriana and Antipholus of Ephesus; and Antipholus of Syracuse's (presumably) approaching marriage is politely but firmly put to one side, as something to be discussed later. He says to Luciana:

What I told you then,
I hope I shall have leisure to make good;
If this be not a dream I see and hear.

(V. i. 373–5)

He is still caught up in the wonder of the family reunion. In Plautus, Menaechmus of Epidamnum sells all his household and returns to Syracuse with his brother; Shakespeare softens the emphasis considerably, but the point is the same: the final image of security is not a wedding dance but a christening feast, a *family* celebration. This may be because of the play's concern with identity: identity is surrendered in love and marriage, but when the original family is recreated, the characters join a comforting social group which asks only that they be their old selves. After the challenges to identity throughout the play the characters—and perhaps the audience—need this kind of comfort, a return to the old and familiar, rather than the start of something new which marriage symbolizes.[15] Even at the end, the characters' disparate lives and experiences are not brought into a total harmony: security is achieved—and this is characteristic of Shakespeare's comedies—by selecting one experience, and fixing on that. Marriage is not brutally dismissed, as in Plautus; but it is quietly placed in the background, and no great hopes are pinned on it.

In the rejoining of the broken family, there is—as in most comic endings—a clear element of wish fulfillment. The play itself is a special, artificial ordering of experience, and, while we are not given the sort of distancing epilogue we find at the end of *A Midsummer Night's Dream* or *As You Like It*, the manner of the play throughout is sufficiently stylized to remind us that it is a work of literary and theatrical artifice.[16] The play is, even for a Shakespearian comedy, unusually full of rhyme, of jingling verse and of comic turns and set pieces—such as the debates on time and falling hair (II. ii. 63–107), and on the respective merits of cheer and welcome (III. i. 19–29); or Dromio of Syracuse's grand description of the fat kitchen wench in terms of European geography (III. ii. 113–37). And the play presents a story starting from a fantastic premise and moving to an almost equally fantastic conclusion. But at the same time, for all its artificiality, it deals with the most normal and intimate relations of life—wives and husbands, parents and children. In comparing the different worlds the Antipholus brothers inhabit, we saw an intersection of the special and fantastic with the normal and everyday—Ephesus as a town of sorcerers, and as a town of merchants. The same intersection of the fantastic and the normal becomes part of the audience's own experience as it watches the play—a strange and stylized fable built out of the most familiar relationships of life. The result of this interweaving of the fantastic and the everyday is to make us see each kind of experience from the perspective of the other—just as Antipholus of Syracuse is brought to see ordinary tradesmen as "Lapland sorcerers," or the Abbess sees the coincidental rejoining of a long-sundered family as an event as natural as childbirth. The comic strategy of the play is one of dislocation, forcing us to see experiences from a fresh perspective, reminding us that no understanding of life is final. The mixed dramatic mode gives shading and variety to what could have been a one-note, mechanical farce; but it also embodies a comic vision of the instability of life itself.

Originally published by Alexander Leggatt, *Shakespeare's Comedy of Love* (London: Methuen, 1974): 1–19. Reprinted with the permission of Methuen and Co.

NOTES

[1] References to *Menaechmi* are to William Warner's translation, in Geoffrey Bullough, *Narrative and Dramatic Sources of Shakespeare*, I (London, 1957). On the likelihood that Shakespeare knew and used this version, see Bullough's introduction, pp. 3–4.

[2] The difference between the characters is summarized by Marion Bodwell Smith, *Dualities in Shakespeare* (Toronto, 1966): Antipholus of Syracuse is the milder and less rash, the more courteous and considerate of the two. Where Antipholus of Ephesus meets obstacles head-on and is with difficulty persuaded by his friends to make the best of a bad situation, Antipholus of Syracuse is more inclined to go with the tide rather fight against it (p. 22).

[3] *The Early Shakespeare* (San Marino, 1967), p. 96.

[4] *Shakespeare's Early Comedies* (London, 1965), pp. 54–5.

[5] See Smith, *Dualities in Shakespeare*, p. 24.

[6] There is a similar silence at the end of *Measure for Measure*, when Isabella says nothing to Claudio, and is given no chance to reply to the Duke's proposal of marriage.

[7] See R.A. Foakes, introduction to his Arden edition of *The Comedy of Errors* (London, 1962), p. xxix.

[8] For a detailed discussion of the loss of identity as a theme in the play, see Harold Brooks, "Themes and structure in *The Comedy of Errors*," in John Russell Brown and Bernard Harris (eds.), *Early Shakespeare* (London, 1961), pp. 55–71.

[9] The contrast between lover-and-mistress and wife-and-husband is reviewed by Charles Brooks, "Shakespeare's romantic shrews," *Shakespeare Quarterly*, XI (summer 1960), p. 355. He takes a more sanguine view of Adriana's marriage than I have.

[10] Bullough, in *Narrative and Dramatic Sources*, includes a passage from Gower's *Confessio Amantis* as a probable source for Aegeon's story.

[11] Here I take issue with the frequently expressed view that Aegeon's account of his misfortunes carries a nearly tragic emotional impact. See, for example, H.B. Charlton, *Shakespearian Comedy* (London, 1966), p. 71; and Derek Traversi, *William Shakespeare: The Early Comedies* (revised edition: London, 1964), p. 12.

[12] According to Marion Bodwell Smith, "In Shakespeare's plays the cry

for "Justice!" is seldom heard without the accompaniment of some sort of irony" (*Dualities in Shakespeare*, p. 23). Cf. also R.A. Foakes, Arden introduction, p. xlviii.

[13] This idea is taken up in the final romances. Pericles refers to his newfound daughter as "Thou that beget'st him that did thee beget" (V. i. 194) and Cymbeline, reunited with his children, exclaims "O, what am I? / A mother to the birth of three?" (V. v. 238–9).

[14] "The argument of comedy," *English Institute Essays, 1948* (New York, 1949), p.60.

[15] Stanley Wells has pointed out the importance of non-sexual love as a "driving force" in the play: see "Shakespeare and romance," in John Russell Brown and Bernard Harris (eds.), *Later Shakespeare* (London, 1966), p. 60.

[16] As Clifford Leech points out, "the multiplication of farcical incident" also achieves a sense of distance. See the introduction to his Arden edition of *The Two Gentlemen of Verona* (London, 1969), p. lxix.

Shakespeare's *Comedy of Errors* and the Nature of Kinds

Arthur F. Kinney

In his extraordinarily helpful study, *Shakespeare and the Confines of Art*, Philip Edwards works from premises that may seem in the abstract not only potentially complex but paradoxical. One of them is this:

> The protean Shakespeare seems to change his being as he moves from the cosmos of *Hamlet* to that of *Othello*, of *Lear*, *Macbeth*, *Antony and Cleopatra*. Our attempts to synthesize and catch the common factors too often hide the more obvious and more important quality of dissimilarity. The characters speak different languages, were brought up in different moral worlds, face entirely new difficulties—just could not belong in the neighbouring play. In each play a different mind seems to be creating a different world.[1]

Yet earlier Edwards has also issued the cautionary observation that, unlike many great poets, "Shakespeare escaped public resistance: his work was not gradually mediated to the public by the discerning few" as we might expect art to be when it keeps changing from play to play; rather, "popular approval slowly moved him towards acceptance by the critics" (6). But to talk about any of Shakespeare's plays—and here I will concentrate on what is putatively his first play, *The Comedy of Errors*—as the Elizabethans would have seen and understood them, Edwards' sense of popular understanding, is to talk of the conventions for plays and entertainments which they had come through long training and experience to expect. It is to talk of the uniqueness of a Shakespearean play, what marks it off from the others, in light of its similarity to existing traditions. It is, as the Tudors would have us do, to speak of Shakespeare's works as redefining the nature of kinds.

For some time we have been doing just this with *The Comedy of Errors* more often perhaps than with any other of Shakespeare's plays. A quarter-century ago, D.A. Traversi wrote that this play is "a farcical work completely in the manner of Plautus"; more recently, Joel Fineman confidently proclaims the play "purely a farce of twins, and a mechanical farce at that."[2] But it is not quite so simple as all that. Given the Tudor perspective, even the very title tells us it is not, for Shakespeare seems to signal his own design by putting *comedy* in the title as he does nowhere else. And, in fact, simply calling the play a farce has created difficulties in reading the text and in producing the play. If we read the play as a farce following such customary definitions and discussions as the well-known one by Eric Bentley, noticing the aggressive, hostile, and violent movement and sensing as a basic theme the destruction of the family and of family values,[3] we shall concentrate on the middle acts and ignore the beginning and ending of the play. Many directors do, and the result is something like *commedia dell'arte*, a contemporary form of comedy in Italy but one posterior to Shakespeare in England. Such productions not only skew meaning but fragment the play: in the New Arden edition, for example, R.A. Foakes cites the anonymous reviewer in the London *Times* who says of a 1905 production that

> We...find certain things in *The Comedy of Errors* out of place in what is mainly, after all, a farce—the impending death of Aegeon, for instance, the love-making of Antipholus of Syracuse to Luciana, and the scene between the Abbess and Adriana before the steps of the priory. These things are not of farce as we understand it....[4]

Just so: the sharp juxtaposition of the play's title and its Plautine elements repeatedly asks us, as it must have asked the early Tudors, whether the play means to stress the absurdity of plot or the human need for family, whether it focuses on circumstances or on estrangement, whether it is controlled by incident or by theme, whether it means to arouse spontaneous laughter or quickened sympathy.

Our first reaction is to think that it means to do all of these things, to combine farce and comedy, yet so far only Alexander Leggatt has made much of this. "Shakespeare gives us a play in a more mixed dramatic idiom," he writes. "The market-place atmosphere of Plautus is still present, but it no longer monopolizes the play; it is varied by suggestions of fantasy and mystery, and the result is a mixture of styles."[5] Leggatt goes on to note the "collisions" (14) of farcical incident with comic themes to explain this "mystery," while others have turned to the exotic setting of Ephesus or the traditions of romance. But again the facts suggest that this is the wrong place to look: the initial staging of the play on Holy Innocents' Day (for a work dealing with innocents and innocence) and with consistent (and overt) Christian references (so that Ephesus takes on Pauline connotations) indicate, rather, that the "mystery" of this play is one shared with something like the *Secunda Pastorum*, the Second Shepherds Play of the "Wakefield Master," which sees something serious in the stolen sheep and something farcical in the act of discovering it. Shakespeare seems, that is, to have understood the ranging resources of kind to which Rosalie L. Colie and Alastair Fowler have called our attention even at the start of his long and varied career as playwright.

I

We *know* now *only* that *The Comedy of Errors* was produced twice, in 1594 at Gray's Inn and in 1604 at the court; *both* performances were on December 28, Holy Innocents' Day. That is no coincidence. This connection with an important feast day of the Elizabethan and Jacobean church—that church which required attendance and whose liturgy became second nature—points to a huge number of liturgical connections which, when pursued, reveal just how bold Shakespeare's brilliant and initial effort in combining Roman farce and Christian belief really was. In superseding the pagan world of Plautus with his own Christian one, Shakespeare emphasizes the precise moment of that catastrophic change as the Elizabethans always perceived it—at the moment of the Nativity. "At Christs birth all [pagan] Oracles were mute, / And put to lasting silence," Thomas Heywood writes,[6] pointing to the miracle of the Incarnation (or the re-incarnation, of and by God) that marked the Christmas season of joy and high spirits. The later John Selden is even more to the point: "Oracles ceas'd presently after Christ, as soon as no body believ'd them. Just as we have no Fortune-Tellers, nor wise Men, when no body cares for them."[7] In a play in which fortune-tellers are displaced by an Abbess, whose miraculous appearance seems permanently to defeat the devilish conjuring in newly holy Ephesus, she invites us to contemplate her "Thirty-three years…in travail" (V.i.400)[8] that by "the calendars of…nativity" can result in a "feast" (V.i.404–05) for "gossips"—that is, a time of baptizing, of "godparenting" (from the Anglo-Saxon *godsibb*). There is no more mistaking these references at the end of the play than the use of *comedy* rather than farce in the play's title. "After so long grief," the Abbess tells us, "such felicity" (V.i.406). This miracle which turns the holy Ephesus of the Holy Bible into a *proper* setting for this initially Plautine play—surely an act of felicity in Shakespeare as strong and as theatrically striking as any—is the mystery ("felicity") of birth, the sacred renewing in this play of the sense of Christ's birth. Indeed, it is the same mystery (and the same felicity) that we (and Shakespeare, drawing on native stage tradition as much as on his Plautine schoolbook tradition) found at the heart of the medieval cycles of mystery plays, those other dramas of the Nativity and of Holy Innocents' Day when unbelievers (like Dr. Pinch in the witch-ridden state of Ephesus in *The Comedy of Errors*) would be replaced by those who had been informed by Christ (such as the Abbess in the newly holy city in the play).

Such hints of this native tradition of church plays and liturgical drama that surrounded Shakespeare as a boy in Warwickshire invoke not simply yet another possible genre in a play which deliberately mixes kinds to establish one of its own, but a tradition which invites us to some extremely helpful ideas about the play, ideas to which Shakespeare himself provides clues so as to direct (or redirect) meaning. *The Comedy of Errors* intends, with one reference following another, to direct us *away* from the farce of a world of men who are foolish in their pursuit of fortune and family when they forget about God and *toward* a sense of comedy such as that conceived by Dante in his own great *Commedia* as providential confusion when wandering and bafflement invite man to contemplate wonder and grace—and achieve, through a kind of rebirth, a baptizing or godparenting, a restructuring of experience which takes the form not simply of union and transformation, but of reuniting, of making parts newly conceived into a whole which they had earlier enjoyed.

Moreover, this mixing of kinds is just what the Tudor imagination, at its best, was setting out to do—in the *Defense of Poesie and The Faerie Queene*, in *The Unfortunate Traveller* and in *Measure for Measure*. We should sense the need, furthermore, because the earlier frames of reference we have used, when pressed into the simplest sort of exacting service, simply will not do. Structurally, for example, The *Comedy of Errors* has no real basis, no deep structure in common with Roman Old Comedy. So, for instance, those plays in which a man and his wife plot against each other (as in *Casina*) or in which we observe the pranks of a parasite (*Curculio*) or a clever slave (*Epidicus*) depend on stories of intrigue and connivance. But there is no trickster in *The Comedy of Errors*, no deliberate intriguer; there is only Antipholus of Syracuse's suspicion of some, calling our attention to the fact that they are simply not there. The force of plot is, rather, the force of fate or providence, not the craftiness of wily man.[9] H.B. Charlton sees these Roman plays somewhat differently—"The outstanding feature of the whole body of Roman comedy is that whilst it is full of sex, it is almost entirely devoid of love...the object is almost invariably illicit"[10]—yet this too points to the enormous gap between the intentions and acts of copulation in Roman plays and the discussions of love that saturate *The Comedy of Errors*, discussions (and definitions) by Egeon, Adriana, Luciana, the two Antipholi, and Emilia, the Abbess. The "hard fathers, foolish mothers, vnthrifty young men, craffie seruantes, [and] sotle bawdes" that Roger Ascham complains of in Plautus, or the moral lessons the representative Tudor translator Richard Bernard finds in the New Roman Comedy of Terence, where we are to learn by knowing laughter "the nature of the fraudulent flatterer, the grimme and greedie old Sire, the roysting ruffian, the minsing mynion, and beastly baud,"[11] the stock stereotypes of farce, are simply not part of Shakespeare's play. Rather, "The study of Adriana's jealous love, the lyrical proposal of Antipholus of Syracuse to Luciana," says Kenneth Muir in his indispensable book on the sources of Shakespeare's plays, results in "bewilderment and horror."[12] Anne Barton agrees: "violence and disorder in Ephesus rise to a pitch that is both funny and frightening."[13] The emphasis on farce in Old Comedy, on plot in New Comedy, and on transformation in romance is replaced in *The Comedy of Errors* by a psychological portrayal of Antipholus of Syracuse and his servant Dromio acting out the fears that Egeon renounces at the beginning of the play, allowing Ruth Nevo, for one, to think of "a schizophrenic nightmare" in which "identities are lost, split, engulfed, hallucinated, imploded."[14]

Barton and Nevo are not merely two twentieth-century sensibilities looking back on Tudor times, but two critics profoundly engaged in the very process of Shakespeare's play when they see, from quite separate starting-points, how dangerously close this drama can seem to come to the apocalyptic. But it is precisely this scraping along the skin and bones of our psyches, this constant return to the basic themes and human fears of estrangement, solitude, and exile—of being alone without family or friend, or being (as one character puts it explicitly) partial, fragmentary, incomplete—that arises directly from the occasion at which it was first staged; for this sense of isolation, of incompleteness was precisely what the Nativity meant, both in simple narrative terms and in only somewhat more complicated liturgical terms, to the churchgoing Elizabethans. Men generally lost a sense of direction, they believed, and God, in order to call His family of man back to Himself, sent part of Himself, His Son, to reconstitute His larger and more complete family. The Nativity of Christ, which cuts like lightning through a moment in human history as the Tudors perceived and received it, awakens the pain of loss and at the same time offers hope of the end to exile. This is the force of the lessons at Christmas-tide, of the prescribed church homilies under Edward VI and Elizabeth I. Strangers made pilgrims in just this way is how Shakespeare's audience would have conceived of nativity and the Nativity on Holy Innocents' Day, and how they would have defined providence. The recent BBC production senses this too, for even among the mountebanks and harlequins of their initial *commedia dell'arte* production, the chief characters with whom we associate wear crosses and crucifixes and, whenever confused or distraught, persistently kneel and genuflect.

Just these concerns are what put us back in touch with Holy Innocents' Day, for which *The Comedy of Errors* was at least twice thought suitable. And so informed, we can see Egeon as the first innocent of many, yet one who seems remarkably, discordantly holy too: he would hazard all, he says, to find his sons. It is faith, rather than weariness, which prompts his acceptance of Ephesian justice at the hands of the Duke as the unexpected ways of a world governed by providence. Egeon's sense of "comfort" (I.i.26) at the threat of imminent death derives from the same sense of faith as Claudio's in *Measure for Measure*—"The words of heaven: on whom it will, it will; / On whom it will not, so. Yet still 'tis just" (I.ii.125–26)—a play more openly Christian in setting, but a play also presented during the Christmas season of 1604, on St. Stephen's Day, two nights before *The Comedy of Errors*. As *Measure for Measure* has its pointer within the text in this early appeal of the Duke to heaven, so *The Comedy of Errors* also has its pointer at the outset of the play in the setting of Ephesus. It was Ephesus, in the Acts of the Apostles, where St. Paul "went into the Synagogue, & spake boldly for the space of thre moneths, disputing & exhorting to the things that *apperteine* to the kingdome of God" (Acts 19:8)[15] but where, as in Shakespeare's Ephesus, he seemed to meet only with witchcraft and sorcery "So that from his bodie were broght vnto the sicke, kerchefs or handkerchefs, and the diseases departed from them, and the euil spirits went out of them" (Acts 19:12). It is St. Paul as the more successive corrective to Dr. Pinch. But there is not only this early, itinerant preacher Paul but the letter-writer Paul, building the New Church: in Paul's other connection to Ephesus, his letter to the Ephesians.[16] Here we find in the Christian New Testament, rather than in Roman farce, the source that inspired *all* parts of *The Comedy of Errors*—that gives it its overall shape and significance, not only mixing with but embodying and transforming Plautine conventions. This summary comes not in the sermon on order and on the directions for husbands and wives, parents and children that has often been cited from Ephesians 6, although this has its part to play in Shakespeare's drama, but in the summary of life's experiences in Ephesians 2 (a text as popular with the Tudors as the later passage). This is a source which has never been cited in connection with *The Comedy of Errors*, but which proceeds from a statement on death not unlike Egeon's through the sin and confusion of the play's chief action and finally to the last transformation of spirit before the priory. "And you *hathe he quickened*," Paul writes,

according to the course of this worlde, & after the prince that ruleth in this aire, *euen* the spirit, that now worketh in the childrē of disobedience,

Among whome we also had our cōuersation in time past, in the lustes of our flesh, in fulfilling the wil of the flesh, & of the minde, and were by nature the children of wrath, as wel as others.

But God which is riche ī mercie, through his great loue wherewith he loued vs,

Euen when we were dead by sinnes, hathe quickened vs together in Christ, *by whose* grace ye are saued,

And hathe raised vs vp together, and made vs sit together in the heauenlie *places* in Christ Iesus,

That he might shew in the ages to come the exceding riches of his grace, through his kindnes towarde vs in Christ Iesus.

For by grace are ye saued through faith, and that not of your selues: it *is* the gifte of God,

Not of workes, lest any man shulde boaste him self.

For we are his workemanship created in Christ Iesus vnto good workes, which God hathe ordeined, that we shulde walke in them.   (2:1–10)

This is the Ephesus the Elizabethans knew by trained instinct, not Shakespeare's. The enforced segregation of Syracusan and Ephesian in the play—like the separation of Jews from Gentiles and Christian from Pharisees in the Bible—results from human sin and hostility which focus on the wrong kind of transgression of the wrong kind of laws. The Elizabethans knew and understood that from childhood. Such divisive acts of fallen men, spurred on by evil lust and Satanic intention in Shakespeare's play, were just those acts that God, Jesus, and Paul meant to heal by *reunion*. Thus the central theme of the letter to the Ephesians, and one which Elizabethan preachers proclaimed with cogency and simplicity, is not only that of order but that of a reuniting—we think of the speeches on reunion as a kind of transformation back into the original state in *The Comedy of Errors*[17]—and the same theme emphasized in the only drama written with Paul as its hero, the non-cycle Digby play known as *The Conversion of St. Paul*. This is a miracle play which has at each of *its* three stations the story of the secular Saul and the reformed—the transformed—Paul. Here too we are taught that life is not a state of permanent separation or loss ("I to the world am like a drop of water / That in the ocean seeks another drop, / Who, falling there to find his fellow forth, [Unseen, inquisitive] confounds himself"), Shakespeare's Antipholus of Syracuse confesses early on (I.ii.35–38), but *of being found*. Chaos and oblivion are destroyed, despite the immediate slaughter of some innocents, in the spreading need and redemptive power of the Nativity ("here we wander in illusions—/ Some blessed power deliver us from hence!" [IV.iii.41–42]). With the patience constantly urged by such disparate characters as Adriana (II.i.32), the Duke's officer (IV.iv.18), and the Abbess (V.i.102), men learn to forget that "guilders...redeem their lives" as the Duke's limited sense of law, of justice and of redemption has it (I.i.8), for this "law" condemns men "to die" (I.i.25). Rather, faith and "sanctuary" (V.i.94) "for God's sake" (V.i.36) are necessary to bring a man "to his wits again" (V.i.96). Thus the customary world of historic time, of farce—of assignations, wedlock, childbirth—is rescued, subsumed, and eventually fulfilled in this play in providential time.[18]

Sensing this deeper organization in a play more integral and traditional than it is to us, the Tudors would see the end of *The Comedy of Errors*, centered as it is on the Abbess, as natural and fitting. Her powers, A.P. Riemer reminds us, heralded by "elevated diction," are "beyond the ordinary through the holiness and virtue conferred upon her by her 'order'" much as Helena will claim all human powers are in *All's Well That Ends Well* (II.i.147ff.).[19] The Abbess says, in Act V of *The Comedy of Errors*,

> Be patient, for I will not let him stir
> Till I have us'd the approved means I have,
> With wholesome syrups, drugs and holy prayers,
> To make of him a formal man again.
> It is a branch and parcel of mine oath,
> A charitable duty of my order. (V.i.102–07)

"The Abbess's powers are sanctioned by religion and morality; she employs natural distillations—syrups, wholesome drugs—accompanied by prayer. The phrase 'charitable duty of mine order' suggests that we have here something other than merely practical, secular medicine; the promise to make Antipholus a 'formal man again' reinforces the particular nature of her skill," Riemer writes (113). But the Abbess, with all her powers, is limited in her power: providence reminds us of the true nature of providentiality. For the Abbess's "control is merely emotional or theatrical: it is events and circumstances that bring about the extraordinary felicity of reunion and salvation," Riemer concludes (114). Human expectations and tested beliefs can help to save: it is a necessary cause in *The Comedy of Errors*, most decidedly, but not an efficient one.

By changing the classical Epidamnum of Plautus' *Menaechmi*, the Old Comedy of separated twins, to the Christian Ephesus associated with Paul, then, Shakespeare decisively if subtly shifts the generic expectations of an Elizabethan audience steeped in Scripture and the liturgical calendar from pure farce to something like a divine comedy in which emotional experiences and intellectual reflections portrayed by the characters are shared simultaneously by the playgoers despite their privileged knowledge of the twinned Antipholi and their twinned Dromios. The comedy works, as Paul Ricoeur claims all comedies work, by moving "from what it says to that about which it speaks."[20] The shape of the travel undergone by Egeon and by Antipholus of Syracuse is like the progress of Pilgrim, but with a double pilgrimage. In both instances, "The pattern of man's individual life coincides with that of Christian history," as Richard Axton writes in reference to the earlier native drama:[21] both Egeon and Antipholus of Syracuse seek that they may find; they lose their present selves to find the fuller selves embodied in their reunited family; they hazard all that they may gain all in a new life that actually restores the old one but with the lessons brought about by faith and heralded by providence. That both characters openly declare this shared philosophy at the outset of the play, one in dialogue, the other in soliloquy, only secures it within the framework of Paul's letter, while the exorcism of Dr. Pinch and the imprisonment of Antipholus of Ephesus, with its allusions to the Harrowing of Hell, confirm, at the play's end, the need for conversion and the desire for salvation. The New Testament and its dramatic outgrowths, as in the *Conversion of St. Paul*, provide what Kenneth Burke calls the "frames of acceptance" of genres[22] in which, here, the past constantly informs the present while the present, in searching for the past, realizes the future. It is this simultaneity of two frames of time—both in the generations represented by Egeon and Antipholus of Syracuse and in the implied past and future—that *The Comedy of Errors* draws its confusion and its resolution. This it shares with the native English tradition of the miracle play, such as the Digby play of St. Paul, the Digby *Mary Magdalene*, and the Wakefield *Secunda Pastorum*.

II

Still this informing shape strikes us at first as startling—perhaps as ingenious—and certainly at some distance from the play as we have come to know it, on the stage or in the study. So much worldliness in the decidedly mercantile environment of Shakespeare's Ephesus, so many set-up scenes such as the confusion with the courtesan and the misunderstanding about dinner, and so many physical beatings and verbal brawls sound nothing at all like the miracle play of St. Paul—or of any of the other examples of the vibrant, abiding medieval drama that has come down to us. But in this instance, I think, our conventional expectations betray us. If we recall Mak and his farcical transformation of sheep for baby as a parallel to the Nativity in the *Secunda Pastorum*, or think of the brawling of Noah's wife or the double-dealing of Cain, events analogous to those in *The*

Comedy of Errors, or the juxtaposition of Egeon's grief alongside the Dromios' antics with the mingling of potential tragedy and lively comedy in the Noah play and the Brome *Abraham and Isaac,* we will be closer to the expectations and realizations of the audiences to whom Shakespeare's first actors played. Much like the language of the *Secunda Pastorum,* in fact, is the language of orthodox Christianity that *The Comedy of Errors* refuses to ignore. Adriana advises her sister, for example, that "A wretched soul bruis'd with adversity, / We bid be quiet when we hear it cry" (II.i.34–35); later she also senses of herself that as "I am possess'd with an adulterate blot, / My blood is mingled with the crime of lust" (II.ii.140–41). Insight, Antipholus of Syracuse tells Dromio elsewhere, is realized only "by inspiration" (II.ii.167).

Indeed, it is a peculiar critical myopia that with Shakespeare's apparent first play—closest in time and experience to the religious drama he saw in childhood—we have been blind to just the kind of influence which some of our best and shrewdest readers have found in much later Shakespearean plays—for the playwright, once launched on this sort of mixed reference (or mixed genres, mixed kinds) alluding to sacred plays even over secular influences, will do it again and again in the plays that follow. Hamlet can speak of out-Heroding Herod and Macbeth's porter can make passing but pointed reference to the Harrowing of Hell in plays written well after the dominance of mystery plays in England. There are numerous other, subtler instances. M.C. Bradbrook and somewhat later O.B. Hardison, Jr. were only the first to see in the tetralogy from *Richard II* to *Henry V* Shakespeare's own Protestant cycle. "When he wrote a cycle of secular history plays, depicting the Fall and Redemption of the English monarchy," Bradbrook comments in *The Growth and Structure of Elizabethan Comedy,*

> Shakespeare was adapting the forms of the old Faith to the glory of the new state, as any good Protestant would do. With the fall of Richard II, the Garden of England is despoiled. With the casting out of the diabolic Richard III, and the triumph of the angelically supported Henry, the ghosts are led out of hell and the curse is annealed. A divine comedy is re-enacted in political terms.[23]

In addition, Emrys Jones points to the Passion play in the mystery cycles as the pattern Shakespeare follows in the tragedy of Humphrey, Duke of Gloucester in *2 Henry VI*, and the play called *The Buffeting* (of Christ) behind the treatment of York in *3 Henry VI*.[24] Lear's humiliation, Coriolanus' exile, Timon's passion, and Caesar's assassination, he tells us, all deliberately hearken back to the plays of Christ's Passion (57, 59, 71–72) while Rosemary Woolf notes the *Massacre of Innocents* play—the true basis for Holy Innocents' Day where Herod ranted, as Hamlet knows—spelled out in Henry V's warning to the citizens of Harfleur regarding the carnage they will experience at England's hands if they do not yield:

> Your naked infants spitted upon pikes,
> Whiles the mad mothers with their howls confus'd
> Do break the clouds, as did the wives of Jewry
> At Herod's bloody-hunting slaughtermen.
>
> *(Henry V*, III.iii.38–41)[25]

Honor Matthews, whose entire book on Shakespeare deals with the marked and essential residue of medieval liturgical drama throughout all of his plays, finds pronounced verbal echoes of the *Ludus Coventriae*'s Cain and Abel in the speeches of Regan and Goneril, lines from *Nature* in Friar Laurence's speeches to Romeo and the *Coming of Antichrist* in the rise of Richard III, to name only three from hundreds of examples.[26] Richard S. Ide notes the slaughter of Duncan as the first of many slaughters of the innocents by Macbeth which lead, in time, to significant redramatizations in that play of the Last Supper, the Harrowing of Hell, and the Last Judgment.[27] Nor were such mystery plays at all remote. The Ashburnham MS of the York Cycle has notations for Elizabeth I by Archbishop Grindal, who examined the Papist script for its use of doctrine, while Matthews records a performance of the Coventry cycle at Kenilworth, neighboring Stratford, in 1575 and A.W. Pollard reports that miracle plays were performed at York at least through 1579, at Newcastle until at least 1589 and at Chester at least through 1600 (last copied in 1607).[28] As for Coventry, of the two extant plays surely from that cycle, one is the Coventry Nativity, performed by the Shearmen and Tailors' guild in Shakespeare's own day, covering the Biblical story from the Annunciation to the Massacre of Innocents, and staged at least until 1580. "As one whose boyhood was spent in Warwickshire," Emrys Jones reminds us, "Shakespeare was exceptionally well placed to catch by the tail the vanishing eel of medieval dramatic tradition" (33).

The form and features of the mystery cycles are pervasive in *The Comedy of Errors*. The cycles began with serious treatments of the fall (and "death") of Adam (needing, like Egeon, to be saved in the per*son* or representative of Christ), moved into knockabout farce with plays on Cain and Abel (much as we witness with the treatment of the two Dromios), and then restored high seriousness in showing how Christ's love conquered travail and sin (as with the increasing seriousness of the final scenes of Shakespeare's play). Some works, like the *Secunda Pastorum*, even collapsed these stages into a single dramatic effort. Audiences expected to see such a varied narrative on a fixed platform with several *sedes* (mansions, rooms, doors) before an unlocalized *platea* or place on the ground swept clean for players to help them suggest and realize plot as pilgrimage. Thus the Digby *Conversion of St. Paul* seems to have been played on a platform which had Damascus at one side and Jerusalem at the other end and the road between a playing place before both, while the *Secunda Pastorum* showed both the shepherds' field and Mak's cottage simultaneously. Like the various "places" in the mystery plays, the moralities, too, had various locations which, if presented first with a kind of shared neutrality, soon took on moral signification as the play unfolded. Most of them, including *The Castle of Perseverance* with its considerable number of places preserved in a diagram in the Macro MS, shows at once both the Hell-mouth and the Hill of Salvation, allowing within the play the presentation of the four stages of the mystery cycle which is also apparent in Shakespeare's play: Innocence; Temptation and Fall; Life in Sin; Realization and Repentance.[29] Following these plays, *The Comedy of Errors* depicts a representative mankind falling into confusion; distracted by worldly things (like a cloak and a chain) of a mercantile world, such as the merchants of Ephesus whom St. Paul addresses; and vulnerable to desire (for an unnamed courtesan or for Luciana) as the witchcraft Paul sees in Ephesus marked the Ephesians. Like the near-contemporary *Everyman*, and like the portrayal of Ephesus in the Acts of the Apostles, *The Comedy of Errors* begins with the Summoning of Death. But like all these religious kinds too, Shakespeare's play shifts from a concern with *ars moriendi*, holy dying, to holy living, *ars vivendi*.[30] (The conclusion of *The Comedy of Errors*, in and before the priory, seems especially close to one of its predecessors, *The Play of the Sacrament*, which, embodying all of the Corpus Christi cycle in one emblematic play, also concludes its pageant of events before the church.) Thus the threatened death of Egeon, finding an early resonance in Herod's threatened slaughter of the innocents, also finds a grim model against which the miracles wrought by providence through the Abbess need to overcome.

Such church plays, acting as what Heather Dubrow suggestively calls "host genres,"[31] transform not only the significance of the situation and the plot but even the borrowed doorways from the Roman stage. It is clear from the entrances, exits, stage directions, and stage business in *The Comedy of Errors* that the three doors are to the Porpentine (an animal known primarily for copulation in medieval bestiaries), the Centaur (the single animal in the bestiaries known for reason), and the Phoenix (a bird, capable of resurrection, that figures Christ).[32] In the play, these signs are for the house of assignation of the courtesan, the inn where Antipholus of Syracuse preserves his worldly goods, and the place where he discovers his "divine" Luciana, or the traditional stations of Hell, Earth, and Heaven of mystery and morality traditions here seen as humanly—as partially, even mistakenly—conceived by the wandering, fallen Antipholus.[33] Pointedly, Antipholus of Ephesus alone enters the Porpentine to conduct business, while Antipholus of Syracuse naturally seeks out the Centaur with his tendency to reason and to common sense. It is Antipholus of Syracuse who foregoes the physical satisfaction of a good dinner at the Phoenix, presumably a great attraction for Antipholus of Ephesus, for the satisfaction of love; and it is when he and his servant Dromio run away from this earthly site of resurrection that they come to the priory (stage direction at V.i.37) in a state of fear and in need of direction. He is explicit about his choices too: "Am I in earth, in heaven, or in hell?" he asks (II.ii.212), calling attention to the three doors of the Plautine stage transformed by Christianity early on in the play into a new set of stations, a new set of choices. And as in the miracle plays Hell here is called a "sty" or "pit" while the great "hall" of the priory suggests the setting of Heaven used in the N-Town cycle.[34] But the priory cannot be the same doorway as the Phoenix as previous critics claim, beginning with E.K. Chambers,[35] for Antipholus and Dromio of Syracuse are running *out* of that *to* the priory; nor can it be the door of the Centaur, for they are running away from their worldly goods to a place of holy sanctuary. The doorway of the priory, then, is the miraculously transformed doorway of the Porpentine; the Courtesan has been displaced, visually and on stage, by the Abbess, and through it she comes to conquer sin and commerce by calling forth the entire cast—the whole world of the play—and transforming them too. "Shakespeare's characters live," Harry Levin says tellingly, "in a Christian ethos."[36]

R. Chris Hassel, Jr. anticipates this understanding of the play when he remarks that "A glance at the liturgical tradition of Innocents' Day makes it even less likely that mere nostalgia or coincidence explains the dual performance of the play on that religious festival." He notes that the proper lesson prescribed for that feast day in the *Book of Common Prayer* is Jeremiah 31:1–17, concerned with "the dispersal and reunion of families. In fact, from such other prescribed passages as...Matt. 2:3–18, Rev. 14:1–5, and Isa. 60, we realize that this theme was a central motif of the liturgical festival." He notes further that

> Jeremiah 31 is insistently parallel to the first and final scene of *Errors*. After the Lord's several promises to gather the remnant of Israel from the coasts of the world, verses 15–17, on the ultimate deliverance of all innocents, seem particularly close to the situation and the sensibility of Egeon and Emilia, parents of their own lost children:
>
> 15 A voice was heard on hie, a mourning and bitter weping, Ra[c]hel weping for her children,...because thei were not.
>
> 16 Thus saith the Lord, Refraine thy voice from weping, and

thine eyes from teares: for thy worke shalbe rewarded, saith ye Lord, and thei shal come againe from the land of the enemie.

17 And there is hope in thine end, saith the Lord, that thy children shal come againe to their owne borders.[37]

Shakespeare's characters, it would seem, like his audiences, could not escape the Christian ethos even if they wanted to.

III

So rhetorically this aporetic play, full of doubts, becomes at its conclusion ecphrastic in the forthright sermon of the Abbess, the overall structure resembling a renewed catechism. The stations derived from the miracle and morality plays are underscored by Christian references throughout the play—to the Dromios' twin births in an inn (I.i.53) following the example of the twin Antipholi (I.i.51), to Antipholus of Syracuse's admission that he is a Christian (I.ii.77) and to his Dromio's plea to his rosary (II.ii.188), to Luciana's litany of God's creatures derived from the Homily on Obedience as well as Acts 19 (II.i.15–25), while Act IV, opening with a reference to Pentecost, leads directly to Dr. Pinch's exorcism chanted in Christian terms (IV.iv.52–55), Antipholus' plea for deliverance (IV.iii.42) and Dromio of Syracuse's concern with Adam and his obsession with prodigality (IV.iii.16ff.),[38] and the Abbess' final speech on Pauline charity (V.i.102–08). Such open terms and echoes cast their light backward on the suggestive language which forms Egeon's autobiography as he reports it to the Duke. Egeon likens himself, it would seem, to the Adam of the Corpus Christi cycle: "Proceed, Solinus, to procure my fall, / And by the doom of death end woes and all" (I. i. 1–2) by showing how his paradoxical response to say what passes the saying can give testimony to those who attend him:

A heavier task could not have been impos'd,
Than I to speak my griefs unspeakable;
Yet that the world may witness that my end

Was wrought by nature, not by vile offence,
I'll utter what my sorrow gives me leave. (I.i.31–35)

His tale, then, is "what obscured light the heavens did grant"
(I.i.66) while his problem, as he knows too well, is his lack of
faith—he became "Hopeless to find" (I.i.135)—and his awareness
of that very loss: "yet loth to leave unsought / Or that or any
place that harbours men" (I.i.135–36). His need for mercy and for
renewed belief is the occasion for mercy from the Duke, who
anticipates the Abbess, and his words, like hers, are far more
Christian than Plautine. Against his crown the Duke places his
soul:

> Against my crown, my oath, my dignity,
> Which princes, would they, may not disannul,
> My soul should sue as advocate for thee;
> But though thou art adjudged to the death,
> And passed sentence may not be recall'd
> But to our honour's great disparagement,
> Yet will I favour thee in what I can;
> Therefore, merchant, I'll limit thee this day
> To seek thy health by beneficial help;
> Try all the friends thou hast in Ephesus,
> Beg thou, or borrow, to make up the sum,
> And live. (I.i.143–54)

That such trust and faith has some possibility even in this
atmosphere of crass materialism and of doom—one famous
production featured a huge clock on stage—is made clear in the
opening lines of the very next scene when a merchant tells
Antipholus of Syracuse of his own fortune while warning him to
keep his citizenship secret (I.ii.1–8). But he is his father's son,
even through the most farcical of the scenes, and money and
doom are abruptly transformed into something else: "I, to find a
mother and a brother, / In quest of them, unhappy, lose myself"
(I.ii.39–40). What looks very much like the possibility of a coming
act of providence, then, in a language popularized in the miracle
and morality plays, seems assured when this Antipholus, lost in
a new city and lost to himself, never loses sight of his faith.

They say this town is full of cozenage,
As nimble jugglers that deceive the eye,
Dark-working sorcerers that change the mind,
Soul-killing witches that deform the body,
Disguised cheaters, prating mountebanks,
And many such-like liberties of sin:
If it prove so, I will be gone the sooner. (I.ii.97–103)

Attracted instead to Luciana, whose name means "light," he is always able to distinguish between women who are worthy and those who are not, as he has apparently taught his own Dromio. When he meets an Ephesian courtesan on the street, both he and his servant are aware of the temptation she represents, and in Christian terms.

Syr. Ant. Satan avoid, I charge thee tempt me not.
Syr. Dro. Master, is this mistress Satan?
Syr. Ant. It is the devil.
Syr. Dro. Nay, she is worse, she is the devil's dam;
    And here she comes in the habit of a light wench, and
    thereof comes that the wenches say "God damn me,"
    that's as much as to say, "God make me a light wench."
    It is written, they appear to men like angels of light; light
    is an effect of fire, and fire will burn; ergo, light wenches
    will burn; come not near her. (IV.iii.46–55)[39]

Both are tested here, and not found wanting, just as Antipholus of Ephesus will be tested by Dr. Pinch and again in the dungeon into which he is thrown. Such temptations and trials here, as in the mystery plays, are what provide a blessed joy. "After so long grief," says the Abbess, "such felicity" (V.i.406),[40] figuring Mary as intercessor and as mother. At the end of the play, the law of the Duke is apparent with his reappearance— actually, only his second appearance—but he is soon made (eternally) subordinate to the Abbess, as Justice is made subordinate to Mercy in numerous scriptural plays.

So many punning and persistent words introduce us, at the end, to The Word. The final petition of the Great Litany in the *Book of Common Prayer* is strikingly appositive in thought and image:

"Thoughe we be tyed and bounde with the chayne of our synnes, yet let the pitifulness of thy great mercy lose vs." The idea is reinforced in the general confession spoken each day at Morning Prayer: "We have erred and straied from thy waies, lyke lost shepe....We have left vndone those thinges whiche we ought to have done, and we haue done those thinges which we ought not to have done, and there is no health in vs." "If we say that we haue no synne, we decyve ourselues, and there is no truthe in vs." But *The Comedy of Errors* does more than give rebirth to general doctrine; it also responds to—and is perhaps partly directed by—the liturgical text for Holy Innocents' Day, making the play a kind of parable for that occasion. The way in which Egeon and his sons seek their own salvation glosses the Scripture assigned that day for morning prayer and not noted by Hassel:

> But this shalbe the couenant that I wil make with the house of Israel. After those daies, saith the Lord, I wil put my Law in their inwarde partes, & write it in their hearts, & wil be their God, and thei shalbe my people.

> And thei shal teache nomore euerie mā his neighbour and euerie man his brother, saying. Knowe the Lord: for they shal all knowe me from the least of them vnto the greatest of them, saith the Lord: for I will forgiue their iniquitie, and wil remember their sinnes no more— (Jeremiah 31:33–34)

as well as the first and second lessons set for that day's evening prayer:

> ARise, *o Ierusalem*: be bright, for thy light is come, & the glorie of the Lord is risen vpon thee.
> For beholde, darkenes shal couer ye earth, and grosse darkenes the people: but the Lord shal arise vpon thee, and his glorie shalbe sene vpon thee.
> And the Gentiles shal walke in thy light, & Kings at ye brightnes of thy rising vp. (Isaiah 60:1–3)

> Babes, kepe your selues frō idoles, Amē. (1 John 5:21)

The Abbess, like the play, draws into narrative those Scriptural passages which Elizabethans heard invariably, year in and year out, on the same day this play was presented, had perhaps just finished hearing that very morning or afternoon; and both move from the painful memory of a slaughter of innocents to the joy of the knowledge of providence which lies through and beyond such bloodshed during the celebration of Christ's birth, the Incarnation of God come to earth.

Such signs and symbols are captured in the *tableaux vivants*, the telling emblem scenes allegorically put forth in *The Comedy of Errors*: in the visual image of the bewildered Antipholus of Syracuse, the maddened (because uninstructed) Dr. Pinch, and, in the final moments, that scene on the steps of the priory that resembles, and is meant to re-embody, something like the Last Judgment. In this, too, *The Comedy of Errors* looks forward to *Macbeth* and especially to *Measure for Measure* where, Ide shows, Vincentio is heralded by trumpets and comes before the gates of the city to distribute rewards and punishments "much like his judicial model at the final compt before the gates of heaven."[41] But whereas that justice is purely retributive (and so goes awry), the judgment and justice of the Abbess are distributive (superbly informed by mercy): she displaces the justice of the Duke. This could not be clearer: "Justice, most sacred duke, against the abbess" (V.i.133) Adriana asks, insisting on the primacy of the law of Ephesus over the law of God, and her husband confirms this request: "Justice, most gracious Duke, O grant me justice" (V.i.190). But such law is at best imperfect; "Most mighty" but not sacred Duke, says the Abbess, "Most mighty duke, behold a man much wrong'd" (V.i.330). It is the Abbess' mercy overcoming human rule: "Whoever bound him, I will loose his bonds" (V.i.339), thereby gaining a husband (V.i.340) and sons (V.i.343, 401) whom she has "delivered" (V.i.402) with the help of God. Thus the Abbess reenacts the host of Judgment plays in the mystery cycles.

The wonders of the religious drama highlight the piling on of wonders that is the concluding movement of *The Comedy of Errors*, yet none is more wonderful than this: that so short a play—actually Shakespeare's briefest—moves all the way from the Nativity to the Last Judgment, spanning not only the life of the Christian but all of Christian history as well. That too is the essential idea behind Paul's letter to the Ephesians and so may also lie behind Shakespeare's choice of scene.

> I Therefore, beīg prisoner in ye Lord, praye you that ye walke worthie of the vocation whereunto ye are called,
> With all humblenes of minde, and mekenes, with long suffring, supporting one another through loue,
> Endeuoring to kepe the vnitie of the Spirit in the bonde of peace.
> There *is* one bodie, and one Spirit, euen as ye are called in one hope of your vocation.
> *There is* one Lord, one Faith, one Baptisme,
> One God & Father of all, which is aboue all, and through all, & in you all....
> Til we all mete together (in the vnitie of faith & knowledge of the Sonne of God) vnto a perfite man, & vnto the measure of the age of the fulnes of Christ,
> That we hence forthe be no more children, wauering & caryed about with euerie winde of doctrine, by the deceit of mē, and with craftiness whereby they laye in waite to deceiue.
> But let vs followe the trueth in loue....
> Be angry, but sinne not: let not the sunne go downe vpon your wrath,
> Neither giue place to the deuil....
> And grieue not the holie Spirit of God by whome ye are sealed vnto the day of redemption.
> Let all bitterness, and angre, and wrath, crying, and euil speaking be put away frō you, with all maliciousnes.
> Be ye courteous one to another, & tender hearted, forgiuing one another, euen as God for Christs sake forgaue you.
> BE ye therefore followers of God, as dere children,
> And walke in loue. (4:1–6, 13–15, 26–27, 30–32; 5:1–2)

The Comedy of Errors is also about the long suffering of those who face the deceit of men, temptations of the devil, bitterness and maliciousness in order to restore the one body of the family, as in one baptism through love. Even the least of the characters, Dromio of Ephesus, realizes this. His recognition ends the play: "We came into the world like brother and brother," he tells Dromio of Syracuse, "And now let's go hand in hand, not one before another" (V.i.425–26). "After so long grief, such felicity." So Hamner. But the Folio text does not say that. It reads, "After so long grief, such Natiuitie"—with a capital N, while Dyce, after Dr. Johnson, makes another choice still: "After so long grief, such festivity." He may not have the word quite right, but surely he has caught the sense of the play too. Seen thus in all its contexts, *The Comedy of Errors* is not merely a mechanical farce, a limp and imitative early play, or even a confusion of kinds, but an excellent play, well digested in the scenes, set down with as much modesty as cunning.

At the close, three couples stand with their servants united in one large family, presenting on stage the very heart of Christian theology in a living icon. It is a profound—and profoundly moving—effect, but actually it is only the last of many. For *The Comedy of Errors* is, from first to last, a *play* of effects—the arrest of Egeon, the tardiness of Antipholus of Ephesus for dinner, the pursuit of Dromio of Syracuse by Nell, the sudden fascination of Antipholus of Syracuse for Luciana, the sudden appearance of the Abbess and her priory—that keeps us actively searching for causes, forcing us into the position of the characters who are likewise searching for causes, and, like them, frustrated, bewildered, and subject to wonder: open as they are to amazement and to grace.

And such searching by us before the play resembles that of Shakespeare behind it. "Shakespeare was not a system-builder: he was an artist, a dealer in dramatic fictions," Philip Edwards writes. "By adjusting the patterns of art, he would seem to be looking for that fictional ordering which could act as a powerful interpretive formula not only for the experience of his audience, but for his own" (14). Edwards has just cited *Twelfth Night, Henry V, All's Well That Ends Well, Antony and Cleopatra,* and *The Tempest,* but we do not need to seek for this motivating force, this secret of Shakespeare's power, in later or major works alone. It is there, coiled up, sprung, and in operation in the earliest of them, where the native, classical, Christian, and Pauline traditions of drama are first exploited and then, in turn, mingled, mixed, and metamorphosed. By bringing his powers of creativity and synthesis to the occasion of Holy Innocents' Day, Shakespeare's peculiar forms and powers of art are visible from the first—and apparent for those of us who, like the early Elizabethans, can understand the signals, the allusions, and the significance of the various natures of kinds.[42]

Originally published by Arthur F. Kinney, "Shakespeare's *Comedy of Errors* and the Nature of Kinds," *Studies in Philology*, 85 (1988): 29–52. Copyright © 1988 by the University of North Carolina Press. Used by the permission of the author and publisher.

NOTES

[1] Philip Edwards, *Shakespeare and the Confines of Art* (London: Methuen, 1968; rpt. 1981), 11.

[2] D.A. Traversi, *An Approach to Shakespeare*, 2nd ed. (London: Sands & Co., 1957), 14; Fineman, "Fratricide and Cuckoldry: Shakespeare's Doubles" in *Representing Shakespeare: New Psychoanalytic Essays*, ed. Murray M. Schwartz and Coppélia Kahn (Baltimore: Johns Hopkins University Press, 1980), 70. This line is the most traditional one. Cf. M.R. Ridley: "It is the best kind of slick prentice work. It is completely artificial, hard, glittering, and exact; but, of its kind, brilliant; it is completely mechanical, 'but it moves,' with the smoothness of well oiled machinery" (*Shakespeare's Plays* [London: The Folcroft Press, Inc., 1937], 53). The most sympathetic and detailed of recent authorities is E.M.W. Tillyard, who writes, in his posthumous *Shakespeare's Early Comedies*, "The core of the *Comedy of Errors* is farce and it is derived from one play of Plautus and some scenes from another" (ed. Stephen Tillyard [London: Chatto and Windus, 1965, 46). Harold Brooks, "Themes and Structure in 'The Comedy of Errors'" in *Early Shakespeare*, ed. John Russell Brown and Bernard Harris (London: Edward Arnold Ltd., 1961), 55–71, and Alexander Leggatt, *Shakespeare's Comedy of Love* (London: Methuen, 1974), chap. 1.

[3] Eric Bentley, *The Life of the Drama* (New York: Atheneum, 1964), chap. 7.

[4] Introduction to *The Comedy of Errors*, ed. R.A. Foakes (London: Methuen, 1962), liii–liv.

[5] Leggatt, *Shakespeare's Comedy of Love*, 3.

[6] Thomas Heywood, *The Hierarchie of the Blessed Angells* (1635), 24; quoted in C.A. Patrides, *Premises and Motifs in Renaissance Thought and Literature* (Princeton: Princeton University Press, 1982), 116.

[7] John Selden, *Table-Talk*, 2nd ed. (1696), 139; quoted in Patrides, 118.

[8] Citations of this and other Shakespeare plays are to the New Arden texts.

[9] See the relevant discussion by Madeleine Doran in *Endeavors of Art: A Study of Form in Elizabethan Drama* (Madison, Wisc.: University of Wisconsin Press, 1964), 152ff.

[10] H.B. Charlton, *Shakespearian Comedy* (London: Methuen, 1966), 52.

[11] Quoted in Kenneth Muir, *Shakespeare's Comic Sequence* (Liverpool: Liverpool University Press, 1979), 3–4.

[12] Kenneth Muir, *The Sources of Shakespeare's Plays* (New Haven: Yale University Press, 1978), 16.

[13] Anne Barton, Introduction to *The Comedy of Errors* in *The Riverside Shakespeare*, ed. G. Blakemore Evans *et al.* (Boston: Houghton Mifflin, 1974), 81.

[14] Ruth Nevo, *Comic Transformations in Shakespeare* (London: Methuen, 1980), 22.

[15] My citations of Scripture are to *The Geneva Bible* (1560) in the facsimile ed. with an introduction by Lloyd E. Berry (Madison, Wisc.: University of Wisconsin Press, 1969).

[16] Biblical scholars now doubt Paul's authorship of this letter, and assign it to the School of Paul; for Shakespeare, however, the letter was authentic.

[17] For example, at II.i.15ff.; II.ii.195–96; III.ii.39–40; IV.ii.19–22,27–28; V.i.270–72.

[18] On these matters, see also Brooks, "Themes and Structure," 66.

[19] A.P. Riemer, *Antic Fables: Patterns of Evasion in Shakespeare's Comedies* (Manchester: Manchester University Press, 1980), 113.

[20] Quoted in Nevo, 10.

[21] Richard Axton, "The Morality Tradition" in *Medieval Literature: Chaucer and the Alliterative Tradition*, New Pelican Guide to English Literature, ed. Boris Ford (Harmondsworth, England: Penguin, 1982), I:347.

[22] Kenneth Burke, *Attitudes Toward History* (Los Altos, Calif.: Hermes Publications, 1959), 43ff.

[23] M.C. Bradbrook, *The Growth and Structure of Elizabethan Comedy* (London: Chatto and Windus, 1963), 21–22; cf. Hardison, *Christian Rite and Christian Drama in the Middle Ages: Essays in the Origin and Early History of Modern Drama* (Baltimore: Johns Hopkins University Press, 1965), 290.

[24] Emrys Jones, *The Origins of Shakespeare* (Oxford: Clarendon Press,

1977), 35–54.

[25] Rosemary Woolf, *The English Mystery Plays* (Berkeley: University of California Press, 1972), 208.

[26] Honor Matthews, *Character & Symbol in Shakespeare's Plays* (Cambridge: Cambridge University Press, 1969), 11, 9. Surprisingly, she pays little attention to *The Comedy of Errors.* I am grateful to Raymond V. Utterback for directing me to Matthews' study.

[27] Richard S. Ide, "The Theatre of the Mind: An Essay on *Macbeth*," *ELH* 43 (1975): 338–61.

[28] Alfred W. Pollard, Introduction to *English Miracle Plays: Moralities and Interludes*, 8th ed. (Oxford: Clarendon Press, 1927, 1965), lxvii.

[29] Such stations are diagrammatically shown for the Anglo-Norman *La Seinte Resureccion* and for *The Castle of Perseverance* in *Medieval Drama*, ed. David Bevington (Boston: Houghton Mifflin, 1975), 122, 796–97.

[30] Some of these remarks paraphrase V.A. Kolve, "*Everyman* and the Parable of the Talents," in *Medieval English Drama: Essays Critical and Contextual*, ed. Jerome Taylor and Alan H. Nelson (Chicago: University of Chicago Press, 1972), 340.

[31] Heather Dubrow, *Genre* (London: Methuen, 1982), 116.

[32] Cf. T.H. White, *The Bestiary: A Book of Beasts*, a trans. of a Latin Bestiary of the twelfth century (New York: Putnam, 1954), 10n., 86, 125ff.

[33] The recent York presentation of the York cycle at the ruins of St. Mary's Abbey has such a stage which shows Hell-Mouth at one end, the Hill of Salvation at another location, and various stations along a front stage for various locations on earth.

[34] See Nelson, "Some Configurations of Staging in Medieval English Drama," in Taylor and Nelson, *Medieval English Drama*, 116–47, esp. 133ff.

[35] E.K. Chambers, *William Shakespeare: A Study of Facts and Problems* (Oxford: Clarendon Press, 1930), 1:307; the idea reappears (without source) in Stanley Wells, Introduction to *The Comedy of Errors*, New Penguin Shakespeare (Harmondsworth: Penguin, 1972), 25, and in Foakes, xxxiv–xxxv.

[36] Harry Levin, Introduction to *The Comedy of Errors*, The Signet Classic Shakespeare (New York: New American Library, 1965), xxviii.

[37] R. Chris Hassel, *Renaissance Drama & the English Church Year* (Lincoln, Neb.: University of Nebraska Press, 1979), 40–41.

[38] In his edition of the play (Cambridge: Cambridge University Press, 1962), 106, J. Dover Wilson notes that "Dromio's mind is full of images from the old miracle and morality plays." Also quoted in A.C. Hamilton, *The Early Shakespeare* (San Marino, Calif.: Huntington Library, 1967), 100n.

[39] For more discussion of this passage, see James H. Sims, *Dramatic Uses of Biblical Allusions in Marlowe and Shakespeare*, University of Florida

Monographs, Humanities No. 24 (Gainesville, Fla.: University of Florida Press, 1966), 30.

[40] "The celebration called for by Aemilia is properly a nativity feast because the central characters are truly reborn; each of them has gained new relationships and thus in the metaphysics of the play transformed his identity." Thomas F. Van Laan, *Role-playing in Shakespeare* (Toronto: University of Toronto Press, 1978), 25.

[41] "Homiletic Tragicomedy and the Ending of *Measure for Measure*," an unpublished essay Ide has shared with me, 10.

[42] This essay, in an earlier form, was the basis for the Annual Shakespeare Birthday Lecture at the University of Edinburgh in 1984.

Commedia Grave and
The Comedy of Errors

Louise George Clubb

Baldwin's *On the Compositional Genetics of "The Comedy of Errors"* accounts exhaustively for every gene of Shakespeare's play, and not one is Italian. Nevertheless, Baldwin states that this comedy is "probably the most fundamentally Italianate play of the English lot, and yet there is not a specific element which can be traced to direct borrowing from the Italian," adding in a note: "It must be evident to anyone who has grasped this development of the type in England that so skillfully complicated a play as *Errors* could not have been constructed before the end of the 'eighties. Even so, it is as remarkable a personal accomplishment for the late 'eighties as Udall's *Ralph Roister Doister* was for the early 'fifties. I have the impression that this point of evolution would be stronger if it were put on the background of the development in Italy of this more complicated form from the simpler form of Plautus and Terence."[1]

Whether this impression, with its apparently subversive effect on the rest of his book, was inserted merely as a protective clause to appease Italianists, only Baldwin knows. But his suggestion is still very much worth taking, though it touches on the sore old question of whether or not Italian Renaissance comedy exercised any significant influence on the Elizabethan drama, especially Shakespeare's.

There are only a few proved connections to support Stephen Gosson's famous complaint that Italian comedies were "ransackt to furnish the Playe houses in London."[2] Some comedies of Ariosto, Grazzini, Aretino, the Intronati, Salviati, Piccolomini, Pasqualigo, Della Porta, and Oddi were translated or adapted in England.[3] From the late 1570s Italian comedy was decidedly chic at Cambridge, where Latin versions were frequently performed.[4] Both of Machiavelli's comedies and four of Aretino's were printed in London in 1588.[5] Royal interest in "comedia italiana" is proved by Queen Elizabeth's request that her courtiers organize a performance of one. There are records of seven visits to England by Italian players between 1546 and 1578, and by 1591 the traffic seems to have been brisk enough to make disguise as Italian entertainers desirable to foreign spies.[6]

But although a handful of facts have been established and analogues have been recorded by several generations of scholars, the investigation of the Elizabethan debt to Italian comedy has been stymied: by the scarcity of documentary proof that there was physical contact or direct borrowing, and by the distractions of the common raw materials, notably Latin comedy and *novelle*.

With regard to Shakespeare the question is especially tantalizing, for half his plays smack of Italian drama, none more than *The Comedy of Errors*. It is generally agreed that the sources of *The Comedy of Errors* are a combination of *Menaechmi* and *Amphitruo*, Gower's version of Apollonius of Tyre, and the account of St. Paul's travels in the Acts of the Apostles; that Shakespeare's handling is more complex than Plautus's; and that the whole is given a serious turn, a touch of spirituality and of horror. It is customary to add that Shakespeare raised the moral tone, cleaned up the meretrix, introduced topics of marriage, courtship, and providence, and developed the themes of madness and sorcery—indeed, Baldwin calls the latter the "chief structural thread."[7]

The Italianate quality of *The Comedy of Errors* has never been met head on. K.M. Lea does not commit herself beyond the suggestion that Shakespeare "seems to have been acquainted with the way the comedy of mistaken identity was exploited on the Italian stage"[8] and points to parallels between the devices for moving and complicating action in *The Comedy of Errors* and those in commedia dell'arte scenarios. Other scholars consider the style of *The Comedy of Errors* a derivation of Gascoigne's and Lyly's ventures into Italianate comedy, attributing the leftover differences to Shakespeare's desire to outcomplicate *Mother Bombie*.[9] Even M.C. Bradbrook, who distinguishes between the "English Plautine" *Mother Bombie* and the "Italian Plautine" *Comedy of Errors*, [10] does not come to grips with the Italian tradition or with the way in which *The Comedy of Errors* is linked to it.

From the time of its definition by Ariosto and his contemporaries, the regular Italian commedia, somewhat misleadingly dubbed *erudita*, was Roman in situation and structure. The Italian way of using the Latin material, however, was never that of simple imitation and expansion, but proceeded rather "by a reasoned synthesis based upon a close analysis of the structure of [Plautus]...analogous materials from other sources...[were] woven into this resulting plan to fill it out. The resultant structure...[was] in general consistent with itself." These words, which could accurately characterize the method instituted in Italy in the first decade of the sixteenth century, come from Baldwin's description of Shakespeare's procedure in constructing *The Comedy of Errors* from *Menaechmi*.[11] For the most part, "other sources" of the Italian playwrights were medieval and contemporary narratives, which exercised on Renaissance comedy an influence equal to that of Plautus and Terence.

Certain features became commonplaces almost at once: the cast of middle-class families and their servants, pedants, soldiers, innkeepers, friars, and courtesans, joined in a series of encounters on the street, in doorways, and at windows; the combination of spatially and temporally restricted farcical intrigue with a potentially romantic antecedent history; the pattern of misunderstanding, disguise, and mistaken identity, kept moving and finally solved by peripeties and recognition. Although the playwrights customarily boasted in their prologues of debts to Plautus, Terence, and Boccaccio, the pieces they borrowed were reassembled to create a total different from the sum of its parts. In the process, they systematically outcomplicated the ancients and strained to do as much to one another.

After professional entertainers came into contact with this regular comedy, the commedia dell'arte appeared, whereupon literary dramatists in their turn began to borrow masks and mannerisms. The relationship was close but not altogether amicable, and by mid-century war had broken out—not, as is sometimes supposed, between amateurs and professionals, but between the regular five-act comedy written along the lines laid down by the generation of Ariosto, and one of the professionals' specialties, the loosely constructed, improvised farce described by Lodovico Dolce as *sciochezze ridicole*, consisting of "Buffoni sciocchi, et confusione vana di lingue, et di attioni poco honeste, nelle scene" (ridiculous inanities...silly buffoons, empty confusion of tongues and indecent actions in the scenes).[12]

In the second half of the century, with Counter-Reformation in the air, the terms of the quarrel were better defined. The shapeless, bawdy zannata ("clownpiece") was challenged by the comedy of reform issuing from such dramatists as Bernardino Pino, Luigi Pasqualigo, Girolamo Bargagli, Raffaello Borghini, Cristoforo Castelletti, Giovanfrancesco Loredano, Giambattista Della Porta, Sforza Oddi, and Giambattista Calderari, to name only those writing before 1589, the earliest likely date for *The Comedy of Errors*. Although historians have usually either ignored the type as such or labeled it, inadequately, "tearful" or "serious" comedy, the practitioners themselves called it *commedia grave*, choosing a term once applied to humanistic comedy in general and recharging it with particular reference to the new seriousness. Castelletti deplored flaccid audiences unable to appreciate *meraviglia, dolore*, and *compassione*: "stimano più una chiacchierata all'improviso... d'un vecchio Vinitiano, & d'un servitor Bergamasco, accompagnata da quattro attioni disoneste...che una Comedia Grave, che vi si serà stentato tre anni a comporla, e sei mesi a recitarla" (they esteem more highly some improvised chatter...between an old Venetian and a Bergomask servant, seasoned with four indecent gestures, than a Grave Comedy that took three years of hard work to compose and six months to rehearse and stage).[13] The gravity being advocated was aesthetic as well as moral and emotional, and the resulting standards of form and matter represented the farthest advances of the sixteenth century in the development of Italian regular comedy.

While writers of commedia grave held one of their purposes to be the defense of regular comedy against the zannate, they were equally determined to improve the regular comedy itself. They preserved the basic situations, characters, and structures of the earlier commediografi, and although there were repudiations like Pino's of "recognoscersi genti incognite, scambiamenti de panni, somiglianza de visi" (recognitions of unknown strangers, exchanging of clothes for disguises, identical facial resemblances),[14] these commonplaces lost none of their currency. Nevertheless, the changes were considerable. The didactic note of Terence, echoed intermittently and without conviction in earlier regular comedy, sounded insistently in late commedia grave, and Pino could advertise on the title page that his *Falsi sospetti* was "Per instruttione de' prudenti Padri di famiglia, d'ubidienti figliuoli, et di fedeli servitori." [15] Dirty jokes were still a necessity, but marriage and the church were treated with new respect. The figure of the corrupt friar disappeared, adultery was cut to a minimum, and even fornication was reduced.

A direct result of the didactic force was discourse on a moral topic growing out of the plot and presented as debate or soliloquy. Not only the time-honored discussions of parental and filial duties but also the questions raised in countless Cinquecento treatises became fashionable matter for set pieces in commedia grave. Along with the debate of love and honor (love usually wins) and that of love and friendship (friendship wins), the nature of feminine honor and the requirements of marriage were favorite subjects. The conclusions were both serious and funny. In *I falsi sospetti* the neglected Bellisaria tots up the score of her marriage and informs her confidante that as the wife of the studious Doctor of law she has become learned but would much rather have become pregnant (1.1). On the oft-invoked principle of "giovare e dilettare" (to be useful and to delight) such scenes were handled with as much wit as their authors possessed, and technically owe more than a little to the practice of the professional actors who memorized passages from various *ragionamenti* and *dialoghi* and used them in improvisation.

As usual in the long history of intimate relationship between regular comedy and commedia dell'arte, the influence was reciprocal. The better professional companies included written plays of all genres in their repertories, and they found already built into commedie gravi the kind of moral, emotional, and intellectual arias that they were wont to introduce into scenarios. Isabella Andreini offers a view of the relationship in her dialogue on comedy, half critical discourse and half love scene, when she echoes the prologues of commedie gravi, emphasizing the dignity of writing comedy and citing as models Piccolomini, Calderari, and Pino. [16] It is noteworthy that the last two wrote very grave comedies, and Piccolomini may be called their precursor by virtue of his occasional romantic and moral themes.

The gravity of the commedia grave was also evident in the increased emotional tensions, the fuller characterization and articulateness of the lovers (another reflection of professional practice), and the sad or sinister direction of the action. The seriousness might consist in additions of flowery love scenes and tender family reconciliations to basic farce, as in Della Porta's *Olimpia*, or in main plots built on nearly tragic contests of love and friendship, with threats of suicide and execution, as in Oddi's three comedies. Whatever the proportions, there was always a mixture of sentiment, pathos, and danger with lively comic action. There was now explicit development of the romantic potential in clichés of exile, conspiracy, trade wars, shipwreck, and kidnaping, and other remembered causes of separation of families. The resemblance of commedia grave to tragedy was pointed out both internally and externally. Hearing of her husband's safe return from a shipwreck, Castelletti's Clarice says: "comincio a prender augurio che la mia lagrimosa tragedia habbia ad haver comico fine" (I begin to see signs that my tearful tragedy is to have a comedy ending).[17] In the opening scene of Oddi's *Prigione d'amore*, Odoardo hopes that the "raro esempio d'amorosa prigione" provided by Flaminio's going to prison to save his friend will prove to be comedy rather than tragedy.[18] The first of two prologues to this play defines it as commedia grave, and the second presents a debate in which the personified figure of Comedia is accused of usurping Tragedia's function and answers, "Nell'amarezza delle lagrime ancora stà nascosta la dolcezza del diletto" (In the bitterness of tears there ever lies hidden the sweetness of delight). Tasso's praise of Pino's *Ingiusti sdegni* takes this form:

> Pino, il vostro leggiadro e vago stile
>> ha fatta in guisa la commedia adorna,
> che fra duci ed eroi talor soggiorna
>> lunge dal riso de la plebe umile.
> Arde e fiammeggia in lei sdegno gentile,
>> e pur bella vergogna in lei s'adorna;
>> e casto amor s'accende, e 'n lei si scorna
>> avaro cor talvolta e scherne il vile.
> E veggendosi tal, ch'ella somiglia

l'alta sorella, ha certo il socco a sdegno,
e 'l coturno da voi prender vorrebbe.
E dice: — Io già non feci il Pino indegno,
ma gloria nei teatri ei già m'accrebbe
ed or move pietate or maraviglia.

Pino, your graceful and pleasing style has so adorned comedy that she dwells betimes with rulers and heroes far from the laughter of humble folk. In her burns and flames noble anger and lovely modesty shines too; and chaste love is kindled in her and oft the miserly heart is ridiculed and baseness is mocked. And seeing herself such that she resembles her loftier sister, surely she disdains the sock and from you would take the buskin. And she says:—I did no dishonor to Pino heretofore [comedy was a creditable genre even before Pino added elements from tragedy] but he has increased my glory and stature in the theaters and moves audiences both to pity and to wonder.[19]

A minor effect of the new principles was visible in the manner of presenting the traditional figure of the courtesan. Although she could trace her origin back to the Roman meretrix, the courtesan of Italian regular comedy had always more closely resembled the ladies of the night in the *Decameron*. It might be expected that the overhauled standards of sexual morality would cause the figure of the courtesan either to appear less frequently or to be treated with greater harshness. Some commedie gravi satisfy these expectations, but in others the courtesan becomes a strikingly more sympathetic figure than she was before. Often, surpassing even Terence's sweetest-natured meretrix, she is shown as an unmercenary, loving girl with an inclination toward fidelity. Sometimes she is nobler of mind than the innamorate. Benedetto Croce admired Oddi's Ardelia for her eloquent loyalty and high concept of love.[20] The most extreme example is Aurelia of *Gli ingiusti sdegni*, who offers to put her lover through school, provide him with room, board, clothing, pocket money, and the company of the most learned men in Rome, to live only with him but in continence, if he prefers, and at the end of a year to retire to a convent and leave him all her wealth. The lover and his avaricious father accept this offer gladly, for different reasons (5.3). For all the dubious morality here, this change in the courtesan is in keeping with the other developments toward general ennoblement and complication, of character as of plot. The commedia grave is romantic in comparison with earlier comedy and with farce, and so is the myth of the good-hearted whore.

But late commedia grave was not defined by content alone; in fact, it was on gravity of structure that the greatest artistry was expended. By mid-Cinquecento the pattern of protasis, epitasis, and catastrophe formed of multiple dramatic and narrative lines had been thoroughly worked over, and writers of commedia grave, inheriting structural aim as well as pattern, found that outcomplicating their predecessors called for intricate complications indeed. They strove to tie still more knots and to untie them with a still greater display of ease. As Ruscelli advised, they avoided imitating the simple plot of the otherwise admired *Mandragola* and made comedies progress from the first act well into the fifth, "sempre crescendo in disturbi, in difficoltà, in intrighi."[21] Crying up the superiority of modern comedy, specifically his own, Della Porta notes that the peripety occurs as if naturally in the course of the fourth act, and that a close observer may also see peripety born of peripety and recognition of recognition.[22]

One way to increase complications was to double characters and misunderstandings, but as Bibbiena and his immediate successors had been no mean hands at the doubling trick, writers of commedia grave had to resort to double doubling. It is common to see several sets of lovers, parents, servants, and comic hangers-on, with as many encounters at cross-purposes as the size of the group makes possible and as may be straightened out with a few well-planned adjustments and revelations. The celebrated *Intrichi d'amore*,[23] a good example of the type's complexity, if not of its quality, includes five couples and an extra man, all loving in the wrong place, half of them in disguises, all standing in unsuspected blood or legal relation to one another; this tangled mess is *meravigliosamente* ordered at the end so that each case is settled satisfactorily, and occasions conceited moralizing in the *congedo*.

More original than the doubling and recomplicating, which simply extended earlier methods of perfecting the form of regular comedy, was the increased use in commedie gravi of governing themes and motifs. Oddi, especially in *L'erofilomachia* and *Prigione d'amore*, uses the conflict of love and friendship as a controlling force working not only on the lovers but on the entire cast of characters, binding them in a web of consistent fiber, as Della Porta does to varying degrees with sibling rivalry in *Gli duoi fratelli rivali*, with love, friendship, and honor in *Il moro*, and with jealousy in *La fantesca*. Everyone in Pino's *Ingiusti sdegni* is unjustly angry with at least one other person at some time in the course of the play. Lovers quarrel over misunderstandings, parents are angry with children for imaginary faults, children blame parents with as little justification, masters erroneously accuse servants, honorable men are suspected of dishonorable dealing, the pedant hates the courtesan as a bad influence on his pupil (when in fact it turns out that her influence is better than anyone else's), and the same pupil's father is violently anti-intellectual, which last injustice calls forth the learned playwright's sharpest style of caricature. Thus the complex pattern of intrigue traditionally built on mistakes gains greater unity by corresponding to an abstract theme, on which variations occur, not consecutively but intertwined, so that the audience may see several variations in action at once. The playwrights' expectation of applause presupposed the kind of courtly and academic audience that supported the regular drama in Italy, made up of the "attenti et avvertiti ascoltatori" (attentive and informed listeners) described by Pino in his *Breve consideratione*. These were spectators who demanded that comedy have "tutte le sue parti soavemente insieme corrispondenti" (all its parts smoothly fitted together), and for whom even the *intermedii* or *moresche* (Morris dances) must therefore be "di materia non molto lontana, ma in guisa del choro molto bene corrispondente et convenevole con l'argomento della favola" (of materials not very distant, but like a chorus closely corresponding and appropriate to the plot).[24] Their taste for a meaning manifested in pattern of action more than in development of individual characterization would be little regarded by later centuries, when comedy of situation seemed merely a mechanical prelude to a superior comedy of character. Our own century, receptive to signifying structure and mistrustful of simple distinctions between form and content, is better prepared to appreciate the grave formal aim of late Italian intrigue comedy.

The motif of supposed magic, specifically sorcery, alchemy, and astrology, which appeared early in Ariosto's *Il negromante* and earlier still in neo-Latin comedy, is tied in late commedia grave more closely than before to language, as well as to whatever happens to be the theme for the variations. Sometimes magic itself is the theme, as in Della Porta's *L'astrologo*; more often it is one of the variations.[25] Belief in sorcery and the powers of divination and transformation associated with it, which had long provided a target for the satire of regular comedy, became in the Counter-Reformation a matter for serious, concentrated attack.[26] The church's campaign against such arts as judiciary astrology underlies the comic playwright's newly biting and deliberate ridicule of charlatan sorcerer, alchemists, astrologers, and their gulls, but it is the dramatists' campaign to crush amorphous zannate and improve regular comedy that underlies the use of sorcery as a unifying structural motif.

The theme of sorcery was frequently used in conjunction with the theme of madness or as a variation on it; this was a favorite with writers of commedia grave. Real madness, supposed madness, assumed madness, fear of madness, and obsessions bordering on madness were familiar both as phenomena and as structural key signatures. The most obvious cause of alienation, in comedy as in epic and lyric poetry, was of course love. Alone, it supported several kinds of insanity, but often other causes were joined to it to create a set of mixed variations on the theme, as in Castelletti's *Stravaganze d'amore*. Here the madness, softened to *stravaganza*, or bizarre eccentricity, consists of several obsessions, and despite the title not all have to do with love. The prologue is a catalogue of stravaganze—of the courtier, the merchant, the alchemist, the miser, the lover. The characters regularly analyze the stravaganze around them, beginning with their own. Orinthia, who for love of Ostilio is disguised as her rival's maid, muses: "Che donne habbiano per amor preso habito d'huomini si è udito infinite volte, & le Comedie ne sono piene. Ma non si è mai inteso, nè letto, che donna nobile, & ricca, habbia tolto forma di vil fante, se non Orinthia... [è da] porgere a Comedie, novo, et Stravagante soggetto" (1.2: That women have put on men's clothes for love has been heard and seen repeatedly in comedies. But it has never been heard of or read that a noble and rich lady has put on the aspect of a lowly maidservant, except Orinthia...this is something to provide comedies with a new and bizarre subject).[27]

In such scenes Castelletti simultaneously links the particular situation to the general theme and mocks the clichés of the genre. Another cliché is ridiculed in the person of Rinuccio, the Platonic lover, whose recommendation of devotion to the lady's mind exclusively is mocked for its stravaganza by Ostilio, a suitor with broader aims (2.1). A third lover, Alessandro, is so stravagante in his passion that he has let his family think him dead and roams disguised as "Dottore Gratian atteggiando, e chiacchierando per questa piazza, come fanno i Gratiani nelle zannate con grandissimo dishonor" (1.1: Doctor Gratian attitudinizing and chattering in the square, as do the Gratiani with the greatest disrepute, in their clownish farces), as his servant puts it. Again Castelletti has a double aim, sketching another variation on the theme while attacking the zannate, as a writer of commedia grave should do. His use of the commedia dell'arte mask of Doctor Graziano, however, shows the interpenetration of the improvised and literary forms at the very moment when they seemed farthest apart. Alessandro's father suffers from a stravaganza on the subject of magic, imagines that malevolent spirits lie in ambush everywhere, and wastes his fortune in hopes of transmuting base metal into gold. The theme is illustrated also by the master plan that brings them together in encounters providing opportunities for other stravaganze. The structure is further tightened by reiteration of the word *stravaganza* and related imagery, and by the intermedio madrigals, each containing the title of the comedy analyzed from a different point of view.

An especially complex and intimate relationship obtained between the theme of Divine Providence and both structure and content of the commedia grave. Earlier regular comedy, like much of the Renaissance literature influencing it, had sometimes included the idea of Fortuna, operating independently of celestial control. But in the second half of the sixteenth century the Counter-Reformers found it necessary to remind Christians of the supremacy of God's providence. In tragedy it became common practice to attach a disclaimer explaining that the use by pagan characters of such words as *fortuna, fato,* and *sorte* does not represent the views of the author, a good Christian who knows that the only real Fortuna is the providence of the Prime Mover.[28]

In comedy there appeared frequent references to Divine Providence, sometimes explicit denials of fortune or stellar influence. More important, the ideas of fortune and providence were used structurally to create meaning, producing a variation on the medieval concept of comedy as metaphor of human life. Borghini's *La donna costante* provides an example of extensive development of the theme.[29] The innumerable peripeties, accidents, and chance encounters in this intrigue plot, based in part on the tale of Juliet and Romeo, are constantly attributed to fortune, the mutability of which is commented on and discussed at every opportunity. The characters invoke Fortuna, bless Fortuna, curse Fortuna, enumerate classical examples of Fortuna's fickleness in the good old medieval way. The intermedi include panoramas of the triumph and decline of the Roman Empire with comments on fortune's constantly changing style. Yet against the idea of fickle fortune is set the title of the play and the characterization of its heroine, Elfenice, whose constancy is firm in all vicissitudes. When at last the difficulties are resolved, she puts the quietus on Fortuna by thanking the "Motore di Cielo" (5.14), and the concluding intermedio neoplatonically praises love, the source of Elfenice's constancy, and defines it as a gift of the "Sommo Motore" (6th *intermedio*). Fortune only seems powerful; Providence reigns supreme, rewards constancy, and plans happy endings.

In few other commedie gravi is the pattern of intrigue governed so relentlessly by the theme of providence. But in play after play, like Castelletti's *Furbo* and Gonzaga's *Inganni,*[30] it is expressly stated that the seeming chaos and confusion of the intrigue are in fact part of a plan above change, a divine pattern, implicitly or explicitly Christian, guiding characters through innumerable *intrichi, inganni, labirinti,* and *errori* to perfect order. The very pattern of seemingly unresolvable complexities worked out to an unexpectedly simple and satisfying conclusion, the structural ideal of the writers of commedia grave, was held to be a reflection of the working of Divine Providence. And just as the theological virtue of hope depends on faith in God's providence, so the meaning of the design was tied back into the tissue of moral lesson. As Oddi says in the second prologue to *Prigione d'amore*, commedia grave teaches people, especially lovers, not to despair, by showing that in times of darkest confusion the pattern of their happiness is taking shape.

It will be noticed that except for certain commonplaces of situation, the plots of the plays used as examples of commedia grave do not resemble that of *The Comedy of Errors*. The time of searching for Shakespeare's immediate sources is past. Many Italian regular comedies are based on *Menaechmi*, but there is no reason to suppose that Shakespeare used any of them or to doubt that his sources were Plautus, Gower, and St. Paul. His choice of elements and his way of blending them, however, give pause. The addition of pathos and a hint of tragedy; the moral de-emphasizing of the courtesan's role to play up the wife Adriana and her sister; the dialogue of these two on the topos of jealousy in marriage; the weaving of multiple sources into a newly complicated pattern of errors with something like a unifying theme in the thread of feared madness and sorcery; Aegeon's evaluation of "the gods" at the beginning, proved false at the end, when maddening errors and nearly fatal sentence become instruments to reunite families and confirm loves—the combination of these elements, characteristic of late Cinquecento commedia grave, could not have been suggested by Lyly or Gascoigne, for both *Mother Bombie* and *Supposes* belong to the earlier type of regular comedy.

Although Geoffrey Bullough recognizes that Shakespeare's addition of pathos and tragic import to his source was anticipated by "some of the Italians," he still accepts E.K. Chambers's statement that Shakespeare was "consciously experimenting with an archaistic form," and he adds, "the remarkable thing is the complexity he wove within the simple outline provided by Plautus' *Menaechmi*."[31] But examining *The Comedy of Errors* against the background of the Italian tradition, as Baldwin suggests, reveals that the form is anything but archaistic. The complexity answers the demands of Italian regular comedy in general, and the character of its unity reflects the late commedia grave in particular. As for the pathos and tragic import, they are not fortuitously anticipated by "some" Italians, but were deliberately developed by a sizable group of theorizing playwrights representing the avant-garde of the day.

It cannot be proved that Shakespeare read Italian plays, or saw commedia dell'arte troupes or Italian amateurs perform commedie gravi at Elizabeth's court, or heard about them from a friend. Nor can *The Comedy of Errors* simply be labeled *commedia grave*, for Shakespeare's Italianate play is still an English one. It is next to certain, however, that the brilliant young upstart crow knew something about the latest Continental fashion in comedy.

From Louise George Clubb, *Italian Drama in Shakespeare's Time* (New Haven: Yale UP, 1989): 49–63; this chapter appeared in slightly different form as "Italian Comedy and *The Comedy of Errors*," *Comparative Literature* 19 (1967): 240–51. Reprinted with the permission of Yale University Press and *Comparative Literature*.

NOTES

[1] T.W. Baldwin, *On the Compositional Genetics of The Comedy of Errors* (Urbana, Ill., 1965), 208.

[2] Stephen Gosson, *Playes Confuted in Five Actions* (London, 1582), D6v.

[3] Ariosto's *Suppositi* in Gascoigne's *Supposes*; Grazzini's *Spiritata* in John Jeffere's (Jefferay's) *Buggbears*; Aretino's *Marescalco* in Jonson's *Epicoene*; the Intronati's *Ingannati* in the anonymous *Laelia*, a Cambridge Latin play; Salviati's *Granchio* in the anonymous *Cancer*, also a Cambridge Latin play; Piccolomini's *Alessandro* in Chapman's *May Day*; Pasqualigo's *Fedele* in Fraunce's Latin *Victoria* and Munday's *Fedele and Fortunio, the Two Italian Gentlemen*; Della Porta's *Cintia* in Hawkesworth's Latin *Labyrinthus*, his *Trappolaria* in Ruggle's Latin *Ignoramus*, his *Sorella* in Brooke's Latin *Adelphe* and Middleton's *No Wit, No Help Like a Woman's*, and his *Astrologo* in Tomkis's *Albumazar*; Oddi's *Erofilomachia* in Hawkesworth's Latin *Leander* and his *Morti vivi* in Marston's *What You Will*.

[4] See F.S. Boas, *University Drama in the Tudor Age* (Oxford, 1914).

[5] By John Wolfe (STC 17158 and STC 19911), who three years later published Guarini's *Pastor fido* and Tasso's *Aminta*. Mere anti-Catholic spirit may have created an English market for the only two well-known writers of comedy banned by the Inquisition, but on the other hand, the plays of Machiavelli and Aretino may have been printed in England

because there was a general demand for Italian drama, in the case of these two not to be satisfied by Italian printers.

[6] K.M. Lea, *Italian Popular Comedy* (Oxford, 1934), 2:362–63, 352ff.

[7] Baldwin, *Compositional Genetics*, 57.

[8] Lea, *Italian Comedy*, 2:438.

[9] William Shakespeare, *The Comedy of Errors*, Arden ed., ed. R.A. Foakes (London, 1955), Introduction, xxxiv; Baldwin, *Compositional Genetics*, 208, 356.

[10] M.C. Bradbrook, *The Growth and Structure of Elizabethan Comedy* (London, 1955), 66.

[11] Baldwin, *Compositional Genetics*, 201.

[12] Lodovico Dolce, *Fabritia* (n.p. [Venice], 1549), Dedication.

[13] Cristoforo Castelletti, *I torti amorosi* (Venice, 1581), Prologue.

[14] Bernardino Pino, *Gli ingiusti sdegni* (Rome, 1553), Prologue.

[15] Bernardino Pino, *I falsi sospetti*, 1st ed. 1579.

[16] *Fragmenti di alcune scritture della Signora Isabella Andreini Comica Gelosa, et Academica Intenta* (Venice, 1620), 60.

[17] Cristoforo Castelletti, *Le stravaganze d'amore*, 1st ed. 1584 (Venice, 1613), V. 7.

[18] Sforza Oddi, *Prigione d'amore* (Florence, 1589), 1.1.

[19] *Le rime di Torquato Tasso*, ed. Angelo Solerti (Bologna, 1902), 4: 190.

[20] Benedetto Croce, "Le commedie patetiche di Sforza Oddi," *Poeti e scrittori del pieno e del tardo rinascimento*, vol. 2 (Bari, 1958).

[21] Girolamo Ruscelli, *Delle comedie elette novamente raccolte insieme, con le correttioni, et annotationi* (Venice, 1554), "Annotationi," 182.

[22] Giambattista Della Porta, *Gli duoi fratelli rivali*, written ca. 1590 (Venice, 1601), Prologue.

[23] *Intrichi d'amore, comedia del Sig. Torquato Tasso. Rappresentata in Caprarola* (Venice, 1604), sometimes considered the joint work of members of the Accademia di Caprarola. Tasso's authorship has been defended by Enrico Malato, "Una commedia poco nota di Torquato Tasso," *Nuova Antologia* 482 (1961): 487–516. Malato has since edited and republished the comedy as Tasso's (Rome, 1976).

[24] Bernardino Pino, *Breve consideratione intorno al componimento de la comedia de'nostri tempi*, 1572, first printed with Oddi's *Erofilomachia* (Venice, 1578), B3. Some integration of intermedio madrigals and plot could be seen in earlier comedies, for example in Giannotti's *Vecchio amoroso*, written between 1533 and 1536.

[25] Only false magic is intended. Real magic, black or white, was reserved in written drama for sacre rappresentazioni, for irregular plays like those of the Congrega dei Rozzi, or for pastoral plays.

[26] In the definitive Roman Index of 1559, for example, Pope Paul IV added magic arts to the list of practices condemned in local indices of

1554 (Venice, Milan), and the decree of Pope Sixtus V in January 1586 condemned judiciary astrology and other forms of divination. See Lynn Thorndike, *A History of Magic and Experimental Science* (New York, 1941), 6:147, 156.

[27] Castelletti, *Le stravaganze d'amore*, 1.2.

[28] See Clubb, *Italian Drama*, chapter 9 "Fate is for Gentiles: The Disclaimer in Baroque Tragedy."

[29] Raffaello Borghini, *La donna costante* (Florence, 1578).

[30] Cristoforo Castelletti, *Il furbo* (Venice, 1584); Curzio Gonzaga, *Gli inganni* (Venice, 1592).

[31] Geoffrey Bullough, *Narrative and Dramatic Sources of Shakespeare*, vol. I (London, 1957): 10, 3, 5.

Dining Out in Ephesus:
Food in *The Comedy of Errors*

Joseph Candido

I

In her fine introduction to *The Comedy of Errors*, Anne Barton reiterates a familiar attitude toward Plautus's *Menaechmi*, calling it "far less complex" than the Shakespearean apprentice piece for which it nonetheless served as the major source. Plautus's drama abounds with "simple and rigidly type-cast" stock characters, and has little "object or concern other than to turn the normal world upside down and to evoke laughter of a simple and unreflective kind."[1] Clearly the critic who goes searching for profound comic insight of a Shakespearean sort in Plautine imitations of Greek New Comedy is inviting scholarly shipwreck. Yet despite the perils involved, I should like to enter Shakespeare's play through Plautus's, considering a rather prominent feature of *The Menaechmi* that, despite its farcical predictability and limited development, appears to have quickened Shakespeare's comic invention as he fashioned his drama.

It is possible that Shakespeare knew in manuscript William Warner's 1595 translation of *The Menaechmi*, a lively and rather faithful version of Plautus's play that contains some suggestive verbal parallels to *The Comedy of Errors*.[2] Warner forsakes the tedious prologue of Plautus and begins instead (after a brief ten-line "argument") with the play proper, specifically the long introductory statement by the ever-hungry Peniculus, the parasite of Menaechmus of Epidamnum. The speech is striking both for its broad and conventional comic buffoonery on the subject of food,[3] and, perhaps less obviously, for what it implies about the centrality of food and dining in helping to define social relationships in the play. For the parasite, whose only object is the exploitation of the unusually generous Menaechmus, food serves as the ultimate tool of male friendship and social control. It matters little to Peniculus that he is fettered by dependency; his utter servility finds full contentment in the maintenance of a sort of male umbilical cord ("belly bands" as one translator puts it)[4] that ensures his version of survival:

> If then ye would keep a man without all suspition of running away from ye, the surest way is to tie him with meate, drink and ease: Let him ever be idle, eate his belly full, and carouse while his skin will hold, and he shall never, I warrant ye, stir a foote. These strings to tie one by the teeth, passe all the bands of iron, steele, or what metall so ever, for the more slack and easie ye make them, the faster still they tie the partie which is in them.... I meane to visit [Menaechmus] at dinner: for my stomacke meethinkes even thrusts me into the fetters of his daintie fare. (p. 13)

No sooner is Peniculus's paean to sycophancy at an end than he meets the irate Menaechmus, fresh from an argument with his wife and determined to abandon "the madbraine scold" at home (p. 13). The talk turns immediately to food. Just as Peniculus defines his bond with Menaechmus in terms of the ties, strings, and fetters of a shared meal in which by some strange rhetorical and psychological alchemy friendship and the full belly serve as metaphors for each other, Menaechmus articulates his alienation from his wife in similar terms. His response to the reopening of a long-standing marital breach is to exact a sort of culinary revenge that goes beyond mere wayward belly cheer: "I mean to dine this day abroad with a sweet friend of mine," Erotium (p. 14). Despite the fact that Peniculus will make a third, the dinner is fraught with psychological and sexual significance. Erich Segal has shown, in a much-criticized yet nonetheless useful book, how centrally *The Menaechmi* turns on the tension between *Industria* and *Voluptas*, or what Freud would call the reality principle and the pleasure principle.[5] Segal has some instructive comments to make on the composition of Menaechmus's proposed dinner, particularly as the foods involved may suggest the psychological importance of the feast to the angry husband:

But the delicacies which Menaechmus orders and all food "along those lines" were specifically forbidden to Romans by the current sumptuary laws. These, according to Pliny, forbade the eating of *abdomnia, glandia, testiculi, vulvae, sincipita verrina*. Not only do these outward items figure prominently on Menaechmus's bill of fare, but Plautus plays with them verbally, concocting dishes like *sincipita-menta*, and the comic patronymics *glandionida* and *pernonida*. Apparently Menaechmus is savoring his words in anticipation of the breaking-of-the-rules banquet. (p. 48)

Thus Menaechmus's choice of *Voluptas* over *Industria* is closely bound up with a distinctly un-Roman release from responsibility as represented visually on stage by the abandoned house and further implied by his temporary absence from the offstage Mart. But his choice of *Voluptas* also suggests a reckless holiday from accepted social norms in which male dependency, marital revenge, and iconoclastic behavior become embedded in banqueting. For Menaechmus the forbidden meal signifies a powerful—if soon disrupted—denial of wife, occupation, and responsibility that crams self- and societal rejection into a voluptuous culinary exercise with parasite and whore.

Part of the "uncomplicated" humor of *The Menaechmi*, of course, involves the ludicrous errors produced when one twin is confused with the other; and it is perhaps no coincidence that the first blunder of this kind is made by Cylindrus the cook, who mistakes the circumspect Menaechmus-Sosicles for his more emotional brother of Epidamnum. The episode plays rhetorical sleight-of-hand with the tripartite association of courtesan, parasite, and food, evoking each of the three in various relations to the others. Warner's translation is particularly good at capturing the scene's compact and suggestive bawdiness: "Thinke ye I have brought meate inough for three of you? If not, ile fetche more for you and your wench, and Snatchcrust your Parasite" (p. 19). And when Erotium appears just afterwards, she addresses the man she mistakenly supposes to be her Menaechmus in language that cements the identification of the illicit feast with adultery. Her sexually symbolic open door, in clear contrast to the shut house of the nameless wife, affords the ultimate in romantic refuge for the alienated husband:

> Let the doore stand so, away, it shall not be shut.... Cover the boord, put fire under the perfuming pannes, let all things be very handsome. Where is hee, that *Cylindrus* sayd stood without here? Oh, what meane you sweet heart, that ye come not in? I trust you thinke yourselfe more welcome to this house then to your owne, and great reason why you should do so. Your dinner & all things are readie as you willed. Will ye go sit downe?   (pp. 19–20)

But the visiting Menaechmus—no innocent himself who resolves selfishly to "coozen" Erotium at dinner (p. 21)—will, unlike his more magnanimous brother, allow no parasite to share his feast. His explicit rejection of his brother's companion ("Ile neither staie for him, nor have him let come in, if he do come" [p. 21]), gets symbolically reenacted when he meets Peniculus after the dinner with Erotium. Peniculus has become separated from Menaechmus of Epidamnum in the course of the day's events, and when he sees the now-sated likeness of his friend coming from Erotium's house he mistakes him for the man he thinks has given him "the slip" earlier in the day (p. 22). When Menaechmus the Traveler insults Peniculus by claiming not to know him ("Away filthie mad drivell, away: I will talke no longer with thee" [p. 23]), the parasite determines to "make this same as unblest a dinner as ever [Menaechmus] eate" (p. 23) by informing the wife of her husband's supposed infidelities. Thus male dependency and marriage dissolve at the hands of the unfed parasite and the selfish brother. Menaechmus of Epidamnum returns from his day of business to an ungrateful friend, to a faithless courtesan (Erotium has not only mistakenly given the wrong brother dinner but also a cloak belonging to Menaechmus's wife), and to a failed marriage:

> Never in my life had I more overthwart fortune in one day, and all by the villanie of this false knave the Parasite, my *Ulisses* that works such mischiefs against mee his king. But let me live no longer but ile be revengde uppon the life of him: his life? nay tis my life,

for hee lives by my meate and drinke. Ile utterly withdraw the slaves life from him. And *Erotium* shee sheweth plainly what she is: who because I require the cloake againe to carrie to my wife, saith I gave it her, and flatly falles out with me. How unfortunate am I?

(pp. 32–33)

Despite the ludicrous intervention on the part of the wife's father to save the marriage (his stern admonitions to his daughter on female subservience and his attempted abduction of his son-in-law for enforced psychological treatment are of no avail), there is no remedy for the union. The play ends cynically on a note of comic alienation rather than marital joy. In response to his brother's plea Menaechmus of Epidamnum will follow his resourceful twin to Syracuse, sell his "servaunts, household stuffe, house, ground and all"—even his wife if anyone is foolish enough to "bid money for her" (p. 39).

As I have already noted, no one could claim that *The Menaechmi* contains the tonal, psychological, or philosophical richness and depth of Shakespeare's play. Anne Barton puts the matter with characteristic succinctness when, in tracing the literary genealogy of *The Comedy of Errors*, she observes that "between Menander's *Epitrepontes* and *Periceiromene* and Shakespeare's play there stretches not only an immense gulf of space and time but also the fact of Christianity with its stress upon the inner life."[6] Indeed, one could easily argue that Shakespeare's play is at least as much Pauline as it is Plautine. Yet despite the essentially farcical nature of *The Menaechmi*—its stock characters, predictable action, and broad humor—the play is clearly not without certain intimations of comic seriousness and depth. There is, for example, in addition to the implied psychological aspects of the episodes I have cited, a vaguely Chaplinesque vulnerability in the reaction of Menaechmus of Epidamnum when, after being rescued by his brother's servant, who mistakenly takes him for his master, he replies: "On mine honestie, I am none of thy maister, I had never yet anie servant would do so much for me" (p. 35). Although the sad poverty of human relationships is implicit both here and at other points in *The Menaechmi*, the idea often recedes in the wake of the play's broad and bumptious humor. But the intimation of a serious comic concern, although only faintly urged in *The Menaechmi*, would have been no less available to Shakespeare on that account. I should like to suggest, then, that Shakespeare, in filling out his Plautine model, seized upon the quietly implied idea of human longing and its connection with food and dining, and that he took what in Plautus had receded behind farce and pushed it into the dramatic forefront of *The Comedy of Errors*.

II

C.L. Barber and Richard P. Wheeler observe shrewdly that in *The Comedy of Errors* "Shakespeare is marvelous at conveying a sense of a world already there," and cite Dromio of Ephesus's first words as illustrating the "routine tensions" of "daily, ordinary life" that pervade the play:[7]

> The capon burns, the pig falls from the spit;
> The clock hath strucken twelve upon the bell:
> My mistress made it one upon my cheek:
> She is so hot, because the meat is cold.   (I.ii.44–47)

The passage is a fine indication of Shakespeare's early genius at dramatic economy, for not only does it catch effortlessly the rhythms of "a world already there," it also points to certain rhetorical and psychological traits that bind the parted Antipholuses and their Dromios together even as the two pairs of twins remain comically at odds throughout much of the play. Dromio's urgent concern over such matters as tardiness for dinner, the condition of food, household plans gone awry, and the anger of his mistress, is by no means exceptional in *The Comedy of Errors*, for voiced attention to the seemingly unremarkable events of day-to-day life occupy the two Antipholuses and their servants with striking regularity. Listen to Antipholus of Syracuse as he first sets foot in Ephesus:

> Within this hour it will be dinner-time;
> Till that, I'll view the manners of the town,
> Peruse the traders, gaze upon the buildings,

And then return and sleep within my inn,
For with long travel I am stiff and weary.   (I.ii.11–15)

The banal itinerary of the tourist tends not to be fit matter for Shakespearean romantic comedy, but in *The Comedy of Errors* bed and board often come abruptly to the forefront of the action. We are seldom unaware of people going to and from dinner or talking about the comforts of food and home. It is perhaps natural enough that the traveling Antipholus of Syracuse—whose sense of aimless nonattachment is so resonantly conveyed by the metaphor of the lone water drop seeking its fellow in the ocean (I.ii.35–38)—should be attracted to the security and solidity implied by the shared meal. He is, to be sure, an earnest seeker of dining companions, oddly receptive, for example, to the sudden feast thrust upon him by total strangers later in the play, and eager to make a dinner engagement with the first native Ephesian he meets. We miss much in the play if we ignore the tentative yet deep longing for connection behind his invitation to the anonymous Ephesian merchant:

What, will you walk with me about the town,
And then go to my inn and dine with me?   (I.ii.22–23)

Coming as it does after Antipholus's admission of frequent "care and melancholy" (I.ii.20), the remark suggests a yearning for the personal and societal integration so sadly absent in the separated twin. Instructive in this regard are the concluding lines of the Ephesian Dromio's previously cited call to dinner, which both elaborate on the servant's urgent request and place the longings of the Syracusan visitor in a wider and more richly suggestive social context:

The meat is cold, because you come not home:
You come not home, because you have no stomach:
You have no stomach, having broke your fast:
But we that know what 'tis to fast and pray,
Are penitent for your default to-day.   (I.ii.48–52)

Dromio's witty admonition points to serious matters that go beyond a mere hunger for food and society; it posits a social reality in which a genuine and strongly felt causal relationship exists between the abandoned meal and intimate moral and marital concerns. The five lines that take us from cold meat to implied sinfulness ("your default to-day"),[8] hinge on the assumption that Ephesus is a place where social ceremonies matter, where the wayward husband's suspected dining away ("having broke [his] fast") has serious consequences for his relationship to wife and home. Antipholus of Ephesus's absence has transformed his house into the social equivalent of a spiritually unprofitable Lent, imposing a penitential fasting on all its inhabitants and eliciting from his wife a resentment that manifests itself in violence to her servant and angry abstinence (I.ii.90).[9]

Before discussing the marital—and expressly sexual—implications of the Ephesian husband's absence from dinner at home, I should first like to review briefly the status of the midday meal for Shakespeare and his audience. William Harrison in his *Description of England* (1577, 1587) has much to say about the importance of the noon dinner for Elizabethans, particularly since this was the central and most elaborate meal of the day. Harrison's moralistic digression on dining habits, although not explicitly related to the action of Shakespeare's play, nonetheless indicates the close relationship between social mores and social morality. He disparages the frequent "odd repasts" of earlier times that included "breakfasts in the forenoon, beverages or nuncheons after dinner, and thereto reresuppers generally when it was time to go to rest,"[10] preferring instead the more enlightened modern habit of eating once, or at most twice, a day. Even this practice, however, is not without the gluttonous abuse of "long and stately sitting at meat" (p. 141): "For the nobility, gentlemen, and merchantmen, especially at great meetings, do sit commonly till two or three of the clock at afternoon, so that with many is an hard matter, to rise from the table to go to Evening Prayer and return from thence to come time enough to supper" (p. 141).

The "supper" to which Harrison alludes was a much lighter evening meal that carried little of the formal or symbolic character of the noon dinner. Lu Emily Pearson and Muriel St. Clare Byrne, both of whom examine in some detail the richly allusive meanings implicit in dinner at the home of a well-to-do Elizabethan, make this point persuasively.[11] Echoing Harrison, Pearson notes how the noon meal could drag on almost to supper with only time for evening prayer between; she then proceeds to underscore the personal and social symbolism implicit in the long repast: "cooking, like ornate architecture or elaborate dress or anything else that might impress one's acquaintances with a display of wealth, became a very important advertisement of a man's financial status.... No one was ever expected to partake of all the dishes but to eat and drink moderately by making a selection from the variety so bounteously offered" (pp. 556–57).

Although Pearson here is describing a somewhat more elaborate dinner than the family meal that Antipholus of Ephesus disregards so casually in *The Comedy of Errors*, even the ordinary dinner prepared for family alone was a matter of some culinary complexity for the housewife. (At least three main dishes were usually served, not including vegetables, bread, and drink, and Dromio mentions capon and pig specifically.) Moreover, Adriana's Elizabethan counterpart could have expected guests on short or no notice—witness the fact that Antipholus of Ephesus approaches his house with Angelo and Balthazar in tow—and her readiness in preparation would have been a sign of her domestic competence as well as her magnanimity as a hostess. Her social role—indeed her identity as wife—was linked in some measure to her success at entertaining, just as her husband's public reputation was linked to the affluence of his board.[12] Along these lines Pearson notes that "even everyday meals were served with due decorum in well-managed homes, and the table was carefully set" (p. 565). Byrne further elaborates on what she calls the "ceremony" observed for daily dinner in "a well-to-do townsman's household":

> a cloth was laid upon the table, and at every place was set a trencher, a napkin, and a spoon. Wine, ale, and drinking vessels, Harrison tells us, stood on the buffet, and the servants filled a clean goblet or Venetian drinking glass when any guest called for liquor. In the kitchen quarters the butler took pains to chip the bread in order to remove

any cinders from the crust, and he also squared each piece neatly before he set it on the board. Finally, the great salt-cellar would be placed on the table, and with basin,[13] ewer, and fine damask towel ready to hand for the diners' ablutions, all was prepared. (p. 30)

Clearly Antipholus of Ephesus's failure to come to dinner on time is a repudiation of more than mere food; his absence from home is the first step in the flouting of an accepted social ceremony that helps define his identity as respected citizen and respectful husband. It is surely no coincidence that in the course of the play he is threatened with the loss of both of these socially and emotionally vital aspects of the self. Reputation and marriage begin to dissolve together when the wrong brother dines at home.[14]

When viewed in this context Adriana's behavior assumes a deeper and more richly suggestive character than the mere ragings of a jealous housewife. Her determination to refrain from eating despite the fact that her husband is two hours late (II.i.3) indicates a serious attempt to maintain personal equilibrium and social bonds in the face of heavy pressures.[15] Adriana is no mere jealous shrew (her readiness to forgive later in the play is too often slighted); rather she is a fiercely combative woman confronting squarely the threat of an imperiled marriage and determined to sustain meaningful ties despite social and personal threats to her identity as wife and Lady. This is, oddly enough, a fact that her didactic and self-assured sister fails to recognize. Luciana's smug suggestion to "let us dine, and never fret" (II.i.6) implies an indifference to her sister's emotional plight that reveals the severe limitations of the unwedded woman's easy aphorisms about marriage (II.i.15–25). Adriana knows better; her rhetoric wisely acknowledges the heavy emotional toll exacted by her husband's absence in terms lost on her sister:

His company must do his minions grace,
Whilst I at home *starve* for a merry look:
. . . .
But, too unruly deer, he breaks the pale,
And *feeds from home*; poor I am but his stale.
(II.i.87–101; emphasis added)

III

When Adriana finally locates the man she believes to be her Antipholus, her first instinct is to reestablish old connections by clarifying the proper relationship of husband to wife. Her moving speech on the mystical Christian notion that the married couple are one flesh evokes longingly an earlier stage of her marriage when identities were stable and rooted securely in the simple ceremonies of everyday life:

> The time was once, when thou unurg'd wouldst vow
> That never words were music to thine ear,
> That never object pleasing in thine eye,
> That never touch well welcome to thy hand,
> That never meat sweet-savor'd in thy taste,
> Unless I spake, or look'd, or touch'd, or carv'd to thee.
> (II.ii.113–18)

Adriana's suggestive use of the Syracusan brother's earlier image of "a drop of water in the breaking gulf" to define marital inseparability (II.ii.126) further implies her sense of identification with the man before her, particularly as he represents—in an almost literal sense—the younger and more innocent version of her husband.[16] Her urgent invitation to the Syracusan twin can thus be seen symbolically as a psychologically necessary act of marital renewal; Adriana's desire for the earlier and untainted version of her husband is symbolically fulfilled as she enacts with the younger twin the meaningful social ceremony that defines for her the basis of a stable marriage. Speaking, looking, and touching—the characteristic intimacies of romantic love—fuse curiously in her mind with carving. Moral realignment and marital recommitment both meet for the anxious wife in the ordered normalcy of the shared meal:

> Come, come, no longer will I be a fool,
> To put the finger in the eye and weep,
> Whilst man and master laughs my woes to scorn.
> Come, sir, to dinner. Dromio, keep the gate.
> Husband, I'll dine above with you to-day,

And shrive you of a thousand idle pranks.
Sirrah, if any ask you for your master,
Say he dines forth, and let no creature enter.   (II.ii.203–10)

The episode is rich with implication. Anthropologists such as Mary Douglas and Claude Levi-Strauss have painstakingly detailed the close association of food with sexual longings and sexual identity.[17] Douglas, in particular, has probed how in various cultures "sexual and gastronomic consummation are made equivalents of one another by reasons of analogous restrictions applied to each" (p. 71), a phenomenon with obvious implications for the marital identity of the couple.[18] Similarly, Adriana's renewed enthusiasm for dinner with the man she thinks is her husband appears to include such psychological concerns. Despite the fact that Luciana will accompany the pair, theirs will be a rather private meal, "above," symbolically located in the living quarters upstairs rather than in the more public business quarters below. Moreover, the exclusivity of the meal is further underscored by Adriana's (unintentionally ironic) instructions to Dromio to tell all callers that her husband dines away, and by her explicit order to the servant to "play the porter well...let none enter, lest I break your pate" (II.ii.211, 218). Clearly there is more at stake here for Adriana than the rearrangement of a disturbed afternoon. Her private family meal serves as a convenient social vehicle for the larger issue of forgiveness, and her insistence on privacy metaphorically links confidential family matters with the equally confidential regenerative power of the confessional: "Husband, I'll...shrive you of a thousand idle pranks." Even Luciana seems to sense what the renewed meal means symbolically for her sister; there is a note of urgency as well as impatience in her enjoinder to the puzzled guest: "Come, come, Antipholus, we dine too late" (II.ii.219).

The arrival of the real husband, of course, throws all into confusion; but as is so often the case in The Comedy of Errors, it is a confusion that abruptly forces characters to clarify identities and locate priorities. As Antipholus of Ephesus approaches his house with Angelo and Balthazar, he exudes a settled complacency with the verities of his mercantile and male-oriented world. He is late for dinner, and although he knows that Adriana "is shrewish when I keep not hours" (III.i.2), he believes that the remedy for her discontent lies in the protective duplicity of his friend the goldsmith: "Say that I linger'd with you at your shop / To see the making of her carcanet, / And that to-morrow you will bring it home" (III.i.3–5). Antipholus's crass gift of the necklace (which in anger he later transfers to the Courtesan) illustrates the immense psychological gap that separates his materialist notion of marriage from Adriana's loftier attitude of Christian idealism. For the inattentive husband, whose response to marital drift is to placate his wife with costly trinkets, the midday meal carries none of the deep-seated marital or sexual significance that it does for Adriana. Indeed, there is every indication that Antipholus sees the dinner as an *exclusively* male concern, an occasion for refined humanist discourse on the relationship of food to friendship, but little more. Any thought of the neglected wife disappears under the somewhat precious and over-embroidered male niceties that precede Antipholus's discovery of the locked door:

E. Ant.   Y' are sad, Signior Balthazar, pray God our cheer
          May answer my good will and your good welcome here.
Balth.   I hold your dainties cheap, sir, and your welcome dear.
E. Ant.   O, Signior Balthazar, either at flesh or fish,
          A table full of welcome makes scarce one dainty dish.
Balth.   Good meat, sir, is common; that every churl affords.
E. Ant.   And welcome more common, for that's nothing but words.
Balth.   Small cheer and great welcome makes a merry feast.
E. Ant.   Ay, to a niggardly host and more sparing guest:
          But though my cates be mean, take them in good part;
          Better cheer may you have, but not with better heart.
          But soft, my door is lock'd; go bid them let us in.
                                     (III.i.19–30)

The stark reality of Adriana's shut door, carrying as it does the same sexual implications as that of the angry wife in *The Menaechmi*, turns Antipholus's dinner of male friendship and ostentation into a marital crisis. By virtue of his denied access to home and wife, the Ephesian brother comes to experience precisely the same feelings of alienation and sexual doubt that he has so casually inflicted upon his wife. But the confusion here produces more than mere psychological tit-for-tat. Antipholus's isolation outside the locked house functions symbolically to define the spiritual divorce he has already produced while at the same time literalizing ominously the ends to which his neglect will lead. In this sense the Ephesian brother joins Adriana, his twin, Egeon, and Aemelia in experiencing the anxieties of isolation and nonattachment, with the significant difference that in his case he alone is to blame. There is a fine irony to the fact that while Antipholus suspects Adriana with another man, his real rival for his virtuous wife is the earlier and idealized image of himself as represented in his younger brother. Adriana *does* love another man—the Antipholus she so longingly evokes as she recalls what her husband once was, the Antipholus she believes she is restoring at dinner in her upstairs room. In an almost literal sense, then, the Ephesian brother is in conflict with himself, thus embodying, in another more resonantly suggestive form, the self-division that is everywhere in the play.[19] As Balthazar wisely points out, Antipholus's unseemly attempt to break into his own house in full view of others is really a senseless act of violence to self:

> Have patience, sir, O, let it not be so!
> Herein you war against your reputation,
> And draw within the compass of suspect
> Th' unviolated honor of your wife.
> . . . .
> If by strong hand you offer to break in
> Now in the stirring passage of the day,
> A vulgar comment will be made of it;
> And that supposed by the common rout
> Against your yet ungalled estimation,
> That may with foul intrusion enter in,
> And dwell upon your grave when you are dead.
>
> (III.i.85–104)

Although the irate husband finally departs "in quiet" (III.i.107), he hardly departs emotionally intact; self-rebellion and self-loathing, not just revenge, drive Antipholus to dinner at the Courtesan's.

The two separate dining experiences of the two identical twins stand in sharp contrast to each other; yet they also reflect each other in curious ways. For Antipholus of Ephesus the dinner with the Courtesan contains many of the same psychological elements as that planned by his Plautine counterpart in *The Menaechmi*. Just as Menaechmus of Epidamnum's choice of *Voluptas* over *Industria* involved a rejection of his wife for male companionship and dinner with Erotium, the Ephesian twin invites his male friends to dine with him at the Courtesan's where he will bestow the necklace "for nothing but to spite my wife" (III.i.118). Obviously Antipholus's rebellious dinner, at which the materialistic sign of his weak marital commitment is to change hands, represents the moral opposite of Adriana's feast of reconciliation. Perhaps less obvious, however, is the way in which the younger Antipholus's behavior at Adriana's dinner unwittingly parallels the unfaithfulness of his brother. As the symbolic embodiment of the younger version of his Ephesian twin, Antipholus of Syracuse reenacts his brother's behavior by forsaking the woman who has welcomed him to the feast and turning his romantic attention to another. In professing love for Luciana he sounds strangely like an only slightly exaggerated version of his older brother:

Your weeping sister is no wife of mine,
Nor to her bed no homage do I owe:
Far more, far more, to you do I decline.   (III.ii.41–43)

And later, when alone, he finds an even more distinctly "Antipholan" mode of expression:

She that doth call me husband, even my soul
Doth for a wife abhor. But her fair sister,
Possess'd with such a gentle sovereign grace,
Of such enchanting presence and discourse,
Hath almost made me traitor to myself.   (III.ii.158–62)

Something very close to this attitude (expressed in strikingly similar rhetoric) lies behind the Ephesian brother's attraction to the "wench of excellent discourse, / Pretty and witty; wild, and yet, too, gentle" (III.i.109–10), at whose home he will dine and to whom he will give his wife's necklace. At both dinners Adriana is rejected by her husband.

IV

Adriana's broken banquet fails to produce its desired ends, but it nonetheless sets in motion a process of moral and social realignment that continues to the end of the play. Critics have generally tended to overlook the rejected wife's response to her failed dinner, particularly her remarks upon hearing that at the meal her supposed husband has tried to woo Luciana:

> He is deformed, crooked, old, and sere,
> Ill-fac'd, worse bodied, shapeless every where;
> Vicious, ungentle, foolish, blunt, unkind,
> Stigmatical in making, worse in mind.
> . . . .
> Ah, but I think him better than I say,
> And yet would herein others' eyes were worse:
> Far from her nest the lapwing cries away;
> My heart prays for him, though my tongue do curse.
> (IV.ii.19–28)

The division here between heart and tongue, feeling and saying, focuses upon yet another pair of forceful oppositions embedded in singleness. Adriana's acknowledgement of her inner divisions not only reflects the outer and more obvious tensions involved in relationships like twinship, sisterhood, marriage, and friendship; it also points implicitly to a means of finding concord in discord. Adriana is a frequent object of others' criticism—her husband, sister, and mother-in-law are only the most vocal examples—yet despite it all she remains the most fully responsive and synthetic character in the play, preferring finally in a crisis to labor at forgiveness rather than to ease into recrimination. If her first significant act of synthesis is her attempted dinner, her second is her readiness to forgive her husband despite its apparent failure. Her recognition of her own divided response to the supposed infidelity of her husband—outward rage and inward love—and her determination to act charitably in the face of it, implies the wise acceptance of a psychological duality in her self and in her husband that is symbolically represented in the two identical yet separate twins. The gold she gives to ransom her Antipholus is the surest sign of her clear-sighted resolve to meet rejection with forgiveness despite warring inner tensions: "Go Dromio...bring thy master home immediately. / Come, sister, I am press'd down with conceit— / Conceit, my comfort and my injury" (IV.ii.63–66). When the younger Antipholus rejects the Courtesan as his older brother should have ("I conjure thee to leave me and be gone" [IV.iii.67]), his behavior ratifies symbolically the process of marital reconciliation that Adriana's charity has begun. But the younger Antipholus's behavior is more than merely symbolic; it also has the practical effect of eroding the Ephesian brother's newly formed relationship with the Courtesan. After being turned away by Antipholus of Syracuse (whom she takes for the Ephesian twin), the Courtesan does an emotional about-face in order to recoup the day's financial losses. Her blatant self-concern—in clear contrast to Adriana's charity—only heightens the emotional poverty of her makeshift meal with the wayward husband:

> My way is now to hie home to his house,
> And tell his wife that, being lunatic,
> He rush'd into my house, and took perforce
> My ring away. This course I fittest choose,
> For forty ducats is too much to lose.   (IV.iii.92–96)

But even Adriana, despite her strenuous attempts to sustain and revivify her marriage, is hardly guiltless of marital neglect. Like her husband, she must endure a harsh public embarrassment that airs private wrongs and forces her to confront squarely her share in the weakened relationship. Her sister's earnest yet commonplace strictures on the superiority of husband to wife (II.i.15–25) pale beside the withering—and more imperiously authoritative—criticism of the Abbess. Unlike Luciana, who relies on traditional and essentially Pauline notions of marriage to upbraid her sister, the Abbess turns her criticism inward to the intimate day-to-day activities of bedroom and kitchen that Adriana sees as her special province. The Abbess is, ironically, not nearly as concerned with theological and religious matters as she is with the practical goings-on inside Adriana's household. In this sense she sounds far less like a cloistered sister than like the concerned mother-in-law that she is. Here is the Abbess just after she learns, from Adriana herself, of the wife's frequent and public criticisms of her husband:

And thereof came it that the man was mad.
The venom clamors of a jealous woman
Poisons more deadly than a mad dog's tooth.
It seems his sleeps were hind'red by thy railing,
And thereof comes it that his head is light.
Thou say'st his meat was sauc'd with thy upbraidings:
Unquiet meals make ill digestions,
Thereof the raging fire of fever bred,
And what's a fever but a fit of madness?
Thou say'st his sports were hind'red by thy brawls:
Sweet recreation barr'd, what doth ensue
But moody and dull melancholy,
Kinsman to grim and comfortless despair,
And at her heels a huge infectious troop
Of pale distemperatures and foes to life?
In food, in sport, and life-preserving rest
To be disturb'd, would mad or man or beast:
The consequence is then, thy jealous fits
Hath scar'd thy husband from the use of wits.   (V.i.68–86)

The speech links two important domestic responsibilities that went hand-in-hand for the Elizabethan housewife, preparing food and ministering to the sick. Popular handbooks of the day such as Sir Hugh Plat's *Delightes for Ladies* (1608) repeatedly spelled out this dual responsibility.[20] Plat's four-part discourse takes up such matters as "The Arte of Preseruing," "Secrets in Distillation," and "Cookerie and Huswiferie," concluding with a detailed section on powders, ointments, and home cures that the good housewife would need to know in order to perform her domestic duties successfully. Here one can find remedies for problems such as yellow teeth, chilblains, pimpled or burned skin, bodily bruises of various sorts, and almost any other commonplace malady of the day. Implicit in Plat's book, particularly its final section, is a recognition of the important role of the housewife as custodian of domestic order and ease. In addition to her skill in the preparation of food (the largest part of the book consists of recipes), the resourceful mistress of an Elizabethan house was expected to produce medical results like that which relieved one "M. *Foster* an Essex man and an Atturney of the Common pleas" of an inflamed face: "Qvilt bay salt well dried & powdered, in double linnen sockes of a prettie bignesse, let the patient weare them in wide hose and shooes day and night, by the space of fourteene daies, or till he be well: euerie morning and euening let him dry his sockes by the fire and put them on againe" (p. 93). It is presumably Adriana's inattentiveness to details such as these to which the Abbess alludes when she speaks of the "huge infectious troop / Of pale distemperatures and foes to life" that characterize the wife's disordered household. Adriana should have paid more attention to Thomas Tusser, whose earnest *Points of Huswifery, United to the Comfort of Husbandry* (1573), also sees attention to food and physic as dual but hardly separate concerns for women like Adriana. Tusser's advice could almost serve as a shorthand introduction to some of the key critical issues in *The Comedy of Errors*:

> Good huswives provide, ere an' sickness do come,
> Of sundry good things, in her house to have some:
> Good *aqua composita*, and vinegar tart,
> Rose-water, and treacle, to comfort the heart.
> Cold herbs in her garden, for agues that burn,
> That over strong heat, to good temper may turn.   (p. 274)

> Use mirth and good word,
>   At bed and at board.
> Provide for thy husband, to make him good cheer,
> Make merry together, while time ye be here.
> At bed and at board, howsoever befall,
> Whatever God sendeth, be merry withall.

> No brawling make,

No jealousy take.
No taunts before servants, for hindering of fame,
No jarring too loud, for avoiding of shame.   (p. 266)[21]

Tusser's cautionary advice could hardly be more apt in Adriana's case. The wife's defense of her jealous accusations is the virtual textbook antithesis of Tusser's admonitions:

It [suspected philandering] was the copy of our conference:
In bed he slept not for my urging it;
At board he fed not for my urging it;
Alone, it was the subject of my theme;
In company I often glanced it;
Still did I tell him it was vile and bad.   (V.i.62–67)

Adriana has indeed acted well in trying to refashion her broken noon meal into a dinner of forgiveness for her supposed husband, but absent from her notion of the shared meal is her own penitence for past wrongs. Now, for the first time, we sense why her husband may have been late for dinner in the first place, for he had little reason to expect anything like the calm repast it was his wife's duty to supply. As the Abbess so pointedly says: "his meat was sauc'd with thy upbraidings: / Unquiet meals make ill digestions." Adriana's repeated unquiet meals have provided more sustenance for Antipholus's "raging fire of fever" and "moody and dull melancholy" than they have for his physical and emotional well-being. Adriana has, in short, forsaken the role of hostess and healer that it was her marital duty to perform. To her credit, however, she responds to this open exposé of her shortcomings, as she always does to a crisis, with admirable clear-sightedness. Her reaction to the Abbess's scathing public denunciation would have made Tusser proud:

I will attend my husband, be his nurse,
Diet his sickness, for it is my office,
And will have no attorney but myself,
And therefore let me have him home with me. (V.i.98–101)

Adriana's suggestive "Diet his sickness" indicates a clear psychological commitment to her twin responsibilities as purveyor of meals and overseer of home remedies. Implicit in her response is the full acceptance of her role as custodian of the day-to-day activities that ensure marital harmony and household ease. In this sense Adriana becomes the willing secular equivalent of the Abbess, the mistress of a religious household, whose "wholesome syrups, drugs, and holy prayers" are "the charitable duty" of her order (V.i.104–107). Religious mother-in-law and secular wife merge psychologically in a mutual determination to ensure "food, sport, and life-preserving rest" for the separate Antipholuses in their care.

V

It is frequently observed that the last act of *The Comedy of Errors*, while suggesting some degree of familial reorientation and renewal, stops short of a full affirmation of marital harmony. This is essentially the view of Alexander Leggatt, who, in an allusive and sensitive essay on the play, points out that there is no explicit reconciliation between Adriana and her husband, leaving the final state of their marriage "an open question." For Leggatt the idea of reconciliation in marriage is not utterly dismissed "but it is quietly placed in the background, and no great hopes are pinned on it."[22] This is true enough, for at the end of the play we have no actual nuptial rite or even the symbolic evocation of one as we sometimes do in Shakespearean comedy. Instead the emphasis here is on the unification of an old family (even its younger members are old enough to have grown apart) rather than on the earnest hope for beginning a new one. But this is not to say that *The Comedy of Errors* is without its own significant—and characteristic—comic closure. When the multiple confusions are finally resolved, the Abbess invites the assembled company into *her* dwelling for a dining experience of a very different sort from those we have seen earlier in the play. This will be a "gossips' feast" (V.i.406), that is, a baptismal banquet at which the whole family assembles to welcome with joy a new member into a social and religious community. As such, it is a time for reestablishing old bonds and reaffirming one's commitment to a set of moral and religious values that impart spiritual significance to the activities of daily life.[23] It is a mended and more comprehensive version of the failed dinners of Adriana and the Courtesan, containing as it does the security and shared spiritual objectives theirs so obviously lack. At the Abbess's feast, in sharp contrast to the dinners planned by Adriana and the Courtesan, participants exist in a stable and recognizable relationship to each other. Indeed, the whole purpose of a baptismal gathering is to ratify collectively the stabilization of one's identity, for it is the baptismal act that fixes a new creature once and for all with a name that denotes both who he is and what one hopes he will become. The Abbess's feast is thus an attempt to reach backward—symbolically at least—to Egeon's and Aemelia's experience with their twin infants on the mast, to begin time again at the key moment when the sacramental stability of a double christening can cancel the psychological division of family shipwreck. Perhaps the surest sign of the need for such stability is the obvious personal and social chaos produced by twin brothers with *identical* names, a consequence that would have been impossible at their joint baptism. Aemelia is at some pains to rectify this problem, at least in psychological terms; and if we cannot see her insistence upon the banquet in the Abbey as a determination literally to re-name her sons, we surely recognize the event as a fit occasion for her to clarify (and codify) who and what they are.[24] Just as in sacramental terms baptism must precede marriage, so too a clear and secure notion of self must precede the hope of marital harmony. It is this process of reclamation that Aemelia begins at her gossips' feast inside the Abbey, a family banquet on which all other feasts—with whatever social, moral, or psychological meaning they may acquire—so heavily depend. After so long marital grief, Aemelia's family needs nothing more than the spiritual nativity and personal stability conferred by the sacrament. It is this need that they ratify in the play's final and most joyously comic banquet.

Originally published by Joseph Candido, "'Dining Out in Ephesus': Food in *The Comedy of Errors*," *Studies in English Literature* 30 (1990): 217–41. Reprinted by permission of *Studies in English Literature 1500–1900*, 30, 2 (Spring 1990).

NOTES

[1] *The Riverside Shakespeare*, ed. G. Blakemore Evans, et al. (Boston: Houghton Mifflin, 1974), p. 80. All references to *The Comedy of Errors* are to this edition. See also Timothy Long, "The Calculus of Confusion: Cognitive and Associative Errors in Plautus's *Menaechmi* and Shakespeare's *Comedy of Errors*," *Classical Bulletin* 53 (1976): 20–23. Long discusses the different categories of error in both plays, finding Shakespeare's representation of experience more complex and true to life than Plautus's.

[2] Geoffrey Bullough, *Narrative and Dramatic Sources of Shakespeare*, 8 vols. (London: Routledge and Kegan Paul, 1966), 1: 3–4, discusses the probability that Shakespeare knew Warner's translation and cites some verbal resemblances between the two works. See also R.A. Foakes's Arden edition of *The Comedy of Errors* (London: Methuen, 1962), pp. xxv–xxvi. Both Bullough and Foakes point out that although Shakespeare possibly knew Warner's text and may have borrowed from it, he also had enough Latin to consult Plautus's original; indeed, whatever borrowing that occurred could have been Warner's (Foakes, p. xxvi). I quote from Warner's version throughout because it is relatively faithful to Plautus and because of its possible connection with Shakespeare's play. Citations of *The Menaechmi* are to Bullough's edition of Warner's text. T.S. Dorsch has challenged the whole idea of *any* connection between Warner's translation and Shakespeare's play. In his edition of *The Comedy of Errors* (Cambridge: Cambridge Univ. Press, 1988), he argues that "no direct connection between Warner and Shakespeare has been established" (p. 9), and attributes the purported verbal parallels between the two works to coincidence or to separate recollection by Warner and Shakespeare of the same literary sources.

[3] On the Parasite in Greek comedy and this character's association with food, see Northrop Frye, *Anatomy of Criticism: Four Essays* (Princeton: Princeton Univ. Press, 1957), p. 175. The comic device of the hungry servant is, of course, a common one on the Elizabethan stage as well, and no doubt the result of Plautine influence. Lyly's *Campaspe* and *Sappho and Phao* both contain examples of the type, as does *The Taming of the Shrew*, a play roughly contemporaneous with The *Comedy of Errors*.

[4] Paul Nixon, trans., *Plautus*, 5 vols. The Loeb Classical Library (Cambridge, MA: Harvard Univ. Press, 1917), 2: 373.

[5] Erich Segal, *Roman Laughter: The Comedy of Plautus*, 2nd edn. (New York: Oxford Univ. Press, 1987), pp. 43–51. Subsequent references to Segal's book are noted parenthetically.

[6] *The Riverside Shakespeare*, p. 81.

[7] C.L. Barber and Richard P. Wheeler, *The Whole Journey: Shakespeare's Power of Development* (Berkeley: Univ. of California Press, 1986), p. 68. See also E.M.W. Tillyard, *Shakespeare's Early Comedies* (New York: Barnes & Noble, 1965), pp. 54–55, and Marvin Felheim and Philip Traci, *Realism in Shakespeare's Romantic Comedies* (Washington: Univ. Press of America, 1980), pp. 14–15.

[8] So glossed in *The Riverside Shakespeare* (p. 85) and in other texts. However, some editors, like Foakes, gloss "default" simply as "offence" or "fault" (p. 15).

[9] For an impressive examination of the connection between food and sexual aggression in Shakespeare see Janet Adelman, "'Anger's My Meat': Feeding, Dependency, and Aggression in *Coriolanus*," in *Shakespeare: Pattern of Excelling Nature*, ed. David Bevington and Jay L. Halio (Newark: Univ. of Delaware Press, 1978), pp. 108–24. See also the Ephesian Dromio's remarks at I.ii.82–90.

[10] William Harrison, *The Description of England*, ed. Georges Edelen (Ithaca: Cornell Univ. Press, 1968), p. 140. Subsequent references to Harrison are noted parenthetically.

[11] Lu Emily Pearson, *Elizabethans at Home* (Stanford: Stanford Univ. Press, 1957); M. St. Clare Byrne, *Elizabethan Life in Town and Country* (Boston: Houghton Mifflin, 1926). Subsequent references to both works are noted parenthetically.

[12] Note, for example, the following lines from Ben Jonson's "To Penshurst," in which the poet praises the hospitality of Sir Robert Sidney, Viscount Lisle, and his wife Barbara Gamage:

> That found King James when, hunting late this way
> With his brave son, the Prince, they saw thy fires
> Shine bright on every hearth as the desires
> Of thy Penates had been set on flame
> To entertain them; or the country came
> With all their zeal to warm their welcome here.
> What (great, I will not say, but) sudden cheer
> Didst thou then make 'em! and what praise was heaped
> On thy good lady then! who therein reaped
> The just reward of her high housewifery;
> To have her linen, plate, and all things nigh,
> When she was far; and not a room but dressed
> As if it had expected such a guest!   (lines 76–88)

[13] Pearson discusses a further "ceremonial" aspect of Elizabethan dining regarding the basin: "If different ranks were not represented at table, one basin was frequently used for a small company, two or three washing their hands at the same time, but if guests of various ranks were present, there must be one basin for each rank, and music between courses. Sir

Francis Drake, for example, liked to live up to his rank even at sea, and besides observing the usual decorum, he had his meals served with the sound of trumpets and other instruments" (p. 565).

[14] The confusion brought about by two sets of identical twins allows Shakespeare to enrich his play in subtly expressive ways. For example, when Antipholus of Syracuse is called to dinner (mistakenly) by the Ephesian Dromio, the Syracusan twin's reaction both expresses his own confusion and restates the *actual* attitude of the brother for whom he is mistaken: "Hang up thy mistress! I know not thy mistress, out on thy mistress!" (II.i.67–68), and "I know...no house, no wife, no mistress" (II.i.71). For an influential study of the way in which the Antipholan twins reflect psychological aspects of each other, see Barbara Freedman, "Egeon's Debt: Self-Division and Self-Redemption in *The Comedy of Errors*," *ELR* 10 (1980): 360–83.

[15] For a provocative study of the fasting of medieval women and its usefulness as a means of criticizing, manipulating, educating, or converting family members, see Caroline Walker Bynum, *Holy Feast and Holy Fast: The Religious Significance of Food to Medieval Women* (Berkeley: Univ. of California Press, 1987), particularly chapters 6 and 7 (pp. 189–244).

[16] The question of the relative ages of the two Antipholuses is a vexed one, since Egeon's comments in I.i on the issue seem to contradict each other. Many editors note Shakespeare's apparent confusion regarding which twin is the elder and, like Foakes, contend that "such conflict in details is not uncommon in Shakespeare and is not noticed on the stage" (p. 9). Addressing the problem critically, Patricia Parker has demonstrated how the "rhetorical crossing" in the relevant passage (I.i.78–85) indicates that the Syracusan twin is consistently referred to as the younger; see "Elder and Younger: The Opening Scene of *The Comedy of Errors*," *SQ* 34 (1983): 325–27. Parker's assumption is shared by most critics; see particularly Freedman (p. 368); Tillyard (p. 567); and Ralph Berry, *Shakespeare's Comedies: Explorations in Form* (Princeton: Princeton Univ. Press, 1972), pp. 28–29. The idea is implied if not expressly stated by Robert Ornstein, *Shakespeare's Comedies: From Roman Farce to Romantic Mystery* (Newark: Univ. of Delaware Press, 1986), p. 30; and by Alexander Leggatt, *Shakespeare's Comedy of Love* (London: Methuen, 1974), pp. 6–7.

[17] Mary Douglas, "Deciphering a Meal," *Daedalus* 101, 1 (Winter 1972): 61–81; Levi-Strauss, *The Origins of Table Manners. Introduction to a Science of Mythology*, 3 vols., trans. John and Doreen Weightmann (New York: Harper & Row, 1978), *passim*, but particularly 3: 54–59 where Levi-Strauss discusses the myth of the "clinging woman" which has certain curious analogies to the relationship between Antipholus of Ephesus and

Adriana. See also, Kurt W. Back, "Food, Sex and Theory," *Nutrition and Anthropology in Action*, ed. Thomas K. Fitzgerald (Amsterdam: Van Gorcum, 1977), p. 31; and Peter Farb and George Armelagos, *Consuming Passions: The Anthropology of Eating* (Boston: Houghton Mifflin, 1980), pp. 4–5; 97–103.

[18] Farb and Armelagos note that "At marriage celebrations in northern Europe during the Middle Ages, it was considered an important moment when the couple ate together" (p. 5).

[19] See particularly Freedman's essay mentioned above, and Berry (p. 176). Also of interest in this regard is William C. Carroll, *The Metamorphoses of Shakespearean Comedy* (Princeton: Princeton Univ. Press, 1985), pp. 68–77.

[20] Sir Hugh Plat, *Delightes for Ladies*, ed. G.E. Fussell and Kathleen Rosemary Fussell (London: Crosby Lockwood & Son, 1948); all references to Plat's work are to this edition and are noted parenthetically. See also Pearson, pp. 213, 403, 409, and 413. Of interest too are the remarks of George Herbert in *A Priest to the Temple or, The Country Parson* (1652) where the necessary characteristics of a good parson's wife are set forth in some detail. Herbert lists three separate qualities that such a woman must possess, among them expertise in "curing, and healing of all wounds and sores with her owne hands; which skill either she brought with her, or he [the parson] takes care she shall learn it of some religious neighbor." See *The Works of George Herbert*, ed. F.E. Hutchinson (Oxford: Clarendon Press, 1941), p. 239.

[21] References to Thomas Tusser are from *Five Hundred Points of Good Husbandry...together with A Book of Huswifery*, ed. William Mavor (London: Lackington, Allen, 1812). Also of interest is George Walton Williams, "Shakespeare's Metaphors of Health: Food, Sport, and Life-Preserving Rest," *JMRS* 14 (1984): 187–202; and Owsei Temkin, "Nutrition from Classical Antiquity to the Baroque," in *Human Nutrition: Historic and Scientific*, ed. Iago Galdston (New York: International Univ. Press, 1960), pp. 78–97. Temkin points out that the concept of "diet" comprised not only food and drink "but also work, sleep, climate of the home, emotions, and sexual life, i.e., what the medieval doctors came to call the six *res nonnaturales*, the six 'non-naturals'" (p. 83).

[22] Alexander Leggatt, *Shakespeare's Comedy of Love* (London: Methuen, 1974), pp. 9, 18.

[23] In *Action Is Eloquence: Shakespeare's Language of Gesture* (Cambridge, MA: Harvard Univ. Press, 1984), David Bevington discusses the theatrical centrality of the banquet in several Shakespearean plays, most notably *Macbeth*, *Timon of Athens*, *Titus Andronicus*, and *Troilus and Cressida*, where the "ceremony of feasting represents not so much God's gift of charity" as a failed ritual of reincorporation that presents a

"disillusioned view of lifeless artificiality" (p. 159). As Bevington notes, the "violence and hypocrisy" underlying banqueting in these plays serves importantly to heighten its moral opposite—the "regular form and sense of hospitable order" that a communal feast implies (pp. 159–60). For an elaboration of the idea of inverted feasting in *Macbeth*, see G. Wilson Knight, *The Imperial Theme: Further Interpretations of Shakespeare's Tragedies Including the Roman Plays* (London: Methuen, 1951), ch. 5 (particularly pp. 134–41).

[24] Elizabethan and Jacobean comedies, of course, abound with concluding banquets (actual or proposed) as symbolic of social harmony and renewal. Shakespeare's *Taming of the Shrew* comes instantly to mind (but see Bevington's modifying remarks here [p. 159]), as do *The Two Gentlemen of Verona, A Midsummer Night's Dream*, and even the end of *The Merchant of Venice*, where, although "It is almost morning," Lorenzo sees Portia and Nerissa as dropping "manna in the way of starved people" (V.i.294–95). The disappearing banquet in *The Tempest* is far too richly allusive to be discussed here, but bears mentioning, as does the proposed feasting at the end of *Cymbeline* (V.v.483). All references to Shakespeare here are to *The Riverside Shakespeare*. Suffice it to say that the motif of the concluding harmonious banquet is so pervasive as to appear in plays as diverse as Peele's *Old Wives' Tale*, Dekker's *The Shoemaker's Holiday*, and Jonson's *Every Man in His Humor* and, most notably, *Bartholomew Fair*.

Figure 3. Scheie production, 1988, Santa Cruz. Antipholus of Ephesus (Bryan Torfeh) looks on from above, Dromio (David Baker), from below, while a demure Abbess (Brad Meyers) meets her shocked husband, Egeon (J. Kenneth Campbell). Used with the permission of D. Scheie.

Rectifying Shakespeare's *Errors*: romance and farce in bardeditry

Charles Whitworth

What in the world can/should/does an editor do to the text of a Shakespeare play?[1] We are reminded by a growing host of performance critics but also, and more significantly, by textual scholars and editors, that play texts are both potential, to be realized in performance, rather than ends in themselves, and, as things in themselves, unstable. We are enjoined to privilege those early texts of Shakespeare—where there exist more than one— which appear to embody his theatrical practice or that of his colleagues, rather than those which represent his first thoughts or a scribe's transcription, and, generally, to have the *play* in mind as we edit the *text*.[2] What then is the role of the textual editor *vis à vis* a Shakespeare play? How can whatever he does make any real difference? He works perforce only with the printed signs of Quartos and Folios. The director and actors of the play may start from the text he or another editor prepares, but they can and do deviate from it, cut it, rewrite it, rearrange it, re-edit it at will, even throw it away, as the actor Richard McCabe—or was it Puck?—did with a copy of the New Penguin edition of *A Midsummer Night's Dream* in the RSC's 1989 production. Some directors go back to the original printed texts, circumventing all subsequent editions. But the vaunted indefiniteness of the dramatic text is not for the editor. He must make choices and fix them in print, however he may equivocate and canvass alternatives in his notes. He must fix that which must remain unfixed, fluid, open, ambiguous, always at the mercy, inspired or banal, of producers.[3] But if that very production, or the totality of all productions, past, present, and future, is the essence of the play, is he not in some quixotic, perverse way engaged in denying that essence? Is not his enterprise both subsidiary and paradoxical, at the same time both prior to and parasitic upon the living business of the theatre? He works for years to produce a printed text, agonizing over accidentals, solving and resolving cruxes, emending, guessing, inventing, admitting defeat, and delivers his text to be printed, bound, and read. But reading is not the activity for which that play was written. Performing is. And his text, over which he sweated for so long, will never be performed as he edited it. It will be reproduced, transformed, literally, in the sweat of rehearsal and performance: Brook's *Dream*, Hall's *Hamlet*, Nunn's *Macbeth*, Warner's *Titus*, not his, the editor's. The edition used as script is rarely even mentioned in the theatre programme.[4] "A poem should not mean but be," said MacLeish. An editor's text cannot mean. Can it be? Certainly there can be no *play* on the editor's carefully constructed page. The editor of a novel or a poem or a treatise has no such anxiety. His text goes to its ultimate consumer, the reader, as he has prepared it, unmediated in its essentials. The play editor's text never goes to its ultimate consumer, the play-goer, as he has prepared it, especially in its essentials.

The editor's quest for his text is, from one perspective, a romantic one. He encounters obstacles, fights giants, dodges between Scylla and Charybdis (who shall remain nameless), comes upon ancient strongholds, smoking ruins, signs of skirmishes, dry bones, dust, the landscape of the editorial history of his text. When it is a Shakespeare play, that landscape is vast, the terrain complicated, with traps for the unwary and the challenges of predecessors, the illustrious and the silly, the flamboyant and the hapless, with many of whom he must pause to do battle. But the quest itself is absurd: he can never succeed. He will think he has it, but like Sir Calidore's Blatant Beast, it will escape again, never be finally pinned down, penned in, tamed. What is worse, all productions of his play will repeatedly release it, in virtually infinite mutations, all of them the play, none of them his play. (Even if he convinces himself that he has got the text, he may have lost, or slain, the play.)

To what or whom is the editor of a dramatic text responsible? To the author? He, in Shakespeare's case, is long dead, and besides, we do not, cannot, know what exactly he wrote or wanted. He is, in a crucial sense, irrelevant. To the reader? To the director, to the actor, all of whom are also readers, but who read to different ends than do the student, the teacher, the literary critic, the "mere" reader? And those to whom the ultimate, infinite re-creations of the play belong, theatre practitioners, amateur and professional, great and small, have no responsibility to any *editor's* text, They may rely upon a single edition, which they will still cut and rearrange as it suits them, or they may work from several, picking and choosing, referring to earlier printed texts, even preferring less reliable texts to more reliable ones.[5] Their responsibilities are various: to that chimera, "the play," in the objectivity of which they sometimes display a touching faith, to the audience, society, the box office, sponsors.

The two activities, reading a printed text and seeing/hearing a performance, are, obviously, radically different.[6] The one thing you cannot do as you read the book is really see and hear a performance (imagination is something else); at a performance, you see, hear, even smell sometimes (as in the 1980 RSC production of *As You Like It* when the most delicious aroma of roast chicken wafted over the stalls as the banished duke and his men sat down to their feast in Act II, scene vii), but you cannot read the printed text of the play, the book simultaneously. To the reader, the medium is print; to the spectator-auditor, the media are many, but print is not normally one of them. The editor provides for the one activity, the director, actors, designer, composer, and others for the other. The editor may hope fervently that his edition is adopted by some director and that his cherished readings will be spoken and thus achieve a fleeting immortality. But he knows that even if that happens, his *text*, what he edited, will be only part of the *play*. He cannot provide for those other essential parts, including the way each phrase and line of his text is delivered. The actor *gives* meaning to words, can indeed give different meanings to the same words, meanings which the editor cannot entertain or even imagine.[7] His text is thus at an even further remove from final or definitive meaning. Whether blueprint or skeleton (or some other, always inadequate, metaphor), his text will be the merest starting-point for the performance, that text which was the goal of his long arduous quest. Not only is it destined to be rehandled in the very act of being realized, it is doomed, even as allegedly fixed, permanent, printed, preserved artifact, to be superseded. The beast breaks out as it is being apprehended.[8]

On the other hand, is it really as hopeless as all that? The writing of a play is an act of literary composition. The editor deals with a literary artifact, written, printed, as any literary work is. Written words are the medium, as they are for a novel or a poem. We cannot edit what is not there, that third dimension: the performance. (Nor should the editor, however much he may yearn to do so, stage the play on the page; to do so is to limit the text's potentiality.) We can only edit that text which is different in its structure and layout—speech prefixes, stage directions, act and scene divisions, and so on, rather than authorial voices, paragraphs, quotation marks, chapters, and so on—but similar in its medium: words. The editor of a dramatic text will always have divided, irreconcilable loyalties: to the written text he works from, the material cause (in Aristotelian terms) of what he aims to make, and to the performed play, the final cause.

These and other related questions have occurred to me, a moderately experienced editor of Renaissance dramatic texts but a relative novice as a Shakespeare editor, as I have worked on an edition of *The Comedy of Errors* for the Oxford Shakespeare. They are, some of them, simple matters, but they are also, I am convinced, fundamental matters. They are theoretical, or rather philosophical, questions about the nature of the editing enterprise where dramatic texts are concerned, and about the nature of those texts themselves. I do not wish to belabour the obvious, nor to over-dramatize harmless drudgery, but I do wish to pose such questions, even the more naive-sounding ones, and to worry, and encourage my fellow-editors to worry, about what we do. This concern has not sprung *ex nihilo*, but neither is there yet any articulated theory of dramatic textual editing that addresses these and related questions. Greg's famous theory of copy-text and the guidelines for editors that were derived from it went unchallenged for a surprisingly long time, such were Greg's stature and authority.[9] But even as editors, the great majority of whom have not considered themselves textual theorists *per se*, have worked, they have recognized the limitations and contradictions in Greg's impressive rationale. Its shortcomings are more clearly seen as the peculiar extra-literary nature of early play-texts, the differences between playwriting and authoring, and the primacy of performance over mere reading emerge and are articulated. I am one of that majority, just an editor, not a bibliographer or textual critic *tout court*, and the questions and sceptical reflections which have arisen in the course of the workaday business of editing a Shakespeare play-text (scepticism has not yet induced paralysis) have led, not to a new theory, but to a preoccupation with the peculiarity of that business.

With these queries pending, or looming, I propose to engage in a sort of quizzical intermittent trialogue with recent Shakespearean textual theory, specifically as enunciated by the editors of the Oxford *Complete Works* and related publications, and by other textual critics, all on one side, and "my" play/text, *The Comedy of Errors*, on the other.[10] On this side too is some limited experience of testing editorial solutions in the arena of performance when I had the opportunity to advise the director Phyllida Lloyd on textual matters as she prepared and rehearsed a production of *The Comedy of Errors* for the Bristol Old Vic.[11] Like Antipholus of Syracuse, I am "smothered in *Errors*." I can only hope that my efforts do not prove me, as he claims to be in the second half of that line, "feeble, shallow, weak" (II.ii.35).

The Comedy of Errors is not a particularly difficult text, compared with others in the Shakespeare canon. It does not raise the "two-text" issue since the Folio of 1623 contains the only early version of the play, and it is not radically corrupt, incomplete, or otherwise maimed. It has its own peculiarities, to some of which I shall return later: a small handful of cruxes, some confusion over characters' names, an occasional vagueness in stage directions, as well as the usual misprints, verse-prose transpositions, unmetrical lines, lacunae, and the like. It is a uniquely Shakespearean amalgam of disparate genres, romance and farce, an early comedy that has more in common with *Twelfth Night* and *Pericles* than with the other plays more nearly contemporary to it, and little of the comedy of young love so prominent in most of Shakespeare's first ten comedies.

I want to discuss here some of the problems and puzzles, critical and editorial, it poses, within the framework of the theoretical and procedural issues adumbrated above. The romance and the farce of editing Shakespeare's plays will, I hope, be both evoked and illustrated in this context, the particular surprises and misprisings, double-takes and double thinking involved in doing the mundane job of editing this text framed, as it were, by the larger questions, as the immediate, hectic business of the farcical comedy is framed and overarched by the mythical, romance motifs of erring, losing, seeking, and finding. The harmless, hopeful drudge sets forth, in the giant shadows of his predecessors, equipped with the tools of the trade, instinct, and some notion of what the achieved thing should be like. He should not deceive himself that he has a perfect idea of the thing-in-itself. Romance versus farce; editing texts for readers versus performing plays for theatre audiences; the editor's need to choose, to set something and not something else down in print, but with space for glosses, collations, explanations versus the performer's need to say one thing and not another, despite the "openness" of the text, with no place for verbal glosses or commentary, but virtually unlimited scope for glossing by gesture, expression, inflection; telling, in narrative and in introductions and commentaries on the page versus showing, in performance, with sets, costumes, and music on the stage; diegesis versus mimesis—these complementary, often contradictory sets of conventions, requirements, and procedures seem to me to be reflected in the play, *The Comedy of Errors*.

Romance is essentially a narrative genre, not a dramatic one. I take it that there are fundamental differences between those two modes, which are more or less identical to Plato's diegesis and mimesis.[12] Drama, as theatre, occurs in the present, is immediate, visual as well as aural; narrative is usually in the past tense, is mediated by a narrator who may or may not be the "author," and nowadays is experienced silently and privately, by reading, though it used more commonly to be experienced aurally and with others. Romance depends upon discursive passages of description, scene-setting, and mood-making, and upon the omniscient narrator's mediation, guidance, information, suspense-building, reassurance, and so on. The time scale is, or can be, vast: "Once upon a time, long ago" is not the dramatist's opening gambit, but it is the essence of the romancer's. Consider

Shakespeare's various ploys to overcome that initial obstacle. He uses prologues and epilogues, choruses, frames (themselves either narrative or dramatic), lumps of narrative within the plays (for example, Prospero, Orlando, the Third Gentleman in *The Winter's Tale*, or Egeon at the beginning of *Errors*), even a real historical poet, Gower, who appears in *Pericles* to tell the story that we are unlikely to credit without his assurances as to its authenticity. Only after forty lines, with references to his book, does Gower hand us over to "the judgement of [our] eye"; not content, he presents dumbshows, refers often to his sources, and in all, appears seven times throughout the play, speaking some 300 lines, including an epilogue, all in order to mediate the romance narrative to a theatre audience, to turn telling into showing. Shakespeare's practice in many of his plays amounts to an inversion, or turning inside out, of Plato's and Aristotle's "mixed mode" (a narrative with some direct dialogue): he writes drama, with a lot of narrative, external and internal, to account for that which is beyond the dramatist's and his audience's reach. An Elizabethan paradigm of this kind of mode-switching is George Peele's marvellous little fantasy, *The Old Wife's Tale*, which announces itself as "tale" but is a play, but a play in which a tale being told turns into a play being performed for an audience which includes the tale-teller herself and her auditors, a play in which several characters tell romance-like tales of travel, hardship, and enchantment.[13] In the vogue of performance studies, we must acknowledge that there are limits to the dramatist's art, even as we claim that his written text is not fully realized until it is performed. Shakespeare's and others' metadrama is a recognition of those limits; it is also a challenge to them, pushing out the circumscribing walls of the wooden O's and concrete caverns in which the performance is confined. There are things the dramatist cannot do, *qua* dramatist, when it comes to story-telling, that the romance narrator can do. But in the theatre the theatrical naturally prevails.

To come to cases: in the theatre, will comedy and its vigorous stepchild, farce, where they are present, inevitably overwhelm, if not subvert, romance? Does romance have a chance where farce pops in its zany face (or arse)? Is *The Comedy of Errors*, romance in its form and in much of its matter, doomed to live *on stage* in a single dimension, that of farce? Is the romance to be left to readers only, while theatre audiences get farce(d) : two works living under one title? Farce is a viewerly, spectator-friendly genre; romance is a readerly, imagination-friendly one. Romance requires imagination, farce leaves nothing to it. As readers of romance, we have to create our own Arcadias and Faerylands, Illyrias, Bohemias, and Ardens (or Ardennes if we are reading the Oxford Shakespeare). Romance is not visual; it is, "to speak metaphorically, a *speaking* picture." Farce has to be seen to be (dis)believed.[14] Is it wrong for directors, designers, and actors to take the farce and let the romance go (or worse, send it up)? Or do the improbabilities of romance pushed further, treated comically on stage, necessarily *become* farcical? That is, is the difference I am talking about one of degree and not of kind? But if so, why isn't *Cymbeline*, of all the outrageously improbable plays, called a farce, or *Twelfth Night*? What is the point of Shakespeare's having encased his "farce"—if that is what it is—in a romance, a story which, on its own, has all the sentiment, pathos, and wonder of *Pericles*? Will we even agree that *The Comedy of Errors*, in its larger dimension, *is* romance? For we are told and have been told for a long time that the play is *a farce*, and theatre practitioners have, it seems, always treated it so.

In 1819, Frederick Reynolds turned the play into an operatic farce. He added songs from other Shakespeare plays, with musical settings by various composers, including Mozart. A reviewer for the *European Magazine* found Reynolds's enormities just the remedy for a silly, incredible play:

> It was attended by the most crowded house since the beginning of the season, and the audience were throughout in a unanimous temper to applaud.... No illusion of the stage can give probability to the perpetual mutations of four persons, paired in such perfect similitude that the servant mistakes his master, and the master his servant; the wife her husband, and the husband his wife. All this so strongly contradicts common experience, that it repels us even in description; but on the stage, with the necessary dissimilarity of countenance, voice, manner, and movement, that occurs

between the actors, however disguised by dress, the improbability becomes almost offensive.[15]

The anonymous reviewer is carried away by his own rhetoric: no husband mistakes his wife, because there are no twin women.[16] Even the farce, let alone what was left of the romance, failed to work for this dyspeptic critic, but whether audiences liked the play or not, farce it was and farce it remained. C.E. Flower, in his preface to the play in the Memorial Theatre acting edition, makes much of the text of the "Comedy, or as we should now call it Farce" being fully restored in the 1881 Stratford production.

Many of us would concur in Dr. Johnson's opinion that "Shakespeare's plays are not in the rigorous and critical sense either tragedies or comedies, but compositions of a distinct kind," accurately reflecting "the real state of sublunary nature" with its "chaos of mingled purposes and casualties."[17] It is well known that Shakespeare drew upon Plautus' comedy, *The Menaechmi,* about twin brothers from Syracuse, accidentally separated in childhood, one of whom journeys in search of the other. It is also clear that in Act III, scene i, he had in mind the first scene of Plautus' *Amphitruo,* in which Jupiter and Mercury impersonate Amphitruo and Sosia, master and servant.[18] But the ingredient that Plautus did not provide was the plot which frames, overarches, and ultimately subsumes the comedy of twins mistook, servants beaten, masters maddened, and merchants thwarted. That plot, which sets *The Comedy of Errors* in another mode altogether, belongs to a different tradition, one which also went back to antiquity, which Shakespeare knew well and turned to again and again, in which he seems to have been more at home than ever he was in the strictly-structured, rule-governed school of classical comedy. Dr. Johnson, keeping to the Folio's tripartite division of the plays into comedies, histories, and tragedies, opined of Shakespeare that "in comedy he seems to repose, or to luxuriate, as in a mode of thinking congenial to his nature...His tragedy seems to be skill, his comedy to be instinct."[19] I would refine Johnson's distinction and suggest that it was particularly *romance* and the dramatic genre that approximates it that were most congenial, even instinctive, to Shakespeare throughout his career. He manifests a peculiar fondness for romance, for old, hoary, much-told tales of wonder and wandering, of storms, shipwrecks, pirates, mistaken identity, oracles and mysteries, treachery and betrayal, bravery and devotion, of parents and children, husbands and wives, brothers and sisters torn asunder and tossed by Fate, but brought together at last against all odds. All of his comedies and tragicomedies contain such elements, some are essentially of that kind.

Just such a tale, of course, is that of old Egeon of Syracuse, his wife, and twin sons and twin servants, shipwrecked, separated, rescued, lost, finally reunited after years of despair and searching, but not before further trials, danger, and anguish. *The Comedy of Errors* begins with it and ends with it, and its dominant moods and motives run right through the farcical comedy, tempering it and transforming it into a new kind of whole which cannot, without distortion, even denaturing, be described or performed simply as "farce." That long discursive opening scene, in which the actors, especially the one who plays Egeon, must grip the audience's attention and imagination with pure tale-telling, holds the cruel promise of execution for the sad, worn-out old man.[20] The comedy which follows must be coloured by it. Johnson may have had in mind that scene, among others, when he complained of the tediousness of Shakespeare's passages of narration:

> He affects a wearisome train of circumlocution and tells the incident imperfectly in many words which might have been more plainly delivered in few. Narration in dramatic poetry is naturally tedious, as it is unanimated and inactive and obstructs the progress of the action; it should therefore always be rapid and enlivened by frequent interruption. Shakespeare found it an encumbrance....[21]

Well, maybe, but he repeatedly brought it upon himself by his choice of romance material. The language of Egeon's narrative is stylized, formulaic, the language of romance: "Once upon a time, long ago..." is the mode; and Egeon's story begins a long time ago, at the beginning of his life, in fact: "In Syracusa was I born...."

Within a few lines of the start of the next scene, we see that the two plots, Plautine comedy and Hellenistic romance, are related, that the promise of doom will not be kept because the elements necessary to avert disaster and to bring about the happy dénouement begin immediately to assemble. Scene ii begins, in sharp contrast to the deliberate narrative tempo of Scene i, dramatically in mid-conversation, in mid-sentence with a friendly local merchant warning the newly-arrived Syracusans of their danger as proscribed foreigners in Ephesus, and pointing the warning with news of another Syracusan who is to be executed that very afternoon. The "wearisome train of circumlocution," the narrative, ends, and the brisk, immediate action of drama begins: *in medias res* takes over from "Once upon a time...." The frequent reminders of the time of day in the play—in eight of its eleven scenes—keep Egeon and his impending fate constantly in mind while he is absent from the stage, in tension with the expectation raised by the romance conventions of the first scene that it will be averted. Shakespeare's observation of the unity of time, here as nowhere else before *The Tempest*, heightens that effect. The theme was rendered visually by the clock in Theodor Komisarjevsky's 1938 Stratford production: its hands moved as the hours ticked away, and sometimes ran to catch up. Reference to Egeon (not by name, of course) in the second scene links his plot to that of Antipholus and Dromio of Syracuse: father, son, and servant, unknown to each other, are in the same place at the same time, aliens all three, despairing seekers for each other and the rest of their family.

Furthermore, the two stories are linked immediately and explicitly by references in both to money. Egeon desperately needs money to save his life; barely half-a-dozen lines after he goes off, "hopeless and helpless," to seek it, Antipholus receives back from the merchant the money he had held in safe-keeping, the very sum, we are soon told (I.ii.81), that Egeon requires. And the place where all of them are, the alien town of Ephesus, is established as one where money counts, and where the making of profit has priority over the taking of pleasure: the merchant excuses himself from accompanying Antipholus on a sight-seeing tour because he has an appointment with "certain merchants/Of whom [he] hope[s] to make much benefit" (I.ii.24–5).[22]

Shakespeare's changing of Plautus' Epidamnus to Ephesus was no doubt suggested by the primary source for his Egeon plot, the famous story of Apollonius of Tyre in Gower's *Confessio Amantis*. It was in Ephesus, where his long-lost wife had been restored to life after shipwreck and become a priestess in the temple of Diana, that Apollonius was reunited with her at last. Egeon finds his long-lost Emilia in Ephesus. Thus, years before he dramatized the story in its entirety in *Pericles*, he seized upon it as the unlikely frame-plot for his most classical comedy. The alteration of Diana's temple to a Christian priory and Diana's priestess to a Christian Abbess are probably due to the prominence of Ephesus and its affairs in St. Paul's New Testament writings, in Acts and the Epistle to the Ephesians, although Gower supplied a hint by referring to Apollonius' wife as an "Abbess." From Paul, Shakespeare would certainly have known about the reputation of Ephesus for strange goings-on, with evil spirits, sorcerers, exorcists, and others who practised "curious arts," as well as its artisans and merchants. Perhaps Demetrius the silversmith in Acts XIX who makes idols for the devotees of Diana suggested Angelo the goldsmith who purveys trinkets for the servants of Venus. Plautus' Epidamnus survives, however, in no fewer than seven references in the play.[23] In his choice of Ephesus, whatever the origin of that choice may have been, Shakespeare gave himself both the strangeness, the menace, and the surreal atmosphere of the typical romance setting, and the urban, mercantile, domestic scene of Roman comedy. The very setting embodies the two primary modes that he fused in this play.

Egeon's story of separation at sea introduces *that* central motif, and sea imagery recurs frequently. Metamorphosis and loss of identity are introduced in the second scene, expressed in the sea image in Antipholus' first soliloquy:

> I to the world am like a drop of water
> That in the ocean seeks another drop,
> Who, failing there to find his fellow forth,
> Unseen, inquisitive, confounds himself,
> So I, to find a mother and a brother,
> In quest of them unhappy, lose myself.   (I.ii.35–40)[24]

Adriana uses the same image later when, ironically, she is pleading with this Antipholus, the wrong one, not to tear himself away from her (II.ii.128–32). Transformation, dissolution, loss of oneself—this related group of states and their various images form a major theme, or super-motif. In Act II, Adriana wonders if age is diminishing her beauty, causing her husband to seek his pleasure in the company of other women; in Act V, when his own son does not recognize him, Egeon exclaims that grief and time must have altered him beyond recognition (both characters use the rare word *defeatures*, its only two occurrences in Shakespeare). Time's ravages, added reminders of the immediate, real time that is passing in the play's day, and related to the transformation and dissolution motif, become the subject of two comic exchanges (II.ii.;IV.ii.). Metamorphosis is mentioned repeatedly, sometimes humorously, sometimes fearfully. The workaday city of Ephesus itself is curiously animate: its very buildings are called "Centaur," "Phoenix," "Tiger," and "Porcupine."

Enchantment continues to work upon Antipholus: someone hands him a gold chain, Dromio brings him a bag of gold. Convinced they are bewitched, he calls upon divine aid—"Some blessed power deliver us from hence"—whereupon a courtesan appears (IV.iii.44) (in Adrian Noble's 1983 RSC production, she rose spectacularly from beneath the floor, scantily clad in red and black). Antipholus and Dromio behold not a heavenly rescuer, but Satan herself. Divine aid will come, and in female form, when the Abbess appears and gives them sanctuary, but not just yet. (Parenthetically, we may notice that Antipholus of Syracuse falls under the spells, as he believes, of a series of enchantresses: Adriana in II.ii., Luciana in III.ii., the courtesan in IV.iii., finally the Abbess in V.i.—one enchantress per act, a neat distribution— with, as prelude, the soliloquy in I.ii. in which he voices his fears of sorcerers, witches, and the like. This underlines his vulnerability and impressionability, and is reminiscent of the case of a famous hero of chivalric romance, Sir Percival, one of the Grail knights of Arthurian legend, whose experiences with women during his quest, including his mother, his sister, and the fiend in female guise several times, similarly underline his susceptibility to error and his innocence. In contrast, Antipholus of Ephesus is always accompanied by men only—his servant, friends, business acquaintances, creditors, the officer who arrests him—until IV.iv., the conjuring scene, when at last he is surrounded by women, who insist that he is mad; his brother thinks *himself* mad, the victim of witches. Another way in which Shakespeare differentiates the brothers, making the Syracusan the romance protagonist while the Ephesian retains the role of the thwarted and irate husband of domestic comedy, is by giving the former no fewer than six soliloquies and asides, totalling fifty lines, while his brother has none.)

A new order, that of genuine divine authority, not Dr. Pinch's sham, intervenes in the person of the Abbess. Her claim to be able to heal the supposedly mad Antipholus and Dromio is the claim of a power superior to those of mere magic, sorcery, even the devil. Now the Duke returns, leading old Egeon to execution. At its height of frenzy, the comical-farcical action, which, as we have seen, is far from being only that, is interrupted by the resumption of the tragicomic one. But its progress is halted too, literally, physically, by the prostrate Adriana, imploring the Duke to intercede with the Abbess and get her husband restored to her. Farce impedes romance temporarily. At this moment, the two plots merge, under the auspices, as it were, of both spiritual and temporal authority, both benign, the Abbess and the Duke. Romance resumes, and subsumes farce. To be sure, the unravelling will take some 300 more lines and there will be further supposes and surprises, even pathos, along the way.

Time, which Dromio claimed had gone back an hour, has now gone back years, to when the family was whole, before the events narrated by Egeon a few hours earlier took place. The boys were infants then, new-born. It is, fittingly, the Abbess, the holy mother, who gives explicit utterance to the metaphor of rebirth, describing this moment as one of nativity, repeating the word (if the Folio is right) for emphasis:

Thirty-three years have I but gone in travail
Of you, my sons, and till this present hour
My heavy burden ne'er deliverèd.
The Duke, my husband, and my children both,
And you the calendars of their nativity,

Go to a gossip's feast, and joy with me.
After so long grief, such [nativity].   (V.i.403–9)

Both Pericles and Cymbeline use similar language when they are reunited with children whom they had believed long dead.[25] The imminent death with which the play began is transfigured into birth: then we met with things dying, now with things, as it were, new-born. That same death-dealing Duke becomes the life-giving lord: "It shall not need. Thy father hath his life." Patron already to one Antipholus, the Duke becomes godfather to both at their re-christening. Even the little coda, with its comic business between the pairs of twins, not yet entirely free from error though beyond its more baleful effects, ends on that note. The Dromios resolve that since they do not know which is elder, but came into the world "like brother and brother," they will now go hand in hand, not one before another, a visual image of recognition and reunion, the joining, not the confounding, of water drops, and a verbal reminder of birth and rebirth. Komisarjevsky's clock should by now have been running furiously backward, whirling away the years, for in the biggest and best of the comedy's errors, Time has indeed gone back, all the way from death to birth, from the intense dramatic final moment to the expansive narrative "Once upon a time," from the end of the play to the beginning of the story. But that, essentially, is what happens in romance.

The editor in his quest may face anything from minor, uncontentious emendations to hopeless cruxes, from mere commas and full stops to be distributed judiciously, to gaping blanks where text should be, and to heaps of text where less, or none, should be. He will be grateful, in the present case, for the relative brevity and relative cleanness of the Folio text of *The Comedy of Errors*, and that there is only the Folio text to contend with, no two-or three-headed monsters. *Errors* is the fifth play in the Folio, following *The Tempest*, *The Two Gentlemen of Verona*, *The Merry Wives of Windsor*, and *Measure for Measure*, all of which were set by the compositors from transcripts made by Ralph Crane. The four plays which follow *Errors*—*Much Ado About Nothing*, *Love's Labour's Lost*, *A Midsummer Night's Dream*, *The Merchant of Venice*—are all reprints of Quartos.[26] *Errors* stands alone among the first nine plays in the Folio in having apparently been set from Shakespeare's foul papers, a genesis it shares with only seven others in the volume. This orthodox view, held by Chambers, McKerrow, Greg, and nearly everyone since, of the nature of the printer's copy for *Errors* has recently been challenged by Paul Werstine.[27] His argument that authorial foul papers might have been used in the theatre, and thus that the standard "foul papers versus prompt copy" dichotomy may not be so rigid after all, is rebutted by Wells and Taylor.[28] Some of the confusions in the text are of the sort usually attributed to unperfected authorial copy: descriptive or narrative stage directions, imprecise distinctions between characters, uncertain or alternate names for characters, missing or imprecise entrances and exits, and so on. All of these require editorial emendation but not all are necessarily problematic for performers.

Take the names, for example. No editor is likely to hesitate before emending "*Iuliana*" and "*Iulia*" in the stage direction and first speech prefix at III.ii. The character in question is clearly Luciana, Adriana's sister, who has already appeared and been named at II.i.3. But the misnamings occur in column *a* of gathering H4, probably the first column of this play set by Compositor C; meanwhile, C's partner, Compositor D, was getting it right seven times—*Luc.*—in column *b* of the same page (this is not to suggest that they were necessarily setting the page simultaneously, side by side). Surely Shakespeare, writing his play seriatim and not by formes, did not forget his character's name between the end of II.ii, where she has the last line, and the beginning of III.ii. Did he on the spur of the moment decide to change her name to "Juliana" to avoid confusion with Luce, who had just made her one and only appearance barely eighty lines before, then revert to "Luciana," the aberration preserved in the foul papers? Compositor D was in no doubt, nor was B, the third *Errors* compositor, and C himself conformed subsequently, though he vacillated between *Luc.* and *Luci.* on three other pages. Such speculation need not trouble even an editor intent on establishing a consistent text; he emends whether it was Shakespeare the composer or C the compositor who erred. A director may never know if he has not seen the Folio text or an apparatus that records such things.

But Luce is a different, more substantial matter. This character, later identified as the kitchen-maid, appears in III.i. and engages in a slanging match with Dromio and Antipholus of Ephesus, who vainly seek entry to their own house, while their twins are inside, enjoying their usurped places. In the Folio, Luce is named once in a stage direction, seven times in speech prefixes, and three times in the dialogue. This is her only scene, though in many productions she returns in the general mêlées in IV.iv. and V.i. (usually taking the small part of the messenger in V.i., which justifies her presence on stage), and to be reunited with the right Dromio as her master and mistress are reunited. John Dover Wilson, in his first Cambridge Shakespeare edition of the play (1922), listed the character as "Luce, or Nell" and he has been followed by many editors since. A few imply that there are two characters, one of whom does not appear. Only the new Oxford edition goes so far as to change the character's name to "Nell," and to give only that in Dramatis Personae, stage directions, speech prefixes, and dialogue. Luce is expunged.

The basis for this emendation is Dromio of Syracuse's reference to the woman in question as "Nell" in his comic set-piece duologue with Antipholus of Syracuse in III.ii. There is no reason to identify Luce, who appears in III.i., with Nell the kitchen-maid described as globular in shape by Dromio in III.ii. But the person who stood behind the door and "reviled" Antipholus of Ephesus, that is, Luce, is identified as the kitchen-maid at IV.iv.75–6. So did Shakespeare begin with a maid called "Luce," then change her name to "Nell," perhaps to avoid confusion with Luciana, or did he originally plan a second maidservant for the second Dromio? If the latter, then he changed his mind before the end where Dromio of Syracuse gratefully relinquishes any claim in the kitchen-maid to his brother (V.i.417–19). In any case, as the text stands in the Folio, the name "Nell" occurs only once, in a set-piece, where Dromio is desperately inventing witty replies to straight-man Antipholus' questions. The scene, with Dromio's (geo)graphic anatomizing of spherical Nell, is the comical counterpart in prose to Antipholus' lyrical wooing of Luciana in rhyming verse in the immediately preceding seventy lines of the same scene; we witness the first wooing, Dromio reports the other, with grotesque embellishment.

"Nell" is an *ad hoc* invention by Dromio; it allows him (and Shakespeare) their harmless necessary pun on "ell": "What's her name?" "Nell, sir. But her name and three-quarters—that's an ell and three-quarters—will not measure her from hip to hip" (III.ii.110–13). He even spells it out to be sure we get it, as bad punsters usually do. The actor might pause momentarily before replying "Nell, sir," as if inventing the name and lining up his gross pun on the spot. This single occurrence of the name in this highly artificial context hardly warrants changing "Luce" to "Nell" eleven times.[29] No editor, to my knowledge, has bothered to mention the name "Dowsabell," let alone proposed that Luce be called that. Yet this same Dromio calls this same woman "Dowsabell" at IV.i.110.

Nevertheless, a director may choose to call the character "Nell," as Phyllida Lloyd did in her 1989 Bristol Old Vic production. She read and was persuaded by the Oxford editors' argument, liked the jingle of "If thy name be called Nell, Nell thou hast answered him well" (III.i.53), and thought the name suited the actress playing the role. My arguments for retaining "Luce" did not prevail; the director simply chose to do otherwise as she was free to do, citing a recent major edition of the play, and no one could protest that the text was grievously violated or directorial whim irresponsibly indulged. The Oxford editors print "Nell," I would print "Luce," and both of us will have done as we did for good reasons. Who will be right? What are the criteria for deciding that question? Shakespeare's intentions? Whatever they were, we cannot recover them, and they may anyway have been one thing at one time, another at another. The beast has not been slain or caught, greasy Nell is forever loose.

Other names and other creatures are less troublesome. The place-name "Epidamium" occurs seven times in the Folio, three on pages set by Compositor C, four on pages set by B. Though minim error is a distinct possibility, the agreement of two compositors makes it more likely that they set what they were reading in their copy. But there was no such place.[30] May an editor rectify Shakespeare's errors? Some would not: the Riverside Shakespeare and David Bevington, in both his last revision of Hardin Craig's edition (1980) and his new Bantam (1988), read "Epidamium." Most editors, however, including the

Oxford, follow Pope in emending to "Epidamnum." But the place in question is Epidamnus, the setting of Plautus' *Menaechmi*. Why the classicist Pope should have chosen the accusative form of the noun (which occurs in various declined forms in *Menaechmi*) is mildly puzzling. Feeling slightly giddy at venturing where no fool editor has ever rushed before, I would propose "Epidamnus," the correct Latin name for the city Shakespeare apparently had in mind. But does it matter? In performance, not a whit. A fictitious place, a mere name on two romance characters' Mediterranean itineraries, that is all it is. But for the editor, it must matter, however insignificant it is: something must be printed and justified against the contending alternatives. In performance, almost anything can be said and no one will blink.

The Courtesan's house is called the Porpentine. This is an archaic spelling of "porcupine," so a modernizing editor should prefer the modern form. Shakespeare used only "porpentine" though "porcupine" was already current; it occurs eight times in his works, five times in *Errors*. But it is a proper name here. Is that then an argument for retaining its archaic form? No. That is to opt for quaintness, a practice that mars the otherwise splendid Riverside edition. A quaintness quotient has no place in a scholarly modernizing editor's set of guidelines. We modernize other spellings, so why not this? Curiously, it has been relatively modern editors, starting with Aldis Wright in the famous nineteenth-century Cambridge Shakespeare, who have reverted to "Porpentine," while Rowe modernized the spelling and was followed by editors until Wright. The Oxford, like eighteenth-century editions, has "Porcupine" (and thus obviates the need for a gloss). No editor, I believe, has retained the Folio spelling "Tyger," another house-name, at III.i.96, nor "Centaure" for the inn where Antipholus of Syracuse lodges at I.ii.9. And in the context of those other recognizable beastnames which abound in the play, "Porpentine" sounds odd in performance as well as looking odd on the page.

Another problem facing editors, but which causes little or no difficulty in the theatre, is the unmetrical line, whether short or long. The New Cambridge editor of *Errors* rhetorically asks *à propos* of one such, "Need we be worried by a line which is metrically short?"[31] Editors, *pace* Dorsch, usually are, assuming that Shakespeare always wrote regular iambic pentameter and that verse lines which contain fewer or more than the standard number of syllables (excluding feminine endings) must be faulty. But perhaps Dorsch is right and the assumption needs re-examining; Shakespeare, like Homer, must have nodded now and then. Metrifying Shakespeare is harder when a syllable or a word is missing than when there are too many; adding something requires that we invent or reconstruct Shakespeare. The line "A meane woman was deliuered" (I.i.54) has been regularized by most editors, usually by adding F2's "poor" before "mean," though some recent editors, from Peter Alexander (1951) to Bevington, leave the line as it stands in F. In performance it is easy and natural for an actor to pause a beat before saying "mean" or to emphasize it to mark the difference between this woman and Egeon's own wife, about whom he has just been speaking, and thus fill out the line. The same holds for many other such lines, short by a mere syllable. A good actor will not chant verse or mark the metre obtrusively anyway (nor will he reduce it to prose), and a missing syllable here and there, provided the sense is clear and the surrounding flow of the verse is maintained, is hardly going to be disastrous. But again, an editor, producing a printed text, may feel the lack more keenly and will probably at least consider whether to supply it, even if he finally decides not to, or writes a note asking whether we need be worried by it.

Gary Taylor's eloquent advocacy of invention by editors must be endorsed with caution and caveat (note 10 above). It will seem to many chillingly like an unrestricted licence. The naturally conservative editor and the naturally, or supernaturally, inventive poet seldom cohabit in one mind, and Taylor is right when he observes: "It is because those who have the facility seldom possess the judgement to restrain their inclination that those with a gift for emendation...invariably indulge in it too often" ("Inventing," p. 43). Though no harm may be done by adding a word to fill out a line of verse, will enough be gained to warrant the in(ter)vention? Taylor's own "mean-born" in the line under discussion seems to me to be a scant improvement over F2's redundant "poor mean." The condition of *her* birth is not relevant, and to refer to it here points away from the birth that is relevant, that of her "burden, male twins" (I.i.55). The point is that she is now "mean," that is poor, of low estate, and so is willing to sell her twin sons to Egeon to be servants to his. If the compulsion to metrify proves too strong, I would favour "A mean young woman was delivèred," but, like many editors, most actors, and any audience, I can live with the Folio's mere nine syllables. In general, editors seem less troubled by F's long "Vnwilling I agreed, alas, too soone / wee came aboard" (I.i.60), which some retain, or the very short one resulting from breaking it up into two: "Unwilling I agreed. Alas, too soon/We came aboard" (following Pope).[32] Sometimes when the latter choice is made, a note solemnly remarks on the rhetorical effect of such a short line at this decisive moment in Egeon's narrative. Such "effect" has been imported by the editor, of course, in breaking up the long line, and an actor can impart rhetorical effect in his delivery by pausing, sighing, whatever, if such an effect seems appropriate at this point, whether or not the line is printed as one or as two in his script.

The inventing editor will find somewhat more fertile ground in Dromio of Syracuse's frantic outburst at II.ii.192–3: "This is the Fairie land, oh spight of spights, / We talke with Goblins, Owles and Sprights." Here is another short line, lacking two syllables this time. The Second Folio, that anonymous first edited text of the First Folio, recognizes the problem, but does not get it right somehow, reading "and Elves Sprights." Pope changed "Elves" to the unmistakably bisyllabic "elvish." Theobald transformed "owls" to "ouphs." Most modern editors, however, have stuck with F's three unmetrical monsters. Even the Oxford retains an octosyllabic line, but modernizes Theobald's "ouphs" to "oafs," a lexically legitimate move all right, but one that creates a misleading and therefore undesirable secondary meaning for modern readers and audiences (as any modernization may run the risk of doing). The short line invites expansion. Is it not plausible that, by haplography, Compositor D conflated "oules and elues and" in his copy to "Owles and"? "We talk with goblins, owls, and elves, and sprites" seems appropriate to Dromio's terrified state, his fevered brain coining monsters pell-mell.[33] But, of course, the actor has even more reason here to pause, engage in business, break the line up, and hence stretch it that extra foot, than was the case with Egeon's line in the first scene discussed earlier. If in performance, where and only where his text can become a play, it does not matter if a word is missing, is the editor justified in indulging the inventing itch? Of course, we edit for *readers*, who can interrupt their reading of the text, who indeed are invited to do so, to jump to the fine print at the bottom of the page where we discuss the options and defend our decisions, as theatre-goers at a performance cannot. For the play editor's peace of mind, the ideal reader of his edition will be a literary reader and not a theatrically-minded one, and will read it as he or she reads a novel, a poem, Johnson's *Dictionary*, or Lawrence's letters. When Shakespeare was but the prince of poets, happy drudges lost less sleep.

Lacunae of a whole line or more, even in a rhyming verse passage where it seems clear that something is missing, are dealt with in performance, while the editor sweats and strains and, maybe, invents iambic pentameter. A case in point occurs in *Errors* III.i., at the height of the furious row between those inside the Phoenix and the rightful occupants and guests outside. In a long rhymed passage, immediately following the line in which Luce's name appears twice, the Folio reads as follows:

ANTI[PHOLUS OF EPHESUS]. Doe you heare you minion, you'll let vs in I hope?
LUCE.   I thought to haue askt you.
S. DRO.   And you said no.
E.DRO.   So come helpe, well strooke, there was blow for blow.

Theobald emended "hope" to "trow" in the first line, producing a triple rhyme, of which there are four others in the passage: lines 19–21, 64–6, 67–9, 76–8. But he produced no more sense. Some modern editors have followed him, including Cuningham, Foakes (new Arden), Wells (New Penguin), Levin (Signet), and Dorsch; the last is peremptory in dismissing Malone's conjecture that a line rhyming with "hope," perhaps ending with "rope," had dropped out (p. 68 n.). Just as many, however, have preferred to retain F's "hope," usually citing Malone's conjecture: Wilson (1922 and 1961), Alexander, Jorgensen (Pelican),

Riverside, Bevington, Tetzeli. Only the Oxford, though, both retains "hope" and leaves a space in brackets to indicate that a line is missing before "Do you hear...I hope?" Gary Taylor admits ("Inventing," p. 43) to not having the temerity to insert his own line into Shakespeare's text in another play, but says further that he would feel no compunction about marking a lacuna and mentioning the conjecture in a note. This he did in the present case, recording "*E. Dro*. Thou wouldst answer well to hanging, if I had a rope." This supplies the rhyme, but leaves Luce's (in the Oxford text, Nell's) "I thought to have asked you" still unattached. What did she think to have asked whom? Bevington thinks the missing line should follow rather than precede the "hope" line, but does not conjecture.[34]

As textual adviser to the Bristol Old Vic production of *Errors* in 1989, I discussed the lacuna with the director, who, while using the Arden edition as her script, studied the text very carefully, consulting several other editions. Prior to one rehearsal, I composed several alternative lines, one of which she might choose to insert in the gap. Alas for my inventions, I arrived to find that she had decided to ignore the lacuna, keep the Arden's "trow," and try to make sense of what was there. The actors had invented business to that end. Nell's and Dromio of Syracuse's half-lines were a resumption of a hypothetical previous conversation, a further sally in the former's attempt to seduce the latter. A little personal drama was simmering away indoors even as the larger, more public drama boiled over outdoors. The large Nell spread-eagled the small Dromio against the door. In the fever of the moment, it worked. Dromio's "And you said—no?" became a plea for mercy. No one gave a further thought to the dread lacuna, which in any case was filled from outside when the other Dromio, in mime, thrust a privy member through the letter slot, and the outraged, frustrated Nell inside applied a vacuum cleaner to it. The audience roared its amusement at the mayhem which ensued, and the rejected inventing editor had, willy-nilly, to join in. An emboldened editor may invent, but if he cannot insert his invention in his text, and performers who know about it do not want or need it, it can only survive as a conjecture, buried in a note. What then is its status or point? Inventing Shakespeare only to lose him in the apparatus seems an unprofitable expense of spirit. Yet Taylor's plea is a powerful one, and it enhances that task of helpful drudgery to which editors earnestly commit themselves. It urges the editor to re-create as well as to recover, to become Shakespeare in some sort, momentarily. That his invention, which may not become text, will *be* only if it is spoken in performance and if it is, will *be* only for an instant, are the absurd odds against which he plays. Taylor's description of such inventive emendation as game is reminiscent of the late Philip Brockbank's advocacy of "festive scholarship." Ludic editing serves Shakespeare, the play, and the reader, not just the black signs on the white pages of F. *Ludus*—the medieval Latin word meant *game* and *play*, as students of medieval drama well know. But games have rules and boundaries, as Taylor reminds us. Because he cannot cheat and write his invention into Shakespeare, the gaming editor offers it and hides it wistfully, playfully, at the same time. It may be in print all right, but it is out of bounds, off stage, below the line. A director like John Barton may write hundreds of lines of "Shakespeare" in his adaptation and they get spoken at every performance. The inspired editor invents, and directs furiously in his head.

May an editor adopt a reading recorded only in acting editions? If we mean what we say about the primacy of performance, why not? A crux or a confusion may be clarified by an actor or director who *has* to get or make sense out of it, and that reading may be passed down in playhouse tradition, unknown to scholarly editors who collate those dozens of other scholarly editions. In *Errors* I.ii., Antipholus of Syracuse speaks his first soliloquy, quoted earlier (p. 238). In the Hull adaptation of the late eighteenth century, revised by John Philip Kemble in 1811, the Folio's "falling" in line 37 is emended to "failing." Thus the parallel drawn by Antipholus between the water drop and himself is exact: it seeks its fellow in the vast ocean, and failing to find it, loses (confounds) itself; he, seeking his family in the wide world, unhappy (unsuccessful) in his quest, loses himself. When this emendation was suggested to Owen Teale who played Antipholus in the Bristol production, he grasped it immediately, perceiving the logic and clarity it achieved. An eighteenth-century theatrical emendation lived again in performance 200 years later. It is a tiny change, to be sure, an *i* for an *l*, and the improvement in sense is slight if real. But should we continue to resist or ignore it in modern editions because an actor not an editor first invented it, and when a simple explanation, compositorial misreading of *i* for *l*, is available anyway? Which reading would Shakespeare have opted for, the actor's, the compositor's, or the editor's? His own—but that begs a few questions.

We have, it would seem, come almost full circle, from making a text by remaking another text which never was, and never will be, what it is meant to be, unless it is performed, and then will be something else quite, to realizing that performance not only makes the play, but can, and often does, make the text itself. Of course, the example just given is a very small one, one word, one letter, in an entire play. We do not edit performance, or base our scholarly editions solely or mainly on texts derived from performance—at least, we do not *say* that we are doing so. But what of those Shakespeare revisions preserved in the Folio? A modern edition of *Hamlet* based on the Folio text may, it would seem, be said to be derived from a performance text. But we as editors unmake and remake that particular early text upon which we base our editions, wherever it emanated from, by modernizing its spelling and punctuation, correcting its obvious misprints, spelling out speech prefixes, adding and expanding stage directions, even reconstructing, as the Oxford editors reconstructed the *Pericles* Quarto, and by emending cruxes, mending lacunae, inventing Shakespeare. In each repeated effort to fix *our* text, pin it down, get it right, we make *the* text more, not less, unstable. For each edition is another text, different from all others, be it by no more than a few commas (it is of course always more than that), as each production is a new text, in that larger sense of the word, as well as enunciating a new text in the narrower sense. Every edition is, and is not, definitive. And each performance of a single production has its peculiarities of rhythm, mood, tempo, "feel," as performers are always telling us.

Actors and directors talk readily about remaking Shakespeare when they do a new production. Indeed, most believe that is what the theatre is about.[35] Editors are more reluctant to acknowledge that they too remake Shakespeare, even when they are engaged in producing diplomatic texts or facsimiles. This implies—and this is no earth-shaking discovery of mine—that that TEXT of Shakespeare which we believed, avowedly or tacitly, it was a duty to attempt to recover *in toto* and exactly, not only is not there to be recovered, that that concept itself is faulty, but that if it were it could never be "restored" in our editions, old- or modern-spelling, diplomatic or inventive. Editors of multi-text plays such as *Hamlet* and *King Lear* have come to realize that, if they have the courage of their convictions, they cannot have all the *Hamlet* or *Lear* that Shakespeare may have written in their edited texts. They cannot print the complete words of *Hamlet* and call it Shakespeare's play. To print all the *Hamlet* that Shakespeare wrote at different times, on first, second and subsequent thoughts, even if one is convinced that he did write all of it, is to produce something under Shakespeare's name that he never invented.[36] We can only edit texts, finally, not plays, not authors. Once we accept that our control-text, be it Folio *Hamlet* or *Errors*, Quarto *Lear* or *Pericles*, is itself only a version, and perhaps a partial one, of Shakespeare's own total *Hamlet, Errors, Lear,* or *Pericles,* and that the very existence of that entity is doubtful and unprovable, we may find ourselves freed from the old idolatry. And if we further accept that all our texts are remakes of versions of uncertain provenance, well, we shall be in no worse company than that of the poets banished by Plato from the commonwealth for making counterfeit copies of imitations of the Forms.

This freedom should in turn help us to overcome the "inhibition of seriousness," as Taylor calls it, the po'-facedness of scientistic textual scholarship which has prevented editors from realizing the playful truth that the object of the quest is given much of its substance and shape by the quester himself. The editor does not return with the captured TEXT in hand, but emerges at the other end of the labyrinthine way with the text that he has found, *trouvé.*[37] Such a concept of the editor's art, partway between setting out to find and retrieve a determinate object that is known to exist *a priori* out there, and the free, frivolous invention, the parlour-game that Taylor, as he predicts, will be accused of encouraging, seems to me a fruitful one. What I find will, of course, be partly determined by what I look for, and it is no game of blind man's buff that I play, or random hunt

I set out upon. Not just any treasure trove will do; ghastly roadside warnings like *The Other Shakespeare* and the deformed corpses of A.L. Rowse's brood litter the way. But what I cannot come back with, however I may "struggle for the vision fair," is the one and only *Comedy of Errors* by Shakespeare.

I might have multiplied the examples of textual puzzles and problems in *The Comedy of Errors*, and proposed or speculated about them at length. I have avoided the most notorious crux in the play, Adriana's speech beginning "I see the jewel best enamelléd" (II.i.108–12). Whatever an editor decides to print in these lines is bound not to be right. The actress Rosie Rowell managed to make the passage sound quite meaningful as it stands in most modern editions when she played Adriana in Bristol in 1989. Editing inevitably complicates such cruxes, while performance, also inevitably, simplifies them: it must. As Stanley Wells suggests, "For some reason—perhaps because an edition can be annotated—one is more willing to confront a reader than a playgoer with nonsense" (*Re-editing*, p. 49). But often, what is nonsense on the page is given sense on the stage, or at least an audience is easily persuaded that it makes sense. The moment comes and goes in seconds, and an audience which is not going to worry whether it is "Epidamium" or "Epidamnum" or "Epidamnus," or fret over Luce or Nell, will be swayed by the gist of what Adriana says as she grieves at her husband's supposed desertion. They will not see the collations and commentaries, or the whole articles devoted to emending and explaining the five lines spoken in fifteen seconds in performance.[38] To return to one of the issues raised at the beginning, it is because he must print this or that but not both that the editor has to resolve cruxes, but he sets about it knowing that he can canvass, collate, comment, and explain also, while the actor has to say it, play it, and be done. Shakespeare, of all people, knew that reading a speech and playing it were worlds apart, that obscurity can evaporate in the action of the stage. May it be that some of the famous cruxes are our own inventions, as readers, critics, and editors? Shakespeare did not count on us getting in the way.

I am not yet sure whether to stick to the Folio's double nativity" in the Abbess's final speech (V.i.403–9, quoted above, pp. 240–1). Double nativity at the end of a play about two pairs of twins lost at sea, separated, then reborn, in the words of their new-found mother, is fitting. Besides the play was performed, probably for the first time, at Christmas 1594. Nativity was seasonal. Johnson proposed "festivity" in the final line, Dyce adopted it and was followed by the Oxford edition, but Hanmer's "felicity" fits the line and sums up the tragicomic action best: "After so long grief, such felicity." Whichever word is spoken in performance, the joy, the felicity, the festivity of comic dénouement and romance rebirth are ambient. Editors will make various decisions; performance will variously fix that particular word at that moment, but will unfix and remake the very text it speaks, playing and showing nativity, festivity, felicity, and more, where the edition can read one of them, collate others, comment on all, but convey none. Text and performance merge, and the printed word, apparently always the same but, as a famous son of ancient Ephesus, Heraclitus, would have known, always in flux, is confounded by the act that gives it being but is itself evanescent, rushing headlong to its own closure, the final curtain.

Romance and farce merge at the end of *The Comedy of Errors*, I have argued. The local absurdities, cruxes, and confusions of the latter are confounded in the eternal improbabilities and incredibilities of the former. Both genres flaunt unlikelihood, the one calling us to witness with our own eyes that it is true, the other telling us even as it shows us that it cannot possibly be true. To attempt to create a coherent whole out of such unlikely components seems doubly unlikely, ludicrous. But Shakespeare brazenly pulled it off. Setting out yet again to edit a Shakespeare play-text may appear an unlikely, quixotic venture, but we do it all the time, put our names to it, package it and sell it—Wilson's, Foakes's, Wells's, Bevington's, Dorsch's, Whitworth's *Errors*—claiming, or at least acquiescing in publishers' claims, that we've got it, the play, right here. Performance too is risky, volatile, ephemeral, over as soon as it is done, and just as brazen, each new show—the Lord Chamberlain's Men's, Kemble's, Komisarjevsky's, Nunn's, Noble's, Lloyd's *Errors*—implying each time that for that time, this one is it, the play, Shakespeare's *Comedy of Errors*.[39] Rectify Shakespeare's *Errors*? Perform

Shakespeare's, the whole of Shakespeare's, and nothing but Shakespeare's *Errors*? Not very likely. Yet on and off we and they go, doing it because it must be done, repeatedly. None of the products of these efforts, the myriad performances, the endless editions, though they stretch out to the crack of doom, can be Shakespeare's *Errors*. All of them, hypothetical and actual, future, present, and past, not one before another, may be so called.

Originally published by Charles Whitworth, "Rectifying Shakespeare's *Errors*: romance and farce in bardeditry," *The Theory and Practice of Text-Editing*, ed. Ian Small and Marcus Walsh (Cambridge: Cambridge University Press, 1991): 107–41. Copyright © Cambridge University Press. Reprinted with the permission of Charles Whitworth and Cambridge University Press.

NOTES

[1] A prior question, in the poststructuralist era, might be to do with how "text" in such a context should be construed. I shall use the term in a conventional sense, to denote the written or printed pages which collectively make up a single work of dramatic literature, a play as it is read in book form. The differences between a play text as edited and read, and a play as performed and seen/heard are crucial to this discussion.

[2] Among the fuller arguments for this general case is Stanley Wells's *Re-editing Shakespeare for the Modern Reader* (Oxford, 1984); one of the most recent and vigorous is T.H. Howard-Hill's "Modern Textual Theories and the Editing of Plays," *Library*, Sixth Series, II (1989), 89–115. Especially pertinent to the concerns of this essay is Howard-Hill's "Playwrights' Intentions and the Editing of Plays," *TEXT*, 4 (1988), 269–78, in which testimony is adduced from an unexpected quarter: C.S. Lewis, half a century ago, anticipated central issues in the current text-performance debate.

[3] I do not mean that an editor should interpret in the text itself. An example of editorial overfixing is the Oxford Shakespeare's "understand" in the speech of Dromio of Ephesus at *Comedy of Errors*, II.i.51–3 (all references will be to the Oxford *Complete Works*, in modern spelling, ed. Stanley Wells and Gary Taylor (Oxford, 1986), unless otherwise indicated). In modern as in Elizabethan English, *understand* is not

hyphenated. To hyphenate it is to interpret reductively, to accord priority, with a nudge and a wink, to the secondary meaning, "stand up under his blows." An editor as annotator may of course do that in his commentary, if he judges it necessary; it is an actor's job to do so in delivering the line, if he judges it necessary.

[4] The New Penguin Shakespeare is the RSC's "house" edition and is frequently mentioned in programme credits. Directors there often use others as well or instead; the Arden is a favourite because of its copious annotation, which, however, actors often admit, can be either an encumbrance or irrelevant to their work. Antony Sher writes that the company used both New Penguin and Arden editions when rehearsing *Richard III* in 1984: "and when there are discrepancies we'll choose whichever is more useful for our purposes" *(Year of the King* [London, 1985], p. 156).

[5] In his 1988/9 production of *Hamlet* for the RSC, director Ron Daniels transposed a scene in accordance with the "bad" Quarto of 1603. He also cut 900 lines from the New Penguin text, itself based on the "good" Quarto of 1604/5, with liberal helpings from the Folio.

[6] On hearing versus seeing a play in Shakespeare's time, see Andrew Gurr, *Playgoing in Shakespeare's London* (Cambridge, 1987), pp. 85–97.

[7] A good example of this occurred in Deborah Warner's 1988 production of *King John*, when Salisbury (Edward Harbour), as he spoke the lines "My arm shall give thee help to bear thee hence, / For I do see the cruel pangs of death / Right in thine eye" (V.iv.58–60), to the mortally wounded Count of Melun, reached behind his back to receive a misericord from his companion Pembroke, with which he put Melun out of his agony. The stage business not only conferred a novel meaning upon "My arm shall give thee help to bear thee hence," but was appropriate in the context, a soldierly act of mercy to a dying, noble enemy who had done the English lords a good turn by warning them of treachery.

[8] At least three noteworthy editions of *The Comedy of Errors* have appeared since I undertook my own in 1985: that in the Oxford *Complete Works*, T.S. Dorsch's New Cambridge (1988), and David Bevington's Bantam (1988). There was a bilingual German-English edition by Kurt Tetzeli von Rosador in 1982, and the script used in the BBC television production was published in 1984. Meanwhile, a variorum edition is in progress in the United States, and the Arden is being revised, etc.

[9] The classic essay "The Rationale of Copy-Text" is reprinted in Greg's *Collected Papers*, ed. J.C. Maxwell (Oxford, 1966), pp. 374–91. Howard-Hill challenges the rationale and the editorial tradition since Greg in the first article cited in n. 2 above.

[10] Besides works already referred to, I would include in this body of

recent work in the immediate light of which my (and others') current editing of Shakespeare is being conducted: Stanley Wells and Gary Taylor, *Modernizing Shakespeare's Spelling, with Three Studies in the Text of "Henry V"* (Oxford, 1979); the same authors' (with John Jowett and William Montgomery) *William Shakespeare: A Textual Companion* (Oxford, 1987) ; Wells, *Shakespeare and Revision*, Hilda Hulme Memorial Lecture, University of London, 3 December 1987 (London, 1988); Gary Taylor and Michael Warren (eds.), *The Division of the Kingdoms: Shakespeare's Two Versions of "King Lear"* (Oxford, 1983), and several articles written in response to this volume; Gary Taylor, "Inventing Shakespeare," *Jahrbuch 1986* (Bochum, 1986), 26–44; Taylor, "Revising Shakespeare," *TEXT*, 3 (1987), 285–304; Taylor, other articles by Taylor and the other members of the Oxford team, and reviews of their books and edition. To these could be added a host of articles, both theoretical and on specific matters relating to the Shakespeare text, such as Folio and Quarto printers and compositors, published in the last decade by such scholars as Fredson Bowers, G. Thomas Tanselle, D.F. McKenzie, Paul Werstine, Howard-Hill, and many others. Among all of these, the Oxford *Textual Companion* is the one for a desert island, or for the editor-errant travelling (moderately) lightly. It is a monumental work of scholarship, and while editions continue to bloom and fade, it will fertilize them and fodder their editors and critics for generations to come.

[11] Preliminary consultations on the text were held in November and December 1988, when Miss Lloyd was Sir Barry Jackson Fellow in the School of Performing Arts, University of Birmingham, with practical work on text and performance with drama students. Several such sessions also took place with the Bristol Old Vic company during rehearsals of the production, which ran from 16 February to 11 March 1989 at the Theatre Royal, Bristol.

[12] Aristotle, typically, complicated this straightforward distinction: for him, in drama, the poet's agents, the actors, imitate for him by taking on the characters of the persons; thus drama is in one sense a mediated form *(Poetics*, 1450a–b). But since for Aristotle action is more important than character, the immediacy of the representation or imitation gives the dramatic genre, tragedy, its superiority over the narrative one, epic (1462a–b). Conversely, Homer is a good narrative poet to the extent that he speaks little in his own person and a great deal in the (assumed) persons of his characters. Another Aristotelian tangent worth pursuing would be the consequences for the subsequent study of drama as *poetry* of Aristotle's relegation of the elements of *performance*—spectacle, music, etc.—to positions of minor importance.

[13] This dimension of Peele's play is discussed more fully in the introduction to my New Mermaids edition (London and New York,

1996), pp. xxvi–xxvii.

[14] I realize that I have oversimplified both romance and farce for the sake of my argument. There can be more to farce than buffets and pratfalls. But critics who label *The Comedy of Errors* "farce" also oversimplify the genre in focussing on those elements, and thus fail to do justice to the play.

[15] Reprinted in Gāmini Salgādo, *Eyewitnesses of Shakespeare* (New York, 1975), pp. 68–9.

[16] But this is as nothing compared with the hash made of the play by one reviewer of the 1989 Bristol Old Vic production. Among other things, he names the wrong actor in the part of Angelo, refers to Adriana's entrance in a swimming pool when it was Luciana who appeared thus, says that the Abbess comes out leading the Ephesian Antipholus, and that Shakespeare unforgivably marries off the Abbess and Egeus (a double howler); that Egeus (again) is "bailed" at the end when, of course, he is pardoned and released unconditionally. Finally, he says, we shall never know which Dromio ends up with Nell (as that production called Luce), when it is perfectly clear a few lines from the end that the Syracusan resigns her with relief to his Ephesian twin (*Financial Times*, 21 February 1989).

[17] Preface to Johnson's edition of *The Plays of William Shakespeare* (1765), reprinted in W.K. Wimsatt (ed.), *Dr. Johnson on Shakespeare* (Harmondsworth, 1969), p. 62.

[18] The fullest, often irksomely exhaustive treatment of sources for the play is T.W. Baldwin's *On the Compositional Genetics of 'The Comedy of Errors"* (Urbana, Illinois, 1965).

[19] *Johnson on Shakespeare*, p. 64.

[20] Phyllida Lloyd, in her 1989 Bristol Old Vic production, had the courage, as most modern directors have not, to put Egeon alone on stage with the Duke for the first scene. Egeon was lit by a single white spot. Some of the Duke's questions were given to recorded voices off, as of a crowd or press corps, but the theatre audience were not distracted, as so often, by a stage audience busily listening and reacting.

[21] *Johnson on Shakespeare*, p. 67.

[22] The word "money" occurs twenty-six times in *Errors*, more than in any other play in the canon. *Marks* and *mart* also occur more times than in any other play. *Gold/golden* are found more times only in *Timon of Athens*; *ducats* and *merchant(s)* more times only in *The Merchant of Venice*.

[23] Plautus, incidentally, set one of his plays, *Miles Gloriosus*, in Ephesus, and another, *Curculio*, in Epidaurus, mentioned in Egeon's narrative; most are set in Athens. Epidamnus was in Illyria.

[24] On the reading "failing" for F's "falling," see above, pp. 250–1. Antipholus' lines about seeking and failing to find his mother and

brother are an abbreviated romance narrative on the same theme as
Egeon's: another link between the plots. The inner plot, the farcical
comedy itself, sounds a romance chord. In *Menaechmi*, the romance story
is told briefly in the Prologue, outside the play.

[25] *Pericles*, xxi.183–5; *Cymbeline* V.vi.369–71.

[26] Wells, Taylor, *et al.*, *William Shakespeare: A Textual Companion*, p. 39.

[27] "'Papers' and 'Prompt Books': Printer's Copy for Shakespeare's *Comedy
of Errors*," *Studies in Bibliography*, 41 (1988), 232–46.

[28] *Textual Companion*, p. 266.

[29] But see the note in its defence (*Textual Companion*, p. 267).

[30] Compositor C also set "Epidarus" at another place on the same page
where "Epidamium" appears twice. F2 corrected the former to
"Epidaurus." But Shakespeare might have gone back and changed it if
he had revised his foul papers, because Emilia later says that she and the
children with her had been picked up by men of "Epidamium," not
Epidaurus (V.i.357).

[31] T.S. Dorsch (ed.), *The Comedy of Errors* (Cambridge, 1988), p. 64 (n. to
II.ii.181).

[32] Henry Cuningham (old Arden) thought "We came aboard ..." an
incomplete line and proposed to complete it thus: "... and put to sea,
but scarce," an intelligent conjecture, if one accepts the short-line
hypothesis.

[33] Gareth Roberts has strengthened the case for "owls" and against
replacing it with "elves," arguing that it is quite plausible for Dromio to
fear being sucked black and blue by a *strix*, a screechowl's body housing
a witch or other malign spirit ("*The Comedy of Errors* II.ii.190: 'Owls' or
'Elves'?," *Notes & Queries*, N.S. 34 (1987), 202–4).

[34] *The Comedy of Errors* (New York, 1988), p. 29n.

[35] Though the kind of informed, sensitive inventiveness that Gary Taylor
urges editors to exercise is sometimes in the theatre, unfortunately,
usurped by directorial arrogance, duncicality, or perversity.

[36] *Ergo*, we cannot edit *Hamlet*, but either the bad Quarto or the good
Quarto or the Folio of *Hamlet*. If *Hamlet* is an eclectic edition,
Shakespeare did not write it. If Shakespeare wrote different versions at
different times, which survive as Quartos and Folio, eclectic editions are
amalgamations and adaptations, misleadingly labelled. A comparable
case-history from Elizabethan nondramatic literature is that of Sidney's
Arcadia(s). He may have written all of the "old" *Arcadia* and all of the
incomplete "new" *Arcadia* which breaks off in mid-sentence in Book III,
but he did not write the composite *Arcadia* published in 1593. That was
constructed after Sidney's death by his literary executors, who also
rewrote some of the "old" *Arcadia* used to piece out the "new," and,
with a link passage by yet another author, Alexander, was the version

read for more than 300 years: the Countess of Pembroke's *Arcadia* more than her brother's, in a significant sense. Yet even after the discovery and publication of the complete "old" *Arcadia* early this century, some editors (e.g. Maurice Evans) and critics (e.g. C.S. Lewis, Walter R. Davis) have edited and written about the composite version, insisting, in some cases, on its primacy (see Lewis, *English Literature in the Sixteenth Century* (Oxford, 1954), pp. 331–3).

[37] As in Provençal *trobar*—find, make, invent, compose, as the *troubadours* did.

[38] The latest and most detailed discussion, of many, is Gary Taylor's "Textual and Sexual Criticism: A Crux in *The Comedy of Errors*," *Renaissance Drama*, N.S. 19 (1988), 195–225. My use of masculine pronouns throughout this essay when referring to Shakespeare editors reflects the fact observed by Taylor at the beginning of his, namely, the virtual absence of women from the field.

[39] I have deliberately excluded film and television from this discussion. They are quite different media from the stage, and Shakespeare's plays were not written for them. Film is a cool medium, its message frozen.

Reading Errantly:
Misrecognition and the Uncanny in
The Comedy of Errors

Barbara Freedman

What in fact is the phenomenon of delusional belief? It is, I insist, failure to recognize, with all that this term contains of an essential antinomy. For to fail to recognize presupposes a recognition, as is manifested in a systematic failure to recognize, where it must obviously be admitted that what is denied is in some fashion recognized.... It seems clear to me that in his feelings of influence and automatism, the subject does not recognize his productions as his own. It is in this respect that we all agree that a madman is a madman. But isn't the remarkable thing rather that he should leave to take cognizance of it? And isn't the question rather to discover what he knows about himself in these productions without recognizing himself in them?

—Lacan, "Propos sur la causalité psychique"

The Comedy of Errors stages denied connections on a variety of levels of imaginative experience. The play is ostensibly about mistaken recognitions and mistaken timing: despite the presence of identical twins within the same town, the two brothers never meet up with each other and so never discover the cause of their confusion. Since these misrecognitions are merely physical, situational errors, they at first seem to bolster our sense of superiority; we know who everyone really is and why these misunderstandings occur. But as the mood darkens, as it oscillates ever more rapidly between comic terror and romance, nightmare and wish fulfillment, we come to identify with the experiences of these erring creatures. We partake in an uncanny fantasy that we recognize at some level but fail to understand.

The Comedy of Errors dramatizes a nightmare vision in comic form—a truly terrifying fantasy of a sudden, inexplicable disjunction between personal and communal accounts of one's identity. Those who are most familiar proclaim one a total stranger, and strangers evince a mysteriously gained familiarity. A recent production of the play emphasized this sense of the uncanny. Egeon's pathetic query—"Not know my voice! O time's extremity, / Hast thou so crack'd and splitted my poor tongue / In seven short years, that here my only son / Knows not my feeble key of untun'd cares?" (5.1.308–11)—was delivered to a winking, snickering crowd onstage, and at each piteous lament the uncomprehending townspeople laughed the louder.

The term *uncanny* aptly describes the mood of *The Comedy of Errors*, since the conflation of the familiar and the unknown is operative at a number of levels of this many-leveled play. Freud maintains that "the uncanny [*unheimlich*] is something which is secretly familiar [*heimlich-heimisch*], which has undergone repression and then returned from it." For this reason, "linguistic usage has extended *das Heimliche* ['homely'] into its opposite, *das Unheimliche*; for this uncanny is in reality nothing new or alien, but something which is familiar and old-established in the mind and which has become alienated from it only through the process of repression."[1]

But *The Comedy of Errors* operates at the level of the uncanny for its critics as well, for as we read the play we continually sense connections that we cannot understand. This comedy insists on its own meaninglessness and yet tantalizes us with the possibility of coherent meaning. The play exhibits a remarkable drive toward closure through a romance plot of the separation and reunion of members of a family, an extensive chain of imagery, an allegorical structure, a morality-based plot, and a permanent stage set. At the same time the play undermines the possibility of closure through a disjunctive double plot that develops only through errors, chance, and miracle. The convoluted logic of this illogical plot progresses from Egeon's mysterious crime and meaningless debt, through his sons' punishment for failure to pay mistaken debts, and finally on to Egeon's miraculous redemption and forgiveness. The patterns of crime-punishment-forgiveness and debt-payment-redemption assert narrative logic; the use of mystery, mistakes, miracle, and a disjunctive double plot deny that logic. Connections that might unite main plot and frame plot, join the father's mysterious crime to the children's mistaken punishment, and relate the twins' payment of mistaken debts to Egeon's miraculous forgiveness are at once forged and denied. The interplay of logic and absurdity, transgression and innocence, punishment and nonsense, may help to explain why a work with such elaborately wrought chains of meaning has been received for centuries as meaningless farce.

Since we have been unable to find a means of uniting these plots—and yet we sense their connection—our own readings display this sense of uncanny connections anticipated and yet denied. Rather than deny this problem we can study the awareness of erring at work in our attempts to deny it, and rethink the reading process itself in terms of erring awareness. The project of reading *The Comedy of Errors* reveals how the identity of the literary work, like the identity of the subject, is uncanny *precisely because of its awareness of its failure to capture awareness*. The value of Shakespeare's comedies may be enfolded within this problem. Given that they repeat within themselves the properties of mind they describe, the comedies are truly *riddled* with meaning. These structural disjunctions suggest ambivalence toward making connections both at the level of interpersonal relations and at the level of meaning. Accordingly, *The Comedy of Errors* is as much "about" its own construction of meaning as it is about the construction or reconstruction of the family. A full articulation of the play's levels of self-awareness is impossible—and this may well be the point. Yet insofar as the play comprehends repression on a variety of levels at once, it functions as an example of the thing it "represents," and so "countenances" its own blindness. And insofar as the play claims to do no more than to articulate splits in subjectivity as a response to the problem of meaning, it frees itself as well as us of the burden of full awareness. What the play "means," then, is as impossible to contain as who we are; the same principle of meaning applies equally to play and player, and the assumption of self-identity in either case no longer applies. *The Comedy of Errors* stages identity as that place where issues of representation and repression, structuration and subjectivity intersect. Identity is treated as a form of knowledge, knowledge as a subset of meaning, and meaning as a process in which repression and recognition vie for mastery.

II

Critics who pose such questions as who is reading or where reading takes place will find *The Comedy of Errors* a convenient vehicle for staging these dilemmas, and for raising many more. When is an uncanny text a canny text? How do we determine a play's level of awareness? Is there any way of speaking about this problem that avoids the pretense that the text is a psyche, split between conscious and unconscious, and so always repressing its own meanings? If we term this text *uncanny*, how do we determine its awareness of its levels of awareness?

The Comedy of Errors is widely considered Shakespeare's most insignificant, unselfconscious, and disjointed play. The degree of critical consensus here would be comforting were it not for the various hints that the play's construction of the knowing subject is a ruse. *The Comedy of Errors* is the only Shakespearean play that turns entirely upon certain knowledge possessed by the audience from the beginning and revealed to the characters only at the conclusion. We know everything; the text knows nothing—*or so we think*. One major critic informs us that this play is "two-dimensional only, unsubstantial, not intended to be taken seriously."[2] Another assures us that "everything which Shakespeare meant by *The Comedy of Errors* is immediately perceptible…. All we have to do is grasp the broadly absurd situation, and follow the ingenious fugue of the plot. To get the point, nothing beyond mental alertness of an easy kind is required."[3] The editor of the Pelican Shakespeare edition complains that "there is left over nothing really to think about—except, if one wishes, the tremendously puzzling question of what so grips and amuses an audience during a play which has so little thought in it."[4] Critics encourage us to value *The Comedy of Errors* as an "assimilation and extension of Plautine comedy," to marvel at its "symmetry and near-flawlessness of plot," and to plumb its rich "harmonic structure" for interrelated themes and patterns of imagery, but warn us to forgo the search for "deeper" meanings.[5]

Scholars frequently regard both the inception and the conclusion of the main plot, derived from Plautus's *Menaechmi* and *Amphitruo*, as arbitrary. According to Paul Jorgensen, the farce of misrecognitions records nothing more than a random "rearranging of human puppets" in an essentially static situation.[6] Harold Jenkins maintains that "the confusion of the twins...[is] little more than an adroit device to bring about a happy ending"; it "is really the result of accidental circumstances and is as accidentally cleared up."[7] And Francis Fergusson muses that "the arabesques of absurdity in *The Comedy of Errors* might continue indefinitely."[8] Although critics acknowledge, following G.R. Elliott, that each character confronts the horror of mistaken identity, they also maintain, with Jorgensen, that "no one learns more about himself or his neighbor as a result of the errors."[9] Since, as Jorgensen complains, "in no other play...is the purpose of the confusion less apparent," he and other critics conclude that the farcical mixup conveys what Larry Champion assesses as "no more and no less than the sheer merriment of controlled confusion."[10]

Directors of this play are less disturbed by these farcical disconnections than by the notorious practical difficulties posed by the frame plot: an illogical situation, an unexpected mood of pathos, seemingly interminable speeches recounting past events, and easily forgettable characters who fail to reappear until the last scene of the play. Scholars generally agree that the frame plot, adapted from *Apollonius of Tyre*, is both poorly integrated into the rest of the play and incompatible with its mood.[11] And yet some critics claim that the frame plot both "humanizes" the farce and adds "emotional tension...to what would otherwise have remained a two-dimensional drama."[12] Despite elaborate New Critical studies of complex themes and patterns of imagery in this play, these problems remain unresolved.[13]

But should they be resolved? And what are the consequences of accepting rather than denying fragmentation and disjunction? One consequence is a recognition of how much we have in common with the characters in the play, since neither characters nor audience seems willing or able to accept disjunction. Our failed attempts to unify *The Comedy of Errors* suggest the unflattering position of the Dromio servants, whose well-meaning attempts to mediate between characters result in disaster. Accordingly, our desire to integrate the plots is far more interesting than any discovery of a means whereby they could be joined. C.L. Barber proposes that one reason for merging the two plots is "that the bonds of marriage, broken in [the parents'] case by romantic accident, are also very much at issue in the intervening scenes."[14] This hypothesis comes closest to offering a unifying principle for the play; yet Barber wisely resists attempting to impose coherence on the fractured plot. And so the characters' plight in attempting to unify their experiences forces us to question our role as readers. Do we need to prove the frame plot intrinsic to the play or the main plot purposive? Must our reading reassemble the text so that what seems out of place has a place—and if so, when does this process properly end?

The Comedy of Errors raises a host of questions concerning levels of awareness in both the text and the reader. In terms of imaginative logic, what is being worked through in this play? At the same time, why, in whom, and on what stage is it denied and repeated, resisted and reenacted? As we trace the play's plotted course, we can explore how the reading process is implicated in the principles of identity and repression we examine. If we cannot fix the identity of the play, we can follow our misreadings to explore how meaning, repression, and recognition intersect. At best, we can hope to identify various levels of awareness at work in our reading and to catch them in moments of interrupting, caricaturing, containing, and escaping one another. Since the etymology of *errors* suggests not only mistakes but wandering, we will move with this play and seek to catch our errors as we make them. The significant misrecognitions are not, finally, those that take place between the characters in the play, but those that occur because of the play of character itself. The telling misprisions include our unquestioning identification with such phantom figures as the omniscient reader of this text or the unified ego of so many other texts. To read *The Comedy of Errors* in this way is to acknowledge the sway of the uncanny in our lives. It is to acknowledge that, insofar as we cannot avoid the principle of errors the play articulates, we can never hope to read the play correctly.

III

For the purpose of engaging critical debate, let us take the play's bait and try on the different reading styles offered by the major characters. To understand Antipholus of Ephesus, for example, is to join him as a reader, to understand a point of view from which understanding is not problematic. Like Malvolio after him (and Oedipus before), he loudly asserts that he knows who he is. And he defines himself through boundaries, hierarchies, repression, and exclusion—through what he owns, and through the servants and women whom he owns. Luciana's set speech affirms this principle of identity: "There's nothing situate under heaven's eye / But hath his bound in earth, in sea, in sky. / The beasts, the fishes, and the winged fowls / Are their males' subjects and at their controls. / Man, more divine, the master of all these, / Lord of the wide world and wild wat'ry seas, / ...Are masters to their females, and their lords" (2.1.16–21, 24).

Almost a caricature of the worst of the New Critics, the Ephesian master is blind to the other readings of events advanced throughout the play. His view of the world is not unlike the chain of command described in Luciana's set speech; he inhabits a closed interpretive universe with a limited number of signifiers and signifieds. Meaning is simply a matter of joining them up according to a principle of right relationship. The sign remains stable, binary oppositions still hold, man is at the center of the universe, and all is right with the world. And the play upholds this mode of reading in its concern with bringing together father and sons, husband and wife, brother and brother into "right relationship"; and in encouraging us to locate meaning that, like the prodigal son, once was lost and at last is found. These strategies suggest a comforting and stable world order which sanctions a reading of the organic unity of both self and text.

The Comedy of Errors also undermines this viewpoint, however, by upholding an opposing reading of identity and meaning. For example, if identity is simply a matter of whom we can dominate, then Antipholus of Ephesus is not himself, for he is neither master in his own home nor his own master. That he is not is demonstrated by his long-lost twin brother, the doppelganger, or denied other within the self, whose actions suggest the phenomenon that Freud termed "the return of the repressed." The prototypical romantic, this twin seeks his identity in whatever he encounters and lacks the boundaries we associate with ego stability. He emerges from the sea only to threaten to drown those ashore; he lends himself to a protean principle of meaning and identity and so takes the shape or place of whatever he encounters. He is all too willing to embrace the other, or the other's point of view, or the other's wife, to the point that madness and chaos finally threaten his existence. Almost a caricature of the worst of the deconstructive critics, this twin champions a principle of the infinite commutability of the signified and celebrates the limitless exchange and transformation of meaning. Insofar as meaning and identity are based not only on privileging some meanings but on repressing the possibility of other meanings that surface in time, this return of the repressed threatens all fictions of closure. By inadvertently challenging the principles of property and repression upon which Western identity is based, this twin adds to a farce of displacement by one's double a fantasy of the endless display and displacement of meaning.

And the play can also be shown to bear out this style of reading. At the level of character, *The Comedy of Errors* keeps multiplying subjects and points of view: it splits its main characters into identical twins, and it splits the male subject into husband and bachelor, homebody and traveler, businessman and poet, sinner and exorcist, servant and master. Further, it splits the female subject into the two holy trinities—angel, devil, nun; and mother, wife, courtesan. At the same time the play proliferates contradictory meanings through games of wit and wordplay and through a dispersal of levels of awareness that haunts any text that would presume to contain this play. That there is no outside to this or any other text is graphically illustrated by the way its multiple levels of awareness imply an infinite regress that in turn rebounds upon itself to collapse those levels. We no sooner consider ourselves superior in awareness to the twin Antipholi than we recall that these "masters" imagine themselves superior to their wives, who in turn enjoy superiority over their servants, who in turn feel superior to "their" women. Yet at any one level, superiority over another is accompanied by a limitation in awareness implied by the level above it. As a result, superiority and inferiority, mastery and bondage, knowledge and errors occupy the same site. The idea of understanding *Errors* is itself called into question by these games with a supposedly omniscient reader.

Even to pose a choice between these two styles of reading is to imply that we can stand outside of them. To attempt to fix or contain the meanings of the play is to deny the principles of repression and representation through which identity and meaning necessarily function. The play contains us in its comedy of errors and encourages us to share the very assumptions it undermines. We contradict ourselves if we assert that the play exhibits ambivalence toward closure, for we thereby imply that we can fix the play's meanings. If we argue that the twin subjects embody authorial intention, we must add that they embody it as that which escapes representational closure. Meaning is staged as subject to a potentially infinite process of splitting and repression. The conflict between repression and representation is enacted both on the stage of the play and within any discourse that would fix the play, close its meanings, and restore its unity.

Before we proclaim Antipholus of Syracuse the master reader, however, we need to consider the limits of his reading style. The traveler's mode of reading all too easily denies the cultural context of any reading and so disowns responsibility for its point of view. It relies upon an unspoken fantasy that we can avoid being displaced by other readings as long as we continually redefine the nature of reading. It suggests that we can remove reading from a context of mastery and truth and innocently envision it as the infinite play of the supplement. Antipholus of Syracuse offers a useful cautionary principle for readers, insofar as his reading style denies that it takes a place. Whereas it calls into question the boundaries between dream and reality, self and other, past and present, order and disorder, it can account for neither these binary oppositions nor the principle of repression they imply.

Where, then, do we stand or wander in this debate? Can we privilege one style of reading over the other? The conclusion of the play at first appears to offer a ridiculously simple solution to this complicated problem. By equating the twin sons with opposing principles of identity and change and then uniting these brothers at its conclusion, the play implies that identity and change are no longer mutually exclusive concepts. As with most of the so-called solutions to Shakespeare's comedies, however, this ending blatantly ignores the complexity of the problems we have been encouraged to entertain. There is no Heraclitean sophistication here, no complex definition of the human animal as that which changes. Since Emilia and Egeon have done nothing to correct the error of over twenty years of separation, the compatibility of these two changed creatures may well strain their imaginations as much as our own.

The concluding nonverbal cues openly interrogate the narrative drive toward closure, as the twin Dromios try to carry out their promise of forevermore going "hand in hand, not one before another" (5.1.426). Are they not comically inept here, as elsewhere, in carrying out their good intentions? Can they always enter every door at precisely the same time? The Dromio servants' recognition that one must go before the other recalls Luciana's sense that identity depends upon a law of priority and place. The exits of the other characters have hardly followed democratic practice, after all. The Dromios have had to wait their turn. They have not been invited to exit at the same time as their masters, nor did the masters exit with "their" ladies, who presumably left the stage before them. Following the comedy's discursive doublespeak, this conclusion underscores the relation between identity and repression.

The limits of both reading styles, as well as the impossibility of either choosing between them or joining them, are graphically portrayed by the Dromio servants. In their clownish efforts to mediate between the twins, the Dromios offer us a mirror image of our own frustrated attempts to unite this play. The funniest moments in *The Comedy of Errors* are the beatings of the Dromio servants. The Dromios never know the cause of their motion and never question the angry beatings they receive upon delivering their messages. Well-meaning but thickheaded, they are the true butts of farce—doomed to err, doomed to disobey their masters' commands, doomed to be beaten but never to know why: "When I am cold, he heats me with beating; when I am warm, he cools me with beating. I am wak'd with it when I sleep, rais'd with it when I sit, driven out of doors with it when I go from home, welcom'd home with it when I return; nay, I bear it on my shoulders, as a beggar wont her brat; and I think when he hath lam'd me, I shall beg with it from door to door" (4.4.32–39).

The function of these perplexed messengers is to act as potential mediators between disjunctive worlds—whether past and present, single and marital personae—with unfailingly disastrous results. These clownish servants convey the sense of helplessness that accompanies the futile attempt to live in mutually exclusive worlds and to meet their contradictory demands. Try as they may to understand a given message and to carry it with all due speed to its proper destination, the Dromios are unable to keep up with the changing worlds of the play. As they automatically give the right message to the wrong person, they offer an image of the self unable to cope with or adapt to the demands of a changing environment. Not only do they remind us of the reader's foolish attempts to join up the play's fragmented parts, they also suggest the binding and purposive ego functions caught in the grasp of an automatic and dysfunctional repetition. Like the ego functions, the Dromios' function is to bring disjunctive selves and worlds together. Continually frustrated in their attempts—beaten, mocked, and scorned by all parties—they graphically depict a situation in which the ego is not master in its own house. If we cannot yet give up our dreams of a unified ego, if we cannot avoid the desire to piece together this play, we must accept that in so doing we are not only playing into the hands of a plot that would prove these efforts impossible, but playing the role of fools.

IV

As persistent messengers, we continue to follow the spirit of the uncanny and to work at the relation of the strange and the familiar. Some of the best treatments of *The Comedy of Errors* have focused on its exploration of the relationship of temporality and identity. Gāmini Salgādo explores "the tricks [*Errors*] plays, in form, language, and action, with what we take to be a normal temporal sequence," and concludes: "If a developed sense of time and a sense of individuality are virtually two aspects of the same thing, this may account for the uncanny and more-than-farcical resonance of the play."[15] When Egeon isn't recognized by his son, he blames "time's deformed hand" (5.1.299) for the mis-recognition. Since the play's humor works through a disruption of "order," and since its wit and wordplay center around the problem of recovering—and denying the recovery of—something lost in time, we might take this fantasy more seriously.

This time, however, we will read from Adriana's point of view. Not surprisingly, the speech that appears to piece everything together is offered by the excluded, discredited voice of a woman. In Act 2, Adriana equates her husband's neglect of marital duties with his own self-estrangement and self-division: "How comes it now, my husband, O, how comes it, / That thou art then estranged from thyself? / Thyself I call it, being strange to me, / That, undividable incorporate, / Am better than thy dear self's better part. / Ah, do not tear away thyself from me" (2.2.119–24). Adriana's reasoning is at least consistent: separation from one's spouse results in a division of the personality into contradictory marital ("thou," "me") and single ("thyself") personae. This elaborate system has the distinction of positing a unified, coherent ideal self, and so holds out the promise of unifying self and text, identity and meaning. Its irrelevance to the situation at hand, however, suggests that we are laboring under another illusion.

The terms of Adriana's equation fail to apply to the man she addresses as her husband, since Antipholus of Syracuse is a bachelor. Nor do they apply to the intended recipient of this speech since, despite Adriana's jealousy, the couple is not yet estranged. The situation does apply to Egeon, however, who has been separated from his spouse, and so from a part of himself, for well over twenty years. As in so many plots based on the usurping double, the sense of closure that we associate with individual identity is eroded, and we experience the phenomenon described as "the second self in time."[16] By reading Egeon's plight as one in which disowned or split-off parts of the self are still recognized by others, we can unite this disjointed plot. But as we take the play's bait, we must remember who and what is being caught.

If Egeon is estranged not only from his wife but from his marital identity, divided into single and marital personae, his twin sons graphically suggest his divided state. The birth of the twins occurs only after Egeon's first separation from his wife, and when his wife comes to see him in Epidamnum. In Adriana's terms, duality is conceived only when Egeon's single identity ("thyself") and marital identity ("thou") confront each other. The twins' symbolic function is further suggested by the correspondence of their opposing characteristics to Egeon's accounts of his marital and postmarital, past and present, unified and divided identities. Antipholus of Ephesus is literally that "part" of Egeon which has remained lost with his wife since the storm first separated the couple. Antipholus of Syracuse is that "part" of Egeon that has remained with him. Like the former Egeon, the Ephesian twin is the settled, respectable citizen; his denied counterpart is drawn in the likeness of the present image of his father—an unhappy sojourner. The Ephesian twin is firmly ensconced in a familial situation; the Syracusan is a wandering bachelor, seeking the domestic stability Egeon has lost. The Ephesian is a businessman, recalled in Egeon's description of his former life to Duke Solinus (1.1.39–40); his brother is an impractical romantic who hazards all in an apparently bootless journey, much like his "hopeless and helpless" father.

Despite some confusion about the order of the twins' births, the married brother is twice referred to and commonly accepted as the elder; this precedence further encourages us to associate him with Egeon's past and his single brother with Egeon's present situation. The Ephesian has no knowledge of his brother; as Egeon's pretempest persona, he cannot anticipate future self-division. The Syracusan, as representative of Egeon's present identity, is aware of his divided condition and seeks to remedy it. Antipholus of Syracuse is further associated with Egeon's divided state when he is advised by a friend to deny his birthplace and to call his home Epidamnum, thereby recalling Egeon's separation from his birthplace, wife, and past when he left for Epidamnum. The Syracusan twin lodges at the Centaur, sign of a divided state; the Ephesian brother who must be recovered lives at the Phoenix, sign of rebirth.

The allegorical schema of the "second self in time" neatly ties together the fragmented plots. It relates the mixup of the twins' identities to Egeon's problem and its resolution in the frame plot. And it suggests that the play enacts a fantasy of confronting and integrating split-off parts of the "self" in time. The tempest that divided Egeon from his wife literally divided his past and present, marital and single identities as well, represented by Egeon's separated twin sons. Antipholus of Ephesus is the stable, secure marital identity of Egeon's youth; Antipholus of Syracuse is Egeon's fragile present persona, the single traveler seeking to recover his other half, to integrate himself, to be reborn: "So I, to find a mother and a brother, / In quest of them (unhappy), ah, lose myself" (1.2.39–40). Egeon's search for a past identity is suggested by his physical separation from Emilia in the frame plot and by Antipholus of Syracuse's search for his long-lost married brother in the main plot. By dividing the personality up neatly into halves, *The Comedy of Errors* holds out the possibility of self-presence. As thematic imagery forges one chain between the fractured plots, the allegorical framework of the second self in time forges an even more stable link, implying that self-redemption can indeed be final and complete.

Were we to stop here, we could conclude that *The Comedy of Errors* is not simply about the physical division and reunion of a family but about the psychic division and integration of the personality. In fact, once this allegorical schema is brought to our attention, hidden "connections" seem everywhere, encouraging us to tie together the play's religious references, its Gray's Inn Christmas performance, its puns on debts and redemption, its emendation of the twins' age from twenty-five to thirty-three, and much more. Yet this reading does not "clinch" the play or supersede other readings. To credit this master narrative, we would have to explain why no one has uncovered it for well over three hundred years. Rather than applaud our own efforts as detectives, we might detect the humor directed at any such stance of mastery. Wasn't C.L. Barber right to stop short of reading the twins as representatives of their father's divided state, since such a reading denies that this is a play about denial? "I deny it not" (5.1.379) is a phrase that we hear and yet deny throughout this curious work. Of more significance than our recovery of a hidden plot is our acknowledgment of its problematic status. Since the play strenuously denies that Egeon was guilty for leaving his wife, any reading of his guilt as something that is worked out or paid for by his sons is simply unwarranted. As we continue to read this play, it is essential that we preserve at the level of meaning the sense of duality and ambivalence which is visually emphasized in the image of identical twins. The uncanny implies a familiar unfamiliarity in relation to time and so both does and undoes the work of repression. Since the uncanny implies a return of the repressed, it offers a comforting sense that what is lost can always be found; since it also points to the inevitability of future repression, it implies that identity and meaning can never be stable. As we continue to err in the direction of allegory, we need to attend to the ways in which the play's ambivalence toward representation and repression troubles any reading.

V

Adriana's desire to pin blame, the twins' desire to punish their servants, Egeon's innocent crime—all betray a curious ambivalence toward guilt and indebtedness. Since the twins are always confused with each other in a way that forces each to mistakenly identify with the other's debts,[17] their indebtedness both evokes Egeon's debt and denies any meaningful relationship to it. Obsessive fantasies of being unable to repay a debt typically suggest guilt regarding an inability to fulfill one's obligations. In this case, the broken marriage bond functions as the debt whose payment alone can retrieve a denied marital persona. But insofar as the play never fully owns up to this debt, the sense of guilt moves symptomatically through the text like a signifier cut loose from its signified—as if by splitting and duplication it could avoid knowing what it knows. In this sense, *The Comedy of Errors* is not only about repression, or even about the return of the repressed, but about the repression of this return. The result is a series of ever more contradictory stories that prevent us from taking any single viewpoint upon them. These elaborate displacements of a situation of indebtedness typify this play's obsessive mode of ordering, fragmenting, and then reordering a highly intricate plot in such a way that it no longer conveys the same meanings at all.

For example, *The Comedy of Errors* actually records two different transgressions: Egeon's violation of Ephesian law in the frame plot and his sons' run-ins with domestic law in the main plot. Not only does the dual status of culprit and crime wonderfully confuse the issue, but the fact that both transgressions are invalidated—whether by ignorance of the law or by mistaken identification of the culprit—renders the punishment either perversely arbitrary or comically absurd. Egeon's debt is actual, obscure, and monetary; his sons' debts are mistaken, meaningful, and marital. On one hand this play is obsessed with confronting, punishing, and forgiving debts; that action follows a logical pattern and is accompanied by significant emotional reaction. On the other hand, the play either invalidates those debts or obscures their content, thereby denying their significance. The question is not what unifies the two debts—for the marital debt does so quite nicely—but at what level of awareness this text is operating in relation to these denials.

We could attribute these contradictions to a functional displacement of meaning and argue that the punishment of unpaid debts is made acceptable by their disguise and denial. But by whom and for whom are these debts and their punishment "made acceptable"? That the play compulsively repeats a situation of indebtedness—adding marital to monetary debts, mistaken debts to actual debts, sons' debts to a father's debt—is undeniable. So is the pattern whereby Egeon's monetary debt is associated with his son's potential monetary debt, equated through replacement with a mistaken marital debt, and so promptly discharged. As the Syracusan twin turns from fear of actual monetary debt to payment for a mistaken marital debt, so his brother turns from fear of an actual marital debt to payment for a mistaken monetary debt. Given such an intricate pattern, as well as the means by which this farcical confrontation of debts results in Egeon's redemption, it would appear that some sort of debt is being repeated and "worked through."

Adriana's copious complaints of marital neglect, coupled with the kitchen maid Nell's equally relentless marital demands, strongly argue for the existence of a valid marital debt—or an odd disjunction between accounts of what constitutes marital obligations in Ephesus. Adriana rightly believes her husband guilty of not returning home that day, and he admits that wrong in considering the jeweler's work on the gold chain to be an excuse for his absence (3.1.1–5). The highlight of Egeon's story is also a failure to return home, regardless of whether this is due to "cruel fate," to business obligations (1.1.41–43), or to personal preference (1.1.58–60).

Since Egeon allows eighteen years to elapse before searching for anyone—and his search is motivated by the loss of his sons—one is tempted to associate the action of "cruel fate" with denied dreams of independence. To do so, however, is to repeat the characters' errors in their attempts to pin blame. By assuming misrecognition as a principle of meaning, the play renders comical any attempt to recognize its meaning from one point of view. Its performance of the subject as erring and divided forces any critical discourse that would master it to confront its own errors—its propensity to locate and unify a given character, author, or the text "itself." As our attempt to pin blame on one character or to thematize the play in terms of a controlling idea fails, as the tendency to speak of the play's author, action, or awareness becomes increasingly less viable, the very terms of critical discourse begin to fragment and turn against themselves.

Psychoanalytic critics have been notoriously guilty of the quest for hidden or denied meanings that would make sense of this play. They have argued loudly and senselessly over whether or not Egeon "meant" to flee his marriage and over whether or not the wish to escape one's wife is the unacceptable, repressed fantasy that the play obsessively repeats in disguised form. Theories that Egeon's punishment is due to his ambivalence toward domesticity, his lust for money, or his repressed oedipal wishes are equally unconvincing.[18] Can a fictional storm punish a fictional character for his disguised wishes?

If *The Comedy of Errors* is taken at face value, Egeon is clearly absolved of any guilt. He was no more aware of the feud between Ephesus and Syracuse than he was in a position to halt the tempest. Although we can "uncover" Freudian slips throughout his copious protests of innocence, the challenge we face as readers is to consider how our readings are implicated in the very process of uncovering and covering up which we would analyze. The challenge we face is neither to pin blame nor to close up the play's meanings but to acknowledge that which resists these efforts. From one standpoint, Egeon's story suggests guilt regarding both the denial of a marital bond and a wish for previous marital separations, and so provides the "missing link" that changes an arbitrary farce plot into a meaningfully directed fantasy. Yet Egeon repeatedly denies any ill will that would affirm this core fantasy, and his resistance is fitting, given a play that never stands in one place regarding innocence or guilt.

Errors resists as it encourages our efforts to fix any of its characters—Antipholus of Ephesus or Syracuse, Dromio of Ephesus or Syracuse, Adriana or Luciana, Luce or Nell—in any final identity. And this resistance forces us to remember that Egeon is not a person and that he has no sons who can re-present him. Egeon is merely a stand-in, in a series of stand-ins, for a sense of guilt that can neither be internalized nor integrated. To argue that the twins re-present Egeon's divided state is therefore as problematic as to maintain that Egeon's disguised wishes motivate the plot, or that the twins are a "part" of Egeon. There is no culprit here, only scapegoats; no crime, only errors. Since this sense of loss and sin lacks a subject in which to ground it, it is passed back and forth within the play, only to find a predictable resting spot in the representation of woman. Guilt drifts almost magically away from Egeon, away from his twin sons, away from the Dromio servants, away from some exorcised fiend, and when all else fails, onto Adriana—guilty, sinful woman. The process of scapegoating follows a typical Shakespearean pattern as guilt gets passed from father to son, from master to servant, and from husband to wife. The play attributes its sense of impending doom to the simple fact that, as one character puts it, "I am due to a woman: one that claims me, one that haunts me, one that will have me" (3.2.81–83). But we can no more accept this fantasy of blame than we can accept any fantasy of an absolute origin.

VI

The theatrical history of *The Comedy of Errors* offers another context for understanding the play's interest in juxtaposing the discourses of court and church, debts and redemption. The first recorded performance took place during the customary Christmas revels at Gray's Inn, and both recorded performances of the play during Shakespeare's lifetime occurred on Holy Innocents Day, which commemorates Herod's slaughter of innocent children in his attempt to destroy the Christ child. The superimposition of a religious narrative of Christian redemption on a simple Plautine farce of physical mishaps works to contain the splits and repressions incurred by debts and so to limit rather than disseminate meanings. The thematics of redemption function to resolve ambivalence toward indebtedness by suggesting that what was lost can be found and that debts can be successfully redeemed.

Perhaps the easiest way to read *The Comedy of Errors* is as an exploration of various definitions of the term *redemption*. The simplest meaning of *redeem*, according to the *Oxford English Dictionary*, is to regain or recover something lost—an obvious and constant subject of this play's learned wit. Antipholus of Syracuse would teach his Dromio that "there's a time for all things" (2.2.65). Dromio would disprove this adage by proving that there is "no time to recover hair lost by nature" (2.2. 102–3) and so "there is no time to recover" (2.2.105) anything at all. Dromio of Syracuse complains that "time is a very bankrout" (4.2.58) and "a thief" (4.2.59), since "time comes stealing on by night and day" (4.2.60). But he admits that sometimes time can "turn back an hour in a day" (4.2.62) and then, as Adriana also acknowledges, "the hours come back" (4.2.55)—"as if Time were in debt!" (4.2.57).

The peril associated with time's movement in this play calls to mind the famous moment in Harold Lloyd's *Safety Last*. Lloyd portrays a man who stays alive by just barely holding on to the hands of a giant clock—as if to make time stand still. The many references to time standing still in *The Comedy of Errors* suggest that the problem of redeeming time is a key source of the play's near paralysis in the form of a senseless repetition of farcical mishaps. Egeon has also been attempting to recover something lost in time but is conveniently interrupted when faced with an insurmountable debt in attempting to cross into Ephesus. The warring towns of Ephesus and Syracuse find their only correlation in this text in the characters of Antipholus of Ephesus and Antipholus of Syracuse. Since the characters are not enemies, the war has meaning only insofar as the twins represent Egeon's contradictory personae. The forbidden boundary between the two towns and the penalty for crossing it suggests the precariousness of a split identity: if the Syracusan and Ephesian twins meet, one or the other must be destroyed. A way out of this dilemma is provided by payment of "a thousand marks .../ To quit the penalty and to ransom him" (1.1.21–22). This debt reminds us that *to redeem* literally means "to buy back," to recover only "by payment of the amount due, or by fulfilling some obligation" (*OED*). The curious financial arrangement implies that Egeon can recover his marital identity only on the condition that he pay the neglected marital debts. This also explains why Antipholus of Syracuse enters Ephesus, is apprehended by Adriana for neglected marital obligations, and dutifully returns home with her. The misidentification of the twins through a series of debts thus serves as a path through which the ideal of self-continuity is forged.

Adriana pays her husband's debt, thereby symbolically freeing him of marital debt. But the play refuses to let him off this easily: he is released by Adriana only to be bound by an exorcist who will purge him of his sins. With the entry of Pinch, the exorcist, the punitive plot threatens to run amok. Only when Antipholus of Ephesus escapes from his bonds and revenges himself upon this pinching, punishing parasite does the play move toward a sense of release and forgiveness. Redemption in the sense of a deliverance from sin takes over the plot when the Syracusan twin escapes into the priory and is offered full protection both from the law and from the scorn of a jealous wife. The movement from father to son, law to mercy, bondage to freedom, separation to reunion, and death to rebirth joins the play's events to its Christmastime occasion: Egeon's sons are freed from bondage, his separated family is reunited, Egeon is released from the penalty of death, and his death is replaced by his sons' symbolic rebirth.

This reading is further strengthened by the change in the twins' age, earlier listed as twenty-five, to thirty-three—the sacred number of the years of Christ's life.[19] Abbess Emilia concludes: "Thirty-three years have I but gone in travail / Of you, my sons, and till this present hour / My heavy burthen [ne'er] delivered" (5.1.401–3). Similarly, the apostle Paul witnesses: "We know that the whole creation has been groaning in travail together until now; and not only the creation, but we ourselves, who have the first fruits of the Spirit, groan inwardly as we wait for adoption as sons, the redemption of our bodies. For in this hope we were saved" (Romans 8:22–24). Still another meaning of *redeem*—"to restore or bring into a condition or state"(*OED*)—prevails when the sons are freed, united, and adopted by their father. *The Comedy of Errors* can therefore be read as a play with and upon redemption: it demonstrates how one redeems (recovers) oneself by redeeming (making payment for) one's debts as one redeems (goes in exchange for) one's alter ego, and how one is thereby redeemed (released) from bondage only to share in the fruits of redemption (as rebirth).

Since this way of thinking about self-division was common to the Elizabethan morality play, which in turn influenced much Renaissance drama, less scholarly audiences than the lawyers at Gray's Inn would be apt to discover some such allegory at work.[20] The grim opening of *The Comedy of Errors* reveals a common man in bondage for sin, facing death, and despairing of mercy, thereby signaling the conventional portrait of natural unredeemed man in the morality plays. Its conclusion also follows a conventional morality-patterned action: Egeon's wife emerges from the priory in time to save him, Egeon is released from bondage, and his sins are forgiven by a merciful judge. The journey of the self toward redemption is figured in the twins' confrontations with the temptation and regeneration offered by the contrasting figures of vice (the courtesan) and of virtue (Luciana). The Ephesian brother's worldly interest in material and physical pleasure is contrasted with the piety of his brother to suggest the warring earthly and heavenly elements in Everyman's nature. The neglected marital identity is portrayed as in need of redemption; the single identity is associated with a spiritual agent willing to undergo penance to redeem its fallen counterpart.

An Elizabethan audience would probably understand the twins on a variety of levels: as long-lost brothers in a family, as dissociated parts of the self, or as warring earthly and heavenly elements in the nature of Everyman. They could read the plot in terms of a romantic comedy formula—as it moves from separation, through bewilderment, to reunion and harmony of family members or lovers; in terms of a psychological formula—as it progresses from repression through confrontation to integration of parts of the self; and in terms of a morality-patterned formula—which charts a development from self-division and bondage through penance to redemption.

Paul's letter to the Ephesians, long accepted as a major source for this play, has never been studied in the context of the second self in time. Scholars have observed that this letter includes such elements as years of wandering, a shipwreck, the Aegean (Egeon) and Adriatic (Adriana) seas, Syracuse, Corinth, Ephesus and its demonic magic, revenge taken upon evil exorcists, and a conflict between law and mercy, bondage and redemption.[21] But its message, for which Paul is being held prisoner at the time, is the union of two hostile nations, Gentiles and Jews, in the body of Christ: "For he is our peace, who has made us both one, and has broken down the dividing wall of hostility, by abolishing in his flesh the law of commandments and ordinances, that he might create in himself one new man in place of the two, so making peace, and might reconcile us both to God in one body through the cross, thereby bringing the hostility to an end" (Ephesians 2:14–3:1). Paul's imagery of the creation of "one new man in place of the two," of one body in which two hostile people are joined in harmony, suggests the problem of joining two hostile identities within one psyche. The two hostile nations are figured in Syracuse and Ephesus and are joined in the body of their common father, Egeon.

It should not be sacrilegious to observe that these gestures of closure are themselves bound to fail, not unlike the characters' attempts to bind themselves to each other or the reader's attempts to bind together various meanings discovered within the play. The problem the play poses is not whether time can turn back but whether we can keep up with the losses we incur as time moves forward—whether we can ever be synonymous with ourselves, pay our debts, or be "redeemed." Our need to unify texts and selves is doomed to err, to travel, to wander, and to fail. Since experience in time creates further splits and fissures in the newly integrated self, how can we believe that Egeon, or the author, or the play, is ever whole? How can we believe that even the most unifying of readings closes discussion of the play, permanently represses all potential readings, is final or complete?

The conclusion of *The Comedy of Errors* offers two interpretations of identity only to mediate between them in a provisional compromise. Adriana defines identity as a composite of internalized relationships with others which is fixed and irreversible: "For know, my love, as easy mayst thou fall / A drop of water in the breaking gulf, / And take unmingled thence that drop again, / Without addition or diminishing, / As take from me thyself and not me too" (2.2.125–29). But Egeon's identity is not simply the sum of his past identifications with others. The Syracusan son is also an essential part of Egeon, born in his denial of his past, nurtured and sustained apart from home and wife. If Egeon is willing to hazard this persona to retrieve his former self, he is unwilling to abandon it completely. Egeon's identity is not found through the actual restoration or the denial of his past relationships with others. Egeon has never set out in search of his beloved Emilia, his "bliss," nor does he mention ever experiencing the desire to do so, despite the twenty-five years they have spent in apparently needless separation. When Emilia finally makes her appearance at the conclusion of the play, Egeon's first words to her are a request for his son. It is not his wife but Antipholus of Ephesus that Egeon "labored of a love to see" (1.1.130); it is only himself (Antipholus of Ephesus) for whom Egeon "hazarded" himself (Antipholus of Syracuse) (1.1.131). Were Egeon to find himself in the renewal of past relationships, this would be tantamount to resolving the identity crisis through the destruction of his present Syracusan identity, rather than through the relation of his present to his past.

The play offers a neat solution to this crisis in its definition of identity as the perception of self-continuity or as the identification and integration of various self-concepts in a time continuum. Of course, the marital reunion celebrated at the conclusion is neither looked for nor, according to some critics, really effected—but this is irrelevant at the end of a comedy.[22] This return of the repressed threatens a return to the repressive, and so is not as stable as critics suppose—but this is not pertinent to the ego's fictions of triumph. That this solution is a virtual impossibility, that it denies the inevitability of future self-division, is only hinted at by the strange doubling onstage. The use of twins undermines the possibility of self-presence by suggesting that identity is a matter of two who can never be one; being is a function of splitting and attempting to recuperate that loss in further splits. Identity is re-presented as grounded in yet prevented by repression and always haunted by the inevitability of a return of the repressed.

VII

Psychoanalytic readings of the comic tend to confirm these narratives of closure. The ostensible goal of the traditional psychoanalytic reading is to reconstruct the denied wish or fantasy at the "core" of the joke or dream. For example, were *The Comedy of Errors* to clarify the connection between father and sons, it is likely that the mistakes of identity and the punishment ensuing from them would fail to be humorous. Instead, these connections are carefully disguised, at once asserted and denied in a way that we associate with the uncanny, so that we sense a significance we never fully understand. This play's sensibility thus exemplifies Eric Bentley's hypothesis that in farce "there is an acknowledgment of absurdity—and...a counterclaim to a kind of sense."[23] Neither, as Bentley notes, ever wins out; meaning and madness battle for priority.

Since farce, like dreams, couples a functional denial of significance with often disturbing and highly significant content, one can read illogic, contradiction, omission, and mistakes as signifiers of a functional dislocation of meaning.[24] Accordingly, one could argue that the aggression directed against the Dromios and their masters displaces aggression "intended" for Egeon, and so the plot is punishing the crime of neglected marital obligations. The punishment of the two Dromios, for example, is never openly associated with any transgression on their part. The play includes but denies Egeon's transgression, focusing instead on random acts of punishment which miraculously result in his redemption. The marital debt is both denied and displaced; only the mistake, the unexpected confusion of the twins' identities, is blamed for all the aggression in the play. The effect of that aggression is similarly denied: Dromio may complain of his beatings or the Ephesian twin of his treatment by Dr. Pinch, but these actions are senselessly delivered and senselessly received. The fast pace, complexity, and extraordinary subject matter of the plot further contribute to this general distortion of the sense of reality, and so are equally vital to our humorous acceptance of this fantasy.

Yet even if we uncover a fantasy behind the play's comic punishment, we cannot say whose it is, what hides it, or how to privilege it. Whether we are analyzing dreams or jokes, the analytic model of fantasy is itself problematic, since it depends upon the illusion of an unchanging reader who works through a single ahistorical fantasy by reading a potentially unified and stable text. We are thus forced to question how aware this play is of the role of denial in the success of its own humor. Since comedy is capable of interrupting and addressing its own production, and since this comedy, in particular, explores the role of the unconscious in the production of meaning, what kind of discourse can under-stand and re-present this? How can we forge a theory of representation in Shakespearean comedy as well as in that comedy of errors known as literary criticism?

More compelling than a reading of the displacement of meaning in farce is the way in which farce subverts meaning, displaces any stable reading, and forces us to rethink such basic terms as *author, play, meaning,* and *fantasy. The Comedy of Errors* suggests less a displaced core fantasy than the impossibility of discovering any single core or fantasy that "governs" a text. Perhaps the best gloss on the play is the definition of the primal scene offered by Jean Laplanche and J.-B. Pontalis: "The original fantasy is first and foremost fantasy: it lies beyond the history of the subject but nevertheless in history: a kind of language and symbolic sequence, but loaded with elements of imagination; a structure, but activated by [certain] contingent elements. As such it is characterized by certain traits which make it difficult to assimilate to a purely transcendental schema, even if it provides the possibility of experience."[25] We can easily analyze the farce play as symptom and uncover hidden transgressions being punished in disguised form. But what is most interesting about farce—of which *The Comedy of Errors* is a variety—is not its repetition of a familiar pattern of wish and defense, but its subversion of that model. What is peculiar about farce and the uncanny alike is not the disguise of a core fantasy but the *recognition* of that disguise.

In farce, plot is more disturbing than content; there is something manic and uncontrolled about the way that the plot unfolds. Bentley explains that although we commonly enjoy illicit fantasies in farce, there is always a disturbing sense of nightmare associated with their fulfillment; we sense that we are driven "from bedroom to bedroom by demons," or we experience a loss of free will and control to something that "bristles with menace," something that in turn threatens to lose control. The more that characters lose control in farce, the more tightly the plot is wound up; the more that characters seek gratification, the more severely the plot punishes them for it. "Melodrama and farce are both arts of escape," argues Bentley, "and what they are running away from is not only social problems but all other forms of moral responsibility. They are running away from the conscience and all its creations."[26] Yet if farce involves running away from the conscience, it appears to reenact that chase with the conscience in the starring role. The characteristic sense of anxiety and menace in a highly elaborate, paranoid plot; the celebrated chase, the hallmark of farce; the series of blows mistakenly delivered—all are signs of a comedy of the superego.

Whereas comedy is concerned with unity, adaptation, purposiveness, and harmony, farce is committed to the discontinuous and the dysfunctional. Its aggression and regression are not in the service of the ego but directly opposed to ego mastery. Accommodation to the reality principle, subservience to the ego—these aims and activities are antithetical to the subversive, rather than festive, spirit of farce. Farce is just the opposite of a neatly disguised fantasy of wish fulfillment and in this sense opposes the adaptive functions of both dream and comedy. As discontinuous, dysfunctional, and demonic form gone wild, farce swings between the extremes of chaotic anti-form and compulsively elaborate plots.

Like nightmares, farce suggests an awareness and interruption of unconscious content. Albert Bermel explains:

The pace and insanity of farce in turn create an atmosphere onstage that approximates the conditions of a dream world or, rather, of a nightmare: the terrors of humiliation—of being, say, unable to remember the simple answer to a leading question; of being found in a stranger's bedroom without pants on; of being taken for a notorious criminal or a lunatic with not a scrap of evidence to support one's identity—such typical dream fears are familiar to audiences. As they recognize them, consciously or unconsciously, they laugh; they are relieved witnesses of somebody else's nightmare.[27]

What is peculiar about farce is not the content of its fantasies but its recognition of fantasy. Farce shares with nightmares the ability to stage the *interruption* of representation itself. The interruption of wishes, the recognition of wishes, the horror of wishes—all imply what we might term a failure of the ego functions.

In this sense, farce is closer to that form of anxiety dream known as the punishment dream. In all dreams, Charles Brenner explains,

the ego anticipates guilt, that is, superego condemnation, if the part of the latent content which derives from the repressed should find too direct an expression in the manifest dream. Consequently the ego's defenses oppose the emergence of this part of the latent content, which is again no different from what goes on in most other dreams. However, the result in the so-called punishment dreams is that the manifest dream, instead of expressing a more or less disguised fantasy of the fulfillment of a repressed wish, expresses a more or less disguised fantasy of punishment for the wish in question, certainly a most extraordinary "compromise" among ego, id, and superego.[28]

More significant than any fantasy content here is the element of "compromise" in the staging of the interruption of staging itself. Like the nightmare and the anxiety dream, the punishment dream suggests a complex reciprocal awareness between levels of psychic functioning that can anticipate, interrupt, represent, and even caricature one another. In farce, as in the punishment dream, the superego not only anticipates and interrupts the representation of wishes by enacting a drama of seemingly absurd punishment but also interrupts, interprets, and recapitulates the representational process. What is terrifying, automatic, and malevolent about plot in farce is an uncanny awareness of the automatic nature of unconscious representation; a quality of the anxiety of the ego under siege spills over onto the representational screen itself, and form becomes both manic and superego-ridden.

Farce not only resists our attempts to fix its meanings but resists meaning itself, as well as a single representational model that could stage it. It caricatures the dream as the "well-made play" and mocks the ego's interest in representations that suggest unity, purposiveness, and integrity. The genre easily accommodates itself to surreal forms, sliding quickly and almost uncontrollably from erotic dream to nightmare. It structures events in a way that implies a caricature of the well-made play; its plots are both controlled and uncontrolled in a way that suggests unconscious processes at work. Michel Foucault comes close to describing this manic tempo when he observes how, in psychological disorders involving temporality, "time is rendered instantaneous by fragmentation; and, lacking any opening on to the past and future, it spins round upon its axis, proceeding either by leaps or by repetitions."[29] If that which is senselessly repeated is that which cannot be remembered, then the uncanny, automatic, and senseless action of farce suggests less a form of mastery than a masterless form. Jean Baudrillard explains this compulsive tempo of repetition: "Affect or representation, every repetitive figure of sense is a figure of death. Only senseless recurrence unleashes pleasure, that which proceeds neither from a conscious order nor an unconscious disorder, but which is a reversion and reiteration of pure form, taking the form of increasing the stakes and challenging the law of contents and their accumulation."[30]

Susanne Langer maintains that "the pure sense of life is the underlying feeling of comedy." She describes this sensibility as that which "sets organic nature apart from inorganic: self-preservation, self-restoration, functional tendency, purpose. Life is teleological, the rest of nature is, apparently, mechanical; to maintain the pattern of vitality in a nonliving universe is the most elementary instinctual purpose."[31] But Henri Bergson comes closer to describing the mood and action of *The Comedy of Errors* when he attributes the comic to "something mechanical encrusted upon the living" or to "that side of a person which reveals his likeness to a thing, that aspect of human events which, through its peculiar inelasticity, conveys the impression of pure mechanism, of automatism, of movement without life."[32] If we read these two definitions against each other, they lead to the hypothesis that farce suggests something closer to a death drive than to the "pure sense of life" celebrated by Western narrative comedy. Unlike comedy, farce shows human beings unable to cope with or adapt to their environments. Instincts that are designed to help us survive are not only dependable but often rigidly mechanical. When these "purposive vital functions" are perceived as dysfunctional, automatic, irrational, and perilously inflexible, then the farcical vision comes into focus. That farce should take the ego as its object, just as objects were once taken for the ego, makes eminent sense from this excentric standpoint.

VIII

The difficulty we experience in reading *The Comedy of Errors* may be attributed in part to the influence of ego psychology on literary theory. The more we try to unify the play according to a model of stability and continuity, the more these attempts fail. Rather than apply psychoanalysis to *The Comedy of Errors*, we might rethink psychoanalytic theory from its fractured standpoint. The Dromios' efforts to bind meaning call to mind Freud's descriptions of the ego as substitute and as flunky, as scapegoat and as body surface.[33] Since these messengers are necessarily substitutes, they suggest a principle of supplementarity that reinterprets identity in terms of the binding and supplementary activity of the ego functions. The ego is best understood as neither present nor unified but as a series of traces seeking to bind or a signifying process of deferral and recuperative activity which works in the spaces between past and future. Like Freud's ego, the Dromios are servile messengers caught between two worlds, accepted in neither, and attempting to control both.

Theater offers an explanation of the ego as the usurping double, as a projection or representation of the body surface. As a screen image that purloins presence, the ego is a gestalt mechanism that passes itself off for those discrete elements it combines and upon which it traces its signature. Theater has always been staging this battle of presence and representation, which explains why Artaud "uncovered" the importance of the figure of the double for theater: "It is the history of the body / which *pursued* (and did not follow) mine / and which, in order to go first and be born, / projected itself across my body / and / was born through the disemboweling of my body / of which he kept a piece / in order to / pass himself off / as me."[34]

What are the implications for psychoanalytic theory of a play that questions the possibility of a stance of mastery outside of it, that takes the ego itself as an object of scorn? What would it mean to implement the play of the ego as supplement in the reading process except to split our reading and explore where it is not our own? At least one lesson we gain from reading psychoanalysis through *The Comedy of Errors* is a paradoxical theory of knowledge based on the *inevitability* of errors and exclusion. *Errors* foregrounds errors, traces levels of misrecognition in its own construction, and in the process represents its own conflicts with repression. The discovery and representation of the unconscious may subvert a static and unified position, but it also makes position possible. The denial of self-presence doesn't negate presence but redefines it as a distancing or spacing we always seek but fail to close. To acknowledge the play of the unconscious is not to deny that we are in a process of dialogue with ourselves and with others, with our splits as we split. Yet it does requires a more dynamic and dramatic model of reading based on the progression of the subject in relation to its discourse—a model of reading based on decentering and positionality, on splitting and attempting to recuperate that loss.

The Comedy of Errors suggests a model of reading based neither on presence nor on absence, neither certainty nor uncertainty. Rather, it requires a model based on *staging misrecognition* and on *staging as misrecognition*—on the inevitability of a repetition that distends and extends being in a splitting that can never be reversed or recovered. Shakespeare's comedies enact the impossibility of self-presence, yet derive identity from this awareness. "I am not what I am" is an assertion of identity through an assumption of misrecognition—in *Oedipus* as in *Errors*, *Twelfth Night* as in *King Lear*. Shakespeare's comedies display this misrecognition, own up to and affirm it, and derive position from the place where we are not. Lacan claims: "It was in fact the so-called Copernican revolution to which Freud himself compared his discovery, emphasizing that it was once again a question of the place man assigns to himself at the centre of a universe. Is the place that I occupy as the subject of a signifier concentric or excentric, in relation to the place I occupy as subject of the signified?—that is the question."[35] Theater derives position from displacement and misrecognition, which is why we think of *Hamlet* here as well as *The Comedy of Errors* and why even Laszlo Versényi's discussion of *Oedipus* sounds a bit Lacanian: "Not knowing what he is, man cannot be what he is; knowing what he is, man cannot bear to exist. Life is *hamartia,* an erring, for to live is to be out of balance, and every effort of the knower to right this balance merely tips the scale toward his doom."[36]

The Lacanian model differs, of course, but similarly posits misrecognition as a condition of subjectivity. Lacan maintains: "It is not simply that the subject is, in a static way, lacking, in error. It is that, in a moving way, in his discourse, he is essentially situated in the dimension of the *making a mistake (se tromper)*."[37] Being is thus a process of dispersal and failed recuperation, a psychic tail-chasing of sorts. Lacan describes the splitting of the ego in the analytic session as similar to the flight of Zeno's arrow: "Half of the subject's *ego* passes over to the other side of the wall that separates the analysand from the analyst, then half of that half, and so on, in an asymptotic procession that will never succeed."[38] In short, Lacan posits a double bind in which the subject confronts language, being confronts meaning, and either option makes the other impossible. Yet out of this double bind, from this recuperative effort, Lacan derives symbolic form.

Inasmuch as psychoanalysis attempts, according to Leo Bersani, to give "a theoretical account of precisely those forces which obstruct, undermine, play havoc with theoretical accounts themselves,"[39] it would appear to be in trouble, and yet it is in less trouble than those discourses that attempt to deny this paradox. *The Comedy of Errors*, for example, encourages us to consider its construction as well as our own on a variety of levels, particularly those levels we either cannot or choose not to consider. Its structure offers a model of how the mind and so how meaning works: we no sooner assert the unity of identity than unconscious splits proliferate and doubles appear; we no sooner loosen ego boundaries and open ourselves up to different points of view than the mind organizes, privileges, represses. What *The Comedy of Errors* finally puts on stage are such basic principles of psychological functioning as splitting, projection, denial, and repression as they haunt our quest for meaning. Since subjectivity is implicated in and predicated upon otherness, identity is itself a product of projection, transference, repression, and internalization. Neither self nor text is ever stable, continuous, or self-present.

To identify where the play finally stands on identity or on any other matter is to join the characters onstage in offering to master events with yet another flawed and arbitrary interpretation. Finally, the play doesn't stand anywhere, which is what makes it so fascinating to under-stand. To attempt closure in discussing a play so ambivalent toward closure is as futile a gesture as it is inappropriate. *The Comedy of Errors* proliferates meanings as a means of escaping containment and at the same time generates narratives that seek to effect closure. It preys upon itself and yet is divided against itself, and we repeat this pattern in our efforts to describe or contain it. Its intricate structure and symbolism, like its elaborate patterns of plot and imagery, betray its compulsive efforts to master meaning and so to repress its own discovery of repression. We can stage this disjunction here only by interrupting and upstaging our own readings; we can only proliferate splits in the play's codes as we attempt to encompass them.

Not surprisingly, Freud denies the importance of automata to the uncanny—or rather, Freud considers, only to dismiss, the importance of objects and events that "excite in the spectator the impression of automatic, mechanical processes at work behind the ordinary appearance of mental activity."[40] And yet "The 'Uncanny'" marks Freud's first connection of repetition compulsions to the superego, and of both to the uncanny, repression, and doubling. Suitably, "The 'Uncanny'" is a fragmented essay that never ties together its insights. As critics have observed, it is as significant for its repressions as for its treatments of the repressed.[41] From such fragmented texts we best glean a sense of the uncanny at work—an awareness of unconscious processes interrupted, observed, and caricatured.

The literature of the uncanny blends the familiar and the strange, makes us feel that we are awake while dreaming, that we see and do not see into our deepest fears and wishes. But such literature also sees that it does not see and where it does not see. It engages representations that do not sufficiently protect us, that do not sufficiently disguise the repressed in the service of the ego, but that mock and subvert the ego's representations. The uncanny recapitulates the processes it exposes: it infiltrates unconscious representation, interrupts it, and stages it. This consciousness of unconsciousness, this representation of interrupted representation, is what makes farce in particular, and the uncanny in general, "significant." Perhaps now we can appreciate Freud's example of the uncanny from Johann Nestroy's farce *Der Zerrisene* [*The Torn Man*], in which "the fleeing man, convinced that he is a murderer, lifts up one trap-door after another and each time sees what he takes to be the ghost of his victim rising up out of it. He calls out in despair, 'But I've only killed *one* man. Why this ghastly multiplication?'"[42]

[1] Freud, "The 'Uncanny'" (1919), *SE*, 17: 245, 241.

[2] Berners A.W. Jackson, Introduction to *The Two Gentlemen of Verona*, in the Pelican Shakespeare (Baltimore: Penguin, 1969), 116.

[3] Francis Fergusson, "*The Comedy of Errors* and *Much Ado about Nothing*," *Sewanee Review* 62 (1954), 37, 28.

[4] Paul A. Jorgensen, Introduction to *The Comedy of Errors*, in *The Pelican Shakespeare*, 55.

[5] Harry Levin, Introduction to *The Comedy of Errors*, in the Signet Classic Shakespeare (New York: New American Library, 1965), xxiii; Jorgensen, Introduction, 56; Harold Brooks, "Themes and Structure in *The Comedy of Errors*," in *Early Shakespeare*, ed. John Russell Brown and Bernard Harris (London: Edward Arnold, 1961), 70–71.

[6] Jorgensen, Introduction, 55.

[7] Harold Jenkins, "Shakespeare's *Twelfth Night*," in *Shakespeare: The Comedies: A Collection of Critical Essays*, ed. Kenneth Muir (Englewood Cliffs, N.J.: Prentice-Hall, 1965), 73.

[8] Fergusson, "*Comedy of Errors* and *Much Ado*," 27.

[9] Jorgensen, Introduction, 57. See also Fergusson, "*Comedy of Errors* and *Much Ado*," 34. This view is strongly expressed by Larry S. Champion, *The Evolution of Shakespeare's Comedy: A Study in Dramatic Perspective* (Cambridge: Harvard University Press, 1970), 13, 19, 61; opposed in D.A. Traversi's *Approach to Shakespeare*, 3d ed., rev., vol. 1 (New York: Doubleday-Anchor, 1969), 64, 68. In "Weirdness in *The Comedy of Errors*," *University of Toronto Quarterly* 9 (1939), 95–106, G.R. Elliott persuasively connects the horror of mistaken identity to the play's strange mood of nightmare.

[10] Jorgensen, Introduction, 57; Champion, *Evolution of Shakespeare's Comedy*, 17.

[11] See Arthur Quiller-Couch, Introduction to *The Comedy of Errors*, in the New Cambridge Shakespeare (1922; rpt. Cambridge: Cambridge University Press, 1962); Champion, *Evolution of Shakespeare's Comedy*; Elliott, "Weirdness in *The Comedy of Errors*"; and H.B. Charlton, *Shakespearian Comedy* (London: Methuen, 1938).

[12] Elliott, "Weirdness in *The Comedy of Errors*," 97; and see Levin, Introduction, xxix.

[13] See especially Brooks, "Themes and Structure in *The Comedy of Errors*"; R.A. Foakes, Introduction to *The Comedy of Errors*, in the Arden Shakespeare (London: Methuen, 1962); William Babula, "'If I Dream Not': Unity in *The Comedy of Errors*," *South Atlantic Bulletin* 38 (1973), 26–33; Vincent F. Petronella, "Structure and Theme through Separation

and Union in Shakespeare's *The Comedy of Errors*," *Modern Language Review* 69 (1974), 481–88; and Barbara Freedman, "Egeon's Debt: Self-Division and Self-Redemption in *The Comedy of Errors*," *English Literary Renaissance* 10 (1980), 360–83.

[14] C.L. Barber, "Shakespearian Comedy in *The Comedy of Errors*," *College English* 25 (1976), 497.

[15] Gāmini Salgādo, "'Time's Deformed Hand': Sequence, Con-sequence, and Inconsequence in *The Comedy of Errors*," *Shakespeare Survey* 25 (1972), 81, 82. For an extended treatment of this problem, see J. Dennis Huston's exciting chapter on *The Comedy of Errors* in *Shakespeare's Comedies of Play* (New York: Columbia University Press, 1981).

[16] C.F. Keppler coined this term in *The Literature of the Second Self* (Tucson: University of Arizona Press, 1972) but failed to note its relevance to this play.

[17] Harold Brooks appears to have been the first to recognize that all the mistaken identifications center around debts; see his "Themes and Structure in *The Comedy of Errors*."

[18] G.G. Gervinus maintains that the family's errors are internal or psychological and stem from a conflict of domestic love and a love of wandering. As proof of ambivalence toward domesticity in this play he cites Egeon's interest in straying from home, Emilia's willful if not jealous plans to follow Egeon, and that the couple's plan to return home was made against Egeon's wishes. See "*The Comedy of Errors* and *The Taming of the Shrew*," *Shakespeare Commentaries*, trans. F.E. Bunnett (London: Smith, Elder, 1863). In "Some Notes on Love and Money in *The Comedy of Errors*," in *Critical Dimensions: English, German, and Comparative Literature Essays in Honor of Aurelio Zanco*, ed. Mario Currelli and Alberto Martino (Cuneo, Italy: Saste, 1978), 107–16, Charles Haines argues that Egeon is guilty of leaving a pregnant wife to attend to business: "To this compelling interest in commerce may be traced all the subsequent accidents in his life and in the lives of his family. All of the breakdowns in human relationship in *Errors* flow from this early evidence of the tyranny of money" (114). In "Shakespeare's Early Errors," *International Journal of Psycho-Analysis* 36 (1955), 114–33, A. Bronson Feldman reads this play as "an apology for Shakespeare's errors in matrimony" (116). Ambivalence toward matrimony is supposedly demonstrated in the fantasy of receiving sexual pleasure without paying for it; in the split figures of the wife; and in an oedipal fantasy that explains the sons' desire for reunion with their mother, Egeon's punishment as a father figure and intruder, and Egeon's release from punishment when the sons regain their mother.

[19] For examples of the symbolic use of the number thirty-three, see Ernst Curtius, *European Literature and the Latin Middle Ages*, trans. Willard

R. Trask (Princeton: Princeton University Press, 1953), 505. We may follow Lewis Theobald in presuming that the twins' age is twenty-five, for Antipholus of Syracuse "at eighteen years became inquisitive / After his brother" (1.1. 125–26) and presumably then set out in search of him, and Egeon twice refers at the conclusion to the seven years that have elapsed since he and Antipholus of Syracuse parted (5.1–310, 321). Theobald's decision to emend Adriana's "thirty-three years" to "twenty-five," however, destroys what appears to be an intentional symbolic reference inserted, perhaps, in honor of the Christmas occasion of the Gray's Inn performance.

[20] Sylvia D. Feldman, *The Morality-Patterned Comedy of the Renaissance* (The Hague: Mouton, 1970).

[21] See R.A. Foakes, Appendices to the Arden edition of *The Comedy of Errors*, 113–15; Geoffrey Bullough, Introduction to *The Comedy of Errors*, in *Narrative and Dramatic Sources of Shakespeare* (New York: Columbia University Press, 1966), 1: 9–10; Richmond Noble, *Shakespeare's Biblical Knowledge and Use of the Book of Common Prayer as Exemplified in the Plays of the First Folio* (New York: Macmillan, 1935).

[22] In "*The Comedy of Errors*: A Different Kind of Comedy," *New Literary History* 9 (1978), W. Thomas MacCary notes that the "entire argument prepares us not for the union of man and wife—its view of marriage is especially pessimistic—but for the reunion of twins with each other and with their parents" (525). He argues that the play was written under indirect influence from the pre-Menandrine tradition and concludes that *Errors* is not romantic comedy but narcissistic, egocentric preoedipal comedy. See his discussion of the preoedipal, narcissistic object-choices in Shakespearean comedy in *Friends and Lovers: The Phenomenology of Desire in Shakespearean Comedy* (New York: Columbia University Press, 1985). Here MacCary more fully explores why the play concludes with no definite marriage plans for Antipholus of Syracuse and Luciana and why the marriage of Adriana and Antipholus of Ephesus is left unreconstructed.

[23] Eric Bentley, *The Life of the Drama* (New York: Atheneum, 1964), 245.

[24] Barbara Freedman, "Errors in Comedy: A Psychoanalytic Theory of Farce," in *Shakespearean Comedy*, ed. Maurice Charney (New York: New York Literary Forum, 1980), 233–43.

[25] Jean Laplanche and J.-B. Pontalis, "Fantasy and the Origins of Sexuality," *International Journal of Psychoanalysis* 49 (1968), 10.

[26] Bentley, *Life of the Drama*, 247–48, 255.

[27] Albert Bermel, "Farce," *The Reader's Encyclopedia of World Drama*, ed. John Gassner and Edward Quinn (New York: Thomas Y. Crowell, 1969), 264–65.

[28] Charles Brenner, *An Elementary Textbook of Psychoanalysis* (1955; rpt.

Garden City, N.Y.: Doubleday-Anchor, 1957), 184.

[29] Michel Foucault, *Mental Illness and Psychology*, trans. Alan Sheridan (New York: Harper and Row, 1976), 51.

[30] Jean Baudrillard, *De la séduction* (Paris: Galilée, 1979), 78.

[31] Susanne Langer, "The Comic Rhythm," *Feeling and Form* (New York: Scribner's, 1953), 326–50, rpt. in *Comedy: Meaning and Form*, 2nd ed., ed. Robert Corrigan (New York: Harper and Row, 1981), 68.

[32] Henri Bergson, "Laughter" (1900), in *Comedy: Meaning and Form*, 331, 332.

[33] Freud, *The Ego and the Id* (1923), *SE*, 19: 26, n.1.

[34] Antonin Artaud, as quoted by Jacques Derrida in "La parole soufflée," *Writing and Difference*, trans. Alan Bass (Chicago: University of Chicago Press, 1978), 181.

[35] Lacan, "The Agency of the Letter in the Unconscious, or Reason since Freud," *Ecrits: A Selection*, trans. Alan Sheridan (New York: Norton, 1977), 165.

[36] Laszlo Versényi, "The Flaw of Oedipus," in *Oedipus Tyrannus*, trans. and ed. Luci Berkowitz and Theodore F. Brunner (New York: Norton, 1970), 206.

[37] Lacan, "Analysis and Truth," *The Four Fundamental Concepts of Psycho-Analysis*, ed. Jacques-Alain Miller, trans. Alan Sheridan (New York: Norton, 1981), 137.

[38] Lacan, "The Function and Field of Speech and Language in Psychoanalysis," *Ecrits*, 91.

[39] Leo Bersani, *The Freudian Body: Psychoanalysis and Art* (New York: Columbia University Press, 1986), 4.

[40] Freud, "The 'Uncanny,'" 226.

[41] See Hélène Cixous, "Fiction and Its Phantoms: A Reading of Freud's 'Das Unheimliche,'" *New Literary History* 7 (1976), 525–48; Samuel Weber, "The Sideshow, or Remarks on a Canny Moment," *Modern Language Notes* 88 (1973), 1102–33; and Neil Hertz, "Freud and the Sandman," in *Textual Strategies: Perspectives in Post-Structuralist Criticism*, ed. Josué V. Harari (Ithaca: Cornell University Press, 1979), 296–321.

[42] Freud, "The 'Uncanny,'" 252.

"Stigmatical in Making": The Material Character of *The Comedy of Errors*

Douglas Lanier

'Tis not alone my inky cloak, good mother,
Nor customary suits of solemn black,
Nor windy suspiration of forc'd breath,
No, nor the fruitful river in the eye,
Nor the dejected haviour of the visage,
Together with all forms, moods, shapes of grief,
That can denote me truly. These indeed seem,
For they are actions that a man might play;
But I have that within which passes show,
These but the trappings and the suits of woe.

(Hamlet 1.2.77–86)

What constitutes Shakespearean character? To the extent that Shakespeareans have continued—with various degrees of discomfort—to labor in the shadow of A.C. Bradley, we have persisted, like Hamlet, in locating Shakespearean character in the workings of an inner self, the elusive "that within" which lies beneath, exceeds or evades its outward "show." Notwithstanding the roses that have periodically been strewn on its grave, this notion of character shows every sign of health. Even the poststructuralist critique of the subject has had the odd effect of redoubling critical attention upon interiority. For although Shakespeareans may no longer be comfortable with unqualified theoretical claims about the autonomy, unity, intentionality, and agency of characters (or, for that matter, people), there remains within much of our critical practice a persistent longing for a not-wholly-demystified self, a subjectivity on or off the stage that is somehow *not* gaps within signification or offered and accepted hegemonic subject-positions. That longing can be glimpsed in a growing impatience in some circles with a critical practice that, so the story goes, again and again unmasks the culturally determined nature of human character: hence the current backlash against the Althusserian determinism of some New Historicist readings. In response, some feminist and political critics have sought to reformulate the private self as a genuine (if nonetheless qualified) site for political resistance.[1] That Shakespearean interiority persists, even in diminished form, in an age of post-essentialist criticism should come as no surprise, for the unique "depth" of Shakespeare's characters has long been one of the centerpieces in his claim to a special place of literary honor. Without the notion of an interiority that "passes show" and prompts our inferences, we would be forced to abandon a long history of audiences' responses, however implicated in ideology those responses might be. Perhaps even more unsettling, we would risk putting ourselves out of critical business.

For that reason, even now Shakespeareans have in large measure continued to give pride of place to those moments where characters seem to give us special access to the depths of the private self in soliloquies, asides and passionate declamations. In the case of genre, this means a continuing stress on the "mature" tragedies. Where that access to interiority has been conspicuously barred or obscured—as in, say, Antonio's pointedly motiveless melancholy at the opening of *The Merchant of Venice* or Leontes' savage jealousy in *The Winter's Tale*—we still set about crafting an explanatory private self from the smallest of textual suggestions. Often, we paper over the gaps by supplying some barely evidenced motive or desire. A longstanding casualty of this procedure has been Shakespeare's early comedies, which, to parrot what has become received doctrine, lack the complex characterization that marks Shakespeare's later achievements. It is a judgment that renders these early plays of interest primarily for what they point toward, not for what they are.[2] One very conspicuous mark of their marginal status is the persistent and damning label "farce."[3]

For the actor, what constitutes Shakespearean character is quite a different matter. For the actor, the problem of character is first and foremost a material one: how to craft and display a set of physical marks—gestures, postures, sounds, costumes—that are legible to an audience and, if not entirely individualizing, at least distinctive. Within the context of performance, character becomes, we might say, a matter of the mechanics of exteriority. Of course, this idea of theatrical character is hardly new: the term "character" itself springs from "χαραττειν," to inscribe or wound. Indeed, a glance at the concordance reminds us that Shakespeare typically understood the word as a distinctive external mark, conceived most often as a kind of inscription, that identifies its bearer's nature, wittingly or not.[4] We owe to the study of acting as a craft and, more recently, to performance studies a renewed appreciation of character's origin in the material mark, something Bradley famously dismissed as inconsequential to a reader's proper understanding of character.[5] This contempt for the study of theatrical character as it makes itself bodily manifest has a long pedigree. Its *terminus a quo* can be found perhaps in Aristotle's disparaging remarks in the *Poetics* about recognition scenes built around physical tokens or marks—"σημείων."[6] Yet even though studies of theatrical craft and of performance have focused new critical attention on historical details of gesture, costume, and spectacle, such studies have rarely considered the parallel history of how identities are physically produced and displayed within Renaissance culture.[7] Although we have come to appreciate that Elizabethan acting is governed by the visual and gestural rhetoric, only relatively recently have we begun to explore the question of how the material conditions and practices of self-display in Elizabethan England relate to crises of self-display faced by Shakespeare's characters.[8] Those crises are, we might observe, often duplicated in the technical challenges posed by performing those roles. In the essay that follows I want to pursue two goals: first, to sketch out in very broad strokes one problematic of self-presentation in Elizabethan England; second, to suggest how *Errors*, by staging disruptions of identity-effects, is preoccupied with interrogating the curious material logic of Renaissance self-presentation. But in addition to these, I will have a third quarry in mind: to suggest how attention to the materiality of Shakespearean character might help us challenge the traditional notion of Shakespeare's artistic "development" and reevaluate the place of the early comedies within his canon.

II

One of the more powerful lessons we have learned from recent accounts of Renaissance culture is the power of display in the construction of Renaissance subjectivity. Because Renaissance hierarchies of being depended upon—indeed were maintained and policed by—rituals of public display, traditionalist interests within Elizabethan culture were particularly uneasy about the public marks of character. In theory, a stable presentational rhetoric of clothing, gesture, mode of address, and style of speech charted one's place in the social matrix. Thomas Elyot locates authority in "majesty," and "majesty" in "a beauty or comeliness in his countenance, language and gesture apt to his dignity, and accommodate to time, place, and company; which, like as the sun doth his beams, so doth it cast on the beholders and hearers a pleasant and terrible reverence."[9] Elizabethan conduct manuals and sumptuary legislation, to take two examples, tended to classify status-coded behavior and clothing with ever more nuance and precision, indicating a larger cultural drive to determine identities by determining the range and meanings of their material manifestations. The aim was, put simply, to insure that who you saw was who you got. In the case of sumptuary distinctions, ideally the cost of a fabric would "naturally" govern its relationship to its corresponding social status, for only a nobleman could afford the sumptuous clothing appropriate to his rank. But, notoriously, the aristocratic burdens of conspicuous consumption and inflation, combined with the wealth of the nouveau riche, seemed to undermine that "natural" relationship. Those who were traditionally entitled to the signs of rank increasingly found them a difficult financial burden; those who could not afford them before, could now purchase them. This, coupled with the opportunities for imposture provided by urban London's exploding size and wealth, rendered the exterior marks of character less reliable, open to quotation and simulation. As Philip Stubbes points out in his disquisition against ostentatious dress in *The Anatomy of Abuses*, who you saw was no longer reliably who you got:

But now there is such a confuse mingle mangle of apparell in Ailgna [i.e., England], and such preposterous excesse therof, as every one is permitted to flaunt it out in what apparell he lust himselfe, or can get by anie kind of meanes. So that it is verie hard to knowe, who is noble, who is worshipfull, who is a gentleman, who is not: for you shall have those, which are neither of the nobylitie gentilitie nor yeomanry, no, nor yet anie Magistrat or Officer in the common welth, go daylie in silkes, velvets, satens, damasks, tafeties and such like, notwithstanding that they be both base by byrthe, meane by estate, & servyle by calling.[10]

It is no coincidence that in his *Anatomy* Stubbes also castigates the theater, for no small part of the anxiety in anti-theatrical polemics sprang from the fact that playing entailed the *citation* of behavior and thereby opened a space between the self fashioned and the self doing the fashioning.[11] In short, play in its various forms disrupted the logic of Elizabethan display. If the general Elizabethan paranoia about dissembling and conspiracy recently chronicled by Lacey Baldwin Smith is any guide, such indeterminacy in the marks of character was felt to be not only epistemologically disorienting but also politically subversive.[12]

In his study of Elizabethan courtesy theory[13] Frank Whigham has argued that, as the socially mobile became increasingly adept at counterfeiting patrician behavior, defenders of aristocratic privilege sought to reassert a monopoly over the display of social rank. They redoubled their efforts to exercise control over public marks of nobility, an impulse obvious in the detailed distinctions of class and clothing in Elizabethan sumptuary laws. As well, they sought to reconfigure a taxonomy of social types and to coordinate those types with stable sets of identifying marks: thus Jonsonian characterization of humours and the revival in the early seventeenth century of the character as a literary genre.[14] Ironically this attempt to subject behavior to detailed classification provided arrivistes with the very material they needed to fashion even more effective simulations of status. In response to the threat of simulation, Whigham argues, defenders of traditional privilege took two steps. First, they subjected displays of character to even more nuanced analysis, looking for the unwitting mistake or telling remark. We can glimpse this emphasis in the challenge Ben Jonson issues in *Timber*, "Language most shewes a man: Speake that I may see thee,"[15] or in the anxiety about rhetorical missteps indicated by Henry Peacham's category "Cautions," included with nearly every rhetorical figure he lists in his *Garden of Eloquence*.[16]

At the same time, Whigham argues, defenders began "to emphasize *manner* rather than matter: others may be found that can do the things a gentleman does, but they cannot do them *properly*" (p. 34). Thus the irony of Peacham's counsel in *The Complete Gentleman* about ostentatious dress, where he instructs his reader to choose "that moderate and middle garb [clothing that is neither ostentatious nor parsimonious] which shall rather lessen than make you bigger than you are; which hath been and is yet observed by our greatest princes, who in [sic] outside go many times inferior to their grooms and pages" (p. 150). Striking in this passage is the studied loosening of the one-to-one correspondence between clothing and rank. Peacham's counsel is but one manifestation of a larger turn in how Renaissance culture conceived of the materiality of identity: a turn toward an interiorization of nobility and value. The link between character and marks of character is reinforced (essential selves still remain determinable from their outward marks), but it is at the same time radically reconceptualized (display comes to reveal rather than to constitute identity). In Peacham's hands the *refusal* to engage in the magnificence to which one is entitled becomes a visible sign of one's superior status: the true "prince" displays that his identity does not depend upon ostentatious display. This presentational strategy appears inimitable, since only those who are already "greatest" can afford the luxury of eschewing visible greatness. Nonetheless Peacham clearly opens it to those who are *not* "our greatest princes." In fact, the passage seems directed toward precisely that mode of self-mystification that demands "the effacement of the traces of production on the [noble subject]."[17] The anxiety is of over-dressing, over-speaking, over-doing, for to overact is to betray that aristocratic character, and authority depends upon counter-theatrical techniques that are nonetheless fundamentally theatrical.

Precisely this anxiety informs Hamlet's declaration that he has, despite his elaborate display of melancholy, "that within that passes show."[18] He contrasts his inviolate and at some level unrevealed character to those "actions that a man might play." Yet how to make "that within" manifest? The paradox is that Hamlet can manifest his interiority only by engaging in a display from which he then must display an inward distance, and he registers this paradox in his opening qualifier, "'Tis not alone." The vehemence with which Hamlet denies "seeming" betrays his recognition that through "seeming" he becomes subjected, opened to Claudius' devices. His visibility reduces him to a fully readable and iterable character, emptied of his secrets and potential. We might locate Elizabethan interiority not only in emergent regimens of hegemonic control (as Francis Barker has argued) but also in essentializing strategies marshalled against self-presentational practices that run the danger of being mimicked or usurped.[19] Yet, as Hamlet's anxiety about his "suits of woe" suggests, there's the rub: this strategy resolves one instability in Renaissance self-display, but in so doing it renders any given characterological mark all the more unreliable. Self-presentation—a condition of being, as Hamlet recognizes, that one can never evade—becomes all the more self-conscious and potentially self-betraying. When all the world's potentially a stage, what is the epistemological status of characterological marks?

III

This cultural crisis of self-representation, if I may inaugurate yet another Renaissance "crisis," clearly fascinated Shakespeare throughout his career.[20] Barry Weller's observation that "much of the action of Shakespearean drama [might be seen] as a struggle, not so much for self-awareness, as for self-representation" (p. 342) is particularly appropriate for the early comedies. Shakespeare's Plautine adaptation *The Comedy of Errors*, for example, takes as its focus the discontinuity between identities and the external marks that display, support, and confirm them. Despite the play's Christian overlay and its extensive references to witchcraft, what has impressed most critics is not its metaphysics so much as its physiques.[21] That is, *Errors* stresses the marks and rituals—faces, clothing, beatings, warts and moles, meals,[22] rings and gold chains—that make characters recognizable, and it demonstrates in copious variety how reliance upon this material evidence leads to unpredictable identity-effects. Like many commentators before and after him, Harold Brooks observes that the play's central issue is relentlessly "made visible, audible, and tangible by 'business'…the gold chain seen, the blows seen and heard, make double the effect they would in narrative."[23] Near its center is an emblem of the play's thoroughgoing focus on corporeality: the grotesquely fat kitchen wench Nell, whose sweating, greasy, swarthy body parts Dromio of Syracuse lavishly details and matches to appropriate countries on the globe.[24] And, as many commentators have noticed, Shakespeare has changed the setting to Ephesus, a commercial center, and obsessively returns to details of trade such as the ubiquitous mart, several merchants added as minor characters, and the central place of exchanges of money and goods in nearly all relationships. Taken together, these changes mark the essentially materialist premises of this world.

Significantly, the plot is set in motion by the duplication of characterological marks, which Shakespeare foregrounds by doubling the single set of twins he found in Plautus's *Menaechmi*. The two Antipholi and Dromios pose a kind of limit case: how might identity be disrupted when the public marks of that identity are not merely counterfeited but *exactly duplicated and possessed by someone else*? Once doubled, those marks become nightmarishly iterable, physically the same but signifying differently, open to a wild variety of preposterous supposes and ultimately leading to near social breakdown. Out of that iterability springs the play's much-remarked imagery of shape-changing. Once Antipholus' and Dromio's faces can point to identities not their own, the play breaks the seemingly necessary correspondence between outer and inner character; a certain self may not necessarily take a certain shape and form.[25] For a culture that places such weight on stable characterological display, the danger to selfhood registers in a threat both spiritual and physical.

In her introduction to *The Comedy of Errors*, Anne Barton raises the central "naive" question, largely dodged in critical discussions, that shapes a viewer's experience of this play: why don't these characters conclude that their myriad confusions are caused not by wandering affections, demons or madness, but by the presence of twins?[26] Their blindness points not, as Crewe has argued (p. 216), to a general failure of reason, nor is it, as Coleridge asserted, simply a *donnée* we must grant his farce. Rather, it makes palpable an ideological blind spot *within a particular kind of logic* that governs the construction of Elizabethan identity: these characters don't come up with the solution "twins" because, as Emilia notes, they all make the same "sympathised one day's error" (5.1.397). They assume that distinct identities are manifest in distinct marks. Crucial to this "local" logic is the role of the viewer, who recognizes those marks and upon whose recognition the character's sense of identity depends. Shakespeare signals the importance of this confirming gaze as early as Egeon's tragic tale of shipwreck in the opening scene, where Egeon tells us that in the midst of a tempest he and his wife Emilia tied their twin sons and servants to a mast:

> My wife, more careful for the latter-born,
> Had fasten'd him unto a small spare mast,
> Such as sea-faring men provide for storms;
> To him one of the other twins was bound,
> Whilst I had been like heedful of the other.
> The children thus dispos'd, my wife and I,
> Fixing our eyes on whom our care was fix'd,
> Fasten'd ourselves at either end the mast. (1.1.78–85)

Egeon and Emilia bind their twins in this way, it seems, so that each parent might gaze upon the child he or she loved better, "Fixing our eyes on whom our care was fix'd."[27] Presumably, each child might do likewise. This odd chiastic arrangement of parent and child is prompted by the logic of the reassuring, recognizing gaze, and it results, with just a little push from Fortune, in the potentially tragic "unjust divorce" of these three pairs. Without understanding their significance, Egeon underlines the importance of paired gazes when he goes on to describe the sun's gaze upon the earth, which literally changes the features of the obscured "face" it looks upon:

At length the sun, gazing upon the earth,
Dispers'd those vapours that offended us,
And by benefit of his wished light
The seas wax'd calm, and we discovered
Two ships from far. (1.1. 88–92)

The demand for another's gaze—for a constant witness—is not Egeon's alone. Antipholus of Syracuse underscores that his quest for his twin brother is motivated by a search for his confirming other:

I to the world am like a drop of water
That in the ocean seeks another drop,
Who, falling there to find his fellow forth
(*Unseen*, inquisitive), confounds himself.
So I, to find a mother and a brother,
In quest of them, unhappy, lose myself.
(1.2.35–40, emphasis added)

Although critics have traditionally (and rightly) understood this passage as evincing a latent fear of self-dissolution (or "weak ego boundaries"), Antipholus' interjected "unseen" suggests a rather precise formulation: the single gaze of his "fellow," a gaze in which he might find himself, is set against the engulfing gaze of the world, a gaze that fails to *see him*.[28] (His musings, we might remember, follow his declaration that he intends to "view the manners of the town, / Peruse the traders, gaze upon the buildings" [1.2.12–13], pointedly as the viewer rather than the one viewed.) Only after recalling his lost brother does he designate Dromio "the almanac of my true date" (1.2.41), as if his servant were a text—the last he has left—in which he can confirm his being. As the confusions mount, Dromio of Ephesus too seeks to confirm who he is by pointing to his apparently rocky relationship with his master. His central exhibits are the bruise marks that function as Antipholus' characteristic signature: "That you beat me at the mart I have your hand to show. / If skin were parchment and the blows you gave were ink, / Your own hand-writing would show you what I think" (3.1.12–14). Here subjectivity ("what I think") becomes quite literally black-and-blue characters on the white flesh. The joke is that the wrong Antipholus does not recognize those "self-evident" marks and so ironically he adds a few of his own.

With Adriana, thoroughly changed from her Plautine source, our attention shifts to yet another mutual relationship. This time the focus falls upon how completely a wife's sense of self depends upon her husband's recognition of her beautiful features:

> His company must do his minions grace,
> Whilst I at home starve for a merry look.
> Hath homely age th'alluring beauty took
> From my poor cheek? then he hath wasted it.
> Are my discourses dull? barren my wit?...
> What ruins are in me that can be found
> By him not ruin'd? Then is he the ground
> Of my defeatures: my decayed fair
> A sunny look of his would soon repair.   (2.1.87–91, 96–99)

In a very important way his look constitutes her sense of identity. As she observes in a later comparison, the enamelled jewel, protected from another's gaze and touch, loses its beauty, yet "the gold bides still / That others touch, and often touching will / Wear gold" (2.1.109–11), a "wearing" that paradoxically produces gold's lustre.[29] With her husband's look and "touch" withdrawn, Adriana's physical features become "defeatures," suddenly susceptible to ruin and unrecognizability.[30] Her insistence upon the "undividable, incorporate" (2.2.122) union of husband and wife, imaged with talk of drops mingled in the ocean and the more traditional image of elms entwined with vines, derives less from the Plautine character-type of the shrew than from the self-presentational symbiosis Adriana needs. She tells Antipholus that he need only "look strange and frown" and "I am not Adriana, nor thy wife" (2.2.110, 112). Egeon, Antipholus, and Dromio have nearly identical moments. It would seem that supposedly self-evident physical distinctions (accounts of faces, warts, bruises, chains, rings) and events (dinners, promises, arrests, beatings) need constantly to be rehearsed and re-rehearsed in order to maintain who's who. Given such characterological instability, it is little wonder that well over a third of the play is taken up with narrating events that have already occurred before the audience's eyes.[31]

This logic of recognition leads to a further uncanny identity-effect: instead of the twins possessing their distinctive marks and thus their identities, those marks (and the identities they carve out) come to possess them. More precisely, because their outward characters are not exclusively their own, identities can be projected upon them from without, an operation that feels to the twins like being inhabited by a spirit. Dromio of Syracuse announces this ubiquitous link between being "defined" and being demonically possessed. When Nell (mis)recognizes the "privy marks I had about me, as the mark of my shoulder, the mole in my neck, the great wart on my left arm" (3.2.141–43), Dromio speaks of her as "one that claims me, one that haunts me, one that will have me" (3.2.80–81). And although he dashes onto the stage seeking confirmation from Antipholus that he is in fact Dromio—"Do you know me, sir? Am I Dromio? Am I your man? Am I myself?" (3.2.72–73)—he later claims that if he had not relied upon an unmanifest manly interiority (his breast of faith and of steel) Nell would have transformed him into a "curtal dog," her emasculated beast of burden. Through knowledge or possession of a self's outward marks, he fears, that self can be possessed, and so he urges his master not to give the courtesan the ring or chain she demands: "Some devils ask but the parings of one's nail, a rush, a hair, a drop of blood, a pin, a nut, a cherry-stone; but she, more covetous, would have a chain. Master, be wise; and if you give it her, the devil will shake her chain and fright us with it" (4.3.69–73). For Antipholus of Ephesus, this trope of possession is literalized to great comic effect. Observing "his heart's meteors tilting in his face" (4.2.6), fiery and sharp looks, ecstatic trembling and propensity to strike, all products of his considerable frustration, Adriana, Doctor Pinch and company all conclude that Satan is "hous'd within this man" (4.4.52). In fact, once Pinch's diagnosis takes hold, Antipholus' protests and grimaces only serve as further "objective" evidence of his demonic possession, a point stressed by Pinch's and Luciana's knowing comments about his "pale and deadly looks" (4.4.91, 106). Here we might notice that the "metaphysics" of this play emphatically does *not* establish some stable supernatural frame of reference. Rather, the allusions to demons, witchcraft, and God's protection are all part of yet another false supposition, generated by the desperate need for these characters to save appearances. In Ephesus the law of the characterological marketplace rules: "possess or be possessed." Indeed, because the twins do not own exclusive rights to the marks of their characters, or to the proliferating interpretations that become attached to those identical yet differing marks, they find themselves again and again self-*dis*possessed.

Given such premises and such unpredictable effects, what's a person to do? Antipholus of Ephesus' experience is that resisting only makes matters worse. Near the center of the play, Luciana voices a second and unexpectedly Machiavellian alternative: accept the identity others seek to project upon you and fashion from it a facade that serves your own interests. If Antipholus must carry on an affair (an erroneous supposition on Luciana's part), then, she declares, he should at least preserve the illusion of his fidelity by faking for Adriana the sunny looks she so craves:

> If you did wed my sister for her wealth,
> Then for her wealth's sake use her with more kindness;
> Or if you like elsewhere, do it by stealth,
> Muffle your false love with some show of blindness.
> Let not my sister read it in your eye;
> Be not thy tongue thy own shame's orator;
> Look sweet, speak fair, become disloyalty;
> Apparel vice like virtue's harbinger;
> Bear a fair presence, though your heart be tainted;
> Teach sin the carriage of a holy saint;
> Be secret-false: what need she be acquainted?...
> 'Tis double wrong to truant with your bed,
> And let her read it in thy looks at board;
> Shame hath a bastard fame, well managed.(3.2.5–15, 17–19)

On its surface, especially considering its source, Luciana's advice has an unexpectedly moral ring: this *would* save Adriana's fragile sense of self. But the passage invokes the very distinctions that would thereby become erased, distinctions between false and true, becoming and being, bearing and heart, saints and sinners, virtue and vice. Such a world of well-managed simulacra, another version of Stubbes's "confuse mingle mangle," would obliterate the world she proffered earlier to Adriana, a world of "natural" distinctions and hierarchies where "there's nothing situate under heaven's eye / But hath his bound" (1.2.16–17). It is a world where, we should notice, those bounds are maintained by public rituals of obeisance. As the scene progresses, Shakespeare twice underscores the dangers of Luciana's counsel, first by having Antipholus misread it as a siren-like come-on to which he instantaneously succumbs, and, second by having Dromio rush onstage to recount his tale of Nell, a tale that terrifyingly illustrates the consequences of accepting a projected identity—castration, servility, beastliness. Just in the nick of time, Antipholus resists becoming "traitor to myself" (3.2.161). Yet Shakespeare cannot leave the scene without also returning our attention (and Antipholus') to the attractions of pretense for profit. For even as Antipholus utters his intention to "stop mine ears against the mermaid's song," Angelo the goldsmith enters and, mistaking him for the other Antipholus, hands him a gold chain. The central scene ends on a note of extraordinary ideological poise, suspended between rejecting and embracing this other-directed world gone wild.

Anxiety about the effacement of one's distinguishing features reaches a climax in the final scene. There Egeon, who has himself mistaken one Antipholus for another, seeks his son's recognition:

> I am sure you both of you remember me....
> Why look you strange on me? you know me well....
> O! grief hath chang'd me since you saw me last,
> And careful hours with time's deformed hand
> Have written strange defeatures in my face.
> (5.1.292, 296, 298–300)

Figuring his unrecognized face as a text rendered illegible by the ill-formed over-scribblings of Time, Egeon seeks desperately for some other distinctive mark of who he is, drawing attention next to his voice. When Dromio and Antipholus shrug that they still just don't recall him, Egeon is thrown into anguished self-doubt:

Not know my voice? O time's extremity,
Hast thou so crack'd and splitted my poor tongue
In seven short years, that here my only son
Knows not my feeble key of untun'd cares?
Though now this grained face of mine be hid
In sap-consuming winter's drizzled snow,
And all the conduits of my blood froze up,
Yet hath my night of life some memory;
My wasting lamps some fading glimmer left;
My dull deaf ears a little use to hear—
All the old witnesses, I cannot err,
Tell me thou art my son Antipholus. (5.1.308–17)

Here Egeon's unrecognized visage runs perilously close to extin-
guishing him, both figuratively ("all the conduits of my blood
froze up") and literally (he can only be saved if his son
recognizes him and pays his ransom). Egeon backs away from
this death by unrecognition by entertaining an alternate
possibility: "but perhaps, my son, / Thou sham'st to acknowledge me in misery" (5.1.321–22). Nonetheless, Egeon's persistent
reliance upon "these old witnesses" fuels this crisis, for
Antipholus can offer equally authoritative "witnesses": "The
duke, and all that know me in the city, / Can witness with me
that it is not so" (5.1.323–24). We see an earlier indication that
these characters occupy different interpretive universes in this
exchange between Dromio of Syracuse and Adriana:

Adr. Tell me, was he arrested on a band?
Dro. Not on a band, but on a stronger thing:
  A chain, a chain, do you not hear it ring?
Adr. What, the chain?
Dro. No, no, the bell, 'tis time that I were gone,
  It was two ere I left him, and now the clock strikes one.
Adr. The hours come back; that did I never hear.
Dro. O yes, if any hour meet a sergeant, 'a turns back for
  very fear.
Adr. As if time were in debt; how fondly dost thou reason!
Dro. Time is a very bankrupt, and owes more than he's
  worth to season...

If 'a be in debt and theft, and a sergeant in the way,
Hath he not reason to turn back an hour in a day?

(4.2.50–58, 61–62)

The puns on "band / bond," "on / one" and "hour / whore"—
duplicated sounds, yet distinct meanings—and the confusion of
referents such as the ambiguous "it" in 1.52 leads to a confusion
about objective clock time. By the end of the passage the
objective world seems to mime Dromio's final punning line.[32] In
the final scene of *The Menaechmi*, one brother, despite the visible
evidence before his eyes, must be convinced in an extended
comic barrage of personal names and remembered details that his
twin brother stands before him; the interpretive universes are
eased into synchronism. In *Errors*, Shakespeare prunes this set
piece. In this case the recognition occurs nearly instantaneously,
in a glance rather than through persuasion. Only when the two
twins are seen standing side by side is some normative frame of
reference reestablished, with all its reassuring social determina-
tions of kinship and rank.

Or is it? Undeniably, the characters' "original" identities have
snapped back into place but, I want to argue, with a crucial
difference. Especially noteworthy is the extent to which these
characters' faith in that final perspective has become much more
provisional. The Duke hardly supplies an authoritative
perspective, for even his lordly eye cannot sort out the myriad
errors. Even after the twins stand side by side before him, the
Duke remains confused: "One of these men is *genius* to the other:
/ And so of these, which is the natural man, / And which the
spirit? *Who deciphers them?*" (5.1.333–35, emphasis added). The
Duke does establish who's who by publicly recalling the tale of
Egeon's broken family, but he still continues to misidentify
Antipholus, and he has to command the twins to "stand apart, I
know not which is which" (5.1.364). This touch of comic byplay
offers a serious blow to those readings that champion the Duke
as an *agent* and guarantor of order. As the remaining characters
unravel their tangle of misrecognitions, their stress is on "if" and
"I think," and they entertain the possibility that they are
dreaming, echoing earlier moments of supposed transformation
(for example, 2.2.195–96, 212–15):

Abbess.	Speak old Egeon, *if* thou be'st the man
	That hadst a wife once call'd Emilia,
	That bore thee at a burden two fair sons? (5.1.341–43)
Egeon.	*If* I dream not, thou art Emilia;
	If thou art she, tell me, where is that son
	That floated with thee on the fatal raft? (5.1.352–54)
Ant.S.	[To Luciana.] What I told you then,
	I hope I shall have leisure to make good,
	If this be not a dream I see and hear.
Angelo.	That is the chain, sir, which you had of me.
Ant.S.	*I think it be,* sir, I deny it not.
Ant.E.	And you, sir, for this chain arrested me.
Angelo.	*I think I did,* sir, I deny it not.

(5.1.374–80, emphasis added)

The Abbess' conventional invitation to a feast signals, as many have observed, the reestablishment of a community and, presumably, each person's place within it. At the same time she signals a symbolic rebirth of her sons: "After so long grief, such Nativity" (V.i.406).[33] Particularly amplified by the context of Holy Innocents' Day (on which the play was twice staged, in 1594 and 1604),[34] the obvious resonance of the Nativity, that unique historical moment in which flesh and ineffable spirit were mysteriously united, serves as an absolute standard of presence. Measured against it, the characters at the play's end come up short. The same ideological poise that closes 3.2 also closes the play as a whole.

As if to clarify this poise, *Errors* is rounded off with a double coda that adds small but unmistakable notes of irresolution to the play's very conventional closure devices. In the first coda Dromio of Syracuse misrecognizes Antipholus of Ephesus. Like the Duke's mistaking of Antipholus earlier in the scene, this moment demonstrates how the characterological conditions and logic that led to the errors in the first place are still in force. Once again errors seem ready to begin anew, implying that the "certainty" about who's who established by this anagnorisis may be less definitive than it first seems. The second coda, a conversation between the Dromios, focuses at first on the relational nature of character. Dromio of Ephesus' comment about his brother underlines how the other serves to verify and provide an ideal shape for the I: "Methinks you are my glass, and not my brother: / I see by you I am a sweet-fac'd youth" (5.1.417–18). The conversation quickly turns to the issue of natural rank, coordinates crucial to Renaissance identity that have supposedly just been resecured:

> Dro.E.   Will you walk in to see their gossiping?
> Dro.S.   Not I, sir, you are my elder.
> Dro.E.   That's a question, how shall we try it?
> Dro.S.   We'll draw cuts for the senior; till then, lead thou first.
> Dro.E.   Nay then, thus:
>   We came into the world like brother and brother,
>   And now let's go hand in hand, not one before
>   another.   (5.1.419–26)

The perspective offered here differs remarkably from that in the first act. There Egeon had distinguished between his sons apparently on the basis of order of birth, Antipholus of Syracuse had been incensed to blows when Dromio seemed to flout his superior rank, and Luciana could speak (however naively) of the natural pre-eminence of some creatures over others. As the play opens characters typically invoke fixed hierarchies of rank to chart their identities and actions. Here, however, hierarchy is invoked precisely so that it might be made a matter of chance, not of God or nature ("We'll draw cuts for the senior"), and then it is postponed ("*till then*, lead thou first"). For the moment at least, these twins dwell in a world where distinctions of degree have *not* yet been established *definitively*: "let's go hand in hand, *not* one before another" (emphasis added). In the opening scene the potentially tragic determinism of fate hung over events, a determinism signalled by Egeon's grim punning on "hap," "happy," and "hope," and his shaping of the narrative of shipwreck. Here in the final scene, it is as if "hap" has become the principle by which characters are (re)created, not destroyed.

My point here is not that the play adopts a kind of social egalitarianism in its final lines. After all, Shakespeare chooses not to use the two Antipholi for this exchange, where the drawing of lots for the senior among men of rank would imply profound, perhaps even revolutionary, social consequences. Rather, the play's final perspective and the identities it supports are subtly but persistently de-essentialized, made pointedly inconclusive and arbitrary. Chance and not any intentional action of the characters initiates the play's scene of recognition. Character, as it emerges from this play, is not co-extensive with its outward marks, but neither is it "that within that passes show." With something of the relentlessness of a nightmare, Shakespeare demonstrates that character is in effect an ongoing inference we make from outward marks, a hypothesis that demands constant interpretive support. And because the marks of character are multivalent, that hypothesis is always vulnerable to competing hypotheses. Of course, by play's end the characters no longer dwell in an *infinitely* mutable world where identity seems as it does to Antipholus of Syracuse, "Known to these, and to myself disguis'd" (2.2.214). But neither, the Dromios stress, do they dwell in a fully stable world where distinctions of degree are conclusively God-given or where erroneous inferences about identity are no longer possible. Although Shakespeare does not yet locate character in interiority, he keeps before our eyes, even after the errors have been sorted out in the play's final scene, how the materiality of character troubles self-presence.

This conclusion may seem hard to accept, particularly since it would appear that the audience has had a privileged, indeed *the* definitive, frame of reference throughout the play. Jonathan Crewe, for example, stresses "the existence of an omniscient perspective on the action, a perspective that the audience is allowed to share up to the final moments and that confers upon the audience a happy invulnerability to the 'errors' by which those onstage are plagued. Only within such a perspective is it possible to characterize as *errors*—that is to say, as wholly illusory—the predicaments of those onstage."[35] This notion of an "omniscient perspective," which reduces onstage action to a kind of "pseudo-action"[36] dispelled in the final scene, accounts for one way the play has been seen: as "sterile," our sympathy or identification with the characters blunted by our God's-eye view. The final frame of reference—the doubled twins—seems all the more "solid" because we as an audience have accepted it as authoritative from the first and the characters have come to share it with us in the end. But there is, I think, reason to believe that this perspective is more complicated than Crewe and others have suggested. This is particularly so if we turn our attention to the most obvious staging problem this play presents: the doubled twins. If we can believe William Drummond's report, Ben Jonson refused to stage Plautus' *Amphitryo* because "he could never find two so like others that could persuade the spectators they were one."[37] Even though we have no reason to believe that Jonson had *Errors* in mind when he made this observation,[38] it does make clear, even if we allow for his notorious critical idiosyncrasies, the special demands this play makes upon its audience's capacity for suspended disbelief. These demands Shakespeare deliberately exacerbated with his decision to double the twins. He could not dodge the problem of verisimilitude by having actors wear masks (as would have been the case in Roman comedy or *commedia dell'arte*). It is extremely unlikely that he would have had access to *two* pairs of twins.[39] If the differences between the actors playing the twins were perceptible (and the relative intimacy of the Elizabethan stage almost assures that to be the case), then the problem of suspended disbelief, the gap between the visual evidence before and the supposition we are encouraged to entertain about it, cannot help but constantly be before our eyes. And it is never more so than when the two sets of twins stand side by side at the play's end. As in the recent movie *Twins*, the obvious differences in appearance would be played for laughs, particularly when the Duke and Dromio continue to misrecognize the Antipholi or Dromio tells his brother "Methinks you are my glass."[40] This discrepancy, certainly significant in a play about mistaken appearances, works to distantiate the "authoritative" perspective from which we view the play's action. Although Crewe is correct that we need that perspective in order to judge the errors as errors, we are not as "happily invulnerable" to perceptual error as might first appear. For our "authoritative" perspective itself depends upon a provisional theatrical illusion particularly *visible* as an illusion. It is an error whose erroneousness the audience is simultaneously encouraged to forget and to recall. The gap between what we see and what we take it to mean draws attention to our own necessary engagement in "supposes" (at a different level of theatricality) and to the aleatory possibilities within the visual logic of character. In *Errors* Shakespeare powerfully interrogates the materiality of character by pushing its logic to its limits. He leaves the characters and the audience in what Peter Berger has called "ecstasy," a state of standing outside oneself looking at one's own social reality, knowing it is real, but knowing also that one has created it.[41] Certainly *Errors* is from first to last a "*play* of effects."[42] But it would nevertheless be an error to think that the effect of such an entertainment, for an audience that notoriously went to the theater to be seen as much as to see, was not also disturbing and profound.

IV

It is an odd historical coincidence that the first recorded performance of *Errors*, at Gray's Inn on December 28, 1594, provided counterpoint and perhaps unwitting commentary for a very different sort of "performance."[43] The Gray's Inn revels seem to have been designed on the model of court ceremonial, the tone (as Philip Finkelpearl notes) uncertainly situated between reverence and gentle mockery. Because such revels were officially justified as part of the Templers' education in aristocratic decorum, it is useful to think of the festivities as a kind of cultural dress rehearsal, in which the revellers strove to (re)produce, often before an audience of actual notables, the ceremonial texture of courtly society, its oratorical style, visual spectacle, ritualized actions, and management of diplomatic challenges. Although the content of that "texture" was of course largely student in-joke and parody, its purpose was apparently not—at least in the early 1590s—to undermine respect for authority or to demystify ceremony. In fact, parody served precisely the opposite goal, that of appropriation: the revels were "intended to be for the credit of Gray's Inn."[44] This structured space of license seems to have encouraged the students to enact the ceremonial forms they were mastering all the more studiously and enthusiastically, and it also placed quotation marks around the entire ritual, blunting its force by explicitly marking it as "non-serious," mere play. Even so, these ceremonial revels were not without consequences, not least because many of the participants expected to take up genuine places at court.[45] The first night's festivities focused presentation of the Prince of Purpoole, Henry Helmes, chosen, the narrator stresses, because he was "fit for so great a dignity." At the center of this presentation was the display of the Prince's coat of arms, an elaborate emblem which had as its center the helmet of Pallas. Significantly, this blazon was an elaboration of Helmes's own family arms, which prominently featured three helmets, so that his personal honor and aristocratic identity—quite literally, his name—was thereby linked to his conduct as the Prince of Purpoole. The narrator's explication of Purpoole's arms makes clear that, despite the ceremony's arch tone, Helmes's acts were to have a certain genuine force: "The Conceit hereof was to shew, that the Prince, whose private arms were three Helmets, should defend his Honour by Vertue, from Reprehension of Malecontents, Carpers and Fools…The Words, *Sic virtus honorem*, that his Vertue should defend his Honour, whilst he had run his whole Course of Dominion, without any either Eclipse or Retrogradation" (p. 15). Helmes's identity, both as a potential courtier and as a gentleman, was bound up in his revels performance, as was the honor of Gray's Inn.

Perhaps for that reason this anonymous account of the *Gesta* seems curiously preoccupied with performative errors or strains. The "Parliament" that should have culminated the opening evening never met, because of "some special Officers that were by necessary Occasion, urged to be absent, without whose Presence it could not be performed" (p. 20). Later, when the Prince returns after Candlemas from his mock diplomatic mission to Russia, the narrator notes in some detail why his welcoming ceremonies were not performed as first conceived:

> the Purpose of the Gentlemen was much disappointed by the Readers and Ancients of the House, by reason of the Term; So that very good Inventions, which were to be performed in publick at his Entertainment into the house again, and two grand Nights which were intended at his Triumphal Return, wherewith his Reign had been conceitedly determined, were by the aforesaid Readers and

Governors made frustrate, for the Want of Room in the Hall, the Scaffolds being taken away, and forbidden to be built up again (as would have been necessary for the good Discharge of such a Matter) thought convenient; but it shewed rather what was performed, than intended. (p. 70)

Material exigencies seem to intrude at nearly every step of the way. Conversely, the narrator seems most delighted when the performance comes closest to the real thing, as in the progress to the Lord Mayor's house and back, a "Shew" that "was very stately and orderly performed" (p. 57). The Prince's progress back home actually fooled some bystanders: "Dinner being ended, the Prince and his Company...returned again the same Way, and in the same Order as he went thither, the Streets being thronged and filled with People, to see the Gentlemen as they passed by; who thought there had been some great Prince, *in very deed*, passing through the City" (p. 57, emphasis added). This extraordinary moment seems offered to stress the transformative potential of the proceedings, providing they are performed correctly. The comments offered to explain the small plot of the concluding *Masque of Proteus*, performed at the Queen's behest, evince an awareness that peppers the narrative. The sports were brief "that Tediousness might be avoided, and confused Disorder, a thing which might easily happen in a multitude of Actions" (p. 76). This account of *Gesta* is informed throughout by the fear of misfires in performance, that anxiety magnified in the last example by the Queen's presence and the potentially catastrophic political consequences.[46] As a cultural rehearsal, *Gesta* focuses the revellers' energies on mastering the arts of courtly display. Through play they learn how to perform the formalities properly and how to improvise deftly over their mistakes.

Errors makes its appearance in this kind of ceremonial space. Apparently, *Errors* served as an on-the-spot substitute for elaborate "Inventions and Conceipts" that were never performed, probably a masque of friendship addressed to the evening's guest of honor, the Ambassador of the Inner Temple. *Gesta* records that in expectation of "some notable Performance," "the multitude of Beholders" which included "a great Presence of Lords, Ladies, and worshipful Personages" became "so exceeding great" (p. 29) that they crowded the performers off the stage. Eager to behold the display of magnificence—the Prince of Gray's Inn and the visiting Ambassador were "very gallantly appointed, and attended by a great number of brave Gentlemen" (p. 29)—and eager themselves to be beheld, the audience at Gray's Inn stole the show. The effect was to blur the line between theater and reality, between an enthusiastic reverence for majesty and a tumultuous disregard for proper decorum, so much so that the audience was "able to disorder and confound any good Inventions whatsoever" (p. 31). To control the crowds, perhaps to impose some sort of visual order on the now chaotic proceedings, and to reserve the sports originally intended "especially for the gracing of the *Templarians*," those in charge resolved only to offer such inconsequential sports as "Dancing and Revelling with Gentlewomen" and "a Comedy of Errors (like to *Plautus* his *Menechmus*)" (p. 31). In the meantime the Ambassador was prompted to leave the evening's genuinely disorderly revels in a huff before these sports even began. Notwithstanding the lightly mock heroic nature of the Gray's Inn Christmas revels, the damage to honor and reputation, the *Gesta* makes clear, was quite real: "This mischanceful Accident sorting so ill, to the great prejudice of the rest of the Proceedings, was a great Discouragement and Disparagement to our whole State." In fact, in the mock charges read two evenings later against the master of these revels, the playing of *Errors* was presented as the crowning indignity of the evening: "And Lastly, that he had foisted a Company of base and common Fellows, to make up our Disorders with a Play of Errors and Confusions." ("To make up" introduces a tantalizing ambiguity in the passage, for it means both "to atone for, recompense" and "to complete.") It is difficult to discern how seriously these charges are intended or, if serious, what precisely the indignity is: was it that the players were "base and common," not gentry? that the play was playhouse fare, not the scheduled "Inventions and Conceipts"? that the subject matter was, given the occasion, poorly chosen? What is clear is that those assembled were scrambling to improvise some ceremony to save appearances.

Shakespeare's play seems to have supplied a kind of gloss to this disruption of ceremonial display: the night was ever afterwards called *"The Night of Errors."* In fact, two nights later, in a vocabulary strikingly reminiscent of Antipholus' anxious conjectures about witches and shapechangers, the Clerk of the Crown read mock judgments "thick and threefold" against a "Sorcerer or Conjurer that was supposed to be the Cause of that confused Inconvenience" (p. 32). The accused answered those judgments, after some conventional mockery of legal knavery, in this way: "that those things which they all saw and preceived [sic] sensibly to be in very deed done, and actually performed, were nothing else but vain Illusions, Fancies, Dreams and Enchantments, and to be wrought and compassed by the Means of a poor harmless Wretch, that never heard of such great Matters in all his Life" (pp. 33–34). Remarkably, the accused restores a sense of order to the revels by drawing the real ceremonial breach two nights earlier back into the realm of the theatrical and non-serious. He redefines it as one of many "vain Illusions," a description that applies equally well to the throng of "worshipful Personages" and Shakespeare's play. Recast as "mere" play, both Shakespeare's and the aristocratic audience's errors simply do not count. Yet whereas *Errors* in the final scene seems to embrace the operations of chance and theatricality in human affairs, in the *Gesta* the concatenation of theatrical frames and rehabilitative mock "supposes" unsettles the Prince's authority rather than reestablishes it.

The Prisoner's extraordinary deconstructive analysis of the proceedings leads almost inexorably to one conclusion: the trial serves only as an obvious case of ceremonial scapegoating. It is designed to draw attention away from the fact that "the very Fault was in the Negligence of the Prince's Council, Lords and Officers of his State, that had the Rule of the Roast, and by whose Advice the Commonwealth was so soundly misgoverned" (p. 34). The response of those assembled suggests the uneasy relationship between "mere" play and its very real consequences. The Prince of Purpoole and his statesmen, we learn, were "not a little offended at the great Liberty that they had taken, in censuring so far of His Highness's Government," and the Prince responded by exercising his "royal" power and relegating the "Attorney, Sollicitor, Master of the Requests, and those that were acquainted with the Draught of the Petition" (p. 34) to the Tower (that is, the stocks). Even in this second evening's entertainment, clearly designed to mitigate the breach of decorum and "utter Discredit of our State and Policy," the ease with which theatricality invades reality and confounds the simple operations of authority is not so much removed as redoubled. A precarious semblance of order is reestablished, but at the price of seeing how interpretively fluid those supposedly stable material practices are. As in *Errors*, there is an end to these "Law-sports," but not before our perception of the bounds of stage and world, aristocratic ritual and farce, actor and person, has been altered.

And yet the end is not here. After these "Law-sports," the men of Gray's Inn turned once again to the task of recovering their lost honor. This time the task took the form of political "reform," better security for performances, and an elaborate ceremony that took as its theme Amity and Friendship. This ceremony, performed before an audience of eminent peers and courtiers, consisted of sacrifices on the altar of the Goddess of Amity, each sacrifice offered by a different pair of famous friends—Theseus and Perithous, Achilles and Patroclus, Pilades and Orestes, Scipio and Lelius. A bright flame and clear smoke signified the Goddess' acceptance of the incense offering. When Graius and Templarius made their offering, however, "the Goddess did not accept of their Service; which appeared by the troubled Smoak, and dark Vapour, that choaked the Flame, and smothered the clear burning thereof" (p. 36). Momentarily it may have seemed to those assembled that a ceremony intended to signify political union had once again been muffed. But the remainder of the ceremony makes the scene clear. For what on first inspection seemed an error is now fully under theatrical control: "Hereat, the Arch-Flamen, willing to pacifie the angry Goddess, preferred certain mystical Ceremonies and Invocations, and commanded her Nymphs to sing some Hymns of Pacification to her Deity, and caused them to make proffer of their Devotion again; which they did, and then the Flame burnt more clear than at any time before, and continued longer in brightness and shining to them, than to any of those Pairs of Friends that had gone before them; and so they departed" (p. 36). "Sorcery" had supposedly disrupted the first ceremony and potentially the relationship between Gray's Inn and the Inner

Temple, but now it now serves the purpose of "magically" recasting the past, making the earlier error seem as if it were part of the larger ritual all along.[47] The Arch-Flamen and his "mystical Ceremonies and Invocations" becomes in this context a metaphor for the resourceful courtier (the Grayan beneath the priestly costume) and the almost supernaturally efficacious art of managed display, here capable of purging a public stigma.

The narrator goes out of his way to stress the ceremony's efficacy and its very real consequences:

> Thus was this Shew ended, which was devised to that End, that those that were present might understand, that the Unkindness which was growing betwixt the *Templarians* and us, by reason of our former Night of Errors, and the uncivil Behaviour wherewith they were entertained, as before I have partly touched, was now clean rooted out and forgotten, and that we now were more firm Friends, and kind Lovers, than ever before we had been, contrary to the evil Reports that some Enviers of our Happiness had sown abroad. (pp. 36–37)

Considering the Prince's personal honor was on the line, little wonder, then, that the Prince should confide in the Templarian Ambassador "that the Shew had contented him exceedingly" (p. 37). But even here, in the hyperbolic assertion that the former performative error "was now *clean rooted out and forgotten*," are we not to see some anxiety that the memory and threat of error nonetheless persisted? Certainly the narrator cannot forget that former Night of Errors, for later in the treatise he returns to it and reminds us once again that it had been thoroughly forgotten: "The Performance of which Nights work *being very carefully and orderly handled*, did so delight and please the Nobles, and the other Auditory, that thereby *Grays-Inn* did not only recover their lost Credit, and quite take away all the Disgrace that the former Night of Errors had incurred; but got instead thereof, so great Honour and Applause, as either the good Reports of our honourable Friends that were present could yield, or we our selves desire" (p. 56, emphasis added). The focus on the careful and orderly handling of the ceremonies is certainly linked with the narrator's anxiety in the *Masque of Proteus* about "confused Disorder, a thing which might easily happen in a multitude of Actions" (p. 76). That anxiety draws our attention once again to what Stephen Orgel has aptly called the illusion of power. Orgel's reversible phrase reminds us, as the narrator of the *Gesta* needed no reminding, of the extraordinary extent to which Renaissance identity depended upon minutely choreographed displays of magnificent surfaces, displays all too prone to going up in dark and troubled smoke.

V

In discussions of Shakespearean farce, it is the word "merely" that damns: farce is "merely" entertainment, "merely" slapstick, pun and sight gag, its characters "merely" stereotypes or "merely" functions of a "merely" mechanical plot. Farce serves in the critical imagination as the soulless *doppelgänger* of "true" theater. It portrays a world not of humanist spirit and motive but a world ruled by the collisions and confusions of things, a rigorous and often alien material calculus. Yet as one student of farce has observed, "farce is no mere medley of inane japes and bacchanalian hoots. Its illogicality is most logical."[48] Farce's logical illogicality is what has prompted traditional character criticism to set Shakespearean farce at the margins of the canon: it returns us to character's status *as a thing*[49] fashioned of bruises or gold chains or crack'd voices or twinned faces or declarations of wifely submission or trappings and suits of woe. It entertains the unsettling possibility that character is perhaps never more (and no "deeper") than a well-managed stage spectacle, a function of theatricality and the logic of marks. Farce is, in effect, the material unconscious of characterological criticism, troubling intentionality, morality, and ego. It is remarkable, then, that the author whose characters have long been cherished as "uniquely lifelike" and "richly interiorized" apparently began his play-writing career by meditating on the materiality of Renaissance character, the troubling contradictions of which may have led him to glimpse the possibility and perils of another kind of character, tentatively, strategically half-seen beneath the actions that a man might play.[50]

Originally published by Douglas Lanier, "'Stigmatical in Making': The Material Character of *The Comedy of Errors*," *English Literary Renaissance*, 23 (1993): 81–112. Reprinted with the permission of Douglas Lanier and *English Literary Renaissance*.

NOTES

[1] See, e.g., Carol Thomas Neely's "Constructing the Subject: Feminist Practice and the New Renaissance Discourses," *English Literary Renaissance* 18 (1988), 5–18, or in a very different vein, Carolyn Porter's "Are We Being Historical Yet?," *South Atlantic Quarterly* 87 (1988), 743–85.

[2] Ironically, one way to "redeem" these plays has been to attribute to them a depth of characterization that other critics have unaccountably "neglected," a critical strategy that only confirms the very critical premises that damn these works in the first place. That is emphatically *not* the approach adopted here.

[3] In "Fear of Farce," Russ MacDonald provides a cogent discussion of the critical reception of Shakespearean farce (in *"Bad" Shakespeare: Reevaluations of the Shakespeare Canon*, ed. Maurice Charney [Rutherford, 1988], pp. 77–79). For some modern examples relevant to the present study, see Larry Champion, *The Evolution of Shakespeare's Comedy* (Cambridge, Mass., 1970), pp. 38–39; R.S. White, "Criticism of the Comedies up to *The Merchant of Venice*: 1953–82," *Shakespeare Survey* 37 (1984), 6–7; and Derek Traversi, *An Approach to Shakespeare*, 2nd ed. (London, 1957). In the case of *Errors* see Arthur F. Kinney's very useful survey in "Shakespeare's *Comedy of Errors* and the Nature of Kinds," *Studies in Philology* 85 (1988), 29–30, esp. 3n; and R.A. Foakes's Arden edition of *Errors* (New York, 1962), pp. xxxix–xl and li. All citations from *Errors* are from this edition. For discussions of the nature of Shakespearean farce, see MacDonald, pp. 77–90; Robert B. Heilman, "Shakespeare's Variations on Farcical Style," in *Shakespeare's Craft: Eight Lectures*, ed. Philip Highfill, Jr. (Carbondale, IL, 1982), pp. 94–112; and Barbara Freedman, *Staging the Gaze: Postmodernism, Psychoanalysis, and Shakespearean Comedy* (Ithaca, NY, 1991), pp. 78–108. See also David Wiles, "Taking Farce Seriously: Recent Critical Approaches to Plautus," in *Farce* (Cambridge, 1988), pp. 261–71.

[4] The entry for "character" in the *OED* suggests a general if irregular movement from the notion of a material inscription or mark to a characteristic (and later a moral) interior state and its representation in the abstract or in art. This general shift in meaning seems to have occurred in the course of the seventeenth century. This movement is elegantly

traced in Amelie Oksenberg Rorty's "A Literary Postscript: Characters, Persons, Selves, Individuals," in *The Identities of Persons*, ed. Amelie O. Rorty (Berkeley, 1976), pp. 301–23. For a useful history of literary character before the Renaissance, see Warren Ginsberg, *The Cast of Character: The Representation of Personality in Ancient and Medieval Literature* (Toronto, 1983). Jonathan Goldberg has produced several extended meditations on the implications of "character" as inscription in Shakespeare; see his "Shakespearean Characters: The Generation of Silvia," in *Voice Terminal Echo: Postmodernism and Renaissance English Texts* (New York, 1986), pp. 68–100, and "Hamlet's Hand," *Shakespeare Quarterly* 39 (1988), pp. 307–27. On the issue of Renaissance interiority, see, in addition to the works listed in n. 8, Patricia Fumerton, "'Secret' Arts: Elizabethan Miniatures and Sonnets," *Representations* 15 (1986), and Anne Ferry, *The "Inward" Language: Sonnets of Wyatt, Sidney, Shakespeare, Donne* (Chicago, 1983). (See also Katharine Eisaman Maus, "Proof and Consequences: Inwardness and Its Exposure in the English Renaissance," *Representations* 34 [1991], pp. 29–52, an article which appeared after I completed this study.) David Bevington, *Action Is Eloquence: Shakespeare's Language of Gesture* (Cambridge, Mass., 1984), pp. 1–98 and passim, and Alan Dessen, *Elizabethan Stage Conventions and Modern Interpreters* (Cambridge, Eng., 1984), discuss Shakespeare's "language" of costume, gesture, and expression from more traditional perspectives.

[5] For Bradley, Barry Weller observes, the actor is of interest "only insofar as he assimilates the emotional state of the character; as soon as he must find technical means for making his understanding external, for mediating between the text and the theatrical audience, he ceases to be of interest. Readers 'do not need, of course, to imagine whereabouts the persons are to stand, or what gestures they ought to use'" ("Identity and Representation in Shakespeare," *ELH* 49 [1982], 341).

[6] *The Poetics*, trans. W. Hamilton Frye, Loeb Classics Edition (Cambridge, Mass., 1923), p. 62; see also p. 58. For a survey of Renaissance commentary on Aristotle's conceptions of anagnorisis, see Terence Cave, *Recognitions: A Study in Poetics* (Oxford, 1988), pp. 55–83; see also his cogent discussion of the "signs of recognition," pp. 242–55.

[7] I have adopted the awkward term "identity-effects" to stress how fully identity depends upon, indeed is largely produced by, its material supports and their recognition by others.

[8] This is not to say that such study has not been undertaken; for examples, primarily from cultural materialist circles, see Catherine Belsey, *The Subject of Tragedy: Identity and Difference in Renaissance Drama* (New York, 1985); Lisa Jardine, *Still Harping on Daughters: Women and Drama in the Age of Shakespeare* (Brighton, Eng., 1983), and Francis Barker, *The Tremulous Private Body: Essays on Subjection* (New York, 1984).

⁹ *The Book Named the Governor*, ed. S.E. Lehmberg (London, 1962), p. 99.

¹⁰ *The Anatomy of Abuses*, facsimile edition (New York, 1972), fol. C2v. It is telling that Stubbes ends his list of usurped social positions with magistrates and officers, for not only are status distinctions in danger but also distinctions of legal authority. In her discussion of Stubbes, Jardine notes that this anxiety about the link between usurpation of marks of character and the erasure of hierarchy extends to anxieties about the erasure of gender distinctions and the *hic mulier* controversy (pp. 151–65). See also N.B. Harte, "State Control of Dress and Social Change in Pre-industrial England," in *Trade, Government, and Economy in Pre-Industrial England*, ed. D.C. Coleman and A.H. John (London, 1976), pp. 132–65.

¹¹ For the context of Stubbes's anti-theatricality, see Jonas Barish's chapter "Puritans, Popery, and Parade" in *The Anti-Theatrical Prejudice* (Berkeley, 1981), pp. 155–90; for his discussion of Stubbes, see 166–67.

¹² This "crisis of self-presentation" has of course been remarked in other works: by Eduardo Saccone in his discussion of "sprezzatura" ("*Grazia, Sprezzatura,* and *Affettazione* in Castiglione's *Book of the Courtier,*" *Glyph* 5 [1979], 35–51); by Jean-Christophe Agnew in *Worlds Apart: The Market and the Theater in Anglo-American Thought, 1550–1750* (Cambridge, 1986), a work that explicitly links the competitive marketplace with the theatrical representation of character; by Lacey Baldwin Smith in *Treason in Tudor England: Politics and Paranoia* (London, 1986), in connection with paranoia and distrust at the Tudor court; and most famously by Stephen Greenblatt in *Renaissance Self-Fashioning: From More to Shakespeare* (Chicago, 1980).

¹³ *Ambition and Privilege: The Social Tropes of Elizabethan Courtesy Theory* (Berkeley, 1984), hereafter noted parenthetically in the text.

¹⁴ Peter Womack sees charactery, rightly in my view, as a technique "for assimilating behavioural difference into the generalised discourse of official culture. The aim in writing is to take the apparently random diversity of observable social behaviours and reduce it to classified gestures which, *because once noted they can be seen as repetitive,* are able to function as signs...to define a person in this way is to exercise power—either the effective power of quasibureaucratic assessment, or the aggressive, unconfirmed power of persuasive rhetoric. To 'characterize' a dramatis persona is not to constitute, but to invade, its interiority, to subordinate it to one's own word, to make it thing-like and knowable" (*Ben Jonson* [London, 1986], pp. 53 and 55, emphasis added). So defined, the seventeenth-century character serves to reconstitute coordinates of social distinction by re-identifying certain marks with certain social types.

¹⁵ *Works*, VIII, ed. C.H. Herford, and Percy and Evelyn Simpson (Oxford, 1925–52), p. 625, ll. 2031–32. Jonson here adapts a rhetorical commonplace from Cicero and, ultimately, Aristotle. He goes on to stress how attending to the details of another's speech allows one to invade the inner recesses

of the self: "It [i.e., language] springs out of the most retired, and inmost parts of us, and is the Image of the Parent of it, the Mind" (Jonson, VIII, 625, ll. 2032–33). One can better sense Jonson's aggressive tone if we compare his remark to a similar passage in Peacham's *The Complete Gentleman* (in *The Complete Gentleman, The Truth of Our Times, and The Art of Living in London,* ed. Virgil B. Heltzel [Ithaca, NY, 1962], p. 54): "Since speech is the character of a man and the interpreter of his mind, and writing the image of that, that so often as we speak or write, so oft we undergo censure and judgment of ourselves, labor first by all means to get the habit of a good style of speaking and writing, as well English as Latin." (Peacham's wordplay on "habit" is noteworthy.) Compare to Jonson's much-quoted comment on language, Peacham's dictum on "following the fashion" in *The Truth of Our Times:* "Ecclesiasticus saith that 'by gait, laughter, and apparel a man is known what he is.' Truly nothing more discovereth the gravity or levity of the mind than apparel" (p. 198). The focus on revealing "the gravity or levity of the mind" suggests that by the mid-seventeenth century, apparel offers Peacham access not so much to social identity as to interior intellectual bearings. The comparison with Freudian examination of parapraxes is almost irresistible.

[16] See also Thomas Wright, *The Passions of the Mind,* ed. William Webster Newbold (New York, 1986), particularly the chapters entitled "Concealing and Revealing of Secrets" and "Feigned Secrets." On p. 166, Wright also discusses the proverb "Speak that I may see thee." For further reading on the material marks and the interpretation of character, see William J. Bouwsma, "Anxiety and the Formation of Early Modern Culture," in *After the Reformation: Essays in Honor of J. H. Hexter,* ed. Barbara Malament (Philadelphia, 1980), pp. 215–46, esp. p. 238; and Margaret Pelling, "Appearance and Reality: Barber-Surgeons, the Body and Disease," in *London 1500–1700: The Making of the Metropolis,* ed. A.L. Beier and Roger Finlay (London, 1986), pp. 89–92, esp. the discussion of bodily tokens of witchcraft on p. 89; and Agnew, *Worlds Apart,* esp. pp. 57–100.

[17] Frederic Jameson, "Marxism and Historicism," *New Literary History* 11 (1979), 57, cited in Whigham, p. 33.

[18] This passage might be compared fruitfully to Hal's rebuke to Falstaff at the end of 2 *Henry IV,* "Presume not that I am the thing I was" (5.5.56), or his soliloquy on "thou idol Ceremony" in *Henry V* (4.1.224–70), in which he struggles to conceive of a royal subjectivity which is not solely constituted by ceremonial practice: "And what have kings that privates have not too, / Save ceremony, save general ceremony?" (224–25). See Richard McCoy's superb discussion of this speech and Elizabethan ceremonial practice in "'Thou Idol Ceremony': Elizabeth I, *The Henriad,* and the Rites of the English Monarchy," in *Urban Life in the Renaissance,*

ed. Susan Zimmerman and Ronald F. E. Weissman (Newark, 1989), pp. 240–66, esp. pp. 257–59.

[19] See Erving Goffman's discussion of recuperative tactics in "Remedial Interchanges," in *Relations in Public* (New York, 1971), pp. 95–187.

[20] On conceptions of "crisis" in Renaissance culture, see Theodore K. Rabb's incisive summary in *The Struggle for Stability in Early Modern Europe* (Oxford, 1975), pp. 3–34.

[21] There are important exceptions, however. Exemplary of the metaphysical line of inquiry are Kinney, and Glyn Austen, "Ephesus Restored: Sacramentalism and Redemption in *The Comedy of Errors*," *Journal of Literature and Theology* 1 (1987), 54–69.

[22] See Joseph Candido's thorough and illuminating discussion of the importance of meals in defining Antipholus' identity as a respected citizen and respectful husband in "Dining Out in Ephesus: Food in *The Comedy of Errors*," *Studies in English Literature* 30 (1990), 217–41.

[23] "Theme and Structure in *The Comedy of Errors*," in *Early Shakespeare*, Stratford-Upon-Avon Studies III (New York, 1961), pp. 58, 60.

[24] Patricia Parker notes the linkage between Nell's "mountain of mad flesh" and the etymology of the term "farce," meaning "fattened, stuffed" (*Literary Fat Ladies: Rhetoric, Gender, Property* [New York, 1987], p. 18).

[25] The names of the two inns to which the Antipholi refer—the Centaur and the Phoenix—seem particularly meaningful in this context. Both are cases in which the creature's identity is indeterminate, the Centaur being visibly both man and beast, the Phoenix, because periodically reborn, being creatures both different and visibly the same. See Jonathan Crewe on "The Phoenix and the Turtle" in "God or the Good Physician: The Rational Playwright in *The Comedy of Errors*," *Genre* 15 (1982), 211.

[26] *The Riverside Shakespeare*, ed. G. Blakemore Evans et al. (Boston, 1974), p. 79.

[27] I here follow Parker's discussion of this crux (pp. 78–80). In 1.1. Egeon tells us that despite the fact that the two sons "could not be distinguish'd but by names" (52), his wife was "more careful for the latter-born," himself "like heedful of the other." Egeon ends up marooned with "my youngest boy, and yet my eldest care" (124), "sever'd from my bliss" (118). His greater care for the elder son no doubt springs from the demands of primogeniture: the elder son is the father's heir and substitute, an image of his authority. Parker notes that the issue of elder and younger returns in the play's final lines.

[28] See, for example, the discussion in Ruth Nevo, *Comic Transformations in Shakespeare* (New York, 1980), p. 26, of this passage and its matching counterpart, Adriana's speech in 2.2.125–29: "Neither sees him or herself as clearly and distinctly autonomous. Neither possesses the detachment of the drop, and both, in consequence, fear oceanic engulfment." Nevo

assumes here, somewhat anachronistically, I believe, that such autonomy is possible and normative within Elizabethan culture.

[29] The linkage Foakes notes with the proverb "Gold by continual wearing wasteth" is potentially misleading, for the sense of the passage hinges on her paradoxical reversal of the adage: here the "wearing" clearly constitutes its beauty. See Gary Taylor, "Textual and Sexual Criticism: A Crux in *The Comedy of Errors*," *Renaissance Drama* 19 (1988), 195–225, for an extended discussion of this interpretive crux.

[30] Adriana's fear of the "defeaturing" action of aging finds its counterpart not only in Egeon's speeches in 5.1 about "time's deformed hand" but also in Dromio and Antipholus of Syracuse's witty exchange in 2.2.63–107 over male baldness. That exchange turns on the fact that the link between a man's hairiness and his wit is haphazard. Adriana's mention of Antipholus' "sunny look" unmistakably and suggestively echoes Egeon's mention of the sun's gaze upon the obscured earth, a gaze that calms the seas and rescues his family at least momentarily from "unjust divorce."

[31] Gāmini Salgādo, "'Time's Deformed Hand': Sequence, Consequence, and Inconsequence in *The Comedy of Errors*," *Shakespeare Survey* 25 (1972), 82.

[32] See Salgādo's discussion of time, as well as Eamon Grennon, "Arm and Sleeve: Nature and Custom in *The Comedy of Errors*," *Philological Quarterly* 59 (1980), 159–60. Climactic scenes of characters talking past one another are a staple of Plautine comedies.

[33] I see no need to emend the Folio reading "Nativitie" to "felicity," as Foakes does. As others have noted in defense of the Folio reading, the repetition and capitalization of "Nativitie" in the Folio and its placement in the mouth of the Abbess draws attention to its scriptural connotations.

[34] See Kinney for a full discussion of the linkages between the liturgical texts for Holy Innocents' Day and the play (pp. 44–51).

[35] Crewe, "God," p. 204. This conception of *Errors* allows Crewe to argue elsewhere for "a certain canonical logic" at work in Shakespeare's earliest comedies, namely the demonstration of "almost alarmingly ostentatious early mastery—and masterfulness" (*Hidden Designs: The Critical Profession and Renaissance Literature* [New York, 1986], p. 134).

[36] Crewe, "God," p. 204.

[37] Jonson, *Works*, I, ll. 420–23.

[38] Nonetheless, the possibility cannot be wholly discounted, for Shakespeare's name came up long enough for Jonson to insist, famously, that "Shakespeare wanted arte."

[39] For a superb discussion of the issues raised by Jonson's comment, see Anne Barton, *Ben Jonson, Dramatist* (Cambridge, 1984), pp. 29–31. Discussions of the play's staging problems rarely focus on this issue: see, for example, Foakes's extensive discussion of staging, pp. xxxiv–xxxix.

[40] In *Twins*, when Arnold Schwarzenegger's character declares that he is Danny DeVito's twin brother, DeVito declares, "The moment I saw you, it was like I was lookin' in a mirror."

[41] Peter L. Berger, *Invitation to Sociology: A Humanist Perspective* (Garden City, NY, 1963), pp. 136–38.

[42] Kinney, p. 51, his emphasis.

[43] For a discussion of this episode, see A. Wigfall Green, *The Inns of Court and Early English Drama* (New Haven, 1931; reissue, Benjamin Blom, 1965), pp. 71–85; Philip J. Finkelpearl, *John Marston of the Middle Temple: An Elizabethan Dramatist in His Social Setting* (Cambridge, Mass., 1969), p. 42; Marie Axton, *The Queen's Two Bodies: Drama and the Elizabethan Succession* (London, 1977), pp. 81ff; and Margaret Knapp and Michal Kobialka, "Shakespeare and the Prince of Purpoole: The 1594 Production of *The Comedy of Errors* at Gray's Inn Hall," *Theatre History Studies* 4 (1984), 70–81. See also the mélange of primary materials collected (if not synthesized) by Basil Brown in *Law Sports at Gray's Inn (1594)* (New York, 1921).

[44] *Gesta Grayorum, or The History of the High and Mighty Prince Henry Prince of Purpoole Domini 1594*, ed. Desmond Bland, English Reprints Series no. 22 (Liverpool, 1968), p. 6. All subsequent quotations will be taken from this text and cited parenthetically. *Gesta* and the other surviving complete Elizabethan Temple Revels, *The Prince d'Amour* (by Sir Benjamin Rudyerd and presented in 1599), were published much later, *Gesta* in 1688 and *Prince* in 1660. The dedicatory letter to *Prince* suggests that the motive for publishing was the remystification of the Restoration monarchy and a related nostalgia for Tudor ceremonial: "A Prince for some yeares past in *disguise*, and a stranger to his Native Soil, is now brought to light; and to you he comes not for *Patronage*, but *welcome*. You will not be backward in giving him an *Honourable Reception*, when you understand that he is *your Prince*, one that owes to you his very *Creation*, and has no other *Historiographer* than an eminent personage of your own Society. His *Raign* was short, but prosperous; the *Genius* of the *Nation* being then heightened by all the accesses *of peace, plenty, Wit*, and *Beauty*, in the exact perfection. They who have been borne as it were out of time, and under the sullen influence of this latter ill-natured Age, who look on the past innocent and ingenious pleasures and divertisements wherewith your *Honourable Society* used to entertain it self and the whole glory and *grandeur of England as Romance* and *Fabulous*, may here read that exaltation of *Wit*, wherewith all eares were charmed, and wish for the return of those blessed days" (*Le Prince d'Amour, or the Prince of Love: With a Collection of Several Ingenious Poems and Songs by the Wits of the Age* [1660], fol. A2–A3).

[45] Marie Axton, *The Queen's Two Bodies*, esp. pp. 150–53. As Axton and other commentators have noted, the Temple Revels also served as a

practice ground for discreetly offering advice to the monarch. Indeed, the much earlier Revels play *Gorboduc* takes this right and art as its theme.
[46] *Gesta* shares with *The Prince d'Amour* some concern to distinguish the mock governments and their ceremonies from the genuine court. *Gesta* ends on this note: "But now our Principality is determined; which, although it shined very bright in ours, and other Darkness; yet, at the Royal Presence of her Majesty, it appeared as an obscured Shadow: In this, not unlike unto the Morning-star, which looketh very chearfully in the World, so long as the Sun looketh not on it: Or, as the great Rivers, that triumph in the Multitude of their Waters, until they come unto the Sea. *Sic vinci, sic mori pulchrum*" (pp. 88–89). In the case of *Prince*, the comparison between the Prince and Elizabeth structures the first day's ceremony: the challenge of the Prince d'Amour's champion is met by that of the Queen's champion, who rises to declare three times that the Prince is an usurper and to "let him herein be as absolute as he can be; yet know, all Lovers are servants; 'tis the beloved hath the Soveraignty; Let him account then his glory to consist in obeying" (pp. 12–13). Both passages offer royal compliments, but both also seem to suggest by way of these seemingly superfluous denials that such mere sports might—as if by ceremonial *ipse dixit*—lapse inadvertently into subversive earnest. Thus the final lines of the *Gesta* in which the play spectacularly erases itself, leaving Elizabeth and her genuine "aura" in its place:

And cullors of false Principallity

Do fade in presence of true majesty...

The Lyons skinn that graict our vanity

Falls down in presence of your Majesty.   (pp. 86–87, ll. 30–31, 5–6)

[47] Precisely this sort of theatrical skill leads Leslie Hotson in *Mr. W.H.* (London, 1964), p. 50, to conclude erroneously that the falling out between Gray's Inn and the Inner Temple was not real but simulated, a calculated prelude to a ceremonial renewing of love between the two societies. This conclusion, I would argue, is precisely what the Grayans are seeking to construct with this ritual.

[48] Jessica Milner Davis, *Farce* (London, 1978), p. 23.

[49] I am here reversing Albert Bermel's observation *Farce: A History from Aristophanes to Woody Allen* (New York, 1982), pp. 25–34, that within farce objects function as characters.

[50] I wish to thank the participants of the 1991 SAA seminar, "Reconstructing Character," and my colleague Elizabeth Hageman for their encouragement and suggestions for revision.

The Comedy of Errors in the Context of the Late 1580s and Early 1590s

David Bevington

The Comedy of Errors is often seen as a work of Shakespeare's "apprenticeship."[1] To what extent is it also a play whose dramaturgy can be understood in the theatrical context of its time? One approach does not preclude the other, of course, but the second does focus attention on Shakespeare's apprenticeship in the theater as distinguished from non-theatrical influences upon him—his reading, the rhetorical bent of what must have been his education, his Warwickshire background, his social class, his observations of London life, and other factors that might be seen as influencing his future development. Even here the distinctions are not hard and fast, since the plays he presumably saw and perhaps helped to perform made plentiful use of rhetorical tropes, romance narratives, classical five-act structure, typed characters, and commentary on the current social and economic scene that Shakespeare might also have encountered in his reading. To study Shakespeare's literary sources (some of them dramatic) and to survey his incessant and only partly digested use of classical citations in a play like *Titus Andronicus* is to acknowledge that he was a great reader. At the same time, to a remarkable extent he could have encountered much of what he needed in the London theater of the late 1580s and early 1590s.

That theater must have come upon him as an astonishing revelation, however much his appetite for theater may have been whetted (and perhaps frustrated) by the mystery cycles and morality plays he presumably encountered in Warwickshire. Moreover, the London theater put before him the materials he needed in dramaturgical form: rhetoric not as pedagogical ingenuity but as living dialogue, Latin not as dusty pedantry of the sort young William doggedly singsongs in *The Merry Wives of Windsor* but as plot narrative, ideas about decorum and copiousness not as the abstractions of Donatus and Puttenham but as effective ways of moving audiences to laughter or tears, language not as sterile schoolboy demonstrations but as confrontational wordplay. This essay will argue that Shakespeare was never more a "man of the theater" than in his earliest and most formative years.

Fortunately, the theater Shakespeare encountered was not polarized into elite and popular traditions, as it was sometimes in France and Italy (though "mixed genres" also met with success in the Italian *Cinquecento*).[2] Most London drama of the 1580s was neither rigorously neoclassical nor predominantly a native theater uninformed by classical precedent. Philip Sidney's genteel animadversions against romantic comedies and hybrid drama that violated all the unities were cheerfully unheeded by dramatists and acting companies that could tell what their audiences wanted, but those same playwrights and actors knew a good thing when they saw it in Senecan horror or in Plautine comedy of outwitting fraudulent figures of authority. Shakespeare's "mixed" genres are an essential feature of his great accomplishment, and they are a product not of his reading so much as of the theatrical expectations he encountered when he came to London.

The point can be made first in relation to the "fable" of *The Comedy of Errors* and how it is constructed. The play is one of Shakespeare's most regularly plotted works in terms of five-act structure. Its action is ostentatiously limited to the daylight hours of a single day, and to a single location; the Duke allows Egeon "this day" to seek the thousand marks that can rescue him from execution as a hated foreigner in Ephesus (1.1.150),[3] and before evening all is reconciled. The regularities of exposition, complication, crisis, and resolution are derived from Shakespeare's main sources, *The Menaechmi* and *Amphitruo* of Plautus, augmented in sturdily neoclassical fashion by the combining of two classical texts, by the amplification of one servant into two, and the like. Ariosto was an important guide here, known to Shakespeare especially in George Gascoigne's lively translation of Ariosto's *I Suppositi* (1509) as *Supposes* (1566, at the Inns of Court), which Shakespeare was to use in writing *The Taming of the Shrew*.[4] Staging requirements are compatible with the familiar Plautine concept of a street scene in front of two or more houses.[5] A neoclassical street scene in perspective need not have been employed, but it would have been feasible, especially for performances at the Gray's Inn in 1594. Nowhere else does Shakespeare employ such a formally neoclassical structure and concept of staging.

At the same time, romantic plotting in the frame plot of Egeon and his two sons opens up vistas of extensive voyaging over a long period of time, separation, loss, and seemingly miraculous reunion in the time-honored tradition of the Greek romance-writer Heliodorus of Emesa (third century A.D.) and of many a medieval saint's life, following the model of St. Paul's travels in the Acts of the Apostles.[6] Although Shakespeare contains this plot of wandering and rediscovery in a narrative form that cleverly does not disrupt the classical unities of dramatic presentation, it is the essence of everything that Sidney found objectionable in drama. Shakespeare's direct source is the story of Apollonius of Tyre, as translated out of the French by Lawrence Twine in *The Pattern of Painful Adventures* (registered in 1576, though no published edition survives prior to 1594-5) or as told earlier by John Gower in his fourteenth-century *Confessio Amantis* (published as early as 1493 by William Caxton, England's first printer).[7]

Shakespeare thus turned to his reading for the frame plot, but in doing so he had ample precedent on the London stage and in the native English tradition it incorporated.[8] Romantic plotting of the sort we find in Egeon's tale is plentifully available, for example, in the late fifteenth-century Digby *Mary Magdalene*, in which the heroine, after her own blessed encounters with Christ, converts the King and Queen of Marseilles to Christianity and encourages them to make a journey to the Holy Land; sailors maneuver a ship into the acting area, land at a rock to rescue its stranded occupant, and much more.[9] Closer to the time of *The Comedy of Errors*, in the anonymous *Clyomon and Clamydes* (c. 1570–83), Clamydes journeys from Suavia to Denmark in pursuit of the hand of the King's daughter and is informed that to win her he must kill the flying serpent in the Forest of Strange Marvels. He subsequently encounters Clyomon, the Danish prince, in Macedon, seeking out glory in the court of the emperor Alexander.[10] *The Rare Triumphs of Love and Fortune* (1582), perhaps by Anthony Munday, tells of Hermione, son of the banished lord Bomelio, who overcomes numerous obstacles to become worthy of Fidelia, daughter of King Phizantius; Bomelio survives his banishment in the disguise of a hermit and then physician until he too is reconciled to the King. The play's title underscores the oscillations of the plot from amorous hope to threatened disaster until Venus and Fortune as presiding deities arrive at a final accommodation.[11] In Robert Greene's *Alphonsus King of Aragon* (1587-8), the title figure is another son of a dispossessed lord, eager to regain the lost title to Aragon. He disguises himself and joins in the defense of Naples; once he has acquired Aragon, he sets his sights on Constantinople and becomes enamored of the great Turk Amurak's daughter Iphigena. As in *Rare Triumphs*, Venus is a presiding deity. This Tamburlainian pastiche, loosely based on the history of Alphonsus I of Naples and V of Aragon, 1385-1454, reveals how an adroit commercial entertainer like Greene could infuse chronicle history and heroic drama with the kind of romantic claptrap that showed itself everywhere on the London stage of the 1570s and 80s.

Shakespeare's frame plot in *The Comedy of Errors* is not close in narrative detail to any of the romantic plays cited here, nor to a host of others one could name, such as George Peele's *The Old Wives Tale* (c. 1588–1594), Greene's *Friar Bacon and Friar Bungay* (c. 1589–92) and *Orlando Furioso* (1588–92) and *The Scottish History of James IV* (c. 1590–1), *George a Greene* (1587–93, perhaps by Greene), *Fair Em*, *The Miller's Daughter* (c. 1589–91, perhaps by Robert Wilson), and various lost romances like *Ariodante and Genevora* (1583) and *Felix and Philomela* (1585). The point rather is that the London theater to which Shakespeare gravitated revelled in romantic plotting and found every imaginable way to incorporate it into other dramatic genres. Shakespeare went to the story of Apollonius of Tyre for his frame material, but his model for the synthesis of romantic adventure with neoclassical farce—a kind of synthesis Ariosto would never have attempted— lay all around him in the stage plays of his generation.

Even in his most neoclassical vein, Shakespeare adapts his plotting to the expectations of his theater. *The Comedy of Errors* expertly stitches together not one but two Plautine comedies. From *The Menaechmi* Shakespeare derived the story of twins separated by the fortunes of sea and now united by chance when Menaechmus the Traveler of Syracuse arrives in Epidamnus (or Epidamnum, as Plautus and Shakespeare spell it) and is mistaken by the courtesan Erotium's cook for Menaechmus the Citizen of that town. Although Shakespeare transforms a single servant, Messenio, into two twin servants, and anglicizes the moral atmosphere of the play by enhancing the roles of the wife and her newly invented sister while conversely eliminating the parasite Peniculus and downplaying the function of the courtesan's cook and maid, he retains and indeed augments Plautus's farcically brilliant plot of mistaken identities. To it he adds, from *Amphitruo,* the business of a husband (Amphitryon) locked out of his own house while his wife (Alcmena), inside, receives a lover (Jupiter) in the guise of her husband, while a servant (Mercury) guards the door in the guise of the husband's slave (Sosia). The real Sosia, like Dromio of Ephesus, approaches the door and is so bewildered by Mercury's inventive wit that he begins to wonder who he really is. Again Shakespeare moralizes the situation in conformity with his audience's expectations:[12] the wife Adriana never commits adultery with her disguised visitor. Indeed one can argue that the sister Luciana is provided expressly so that Antipholus of Syracuse's amorous desires can be deflected onto a woman who is free to be his wife. Similarly, the comic business of doorkeeping finds a suitable dramatic function for Dromio of Ephesus, one of the characters in *The Comedy of Errors* not found in *The Menaechmi;* arguably, the device of two comic servants mistaken for each other is taken from *Amphitruo,* rather than being simply a duplication of the situation in *The Menaechmi.* Shakespeare's conflation of two Plautine comedies is admirably skillful; an audience has no sense of being passed from one narrative to another, for the business of mistaken identities links the two stories together, and the character types of citizen husband and comic servant are so compatible that one can only guess at Shakespeare's thought processes as he wove the two plays together.

Two points can be made here about Shakespeare's response to the theater of the late 1580s and early 90s. The first is that his impulse toward an anglicizing moralization, however much it may or may not have accorded with his own temperament and artistic instincts, is wholly in accord with the practices of dramatists like Greene, Peele, Wilson, and the rest. Greene's Margaret of Fressingfield, in *Friar Bacon and Friar Bungay*, is invincibly decent and English. She affirms her loyalty to her rural companions and maneuvers her way past the ardent advances of the crown prince of England, choosing instead to marry the Earl of Lincoln in a double ring ceremony with that of the Prince and his Spanish bride. The improbabilities of such a rank-levelling match underscore the extent to which Greene knew how to cater to pipe-dreams of his spectators. Greene's heroines are generally cut from the same cloth, as in *James IV* and *George a Greene*. Somehow they manage to be wholesomely appealing and devoid of prudishness even while insisting that erotic love and marriage are to be indissolubly linked. Not surprisingly, the instances we find in Greene focus on women as they prepare to marry, as though in direct response to the Plautine typing of the courtesan.

Shakespeare's adaptation of Greene's model in Adriana and Luciana is thus part of a theatrical trend, one to which other dramatists contributed as well. The title character in *Fair Em, The Miller's Daughter* (1589–91) and the Countess of Salisbury in *Edward III* (c. 1590–95) provide further examples. In the boys' more exclusive and courtly private theater, the cult of Elizabeth (complicated by male resentment of her authority) led to many invocations of Diana and of chaste propriety, as in John Lyly's *Gallathea* (1584–8). The linking of erotic love and marriage in English popular drama and in much nondramatic literature (such as Spenser's *Epithalamion*) reflected concerns of the English church as it undertook to strengthen and deepen the mutual responsibilities of marriage. Shakespeare's treatment of love and marriage, like Greene's, attempts to come to terms with the misogyny that is so characteristic of Lyly and of many male courtiers who served restively under the rule of a female monarch.[13]

The second point about Shakespeare's astute mingling of his sources and plots in *The Comedy of Errors* is that it conforms to theatrical fashions in multiple plotting that Shakespeare plentifully encountered when he first came to London. *Friar*

Bacon and Friar Bungay weaves together the story of a scholarly friar-magician with that of the wooing of Margaret of Fressingfield, and shows how the plots can be linked by giving Prince Edward a function in both. *The Comedy of Errors* is more decorously neoclassical, but it does achieve its linkage of the *Menaechmi* and the *Amphitruo* plots in a similar fashion, by locating Antipholus of Ephesus and the two Dromios in two plots that intersect when Antipholus is locked out of his house. Shakespeare uses this kind of intersection often, as in *The Taming of the Shrew*, where Kate and Bianca as sisters form the centers respectively of the taming and the *Supposes* plot, or *A Midsummer Night's Dream*, in which Bottom is both the lover of the Queen of Fairies and the leading thespian of the band that performs in Theseus's presence, or *Much Ado about Nothing*, where Hero and Beatrice as cousins and Claudio and Benedick as fellow officers bring together the two main plots of that play. Similar linkages occur earlier and were thus potential models for Shakespeare, as in *Doctor Faustus* (c. 1589), in which Faustus himself, his servant Wagner, and Mephistopheles all interact with characters in the raucous scenes of "low" comedy, or Henry Porter's *The Two Angry Women of Abingdon* (c. 1585–9), with its extensive antithetical balancing of the tribulations of two neighborly families and their sons, Frank Goursey and Philip Barnes.

Characterization in *The Comedy of Errors* certainly reveals the intensity of Shakespeare's reading in Plautus and in neoclassical comedy. Clever servants and their masters are at the center of the plot.[14] Yet the cast is very English, for all the play's being set in Ephesus, and manifests a concept of character that is compatible with the London stage of the late 1580s and early 90s. The parasite is gone, and the courtesan is given a reduced role and retinue. The conventional doctor, Medicus, becomes the zany Pinch, a schoolmaster and a conjurer whose attempts to exorcise Satan from Antipholus of Ephesus add hilariously to the play's fascination with magic, dreaming, and witchcraft (see 4.3.77, for example). Whereas *The Menaechmi* refers to a goldsmith, to whom the courtesan's maid carries a chain for mending, Shakespeare brings on a goldsmith named Angelo, presenting him as one who might well belong to the London guild of goldsmiths. Three merchants, one named Balthasar, augment the play's mercantile and bourgeois ambience. An officer and a messenger supplement the atmosphere of civic officialdom. Luce is a brilliant translation into the English domestic household of the courtesan's maid and cook. Duke Solinus, Egeon, and his wife the Abbess Emilia come from a world apart from those worlds created by Plautus, even if Plautus, Terence, and Menander rely, as does Shakespeare, on theatrical concepts of role-playing. And, as we have seen, Adriana and especially Luciana are more English than Roman in their views on domestic harmony. On balance, most of the play's characters are not essentially Plautine. They are, on the other hand, highly recognizable in terms of London's theatrical environment.

Shakespeare's concept of characterization admirably fits his anglicizing of the comedy. The play's characters are defined by their roles, in the social structure and in the family. Antipholus of Ephesus is a householder, a patriarch, a husband, a master of servants, a brother, a commercial trader, a worthy citizen of the town.[15] All that he does can be explained in terms of the decorums and responsibilities of these roles; comedy arises out the conflicting demands of these roles generated by mistaken identities. We laugh to see a master shut out of his own house, denied entrance by his own servant. We laugh to see a servant told that he may not enter the house because it is already provided with servants. The comedy of mistaken identity depends upon the concept of role. The recurring conundrum of this play, nightmarish to its participants and hilarious to us, is one of misplaced identity in which a character is led to wonder if he has any role and hence any identity.[16]

Shakespeare shows later how brilliantly he can treat the subject tragically, as when King Lear is denied in succession his roles as king, father, master, judge, and sane human being. Here in *The Comedy of Errors* Shakespeare explores the dark potentials of illusion and misrepresentation as well;[17] yet the theme remains comic in that it questions but ultimately does not disrupt identity. The play's resolution is to restore to Antipholus of Ephesus his wife, his brother, his loyal servant, his commercial integrity, and his place in the *polis* as a good subject of the Duke. Other less comfortable roles, like that of patronizing the local courtesan, assume the character of the midsummer madness that has seized for a time the citizens of Ephesus, and that has been discarded now that sanity and status are restored. So too with Antipholus's brother, whose role of seeker is ultimately confirmed; with the servants, who at the last see in each other as in a mirror the portrait of one who is fulfilled by being a servant; with the women, who recover or discover their identities as loyal and patient wives; and even with Luce, the "fat friend" who is now to be Dromio of Ephesus's wife and the other Dromio's sister-in-law (5.1.415–7).

Examples of this comic treatment of role-playing are not hard to find in Shakespeare's contemporary theater. Luce's below-stairs flirtations with the Dromios, parodying the quarrels and misunderstandings of their social betters, are not unlike the bantering that goes on in Lyly's *Endymion* (1588), for example, between the pages Dares and Simias and the maids-in-waiting Scintilla and Favilla, or between the pages Criticus and Molus and the ladies of Sappho's court in *Sappho and Phao* (1584). The invention of Luciana gives to Shakespeare the opportunity for a debate between two sisters as to how women should respond to marital infidelity. The plot of mistaken identities allows the audience to explore vicariously a fantasy of infidelity as it watches Adriana flirt with her husband's twin brother (as in many similar fantasies about making love to twins), and yet Adriana does all this unknowingly; the device explores disloyalty as a kind of reciprocity for Antipholus of Ephesus's waywardness without in fact making Adriana guilty of anything. The portrayal is not deeply motivated in psychological terms, but is instead a farcical comic manipulation of Adriana's conventional roles as shrew and beleaguered wife.[18] None of this is in Plautus, but it does resemble, for example, the comic conflict in Porter's *The Two Angry Women of Abingdon*, where the amity between two neighborly women, Mrs. Goursey and Mrs. Barnes, is tested by Mrs. Barnes's fear that Mrs. Goursey is more interested than she should be in Mr. Barnes. When Mr. Barnes tells his wife to rule her tongue and be hospitable to their friend, she turns on him angrily, prompting Mrs. Goursey to flare up at her erstwhile friend. The men, seeing they are both saddled with curst wives, resolve to patch things up if they can, but things are not made any better when Mr. Barnes scolds his wife for being at fault in the quarrel. His role-conscious criticism is that she has violated rules of neighborliness out of womanly willfulness. She for her part sees her role as that of the justly jealous wife. The strife between the families worsens until finally a Justice of the Peace, Sir Ralph, plays the role of Duke Solinus (or Duke Escalus in *Romeo and Juliet)* in urging all to a peace.

The suddenness and arbitrariness of falling into a complicated and sometimes guilty love relationship, destined to become a hallmark of Shakespearean romantic comedy, is not absent from the concept of character in *The Comedy of Errors*, especially in the wooing of Luciana by Antipholus of Syracuse and parodically in the below-stairs antics of Luce and the Dromios. Plautus, in his *Amphitruo* and *The Menaechmi*, shows little interest in the phenomenon (though it does surface elsewhere in New Comedy, especially in Terence). Shakespeare's English theatrical resources, on the other hand, were rich in opportunities, as found also in the narrative materials on which the plays were based. *Fair Em* gives us William the Conqueror falling in love with the mere picture of Blanch, daughter of Sweyn, King of Denmark, much as King Henry VI is to do when he sees a picture of Margaret of Anjou in *1 Henry VI.* Blanch falls for William at once when he comes to Denmark, even though he is in disguise. Meantime, Mandville, a gentleman of Manchester, berates himself for falling in love with a seeming miller's daughter, Em, but is unable to control his own feelings of rivalry with Trotter, the comical servant who seems more socially suited to be Em's suitor until her father is revealed to be the disguised Sir Thomas Goddard, in hiding in the wake of the Norman Conquest. In Anthony Munday's *John a Kent and John a Cumber* (c. 1587–90), the Prince of South Wales (Sir Griffin Meriddock) and Lord Geoffrey Powis enlist the help of a Welsh magician, John a Kent, to abduct Llwellen's daughter Sidanen and the Earl of Chester's daughter Marian from arranged and loveless marriages. Examples could easily be multiplied, from Greene's *James the Fourth*, where the King falls in love with the virtuous Ida in betrayal of his vows to Dorothea, daughter of the King of England, and is eventually recalled to his duty; or *John of Bordeaux* (1590–94), perhaps by Greene and revised by Henry Chettle, in which the Emperor's son Ferdinand falls guiltily in love with Rossalin, the wife of the title figure; or *Friar Bacon and Friar Bungay, Mucedorus* (1588–98), and a host of other contemporary plays.

Shakespeare's dialogue in *The Comedy of Errors*, as Robert Y. Turner has shown,[19] is fashioned out of the rhetorical tropes that he learned in school, but it is also noteworthy that Shakespeare's "apprenticeship" in this regard points to many examples from his dramatic contemporaries and immediate predecessors. John Lyly above all other dramatists showed how the pedagogical and theatrical could be brilliantly combined by putting on stage juvenile actors and inviting them to capitalize on their familiarity with rhetorical word games. Sir Tophas in *Endymion*, afflicted by love melancholy, complains to his page Epiton that he is "but three quarters of a noun substantive" and is little more than a "noun adjective" because he cannot "stand without another," that is, cannot survive without Dipsas's love (3.3.16–19).[20] His lame witticism plays on the familiar Renaissance definition of a noun as enunciated in Lily and Colet's famous *A Short Introduction of Grammar*, sig, A5: "A noun is the name of a thing, that may be seen, felt, heard, or understande[d]," and also on that same book's definition of a noun substantive, or what we would call simply an adjective (as in "a *black* coat," where *black* is abstractly a nominative for a certain color but here used to modify "coat"): "A noun adjective is that cannot stand by itself, but requireth to be joined with another word." Tophas's "stand" thus comes to mean (a) "stand alone in a sentence," (b) "survive," and (c) "be erect."

Argumentation and use of syllogism come in for a fair amount of fun in Lyly, as in *Sappho and Phao*, where the pages Criticus and Molus end their first scene of wordplay in the following exchange:

> *Criticus.* Soft, *scholaris*, I deny your argument.
> *Molus.* Why, it is no argument.
> *Criticus.* Then I deny it because it is no argument.
>
> (1.3.44–6)

To Molus's insistence he was not intending to use syllogistic argument in what he has just been talking about, Criticus replies in effect that if it was not syllogistically constructed then it was invalid. Marlowe or his collaborator exploits a similar jest when Dr. Faustus's cheeky servant Wagner uses schoolboy choplogic to rebuke the Doctor's two scholarly friends for their inquiries into the Doctor's whereabouts *(Doctor Faustus*, 1.2).

This pattern of adolescent wit combat onstage gave Shakespeare what he needed to write the dialogue of the Syracusan Dromio when he inquires of his master why he has been beaten:

> *S. Antipholus.* Shall I tell you why?
> *S. Dromio.* Ay, sir, and wherefore; for they say every why hath a wherefore.
> *S. Antipholus.* "Why," first—for flouting me; and then "wherefore"— for urging it the second time to me.
> *S. Dromio.* Was there ever any man thus beaten out of season,
> When in the why and the wherefore is neither rhyme nor reason?　　　　　　　　　　　　　　　　　(2.2.42–8)

The wit resides in the tension between logic and violence, between the rationality that ought to be accessible through reasoning and the seeming inexplicability to Dromio of what is happening to him. Much the same kind of humor resides in Dromio's syllogistic attempt to deny his master's proposition that "There's a time for all things" through appeal to the bald pate of Father Time and to the impossibility of recovering hair once lost to natural baldness (2.2.64–106); the language of comic exchange here is rife with logical signposts such as "Your reason?" and "By what rule?" and "For what reason?" The two Dromios' summing up of the dubious attractions of Luce is structured like a secular catechism, with questions like "What claims lays she to thee?" and "What complexion is she of?" and "Where Scotland?"

As Turner observes, the verbal exchanges take various forms of word games, twisting a central word from the opponent's statement into a new context in an act of verbal power, repeating and then reversing the preceding statement, turning a literal statement into a metaphorical one, engaging in riddle to prove the impossible (as when time is "proven" to go backwards at 4.2.53–5), and the like. Surprisingly, perhaps, we find essentially the same verbal pattern of wit combat in an early "serious" play like *1 Henry VI*.[21] This was an essential means through which Shakespeare learned to solve the problem of dialogue, in its pacing and development of character. He undoubtedly brought to the task his schoolboy training in rhetoric; he also lived and breathed it in the theater he saw in London.

Staging, finally, is an aspect of *The Comedy of Errors* over which contemporary theatrical practice has considerable influence, despite the play's adherence to neoclassical precedent. Even if the play seems to call for the traditional street scene flanked by *domus*, Shakespeare is entirely comfortable with an "open" scene that allows the actors' location to be fluid and unspecific. Act 3 scene 2, for example, begins with a domestic scene that plausibly belongs indoors at the house of Antipholus of Ephesus. Luciana is being wooed by the person she takes to be her own sister's husband, though we know him to be Antipholus of Syracuse. The conversation is intimate and domestic, like other scenes seemingly located in the house, especially the conversation of the two sisters about marital duty in 2.2 and their later worried consultation as to what they ought to do about Antipholus of Ephesus's seeming fascination for his sister-in-law in 4.2. Although Shakespeare provides occasional directional remarks that are consistent with a location on the street in front of the house ("Then, gentle brother, get you in again," 3.2.25, "I'll fetch my sister, to get her good will," 3.2.70, "Go fetch it [the money to redeem Antipholus], sister," 4.2.47), these exhortations are also plausible if one imagines an interior location from which characters depart into other rooms to find someone or something. Yet by the end of 3.2 we certainly must imagine the scene to be outdoors, since the goldsmith Angelo shows up unannounced with the chain that has been ordered. A scene that begins in domestic intimacy ends in vigorous outdoor farcical action.

John Lyly offers apt illustrations of this kind of fluidity amid a set calling for certain fixed symbolic locales, ambiguously neoclassical and native English. In *Sappho and Phao*, for instance, two "houses," antithetically opposed to represent the cave of Sibylla and the bedchamber of Sappho, are separated by a neutral playing space that can varyingly represent Phao's ferry location and Sappho's court, all comprising Syracuse and its environs. Phao need only make a short symbolic journey across the open stage to arrive at Sybilla's cave; pages and court ladies can converse in the open, allowing us to understand that they are going to see Phao at his oarsman's location or are in the vicinity of the court. Cave and bedchamber open onto the stage so that the speakers need not be hidden within some stage structure. Neutral stage space foreshortens distance and signals the metaphorical import of various journeys.[22] Other locations in Syracuse are invoked as offstage, much as *The Comedy of Errors* alludes repeatedly to such inns as the Centaur (1.2.9), the Tiger (3.1.95), and the Porcupine or Porpentine (3.2.166). (The Phoenix, located at Antipholus's house, 1.2.75, is presumably associated with one stage door; the Porcupine, the dwelling of the Courtesan, need not require any such fixed sense of locale, though we do need one door to represent the Abbey for the moment of reversal in 5.1 when the Abbess enters with Antipholus and Dromio of Syracuse. None of these requires any stage structure.)[23] Many of these tricks of stage illusion are ambivalently neoclassical and indigenous. Lyly was the theatrical genius preeminently able to synthesize the two in his plays designed for Blackfriars (like *Sappho and Phao* and *Campaspe*, both in 1584) or for the location known as "Paul's" (*Gallathea* and *Endymion*, both first performed in 1588), with the requirements of Whitehall and other royal palaces also in mind. It is perhaps not coincidental that *The Comedy of Errors*, so akin to Lyly in staging method, was acted at the Inns of Court in 1594. (*Love's Labor's Lost*, often justly called Shakespeare's most Lylyan play because of its juvenile wit combat, can similarly be antithetically staged in such a way as to juxtapose the ladies' tent with the gathering-place of Navarre and his fellow lords, all within the purviews of Navarre's park.)

The central action of denying Antipholus of Ephesus his own house, derived from Plautus's *Amphitruo*, nicely demonstrates how Shakespeare, at the Inns of Court and probably in a public theater as well, adapts an ancient Roman script lacking authentic stage directions to the practicalities of his stage or stages.[24] The very likelihood of multiple performance in varying locations and before audiences of differing social makeup obligated

Shakespeare to be adaptable, just as Lyly, Marlowe, and others learned to be versatile. As Act 3 scene 1 commences, Adriana bids her seeming husband in to "dine above" (2.2.206), presumably on the second floor above Antipholus's shop. They presumably exeunt into the tiring house, though the Folio text gives no stage direction to separate 2.2 from what is plainly marked as "*Actus Tertius. Scena Prima.*" The absence of an exeunt may encourage us to speculate that Dromio of Syracuse remains visible somewhere onstage as porter, and that the scene is in effect continuous. Certainly the action works well if Antipholus of Ephesus and his Dromio then approach the stage door, knock, and are answered by Dromio of Syracuse from some location where he is visible and audible to the audience. The expedient of erecting some door onstage seems unnecessary and unlikely in the fast-paced Elizabethan theater. Alternatively, Dromio of Syracuse could remain offstage behind the stage door, bellowing his lines.

In any event, it seems likely that Luce, who is directed to "*enter*" at 3.1.47.1, does so above, by way of signaling that she is within the house in the upstairs dining room with Antipholus of Syracuse and with her mistress, the latter being similarly directed to "*enter*" at line 60.1.[25] Both women might well then be easily seen and heard by the audience and yet be understood to be invisible to those at the door. These devices are not unlike those used by Marlowe, for example, in *The Jew of Malta* (c. 1589-90), when Abigail throws down her father's treasure to him at his house that has been converted to a nunnery, or *Doctor Faustus*, in which the protagonist is first seen "*in his study*" (A-text) and yet can move beyond any constricted sense of location without a scene break, or later in Shakespeare's *Romeo and Juliet*, where in one remarkable scene (3.5) Juliet is able to bid a tearful farewell to Romeo at her "window" in the upper acting gallery and then exit above to join her mother on the main stage, with no scene break and seemingly without her having left her chambers.

Staging thus expresses visually what is so evident throughout *The Comedy of Errors*: Shakespeare's responsiveness to his immediate theatrical environment in every aspect of his modifying his classical sources. At the same time, the play shows the daring of his achievement.[26] Far from being the imitative "apprenticeship" exercise as it has been viewed by so many critics, this early work shows how a creative reconfiguration of classical sources in the rich environment of the contemporary London theater could move Shakespeare rapidly in many directions that his subsequent work would take.

NOTES

[1] Robert Y. Turner, *Shakespeare's Apprenticeship* (Chicago and London: University of Chicago Press, 1974). This is a book worth rediscovering; I am indebted to it for many insights. See also T.W. Baldwin's *William Shakespeare's Small Latine & Lesse Greek*, 2 vols. (Urbana: University of Illinois Press, 1944), and E.C. Pettet, *Shakespeare and the Romance Tradition* (London: Staples, 1949).

[2] Louise Clubb, "Italian Comedy and *The Comedy of Errors*," *Comparative Literature*, 19 (1967), 240–51.

[3] Textual citations are from David Bevington, ed., *The Complete Works of Shakespeare*, 4th ed. (New York: HarperCollins, 1992).

[4] Clubb, "Italian Comedy and *The Comedy of Errors*," 240–51, argues for Italian influence on English Renaissance comedy in terms of increasing complication, doubling of characters, didactic discourse on moral topics, and still more, pointing to Cristoforo Castellati and Curzio Gonzaga, among others, besides Ariosto. See also K.M. Lea, *Italian Popular Comedy*, II (Oxford, 1934), pp. 362–3 and 352 ff.

[5] See note 20 below, and accompanying text, on the staging of the play and on the lack of necessity for a specific *domus* labelled the Porcupine or Porpentine.

[6] Gāmini Salgādo, "'Time's Deformed Hand': Sequence, Consequence, and Inconsequence in *The Comedy of Errors*," *Shakespeare Survey*, 25 (1972), 81–91, aptly contrasts the two different aspects of time that govern the frame plot and the play proper. See also C.L. Barber, "Shakespearian Comedy in *The Comedy of Errors*," *College English*, 25 (1963–4), 493–7, who sees Shakespeare's "sense of life and art" asserting itself in the way the play combines "Gower's narrative with Roman dramatic form," merging a narrative of reunion over long distances and time with one of restoration of domestic harmony.

[7] See T.W. Baldwin, *On the Compositional Genetics of* The Comedy of Errors (Urbana: University of Illinois Press, 1965). A.C. Hamilton, *The Early Shakespeare* (San Marino, CA: Huntington Library, 1967), makes a case for Shakespeare's use also of Ovid's *Metamorphoses*. John Dover Wilson, ed., *The Comedy of Errors*, 2nd ed. (Cambridge: Cambridge

University Press, 1962), p. 106, points out that the old miracle and morality plays come into use, especially in Dromio of Syracuse's ravings about Tartar Limbo and a devil who "carries pour souls to hell" (4.2.32–40).

[8] Leo Salingar, *Shakespeare and the Traditions of Comedy* (Cambridge: Cambridge University Press, 1974), p. 30, speculates on Shakespeare's choosing romantic plots for his early comedies because of the plays he had seen as a boy. He points out further (pp. 64–5) that Shakespeare could have found in *The Golden Legend* the stories of St. Clement and St. Eustace, with their narratives of the extraordinary reunion of twin brothers.

[9] Salingar discusses *Mary Magdalene* on p. 68.

[10] Salingar, pp. 33–5 and 69–71. His discussion of *Common Conditions* on pp. 35–7 is also pertinent.

[11] Salingar, pp. 37–8.

[12] See Alfred Harbage, *As They Liked It* (New York, 1947). The cleaning up of New Comedic action was everywhere characteristic of English appropriation of Italianate neoclassical drama, as observed by Salingar, *passim*, T.W. Baldwin, *Compositional Genetics*, Bruce Smith, *Ancient Scripts and Modern Experience on the English Stage 1500-1700* (Princeton: Princeton University Press, 1988), and others.

[13] Mary Beth Rose, *The Expense of Spirit: Love and Sexuality in English Renaissance Drama* (Ithaca: Cornell University Press, 1988); Louis A. Montrose, "'Shaping Fantasies': Figurations of Gender and Power in Elizabethan Culture," *Representations*, 2 (1983), 61–94, rpt. in *Representing the English Renaissance*, ed. Stephen Greenblatt (Berkeley: University of California Press, 1988), pp. 31–64; and Montrose, "A Kingdom of Shadows," *The Theatrical City: Culture, Theatre and Politics in London, 1576-1649*, ed. David L. Smith, Richard Strier, and David Bevington (Cambridge: Cambridge University Press, 1995), pp. 68–86. See also Montrose, *The Purpose of Playing: Shakespeare and the Cultural Politics of the Elizabethan Theatre* (Chicago: University of Chicago Press, 1996), and Philippa Berry, *Of Chastity and Power: Elizabethan Literature and the Unmarried Queen* (London: Routledge, 1989).

[14] Salingar, pp. 78–9, argues cogently that English imitations of Plautus and Terence were generally farces of trickery, as in *Ralph Roister Doister* and *Gammer Gurton's Needle* from the 1550s down through Lyly's *Mother Bombie* (c. 1589).

[15] Turner, *Shakespeare's Apprenticeship*, pp. 156–7, and Thomas F. Van Laan, *Role-Playing in Shakespeare* (Toronto: University of Toronto Press, 1978).

[16] On loss of identity, see Harold F. Brooks, "Themes and Structure in *The Comedy of Errors*," *Early Shakespeare*, ed. John Russell Brown and

Bernard Harris, Stratford-upon-Avon Studies 3 (London, 1961), pp. 55–71, and Barbara Freedman, "Egeon's Debt: Self-Division and Self-Redemption in *The Comedy of Errors*," *English Literary Renaissance*, 19 (1980), 360–83.

[17] Harry Levin, "Two Comedies of Errors," *Refractions: Essays in Comparative Literature* (New York: Oxford University Press, 1966), 128–50.

[18] Charles Brooks, "Shakespeare's Romantic Shrews," *Shakespeare Quarterly*, 11 (1960), 351–6, argues for a psychological reading of shrewishness in this play; but see Turner, *Shakespeare's Apprenticeship*, pp. 146–62, and E.M.W. Tillyard, *Shakespeare's Early Comedies* (London: Chatto & Windus, 1966), pp. 46–72.

[19] Turner, *Shakespeare's Apprenticeship*, pp. 11–27 and 201–14.

[20] John Lyly, *Endymion*, ed. David Bevington, *The Revels Plays* (Manchester: University of Manchester Press, 1996).

[21] Turner, *Shakespeare's Apprenticeship*, pp. 12–27, 204–7.

[22] John Lyly, *Campaspe* and *Sappho and Phao*, ed. George K. Hunter and David Bevington, *The Revels Plays* (Manchester: University of Manchester Press, 1991), pp. 184–8.

[23] E.K. Chambers, *William Shakespeare: A Study of Facts and Problems*, 2 vols. (Oxford: Clarendon, 1930), I.307, is not alone in supposing that three, not two, houses are represented at the back of the stage: the Priory, the Courtesan's house at the sign of the Porcupine or Porpentine, and, in the center, the house of Antipholus of Ephesus at the sign of the Phoenix. Indeed, a stage direction at 4.1.131–2 does specify that Antipholus and Dromio of Ephesus enter *"from the Courtesan's."* But since the Courtesan herself is not present at this moment, and appears only in the crowd scene of Act 5, no special door need be required at 4.1.131–2; the stage direction may indicate simply that the audience is to understand that Antipholus and Dromio have just come from the Courtesan's and that Antipholus has left there the chain he originally intended for his wife. The dialogue makes no mention of the Courtesan's, so that the audience is given no apparent way of making a visual connection unless we posit a signboard. Hamilton, *The Early Shakespeare*, p. 103, accepts Chambers's account without argument. R.A. Foakes, ed., *The Comedy of Errors*, Arden Shakespeare (London, 1962), pp. xxxii–xxxv and xxxix, discusses the staging in some detail.

[24] Robert Miola, to whom I am indebted for a thorough and learned reading of an earlier draft of this essay, points out to me that the lock-out scene of the *Amphitruo* was garbled in the surviving texts and was reconstructed in erudite notes in Latin editions of Plautus.

[25] G.R. Elliott, "Weirdness in *The Comedy of Errors*," *University of Toronto Quarterly*, 9 (1939–40), 95–106, discusses this scene thematically in terms of its contrasts between love and pathos on the one hand and farcical

rage and frustration on the other. Alexander Leggatt, *Shakespeare's Comedy of Love* (London: Methuen, 1974), pp. 1–19, argues similarly in this scene and in the play for a contrast between mundane materiality versus magic and danger. The two brothers are similarly polarized: one is showered with gifts, women, and money, while the other is locked out of his house and later tied up as a lunatic.

[26] Stanley Wells, ed., *The Comedy of Errors* (Harmondsworth: Penguin, 1972).

The Girls from Ephesus

Laurie Maguire

In adapting Roman source material (Plautus' *Amphitryo* and *Menaechmi*) for *The Comedy of Errors*, Shakespeare made two particularly significant changes: he doubled the number of twins, and he changed the setting from Epidamnus to Ephesus. Critics frequently observe the effects of these changes. The first increases "the incidents of error in the play from seventeen to fifty"[1] for, although the resident twin in *Menaechmi* can be mistaken, there is no one whom he can mistake; and the second introduces the occult, Ephesian deception, sorcery, "emphasizing witchcraft instead of Plautine thievery."[2] Both changes seem to me to be linked, relating to Shakespeare's investigation of duplicity (in both its literal sense of doubleness and its metaphoric sense of deceit), and his analysis of marriage, that institution in which "two become one flesh" (*Ephesians* 5:31).

Although my departure point is source material (Shakespeare's decision to change location and double the twins), my destination is women and marriage in *The Comedy of Errors*, for Ephesus is associated with a pair of models for female conduct (one independent, one submissive) whose polarity resonates throughout the play in the characters of Adriana and Luciana. I want to approach this subject through a survey of binaries in *Errors* in order to accentuate a critical mode (thinking and seeing with double vision) which may prove useful in my subsequent discussion of Ephesian women. In considering the conditions of Adriana's marriage, and the thematic double to which they lead—the "double standard," which Adriana protests against in her rhetorical question, "Why should their liberty than ours be more?"—this essay will also focus on twentieth-century stage treatments of Adriana and her society. My subject, then, is not "the boy(s) from Syracuse" (although the play is presented from the viewpoint of the Syracusans)[3] but "the girls from Ephesus."

I. DOUBLE VISION

It is impossible to talk about *The Comedy of Errors* without invoking duality, polarity, antithesis, symbiosis, fusion, binary oppositions. Shakespeare combines Pauline and Plautine sources, mixing one of antiquity's most spiritual writers with one of its most salacious. He gives us two kinds of supernatural power, the prestigidatory exorcisms of Dr. Pinch and the holistic religion of the Abbess. He explores two kinds of personality loss, the negative in the fragmentation caused by grief, the positive in the sublimation of love.[4] Lodgings are characterised by division and duality: the Centaur (half man, half beast) and the Phoenix (death and rebirth). There are two lock-out scenes, one each for husband (Antipholus of Ephesus) and wife. Emendations by Hanmer and Johnson notwithstanding, the play ends most fittingly, as it began, with a double birth:

> And you, the calendars of their *nativity*,
> Go to a gossips' feast, and go with me—
> After so long grief, such *nativity!* (5.1.405–07; my italics)[5]

"Who deciphers them?" asks the Duke of the two Antipholi (5.1.335), adopting a verb from reading practice, the compare-and-contrast exercise of the interpretive critic, the collation work of the editor. The characters come only belatedly to a critical mode forced upon the audience from the beginning.

Egeon's romance narrative frames the central scenes of farce, prompting Charles Whitworth to describe the generic hybrid as "two works living under one title."[6] The Antipholus twins (also, we note, two works living under one title[7]) have antimeric experiences: Antipholus of Syracuse has a "delightful dream," Antipholus of Ephesus a "nightmare";[8] Antipholus of Syracuse is afraid of foreigners, Antipholus of Ephesus is disoriented by a domestic threat; Antipholus of Syracuse is welcomed and recognized, Antipholus of Ephesus is rejected and denied. These inverse parallels also find expression within individual characters. Thus, Adriana catalogues her husband's faults but concedes, "I think him better than I say" (4.2.25); Luciana has two speeches on marital relations, the first of which offers a text-book defence of female subservience, the second "a picture less of cosmic determinism than circumstantial pragmatism."[9]

Appropriately, the linguistic medium of this play is paradox and the pun (those figures wherein two opposites co-exist) and duplication. Antipholus of Syracuse decides to entertain "sure uncertainty" (2.2.185) and employs, as Karen Newman points out, antithesis, anaphora, chiasmus.[10] Adriana finds conceit to be both her "comfort and [her] injury" (4.2.66). Egeon is asked to "speak...griefs unspeakable," and gives a narrative filled with paradox: pregnancy is a "pleasing punishment,"[11] marine disaster separates the family leaving husband and wife "what to delight in, what to sorrow for" (1.1.32, 46, 106). Dromio of Syracuse offers the sage tautology "every why hath a wherefore" (2.2.43–4), only to find his master responding in kind: he beats Dromio twice, "first—for flouting me, and then.../ For urging it the second time" (2.2.44–6). The puns, so often dismissed as the rhetorical embellishments of a youthful Shakespeare, are, as Grennan points out, the linguistic equivalents of the play's dual subjects; thus, when identity is reestablished and family reunited in Act 5, the puns all but disappear and language is "restored to a happy singularity."[12]

It is fitting, if only serendipitously so, that the textual cruces, such as they are, in this single-text play (the only authority for which is the Folio) relate to duplicity (see note 5) and division. Adriana's sister is given two names (*Iuliana* in stage direction [speech prefix: *Iulia.*] on her appearance in 3.2 (TLN 786–7), *Luciana* elsewhere). The first is possibly a compositor's misreading of the second, or an authorial change of mind; whatever the cause, the Folio text preserves a divided identity for Luciana, as for her sister, brother-in-law, and future husband. Adriana's kitchen-maid has also made division of herself. Introduced as "Luce" on her first appearance at 3.1.47 (TLN 670), she is elsewhere rechristened "Nell," apparently for the sake of a pun at 3.2.109–10 (TLN 900–901); this, like the later "Dowsabel" (4.1.110), is most plausibly a local improvisation of Dromio's and, appearing only in dialogue, does not confuse.[13]

Following McKerrow's "Suggestion," textual critics have long confidently believed that the manuscript copy underlying the printed text of *Errors* is authorial "foul papers."[14] The titles which distinguish the Antipholi vary (and are easily confused with the consistent titles which distinguish the Dromios) before settling into consistency in Act 3; furthermore stage directions provide narrative information unnecessary for a prompter (e.g. "*Enter...a Schoole/master, call'd Pinch*"; TLN 1321–2) and hence assumed to be the literary explanations of an author. Paul Werstine has recently disputed this assumption, showing that when "one addresses the stage directions of *Comedy of Errors* with questions about whether their *origin* is authorial or theatrical, one finds that they offer *divided testimony*."[15] "Foul papers" and "promptbooks," it seems, like the Antipholi, may be mistaken for each other. Confusion and duplication are inherent in all aspects of this play.

Needless to say, productions capitalize on such doubling, underlining the thematic with the visual. In the Regent's Park production in 1981 (directed by Ian Talbot), Dr. Pinch was cast against the text[16]: a stocky actor, described as a "lean-fac'd villain," a "mere anatomy," a "needy hollow-ey'd, sharp-looking wretch," a "living dead man" (5.1.238–42) served as a reminder that, as in the case of Antipholus of Syracuse, verbal identification may be at odds with reality. The Luce of the Folio became two maids in Trevor Nunn's 1976 RSC production, a spherical kitchen-maid (Nell), affianced to Dromio of Ephesus, and a tall, slim maid (Luce), servant to Adriana, who was subsequently paired off with Dromio of Syracuse. In the 1990 RSC production (directed by Ian Judge), the First Merchant (1.2) was not one but two, dressed identically, sharing lines and speaking in unison. In the same production the Antipholi and the Dromios became one, "each pair...played...by one actor in two minds about the whole thing" (*Daily Express*, 30 April 1990), although a double was necessary for the reunion of the last scene.[17] This production presented Dr. Pinch as a fairground performer who encased the "possessed" Ephesian master and man in wooden boxes and sawed them in half. Thus, in demonstrating his showmanship, Dr. Pinch inadvertently symbolised the twins' divided states.

Productions also draw attention to the similarities between *Errors* and the late plays. The Manchester Royal Exchange production in 1993 had the enthroned Duke descend from on high to hear Egeon and pronounce sentence: one felt as if one were hearing an early Shakespearean comedy but watching a late Shakespearean romance. Romance is, as often observed, a narrative genre, and in *Pericles*, for example, the characters themselves frequently resort to story-telling as if narration will alleviate their woes. Thus Cleon asks his wife

> My Dionyza, shall we rest us here,
> And by relating tales of others' griefs,
> See if 'twill teach us to forget our own? (1.4.1–3)

The Comedy of Errors has several narrative high-spots—the woes of Egeon, Adriana, and Antipholus of Ephesus, for example (1.1.31–139; 5.1.136–160; 5.1.214–54). In most productions it is clearly the power of Egeon's narrative which motivates the Duke's (relative) leniency in 1.1.[18] Dromio of Ephesus also has an opportunity to relate his griefs (4.4.29–39). In Clifford Williams' 1962 production for the RSC, Dromio addressed his complaint to the officer, who sat down leisurely to hear this latest narrative.

Williams' production also showed itself most fully aware of the conventions of the romance dénouement with its reliance on an item of personal jewellery to clear up confusions. Antipholus of Ephesus seized gratefully on the Courtesan's introduction of the ring: "'Tis true, my liege, this ring I had of her" (5.1.278). The action was halted for relieved exclamations, examination of the ring, and attendant stage business, all of which clearly had the status of conclusion for Antipholus. Only when the Courtesan introduced the new complication—that she had seen Antipholus enter the Abbey—did the tone change, the happy ending vanishing as Antipholus fainted.

Thus, productions, sources, text, language, genre, and theme combine to make sure that we view *Errors* with double vision, that we look both back and ahead, that we think in duplicate, seeing *Pericles* as we watch *Errors*, hearing St. Paul as we see Plautus, observing language, identity, families, and genres fragment and unite. Although confusion is inherent in Shakespeare's Plautine sources, duplication on this scale is not.

Nowhere are the duplications and polarities more evident than in the play's discussion of marriage, an institution which is both spiritual and social, sometimes both romantic and farcical;

an institution which cruelly reverses the rhetoric and power of courtship, transforming the worshipping male servant into household master and the female mistress into obedient conjugal servant; an institution in which personalities may struggle for individuality or unity (or both); an institution in which one's most intimate companion can sometimes seem a stranger. Adriana inhabits a society which does not permit her the wry bluntness of the twentieth century ("Marriage is a wonderful institution, but who wants to live in an institution?"), but she anticipates this image of restraint in her dialogue with Luciana:

Luciana. [H]e [Antipholus] is the bridle of your will.
Adriana. There's none but asses will be bridled so. (2.1.13–14)

Adriana's marital predicament, in which "bridal" doubles with "bridle," is clearly another of the play's dominant binaries, but it has received less attention than it deserves. Wells dismisses it in a generalisation ("the wife is brought to an understanding of flaws in her relationship with her husband") and Ralph Berry makes it but an introduction to another subject: "There is domestic drama, certainly, in the tensions between Adriana and her husband.... *More interesting*, perhaps, is the master and servant relationship."[19] C. L. Barber and Germaine Greer are in a critical minority in articulating the complex dualities in the topic: marriage's "irritations and its strong holding power" (Barber), the difficulty of "creating a durable social institution out of volatile material of lovers' fantasies" (Greer).[20] Before considering this "social institution" it will be necessary to examine the society in which Shakespeare chooses to locate Adriana's marriage: Ephesus.

II. EPHESUS

Errors is often compared with *The Tempest*, these being the only two plays in which Shakespeare observed the classical unities, but the plays also invite comparison by contrast. *The Tempest* is notable for its lack of female characters, Miranda being the sole representative of womankind;[21] *The Comedy of Errors*, by contrast, provides a range of examples of womankind: wife, sweetheart, kitchen maid, courtesan, mother/nun/priestess. Whereas in *The Tempest* marine travel and shipwreck lead to isolation, an anonymous, uninhabited isle, in *The Comedy of Errors*, the "consequences of shipwreck are teemingly social" (*Independent*, 9 March 1993), a point usually well brought out in production. The nineteenth-century Italian setting of the 1981 Regent's Park production was plastered with posters for "La Favorita" and Garibaldi. Trevor Nunn's 1976 Greek island setting was characterised by tavernas and souvenir stalls, all cameras and postcards, newspapers and straw hats, tables and sun-umbrellas; waiters and prostitutes hovered to serve the on-stage native and tourist population. The bare stage of Clifford Williams' 1962 production conveyed a similar atmosphere: the decision of Antipholus of Syracuse to leave Ephesus was followed by a procession of removal men carrying his belongings shipwards—belongings which included exotic souvenir purchases: an erotic Greek statue, a dried crocodile skin, a live snake.

Certainly, for Shakespeare, Ephesus is synonymous with a social life of revels. In *2 Henry 4* Falstaff roisters in a tavern with "Ephesians, my lord, of the old church" (2.2.150) and in *The Merry Wives of Windsor* the Host of the Garter Inn characterises himself as Falstaff's "Ephesian" (4.5.18)[22]; yet both *1* and *2 Henry 4* also associate Ephesus with spiritual regeneration, dramatising imagery from *Ephesians* 5:16 and 4:22–4, making Paul's metaphor for Christian renewal ("putting off the old man and putting on the new") actual and visual.[23]

Such duality is inherent in the history of Ephesus. Ephesus was a major commercial centre, connecting with the West via the sea routes of the Adriatic (the term used loosely for the Aegean, Ionian, Eastern Mediterranean, and Adriatic seas) and with the East via excellent road communications. Ephesus as St. Paul found it when he arrived in 54 A.D. was, however, a city with a divided identity. Greeks and Jews struggled to live together as fellow-citizens; the theme of Paul's subsequent letter to the Ephesians was the transformation of racial difference into racial unity, the removal of the metaphoric wall of division through Christianity. Although Paul converted the Ephesians to Christianity, pagan beliefs continued (and were tolerated) alongside the new religion well into the fourth century A.D. Thus, Ephesus retained its former pagan reputation for occult magic while developing renown as a Christian centre. Magicians continued to sell oracles and tell fortunes;[24] extant pottery lamps from late antiquity bore more mythological than Biblical scenes;[25] and, in an ironic inversion which would not be thematically out of place in *Errors*, the philosophy teacher of the young Julian (Emperor 361–363 A.D.), seeking to expose the beliefs of Ephesian theurgists as "specious and meretricious," inadvertently converted his charge to magic. "He described how Maximus [a native Ephesian and a teacher] had performed the theatrical miracle of causing a statute of Hecate to smile and laugh, and the torches in her hand to burst into flame....The narrative so impressed Julian that he immediately left for Ephesus to study with Maximus."[26] Even as Christianity became the dominant religion, Ephesian history was still characterised by religious division. The second Council of Ephesus (449 A.D.) debated "whether the Divinity had a singular or dual nature." Eusebius, the losing bishop in the debate, was punished appropriately for his beliefs: "let him be torn in two. As he divides, let him be divided."[27]

Maximus' magic, as Eunapius describes it, is at once awesome and frightening. To the non-hierophant, however, magic is simply a species of duplicity: it is illusion, sleight of hand, *trompe l'oeil*, trickery. The brother of the love-sick Aurelius in Chaucer's *The Franklin's Tale* knows the impossibility of granting Dorigen's request that Aurelius clear the rocks from the coast of Brittany. But he is confident that "ther be sciences / By whiche men make diverse apparences" (1139–40). Accordingly, the magician whom he hires performs magic in which the coast only appears to be cleared: "But thurgh his magik, for a wyke or tweye, / It *semed* that alle the rokkes were aweye"' (1295–6; my emphasis). Although accredited as "magik," performed by a "magicien," the act is explicitly linked with "swiche *illusiouns* and swiche meschaunces / As hethen folk useden" (1292–3; my emphasis).[28]

Magic's property is that of duplicity, of juxtaposing appearance and reality: one does not know how the rabbit vanishes, how the sea appears rockless, how the statue of Hecate smiles and laughs; one does not know how the women know one's name and that of one's servant. Stage magic and party tricks might arouse the audience's admiration of the (unknown) technique but, in real life, magic arouses fear. Antipholus and Dromio of Syracuse "wander in illusions"; "everyone knows [them], and [they] know none" (4.3.44; 3.2.156). Clifford Williams' production presented Dromio of Syracuse on his knees, cowering in fright as he lamented:

> We talk with goblins, owls, and sprites;
> If we obey them not, this will ensue:
> They'll suck our breath, or pinch us black and blue.
>
> (2.2.190–2)

His worst fears were realised instantly as Luciana, approaching from behind, pinched him to attract his attention: "Why prat'st thou to thyself, and answer'st not?" (2.2.193). For the victim of the illusion, magic is fearful.[29]

Not surprisingly, given the duality of Ephesus' fame as a centre of commerce and of magic, "possession" in *Errors* has both a commercial and a demonic meaning. Trevor Nunn's production stressed the demonic side of possession. St. Paul believed that immorality was partly the result of demonic powers (*Ephesians* 2: 2–3).[30] Judi Dench's Adriana terrified the onstage audience with her eldritch confession "I am possess'd" before continuing, conversationally, "with an adulterate blot" (2.2.140). This reading fits logically in a text where everyone's first reaction to a character's unexpected behaviour is to assume madness (3.2.53; 4.1.93; 4.3.81).[31] The production further capitalized on Ephesus' reputation for magic: on arrival in the city, Roger Rees' Antipholus of Syracuse consulted his *Blue Guide* to read that Ephesus "is full of cozenage" (1.2.97).

The financial fame of Ephesus, and its related motif in *Errors* (where a merchant places the fiscal profit of business before the spiritual profit of friendship; 1.2.24–9) were also effectively to the fore in Nunn's production. Angelo, the goldsmith, wore an ostentatious gold pendant with a large fish (the symbol of Christianity); this prominent prop suggested that Angelo had shrewdly found a way to change his spiritual allegiance without compromising his business interests, unlike the Demetrius of the New Testament who made a lucrative living by selling silver idols of Diana and so protested against St. Paul's teachings on the grounds of prospective financial ruin (*Acts* 19: 24–27).[32]

Ephesus united its commercial and spiritual identities in the Temple of Diana, which functioned as "a kind of bank for the province."[33] One of the wonders of the ancient world, the Temple of Diana was a triumph of beauty, finance, architectural technique, and human endeavour, the product of "the arts of Greece and the wealth of Asia" as Gibbon expressed it in 1780.[34] "The beauty of Ephesus is the Temple of Diana" reads William Warner's translation of Solinus' *Excellent and Pleasant Works* (1587).[35] "*Ephesus* was renowned for the great temple of *Diana*, one of the Wonders of the World, 425 feet long, 220 broad, hauing 127. pillars the workes of so many Kings, 220. Yeares in building" explains Sampson Price in a Paul's Cross sermon of 1615.[36] Edward Chaloner describes the Temple of Diana as "a place so magnificent for the structure"[37]—a structure so magnificent that Xerxes spared it when he destroyed all the other temples of Asia. Pericles' journey ends, like Egeon's, in Ephesus, and it is logical to conclude that the "Abbess" and the "priory" of *Errors* Act 5 are but superficially Christianised references to the pagan Temple of Diana. In fact, Gower's *Confessio Amantis* (one of the sources of *Pericles*) contains a version of the story of Apollonius of Tyre in which Lucina dedicates herself to "religion," becoming "Abbesse" in the temple at Ephesus, so that, as R.A. Foakes explains, "the change from temple to priory was already half-made."[38]

Ephesus was allegedly founded by Scythian Amazons and it is they who are responsible for the Temple (as Solinus, Heywood, Raleigh, and others tell us[39]), dedicated to Artemis. The renown of Ephesus and its temple derives in part from this presiding goddess, a colourfully active participant in the life of the city (she allegedly helped the suicidal architect of her temple erect the lintel over the entrance).[40] The Greek travel writer Pausanius (second century B.C.) explains that

> all cities [in Greece] worship Artemis of Ephesus, and individuals hold her in honour above all the gods. The reason, in my view, is the renown of the Amazons, who traditionally dedicated the image[.][41]

The polymaste Amazon Artemis (probably a fertility goddess) resembles the Greek Artemis in name only, but became identified with Artemis, the twin sister of Apollo, when Ephesus came under Greek rule. It was believed that the twins of Zeus and Leda were born in Ephesus, whither Leda had fled to avoid Hera's wrath. The Temple of Artemis became the Temple of Diana under Roman hands. "Great is Diana of the Ephesians" chant the rioting silversmiths in *Acts* 20. That the Greek Artemis, goddess of maiden purity, the Roman Diana, should develop from an Amazon fertility goddess is ironic, and that Ephesus should be associated with twins from its early history is doubtless coincidence, but the opposition and the doubling are undeniably appropriate.

Myths of Ephesus' founding, like those of so many ancient cities, credit it with multiple foundations: the founding by Scythian Amazons and a subsequent refounding by the Emperor Hadrian. (Hadrian's interest in Ephesus stemmed from his fascination with the occult.)[42] The Elizabethans were profoundly alarmed by Amazons, primarily because of the tribe's refusal to accept the female state of obedience. "They disdained to marry with their neighbours calling it rather a seruitude than Wedlock. A singular example to all ages" writes Heywood sternly in 1624, reiterating this point, but moderating his disapproval, in 1640: "finding the sweetnesse of liberty...they refused to take Husbands,...accounting Matrimony, no better then a miserable servitude."[43] Antonio in the induction to *Antonio and Mellida* expresses anxiety over his role as an Amazon, "an hermaphrodite, two parts in one," only to be reassured by Alberto: "Not play two parts in one? away, away; 'tis common fashion."[44] The Amazon, like the actor, is both male and female. It is hard to dissociate Adriana, that "warrior against double standards" (the phrase is Ruth Nevo's[45]) from her Amazon forebears in Ephesus, and one cannot but wonder whether her name—the female form of Hadrian, the Ephesian patron—is coincidental.[46]

Certainly in changing the Epidamnus of Plautus to Ephesus, Shakespeare chose a city whose history added thematic resonance to his dramatic topoi. From its legendary Amazon foundation (the Amazons had two queens, one each for military and domestic rule), its reigning goddess Artemis/Diana, and its Pauline themes of separation and division to its fame as a centre for commerce and religion (whether pagan or Christian), binaries/duplication/twins have a long association with Ephesus.[47]

III. MARRIAGE

Given the thematic emphasis on twinning, doubling, fusion, it is appropriate that Paul's letter to the Ephesians contains advice about marriage, that state in which "two become one flesh" (*Ephesians* 5:31). Identical twins, separate but the same, provide an ideal metaphor for the theme of division and reconciliation, not just of two pairs of siblings but of two pairs of marriage partners. One marriage (that of Egeon-Emilia) is disrupted by external hostility (shipwreck), the other by internal (domestic) strife; both marriages are characterised by separation (Egeon is a Renaissance commercial traveller, Antipholus a straying husband), and both wives object to their husbands' absence (Emilia makes provision to follow her spouse [1.1.47–8], Adriana protests).

Marriage is a difficult business to negotiate (I use both noun and verb advisedly). Both Adriana and Antipholus refer to their marriage as an arranged marriage. Antipholus describes Adriana as the woman "whom thou [the Duke] gav'st to me to be my wife" (5.1.198), a reference made independently by Adriana: "Antipholus my husband, / Who I made lord of me and all I had, / At your [the Duke's] important letters" (5.1.136–8). Adriana, it is implied at 5.1.161–4, was the Duke's reward to Antipholus for military service.

Marriage may be a transaction, the woman an object traded by men, but it also, paradoxically, as far removed from transaction as is possible: a holy union, characterised by mutual spiritual giving. Thus St. Paul: "Be subject to one another out of reverence for Christ" (*Ephesians* 4:21). The commercial and the spiritual seem strange bedfellows (as it were) but they are no more paradoxical than the dramatic hybrid which results from Shakespeare's Pauline and Plautine sources. Shakespeare negotiates the thematic and generic tensions in his disparate source material to create a successful partnership.[48] Adriana has more trouble synthesising polarities.

Adriana's difficulty derives in part from a duality in Renaissance attitudes to women. Viewed as both divine and dangerous, women and their beauty could lead men to an appreciation of higher things (the spiritually beautiful, the celestial) or to physical temptation (lust, gratification, damnation). Both extremes of these female stereotypes are represented in *Errors*. The love-stricken Antipholus of Syracuse employs the vocabulary of the worshipping Petrarchan wooer: "your grace," "more than earth divine," "Are you a god?" are the terms he uses for the resisting Luciana in 3.2. In the contrasting episode, which follows immediately, Dromio of Syracuse describes his pursuit by the sexual Luce in the language of demonology: Luce "haunts" him, she is a "diviner" [witch], she knows "what privy marks" he has, so that he "amaz'd, ran from her as a witch" (3.2.144). The common root of these two women's names (Luce and Luciana) shows that the demonic female (the diviner who would possess the male) and the divine female (the goddess whom the male wishes to possess) are but two sides of the same female stereotype.

This duality is pushed further in *Errors* with the representation of the demonic and divine two female stereotypes by the professional extremes: by the Courtesan (whom Antipholus and Dromio of Syracuse characterize as "Sathan," "Mistress Sathan," "the devil," "the devil's dam": 4.3.48–51)[49] and by the Abbess (characterized in dialogue as "a virtuous and a reverend lady": 5.1.134). Emilia's dual role as procreative mother and chaste Abbess (during a surely significant period of thirty-three years, the number of years Christ lived on earth[50]) links her even more obviously with that other chaste mother, the Virgin Mary. Adriana attempts to unite both extremes, attending to her husband's body and soul: she offers dinner/sex and confession ("Husband, I'll dine above with you to-day, / And shrive you of a thousand idle pranks"; 2.2.207–08).

Whether Adriana offers Antipholus of Syracuse dinner or sex is, in fact, a moot point. Stanley Wells views the rendezvous as innocent: "Shakespeare raises the moral tone by substituting the dinner party of *Menaechmi* for the bedroom setting of *Amphitruo*."[51] However, there is an association between food and sex (the former a metaphor for the latter) in the brothel scene in

Pericles,[52] and Ralph Berry suggests that the "audience would...receive the impression of sexual congress behind locked doors."[53]

"Your cake here is warm within: you stand here in the cold" says Dromio of Ephesus to his master (3.1.71), where "cake" euphemistically indicates "woman," and the scene concludes with "standard slang for sexual entry," Antipholus' decision to "knock elsewhere" since his "own doors refuse to entertain [him]."[54]

Certainly, the argument from stage symbolism is persuasive: "the house [was] perceived from earliest times as the coding for woman, and the knocking at the gates, the male attempts at entry."[55] This is the symbolism in plays as diverse as *Lysistrata* (where the women deny their husbands sex, and lock themselves in the Acropolis only to be threatened by phallic weapons) and *Henry 5* where Henry's invasion of France is analogous to his conquest of Catherine. "Enter our gates, dispose of us and ours, / For we no longer are defensible" says the yielding Governor on the walls of Harfleur (3.3.49–50) in a line no less appropriate to the Princess. However, practical considerations may support the notion of culinary rather than sexual offerings. Luciana chaperones the meeting; given Antipholus of Syracuse's fear of Adriana and love of her sister, it seems unlikely that he would engage in sexual intimacies with his hostess; and in the Shakespeare canon adultery is not the comic matter that fornication is.[56] What is clear is that Adriana's attempt to unite female physicality and divinity involves ministering to her supposed husband's body and soul: she provides dinner (or its less euphemistic equivalent) and confession. For Adriana, wifehood is a fusion of two opposing female stereotypes.

"Why should their liberty than ours be more?" Adriana protests in 2.1, the noun subtly hinting at the kind of freedom men enjoy, that in which they visit the Liberties.[57] Elizabethan marriage may be a mixture of otium (the social niceties of leisurely dinners) and negotium ("If thou didst wed her for her wealth"), but Antipholus looks elsewhere for Erotium. I choose the word deliberately, for Shakespeare elects not to: Erotium is the name of the Courtesan whom the resident twin visits in *Menaechmi*. In *The Comedy of Errors* the Courtesan is "pretty and witty; wild" (3.1.110), a provider of hospitality ("thanks for my good cheer": 5.1.393), a woman "of excellent discourse" (3.1.109). Critics remind us that discourse is not what courtesans were renowned for; but in Greek society hetairai certainly were. High-class escorts ("hetaira" literally means "companion"), distinct from concubines, prostitutes in brothels, or streetwalkers, hetairai provided intellectual conversation as equals, socialising with men at dinner and drinking parties.[58] By turning Antipholus' sexual and social needs into a business, the Courtesan in *Errors* achieves outside marriage what Adriana has not managed within: the fusion of otium, negotium, erotium.

Lest we be in danger of admiring her for this, Shakespeare qualifies the Courtesan's triumph in two ways: he makes her the only deliberate deceiver in a play of chance; and he denies her a name. The play concludes with baptism, that act of naming which bestows identity, strengthens family, celebrates society. For as long as she is nameless, the Courtesan is kept outside that society.

Onomastics in *The Comedy of Errors* are not without thematic or character relevance. "Egeon" recalls the father of Theseus who gave his name to the Aegean Sea, drowning himself from grief at the (supposed) loss of his son. Luciana is associated with light (from the Latin *lux*) and Lucian, that exposer of follies (cf. the role of Lucian in *Titus Andronicus*). Angelo is an apt name for a goldsmith, angels being gold coins. Adriana, as indicated above, is the female form of Hadrian, the Roman ruler from whom the Adriatic Sea takes its name; Adriana also appears in Chaucer and Gower as a variant of Ariadne, the princess whom Theseus abandoned on Naxos and Dionysus subsequently wed.[59] Ariadne thus has a dual aspect—the mourner and the joyful bride—a duality inherent in another etymology of Adriana as the female form of Janus, the two-faced god.

The kitchen-maid Luce, as we have seen, is also referred to as "Nell."[60] Although Shakespeare uses "Nell" as an abbreviation for Eleanor in *2 Henry 6*, he also views it as an abbreviation for Helen: Paris twice calls Helen of Troy by this homely diminutive in *Troilus and Cressida*. There are more Helens in Shakespeare than there are Eleanors, and they may provide a clue as to how to view the kitchen-maid in *Errors*. One dominant pattern stands out, that of the sexually assertive female who pursues her chosen mate. Helena in *A Midsummer Night's Dream* trails Demetrius through the wood outside Athens, a role reversal of which she is only too aware: "Your wrongs do set a scandal on my sex. / We cannot fight for love, as men may do./ We should be woo'd, and were not made to woo." (*MND* 2.1.240–2). This generalisation, in which she moves from the impropriety of her own behaviour to that of all women, illustrates her awareness of society's automatic reaction in which her weakness "will be taken as female weakness rather than as an individual weakness."[61]

The link between individual transgression and female transgression was, in fact, already implicit in the Renaissance in the name Helen, by association with Menelaus' Helen, who accompanied Paris to Troy (whether by force or choice is open to doubt, but the Renaissance assumed her willing compliance). In *Troilus and Cressida* Thersites presents Helen in unflattering terms (a "whore," a "placket") and Shakespeare continually associates the name with female sexual eagerness. Critics note that Helena in *All's Well That Ends Well* seems more eager to lose her virginity than is deemed proper for a heroine. In conversation with Parolles she defends the female right to have and enjoy sex, and subsequently engages in a marathon cross-country pursuit of a man who does nothing to encourage her: she follows Bertram to Paris (a destination with classical overtones), before conveniently arriving in Florence (where Bertram is) despite her intention of travelling to the shrine of St. Jacques le Grand in Spain. To this sexually assertive trio—the Helens of *Midsummer Night's Dream*, *Troilus and Cressida*, *All's Well That Ends Well*—we must add another Helen, Mistress Quickly ("Nell") of *Henry 4* and *5*, whose vocabulary is full of unintentional sexual innuendo. Shakespeare's Helens/Nells are cast in the same mould. To Shakespeare, it seems, all Nells are loose; in *The Comedy of Errors* Nell is both loose and Luce.

The *dramatis personae* in *Errors* are aware of the way in which name confers identity. Dromio of Syracuse reacts noticeably to his finding out the name of the kitchen-maid; he comments on her name and uses it immediately in apostrophe: "if thy name be called Luce—Luce, thou hast answer'd him well" (3.1.52–3). Dromio's master, Antipholus of Syracuse, reacts similarly to *not* finding out the name of Luciana. His opening apostrophe and ensuing comment ("Sweet mistress—what your name is else, I know not"; 3.2.29) implies that he would use her Christian name if he could. The fact that Adriana identifies the Syracusans by their names is taken as proof that she does recognize and know them ("How can she thus then call us by our names, / Unless it be by inspiration?": 2.2.166–7) although, as confusions escalate, both Antipholus and Dromio of Syracuse grow more hesitant in assuming that name and identity are synonymous. "Do you know me, sir? Am I Dromio? Am I your man? Am I myself?" asks Dromio in anguish at 3.2.73–4. His master reassures him "Thou art Dromio, thou art my man, thou art thyself" (75) but just 100 lines later he is unable to apply the same confidence to his own situation. "Master Antipholus," hails the goldsmith at 3.2.165; "Ay, that's my name" is Antipholus' guarded response.[62] In a play which is sensitive to names—their meanings and their confusions—the anonymity of a courtesan who is named in the source is conspicuous.

In the reunion of Act 5 Antipholus of Syracuse immediately identifies his father as Egeon, and Egeon and Emilia exchange first names five times in their first six lines of dialogue (5.1.342–7). Antipholus of Ephesus and Adriana have no opportunity to use Christian names in the last scene, as Shakespeare does not provide them with a dialogue opportunity for reconciliation. Their marriage is, as Leggatt observes, "quietly placed in the background and no great hopes are pinned on it."[63]

The only grounds for optimism lie in the Courtesan's anonymity in a play whose conclusion stresses rebirth and baptism, a gossips' feast, and in the fact that the Courtesan is not included in the final pairing-off (although the BBC production does match her with the Duke). Any optimism is necessarily limited, however, by the fact that Antipholus of Ephesus has more to say to the Courtesan than he does to his wife: he addresses the Courtesan in ten words ("There take it [the ring], and much thanks for my good cheer"), of which the last six may be a termination of a relationship, a salacious reminiscence, or a genuine expression of gratitude. The husband-wife reunion must be realised on stage wordlessly, if at all.

Directors rise to this interpretive challenge. A happy ending is most easily suggested by the simple expedient of Antipholus giving his wife the promised chain so that objects, as identities, are restored to their rightful owners. (Although the BBC Antipholus does give his wife the chain—a large, heart-shaped pendant—his emotional discomfort at the family reunion is made clear by the uncertain looks which pass between himself and Adriana.) Adriana's question, "And are not you my husband?" (5.1.371) is addressed not to her husband but to her dinner companion, Antipholus of Syracuse. She posed the question in resigned sadness in Clifford Williams' production, already aware of the negative answer she would receive, and in urgent desperation in the 1983 RSC production, willing the answer to be positive. This latter production gave Antipholus of Ephesus and Adriana an embrace into which Adriana drew Dromio of Ephesus, showing the importance of servants to the family unit in early modern England. Adriana then moved to exit with her sister; Antipholus pulled his wife back to him but she slowly propelled her husband in the direction of his twin. Deliberately eschewing or postponing a marital reunion, this Adriana showed (as does Shakespeare's dialogue) that the reestablishment of the family unit—parents/ children, sibling/sibling—was to take precedence over conjugal communion. Her actions with servant and husband left her firmly, if a trifle regretfully, in control of tone.

This Adriana's inclusion of Dromio in the embrace reminded us, albeit in an affectionately twentieth-century way, that the Elizabethan household was an extended family unit. The master-husband held sway over a group of social subordinates: wife, children, servants. The link between the treatment of wives and servants is seen in the linguistic instruction offered by a husband and a ruler in an early comedy and a late romance, respectively. In *The Taming of the Shrew* 4.5 Petruchio "teaches" his wife the difference between the sun and the moon.[64] In *The Tempest* Prospero gives his slave Caliban the same lesson. He teaches Caliban "how / To name the bigger light, and how the less, / That burn by day and night"; as a result, Caliban tells him, "I lov'd thee" (1.2.335–6).

Marriage may be a spiritual world-without-end bargain, a selfless service; but it may also be little better than slavery. As More's Raphael reminds us, the difference between service and servitude "is only a matter of one syllable."[65] In *The Tempest*, Ferdinand, in service to Prospero, takes pleasure in a "mean task" which would be as "heavy...as odious" were it not for Miranda's sympathy and love (3.1.1–15); his heart is a willing "slave" to Miranda (3.1.66). This love leads Ferdinand to enter Miranda's service in marriage, paradoxically "with a heart as willing / As bondage e'er of freedom" (3.1.88–9). Miranda, reciprocating Ferdinand's feelings, mirrors his vocabulary: "I'll be your servant" (3.1.85). In contrast, Helen in *All's Well That Ends Well* does not enjoy reciprocal love, and the consequences are voiced by Diana: "'Tis a hard bondage to become the wife / Of a detesting lord" (3.5.64–5). Thus, marriage may be a pleasurable bondage or a hard bondage, service or servitude.

In *Errors* Luciana counsels her sister in obedience, patience, and the domestic hierarchy which makes men "masters to their females" (2.1.24); Adriana responds with sisterly sarcasm, "This servitude makes you to keep unwed." Servitude, asses, bridled: these are the terms Adriana associates with married life. Renaissance matrimony can indeed be "hard bondage" for the female because Renaissance culture associates wives with servants. In the letter in which Paul counsels wives to be obedient to husbands, he also advises servants to be obedient to their masters (*Ephesians* 6:5–9). Claudius Hollyband links the two social inferiors in a succinct aphorism: "he is happie which hath a good servant, and a good wife."[66] Before continuing with Adriana we need to consider servants and service.

IV. SERVANTS

The Elizabethan household, like Elizabethan life, was hierarchical. Husbands ruled over wives who ruled over children; at the bottom of this pecking order came servants. However, my generalisation distorts, flattening as it does the permutations possible. Thus in many instances servants were viewed as a variant of children, not inferior beings but dependents. In Claudius Hollyband's dialogue, *The Citizen at Home*, the Father's admonition to his servant William reminds one more of parental frustration than employer's dissatisfaction: "William, give here some bread...you will never learn to serve; why do you not lead it with a trencher plate, and not with the hand? I have told it to you above an hundred times."[67] At the other extreme is the treatment which William Gouge describes: "Sometimes Masters offend in the quality of that foode which thay give to their servants, as when it is kept too long, and grone musty, mouldy, or otherwise unsavory: or when the worst kind of foode, for cheapnesse sake, is bought, evene such as is scarce fit for mans meat."[68] Given an inferior diet, servants were thus daily reminded that they "did not belong to their employer's family."[69] Although masters were expected to care for their servants, attending to their physical and spiritual needs and caring for them when ill, Thomas Becon's admonition makes it clear that many masters did not behave in this way. Becon corrects those who "curse, and lame them [servants], cast dishes and pots at their heads, beat them, put them in danger of their life."[70] Compare Vives, whose discussion of the treatment of wives by husbands illuminates the treatment of servants by masters: "some [husbands] there be, that through evyll and rough handelynge and in threatenynge of their wives, have them not as wives, but as servauntes."[71]

The Elizabethans understood the term "family" more in the sense of domestic household than sentimental attachments. The components of this household are made clear in Gouge's *Treatises on Domestical Duties* (an exegesis on *Ephesians*) which outlines the duties of three sets of people: Wives-Husbands, Children-Parents, Servants-Masters. Treatise 7, "Duties of Servants," stresses the importance of obedience, referring the reader to the previous treatises on wives and children for the reasons why obedience is desirable: "The reasons alleged to move wives and children to obey, ought much more to move servants" (p. 613). In section 36 (p. 645), "*Of servants endeavour to make their judgement agree with their masters*," the reader is referred to Gouge's precepts for other inferiors since the same principle applies. Antipholus of Syracuse corrects his man's behaviour, reminding Dromio that the servant should "fashion [his] demeanor to my looks" (2.2.33), a classic textbook rule for wives: "it beseemes an honest wife to frame her selfe to her husbands affect, and not to be merry, when he is melancholy, not iocund when he is sad, much less fliere when hee is angry."[72]

Although social historians are unsure about the extent of the similarity between the roles of servant and wife in the early modern period, in one startling criminal category servants and wives were yoked together. Husband-killing and master-killing were both classified as petty treason. Masters feared betrayal from within, insubordination by servant or wife, those whom Frances E. Dolan characterises as "dangerous familiars." Petty treason embodies the fear "that the other and the enemy might be the person who makes your fire, prepares your food and lodges in your own cell."[73]

Antipholus of Ephesus perceives himself as betrayed by both wife and servant. His wife bars him from the house, *his* house. His servant purloins a bag of gold, *his* gold. And both servant and wife compound the villainy by denial. Adriana: "I did not, gentle husband, lock thee forth"; Dromio of Ephesus: "And, gentle master, I receiv'd no gold" (4.4.98–9). Adriana transgresses, albeit unknowingly, by inviting a lover and a strange servant into the marital home; she commits infractions of *mensa* and possibly of *thoro*, welcoming the ersatz husband to her table and, perhaps, her bed. Alice Arden did as much and was burned at the stake for her sins.

But Shakespeare is not interested in petty treason—this is a comedy of errors, not of murders[74]—so much as he is in the parallels between two sets of relationships: master-servant and husband-wife. We see more of the former relationship than we do of the latter; this is perhaps why Ralph Berry views the master-servant relationship as of more interest (see note 19). Berry fails to realize, however, that we are invited to consider Antipholus-Adriana by analogy with Antipholus-Dromio. Which Antipholus-Dromio? Both. The two Antipholus-Dromio relationships, very different, provide us with two possible paradigms of marriage.

If the literature of the period associates wives with servants, the language of *Errors* links Adriana with Dromio (either and both). Both Dromios are called "ass." Luciana insults Dromio of Syracuse so, and he agrees: "'Tis true she [Adriana, or possibly Luciana] rides me and I long for grass. 'Tis so, I am an ass" (2.2.200–01). In the next scene Antipholus of Ephesus, applies the insult to Dromio of Ephesus who also agrees: "Marry, so it doth appear / By the wrongs I suffer, and the blows I bear. / I should kick, being kick'd, and being at that pass, / You would keep from my heels, and beware of an ass" (3.1.15–18). In 4.4 Dromio of Ephesus expands on the motif, summarising his sufferings at the hands of his master: "I am an ass indeed; you may prove it by my long ears. I have serv'd him from the hour of my nativity to this instant, and have nothing at his hands for my service but blows" (4.4.29–32). Although in all three cases the insult from master/mistress to man could be left as a one-line criticism, on each occasion the analogy is expanded. It is difficult, then, not to be reminded of the earlier dialogue between Luciana and Adriana:

> Luciana. O, know he is the bridle of your will.
> Adriana. There's none but asses will be bridled so. (2.1.13–14)

Wives, like servants, like asses, endure wrongs and blows from the master whom they serve.

It is noticeable in reading, and particularly marked in production, that the Antipholi enjoy different relationships with their respective Dromios. The Syracusans are friendlier, less hierarchical, more supportive of each other. In one sense this equality is the result of the circumstances in which they find themselves, strangers in a strange land; as the BBC production showed, they "cling to each other for support."[75] The affectionate relationship between Antipholus of Syracuse and Dromio of Syracuse was established from the first in the Clifford Williams production, to the evident perplexity of the Merchant. Thus, Antipholus' "A trusty villain, sir, that very oft, / When I am dull with care and melancholy, / Lightens my humour" (1.2.199–201) was delivered as a half-apologetic explanation. The Merchant's refusal of the dinner invitation was due to his desire to get away from the strange duo, his "I commend you to your *own* content" (1.2.32) emphatic, terminative, relieved at his success in extricating himself.

In this production Dromio's concern for his master was tellingly shown. To Antipholus' reprise of Dromio's alleged misdemeanours—"thou didst deny the gold's receipt, / And told'st me of a mistress, and a dinner" (2.2.17–18)—Dromio looked (understandably) uncomprehending, before reacting in delight at this evident example of his master's recovery from depression : "I am *glad* to see you in this merry vein" (2.2.20).

Later Dromio anxiously felt his master's forehead when Antipholus of Syracuse asked him about the bark. "Why, sir, I brought you word an hour since" replied Dromio (4.3.37–8), concerned that his master might be running a fever. In the 1983 RSC production Antipholus' "As you love strokes, so jest with me again" was a genuine invitation to his man to replay his earlier absurd answers, each question followed by a pause for Dromio's anticipated (but not forthcoming) music-hall reply (2.2.8–10). I reline:

You know no Centaur? (Pause)
You receiv'd no gold? (Pause)
Your mistress sent to have me home to dinner? (Pause)

In contrast to his Ephesian brother, Antipholus of Syracuse describes his man as a "heedful slave" (2.2.2) who acts "in care" of him (2.2.3), and he acknowledges his "love" for the servant (2.2.28). As Alexander Leggatt points out,[76] both Antipholus of Syracuse and Dromio of Syracuse are willing to sacrifice their own happiness and safety for the sake of the other (3.2.145–9; 4.4.151–3), an example of mutual selfless love, the kind that ideally characterises marriage.

Very different is the relationship between Antipholus of Ephesus and his Dromio, who are never alone on stage together and are thus denied the intimate friendly chats of their respective siblings. In production, as in the text, Antipholus of Ephesus is clearly a more violent man than his brother. Although both masters beat their servants, productions differentiate the types of beatings. In Trevor Nunn's production, Antipholus of Syracuse used only a rolled-up newspaper to hit his man; the BBC Antipholus of Syracuse employed a soft Tudor bonnet; in both productions Antipholus of Ephesus hit his man with the flat of his hand or with the property rope. This distinction motivated a moment of amazement in the BBC production when Syracusan Dromio's news of the bark in port, delivered to the wrong Antipholus, met with a slap across the face; the close-up of the servant showed his emotional, rather than his physical, pain at this uncharacteristic behaviour, a betrayal of unwritten rules. It is, appropriately, Dromio of Ephesus who is given the comic-poignant testimony about his life history of beatings.[77] In *Menaechmi* Plautus also differentiates the two master-servant relationships. The resident twin, astonished by the magnanimity of the unknown slave who saves him, rejects the servant's explanation that he is Menaechmus' man: "I had never yet anie servant would do so much for me."[78]

It is tempting to argue that Adriana seeks in marriage the symbiotic friendly "service" of the Syracusans, but finds that Antipholus of Ephesus offers her only servitude. However, the play does not permit such simple thematic bifurcation. Before deciding what kind of marriage Adriana wants to have, we must first consider what kind of woman Adriana wants to be.

V. "TWO PARTS IN ONE"

Historically, as we have seen, Ephesus offers two female role models: the independent pagan Amazon and the submissive Christian servant. At the beginning of the play Adriana is clearly equated with the former, Luciana with the latter. Adriana chafes at the restrictions marriage imposes on women; she questions the male right to have geographic freedom, desiring equal liberty for husbands and wives. Critical and resentful of her husband's greater freedom, she expresses herself in actions as well as words, granting herself permission to circulate out of doors. Her *quid pro quo* independence has not been well received: "Look when I serve him so, he takes it ill" (2.1.12). Desiring "the sweetnesse of liberty," viewing marriage as rather a "servitude than wedlock," Adriana is exactly the kind of woman who so alarmed Heywood and appalled the Renaissance male. Playing "two parts in one"—the male and the female—she is in the tradition of the Ephesian Amazon.

It is because of Ephesus' tradition of non-submissive women that St. Paul directs his letter about wifely submission not to the Galatians, Corinthians, or Colossians, not to the Philippians, the Hebrews, or the Romans, but to the Ephesians. It is the Ephesians who are most in need of Paul's advice:

Be subject to one another out of reverence for Christ.
Wives should be subject to their husbands as to the Lord,

since, as Christ is head of the Church and saves the whole body, so is a husband the head of his wife; and as the Church is subject to Christ, so should wives be to their husbands in everything. Husbands should love their wives, just as Christ loved the Church and sacrificed for her to make her holy...; and let every wife respect her husband. (*Ephesians* 5: 21–33)[79]

Concerned to establish domestic harmony through domestic hierarchy, Paul is explicit in his message: husbands must love their wives, but wives must be subject to their husbands.

Luciana knows Paul's lesson by heart:

There's nothing situate under heaven's eye
But hath his bound in earth, in sea, in sky.
The beasts, the fishes, and the winged fowls
Are their males' subjects and at their controls:
Man, more divine, the master of all these,
Lord of the wide world and wild wat'ry seas,
Indu'd with intellectual sense and souls,
Of more pre-eminence than fish and fowls,
Are masters to their females, and their lords:
Then let your will attend on their accords...
Ere I learn love, I'll practice to obey. (2.1.16–25, 29)

The lines are Luciana's but the sentiments are Paul's: Luciana is merely paraphrasing *Ephesians* 5:21ff.[80]

Having introduced this opposition between the Amazon and the Pauline female, the play immediately begins to deconstruct it. Adriana can hardly be an independent woman since, as a wife, she has technically espoused submission, while Luciana, who preaches submission, can do so only because (as Adriana points out), she is independent:

thou, that hast no unkind mate to grieve thee,
With urging helpless patience would relieve me;
But if thou live to see like right bereft,
This fool-begg'd patience in thee will be left. (2.1.38–41)

The identities of Adriana and Luciana, like those of the twins, begin to merge, become confused. Despite her rhetorical question, "Why should their liberty than ours be more?", Adriana seems to want not liberty but the right to love and be loved as a wife. No Moll Cutpurse, she. When next we meet the women it is Adriana who has the long Pauline speech on marriage as she lyrically, passionately tells Antipholus that husband and wife are "undividable incorporate" (2.2.122). Luciana's subsequent speech on marriage is strangely unspiritual, full of knowing advice to her (supposed) brother-in-law about how to conduct an extra-marital affair:

> Look sweet, speak fair, become disloyalty;
> Apparel vice like virtue's harbinger;
> Bear a fair presence, though your heart be tainted;
> Teach sin the carriage of a holy saint:
> Be secret-false. (3.2.11–15)

Instead of husband and wife being one, as Paul counsels, the wife is to be kept ignorant of the husband's infidelity: "what need she be acquainted?" Paul's letter to the Ephesians was about breaking down the wall of division; Luciana's advice here is about how to paper over that wall.

The contradictions and cross-overs in female identity become increasingly obvious. Despite the feminist vigour of her conversation with Luciana, Adriana plays a more (al)luring role with her husband, while Luciana the good (wearing, in the BBC version, a necklace with a large crucifix) is involved in a disturbing dialogue with her supposed brother-in-law (3.2). One wonders if Luciana's behaviour is not slightly flirtatious. Despite some valiant attempts to redirect Antipholus' attentions ("Why call you me love? Call my sister so": 3.2.59; and cf.57, 60, 65), Luciana concludes the dialogue with an ambiguous line: "hold you still; / I'll fetch my sister to get her good will" (70).

The line may be a desperate excuse to exit (after all, the situation is now dangerously physical, Antipholus having asked to hold Luciana's hand; and his love talk is clearly out of control since he has just proposed marriage). Both the BBC production and the 1983 RSC version played the line as an impetus to exit.

In the 1962 RSC version, however, Luciana succumbed to Antipholus, giving him her right hand in a waltz gesture (repeated in more legitimate circumstances at 5.1.375–7) while her left hand caressed his hair. Although she quickly removed her hand, aghast at herself, her exit line was a helplessly loving acceptance of the situation. In Ian Judge's 1990 RSC production Luciana's acceptance of Antipholus was less passive. "I'll fetch my sister to get her good will" was a spirited decision to face the music, Luciana having agreed to love Antipholus. Her later recounting of the conversation to Adriana was triumphant, not apologetic:

> That love I begg'd for you [gleeful laugh], he begged of me. First he did praise my beauty [gleeful laugh], then my speech. (4.2.12; 15)

In Act 5 the Abbess touches a sore spot when she questions Adriana about the possibility of her husband's "unlawful love." The BBC close-up of the Courtesan at this moment showed the rival suspected by Adriana. However, in Adrian Noble's production (1983) Adriana's admission that "some love...drew him oft from home" (5.1.56) was accompanied by a glare at Luciana. In Adriana's eyes the submissive sister was not as innocent as she appeared.

By Act 5, then, the identities of Adriana and Luciana are as confused as those of the Antipholi. Adriana the independent meekly submits to the Abbess's rebukes, even though the Abbess's claim (that Adriana's jealousy has caused her husband's madness) is unfounded, as Acts 1 through 4 show. Luciana the submissive objects vociferously on behalf of her sister (5.1.87–8) and encourages Adriana to resist: "Why bear you these rebukes and answer not?" (5.1.89). In the play's conclusion the Antipholi are distinguished, returned to their separate identities, but their partners are not.

This duality seems to be deliberate. Throughout *Errors* we see Adriana and Luciana trying to work out which type of Ephesian woman to be (pagan or Christian, independent or submissive), and experimenting with whether it is possible to be both. Can women play "two parts in one," being both divine (goddess) and "diviner" (witch)? Shakespeare juxtaposes this adjective and noun in the play's structural centre, Act 3, scene 2, where Antipholus' romantic approaches to Luciana are followed by Dromio's narrative about her onomastic relative, Luce. Luciana the goddess, "more than earth divine," is followed by Luce the "diviner" (140); the advocate of wifely submission in marriage, the woman who will be subservient to her husband, is followed by a more assertive type of servant. But the scene begins with the goddess sanctioning sin and ends with the witch seeking holy marriage. This is hot ice and wondrous strange snow.

Opposites can co-exist, however, as the name Luce/Luciana implies and as Adriana's attentions to her "husband"'s body and soul at 2.2.207–08 specifically show. And if in *Errors* Shakespeare can combine the pagan and the Christian in Ephesus, why can not the women do so too?

In this duality Adriana resembles Lysistrata, that other independent heroine who staged a lock-out scene. Lysistrata's lock-out tactic was deliberate, Adriana's unwitting, but the motive was the same: domestic harmony. The women in *Lysistrata* do not want peace *qua* peace but as a guarantor of normal domestic life: uninterrupted market shopping, regular sexual relations. Adriana similarly regrets the demise of domestic activities: carving, speaking, looking, touching (2.2.113–18). Like Adriana, although for a different reason, Lysistrata has no reconciliation with a partner.[81] Instead, in a dénouement unusual in Greek drama, the divided chorus of old men and old women come together, celebrating the resumption of interrupted relations. In *Lysistrata* as in *Errors* it is the older couple(s) who are depicted most harmoniously. Adriana is left dramatically in the cold by Shakespeare, and perhaps by Antipholus; she and her husband have some voyaging still to do.

If the ending seems inconclusive, the marital future uncertain, it is not because of Adriana but because of her husband. Three of the four main protagonists in *Errors* not only experience mistakes of identity but initiate their own experiments with opposing and complementary personalities, doubles, binaries, paradoxes. Antipholus of Syracuse seeks his twin in order to make himself whole again, but, before achieving this goal, he finds himself by losing himself to Luciana. Adriana and

Luciana synthesise two extremes of female behaviour. Only Antipholus of Ephesus clings tenaciously to his original identity (5.1.214–54). Act 5 provides the end of a journey for all but him; it is now his turn to explore personality. Ephesian Antipholus must now embark on a quest for self- and family-identity just as Syracusan Antipholus embarked in Act 1.[82]

The straying husband, the errant Antipholus of Ephesus, thus becomes errant in a different way: like his twin at the beginning of the play, he is *erraticus*.[83] He too may eventually unite opposites, telling his wife "I am thee" (3.2.64). In the spirit of doubling and repetition which is this play's dominant mode, we may hope that Adriana's marriage, like that of her mother-in-law, will be a remarriage. But that is for the future. Adriana inhabits a world where the thaumaturge is Pinch not Prospero, and the one magician—the dramatist—who could give her (and us) a happy ending, declines to do so. Although the play ends, as comedies should, with marriage, Shakespeare leaves us with but the appearance of a happy ending. Not all illusions are dispelled: Ephesus' reputation for duplicity is still in evidence.[84]

NOTES

[1] Robert S. Miola, *Shakespeare and Classical Comedy* (Oxford: Clarendon Press, 1994), p. 22.

[2] *Ibid.*, p. 26.

[3] *Menaechmi*, by contrast, is told from the resident twin's point of view.

[4] Stanley Wells, ed. *The Comedy of Errors* (Harmondsworth: Penguin, 1972), p. 30.

[5] Unhappy with the repetition of *nativity* in line 407 (TLN 1896), which they viewed as compositorial eyeskip from line 405 (TLN 1894), Hanmer and Johnson emended to *felicity* and *festivity*, respectively. The duplication of *nativity* may indeed be an error. George Walton Williams (personal communication) points out two other textual cruces that involve repetition: "To seek thy *helpe* by beneficiall *helpe*" (1.1.151; TLN 154; Dover Wilson emends the first *help* to *helth*, Rowe to *life*, Cunningham (Arden) to *pelf*), and "Besides *her* vrging of *her* wrecke at sea" (5.1.360; TLN 1835; the New Oxford *Complete Works* (Oxford: Clarendon Press, 1986), following Collier, emends the first *her* to *his*). Compositorial anticipation, in which the second item (which is correct)

drives out the first, may well explain the double *nativity* of 5.1. All quotations from Shakespeare's plays come from the Riverside edition, edited by G. Blakemore Evans (Boston: Houghton Mifflin, 1974) and are included parenthetically in my text; T[through] L[ine] N[umbers] come from Charlton Hinman's facsimile of the First Folio (New York: W.W. Norton, 1968).

⁶ Whitworth, "Rectifying Shakespeare's *Errors*: Romance and Farce in Bardeditry" in *The Theory and Practice of Text-Editing*, ed. Ian Small and Marcus Walsh (Cambridge: Cambridge University Press, 1991): 107–41 (p. 114).

⁷ Egeon describes his offspring as being so alike that they could not be distinguished "but by names" (1.1.53), yet when we meet them they are onomastically identical. Plautus, aware that the farcical confusions of *Menaechmi* require a set of identical twins with identical names, gives elaborate background reasons for such double nomenclature: "He changed the name of the surviving brother / (Because, in fact, he much preferred the other) / And *Sosicles*, the one at home, became / *Menaechmus*—which had been his brother's name." (*The Brothers Menaechmus*, in Plautus, *The Pot of Gold and Other Plays*, trans E.F. Watling (Harmondsworth: Penguin, 1965), p. 104). William Warner's translation (1595), which may have been available to Shakespeare, is more succinct: *"The first his Father lost a little Lad, / The Grandsire namde the latter like his brother"* (I quote from the version printed in Geoffrey Bullough, *Narrative and Dramatic Sources of Shakespeare*, vol. 1 [London: Routledge and Kegan Paul, 1957], p. 13). Shakespeare, as Alexander Leggatt notes, "provides *two* sets of twins with the same name and not a word of explanation" (*Shakespeare's Comedy of Love* [London: Methuen, 1974], p. 3).

⁸ A.C. Hamilton, *The Early Shakespeare* (San Marino, CA: The Huntington Library, 1967), p. 96.

⁹ Eamon Grennan, "Arm and Sleeve: Nature and Custom in *Comedy of Errors*," *PQ* 59 (1980): 150–64 (p. 151).

¹⁰ Karen Newman, *Shakespeare's Rhetoric of Comic Character* (New York and London: Methuen, 1985), p. 81.

¹¹ The raised eyebrows and rolled eyes of the listening prostitutes in Trevor Nunn's 1976 RSC production showed that these women questioned the paradox, agreeing with the noun more than the adjective.

¹² Grennan, "Arm and Sleeve," p. 162.

¹³ See Paul Werstine, "'Foul Papers' and 'Prompt-Books': Printer's Copy for Shakespeare's *Comedy of Errors*," *SB* 41 (1988): 232–46 (p. 240). The Oxford *Complete Works* (gen. eds. Stanley Wells and Gary Taylor [Oxford: Clarendon Press, 1986]) over-helpfully reduces this protean character to the singular consistency of "Nell," an emendation based on the belief

that "Nell" represents an imperfect revision by Shakespeare to avoid confusion of Luciana/Luce. For arguments in favour of retaining "Luce" see Whitworth ("Rectifying Shakespeare's *Errors*," p. 124) and Werstine ("'Foul Papers'"). R.A. Foakes (ed., *The Comedy of Errors* [London: Methuen, 1963]) suggests that Shakespeare may initially have "thought of taking over into his play [from Plautus' *Menaechmi*] both the maid and a figure corresponding to the cook, Cylindrus" (p. xxv, n.1).

[14] See Werstine, "'Foul Papers'" for analysis of the unsatisfactory use of this term.

[15] Werstine, "'Foul Papers,'" p. 233, my italics.

[16] The role may originally have been played by John Sincler (Sincklo), an actor in Strange's or Admiral's Men c. 1590–1, and later in the Chamberlain's Men, whose thinness was commemorated in the Induction to *The Malcontent* (1604).

[17] As Robert Smallwood rightly objected, the introduction of a *Doppelgänger* reduced "the audience's participation in the joy of recognition and reconciliation...to simple curiosity about how the trick was done" ("Shakespeare at Stratford-upon-Avon, 1990," *SQ* 42 (1991): 34–59 [p. 35]). Carlo Goldoni's *I Due Gemelli Veneziani* (1748) shows the very different dramatic effects which result when *Menaechmi* is adapted with the aim of one actor playing two twins.

[18] In the BBC production the Duke's invitation for a *brief* synopsis is a response to the audible pity of the crowd; his two subsequent invitations to Egeon to continue are due to his increasing involvement with the tale. The on-stage crowd in the 1983 RSC production emulated and so reinforced the gestures with which Adriana accompanied her narrative (5.1.136–60), aware of the performance pressure in her tale. In the 1976 RSC version Antipholus and Dromio of Ephesus presented their material (5.1.214–54) as if in a court of law, conferring, consulting notes, and taking exhibits (such as the rope) from a briefcase.

[19] Wells, ed., *The Comedy of Errors*, p. 28; Berry, *Shakespeare and Social Class* (Atlantic Highlands, NJ: Humanities Press, 1988) p. 22 (my italics). Elsewhere Berry is more astute: "Certainly Adriana has overdone her complaints....But this is not the same thing as saying she has no grounds for complaint" (*Shakespeare's Comedies* [Princeton, NJ: Princeton University Press, 1972], p. 32).

[20] C.L. Barber, "Shakespearian Comedy in *The Comedy of Errors*," *College English* 25 (1964): 493–7 (p. 497); Germaine Greer, *Shakespeare* (Oxford: Oxford University Press, 1986), p. 119.

[21] Casting exigencies in the 1995 RSC *Tempest*, directed by David Thacker, forced the metamorphosis of "Adrian" into "Adriana," a tantalising link with *Errors*, although in production it proved a thematic cul de sac.

22 Mike Gwilym's Ephesian Antipholus (RSC, 1976) smoked, played cards, rolled dice, and consorted with a Mafioso merchant.

23 See D.J. Palmer, "Casting off the Old Man: History and St. Paul in *Henry IV*," *Critical Quarterly* 12 (1970): 26–83, and Palmer, *Ephesians*, in David Lyle Jeffrey, gen. ed., *A Dictionary of Biblical Tradition in English Literature* (Grand Rapids, MI: Eerdmans, 1992).

24 Bluma L. Trell, "The Temple of Artemis at Ephesos" in *The Seven Wonders of the Ancient World*, ed. Peter A. Clayton and Martin J. Price (London: Routledge, 1988), pp. 78–99 (p. 82).

25 Clive Foss, *Ephesus after Antiquity. A Late Antique, Byzantine and Turkish City* (Cambridge: Cambridge University Press, 1979), p. 11.

26 Foss, p. 23. The story is told by Eunapius in *Lives of the Philosophers*. See Philostratus and Eunapius, *The Lives of the Sophists*, trans. W.C. Wright (London: Heinemann, 1952), pp. 433–35.

27 Foss, p. 41.

28 *The Riverside Chaucer*, gen. ed. Larry D. Benson (Boston: Houghton Mifflin Company, 1987).

29 For this reason, productions of *Errors* which present the Dromios as circus clowns seem to me to miss the point. Clowns inhabit a world where crazy, illogical, violent, "magical" events are expected; the Dromios do not. Dromio of Syracuse and his master (like Vincentio in *The Taming of the Shrew*) are ordinary people going about their business; they unwittingly find themselves involved in an illusion. "Thus strangers may be haled and abused/bemused."

30 See also A.E. Harvey, *Companion to the New Testament* (Oxford University Press and Cambridge University Press, 1970).

31 In this same production Adriana's reaction to the news that Antipholus has maltreated the exorcist was delivered slowly, in a tone both condescending and soothing: "Peace, fool, thy master and his man are here, / And that is false thou dost report to us" (5.1. 178). The implication was that the kitchen-maid (who here delivered the Messenger's speech) was mad.

32 Whereas Nunn chose to underline the alliance of commercial and Christian in his choice of goldsmith's wares, the 1993 Manchester Royal Exchange production stressed the commercial and the pagan in its presentation of a modern-day Ephesus, epitomised by "port and terminus scurry as an eclectic hive of travellers—including *a City type carrying a Zulu spear and shield*—queue and hurry and squint at directions" (*Independent* March 9, 1993; my italics).

33 Guy MacLean Rogers, *The Sacred Identity of Ephesus* (London: Routledge, 1991), p. 11.

34 Edward Gibbon, *The Decline and Fall of the Roman Empire* (4 volumes. Reprinted London and New York: Frederick Warne and Co, 1894), vol.

1, p. 207.

[35] Sig. Aa3v. This work may have provided Shakespeare with the name of the Duke, Solinus, in *Errors*. See Foakes, ed., *Comedy of Errors*, p. xxx.

[36] *Ephesus Warning before Her Woe. A Sermon Preached at Pauls Crosse on Passion Sunday, the 17. of March last by Sampson Price* (1616).

[37] Edward Chaloner, *Ephesus Common Pleas* (a sermon preached in 1618, published 1623).

[38] Foakes, ed., *The Comedy of Errors*, p. xxxii.

[39] Solinus, translated by Warner, *Excellent and Pleasant Works*, sig. Aa3v; Thomas Heywood, *Gunaikeion* (1624), pp. 218–24; Walter Raleigh, *History of the World* (1614), p. 196.

[40] Trell, "The Temple of Artemis," pp. 82–3.

[41] Pausanius, *Description of Greece*, trans. W. H. S. Jones *et al.* (6 vols. London: Heinemann, 1918), Book IV, *Messenia* xxxi, para. 8 (p. 345). Although tradition has it that the temple "was founded by the Amazons during their campaign against Athens and Theseus," Pausanius tells us that the Temple of Artemis predates the Amazon association (pp. 175–7). Aparently the Amazons sought sanctuary in the temple, hence their association with it. This association led to their being credited with the founding of the temple. In the fifth century, four bronze statues of Amazons were chosen to decorate the temple pediment.

[42] See, for example, Philostratus, *The Life of Apollonius of Tyana* (2 vols. London: Heinemann, 1927), p. vi.

[43] *Gunaikeion* (1624), p. 220; *The Exemplary Lives and Memorable Acts of Nine the Most Worthy Women of the World* (1640), p. 220. Simon Shepherd deals with stage depictions of Amazons in *Amazons and Warrior Women* (Brighton: Harvester Press, 1981). For analogous discussions, see Susanne Woods, "Amazonian Tyranny: Spenser's Radigund and Diachronic Mimesis" in *Playing with Gender*, ed. Jean R. Brink, Maryanna C. Horowitz, and Allison P. Coudert (Urbana and Chicago: University of Illinois Press, 1991): 62–81; Margaret M. Sullivan, "Amazons and Aristocrats: The Function of Pyrocles' Amazon Role in Sidney's Revised *Arcadia*" in *ibid.*, 52–61; Priscilla Martin, *Chaucer's Women: Nuns, Wives and Amazons* (London: Macmillan, 1990); and Dympna Callaghan, "Cutting Up: Female Impersonation on the Early Modern Stage" (forthcoming in *Journal of Medieval and Early Modern Studies*, special issue on psychoanalysis). See also Celeste T. Wright, "The Amazons in Elizabethan Literature," *SP* 37 (1940): 433–56, and the entry under "Amazon" in Thomas L. Berger and William C. Bradford Jr, *An Index of Characters in English Printed Drama to the Restoration* (Englewood, CO: Microcard Editions, 1975).

[44] John Marston, *Antonio and Mellida*, ed. W. Reavley Gair (Manchester and New York: Manchester University Press, 1991), induction, ll. 70–1,

77–8.

[45] Nevo, *Comic Transformation in Shakespeare* (London and New York: Methuen, 1980), p. 25.

[46] The dress worn by Adriana in the second half of the BBC version had two circular gold/black bodice cups reminiscent of a military breastplate, while the tiara head-dress she wore throughout gave her a regal air.

[47] We might note here that Paul's departure from Ephesus in 57 A.D., plagued by storm and shipwreck, led to an attempt to winter in a Cretan harbour called Phoenix, and a voyage in a ship whose figurehead was the Twins (*Acts* 27 and 28). Furthermore, Paul, like many apostles, Jews, and Eastern peoples, adopted a name familiar in the Greco-Roman world, changing his identity from Saul to Paul.

[48] Lock-out scenes are not the prerogative of Plautus alone; one also appears in a Pauline epistle, describing an event that took place in Ephesus. In *Acts* some itinerant exorcists "planned to experiment by using the name of the Lord Jesus." The incantation they chose was "I adjure you by Jesus, whom Paul preaches, to come out!" They tried this on a possessed Ephesian, but the demon replied "I know Jesus and I know Paul, but who are you?" The possessed man then pounced on two of his exorcists and drove them out of his house into the street (19:13–16).

Similarly, Plautus does not have the monopoly on disguise and mistaken identity. In his sermon on *Ephesus Common Pleas* (see note 37), Edward Chaloner compares the devil's theatrical use of disguise to a scene from Plautus' *Amphitryo*, invoking *Acts* 14:12 in which the crowd compares Barnabas to Jupiter and Paul to Mercury. Chaloner's marginal reference further stresses the Pauline/Plautine connection. (A divine at Oxford, Chaloner had presumably seen college productions of Plautus.)

[49] The Courtesan in the 1983 RSC production ascended from beneath the stage, clad in red. To the typical (physical) stereotypes of the buxom, callipygian prostitute was thus added another (more ethereal) stereotype: the scarlet woman, the Whore of Babylon, rising through the stage trapdoor, the area associated on the Elizabethan stage with Hell.

[50] The text is inconsistent in the ages of the Antipholi who are presented as twenty-five (1.1.125; 5.1.321) and thirty-three (5.1.401).

[51] Wells, ed., *The Comedy of Errors*, p. 17.

[52] See Anthony J. Lewis, "'I Feed on Mother's Flesh': Incest and Eating in *Pericles*," *Essays in Literature* 15 (1988): 147–63.

[53] Berry, *Shakespeare and the Awareness of the Audience* (London: Macmillan, 1985), p. 39. This was indeed the impression in Trevor Nunn's production where Adriana's naked arm and shoulder emerged to close the shutters, and her red espadrille dropped from the balcony

(the shoe was later presented by Antipholus of Ephesus as "evidence" in his deposition of 5.1: see above, n.18). Antipholus of Syracuse subsequently departed shoeless, a red carnation between his teeth, clearly sexually exhausted. In the 1983 RSC production Adrian Noble made the "dinner" arrangements equally clear by concluding Adriana's invitation to the wrong husband in 2.2. with a clinch which Antipholus increasingly enjoyed: Dromio functioned as a chair for the embracing couple but such was Antipholus' ardour that he and Adriana collapsed in passion on the ground. The offstage intention was unambiguous.

[54] Berry, *Shakespeare and the Awareness of the Audience*, pp. 39–40. (Desmond Barritt's Antipholus in the 1990 RSC production made the double entendre clear in his slightly self-conscious announcement "I'll—ahem, 'knock'—elsewhere": 3.1.121.) Joseph Candido contrasts the Courtesan's "sexually symbolic open door" with the "shut house of the nameless wife" in *Menaechmi*. See "Dining Out in Ephesus: Food in *The Comedy of Errors*," *SEL* 30 (1990): 217–41 (p. 219).

[55] Berry, *ibid.*, p. 40.

[56] I am grateful to George Walton Williams for these caveats.

[57] Antipholus of Syracuse concludes his list of Ephesian iniquities with the summation "many such-like liberties" (1.2.102). Productions often illustrate this phrase with stage business that links it with sex, and hence with Adriana's rhetorical question. In the 1962 production Antipholus accompanied the phrase with hand gestures which indicated a female bosom; in 1976 Antipholus rotated his *Blue Guide* to admire what was obviously a centre-fold pin-up. Ephesus in the first century A.D. was renowned for self-indulgent leisure: "bordellos, singers, actors, playboys, whores" (Trell, "The Temple of Artemis," p. 86).

[58] See Roger Just, *Women in Athenian Law and Life* (London: Routledge, 1989) and Sarah B. Pomeroy, *Goddesses, Whores, Wives and Slaves* (New York: Schocken Press, 1975).

[59] For Ariadne in Chaucer and Gower see Wolfgang Riehle, *Shakespeare, Plautus, and the Humanist Tradition* (Cambridge: D.S. Brewer, 1990), p. 179.

[60] Nell is also the name of a kitchen-maid in *Romeo and Juliet*, who is requested to enter with Susan Grindstone (1.5.9).

[61] Juliet Dusinberre, *Shakespeare and the Nature of Women* (London: Macmillan, 1978), p. 55.

[62] Onomastic identity and malleability are very much to the fore in *Menaechmi*, *Amphitryo*, and the Tudor adaptation of *Amphitryo*, *Jack Juggler*. "And what's your name?"—"Any name that suits you" (*Amphitryo*, p. 243). "You can be Sossia as much as you like when I don't want to be. At the moment I am Sossia." "[D]id ye never heare why the Grecians termed *Hecuba* to be a bitch?...Because...she railed, and

therefore well deserved that dogged name" (*Menaechmi* in Bullough, p. 29). "For ought I se yet, betwene erneste and game, / I must go sike me an other name" (*Jack Juggler*, p. 79). Such flexibility extends even to geography, where the same stage represents different locations at different times. The prologue to *Menaechmi* (not included in Warner's translation) explains that the play's location is Epidamnus but when another play is performed on the same stage the location will be some other city (ed. Watling, p. 104). I cite *Amphitryo* from the translation by E.F. Watling (Harmondsworth: Penguin, 1964, reprinted 1972), and *Jack Juggler* from *Three Classical Interludes*, ed. Marie Axton (Cambridge: D.S. Brewer, 1982).

[63] Leggatt, *Shakespeare's Comedy of Love*, p. 18.

[64] Whether his attitude is playful or imperative is not relevant to this discussion; but if playful he is parodying by exaggeration conventional imperious behaviour.

[65] He refers to the Latin *servias/inservias*. See Thomas More, *Utopia*, trans. Robert M. Adams (1989) in *The Norton Anthology of English Literature*, sixth edition (New York: Norton, 1993), vol. 1, p. 418.

[66] *The French Schoolmaster* in *The Elizabethan Home Discovered in Two Dialogues by Claudius Hollyband and Peter Erondell*, ed. Muriel St. Clare Byrne (London: Etchells and Macdonald, 1925), p. 24.

[67] *Ibid.*, p. 28.

[68] William Gouge, *Treatises on Domestical Duties*, Treatise 8, para.23, p. 680. I quote from the edition of 1634; the first edition is 1622 (SR 1620).

[69] Ralph A. Houlbrooke, *The English Family 1450–1700* (London: Longman, 1974), p. 176.

[70] Thomas Becon, *The Catechism...with other pieces written by him in the Reign of Edward the sixth*, ed. John Ayre. *Parker Society* (Cambridge: Cambridge University Press, 1844), p. 362.

[71] Juan Luis Vives, *The Office and Duetie of an Husband* (1550), sigs. Kviiiv–Li.

[72] R.S. [Robert Snowse], *A Looking-Glass for Married Folkes* (1610), p. 54.

[73] Frances E. Dolan, *Dangerous Familiars* (Ithaca, NY: Cornell University Press, 1994), p. 67.

[74] *Arden of Faversham* combines both, creating a hybrid genre even more marked than that of *Errors*.

[75] BBC TV *Comedy of Errors* (London: BBC Books, 1984), p. 25.

[76] Leggatt, *Shakespeare's Comedy of Love*, p. 13.

[77] Robert S. Miola demonstrates the classical, comic antecedents of this testimony (*Shakespeare and Classical Comedy*, p. 23); but traditions of classical comedy have not stopped the narrative from being delivered seriously in production.

[78] Bullough, *Narrative and Dramatic Sources*, vol. 1, p. 35.

[79] *The New Jerusalem Bible* (London: Darton, Longman, and Todd, 1985).

[80] Trevor Nunn's production had Luciana read the speech from a book in which she showed her sister the relevant passage, indicating that the subject is non-negotiable.

[81] It is unclear whether Lysistrata is married or not; some translations have her refer to her husband, others to her "man" (the original Greek is clearly ambiguous). Peter Hall's production for the Old Vic (1993) paired her off with the Magistrate. Critics who view Lysistrata as married cite the improbability of the Athenian women agreeing to a sex-strike if the initiator were not imposing similar deprivation upon herself; those who view Lysistrata as single find a thematic parallel between Lysistrata, the guardian of Athens, and Athens' mythological protectress, the chaste, unmarried Athena.

[82] This point was made most intriguingly in the BBC production in the reassignment of a line which is marked for alteration but not reassignment in the published text; nor indeed can its reassignment be justified. In the Folio text Antipholus of Ephesus explains his origins: he was, he tells Duke Solinus, brought to Ephesus by "that most famous warrior, / Duke Menaphon, your most renowned uncle" (5.1.368–9). In the BBC film Solinus is given the line "Menaphon your most renowned uncle" (the deleted "Duke" showing that the reassignment is not accidental, although, perplexingly, the BBC *text* still assigns the line (minus the "Duke") to Antipholus). On screen Solinus delivers the line with epiphanic fervour as if realising that one more member of the family still remains to complete the reunion. Antipholus of Ephesus' roll of the eyes at the mention of Menaphon suggests that family (whether uncle/nephew, father/son, husband/wife) is not a concept with which he is at ease: he has deliberately ignored the ties that his brother has been so anxious to seek. (This at least is the only explanation I can give for a moment which has no authoritative textual basis. George Walton Williams astutely suggests that the reassignment is an error: in preparing the filmscript from the Alexander text someone interpreted the "Duke" of line 369 as a speech prefix and reassigned the ensuing words accordingly.)

[83] In the stage directions to 1.2 and 2.2 the Folio presents Antipholus of Syracuse as *Erotes* and *Errotis*, which editors take to be misreadings of *Erraticus* (wandering).

[84] I am grateful to David R. Carlson and to Robert S. Miola for generously sharing with me their classical and Shakespearean expertise, and to George Walton Williams for his careful scrutiny of textual details.

Figure 4. Williams production, 1962, Stratford-upon-Avon, RSC Theatre. Antipholus of Syracuse (Alec McCowan) wooing Luciana (Susan Maryott). Used with the permission of the Shakespeare Centre Library, Stratford-upon-Avon.

The Errors of the Verse:
Metrical Reading and Performance of
The Comedy of Errors

Brennan O'Donnell

> Music is to be fetched from the passed world.
> —Peter Ackroyd, *English Music*

1.

At least two peculiarities immediately face a reader or performer who tries to make sense of the versification of *The Comedy of Errors*. First and most obvious is the variety of kinds. The play shifts frequently and unpredictably back and forth from blank verse to rhymed iambic pentameter, prose, and, most disruptively, a widely variable non-iambic rhymed form that is commonly (and not very helpfully) labelled doggerel. Until fairly recently, this mingling of measures—and especially the co-presence of iambic and non-iambic verse—was taken as evidence of the uncertainty of the young Shakespeare's grasp of technical matters, or of multiple authorship of the play. As an eighteenth-century commentator put it, patches of "silk" alternate with swatches of "worsted."[1] The lyrical, perfectly "correct" iambic pentameter quatrains spoken by Antipholus of Syracuse and Luciana in act 3 scene 2 come on the heels of scenes dominated by "long hobbling verses" that are reminiscent of the antiquated versification of *Ralph Roister Doister*, *Gammer Gurton's Needle*, and other earlier adaptations of Roman comedy in English:

> Was there ever any man thus beaten out of season,
> When in the why and the wherefore is neither rhyme
> > nor reason?[2]

This kind of verse virtually disappears from Shakespeare's canon after *The Comedy of Errors*, *The Taming of the Shrew*, and *Love's Labour's Lost*. And, except for *Love's Labour's Lost* and *A Midsummer Night's Dream*, no play uses rhyme as extensively as does *The Comedy of Errors*.[3]

The second peculiarity is the blank verse, which lacks the kind of subtle variety that the adjective Shakespearean usually calls to mind. Considered alongside the verse of *King Lear* or *The Tempest*, the blank verse of *The Comedy of Errors* is relatively unindividuated. As George T. Wright has most recently and convincingly shown, much of the power of Shakespeare's later verse derives from the basic aesthetic tension between a simple metrical pattern—the ten-syllable line with five alternating beats and offbeats that we call iambic pentameter—and an astoundingly complex array of syntactic and phonetic structures.[4] At its most impressive, this blank verse can amass so many departures from its conventional "rules" in so short a span that it seems almost to operate on a level beyond its metrical pattern, as if it depended for its shape and structure on nothing except the individuated expression of a speaker's passion. Wright points to Prospero's speech in act 5 scene 1 of *The Tempest* as a particularly rich example of Shakespeare's metrical art. (Only those metrical feet that exhibit obvious kinds of departures from the norm are marked; - = unstressed, / = stressed, \ = secondary stress):

> I have bedimm'd
>
> The noontide sun, | call'd forth | the mutinous winds,
>
> And 'twixt the green | sea and | the azur'd vault
>
> Set roaring war; | to the | dread rat | tling thunder
>
> Have I given fire, and rifted Jove's | stout oak
>
> With his | own bolt; | the strong-base'd promontory
>
> Have I made shake, and by the spurs | pluck'd up
>
> The pine and cedar. Graves at my command

Have wak'd their sleepers, op'd, and let 'em forth

By my | so po | tent art....   (*Tempest*, 5.1.41–50)

Sentences overflow line endings, so that the paragraph, not the line, becomes the basic aesthetic unit; mid-line pauses fall in varied places in successive lines; eleven-syllable lines with unstressed (or feminine) endings occur frequently; lines are slowed by spondaic patterns or quickened by leveling or omission of expected stresses.

There is nothing in the blank verse of *The Comedy of Errors* to match this. But then there is nothing like this in *any* English drama before Shakespeare developed the blank verse of the great tragedies and romances. Unrhymed iambic pentameter was a fresh and still largely unexplored medium on the English stage in the early 1590s, when *The Comedy of Errors* appeared. The verse that Shakespeare and his audiences might have heard in works by Sackville and Norton, Kyd, Peele, and others was not nearly so flexible a medium as that through which Shakespeare was later to make his indelible mark on English verse music. Even Marlowe, the most metrically daring and accomplished of dramatic poets before Shakespeare, shows little of the kind of potent art out of which the distinctive voice of a Prospero would emerge. Marlowe's mighty *line* is the chief unit of organization, and that line's solid structure tends to make itself felt even in so thematically adventurous and restless a speech as that of Tamburlaine at the height of his ambition:

Our souls, whose faculties can comprehend
The wondrous architecture of the world,
And measure every wandering planet's course,
Still climbing after knowledge infinite,
And always moving as the restless spheres,
Until we reach the ripest fruit of all,
That perfect bliss and sole felicity,
The sweet fruition of an earthly crown.[5]

Shakespeare's early blank verse style, though decidedly not monolithic, is much closer to this than it is to the style of *The*

Tempest. The subtle shifts of pace and complex interplay of phrase and line that mark the great speech of Prospero are not frequently on display here. Instead, the line itself tends to be preserved as an important element of structure, as in this passage from Egeon's opening narration:

> Five summers have I spent in farthest Greece,
> Roaming clean through the bounds of Asia,
> And, coasting homeward, came to Ephesus—
> Hopeless to find, yet loath to leave unsought
> Or that or any place that harbors men.
> But here must end the story of my life,
> And happy were I in my timely death
> Could all my travels warrant me they live. (1.1.132–139)

Study of the verse of the play, then, begins with an acknowledgment that its rhythms and its metrical varieties are, like the play's observation of the neo-classical unities of time and place, not what we have come to expect from Shakespeare. Wolfgang Riehle has tried to account for the play's metrical peculiarities by arguing that Shakespeare would have considered metrical "liberty" as a generic requirement of Plautine comedy. Editions of the Roman comic playwrights emphasize the variety of meters and the relationship of the plays to music, and works such as Erasmus's *De Ratione Studii* advise schoolmasters to "be careful to point out the type of meter" to students reading Roman comedy.[6] Others, noting that elaborately varied and rhymed verse cuts across genres in Shakespeare's work of the earlier 1590s (in *Love's Labour's Lost, Richard the Third* and *Romeo and Juliet,* for example), would advance more broadly biographical explanations. Plague suspended theatrical activity for a time in 1592–3; Shakespeare turned to rhymed poetry to make his living (in *Venus and Adonis* and *The Rape of Lucrece*); the habit of rhyme carried over into the plays of this period.[7] Whatever Shakespeare's motivation, the fact is that the versification of *The Comedy of Errors* clearly manifests the same kind of "virtuoso... exhibitionism" that Wells and Taylor see in the diction and figures of the play.[8] Conditioned as we are by Shakespearean metrical subtlety, recovering the "other" music of this exhibitionist Shakespeare may require some close analytic attention and some imaginative effort.

2.

The most obvious displays of exhibitionist versification occur in the mingling of passages in rhyme—in pentameter couplets, quatrains, and non-iambic couplets—with blank verse. If shifts from unrhymed to rhymed verse tend to foreground the verse of a predominantly blank-verse play, then the verse of *The Comedy of Errors* is very frequently on display. The play begins with a couplet, which, along with another couplet at lines 26–27, frames a blank-verse speech in which the Duke sentences Egeon. After Egeon's long blank-verse narrative of his woes, the Duke's second speech ends with an ominous rhyme on the words "custody" and "die." The scene ends with yet another couplet, spoken by Egeon. The rhymes and heavy alliteration of Egeon's couplets emphasize endings and, like a tolling bell, sound the key theme of the old man's impending doom:

Proceed, Solinus, to procure my fall
And by the doom of death end woes and all.   (1.1.1–2)

...

Yet this my comfort, when your words are done
My woes end likewise with the evening sun.   (1.1.26–27)

...

Hopeless and helpless doth Egeon wend,
But to procrastinate his lifeless end.   Exeunt.(1.1.157–58)

Punctuating a scene dominated by a legal pronouncement and a past-tense narrative of the fatal voyage that began Egeon's woes, the closed rhymes emphasize the scene's restriction of speech chiefly to its delimiting or prohibitive functions: the scene sounds repeatedly the elegiac theme of "never again" and the legal injunction "thou shalt not," the two themes against which the main energies of the comedy will strain. Whenever the bell tolls or reference is made to the passing of time, it may be heard to echo these pat, rhymed summations and the intractable sentence uttered here by the Duke:

>...thou art adjudged to the death,
>And passed sentence may not be recalled.   (1.1.146–147)

The scene sounds the keynote that reminds its audience what is at stake in the erring twists of the plot. Its metrical structures suggest summation and closure even before the action begins, emphasizing the irony of an opening scene that looks like an ending.

Stanley Wells is right, I think, to call attention to the "adagio" pace of act 1 scene 1 as crucial to any performance of the play. The doom-sounding couplets help to reinforce the tendency of the blank verse toward a slow and serious presentation, and Egeon's entire *narratio* acts as a rhythmic foil, setting off the "vivacity of the action that is to follow."[9] The rhythmic and sonic qualities of the blank verse spoken by Egeon do not allow rapid or glib presentation, and directors who would play the scene lightly, undercutting the dignity of Egeon and the seriousness of his predicament, must strain against the scene's intrinsic prosodic features. Verse as heavily end-stopped and as rhetorically measured as Egeon's simply cannot be performed rapidly without doing violence to its integrity. Egeon utters "what [his] sorrow gives [him] leave" in short phrases with frequent pauses:

>Yet the incessant weepings of my wife,
>Weeping before for what she saw must come,
>And piteous plainings of the pretty babes,
>That mourned for fashion, ignorant what to fear,
>Forced me to seek delays for them and me.   (1.1.70–74)

The single sentence—her "weepings...forced me to seek delays"—is measured out over the five lines, one end-stopped clause at a time.

The slow pace also allows for emblematic, as well as expressive, effects, as Shakespeare develops in these opening speeches a number of fairly complex and thematically significant sonic patterns. Note, for example, how a clever balancing of line-beginning and line-ending sounds underpins Egeon's presentation of an image, crucial to the plot, of the polarization and eventual division of the household into equal parts. Expecting shipwreck, Egeon and Emilia each fasten one of the

twin children and one of the twin servants to either end of a
"spare mast":

> The children thus disposed, my wife and I,
> / -   - /   -   /   - /   - /
> Fixing our eyes on whom our care was fixed,
> / -   - /   - / - /   - /
> Fastened ourselves at either end the *mast*
> And, floating straight, obedient to the stream,
> Was carried towards Corinth.... (1.1.83–87; italics added)

The exact rhythmic parallel of lines 84 and 85 emphasizes the
presence of duplicated (fixing/fixed) or rhymed (fast/mast)
syllables at "either end" of the lines, creating a kind of structural
integrity that functions as an aural emblem of the impending
divorce or wife from husband, brothers from brothers. Evidence
that this kind of sonic play is part of Shakespeare's metrical
repertoire is provided by a similarly emblematic use of mid-line
pause in the line that tells of the immediate aftermath of the
fateful encounter with the "mighty rock" that "splitted" the mast
"in the midst":

> So that, in this unjust divorce of us,
> Fortune had left to both of us alike
> / - - / - (x)   / - / - \
> What to delight in, // what to sorrow for. (1.1.104–106)

Five syllables fall before the pause; five fall after. The weak stress
("for") before the full stop at line's end echoes the unstressed
syllable ("in") before the strong mid-line pause. Two strong
stresses in the first half are answered by two in the second.
Grammatically and metrically parallel clauses articulate the
paradox that each parent, in having what the other has not, has
both his or her chief delight and chief sorrow.

This elaborately stylized verse has been called "wooden,"
which I understand to mean lacking verisimilitude as imitated
speech adapted to the precise dramatic moment.[10] So it is. But
such woodenness can be effective in its own way. The slow pace
and elaborate architectonics create a distinctive texture that will
be associated throughout the play with Egeon's fate. In a set of

speeches denotatively dominated by endings, by the limits imposed by time, fate, and legality, the almost schematic formality of Egeon's speech is an expression of his own sense that his well-worn story is at an end:

> Hopeless and helpless doth Egeon wend,
> But to procrastinate his lifeless end. (1.2.157–8)

At the same time, other elements of the *narratio* tend to hint at more in Egeon's story than he at present is prepared to see (or hear, or let us hear). The key motifs of his tale—coincidental births, a sea voyage, a fateful storm, a divorcing rock, a rescue by Corinthian fishermen—are, as Robert Miola suggests, charged with a kind of double agency. In his narrative, these add up to a long chain of baffling contingencies culminating in his being condemned to death. At the same time, Egeon seems to sense, though "dimly," that these same elements may form a very different chain of evidence. Not all the "hap" he narrates is bad, and the "heavens" have been merciful. Instead of meaningless wanderings leading inexorably to misfortune, the events in his narrative may be signs of "a mysterious order," "hints of some unfathomable chain of command and obedience, of some providential order."[11] Egeon's "wooden" tone, with its settled formality and insistent (and slightly too pat) rhymes, then, registers that he is reading the signs of his own narrative with an emphasis on its more dismal interpretation. Coming as it does at the beginning of a play, and in a speech that offers so many hints of that "mysterious order" that Egeon only dimly glimpses, however, the incongruous finality of his tone may direct an audience to those submerged possibilities to which he cannot, yet, give voice. Solinus's irrevocable sentence surely cannot be the last word.

The versification of the rest of the play features departures from the pace and pattern of this opening scene so frequent, various, and extreme that one might well suspect an emblematic purpose behind Shakespeare's art. Shifts from one kind of blank verse to another—and from blank verse to couplets, quatrains, prose and non-iambic long lines—help to make of the sound texture of the play an embodiment of its main paradox: that wandering leads to destined ends, that error embodies an order more rich and strange than that comprehended by the laws of Ephesus. The first of many extreme shifts in pace coincides with the first of many errors of the plot, when Dromio of Ephesus mistakes Antipholus of Syracuse for his master, and proceeds to harangue him. The passage is a metrically simple, rhetorically elaborate *tour de force*, a textbook example of what Puttenham calls "clymax" or "the marching figure":[12]

> Returned so soon! Rather approached too late:
> The capon burns, the pig falls from the spit;
> The clock hath strucken twelve upon the bell
> My mistress made it one upon my cheek.
> She is so hot because the meat is cold;
> The meat is cold because you come not home;
> You come not home because you have no stomach;
> You have not stomach, having broke your fast.
> But we that know what 'tis to fast and pray
> Are penitent for your default today.   (1.2.43–52)

This is blank verse, but of a very different kind from that employed to create the elegiac tones of Egeon. It is also very different from the verse on display in the immediately preceding meditative soliloquy of Antipholus of Syracuse:

> I to the world am like a drop of water
> That in the ocean seeks another drop,
> Who, falling there to find his fellow forth,
> Unseen, inquisitive, confounds himself;
> So I to find a mother and a brother,
> In quest of them, unhappy, lose myself.   (1.2.35–40)

Antipholus's tones here announce him as very much his father's son. Note, for example, the slow pace (created in part by the nine monosyllabic words of the first line, and the multiple pauses in the fourth and sixth verses), the short phrases, the fairly subtly patterned sound in the alliteration of "falling...find...fellow forth," the internal rhyme on nouns denoting key relationships (mother/brother), and the line ending *homoeteleuton* in himself/myself, which is the first of many sonic plays on pronouns, those thematically crucial parts of speech.

Directly following this, Dromio's metrically elementary and rapid play on words should provide an audience (as it surely does the mournfully contemplative Antipholus) with a rhythmic jolt. Dromio bewilders Antipholus both because his words are incomprehensible and because his tone (marked in part by rhythm) is inappropriate to the serious situation. Word play is maddening to a man bent on finding himself, and Dromio's playful and punning verbosity leads Antipholus first to suspect he is being "flouted" (that is, played like a flute) and then by the end of the scene to wonder if Ephesus is bewitched. The genius of the scene is, of course, that nothing has been said that does not make perfect sense, in its proper context. No deliberate deceit, no "cozenage," bewilders Antipholus.[13] Dromio gets a beating and Antipholus is left shaken because the plot has contrived a linguistic situation in which speakers are doomed to have their words mean other than what they intend.

Hence the important role of puns throughout the play. Puns function despite our attempts at control ("no pun intended") to remind us how precarious the relationship of thought, word, and thing really is, how dependent it is on conventional assumptions and extra-linguistic contexts. Puns are tiny eruptions of coincidence that challenge our belief that we can say what we mean, and mean what we say. The oscillation of mind between denotative and figurative meanings, serious and frivolous connotations, and rationally directed and anarchic speech motives can cause delight (a small, poetic, shock of surprise at a loophole in the web of language) or annoyance (the groan that usually accompanies a pun in otherwise rational conversations). In this play, puns are the linguistic equivalent of the visual doubling of the two sets of twins.[14] We groan at visual and phonetic misapprehensions both, insofar as they work against our desire for order. At the same time, we are led to understand, with delight, that these mistakes are also the effects of (and therefore clues to) an underlying reality that no character yet can grasp, but that will force Solinus in the end to do the impossible—to revoke the irrevocable "passed sentence" (1.1.146–147). The Ephesian Dromio's speech is incomprehensible wind to

Antipholus of Syracuse only because Antipholus does not yet see what we see—that he has come to the end of his search. Once he has come face-to-face with this "calendar" of both his own and his brother's nativity, however, it is only a matter of time before the visual mistakes are rectified, and speech once again is contextualized within the renewed relationships of Egeon's household. Error begets the possibility of a transformation of time from the agent of separation and irrecoverable loss it seems to be in act 1 ("so long grief") to the source of reconciliation, new life, and joy that it becomes in act 5 ("such nativity!"). The rhythmic and phonetic disruptions that accompany and embody error, then, may be understood paradoxically as aural markers of progress toward comic ends.

If rhythms that depart from the relatively static sonorities of the opening scene mark progress, then the lockout scene (act 3 scene 1) is a lurch forward. This is where the largest patch of "worsted" appears in the midst of the play's "silk." Eighteenth-century critics were right to describe the verse of the lockout scene as startlingly different from the rest of the play. To understand what might have been the dramatic use or effect of that difference, however, we need to go beyond the metaphoric contrast of crude and refined, and beyond subsequent dismissals of the verse as mere "doggerel."

The "doggerel" of act 3 scene 1 is actually a kind of accentual or strong-stress verse, probably derived from the native English alliterative line.[15] Occurring commonly in drama of the earlier sixteenth century, strong-stress verse all but disappeared from the English stage once blank verse appeared.[16] Iambic and strong-stress verse did not share the same stage for long because the two kinds embody antithetical prosodic systems. Martin Halpern has argued that all non-iambic verse in English, including trochaic, anapestic, dactylic, and the kind of syllabically variable verse that Shakespeare uses in this scene, differs from iambics chiefly because it tends to enforce *isoaccentual* and *isochronic* performance. This means that each accented syllable is perceived as bearing approximately the same stress as all other accented syllables (*isoaccentual*) and that these generically strong stresses are felt to fall at regularly timed intervals (*isochronic*).[17] These meters tend to enforce a metronomic movement from stress to (equivalent) stress, even at the expense of recalcitrant syllables, which tend to be demoted or promoted to fulfill the insistent pattern:

    /   /   /   /
Tyger, tyger burning bright
In the forests of the night

The first line of Blake's poem starts a metrical beat that will dominate the entire poem. Within its metrical context, the second line cannot be given its natural pronunciation:

 -   - / -   -   - /
In the forests of the night

It must conform to the pattern, and the normally unstressed syllables "in" and "of" are promoted to full stresses:

 /   /   /   /
In the forests of the night

This fitting of phonetic material to an insistent meter is common in the kind of strong-stress verse that dominates English drama of the early sixteenth century, in which the number of syllables between strong stresses varies widely:

   /   /   /   /
As Gammer Gurton with many a wide stitch
   /   /   /   /
Sat piecing and patching of Hodge her man's breech,
   /   /   /   /
By chance or misfortune as she her gear tossed
   /   /   /   /
In Hodge's leather breeches her needle she lost.[18]

In such verse, promotion of normally unstressed syllables in full-stress (ictic) positions and demotion of normally stressed syllables in unstressed (non-ictic) positions is accompanied by a tendency to bundle various numbers of syllables together for isochronic performance: such rhythmic units as the first part of the first quoted line [As Gam-] and the ending of that same line [-ny a wide stitch] are experienced as equivalent sequences in time, despite their very different syllable counts. This last effect probably encourages elision wherever possible among the unstressed syllables, and helps account for the sense of spontaneity and rapidity that these long lines (paradoxically) are frequently able to create:

$$\acute{S}ay \ what \ you \ w\acute{i}ll, \ sir, \ but \ I \ kn\acute{o}w \ what \ I \ kn\acute{o}w.$$

That you beat me at the mart, I have your hand to show

$$[me \ a'th'mart?] \qquad [your \ 'an't'show?]$$

(*Errors* 3.1.11–12)

This meter, like the native alliterative verse to which it is related, also tends to enforce a fairly uniform placement of pause, drawing upon a natural tendency in all speech to gravitate toward simple binary rhythms and hierarchies based upon such rhythms.[19] The basic alternation of stress and unstress in speech is binary. These binary groups tend in popular verse to be echoed at the level of the line's structure, so that a line will in effect be two equivalent half-lines, with the pause falling in the middle:

E. DROMIO
                               (x)
    What patch is made our porter? // My master stays in the
                                               street.

S. DROMIO
                                 (x)
    Let him walk from whence he came, // lest he catch cold
                                          on 's feet
                                       (3.1. 36–37)

Note, too, that alliteration frequently serves as a kind of internal timing device, marking key stresses (patch/porter; stays/street; came/cold).

Iambic verse breaks free of isoaccentual and isochronic constraints, allowing what prosodists call the relative-stress principle to function. In iambic verse, syllables are not heard or felt as absolutely stressed or unstressed, but as stressed relative to the unstressed syllables with which they are in regular alternation, and in degrees that vary from other stresses in a line or passage (numbers above the line approximate degrees of stress required by syllables in ictic positions, 4 = strongest; 1 = weakest):

E. ANTIPHOLUS

<pre>
 4   4   1   3   4
But here's a villain that would face me down

 3   1   3   1   4
He met me on the mart, and that I beat him

 4   1   3   4   4
And charged him with a thousand marks in gold,

 2   3   4   4   4
And that I did deny my wife and house.

 4   4   3   4   3
Thou drunkard, thou, what didst thou mean by this?
</pre>

(3.1. 6–10)

The relative-stress principle accounts in large part for the dramatic adaptability of blank verse. The numbers assigned above to stressed syllables show how variously individual lines may be stressed. They also suggest how open to interpretive modulation any of these stresses might be in any one performance. Is "mean" in the last line really a "4"? Might it be a "3" and the final syllable—"this"—a "4"? Even if one posits only four degrees of stress, a single line of iambic pentameter has theoretically 4^5 or over one thousand different possibilities for its stress contour. The five-stress line, too, allows the poet to break free from the pull of binary grouping when it comes to placement of pause. The uneven number of stresses allows for great flexibility in stress grouping, which in turn provides opportunities for great variety in the pace of a line. Add to this the subtle variations that may be effected through enjambement, and the attractiveness of blank verse as a medium for presentation of individualized dramatic voices expressing a range of emotions becomes apparent.

If the blank verse of *The Comedy of Errors* does not exploit these possibilities as fully as would Shakespeare's later verse, it nonetheless allows for much greater modulation of voice and dramatic propriety than would be possible in the isoaccentual and isochronic verse of act 3 scene 1. The poet who could write the exchange between Antipholus and Dromio in act 1 scene 2 could not have been insensitive to what he lost by reverting to the already outdated strong-stress measures of the 1550s, 60s, and

70s. The effect in the theater must have been something like watching Cary Grant and Katharine Hepburn suddenly transformed into silent-film comedians in the middle of *The Philadelphia Story*. The question becomes, then, what did he gain?

Appropriately for the *The Comedy of Errors*, with its emphasis on identity and especially on finding oneself by losing oneself, Shakespeare gained precisely what he lost in writing such strangely unwieldy verse. Adopting the antiquated measures of the knock-about farces of popular theater, he emphatically homogenized the individual voices of the scene. The meter and rhyme, like a mask that transforms distinct voices to its own tone, or like some acoustic equivalent of the effect of darkness on visual perception, makes all voices sound virtually identical. The presentation of homogeneous voices creates an acoustic anarchy that helps to bring the complexities of the double plot to the "very pitch," in Harry Levin's words, of "dramatic subversion."[20] The outsider is inside and the insider has been excluded. Servants exert power over masters. Twin brother echoes twin brother. Note how the Syracusan Dromio picks up not only the meter, but the pauses and the alliteration of his brother:

E. DROMIO
    Maud, Bridget, Marian, Cicely, Gillian, Ginn!

S. DROMIO [*Speaking from the other side of the door*]
    Mome, malt-horse, capon, coxcomb, idiot patch
    Either get thee from the door or sit down at the hatch.
                            (3.1.31–33)

Servant berates master in shared lines and couplets that give the underling the last words:

E. ANTIPHOLUS
  Thou baggage, let me in.
LUCE   Can you tell for whose sake?
E. DROMIO
  Master, knock the door hard.
LUCE   Let him knock till it ache.

E. ANTIPHOLUS
You'll cry for this, minion, if I beat the door down.
                                              [*He knocks.*]
LUCE
What needs all that, and a pair of stocks in the town?
                                              (3.1.57–60)

Wife repulses husband with a line that mimics his speech rhythm and closes the couplet with a brilliant trisyllabic rhyme. The sound of the line makes it the verbal equivalent of a slammed door:

E. ANTIPHOLUS
Are you there, wife? You might have *come before*
ADRIANA
Your wife, sir knave? Go get you *from the door.* (62–3)
                                              [*Exit with Luce.*]

In the course of this extremely fast-paced exchange, characters become linguistic puppets in a scene of hilarious confusion. The devolution of the relatively subtle rhythmic expression of the first two acts into this gaggle of echoic repulses serves as an aural correlative to the baffling loss of identity that each character is undergoing.

Shakespeare continues to exploit relationships between the rhythms of his speakers' voices and their progress toward the new identities required by his comic order in the very next scene, when Antipholus of Syracuse finds himself swept away by Luciana. As the scene shifts inside, the music of the play undergoes a complete transformation. The quatrains that Luciana speaks and to which Antipholus responds in kind are as lyrically modulated and richly textured as the tumbling verse of the lockout scene is boisterous and uncouth:

And may it be that you have quite forgot
 A husband's office? Shall, Antipholus,
Even in the spring of love, thy love springs rot?
 Shall love, in building, grow so ruinous?
If thou did wed my sister for her wealth,
 Then for her wealth's sake use her with more kindness;

Or if you like elsewhere, do it by stealth;
Muffle your false love with some show of blindness.

                                                                    (3.2.1–8)

The alternate rhyme of the quatrain and the variable stresses and pauses permitted by the pentameter encourage and accommodate longer, more elaborate, syntactic structures than the four-stress couplets of the lockout could accommodate. The slow pace allows Antipholus (and the audience) time for appreciation not only of the argument but of its aural sensuousness. Note, for example, the sonic chiasmus in the third line, where the reversed repetition of sound in "spring of love" and "love springs" emphasizes the witty play on "spring." Notable, too, is the use of disyllabic (feminine) rhymes both in the passage quoted (kindness/blindness) and throughout the scene (tainted / acquainted [ll. 13,15], love us / move us [ll. 22,24]). Their heightened sensuality helps to give Luciana's speech and the entire scene overtones of a slightly Italianate lyricism and eroticism.

As the scene progresses, it becomes clear that the identity of the Syracusan Antipholus is no less imperiled by his having been taken into the house (and its linguistic universe) than his brother's was in being shut out in the noise of the street. The single Antipholus finds himself alone with a woman who acts in unaccountable ways. She and her sister have practically dragged him into their home, and now she counsels him in the ways of love and deception in the lush rhythms and tones of a courtly lyric. As he responds in kind, adapting his speech to her measures, the sound of his speech becomes a chief support of his claim to be, quite literally, enchanted:

Teach me, dear creature, how to think and speak;
Lay open to my earthy-gross conceit,
Smothered in errors, feeble, shallow, weak,
The folded meaning of your words' deceit
        . . .
Are you a god? Would thou create me new?
Transform me, then, and to your power I'll yield.

                                                        (3.2.33-36, 39–40)

Transported out of himself by Luciana's singing, he goes on to figure her as a mermaid or siren and himself as a mariner in danger of drowning:

> O, train me not, sweet mermaid, with thy note,
> To drown me in thy sister's flood of tears!
> Sing, siren, for thyself and I will dote.
> Spread o'er the silver waves thy golden hairs...
> And as a bed I'll take them and there lie
> And in that glorious supposition think
> He gains by death that hath such means to die.
> Let Love, being light be drownèd if she sink! (3.2.45–52)

The imagery harks back to his first soliloquy, in which he compares himself to a drop of water in danger of losing itself in the sea: "I to the world am like a drop of water / That in the ocean seeks another drop" (1.2.35–36). The difference between that measured, sorrowful and elegiac blank verse and the agitated quatrains here marks rhythmically how far Antipholus has moved into that ontological no-man's land through which Shakespeare's bewildered characters move. Shakespeare transforms the poetics of his character's speech from the elegiac to the erotic, hinting through a suggestion of an impending generic shift the character's movement from death-in-life to the possibility of his rebirth through love.

Nor is Luciana free from peril. She has been characterized as a *raisonneuse*—a "mouthpiece of moderation" and the "voice of reason and tolerance."[21] The prosody of her first extended speech, in which she counsels Adriana on the boundaries of women and the due subjugation of wives to their husbands, certainly supports such a characterization. In that scene, Shakespeare gives Luciana's speech an almost neo-classical feel. Closed couplets, syntactic parallelism, and rhetorical sophistication give her speech epigrammatic force. Parts of it would not be out of place in the *Essay on Man*:

> There's nothing situate under heaven's eye
> But hath his bound, in earth, in sea, in sky.

The beasts, the fishes, and the wingèd fowls
Are their males' subjects and at their controls.   (2.1.16–19)

Trevor Nunn's decision to play this speech as if Luciana were reading from a book of *sententiae* shows a good ear for their studied artificiality (while, incidentally, diminishing Luciana by suggesting that she could not achieve such wise and pointed speech unaided). The couplets stand out as evidence of Luciana's effectiveness as *raisonneuse* and rhetorician.[22] They also provide a form of rhythmic order against which the prosodic disruption of her sister's two main speeches may better be appreciated:

What ruins are in me that can be found
By him not ruined? Then is he the ground
Of my defeatures...
...
So he would keep fair quarter with his bed!
I see the jewel best enamelèd
Will lose his beauty; yet the gold bides still
That others touch, and often touching will
Wear gold...   (2.2.95–97, 107–111)

Shakespeare breaks the couplet three times in the span of sixteen lines, including a back-to-back occurrence in the last four lines of the quotation. The last couplet employs an especially strained enjambement, breaking in the middle of the verb: "still / ...will / Wear gold." Adriana's speech is as uncomfortably situated athwart the moderating measures of the couplet as her sister's is at home within them.[23]

Throughout the scene, Luciana supplies not only the answers, but the answering rhymes, to her sister's complaints, repeatedly turning the implications of her sister's impatient queries back upon her and creating out of Adriana's desperation a catechism of wifely forbearance:

ADRIANA
But, were you wedded, you would bear some sway.
LUCIANA
Ere I learn love, I'll practice to obey.

ADRIANA
How if your husband start some other where?
LUCIANA
Till he come home again, I would forbear.

(2.1.28–31)

Her scene-ending line is particularly effective in this regard. Adriana believes she has summed up the issue with a couplet as formally overwrought as it is lugubriously morbid. (Note the assonance and internal rhyme—*please* / *weep* / *weeping*, the alliteration on *w*, and the pathetic effect of the late pause in the second line):

Since that my beauty cannot please his eye,
I'll weep what's left away, and weeping die.

(2.1.113–114)

Luciana's single line undercuts both the thematic and formal closure here. In opening up the couplet into a triplet, she ends the scene by transforming Adriana's speech from a pathetic lament to an *exemplum* of foolishness:

How many fond fools serve mad jealousy.   (2.1.115)

From first to last in this scene, Luciana's ability to make the sound the echo of the sense is part of her characterization as a moderating figure.

But if music can moderate and calm, it can also move to passionate action. Like the Ephesian Dromio's innocently cheerful greeting of Antipholus of Syracuse (in act 1 scene 2), which fetches him a beating and leaves Antipholus suspecting "cozenage," Luciana's plea to Antipholus on behalf of her sister turns in its listener's ear into something very different from what was intended. The intent of her speech is, like her homily to Adriana, to chasten and correct the listener. The beauty of its versification, however, works as a kind of aural equivalent of a cinematic soft focus; we hear her voice as the smitten and bewildered Antipholus may be supposed to hear it. The counsel of a sister-in-law is heard as the seduction of a lover.

In the lines that follow Antipholus's lyrical lovemaking, the use of couplets signals a turning of tables on Luciana. Now it is she who has the impulses of her speech diverted to other ends than she intended, as Antipholus supplies the answering rhymes:

LUCIANA
What, are you mad, that you do reason so?
ANTIPHOLUS
Not mad, mute mated—how, I do not know.

(3.2.53–54)

Antipholus's verbal flanking action is perhaps most impressively exemplified in lines 59–61, where he answers Luciana's protests twice within a single line:

LUCIANA
Why call you me "love"? Call my sister so.
ANTIPHOLUS
Thy sister's sister.
LUCIANA
That's my sister.
ANTIPHOLUS
No,
It is thyself, mine own self's better part.

The tripartite shared line (the only such instance in the play), ending with Antipholus's couplet-closing rhyme, marks the complete transformation of Luciana's speech. Misheard by the enchanted Antipholus, her counsel is echoed back as an imperiling proposition. His phonological linkage of "self" with "self" in the final quoted line suggests possibilities that force her to flee the stage. If the dialogue between Luciana and Antipholus is played with sensitivity to just how enchanting the sound of her voice is to him, this later exchange (in 4.2), in which Luciana is recounting to her sister Antipholus's strange proposal, should get a laugh:

LUCIANA
First he did praise my beauty, then my speech.

ADRIANA
  Didst speak him fair?   (4.2.15–16)

Adriana asks a fair question. Luciana's chastisement has *sounded*
like seduction.

3.

Such examples of metrical sophistication suggest that much
of what happens in *The Comedy of Errors* happens in the ear. The
shifts among varieties of verse, the insistent use of puns, rhyme,
assonance, alliteration, and other devices of sound make the play
one of the noisiest in Shakespeare's corpus. This play seems
particularly aware that an audience is an *audience*, not an
assembly of onlookers. When Antipholus blurts out the question
that articulates the key aesthetic figure in the play, he pointedly
extends the theme of illusion to the ear: "What error drives our
eyes and ears amiss?" Vocal exhibitionism of all kinds does for
the audience's ears what the double twinning of man and master
does for the eyes. Nobody wears a disguise, yet everyone
misidentifies someone; nearly all of the speeches are spoken
without any intent to deceive, yet almost every speech drives
someone to suspect that sorcery, enchantment, or "cozenage" is
afoot.

The theme of miscommunication, of sense experience
transformed through coincidence, is pursued with delight
throughout the play, but not without serious overtones. The clock
that has been ticking since the first act becomes more and more
insistently present to an audience's senses as the play approaches
its end. Each twist of the plot, each wandering from the
inexorable march of events, has been charged both with a sense
of the possibility of liberation from the iron rule of Ephesian law
and with a reminder of the debt that is to be paid if error
remains only error, failing to come together finally in some
satisfying whole.

In this connection, Shakespeare's use of the chain is a
brilliant piece of stage business, both visually and aurally, as
prop and as repeated phonetic element. The chain appears on
stage at key points as a visual marker of several relationships—

between Antipholus of Ephesus and Adriana, Antipholus and Angelo, Antipholus and the Courtesan, and, eventually, Antipholus and Antipholus. Its symbolic associations with the key thematic issue of binding and loosing are obvious, and are used with double-edged significance.[24] It is the price of the chain that binds Antipholus of Ephesus to the law, and it is the physical evidence of the chain that finally frees him, reestablishing his marriage bond with Adriana and clearing the way for the multiple reunions in act 5. For every sighting of the chain in the play, Shakespeare provides multiple soundings, many of which seem calculated to make the syllable itself resonate with meaning. In act 2 scene 1, he rhymes it, wittily, with "detain." (ll. 105–106). In act 3 scene 1, the locked-out Antipholus of Ephesus plans to give the chain to the Courtesan, effectively using it as a punishment for Adriana (and thereby linking it figuratively with the rope end of act 4 scene 4). Antipholus repeats the word "chain" twice in three lines of blank verse, and then picks up its sound in a speech-ending (and attention grabbing) disyllabic rhyme three lines later:

> Since mine own doors refuse to enter*tain* me
> I'll knock elsewhere, to see if they'll dis*dain* me.
>
> (3.1.120–121)

Later, assonance links the chain with the thematically crucial issue of naming, when Angelo addresses the Syracusan Antipholus:

ANGELO
> Master Antipholus

ANTIPHOLUS
> —Ay, that's my *name*.

ANGELO
> I know it well, sir. Lo, here's the *chain*.   (3.2.164–65)

The word is subsequently sounded three more times, once as a rhyme word, before the end of the scene. Repetition of the sound reaches almost absurd proportions in act 4, where during the argument over payment for the chain between Angelo and the

Ephesian Antipholus it occurs thirteen times in a space of some forty lines. This scene includes a metaphorically interesting punning usage by Antipholus:

> I promised your presence and the *chain*,
> But neither *chain* nor goldsmith came to me.
> Belike you thought our love would last too long
> If it were *chained* together, and therefore came not.
>
> (4.1.23–26)

It also includes an instance of an identical rhyme on the syllable. The identity of sound marks aurally the fact that the argument is at loggerheads, and leads directly to the binding of Antipholus for debt:

> ANGELO
> The money that you own me for the chain.
> ANTIPHOLUS
> I owe you none till I receive the chain.   (4.1.63–64)

By the time that Adriana's error and Dromio's penchant for puns link the sound of this word explicitly with time, the most ominous of all the chains in the play, the syllable has become an aural motif, chiming like a bell in a play increasingly pressed for time:

> ADRIANA
> Tell me, is he arrested on a band?
> S. DROMIO
> Not on a band, but on a stronger thing:
> A *chain*, a *chain*! Do you not hear it ring?
> ADRIANA
> What, the *chain*?
> S. DROMIO
> No, no, the bell. 'Tis time that I were gone.
> It was two ere I left him, and now the clock strikes one.
>
> (4.2.49–54)

Legal bands, the physical binding of Antipholus of Ephesus, the bell tolling the approach of Egeon's death, and the chain coalesce in a brilliant moment in the play's music. And just in case we missed it, Shakespeare takes advantage in act 4 scene 3 of the acoustic potential of another prop—the Courtesan's ring—to ring even more changes on the theme. Three times in the space of seventeen lines the Courtesan repeats some form of her demand: "I pray you sir, my ring, or else the chain" (4.3.74). So pervasive is the sound "chain," especially in the later stages of the play, that I would venture to suggest that the word's acoustic value was a chief consideration in Shakespeare's departure from his source in his choice of props. The "spinter" or bracelet used by Plautus in the *Menaechmi* may not have had, as commentators have noted, the visual prominence of a large Elizabethan gold chain.[25] It certainly would not have lent itself to the brilliant and thematically linked sonic changes that Shakespeare rings on the word "chain" in the final acts of the play.

In a context in which sound is given so prominent and so double-edged a role in the manifestation of character and the development of plot, Egeon's speech upon his return to the stage in act 5 is particularly charged with significance. Bound by officers of the law, acknowledging that grief and time may have "written strange defeatures in [his] face," he depends upon his voice to be more resistant to the deforming changes he has undergone: "O, grief hath changed me since you saw me last… / But tell me yet, dost thou not know my voice?" Egeon's trust in his voice echoes a long tradition pitting the untrustworthy eye against the more constant ear, the superficiality of appearances against the interiority of voice, ease of visual disguise against the revelatory power of vocal sound: "Sight is often deceived, hearing serves as guaranty" (Saint Ambrose).[26] The crushing disappointment that results from his having addressed himself, deceived by his eyes, to characters who cannot distinguish him visually or aurally issues in a speech that an audience may hear, ironically, as clearly manifesting Egeon's own distinctive voice. The "genuine if somewhat dated eloquence" of this blank verse marks a return to the adagio tone and pace of the opening scene:[27]

Not know my voice! O time's extremity,
Hast thou so cracked and splitted my poor tongue

In seven short years, that here my only son
Knows not my feeble key of untuned cares?   (5.1.308–311)

It is one thing to watch and hear Antipholus of Ephesus, his voice made indistinct through the vocal mask of the strong-stress verse, repulsed by Luce or Adriana, and quite another to listen to Egeon here. His fears of being "untuned" take the theme of misperception and the loss of identity that it threatens perhaps as far as Shakespeare could take it. It is Egeon's voice that began the play, sounding its keynote, and it is in relation to Egeon that all characters will reestablish their identity at play's end, enabling them once again to engage in reasonable and purposeful speech. Egeon untuned threatens to untune the play itself.

Shakespeare's placement of this speech some eleven lines before the entrance of Amelia and the rapid resolution of the plot makes act 5 a recapitulation of the rhythmic development of the entire play. Once again, the bedazzled eye creates the context for excited vocal exchanges. But this time, the stichomythic exchanges, rhymes, and rhythmic variety mark not confusion, but an appropriately joyful response to the fact that time has been transformed:

After so long grief, such nativity!   (3.1.407)

The music of the play pervades even the individual lines. The five syllables before the pause are drawn out:

2   4 3   4 (x)
After so long grief, // such nativity!

The three monosyllables, all bearing stress, require distinct emphasis, slowing the line down. The strong stress in the (normally unstressed) fifth position makes the pause at mid-line particularly emphatic. The long vowels of "so" and "grief," along with the contiguous gutturals "long grief" contribute to making the half-line extraordinarily slow. By comparison, the second half of the line trips by in less than a blink of an eye:

4   4 1
After so long grief, such nativity!

The line labors, then dances. Reunion transforms elegy to celebration, as a sentence of death gives way to new life. Time's slow-chapped power brings forth a feast.

The peculiarity of the verse of *The Comedy of Errors*—its variety, changes of pace and rhythm, its foregrounding of sound through rhymes, puns, figures of speech, and other means—may help to explain in part why so many directors from the early nineteenth century to the present have seen fit (in Kenneth Muir's words) to "jazz it up."[28] The play is, as has been argued here, a virtuoso display of the phonetic resources of the language. It insists on putting eye and ear in tension with one another, and therefore creates many of its effects through what may be described as an embarrassment of aesthetic riches. So it is not surprising to find the play turned into a libretto for one or another kind of musical performance—from the 1819 operatic production at Covent Garden to Trevor Nunn's delightfully raucous 1976 Stratford production and beyond. And the circus or carnival atmosphere of many productions (I'm thinking here especially of Robert Woodruff's 1983 and 1987 productions featuring the juggling of the Flying Karamazov Brothers) reflects an aesthetic generosity of spirit that is indeed in the play. Read or performed with some attention to the precise nature of its exhibitionist versification, however, *The Comedy of Errors* reveals a surprisingly sophisticated internal musicality. It was already jazzed up when Shakespeare wrote it.

NOTES

[1] Arguments that the play's metrical peculiarity suggests apprentice work or multiple authorship are legion. Ritson, the source of the "silk and worsted" remark, concludes that Shakespeare could not have written the "long hobbling verses" (quoting William Blakestone) of act 3 scene 1 and elsewhere. See the comments from George Steevens, *et al.*, *The Plays of William Shakespeare* (1793) in *Shakespeare: The Critical Heritage*, edited by Brian Vickers (London, 1974—81), Vol. 6, p. 588.

[2] William Shakespeare, *The Comedy of Errors*, edited by David Bevington (New York, 1988), act 2 scene 2, ll. 47–48. All further quotations of Shakespeare's play are from this text.

[3] For an overview of Shakespeare's use of rhyme and non-iambic verse, see the tables provided by Stanley Wells and Gary Taylor, in *William Shakespeare: A Textual Companion* (Oxford: Clarendon, 1987), especially pp. 116–117.

[4] George T. Wright, *Shakespeare's Metrical Art* (Berkeley, California, 1988).

[5] Christopher Marlowe, *Tamburlaine the Great*, Part I, in *Drama of the English Renaissance*, Vol. I: *The Tudor Period*, edited by Russell A. Fraser and Norman Rabkin (New York, 1976), act 2, scene 7, ll. 21–28.

[6] Wolfgang Riehle, *Shakespeare, Plautus and the Humanist Tradition* (Cambridge, 1990), pp. 155–56. Riehle also cites the following comment by Erasmus from a 1534 Cologne edition of Terence: "Comici Latini multam libertatem sibi usurparunt in uersibus, sed nemo largius Terentio" (*P. Terentii Afri Comoediea ex D. Erasmi et Jo. Rivii Attendoriensis Castigationibus* [Cologne, 1534], f. III.; cited Riehle, 155). Chapter 6 of Riehle's study relies heavily on A.J. Tobias, *Plautus' Metrical Characterization* (diss. Stanford, 1970) in an attempt to elucidate motives behind shifts from one kind of verse to another. While his chapter rightly notes that the verse of the play has been unduly neglected, to my mind the best parts of the argument are those that show not how Shakespeare may or may not have been following the lead of Plautus, but how metrical shifts serve the internal logic of Shakespeare's comedy.

[7] Wells and Taylor, *William Shakespeare: A Textual Companion*, p. 95.

[8] Wells and Taylor, *William Shakespeare: A Textual Companion*, p. 97.

[9] Stanley Wells, Introduction to *The Comedy of Errors* (New York, 1972), p. 21.

[10] On the woodenness of Egeon's verse, see, for example, F.E. Halliday, *The Poetry of Shakespeare's Plays* (London, 1954), pp. 24, 184.

[11] Robert S. Miola, *Shakespeare and Classical Comedy* (Oxford, 1994), pp. 24–25.

[12] Frederic W. Ness points to many such uses of well-worn rhetorical figures in *The Use of Rhyme in Shakespeare's Plays* (New Haven, 1941); see p. 31 for his comments on this example of *clymax*.

[13] See Harry Levin on the nearly complete absence of deceit in the play, a remarkable fact in a comedy of the kind that Shakespeare is writing. Levin notes, for example, that Shakespeare drops from his play "the sole Plautine character who acts out of self-interest, the Parasite." *Playboys and Killjoys: An Essay on the Theory and Practice of Comedy* (New York, 1987), p. 80.

[14] For discussions of puns in the play, see Harry Levin, "Two Comedies of Errors," in *Refractions: Essays in Comparative Literature* (New York, 1966), p. 143: twinship of the Antipholuses is "a sort of human pun." Levin makes a similar point in *Playboys and Killjoys*, p. 82: "now, a twin

is regarded as a kind of human pun." Russ McDonald discusses the importance of puns as showing the "enormous possibilities for error" afforded by words. See his "Fear of Farce," in *"Bad" Shakespeare: Revaluations of the Shakespeare Canon* (Toronto, 1988), pp. 77–90. Eamon Grennan argues that "the pun recognizes the refusal of language to be confined within its conventional borders" in "Arm and Sleeve: Nature and Custom in *The Comedy of Errors*," *Philological Quarterly* 59 (1980): 150–64.

[15] On the provenance and history of this measure, see Jakob Schipper, *A History of English Versification* (Oxford, 1910), pp. 117–19, 231.

[16] Jules Eugene Bernard, Jr. presents tables that trace the disappearance of strong-stress verse from English drama in *The Prosody of the Tudor Interlude* (New Haven, 1939; rpt. Hamden, Conn., 1969), see esp. p. 210.

[17] Martin Halpern, "On the Two Chief Metrical Modes in English," *PMLA* 77 (1962): 177–86.

[18] [William] S[tevenson?], Prologue to *Gammer Gurton's Needle*, in *Drama of the English Renaissance*, Vol. I: *The Tudor Period*, edited by Russell A. Fraser and Norman Rabkin (New York, 1976).

[19] On binary arrangement, see Joseph Malof, *A Manual of English Meters* (Bloomington, Indiana, 1970), esp. chapter 4; and Derek Attridge, *The Rhythms of English Poetry* (London, 1982), esp. pp. 80–96.

[20] Harry Levin, "Two Comedies," p. 145.

[21] Levin, "Two Comedies of Errors," p. 140; Anne Barton, Introduction to *The Comedy of Errors* in *The Riverside Shakespeare*, edited by G. Blakemore Evans (Boston, 1974), p. 81.

[22] On the sources of this speech, see T.W. Baldwin, *On the Compositional Genetics of* The Comedy of Errors (Urbana, Illinois, 1965): 166–9. Baldwin calls the speech Luciana's "homily."

[23] It should be acknowledged here that the text of this passage is, in David Bevington's words, "evidently corrupt" (*The Comedy of Errors* 17n), and that its corruption may account for some of its disruptive metrical character. The contrast created by the broken couplets, however, is entirely characteristic of Shakespeare's exuberant metrical shifts throughout the play.

[24] Richard Henze argues for the chain as a "complex symbol of the recommended norm of the play, the binding of headstrong freedom and wandering individualism," in *"The Comedy of Errors*: A Freely Binding Chain," *Shakespeare Quarterly* 22 (1971): 35–41. Henze's article does not treat the phonetic element that is my focus here.

[25] R.A. Foakes notes that Warner's 1595 translation also changes Plautus's "spinter" (*Menaechmi* 527, 530) to "chain," saying that it is probably "a coincidence, and due to the popular fashion of the time of wearing chains of gold or jewels round the neck, as well as to the

greater prominence of a chain on the stage." T.W. Baldwin agrees, suggesting that Shakespeare chose the chain out of a need for a more "stagey" device than a bracelet. Foakes, ed. *The Comedy of Errors, The Arden Edition of the Works of William Shakespeare* (Cambridge, Massachusetts, 1962), p. 25. Baldwin, *Compositional Genetics*, pp. 194–95.

[26] Saint Ambrose, *Commentary on St. Luke*, iv. 5: "Everything that we believe, we believe either through sight or through hearing. Sight is often deceived, hearing serves as guaranty." Cited in Walter J. Ong, S.J., "Voice as a Summons for Belief: Literature, Faith, and the Divided Self," in *The Barbarian Within* (Macmillan, 1962), p. 49.

[27] Wells, Introduction to *The Comedy of Errors* (New York, 1972), p. 13.

[28] Kenneth Muir, *Shakespeare's Comic Sequence* (New York, 1979), p. 22.

III *THE COMEDY OF ERRORS* IN PERFORMANCE

The *Gesta Grayorum* Account
[at Gray's Inn, 1594]

The next grand night was intended to be upon Innocents-Day at night; at which time there was a great presence of lords, ladies, and worshipful personages, that did expect some notable performance at that time; which, indeed, had been effected, if the multitude of beholders had not been so exceeding great, that thereby there was no convenient room for those that were actors; by reason whereof, very good inventions and conceits could not have opportunity to be applauded, which otherwise would have been great contentation to the beholders. Against which time, our friend, the Inner Temple, determined to send their ambassador to our Prince of State, as sent from Frederick Templarius, their Emperor, who was then busied in his wars against the Turk. The ambassador came very gallantly appointed, and attended by a great number of brave gentlemen, which arrived at our court about nine of the clock at night. Upon their coming thither, the King at Arms gave notice to the Prince, then sitting in his chair of state in the hall, that there was come to his court an ambassador from his ancient friend the state of Templaria, which desired to have present access unto his Highness; and showed his Honour further that he seemed to be of very good sort, because he was so well attended; and therefore desired that it would please his Honour that some of his nobles and lords might conduct him to his Highness's presence, which was done. So he was brought in very solemnly with sound of trumpets, the King at Arms and Lords of Purpoole making to his company, which marched before him in order. He was received very kindly of the Prince, and placed in a chair besides his Highness to the end that he might be partaker of the sports intended. But first he made a speech to the Prince, wherein he declared how his excellent renown and fame was known throughout all the whole world; and that the report of his greatness was not contained within the bounds of the ocean, but had come to the ears of his noble sovereign, Frederick Templarius, where he is now warring against the Turks, the known enemies to all Christendom; who, having heard that his Excellency kept his court at Graya this Christmas, thought it to stand with his ancient league of amity and near kindness, that so long hath been continued and increased by their noble ancestors of famous memory and desert, to gratulate his happiness and flourishing estate; and in that regard had sent him his ambassador, to be residing at his Excellency's court in honour of his greatness, and token of his tender love and good will he beareth to his Highness; the confirmation whereof he especially required and by all means possible would study to increase and eternize: which function he was the more willing to accomplish, because our state of Graya did grace Templaria with the presence of an ambassador about thirty years since upon like occasion.

Our Prince made him this answer: that he did acknowledge that the great kindness of his Lord, whereby he doth invite to further degrees in firm and loyal friendship, did deserve all honourable commendations and effectual accomplishment that by any means might be devised; and that he accounted himself happy by having the sincere and steadfast love of so gracious and renowned a Prince as his lord and master deserved to be esteemed; and that nothing in the world should hinder the due observation of so inviolable a band as he esteemed his favour and good will. Withal he entered into commendations of his noble and courageous enterprizes in that he chooseth out an adversary fit for his greatness to encounter with, his honour to be illustrated by, and such an enemy to all Christendom as that the glory of his actions tend to the safety and Liberty of all civility and humanity; yet, notwithstanding that he was thus employed, in this action of honouring us he showed both his honourable mindfulness of our love and friendship and also his own puissance that can afford so great a number of brave gentlemen and so gallantly furnished and accomplished. And so concluded, with a welcome both to the Ambassador himself and his favourites for their lord and master's sake and so for their own good deserts and condition.

When the Ambassador was placed as aforesaid and that there was something to be performed for the delight of the beholders, there arose such a disordered tumult and crowd upon the stage that there was no opportunity to effect that which was intended. There came so great a number of worshipful personages upon the stage that might not be displaced; and gentlewomen, whose sex did privilege them from violence, that when the Prince and his officers had in vain a good while expected and endeavoured a reformation, at length there was no hope of redress for that present. The Lord Ambassador and his train thought that they were not so kindly entertained as was before expected, and thereupon would not stay any longer at that time but in a sort discontented and displeased. After their departure the throngs and tumults did somewhat cease, although so much of them continued as was able to disorder and confound any good inventions whatsoever. In regard whereof, as also for that the sports intended were especially for the gracing of the Templarians, it was thought good not to offer any thing of account, saving dancing and revelling with gentlewomen; and after such sports, a Comedy of Errors (like to Plautus his Menechmus) was played by the players. So that night was begun and continued to the end in nothing but confusion and errors; whereupon, it was ever afterwards called, The Night of Errors.

This mischanceful accident sorting so ill, to the great prejudice of the rest of our proceedings, was a great discouragement and disparagement to our whole state; yet it gave occasion to the lawyers of the Prince's council the next night after revels to read a Commission of Oyer and Terminer, directed to certain noblemen and lords of his Highness's council and others, that they should enquire or cause enquiry to be made of some great disorders and abuses lately done and committed within his Highness's dominions of Purpoole, especially by sorceries and enchantments; and, namely, of a great witchcraft used the night before, whereby there were great disorders and misdemeanours by hurly-burlies, crowds, errors, confusions, vain representations and shows, to the utter discredit of our state and policy.

The next night upon this occasion, we preferred judgments thick and threefold, which were read publicly by the clerk of the crown, being all against a sorcerer or conjurer that was supposed to be the cause of that confused inconvenience. Therein was contained how he had caused the stage to be built and scaffolds to be reared to the top of the house to increase expectation. Also how he had caused divers ladies and gentlewomen and others of good condition to be invited to our sports, also our dearest friend, the state of Templaria, to be disgraced, and disappointed of their kind entertainment, deserved and intended. Also that he caused throngs and tumults, crowds and outrages to disturb our whole proceedings. And lastly, that he had foisted a company of base and common fellows to make up our disorders with a play of errors and confusions; and that that night had gained to us discredit, and itself a nick-name of Errors. All which were against the crown and dignity of our sovereign Lord, the Prince of Purpoole.

Under colour of these proceedings were laid open to the view all the causes of note that were committed by our chiefest statesmen in the government of our principality; and every officer in any great place that had not performed his duty in that service was taxed hereby, from the highest to the lowest, not sparing the guard and porters, that suffered so many disordered persons to enter in at the court-gates. Upon whose aforesaid indictments the prisoner was arraigned at the bar, being brought thither by the Lieutenant of the Tower (for at that time the stocks were graced with that name); and the Sheriff impanelled a jury of twenty-four gentlemen that were to give their verdict upon the evidence given. The prisoner appealed to the Prince his Excellency for justice and humbly desired that it would please his Highness to understand the truth of the matter by his supplication, which he had ready to be offered to the Master of the Requests. The Prince gave leave to the Master of the Requests that he should read the petition; wherein was a disclosure of all the knavery and juggling of the Attorney and Sollicitor, which had brought all this law-stuff on purpose to blind the eyes of his Excellency and all the honourable court there, going about to make them think that those things which they all saw and perceived sensibly to be in very deed done and actually performed, were nothing else but vain illusions, fancies, dreams and enchantments, and to be wrought and compassed by the means of a poor harmless wretch, that never had heard of such great matters in all his life. Whereas the very fault was in the negligence of the Prince's council, lords and officers of his state, that had the rule of the roast, and by whose advice the Commonwealth was so soundly misgoverned. To prove these things to be true, he brought divers instances of great absurdities committed by the greatest; and made such allegations as could not be denied. These were done by some that were touched by the Attorney and Sollicitor in their former proceedings, and they used the prisoners' names for means of quittance with them in that behalf. But the Prince and statesmen (being pinched on both sides, by both the parties) were not a little offended at the great liberty that they had taken in censuring so far of his Highness's government; and thereupon the prisoner was freed and pardoned, the Attorney, Sollicitor, Master of the Requests, and those that were acquainted with the draught of the petition were all of them commanded to the Tower; so the Lieutenant took charge of them. And this was the end of our lawsports, concerning the Night of Errors.

When we were wearied with mocking thus at our own follies, at length there was a great consultation had for the recovery of our lost honour. It was then concluded, that first the Prince's council should be reformed and some graver conceits should have their places, to advise upon those things that were propounded to be done afterward. Therefore, upon better consideration, there were divers plots and devices intended against the Friday after New Year's day, being the 3d. of January. And to prevent all unruly tumults and former inconveniences, there was provided a watch of armed men to ward at the four ports; and whifflers, to make good order under the four barons; and the Lord Warden to oversee them all, that none but those that were of good condition might be suffered to be let into the court. And the like officers were everywhere appointed.

Republished by The Malone Society, *Gesta Grayorum* (Oxford University Press, 1914): 20–4. Reprinted with the permission of The Malone Society.

Shakespeare and the Prince of Purpoole: The 1594 Production of *The Comedy of Errors* at Gray's Inn Hall

Margaret Knapp and Michal Kobialka

An investigation of the scholarship concerning the production of Shakespeare's plays at the Globe Theatre reveals that in recent years there seems to have been something of a cease-fire among theatre historians, perhaps a tacit admission that in the absence of additional evidence about inner stages, discovery scenes, etc., further speculations about staging are useless. One result of this cease-fire has been that historians have turned their attention to the search for evidence concerning other Elizabethan and Jacobean public, private, and court theatres. Surprisingly, there has been little recent investigation of a group of buildings closely connected with, and often converted to, Elizabethan theatres—the Inns of Court.[1] The neglect of the Inns in relation to theatre is all the more startling when one considers that there is evidence that at least two, and possibly as many as six, of Shakespeare's plays were performed in the great halls of the Inns of Court during his lifetime.[2]

Previous scholarship about the staging of plays at the Inns has assumed that performances there were analogous to performances in the great halls of Tudor homes, palaces, and universities.[3] According to this view, a temporary stage would be placed across one end of a hall, in front of the hall screen. The two doors in the screen would serve as convenient entrances and exits for the actors, and the musicians' gallery, an amenity often built into the upper part of a screen, would be used for scenes requiring an upper level. As sensible as this hypothetical arrangement may seem to the modern theatre scholar or practitioner, it does not take into account the variety of theatrical entertainments offered in halls, nor does it acknowledge the tendency of the Elizabethan period to value tradition, symbolism, and diplomacy over convenience and logic. A careful examination of the conditions under which *The Comedy of Errors* was performed at Gray's Inn hall in 1594 reveals that the physical arrangement of the hall and the nature of the entire Christmas Revel celebration dictated a method of staging that differed markedly from presently accepted ideas about the performances of plays in great halls.

The Inns of Court were, and still are, the major law schools of England. Begun in the Middle Ages, they were by the Elizabethan period substantial organizations occupying numerous buildings in central London. The four main Inns of Court were Middle Temple, Lincoln's Inn, Inner Temple, and Gray's Inn. There were also several less important schools called the Inns of Chancery. The Inns were far more than law schools in the modern sense. Their students were largely limited to the sons of important and influential families. Most had completed a university education at Oxford or Cambridge. The curriculum at the Inns was flexible, largely voluntary, and covered a wide variety of subjects in the arts and humanities as well as law. The ultimate purpose of the Inns was to develop future statesmen, justices, and scholars, and therefore the students' time was taken up not only with the study of legal subjects, but also with the development of such courtiers' skills as dancing, fencing, writing poetry, and acting in plays and masques.

In Elizabeth's time the Inns were major contributors to the development of literature and drama. One has only to note that the Inns of Court produced the first English tragedy (*Gorboduc*), possibly the first English adaptation of a Greek tragedy (*Jocasta*), the first English prose comedy (*The Supposes*), the oldest extant English play based on an Italian novella (*Gismonde of Salerne*), and the first play to use the Arthurian legend for its subject matter (*The Misfortunes of Arthur*), to understand the central role that the Inns played in the development of Elizabethan drama. The Inns also presented many masques, some written by their own members and others by professional playwrights. The Inns are credited with the production of the most spectacular and most expensive masque of the pre-Commonwealth period, James Shirley's *The Triumph of Peace*, which cost an estimated £21,000–24,000 to produce.[4] In addition to their own involvement in theatrical productions, the Inns sponsored many other events such as feasts and disguisings, and would often hire a professional acting company to give a play as part of the entertainment. One such occasion was the performance of *The Comedy of Errors* at Gray's Inn hall in 1594.

In reconstructing a performance of a Shakespearean play during the Elizabethan period, scholars generally search for three kinds of evidence: the playscript, the theatre space in which the play was performed, and eyewitness accounts, both written and pictorial. Each of these forms has its advantages and disadvantages. A playscript's value as evidence for a particular performance of a play is often questionable, since theatre companies constantly revised their promptscripts to adapt to such changed conditions as a new theatre, a new actor, or the need for touring. *The Comedy of Errors* first appeared in print in the First Folio of Shakespeare's plays, published almost thirty years after its performance at Gray's Inn. In the intervening time, it was performed at Court,[5] and perhaps also at Burbage's Theatre, the First and Second Globes, Blackfriars, and on tour. Therefore, the stage directions and indications in the dialogue of scenery, entrances and exits, and stage business may reflect the practices at any or all of the theatrical venues in which the play was presented. For this reason, the play itself is an unreliable guide to its staging at Gray's Inn.

With the second type of evidence, the theatre space, we are on firmer ground. Gray's Inn hall still exists, and although it has been renovated from time to time, the basic dimensions of the hall remain the some. Moreover, through a variety of sources it is possible to reconstruct its configuration in Elizabethan days. There is no evidence for the year in which the hall was first erected, but *Gentleman's Magazine* states that it had been built in the reign of Queen Mary and, until the repairs in 1826, was almost a perfect specimen of the architecture of the Tudor period.[6] The seventeenth-century historian William Dugdale, quoting from records of the Society of Gray's Inn which are no longer extant, asserts that in 1551 "the old hall was seiled with 54 yards of wainscot at 2 s. a yard, and in 3 and 4 Philip and Mary (1556) the Society began the re-edifying it."[7] The hall itself is seventy feet in length, thirty-four feet, eight inches wide, and forty-seven feet high.[8] On its southern side, above the wainscoted walls, there are five mullioned and transomed windows. On the opposite, northern side, are four similar windows and a big Tudor-style bay window which sheds light onto the dais, located in the western part, or high end, of the hall. At the low end of the hall, that is, the eastern side, there is the music gallery, which was erected between 1555 and 1560, below which there is a hall screen with two openings serving as entrances to the hall.[9] At the high end of the hall on the dais, or half-pace (elevated some six inches from the floor), the high table is located. In front of it, on the floor, there was in former times a table for the Ancients, those senior members of the Inn who "could not conveniently have place at the upper table."[10] A few feet away from the Ancients' Table was a fireplace, also referred to as the andirons, which was in the lateral center of the floor but longitudinally closer to the upper end of the hall than to the lower end, being directly under the smoke louvre in the roof above.[11] Near the fireplace there stood a cupboard called in the Latin entries the *Abacus*.[12] The rest of the space in the hall was taken by students' tables which were placed parallel to the side walls in such a way that "no fellow of the Society [would] stand with his back to the fire."[13] A manuscript of 1586 preserved among the Burgley papers states that Gray's Inn was the most prosperous of all the Inns of Court. The number of students attending there and dining in the hall was 336 during the term and around 229 during the vacation period.[14] These figures give some indication of the capacity of the hall and the possible size of the festivities which were held there during the Christmas Revels of 1594/5.

The third form of evidence for the performance of a play in Shakespeare's time, the eyewitness account, is often a mixed blessing in Elizabethan studies, for the recollections of foreign travelers and the second-hand drawings with Latin tags often give rise to more problems than they solve. In the case of the 1594 performance of *The Comedy of Errors*, however, there exists a unique eyewitness account, a description of the entire

Christmas Revel festivities at Gray's Inn in 1594/5. This document, called the *Gesta Grayorum*, was published anonymously in 1688, but despite its late date it is clearly an account written by someone who had taken part in the 1594 festivities.[15] The paragraph of the *Gesta* directly relating to *The Comedy of Errors* has been quoted in many places,[16] but to date no one has published an analysis of the many other references in the *Gesta* that relate to the conditions under which theatrical entertainments were given at Gray's Inn. (A list of the events that took place during the Revels of 1594/5 is appended to this article.)

The Christmas Revels, a tradition of the Inns dating from the medieval Feast of Fools and the Lord of Misrule, was a period running from 20 December (the Eve of the Feast of St. Thomas) to Shrovetide (the day before Ash Wednesday) during which the students organized a series of events for their own entertainment. The Inns elected one of their number to preside over the festivities; at Gray's Inn this ruler was known as the Prince of Purpoole, a corruption of Portpool, the parish in which Gray's Inn was located. The extent of the festivities held during the Christmas Revels varied from Inn to Inn and from year to year, but at certain times one of the Inns would plan its revels on a grand scale. The author of the *Gesta* maintains that the elaborate revels at Gray's Inn during the Christmas vacation of 1594/5 resulted from a combination of an exceptionally large number of students remaining in residence at the Inn during the vacation, and the fact that revels had been cancelled in the previous three or four years because of the plague (p. 1).

It is clear from several references in the *Gesta Grayorum* that alterations were made in the hall for the Christmas festivities. For example, on 29 December charges were leveled against the supposed perpetrator of the previous evening's disorders. Among the charges was: "How he had caused the Stage to be built, and Scaffolds to be reared to the top of the House, to increase Expectation" (p. 23). Clearly, all the tables must have been taken away and the stage and scaffolds put into place at an early date, their presence no doubt adding to a sense of anticipation. The scaffolds were considered essential to the Christmas festivities, for when the Prince of Purpoole was due to return from Russia on 28

January the students planned "two grand Nights" which had to be cancelled "for Want of Room in the Hall, the Scaffolds being taken away, and forbidden to be built up again (as would have been necessary for the good Discharge of such a Matter)" (p. 53).

The scaffolds seem to have provided temporary seating for both the members of Gray's Inn who were not directly participating in the Revel, and for outside guests. They were probably located at the sides of the hall, leaving the space in the center of the floor for dancing and other uses. At least this was the practice at the Inner Temple, where, for the Banqueting Night during the Christmas Celebrations, "The hall is to be furnished with Scaffolds to sit on, for the ladies to behold the Sports, on each side."[17]

Before discussing the location of the stage it is necessary to clarify the nature and use of the dais. According to the *Gesta Grayorum*, on 20 December the Prince of Purpoole marched from his lodgings in the hall in the company of his train of followers, about 112 people excluding trumpeters, "townsmen in liveries," the family, and followers (pp. 7–8). The Prince took his place on his throne under a rich cloth of state at the high end of the hall, that is, on the dais. "His Counsellors and great Lords were placed about him, and before him; below the Half-pace, at a Table, sate his learned Council and Lawyers; the rest of the Officers and Attendants took their proper Places, as belonged to their condition" (p. 9). Thus, it is possible to estimate that on the dais, in the space of about fourteen feet by thirty-four feet, there were approximately seventy people, with additional people seated at the table below the dais.

The area in the middle of the hall, that is, bounded on the north and south by scaffolds, on the east by the hall screen, and on the west by the fireplace, was probably left open, since there had to be room there for at least thirty couples to dance, and since on 20 December the Prince's Champion rode into the hall on horseback and rode around the fireplace before issuing his challenge (pp. 9, 20).

The evening of 28 December (Innocents' Night) is of central significance to this discussion. Because the earlier Revels had been so successful, the author of the *Gesta* claims that "the common Report amongst all Strangers was so great, and the

Expectation of our Proceedings so extraordinary, that it urged us to take upon a greater State than that was at the first intended: And therefore, besides all the stately and sumptuous Service that was continually done the Prince, in very Princely manner; and besides the daily revels, and such like Sports, which were usual, there was intended divers grand Nights, for the Entertainment of Strangers to our Pass-times and Sports" (p. 20).

As a result, on Innocents' Night there was an unexpected influx of guests, "Lords, Ladies, and worshipful Personages, that did expect some notable Performance at that time; which, indeed, had been effected, if the multitude of Beholders had not been so exceedingly great, that thereby there was no convenient room for those that were Actors" (p. 20). The term actors here seems to refer to members of Gray's Inn who had prepared an entertainment, possibly a masque, for the Prince and his special guests, the Ambassador from the Inner Temple and his train of followers. After entering the hall, the Ambassador exchanged speeches of greeting with the Prince, and then was also seated on the dais with his train. By now, the crowd must have been immense and unruly, for

there arose such a disordered Tumult and Crowd upon the Stage, that there was no Opportunity to effect that which was intended: There came so great a number of worshipful Personages upon the Stage, that might not be displaced; and Gentlewomen, whose Sex did privilege them from Violence, that when the Prince and his Officers had in vain, a good while, expected and endeavoured a Reformation, at length there was no hope of Redress for that present. The Lord Ambassador and his Train thought that they were not so kindly entertained, as was before expected, and thereupon would not stay any longer at that time, but in a sort, discontented and displeased. After their Departure the Throngs and Tumults did somewhat cease, although so much of them continued, as was able to disorder and confound any good Inventions whatsoever. In regard whereof, as also for that the Sports intended were especially for the gracing of the Templarians, it was thought good not to offer any thing of Account, saving Dancing and Revelling with Gentlewomen; and offer such Sports, a Comedy of Errors (like to Plautus his Menechmus) was played by the Players. So that night had begun, and continued to the end, in nothing but Confusion and Errors; whereupon, it was ever afterwards called, The Night of Errors. (p. 22)

One can imagine from this description a crowd of important people (the so-called "worshipful personages") pushing onto the dais, and when there is no more room there because of the Prince, his train, the Ambassador, his train, and the many outside guests, the overflow seems to have spilled onto the stage, thereby obstructing the performance planned by the members of the Inn.

Where was this stage and why were so many "worshipful personages" trying to sit on it? If it were in front of the hall screen, as it is usually conjectured to be, it would be at the opposite end of the hall from the Prince, and therefore not very tempting as a seat for important guests. Nor could the stage be in the middle of the floor below the fireplace, for it would restrict the dancing and make the Champion's entrance on horseback impossible.

The stage must have been located in front of the dais, in the space between the dais and the fireplace. Further evidence for this location comes from the *Gesta Grayorum*'s account of the events of 3 January. After the masque, the knightings, and the running banquet, "there was a table set in the midst of the Stage, before the Prince's Seat; and there sate six of the Lords of his Privy Council" (p. 31). We know that the Prince's seat was located on the dais, and that the Privy Council had previously sat at the table below, that is, in front of, the dais. Moreover, given the length and literary sophistication of the six councillors' speeches (reportedly written by Francis Bacon), the speakers must have been in close proximity to the Prince. Therefore, the phrase "in the midst of the stage, before the Prince's seat" must refer to a stage that was directly in front of the dais, in the space between the dais and the fireplace. This area could be about nine feet deep and as wide as the hall, that is, thirty-four feet, eight inches.

How could this area function as a stage for the performance of *The Comedy of Errors*? Obviously, the stage is wide and shallow, with the audience seated on at least two, and possibly all four, sides. Entrances and exits could have been made through the door at the back of the dais, or through the open space in front of the stage, which led back to the doorways in the hall screen. Such entrances and exits through the hall would have brought the audience seated in the scaffolds into the action of the play. If scenery were employed at all, it could have taken the form of booth-like medieval mansions set up in front of the walls on either side of the stage. In short, if this is the stage on which *The Comedy of Errors* was given, the performance would have differed greatly from one in a public theatre with its deep thrust stage backed by a tiring-house facade.

Two other pieces of evidence should be mentioned in relation to the location of theatrical performances at the Inns of Court. A description of a feast held in 1577 at the Middle Temple asserts that "at the high end of the hall, which is somewhat raised, both to signify the exalted status of the Benchers and for the convenience of play actors, are seated the members of the Privy Council and the peerage."[18] In this case, it seems as if the dais itself were used for the staging of plays.

The other piece of evidence comes from the *Gesta Grayorum*. It is a description of *The Masque of Amity*, performed on 3 January as an apology to the Ambassador from the Inner Temple for the disorders and tumults of Innocents' Night. In the course of his account, the author of the *Gesta* states that "at the side of the Hall, behind a Curtain, was erected an Altar to the Goddess of Amity" (p. 25). He then proceeds to describe the action of the masque, all of which takes place around the altar (the curtains were opened at the beginning and closed at the end). Where was the curtained altar at the side the hall? It could have been in the bay window, which could easily have been curtained off, or it could have been a makeshift arrangement on one of the scaffolds. In either case, the reference to "the side of the hall" suggests still another location for theatrical performances at the Inns of Court.

To summarize, an examination of the *Gesta Grayorum* and related evidence leads to the following conclusions: first, the performance of *The Comedy of Errors* was only one event in a lengthy and complex Christmas Revel celebration. Second, since the stage and scaffolds were erected for a variety of uses during the Revels, the professional players would have been forced to adapt their performance of *The Comedy of Errors* to existing conditions, that is, to a stage erected directly in front of the dais. Third, since additional evidence documents instances when either the dais itself or the side of the hall was used for a theatrical performance at the Inns of Court, there could not have been a single, universally used method for staging plays at the Inns. In light of these points, it would seem that the assumption of a typical or composite method for reconstructing the staging of plays in Tudor halls may be a dangerous generalization. Adaptability and flexibility, rather than typicality, seem to have been the hallmarks of Elizabethan acting companies, especially when they visited the Inns of Court.

The 1594/5 Christmas Revels at Gray's Inn Hall As Recorded in the *Gesta Grayorum*

20 December:
The Prince arrives in the Great Hall of Gray's Inn with a train of over 140 followers.
The King at Arms proclaims the Prince's style and titles.
The Prince's Champion enters the hall on horseback and challenges the Prince's enemies.
The King at Arms blazons the Prince's coat of arms.
The Prince's Attorney and Solicitor give speeches.
The Names of those who hold lands, lordships, privileges, etc., from the Prince are read.
[A plan to hold a parliament is cancelled because important figures are absent.]
The Prince's Pardon and exceptions to it are read.
The Prince gives a short speech.
Dancing—thirty couples of gentlemen do traditional dances.
21–27 December:
Daily revels "and such like sports" are held.
28 December [Innocents' Day]:
The Prince arrives in the hall and is seated on his throne.
The Ambassador from Inner Temple arrives with his

train.

A speech is given by the Ambassador and the Prince replies.

A "Tumult" breaks out, resulting in no room for the performance of the "good inventions" planned by the members of the Inn.

The Ambassador departs in anger at the tumult.

Dancing and reveling are held.

The Comedy of Errors is performed by the players.

29 December:

Revels are held.

After revels, a "Commission of Oyer and Terminer" is appointed to investigate the previous night's disorder.

30 December:

"Judgments thick and threefold" are preferred against the (fictional) authors of the disturbance on Innocents' Night.

31 January:

Important guests from Queen Elizabeth's court are invited to attend the revels for this night.

The Prince of Purpoole enters the hall with his train.

The Ambassador from the Inner Temple enters with his train.

A *Masque of Amity* is offered as an apology to the Ambassador.

The Prince knights the Ambassador and his followers and some of his own men.

The King at Arms reads the order [rules and regulations] of the knighthood

A consort of music is presented.

A running banquet is served.

Six lords of the Privy Council make speeches (by Francis Bacon?) advising the Prince on the proper pursuits of a monarch.

The Prince replies to the speeches.

Dancing.

4 January:

The Prince and the Ambassador and their followers (80 in all) mount horses and make a progress to the house of the Lord Mayor of London.

The Prince, the Ambassador and their followers dine at the

Lord Mayor's.

6 January [Twelfth Night]:

The Prince takes his place in the hall.

A masque is presented concerning His Highness' State and Government.

Dancing.

Arrival of an Ambassador from the Emperor of Russia and Muscovy.

The Ambassador makes a speech asking for the Prince's help. The Prince replies that he will bring an army to aid the Emperor.

A running banquet is served.

Letters from diverse parts of the kingdom advising the Prince on the results of sea battles, etc., are read.

Dancing.

7 January:

The Prince leaves for Russia with the Ambassador.

28 January:

During dinner in the hall [everyone is back for the term), a trumpet sounds.

The King at Arms announces the Prince's return from Russia and informs officers of the Prince's court that they must attend him at Blackwall on 1 February.

1 February:

Officers of the court meet the Prince and his train at Blackwall.

The Prince and his court ride downriver in fifteen barges decorated with flags, banners, etc., and carrying musicians and trumpeters; some of the barges shoot off ordnance.

The Prince debarks at the stairs to Queen Elizabeth's palace at Greenwich, sends a message to Sir Thomas Heneage apologizing for not calling on the Queen, and promising he will come to her at Shrovetide. The Queen sends an answer forgiving the Prince for not calling and saying that she will welcome his visit.

The Prince continues on to the Tower of London, where, by the Queen's order, a volley of great ordnance is shot off in the Prince's honor.

At Tower Hill, the Prince joins 100 of his men waiting on

horseback to escort him to Gray's Inn.

The Prince and his company ride through the streets of London; large crowds gather to see them.

At St. Paul's School, one of the scholars gives an oration in Latin in the Prince's honor.

The Prince arrives at Gray's Inn.

Dinner is served, and is followed by dancing.

2 February:

More dancing and reveling.

Shrovetide:

The Prince and his followers attend Queen Elizabeth at court, where they present *The Masque of Proteus*.

The Next Day:

The Prince and his followers are presented to the Queen.

That night, members of Elizabeth's court arrange for fighting at barriers; the Prince of Purpoole is asked to join them. He acquits himself well and is given a gift.

Shrove Tuesday:

The revels end.

Originally published by Margaret Knapp and Michal Kobialka, "Shakespeare and the Prince of Purpoole: The 1594 Production of *The Comedy of Errors* at Gray's Inn Hall," *Theatre History Studies* 4 (1984): 71–81. Reprinted with the permission of *Theatre History Studies*.

NOTES

[1] To date, the only book-length study of the subject has been A. Wigfall Green's *The Inns of Court and Early English Drama* (New Haven: Yale University Press, 1931).

[2] In addition to *The Comedy of Errors* and *Twelfth Night*, for which there is external evidence of an Inns performance, scholars have argued that *Troilus and Cressida, Love's Labours Lost, Timon of Athens*, and *Measure for Measure* were also performed at the Inns of Court.

[3] See, for example, Richard Hosley's comparison of the Hampton Court hall screen, the Middle Temple hall screen, and the Swan drawing in "The Origin of the Shakespearian Playhouse" in *Shakespeare 400*, ed. James G. McManaway (New York: Holt, Rinehart and Winston, 1964),

pp. 29–39. On the other hand, Richard Southern's study of performances of Tudor interludes in halls, *The Staging of Plays before Shakespeare* (New York: Theatre Arts, 1973), excludes productions at the Inns of Court because they do not fit into his developmental theory.

[4] Green, *The Inns of Court*, pp. 14, 17.

[5] The Revels Accounts of 1604/5 record a performance of *The Comedy of Errors* at Court on Innocents' Night 1604, exactly ten years after the performance at Gray's Inn hall. See Gāmini Salgādo, ed., *Eyewitnesses of Shakespeare* (Sussex: Sussex University Press, 1975), p. 24.

[6] *Gentleman's Magazine*, 96 (1826), 109.

[7] William Dugdale, *Origines Juridiciales* (London: Thomas Newcomb, 1671), p. 273.

[8] All of the measurements were done at Gray's Inn by Michal Kobialka. We would like to thank Mrs. Theresa Thom, the Librarian of Gray's Inn, for her help in conducting the research.

[9] The first reference to the hanging of doors in the hall screen openings is a carpenter's contract of 1826 preserved in the Library of Gray's Inn that provides for a "folding door hung with two pair of four inch iron butts a strong copper warded iron rim lock with 4 knobs."

[10] J. Fletcher, ed., *The Pension Book of Gray's Inn* (London: Chiswick Press, 1901), vol. 1, entry from 5 February, 35 Elizabeth (1593).

[11] W.R. Douthwaite, *Gray's Inn: Its History and Associations* (London: Reeves and Turner, 1886), p. 113. The fireplace remained in the middle of the hall until 1743, when, according to a carpenter's contract preserved in the Gray's Inn Library, the floor of the hall was removed and replaced. During the Elizabethan era, the fire was symbolic of both the sun and the law, and an emblem of it was worn on garments, particularly on collars. See Green, *The Inns of Court*, p. 62.

[12] J. Bruce Williamson, *The History of the Temple, London* (New York: E.P. Dutton, 1924), p. 118.

[13] Dugdale, *Origines*, p. 291.

[14] Williamson, *The History of the Temple*, p. 244.

[15] *Gesta Grayorum* (London: W. Canning, 1688). For a recent edition, see D.S. Bland, ed., *Gesta Grayorum*, English Reprints Series (Liverpool: Liverpool University Press, 1968). Subsequent page numbers in the text refer to the 1688 edition.

[16] See, for example, Salgado, ed., *Eyewitnesses of Shakespeare*, p. 16.

[17] Dugdale, *Origines*, p. 157.

[18] Quoted in George Godwin, *The Middle Temple* (London: Staples Press, 1964), p. 53.

PLAN OF GRAY'S INN HALL
DURING THE TERM

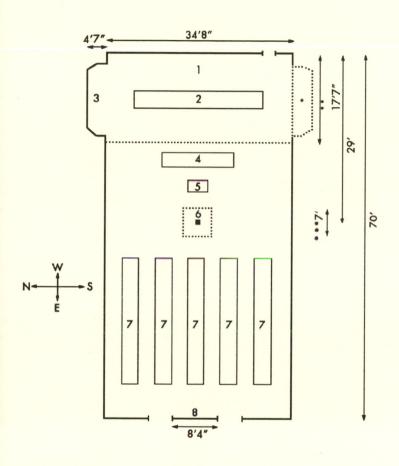

1 Dais (Half-pace)   4 Ancients' Table   7 Students' Tables
2 High Table   5 Abacus   8 Hall Screen
3 Bay Window   6 Fireplace

*   the bay window on the southern side was built after World War II.

**   17'7" refers to the modern length of the dais. However, as numerous primary sources indicate, the dais was shorter in the past.

***   the possible size of the fireplace was estimated by the approximate size of the louvre.

The Elizabethan Stage Society Production at Gray's Inn, 1895

George Bernard Shaw

And yet there is more talent now than ever—more skill now than ever—more artistic culture—better taste, better acting, better theatres, better dramatic literature. Mr. Tree, Mr. Alexander, Mr. Flare, have made honorable experiments; Mr. Forbes Robertson's enterprise at the Lyceum is not a sordid one; Mr. Henry Arthur Jones and Mr. Pinero are doing better work than ever before, and doing it without any craven concession to the follies of "the British public." But it is still necessary, if you want to feel quite reassured, to turn your back on the ordinary commercial West End theatre, with its ignoble gambling for "a catch-on," and its eagerly envious whisperings of how much Mr. Penley has made by Charley's Aunt, to watch the forlorn hopes that are led from time to time by artists and amateurs driven into action by the starvation of their artistic instincts. The latest of these is the Elizabethan Stage Society; and I am delighted to be able to taunt those who missed the performance in Gray's Inn Hall with being most pitiably out of the movement. The Lyceum itself could not have drawn a more distinguished audience; and the pleasant effect of the play, as performed on the floor of the hall without proscenium or fittings of any kind, and played straight through in less than an hour and a half without any division into acts, cannot be as much as imagined by any frequenter of our ordinary theatres. The illusion, which generally lapses during performances in our style whenever the principal performers are off the stage, was maintained throughout: neither the torchbearers on the stage nor the very effective oddity of the Dromio costumes interfering with it in the least. Only, the modern dresses of the audience, the gasaliers, and the portrait of Manisty next that of Bacon, were anachronisms which one had to ignore. The stage management was good as regards the exits, entrances, and groupings—not so good in the business of the speeches, which might have been made more helpful to the actors, especially to Adriana, whose best speeches were underdone. On the whole the acting was fair—much better than it would have been at an average professional performance. Egeon, one of the Dromios, and the courtezan distinguished themselves most. The evening wound up with a Dolmetsch concert of lute and viol, virginal and voice, a delectable entertainment which defies all description by the pen.

Originally published by G. Bernard Shaw, *Our Theatres in the Nineties*, 3 vols. (1932; rpt. London: Constable and Co., 1948), vol. 2: 274–5. Reprinted with the permission of The Society of Authors on behalf of the Bernard Shaw Estate.

Die Irrungen:
The Comedy of Errors in Germany

Günter Walch

One of the perennial clichés in German criticism of *The Comedy of Errors* tells us that the play "very rarely appears on a German stage." That statement was made in 1911.[1] There is occasional implicit disagreement with that pre-World War I voice, as when a theatre critic declared in 1934 that this extravagant play of mistaken recognitions had often before been "ventured" in Berlin.[2] Whether Berlin had really seen more productions than was usual in that period of fatal errors, or whether the critic's impression happened to be rather subjective, is hard to say. The influential *Shakespeare-Handbuch* also maintains that in the German-speaking countries "*The Comedy of Errors* is one of Shakespeare's most frequently performed comedies."[3] In the view of most critics, however, the play has been "relatively seldom given in Germany" (1944),[4] "only rarely played, and rightly so," as the late Friedrich Luft, a very famous Berlin theatre critic hastened to add in 1983,[5] or "comparatively rarely performed" (1991).[6]

That *The Comedy of Errors* has attracted relatively little attention in this country is corroborated by German academic criticism. Thus Kurt Tetzeli von Rosador in his bilingual 1982 edition points out, in his discussion of the history of critical writing about the play generally, that scholars began taking a sporadic interest in *The Comedy of Errors* only in the nineteenth century, and that in Germany this took the characteristic positivist form "almost exclusively" of source hunting.[7] Encouraged by the early stage practice of performing only radical adaptations, the play was considered an immature early work. Only few specific approaches were developed towards the peculiar character of this play. For this reason the literature remains surveyable to this day, a rare case in Shakespeare studies, as Tetzeli adds.[8]

What are we to make of these confident yet contradictory views? Has *The Comedy of Errors* been staged and critically discussed very rarely or very frequently in Germany?

The answer seems to lie in the relativity which is implied in quite a few of these statements. *The Comedy of Errors* has never been so overwhelmingly successful a comedy in Germany as *A Midsummer Night's Dream*, *The Merchant of Venice* or *Twelfth Night*. Nor has it ever equalled the even more stunning success of some of the tragedies, privileged in this country over the comedies until the second half of our century. "If a German had created Hamlet, I would not have been at all surprised," wrote the poet Ludwig Börne in 1828.[9] In fact, many German intellectuals in the nineteenth century, amid the political malaise of their country, identified to an amazing degree with the philosophical and inactive Danish prince. But to my knowledge no one ever identified what was going on in Germany with the action in *The Comedy of Errors*, that uproarious and uncanny play on the loss of and search for identity, with mistaken recognition, with the drive toward meaning and closure which is perpetually undermined, although a nice literary case might be made for such an identification.

The answer to the question for place of *The Comedy of Errors* in German culture seems to be that it was *Hamlet* and *A Midsummer Night's Dream*, not *The Comedy of Errors*, which played the central role in the German imagination, both academically and theatrically. *The Comedy of Errors* was performed fairly regularly and has been to the present day, but not as frequently as some other plays by Shakespeare. A look at an historical record of Shakespeare performances in a German dissertation of 1934[10] may provide an indication of *The Comedy of Errors* career. The survey starts in 1875, only a few years after the foundation of the second German Reich, and covers nearly sixty years, up to 1933. It shows *The Comedy of Errors* given at least a few performances every year, with the exception of 1886. We cannot tell the number of productions, since only actual performances are counted. The small numbers, only one performance in the 1876–1877 season, or two each in 1874–1875 and 1875–1876, may seem odd. But that was the time before the invention of the modern director and *Regietheater*. Shakespeare's plays, always several and sometimes as many as twenty-five or so, were in the repertory of practically all of Germany's 180 theatres in the early twentieth century. Almost at the bottom of the popularity scale in the first season (and again, curiously, in 1926), *The Comedy of Errors* rose steadily in the spectators' favour to attain a record fifth place among all twenty-six Shakespeare plays performed in 1927.

Figures such as these, selective though they may be, do give us some idea of the dramatist's standing in Germany. But what is the stage and critical history behind such figures? What can be shown in a paradigmatic sketch of this history is, first of all, that interest in *The Comedy of Errors* actually developed *before* the nineteenth century. In fact, the process of the play's reception in this country is generally speaking not dissimilar to that in England.

It has become a commonplace that the history of German Shakespeare criticism reflects the development of poetological thinking in the eighteenth and nineteenth centuries. The ground had been prepared by Gotthold Ephraim Lessing in the 1750s and 1760s. Only a few of the great men of letters of the time who were then discovering Shakespeare wrote about *The Comedy of Errors*. One who did was Heinrich Wilhelm von Gerstenberg (1737–1823), an early defender of the English "genius."[11] Although he initially seems to have shared the Enlightenment mixture of stern reproval of Shakespeare's "lack of rules" and fascination with an almost exotic genius, he came to hold a mediating position between the Enlightenment, Storm and Stress and Romanticism.[12] Thus even the early Gerstenberg becomes sceptical of rationalist classifications. To him, "Schakespear's" lack of "rule" is counterbalanced by his treatment of "character": The English generally, he believes, know human nature better than the French, and therefore it is less formal artistry that matters than the poetic revelation of hidden human nature by the eye of the genius who penetrates the surface of life. Distinctions between tragedy and comedy, very often so painfully blurred in Shakespeare's plays to the thinking of stern Enlightenment critics, matter less to him than Shakespeare's higher intention of an image of ideal life, the creation of a second reality, "eine zweyte dichterische Natur"—views quite close to those of Goethe. In accordance with German Romantic aesthetics, Gerstenberg comes to defend Shakespeare's blending of the tragic and the comic, rejecting the idea of wild, "natural creation," just as August Wilhelm Schlegel was to reject the idea of Shakespeare as "a drunken wild man"[13] whose artistic sublimity can only be guessed at under a heap of rubble and ruins. Instead, Gerstenberg praises Shakespeare's wise design and deftness of composition. Where in his earlier writings he can be seen to apply classicist standards to Shakespeare's plays, actually with moderation but blaming him for his grave mistakes concerning the neglect of the unities, the underlying holistic idea is modified in *Briefe über die Merkwürdigkeiten der Litteratur* of 1766. Now, the artistic whole of the dramatic composition is considered to justify each detail. There is "not a single superfluous scene" in Shakespeare.[14]

In the seventeenth of his *Briefe über die Merkwürdigkeiten der Litteratur*,[15] Gerstenberg sets out to prove the dramatist's stature and in particular to demolish the "general prejudice that Shakespeare is lacking art." He promises a detailed analysis of *The Comedy of Errors*, tells the story, and praises Shakespeare's lack of "affectation" and the wealth of his imagination. To him, there is so much material in the play that another poet would have used it to make "seven or eight comedies" out of the one. Gerstenberg's discussion of *The Comedy of Errors* can thus be seen roughly to follow Dryden's ancients versus moderns debate, which became so important also to German literary criticism later. That *The Comedy of Errors* is indeed a comedy rather than a farce, a recurring problem in later discussions, does not seem to him in the least doubtful.

Gerstenberg also seems quite familiar with English scholarship and enters into an argument with Warburton's rejection of Shakespeare's authorship on the grounds of the farcical plot and doubtful diction, citing Edwards, Upton and Warton in support of his own positive answer to the open question.

If in Germany *The Comedy of Errors* was first discussed by eighteenth-century men of letters in terms similar to those current in Augustan England and the English Romantic period, the play's stage history also has strong similarities to that in its country of origination.[16] But that was only after a long process of making seventeenth-century Germans acquainted with some of the achievements of the contemporary English theatre. At a time when the Elizabethan and Jacobean theatre had reached its astounding peak, German theatre culture resembled that of England in the early sixteenth century. Classical and neoclassical plays in Latin were recited at schools and universities, simple Shrovetide plays were regularly shown at private mansions and the courts of princelings, and religious plays were performed in churches and public squares. But, as in England before the advent of its brilliant Renaissance theatre, the plays were crude, and the acting was not yet professional. This situation goes far to explain the great success of the English acting companies who were driven across the Channel by unemployment, poverty and plagues during the time of *The Comedy of Errors'* first performances in London in (1594 and 1604). Although the English found well-equipped theatres in which to perform, their German audiences were exposed for the first time to the marvel of their rich costumes and properties, and, above all, to their professional acting. The language barrier foregrounded pantomime, dance, song, slapstick and action-packed melodrama. Although this does not seem to have noticeably lessened the audiences' enjoyment of these shows, it did for a long time prevent the staging of the original texts.

Thus the little evidence that we have of any familiarity with *The Comedy of Errors* in the seventeenth century takes the form of some echoes in the work of Jacob Ayrer of Nuremberg, better known for *Die Schöne Sidea*, which has strong plot resemblances to *The Tempest*. Also, there are records of performances of *The Comedy of Errors* in the later seventeenth century.[17] With the very serious interruption by the ravages of the Thirty Years' War, English plays, *The Comedy of Errors* among them, continued to be performed, in whatever bizarre form, throughout the seventeenth century. Crude though they may have been in the initial stages, these shows began to create a new theatrical awareness and prepared the way for deflecting literary and dramatic attention from the French theatre in the direction of the English theatre.

Yet even in the eighteenth century, at a time when this process was beginning to bear fruit, the plays continued to be performed in adapted form. As in England, *The Comedy of Errors* was considered an apprentice work dashed off for light entertainment and in need of improvement according to current taste. Consequently, the farce and sentimental interests were emphasized in highly successful English adaptations like *Every Body Mistaken* (1716), *See If You Like It* (1734) or *The Twins* (1762, 1808), which were paralleled in Germany by a text like G.F.W. Großmann's *Die Irrungen*, first performed in 1777 and printed in the same year,[18] obscure enough but worthwhile looking at both for its similarities to its English counterparts and for its German specificity.[19]

The most immediately visible difference from the original text is that the frame story has been abandoned. Consequently, the sombre tone deemed necessary in order to create comedy by authorities like Donatus and obviously by Shakespeare himself, acknowledging the link with classical comedy as he does in the title, is not established in Act I. This is of course standard procedure of theatres everywhere eager to provide light entertainment. As will be shown, it has been employed in Germany, too, well into our own time.

Die Irrungen makes no bones about its concern with what is very often advertised as theatrical effectiveness. Its title page first defines the play as "Ein Lustspiel," a comedy, only to add that it is "No more and no less than a farce." As was traditionally done in Germany with Shakespeare's plays in the seventeenth century, initially for sheer necessity, the fine linguistic flights are also sacrificed. The set pieces have been cut more or less to a functional minimum. The blank verse is reduced to flat German prose. Even the servants' invective is rather less imaginative, while the puns, a perennial problem in German Shakespeare translation, are either lost or somewhat pedantically adapted.

However, the main story is followed quite faithfully. One formal difference is that each character entering the stage starts a new scene. Thus we have nine scenes (instead of the two) to Act I, seven to Act II, ten to Act III, eighteen to Act IV and another eighteen to Act V. Some of these scenes comprise only a few lines.

The characters have been given homely German names, a move indicative of a change in the play's mode or in the general atmosphere of this neoclassical age, or possibly both. The Antipholi have become the Reichard twins, one a resident of Berlin where the scene is laid, the other from Hamburg. Both are rich merchants. The sums of money involved have been increased. A sum of three thousand marks is at stake instead of the one thousand. The merchants' meeting place here is the exchange ("Börse"), not "upon the mart" (I,ii,27). Since both are "reich," rich, "Reichard" would seem a suitable name. The Dromios bear the traditional German servants' name of Johann.

Adriana has become Henriette, her sister Luciana, Wilhelmine. A little surprisingly for late eighteenth-century Germany, Adriana's emancipatory talk in CE II,i has been fairly fully preserved, and Wilhelmine is actually less conciliatory than Luciana, suggesting in no uncertain terms that the gentlemen should be reminded of their duties lest the ladies lose their grip of them.[20] There are also several additional characters. Reichard of Berlin has a little daughter, Louischen, a tribute to the unwaning popularity of children (and animals) on stage as well as to sentiment. Little Louise, or Louischen, seriously aggravates the identity crisis of Reichard of Hamburg, who now finds himself assailed by the emotional demands of a small daughter as well as a surprise wife. Then there is Mauskopf (Mousehead), the tailor, a new creation probably due to the availability of a popular comic actor. The *Theater-Journal für Deutschland* gives a brief description of the "Seylersche Schauspielgesellschaft," which was performing in the Rhein area late in 1777, and mentions that a certain "Herr Helmuth" had performed most attractively of all the company as Mauskopf the tailor in *Die Irrungen*.[21] In the text Mauskopf is given an atrocious stammer, which at one point is parodied by Johann of Berlin. Herr Großmann seems to have been only too happy to cater to the taste of his audience.

However, just as in England at the time, audiences were fond of music, of which a fair amount was built into this show. That also had the virtue of helping to solve the somewhat ticklish problem of the original courtesan, who kept some Germans worrying quite a bit.[22] Here, the Courtesan is transformed into Madame Hellsang, a very respectable singer. Reichard of Berlin, a chastened Antipholus of Ephesus, turns out to be a cultivated friend of the muses who has a long conversation with Madame Hellsang[23] about Italian vocal music, which both of them consider vulgar and superficial. When Reichard still wishes that, with her talent, she had been born Italian, she objects, and we are offered a taste of frustrated early German nationalism. "I am proud to be German," protests Madame Hellsang. She then blames all the arts for not serving the honour and enlightenment ("Aufklärung") of the German nation, and in particular the craze to adore everything foreign, to prefer foreign to German art and fashion, and to spend good German money abroad rather than at home.

After this vigorous overture Madame Hellsang obliges and sings an aria by Sarti. Another song is not immediately granted for artistic reasons. Fortunately, another newcomer to the play happens to be present, the singer's sister, Rosine. Reichard is duly impressed by the revelation that she is a flautist: "I stand amazed! A woman, the flute?" It is important to all present that she plays a concerto by a German composer, "Kleinknecht in Anspach."[24] To demonstrate the wealth of German music, Madame Hellsang, accompanied by her sister on the flute, sings another song, a composition by "Benda the younger."[25]

The eighteenth century German version of *The Comedy of Errors* is thus used for a celebration of superior German culture, culminating in a regular concert performance. After the concert the small party go to drink coffee in the garden after the German fashion. There are of course many other reflections of German conditions. The Abbess's dramatic job, involving a diagnosis of Antipholus of Ephesus' supposed madness, is given to a prototypical town clerk. The Duke has become a president. His house provides the Berlin Reichard's asylum of Act V. The "Herr Präsident" is responsible to the King, who does not appear in person but lurks in the background. The Präsident graciously offers Reichard of Hamburg half of his late father's considerable fortune plus interest on condition that he settle down in Berlin. It would be "offending the King's will" if such a considerable fortune were allowed out of the city. The dénouement tries to root *Die Irrungen* even more firmly in continental Europe, the complex migrations of the Reichard family finally revealed to involve not only Berlin and Hamburg, but also Königsberg and Moscow.

In 1762 the poet Christoph Martin Wieland began to publish reliable prose translations of twenty-two of the plays, and these have retained their unadorned charm to this day. Wieland completed his task in 1766.[26] *Die Irrungen, oder Die doppelten Zwillinge, ein Lustspiel* was contained in volume IV (1764).[27]

Wieland's work provided German theatres as well as commentators with a body of easily available texts.[28] Johann Joachim Eschenburg completed Wieland's work and between 1775 and 1782 published the first German edition of all the plays, also in prose. *The Comedy of Errors* was not one of the original seventeen translations of Shakespeare's plays, in appropriate verse as well as prose, contained in the classical work by the leader of the Romantic movement in Germany, August Wilhelm Schlegel. *Die Komödie der Irrungen* was provided by Graf Wolf Heinrich Baudissin, who together with his wife, Johann Ludwig Tieck's daughter Dorothea, completed the whole body of translations between 1825 and 1833 under Tieck's supervision, adding nineteen plays. This body of translations has since played an outstanding rôle in the history of Shakespeare reception, idolatry and debate. That rôle has not remained unchallenged, partly because of later philological discoveries unknown during the period of the Schlegel and Tieck team, partly for the literary rather than theatrical nature of their diction, and partly for their "Victorian" prudery. In one count, near to a hundred translators were competing with the "Schlegel-Tieck Edition" in the nineteenth century, and another eighty or so more in the twentieth,[29] in an effort to provide texts appropriate to changing needs and attitudes.

In the second half of the nineteenth century an increasing number of reliable texts were thereby becoming available and performed. In the theatre, too, new forms of historicist attention to detail were emerging. Thus the Meiningen court theatre developed a new desire for verisimilitude, insisting on the accuracy of historical costume and scenery, but during its peak period also on carefully staged, integrated ensemble acting, with special attention to small parts and mass scenes. *The Comedy of Errors* was one of five Shakespeare plays performed between 1860 and 1866. That was the time just before Duke Georg II of Saxe-Meiningen came to the throne, although he was already influencing affairs from behind the scene as crown prince while not daring to step in openly while Duke Bernhard was still in charge.[30]

Yet in spite of all these aspirations after textual and theatrical historicity, which at times tended to become ends in themselves, adaptations remained common practice. These were justified in theory by a need to cleanse Shakespeare of the aesthetic faults attributable to the primitivism of his own age and nation—his "indecent puns, euphuistic mannerisms, and poor motivation of (the) characters' actions." At the time before and following the first German unification and the foundation of the Second Reich of 1871, the idea was to Germanize Shakespeare even more thoroughly than before by performing his plays as he would have written them "had he had the good fortune to live in an age (and in a nation) more advanced than his own."[31]

That idea of improving on the effectiveness of Shakespeare's plays persisted in the twentieth century, although after World War I the nationalist motivation waned. Nevertheless a man like Hans Rothe managed to stir a national scandal when, starting in 1918, he adapted Shakespeare for the modern German stage. He believed that in order to capture the spirit of the Elizabethan theatre the plays could not be performed pure and simple but had to be massively changed. He, too, purged them of alleged mannerisms, in fact of anything that seemed to stand in the way of slick entertainment, and generally streamlined the plots and dialogues for immediate effect. Thus in *The Comedy of Errors* he continued the old tradition of cutting the frame story. To Rothe, *The Comedy of Errors* was an apocryphal play. He believed that Shakespeare's only original contributions were the Abbess and, perhaps, the narrative parts of the dénouement. According to Rothe, Shakespeare had taken even the double Dromios from Plautus' *Amphitruo*, and *The Comedy of Errors* was an unfinished text, certainly no masterpiece. For him, it represented a potential, "a monument of the incomplete,"[32] to be finished by a kindred spirit with a thorough understanding of the spirit of the Elizabethan period and of the theatre generally.

Rothe's adaptations were widely played for many years. His *Komödie der Irrungen* was even translated into English by Ashley Dukes and performed in London and in the United States.[33] One production of his *Komödie der Irrungen* stands out for the attention it attracted when it came out in Berlin at the Schauspielhaus am Gendarmenmarkt in April, 1934, early in the second year of Nazi rule in Germany. It marked a special occasion in Berlin's theatrical life because the Schauspielhaus had recently been taken over by the now legendary Gustav Gründgens as intendant, and director Lothar Müthel was generally praised for presenting very lively entertainment, as promised by being set right at the beginning in the spirit almost of Mozart, of a "rococo opera."[34]

Critics were in agreement that, as one of them put it, "the Schauspielhaus has scored its spring hit," to the vehement and cordial applause and laughter of the audience.[35] But with the notable exception of O.E.H.,[36] critics were also unanimous in their ambivalent attitude towards Rothe's text. Carl Weichardt at first seems unambiguous in his praise of Rothe's version. Since the English literary historian J.M. Robertson has recently proved, he says, that Shakespeare used a play by his brilliant predecessor Marlowe for *The Comedy of Errors* and himself contributed even less than was hitherto thought, "Rothe is right not to believe he has to stick to Shakespeare's text with philological anxiety for his new version now used by the Schauspielhaus, but instead unrestrainedly to improvise again, using his own imagination."[37] "All that's superfluous has been dropped,"[38] the language and allusions have been modernized for effects which have been richly exploited. "For the theatre this new version is of great benefit, even though people will continue to prefer to read the original or Tieck's translation in the privacy of their own home."[39] The majority of critics make a recurring similar distinction. On the one hand they applaud what they see as Rothe's dramaturgical skill, usually mentioning his concluding invention of a ménage à trois involving Nell/Luce and the Dromios. And on the other hand they blame him for vulgarizing Shakespeare's language.

There is nothing overtly reminiscent of the new Nazi rule in these reviews, except for one thing. A closer look reveals a pervading enthusiasm on the part of all critics regarding the youthfulness of both sets of twins, the young women, and the youthful spirit of the production generally. The Berlin Schillertheater had been closed down some time before (as in fact happened again for lack of funds in 1993), and some of the unemployed young actors had been given jobs in this production.[40] On the other hand, the almost obsessive references to the vivacity and beauty of the young actors, and their young voices, shining faces and flashing teeth reflect a cult of youth which had been evident in Germany for some time, ready to be exploited by the

Third Reich once it had taken over. It is something that tells us more about the tragicomedy of the time than about *The Comedy of Errors*. Almost forgotten today, that German cult of youth was incidentally observed by Thomas Mann who made one of the characters in his novel *Doktor Faustus*, the Berlin pastor Deutschlin, remark on it, speaking in 1932:

> The idea of youth is a prerogative and a mark of excellence of our, the German people,—the others hardly know it, youth as an intrinsic value is all but unknown to them , they marvel at the behaviour of German youth, with its emphasis on character and formed by the higher age classes, and even at their unbourgeois costume. Let them do so. German youth represents, precisely as youth, the very spirit of the people, the German spirit, which is young and full of the future,—immature if you will, but what does that signify! German deeds have always come from a certain violent immaturity, and we are not the people of the Reformation for nothing.[41]

Rothe left Germany in 1934. Public discussion of Shakespeare translations was stopped by Goebbels himself, who decreed that henceforth only the "Schlegel-Tieck" translations were to be performed by German theatres.[42] *The Comedy of Errors* continued to be put on even during World War II. A production at the Dresden Theater des Volkes is on record as late as April 1944.[43]

That was not the end of the story. In 1960, Hans Schweikart directed *The Comedy of Errors* for the Munich Kammerspiele, once again using Rothe's version. Once more there was a scandal pretty much along the lines of the 1934 Berlin performance, showing that the scene could still be shaken by the Bard in post-war Germany. But this time academics publicly tore the version to pieces. Above all, the Bavarian Academy of Fine Arts condemned it as a serious offence against common decency, since it deceived the public into believing that this banal farce was by Shakespeare, who had in reality been plundered and depraved by Rothe. Rothe, who was sixty-six at the time and living in Florence, was actually somewhat surprised at the vehemence of the excommunication. The version so harshly condemned was after all the old one first performed in 1932 in Breslau, then in Berlin and elsewhere, and put on by about thirty theatres since the end of the war. Rothe announced he would take legal action against the Academy.[44]

The alleged aesthetic inferiority of *The Comedy of Errors* as an early apprentice work has long bothered German intellectuals. To Herrmann Conrad, writing in 1910, *The Comedy of Errors* was "even more insignificant" than *The Taming of the Shrew*;[45] to Hermann Kienzl in 1911 it was "a naive jest," "a preliminary study,"[46] the sort of thing which made yet another critic hope that *The Comedy of Errors* might not be by Shakespeare after all; even director Werner Schröter, Benjamin Henrichs reports, thought the play he had just staged rather poor.[47]

Rothe named the "many improbabilities" of the frame story as his principal justification for his decision to eliminate those parts of the text.[48] Long before Rothe, August Wilhelm Schlegel had suggested that the actors involved in the incredible misrecognitions should always wear masks, "to endow them at least with a measure of sensual truth, and this is something the poet will have observed himself."[49] Hellmut Kotschenreuther, also reviewing the Schroeter production at the Berlin Freie Volksbühne of 1983, thought the actors on stage pushed into the rôle of blind people or blockheads since the play was expecting them to keep mixing up people who could not possibly be mixed up.[50]

It was relatively late before theatre critics and academics realized what had been experienced by audiences all along in any even moderately successful staging of *The Comedy of Errors*, namely that this comedy and anyone performing it can rely for its stage success not on some sort of realism of representation, but on the very improbabilities themselves which had been the cause of so many critical headaches. And so Doris Eisner, reviewing a Vienna production of 1949 based, incidentally, on Rothe's text, describes in passing how, in spite of lack of rehearsal and inadequately trained actors, the show had succeeded through foregrounding the tumult and madness of events, highlighting them by means of parodistic elements.[51] In a review of the 1960 production at the Berlin Volksbühne, Dieter Kranz says the same in reverse: "The more lifelike, the more 'probable' one makes the story of the separated twin brothers, the more incredible does it basically become."[52] "No one thinks of inquiring into probability," is Hugo Zehder's comment on the same production.[53]

The performance, the reviewer continues, even made people laugh who had come determined not to laugh, and the story "did not even lack the spicy nuance of possible suspiciousness to the mind of the censor. For it assumes man to be as he or she happens to be, namely incorrigible."[54] An East Berlin *Comedy of Errors* production was here being reviewed for a Western newspaper by an observer from the West. It did not occur to ordinary Germans at the time that the two sides, East and West, would be physically separated from each other by The Wall a little over a year later. But the political separation had been an accomplished fact for years. Side effects of the cold war division of Germany can be glimpsed occasionally even from a random selection of texts relating to *The Comedy of Errors*.[55] Zehder in 1960 was alluding not only to the fact of censorship in the East, he was also implicitly referring to the régime's ideological mainstay of a belief in the perfectibility (and hence superiority) of socialist man no longer subdued to the rule of money, a Utopia, but also an alibi, especially attractive to many intellectuals in the early years, before disillusion with the realities of life set in.

Shakespeare's concern with the corrupting influence of money on human relations had of course been a scholarly subject for a long time, and not only in *Timon of Athens*, and not only among Marxists. In his review of the 1960 production quoted above, Dieter Kranz referred to the destructive power of money.[56] In 1964, the East German doyen of Marxist Shakespeare studies, Anselm Schlösser, applied the topos to *The Comedy of Errors* in a seminal article, referring to it in the title by the German equivalent of the philosophical term of "alienation."[57] Whether or not they were influenced by Professor Schlösser's article, subsequent East German productions of *The Comedy of Errors* gave considerable emphasis to the alienating rôle of money. Anneliese Priewe, in a close and thorough review of a 1974 production at Neustrelitz, quotes Marx's dictum that "everything becomes saleable and purchasable"[58] as the motto underlying the production and making it both more profound and more entertaining.[59] Eva and Günter Walch's coverage of several 1978

Shakespeare productions for *Shakespeare Quarterly* included a piece on *The Comedy of Errors* in which they intimated that the production was transcending the rigid boundaries of the official alienation topos:

> *The Comedy of Errors* was given an elegant and witty performance in Weimar. Obviously inspired by the eminent Shakespeare scholar Anselm Schlösser's analysis of the play in the light of "unjust divorce," the company made visible through the turbulence of the stage-business the underlying insecurity and vulnerability of human existence. Even time itself, symbolized by a huge handless clock whose pendulum was pulled up out of sight at the beginning of the play, ceased to be something to be relied upon. Romanian director Sorana Coroama, doing her second guest production for the *National theater Weimar*, made the two Antipholuses and Dromios search desperately for an identity whose gradual loss was visibly driving them mad.[60]

Just as, in Hugo Zehder's 1960 observation in East Berlin, characters were presented as beset by the weaknesses of the human condition, East or West, the Romanian director against the background of her own national experience was staging "the underlying insecurity and vulnerability," not just of life under capitalism, but "of human existence" altogether.

While specially encoded stage language was being used in this way by directors in the East several years earlier, in West Germany the Kassel theatre based a 1971 production of *The Comedy of Errors* on the same basic idea of alienation. Georg Hensel disliked the result. The anticapitalist emphasis was too obviously pregnant with significance and generally heavy-handed to survive as entertaining comedy. Shakespeare had used the money to endow *The Comedy of Errors* with significance, the director was using *The Comedy of Errors* to bestow significance on money.[61]

After The Wall was torn down in 1989 and Germany was reunited in 1990, *The Comedy of Errors* was one of the first Shakespeare productions to be shown in Berlin, once again at the Volksbühne theatre in East Berlin, the site of the play's previous successful runs. The potentially tragic beginning was emphasized, for example, with a huge symbolical guillotine mounted above the stage. As so often before in Germany, a new translation played a prominent rôle in the production and in the reviews, most of which underlined its theatrical viability.[62] Critic Ernst Schumacher, an academic and an expert on Brecht, stressed the contemporary uses of metaphor in the new translation but criticized the production as too lightweight. In making this point, he reflected the new situation that had emerged in the country after the first reunification euphoria had evaporated. In his view, the Volksbühne, offering a fun show and obligingly taking people's minds off the misery of everyday life, had once again yielded compulsively to an attempt to save itself in the ideologically confused and economically shaken situation in the new federal states.[63]

It is easy to predict that there will be more productions of *The Comedy of Errors* in Germany, that the text will be used in old and new, surprising ways in a theatre which, many believe, is in deep crisis. It is a crisis which is financial, philosophical and aesthetic. It is a crisis, some believe, in which the theatre has been actually been for centuries. It is also felt by many to be a crisis caused by omnipotent directors driven by "the urge to do something 'differently,' something different from that done by A and B and—in this age of the cult of personality and individuality—different from what one did oneself the day before yesterday."[64] But that, too, is an old complaint, already expressed by Herrmann Conrad in 1910.[65]

NOTES

[1] Hermann Kienzl in *Bühne und Welt*, 13 (1911), p. 86: "taucht sehr selten auf einer deutschen Bühne auf." All translations are my own unless otherwise stated.

[2] Erik Krünes, "Shakespeare errötet. *Komödie der Irrungen* inszeniert von Lothar Müthel," *Berliner Illustrierte Nachtausgabe*, 27 April 1934.

[3] Hans Heck and Monika Müller, "Die Komödien," in Ina Schabert (ed.), *Shakespeare-Handbuch. Die Zeit. Der Mensch. Das Werk. Die Nachwelt*, Stuttgart: Kröner, 1972, p. 398.

[4] Alexander Reschke, "*Komödie der Irrungen*. Shakespeares Lustspiel seiner

ersten Schaffenszeit in Theater des Volkes," *Pirnaer Anzeiger*, 28 April 1944. The critique refers to a production at the Dresden theatre, a year before the end of the Second World War.

[5] Friedrich Luft, "Ein Fest ist noch kein Spaß," *Berliner Morgenpost*, 4 Sept. 1983.

[6] Volker Oesterreich, "Shakespeares Software paßt zur Volksbühnen-Hardware," *Berliner Morgenpost*, 17 Feb. 1991.

[7] William Shakespeare, *The Comedy of Errors. Die Komödie der Irrungen*. Englisch-deutsche Studienausgabe. Textausgabe, deutsche Prosafassung, Anmerkungen, Einleitung und Kommentar von Kurt Tetzeli v. Rosador, Berlin und München: Francke, 1982, p. 25. Tetzeli cites Paul Wislicenus, "Zwei neuentdeckte Shakespearequellen," *Shakespeare Jahrbuch*, 14 (1879) pp. 87–96; and, as examples of a persistent tradition, M. Labinski, *Shakespeares "Komödie der Irrungen." Das Werk und seine Gestaltung auf der Bühne*, Diss. Breslau, 1934, pp. 16–38, and W. Born, *Shakespeares Verhältnis zu seinen Quellen in "The Comedy of Errors" und "The Taming of the Shrew,"* Diss. Hamburg, 1955. I would add Joh. Groene, "Zwei neu entdeckte Quellen zu Shakespeares Komödie der Irrungen," *Shakespeare Jahrbuch*, 29/30 (1894), pp. 281–287.

[8] Tetzeli, p. 25.

[9] Wolfgang Stellmacher (ed.), *Auseinandersetzung mit Shakespeare. Texte zur deutschen Shakespeare-Aufnahme 1790–1830*, Berlin: Akademie-Verlag, 1985, p. 279.

[10] Marianne Labinski, *Shakespeares "Komödie der Irrungen." Das Werk und seine Gestaltung auf der Bühne*, Diss. Breslau 1934, pp. 84–85.

[11] See Karl Schneider, "Gerstenberg als Verkünder Shakespeares," *Shakespeare Jahrbuch*, 58 (1922), pp. 39–45.

[12] Karl S. Guthke, "Richtungskonstanten in der Deutschen Shakespeare-Deutung des 18. Jahrhunderts," *Shakespeare Jahrbuch*, 98 (1962), pp. 64–92.

[13] That the work of the Englishman "von einem besoffenen Wilden herzurühren scheine." Guthke, p. 82.

[14] "Nicht eine einzige unnötige Scene." Heinrich Wilhelm von Gerstenberg, *Briefe über die Merkwürdigkeiten der Litteratur* (1766), ed. Alexander von Weilen, Stuttgart 1890, p. 102.

[15] "Des allgemeinen Vorurtheils…daß es Shakespearn an Kunst fehle." *Merkwürdigkeiten*, p. 156.

[16] For the English stage history see R.A. Foakes (ed.), William Shakespeare, *The Comedy of Errors. The Arden Edition*, London: Methuen, 1968, pp. 51–55.

[17] See Ernest Brennecke, "Germany," in Oscar James Campbell (ed.), *A Shakespeare Encyclopaedia*, London: Methuen, 1974 (1966), p. 256.

[18] G.F.W. Großmann, *Die Irrungen. Ein Lustspiel in fünf Aufzügen nach dem Shakespear. Nichts mehr und nichts weniger als eine Farce*. Frankfurt, gedruckt mit Diehlischen Schriften, und zu finden bey dem Kassierer

Sprenkel, 1777. One other adaptation was that by F.L. Schröder, who from 1776 on did much to establish Shakespeare in the classical repertory of the German stage by performing, and appearing in, his versions of about ten of the plays. His script for his Garrick-like version of *Hamlet* for example, "was his own adaptation of Heufeld's reduction and regularized adaptation of Wieland's prose translation." Werner Habicht, *Shakespeare and the German Imagination*. International Shakespeare Association Occasional Paper No. 5, Hertford: Stephen Austin and Sons Ltd., 1994, p. 5.

[19] E.L. Stahl, *Shakespeare und das deutsche Theater* (Berlin, 1947) gives 28 November 1777 as the date of the first night. The *Theatralisches Wochenblatt* (Hamburg, 1774/1775, p. 187) registers a performance of a play called *Die Irrungen* by the "Ackermannsche Gesellschaft" in Hamburg on 15 November 1775.

[20] "Die Herren wachsen uns sonst über den Kopf," *Die Irrungen* I, ix.

[21] See *Theater-Journal für Deutschland*, Gotha 1778, 7. Stück. Repr. München 1981, p. 41.

[22] Thus the scholar Theodor Eichhoff, writing in 1903, takes exception to a number of aspects of *The Comedy of Errors*, first of all to what he believes to be Shakespeare's adapters, then to booksellers, clowns, and the deplorable taste of Shakespeare's audiences. And he objects very much to the Courtesan. What upsets him as scandalous is not just the Courtesan's "unnatural" ("unnatürlich") profession, but that "ladies and gentlemen of superior rank" and even a duke and an abbess should be seen conversing with her as if that were quite natural ("daß sie sich in der Gesellschaft vornehmer Männer und Frauen, ja des Herzogs und der Äbtissin ungeniert bewegt"). "Such a person as depicted in the *CE* cannot be a legitimate subject of artistic treatment at all and is an insult to the other persons of the play as well as to the audience" ("Eine solche Person, wie sie in der CE geschildert wird, ist überhaupt keiner künstlerischen Behandlung fähig und bedeutet eine Beleidigung für die anderen Personen des Stücks wie für das Publikum"). He blames Shakespeare's alleged corrupters, deplorable audience taste but also Plautus for the scandal. But he, too, has a solution to the problem. The Courtesan "does not belong in the play" ("gehört nicht in das Stück hinein"), she is actually an entirely different sort of person altogether, "a nice, proper hostess" ("Wir haben es also mit einer netten, feschen Wirtin zu tun"), who presides over a fashionable inn much frequented by Antipholus of Ephesus who wants to give her the gold chain as a present. Why? One wonders. See Theodor Eichhoff, "Unser Shakespeare." *Beiträge zu einer wissenschaftlichen Shakespeare Kritik*. Halle: H. Niemeyer, 903, pp. 54–55. Eichhoff's (and others') theory of interpolation was attacked in 1910 by Friedrich Brie. See Friedrich Brie, "Bearbeitungen von Dramen Shakespeares," *Shakespeare Jahrbuch*, 46 (1910), p. 13.

[23] See *Die Irrungen* III, ix.

[24] "Ich erstaune! Ein Frauenzimmer, die Flöte?" Kleinknecht came from a family especially well known in southern Germany which produced three generations of talented musicians. The K. whose concerto is performed and who is praised by Rosine for his musical skill probably is Jakob Friedrich K. (1722–1794), a member of the Bayreuth court orchestra and its chief conductor after it had been moved to Ansbach in 1769. He was admired for the quality of his compositions, among them several flute concertos. See Friedrich Blume (ed.), *Die Musik in Geschichte und Gegenwart*. Allgemeine Enzyklopädie der Musik. Kassel: Bärenreiter, 1958, vol. 7, cols. 1209–1210.

[25] There was a profusion of musical Bendas in eighteenth century Germany. The second composer, referred to by Madame Hellsang also as the "young artist, worthy son of a great father," was in all probability Friedrich Ludwig B. (1746–1792), violinist, conductor, composer of oratorios, a *Barber of Seville* opera, operettas, etc. He was the son of the famous Georg Benda (1722–1795), who, like many other musicians, originally came from Bohemia. See *Riemann Musik Lexikon*. Personenteil A-K. Mainz: B. Schott's Söhne, 1959, p. 127.

[26] The rich tradition of German Shakespeare translation was begun by Baron von Borck, Prussian ambassador to London, who published the very first German translation of an actual text by Shakespeare in 1741. He rendered *Julius Caesar* in Alexandrine verses, attracting immediate critical attention.

[27] Ernst Stadler (ed.), *Wielands Gesammelte Schriften*. 2. Abteilung: Übersetzungen, Zweiter Band. Berlin: Weidmannsche Buchhandlung, 1909.

[28] Wieland used Pope and Warburton's 1747 edition, occasionally those by Theobald and Johnson. See Kyösti Itkonen, *Die Shakespeare- Übersetzung Wielands (1762–1766)*. Ein Beitrag zur Erforschung englisch-deutscher Lehnbeziehungen. *Studia Philologica Juväskyläensia VII*, Jyväskylä, 1971.

[29] See Habicht, p. 16. Well-known translations of *The Comedy of Errors* were contributed by Johann W.O. Benda (1825), Ernst Ortlepp (1842), Karl Simrock (1871), Friedrich Dingelstedt (1878), Georg Herwegh (1880), Friedrich Gundolf (1921), Richard Flatter (1954) and Rudolph Schaller (1961). Erich Fried, one of the best-known post-war translators of Shakespeare, did not translate *The Comedy of Errors*.

[30] See Ann Marie Koller, *The Theater Duke. Georg II of Saxe-Meiningen and the German Stage*. Stanford: Stanford University Press, 1984, p. 58. The other Shakespeare plays put on were *Hamlet*, *The Taming of the Shrew*, *Twelfth Night* and *Henry IV*. See ibid., p. 227.

[31] Habicht, p. 12.

[32] "(E)in Monument der Unvollendung." Hans Rothe, *Shakespeare als Provokation. Sein Leben und Werk. Sein Theater und seine Welt. Seine Freunde und Feinde*. München: Langen, Müller, 1961, p. 200.

[33] See Rothe, p. 201.

[34] "Schon das erste Bühnenbild Traugott Müllers läßt erkennen, wie diese

Aufführung verlaufen wird. Als ein buntes Puppenspiel, als Rokoko-Oper, als Mozartsches Septett." H.P., *"Komödie der Irrungen* im Staatstheater am Gendarmenmarkt," *Das 12 Uhr Blatt,* 27 April 1934.

[35] "Das Schauspielhaus hat sein Frühlings-Erfolgsstück." "Der Beifall was so heftig und herzlich, wie in allen Szenen das Lachen." Dr. Carl Weichardt, *"Komödie der Irrungen* im Schauspielhaus am Gendarmenmarkt," *Berliner Morgenpost,* 28 April 1934.

[36] See O.E.H., "Von Plautus zu Hans Rothe. Shakespeares *Komödie der Irrungen* im Staatstheater," *B.Z. am Mittag,* 27 April 1934: Rothe's "translation turns out to be much more than a translation...: it is a fresh rendering which deepens, beautifies, spiritualizes and so inspires the play of mistakes in such a way that theatre playing has become a game of jesting, irony and real significance." (Rothes "Übersetzung ist mehr als eine Übertragung...: sie ist eine Neugestaltung, die das Verwechslungsspiel vertieft, verschönt, vergeistigt und so beseelt, daß die Theaterspielerei zu einem Spiel aus Scherz, Ironie und wirklicher Bedeutung geworden ist."

[37] "Hans Rothe (hat) recht, wenn er in seiner Neufassung, die das Schauspielhaus jetzt spielt, sich nicht mit philologischer Ängstlichkeit an Shakespeares Text glaubt halten zu müssen, sondern selber noch einmal frisch drauflos phantasiert." Weichardt, ibid.

[38] "Alles Überflüssige ist unter den Tisch gefallen." Weichardt, ibid.

[39] "(F)ürs Theater ist diese Neufassung ein großer Gewinn, wenn man auch im stillen Kämmerlein nach wie vor lieber zum Original oder zur Tieckschen Uebersetzung greifen wird." Weichardt, ibid.

[40] See Erik Künes, "Shakespeare errötet. *Komödie der Irrungen* inszeniert von Lothar Müthel," *Berliner Illustierte Nachtausgabe,* 27 April 1934. The title would translate as "Shakespeare blushes," punning on "Rothe," "red."

[41] Thomas Mann, *Doktor Faustus. Das Leben des deutschen Tonsetzers Adrian Leverkühn, erzählt von einem Freund,* Stockholm: Bermann-Fischer Verlag, 1947, p. 184.

[42] See Habicht, p. 17.

[43] See Alexander Reschke, *"Komödie der Irrungen.* Shakespeares Lustspiel seiner ersten Schaffenszeit im Theater des Volkes," *Pirnaer Anzeiger,* 28 April 1944; G. Stolte-Adelt, "Tiefer Sinn im heiteren Spiel. *Komödie der Irrungen* im Theater des Volkes," *Dresdner Zeitung,* 28 April 1944.

[44] See Reinhold Grimm, Willy Jägy, Hans Oesch (eds.), *Der deutsche Shakespeare. Theater unserer Zeit,* vol. 7. Basel, Hamburg, Wien: Basilius Press, 1965, with contributions to the Rothe controversy by Rudolf Franke, Rudolf Stamm, and others. See also *Der Spiegel,* 44 (1960), pp. 84, 87.

[45] "(N)och unbedeutender." Herrmann Conrad, "Theater-Korrespondenz. Shakespeares *Komödie der Irrungen* in den Kammerspielen des Deutschen Theaters," *Preußische Jahrbücher,* 142 (1910), p. 359.

[46] "(N)aiver Scherz," "Vorstudie." Hermann Kienzl, review of *Die Komödie*

der Irrungen at Reinhardt's Kammerspiele, *Bühne und Welt*, 13 (1911), p. 86.
[47] "(E)in bißchen kümmerlich." Benjamin Henrichs, "Botschaften aus dem Wrack", *Die Zeit*, 9 September 1983. Kurt Schlüter supported the assessment of *The Comedy of Errors* as generally inferior, comparing Shakespeare's handling of the narration of the characters' previous history in *The Comedy of Errors* with that in *The Tempest*. Kurt Schlüter, "Die Erzählung der Vorgeschichte in Shakespeares Dramen," *Shakespeare Jahrbuch*, 90 (1954), pp. 108–123.

[48] "Die Rahmenhandlung mit ihren vielen Unwahrscheinlichkeiten wurde in der Neufassung nicht wiederbelebt." Rothe, p. 200.

[49] "Es versteht sich, daß in dergleichen Stücken, um ihnen wenigstens eine sinnliche Wahrheit zu geben, die Rollen, welche das Mißverständnis verursachen immer mit Masken gespielt werden sollten, und so wird es auch der Dichter beobachtet haben." August Wilhelm von Schlegel, *Vorlesungen über dramatische Kunst und Litteratur*, Leipzig: Weidmannsche Buchhandlung, 1846, p. 214.

[50] "Die Handlungsträger, die immer wieder Menschen verwechseln müssen, die nicht zu verwechseln sind, werden in die Rollen von Blinden beziehungsweise Dummköpfen gedrängt." Hellmut Kotschenreuther, "Schließlich glaubt man keinem mehr. Berlin: Schroeter inszeniert Shakespeares *Komödie der Irrungen*," *Abendzeitung*, 6 September 1983.

[51] See Doris Eisner, "Sieben Jahre Shakespeare in Österreich 1945–1951," *Shakespeare Jahrbuch*, 87/88 (1951/52), pp. 195–196.

[52] "Je lebensechter, je 'wahrscheinlicher' man nämlich die Geschichte von den getrennten Zwillingsbrüdern darstellt, desto unglaubwürdiger wird sie imgrunde." Dieter Kranz, "Im Geiste Shakespeares. *Komödie der Irrungen* in der Volksbühne Berlin," *Theater der Zeit*, 19 (1960), p. 80.

[53] Hugo Zehder, "Wahrscheinlichkeit ist suspendiert. Shakespeares *Komödie der Irrungen* in der Volksbühne," *Der Tag*, 13 January 1960.

[54] The story "entbehrt nicht einmal der pikanten Nuance der Zensurbedenklichkeit. Es nimmt nämlich den Menschen mit seinen Schwächen wie er ist, als unverbesserlich." Zehder, ibid.

[55] In the East, the Soviet Union was elevated to the highest authority in all questions. Thus, reviewing a production of *The Comedy of Errors* in 1954, still the height of Stalinism, Dr. Walter Pollatschek praises the Maxim Gorki Theatre for "having won Shakespeare for us the Stanislavski way" ("daß das Maxim-Gorki-Theater uns auf dem Stanislawski-Wege Shakespeare gewonnen hat"). *Neues Deutschland*, 23 October 1954). Reviewing the identical production (*Tägliche Rundschau*, 30 September 1954), Horst Reinecke quotes Soviet scholar A. Smirnov: "Under the guise of seemingly thoughtless mirth, the characteristic expression of the Renaissance acceptance of life, Shakespeare in these comedies touches upon great social problems and conflicts." ("Unter der Hülle scheinbar gedankenloser Heiterkeit, dem

charakteristischen Ausdruck für die Lebensbejahung der Renaissance, rührt Shakespeare an große gesellschaftliche Probleme und Konflikte.")

[56] Dieter Kranz, "Im Geiste Shakespeares," *Theater der Zeit*, 19 (1960), p. 80.

[57] Anselm Schlösser, "Das Motiv der Entfremdung in der *Komödie der Irrungen*," *Shakespeare Jahrbuch* (Weimar), 100/101 (1964/65), pp. 57–71. Georg Seehases, "Ein verwirrter Handel? Zur Dialektik in Shakespeares *Komödie der Irrungen*," *Shakespeare Jahrbuch* (Weimar) 117 (1981), pp. 55–61, elaborates on Schlösser's approach sociologically (individual and society, official and "plebeian" plot levels) and generically (comedy and tragedy). The question of genre is discussed along traditional lines, i.e. *The Comedy of Errors* as a comedy artistically enriched by tragic elements: "Aus den Bausteinen Tragödie und Komödie ist in der künstlerischen Synthese eine Komödie geworden" (see p. 56). Farce is not even mentioned. The generic problem of farce has of course been given attention in Germany, too. See e.g. Manfred Pfister, *Studien zum Wandel der Perspektivenstruktur in elisabethanischen und jakobäischen Komödien*, München, 1974. See also Kurt Tetzeli v. Rosador, who in his English and German student edition of *The Comedy of Errors* does mention the problem of genre, including farce, although very briefly. He also discusses the play's gold, money and chain imagery, but in the context of a critique of the New Criticism. He quotes a whole range of interpretations. See William Shakespeare, *The Comedy of Errors. Die Komödie der Irrungen*. Ed. Kurt Tetzeli v. Rosador. Berlin und München: Francke, 1982, pp. 24–29. For a recent stimulating discussion of farce see Barbara Freedman's *Staging the Gaze. Postmodernism, Psychoanalysis, and Shakespearean Comedy*. Ithaca and London: Cornell University Press, 1991, pp. 78–113, especially pp. 105–108.

[58] "Alles wird verkäuflich und kaufbar."

[59] Anneliese Priewe, "Shakespeare contra Schiller? Ein junges Ensemble arbeitet mit dem Erbe," *Theater der Zeit*, 33 (1974), No. 10, pp. 22–25.

[60] Eva and Günter Walch, "Shakespeare in the German Democratic Republic," *Shakespeare Quarterly*, 31 (1980), pp. 408–410.

[61] "Bei Shakespeare jedoch scheint mir das Geld nur wichtig, um den Verwirrungen ihre Bedeutung zu verleihen; bei Dieter Reible aber sind die Verwirrungen wichtig, um dem Geld seine Bedeutung zu verleihen." Georg Hensel, "Geldnöte? *Komödie der Irrungen* in Kassel," *Theater heute*, 12 (1971), No. 4, p. 23.

[62] Translation by Eva Walch. For some reviews see Christoph Funke, "Schmerzhafter Verlust von Identität. Shakespeares *Komödie der Irrungen* in der Berliner Volksbühne am Rosa-Luxemburg-Platz," *Der Morgen*, 18 February 1991. Volker Oesterreich, "*Die Komödie der Irrungen* am Rosa-Luxemburg-Platz. Shakespeares Software paßt zur Volksbühnen-Hardware," *Berliner Morgenpost*, 17 February 1991.

[63] "Sich ja gefällig zu machen, indem man Spaß macht, um von der Tristesse

des Alltags abzulenken-diesem schon zwangshaft gewordenen Selbstrettungsversuch des Theaters in den weltanschaulich konfusen und ökonomisch gebeutelten neuen Ländern gibt die Volksbühne am Luxemburg-Platz ein weiteres Mal mit der Inszenierung von Shakespeares *Komödie der Irrungen* nach." Ernst Schumacher, *"Die Komödie der Irrungen. Shakespeare in der Volksbühne,"* Berliner Zeitung, 18 February 1991.

[64] "Das Verlangen, etwas 'Anderes' zu machen, etwas anderes, als A und B gemacht haben und—in dieser Zeit des Persönlichkeits—und Individualitäts-Kultus!—als man selbst vorgestern gemacht hat."

[65] See Herrmann Conrad, "Theater-Korrespondenz," p. 23. Cp. note 44.

Stimulating Komisarjevsky Production: Stratford's Best, 1938

M.F.K.F.

"C'est magnifique, mais ce n'est pas le Shakespeare." Or, to vary a familiar advertisement slogan, we thought modern-dress Shakespeare advanced until we saw the Komisarjevsky production of *The Comedy of Errors* at Stratford, last night. Mr. Komisarjevsky, in his costume and scenic designs, shows us not only the shape of things present and past, but also the shape of things to come—a gloriously undisciplined conglomeration of styles, yet a perfect harmony of colour.

Sartorially, it is the apotheosis of the bowler hat, with a sop to the flat-brimmed topper. Mr. Komisarjevsky has "rung the changes" on the Derby, as the Americans call it, in all the 57 varieties, and in every colour of the rainbow. With it, some of his characters wear quite modern suits, carry umbrellas, and so on. Others are formally clad in stylised versions of classic costumes; others again display the fashions of 2038, or a natty mixture of those from the year Dot to the year Infinity.

Dramatically, Mr. Komisarjevsky uses Shakespeare's rhyming couplets and long-winded explanations as the skeleton of a script for the maddest, merriest farce imaginable. It all takes place in the Square at Ephesus, a sun-drenched plaza in which the unities of time, place and action are ruthlessly observed—with the aid of a clock which advances briskly through the hours to mark the intervals between scenes. Here the piteous story of old Aegeon is perfunctorily related and brusquely relegated to the background, while the farcical misadventures consequent upon the resemblance each to each of the Antipholus and Dromio brothers are joyously unfolded. When things look like becoming tedious the townsfolk change their sober paces into the steps of a descriptive ballet, or burst into concerted song in the village choral society manner—and to music, if you please, by Handel as well as by Mr. Anthony Bernard!

Eventually, Aegeon, whom we have quite forgotten, returns to be rescued from a grisly end (much to the disappointment of the simple Ephesian citizens), by an extremely masterful Abbess who turns out to be his long-lost wife. Other confusions are briskly resolved, and the curtain falls on the most audacious, stimulating, rare and entirely delightful production in Stratford's memory.

A SPLENDID RESPONSE

The company, without exception, respond splendidly to their producer's call for a blend of the formal and the farcical in their acting. They carry out their work in the true spirit of burlesque, and with the seriousness which makes for the full amusement. There are excellent "doubles": Mr. Dennis Roberts and Mr. Andrew Leigh as the Dromios, on whom the burden of the more obvious clowning falls; and by Mr. James Dale and Mr. G. Sheldon Bishop, who strike an effective contrast between the shocked puzzlement of the visiting Antipholus and the choleric good-humour of his townee brother.

Miss Valerie Tudor makes a charming spitfire as Adriana, with an equally charming sister in Miss Pauline Letts. The Duke is cleverly rendered by Mr. Michael Goodliffe in the vein of bored tolerance, while Mr. Donald Layne-Smith apes his manners nicely as his exquisite servant. A firm, shrill-tongued rendering of the Abbess is given by Miss Ethel Griffies, whose version of the part adds the final touch of unexpectedness to the production.

Again one must compliment Miss Peggy Livesey for an outstanding performance in a part of no great dimensions. The Courtesan, indeed, has little to do in the conventional renderings, but in this lighthearted burlesque she is always there or thereabouts, in the sauciest imaginable clothes and with an infinitely expressive range of gesture and aside. It is not so much what she says as what she does and how she looks, but when she has anything to say she gives point to every syllable.

The crowd work is superb. In all sorts of disguises from something approaching American sailors on leave (complete with hornpipe) to the dead images of Viennese musical-comedy policemen, members of the company, too numerous to specify, makes a perfect chorus and commentary on the ludicrous events of the main theme. They cannot be too high praised.

Originally published by M.F.K.F., *The Birmingham Mail*, 13 April 1938. Reprinted with the permission of Birmingham Mail & Post Ltd.

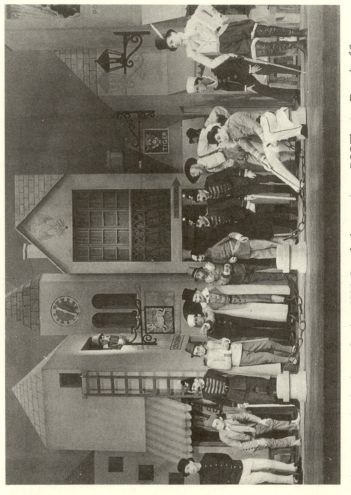

Figure 5. Komisarjevsky production, 1938, Stratford-upon-Avon, RSC Theatre. Dromio of Syracuse (Dennis Roberts) in window; Dr. Pinch (C. Rivers Gadsby) in center with black beard. Used with the permission of the Shakespeare Centre Library, Stratford-upon-Avon.

The Comedy of Errors:
Russian Producer's Merry Pranks, 1938

C.

The Comedy of Errors is a play of Shakespeare that has not until now been seen at the new Memorial Theatre of Stratford-upon-Avon. It has been looked upon as one of the least important plays that its author ever wrote, and as a rule it is ignored. But it responds to treatment; and Mr. Theodore Komisarjevsky, who has such bold ideas about the treatment of Shakespeare, produced it on Tuesday (the second night of the Shakespeare Festival of 1938) in a manner that endowed it with a new life as one of the maddest and merriest jests ever perpetrated by Shakespeare or any other writer.

The comedy, as all Shakespeareans know, concerns the confusion raised by the exact resemblance of twin brothers, a confusion increased by the exact resemblance between their servants. It opens sombrely with a provisional sentence of death upon Aegeon, the Syracusan merchant stranded in hostile Ephesus, and (as we learn later) the father of the twins.

A LIVELY START

But Komisarjevsky is not going to have any sombreness about this business. The play opens with a comic ballet (to Handel's music), as gorgeously and convulsively funny as if the theatre had been invaded by the Marx Brothers. The main idea of the costumes is that the wearers should be figures of fun, but each costume has a tinge of the wearer's status and occupation. The place is Ephesus, but it might be anywhere, given sunshine and colour and gaiety. After this keynote has been sounded, the trial of Aegeon (in robes and top-hat) by the Duke of Ephesus (in Waterloo uniform and a bowler hat with a huge feather) falls into its place as one of the play's jokes, a parallel to the Mikado's judgment on Ko-Ko and the others. And this vein of daft glorious merriment lasted throughout the piece. The theatre rocked with laughter; never has a Shakespeare Festival been so festive as this.

But was all this fantastication to the detriment of the play? Just at first one was doubtful on the point, but the doubts were cleared as the essence of the piece, which is of course farcical in its whole intent, was seen to stand out clearly amid the whirligig. The misadventures of the two Antipholuses and their servants the Dromios were revealed in word and deed as their author had designed. The mystery of how the two pairs, belonging to different cities, could be exactly alike not only in form but in costume, was solved with a neat stroke of ingenuity. The Syracusan pair, finding themselves in unfriendly Ephesus, changed their clothes (on the stage) for others in the Ephesian mode; so that both Antipholuses looked something like bullfighters, while each Dromio was attired in an *ensemble* reminiscent of Max Miller.

"CRAZY GANGS" SURPASSED

The Syracusan pair have most of the fun, and Mr. James Dale and Mr. Dennis Roberts revelled in it, but Mr. S. Sheldon Bishop and Mr. Andrew Leigh were not behindhand as their Ephesian doubles. Though the resemblances were remarkably close, the audience was in no danger of being mixed; the words Shakespeare gave the characters instantly betrayed their identities. The company as a whole flung themselves whole-heartedly into the revelry; no habitual crazy gang could have given a better show. Some of the characters hurried their speech now and then to a degree of indistinctness; the hot pace must have been too much for them. That is an explanation, not an excuse.

One enjoyed, especially, the grotesque comicality of Mr. C. Rivers Gadsby as Doctor Pinch, the delicious effrontery of Miss Peggy Livesey as the Courtezan, the snappiness of Mr. Kenneth Wicksteed as Angelo, and the skill with which Miss Ethel Griffies turned the rather serious part of the Abbess to the service of comedy. All sorts of mirthful ideas keep cropping up as the play goes on. It was a great moment when the company took the last line of the first part and sang it in the manner of an oratorio.

And the clock—it kept pace with the action in a series of sudden and unexpected jerks; time itself joined in the sport.

One wonders whether any of those present had ever seen a gayer and giddier two hours' traffic of the stage than that afforded them by the author of "Hamlet," assisted musically by the composer of "The Messiah," and under the guidance of a very modern producer from Russia. The *comédie-ballet* of Molière contributed something, no doubt, to Mr. Komisarjevsky's treatment of the subject, but with all its daring innovations this version of "The Comedy of Errors" was fundamentally true to the Shakespearean spirit, which was on occasion a very merry spirit in Shakespeare's own days, and can by bold and right interpretation revive the joy of life in these times of our own, which so badly need its revival.

Originally published by C., *The Sheffield Daily Telegraph*, 14 April 1938.

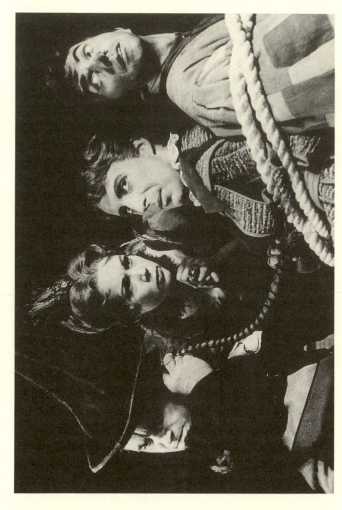

Figure 6. Williams production, 1962, Stratford-upon-Avon, RSC Theatre. Dr. Pinch (James Booth) and Adriana (Diana Rigg) with the bound Antipholus of Ephesus (Ian Richardson) and Dromio of Ephesus (Ian Hewitson). Used with the permission of the Shakespeare Centre Library, Stratford-upon-Avon.

The Act of Uniformity:
Williams Production, 1962

Edmund Gardner

Clifford Williams's fluorescent production of *The Comedy of Errors* (Royal Shakespeare Theatre) opens with a stage bare but for a terrace of rostrums for'ard of a blue cyclorama pierced by a single arch.

With a choreographed, military precision, the Stratford contingent of the Peter Hall dramatic battalion falls in for general inspection by the audience. For this production at least, the company have acquired a uniform: grey, high-buttoned overalls (RFC c.1916) and drab-grey dresses. Having paid their respects, the actors depart to garb themselves for the play proper.

The motivation for these balletic and sartorial rites is, presumably, to demonstrate a uniformity of style. And demonstrated it is. The skin-tight, integrated display of ensemble work which follows is the best to be seen by the Avon this season—if not the best since Peter Hall took command.

It has taken 24 years for *The Comedy of Errors* to be resurrected at Stratford. The last time the twin sets of twins hurtled round this stage was in 1938 when Komisarjevsky—if one can believe all one hears—whipped up such goings-on that the team had to be called in to do a re-play in 1939.

(As a point of interest, one of that original company—Pauline Letts—plays the Abbess in the present production; while another, Donald Layne-Smith, is doing the grand tour with the RSC up north.)

But it is easy to see why successive Stratford directors have kept this piece at folio length and refused it a place in recent seasons. It demands the highest standard of that kind of acting which mixes physical slickness with complete understanding of comedy's vocal nuances.

In plain language it needs superlative team-work.

Though Shakespeare was still relatively an apprentice craftsman when he knocked it off, *The Comedy of Errors* is an essay in brash, uneasy farce. Modern *farceurs* complain of the difficulty of handling, theatrically, one simple case of mistaken identity; yet here Shakespeare takes the complex joke of a double set of doubles, unaware of each other's proximity, and sustains the countless permutations of the situation with meticulous stagecraft—it matters little that he pinched the whole plot.

Though the long, explanatory opening—old Aegeon trembling through his unlikely autobiography—is tortuously inept, the guts of the play run with glittering smoothness on wheels greased with the most slippery of banana skins. At each new twist, Shakespeare leads his audience with care, knocking away with sledgehammer cross-talk, word-juggling as bright and hard as a cluster of diamonds, and chestnut gagging. It is early, flawed and unsubtle stuff yet it still works.

Mr. Williams and the company happily show complete faith in their author. The comic business finds its source in the text (with the possible exception of some smoky decoration to the abortive conjuror, Pinch), and the belly-laughs belch out as reactions to the sly, mocking delivery of lines, and not to overlaid directorial fancies.

LEANING GENTLY

The company lean their shoulders gently on Shakespeare's intention, grin at it, and manage to do the most difficult thing in the whole range of playing comedy—by fractional timing, steady pace and the look wry, they make the whole thing appear to be as easy as falling off a proscenium arch.

As each Antipholus, Alec McCowen (Syracuse) and Ian Richardson (Ephesus) convey just enough frustrated bewilderment to allow one a momentary belief in the preposterous situation (even though we have seen them meet as actors, before the play, sorting out their costumes). Ian Hewitson and Barry MacGregor—spry puppet-nosed Dromios—present near-hysterical servile acceptance of the madness which seems to be exploding around them.

What else? Mr. Williams has peopled Ephesus with masked fantasticks, clowns and strumpets who all have close kinship with the *commedia dell'arte*. Tony Church battles lucidly with the near-doomed bore Aegeon; Tony Steedman—a natural, it seems, for Establishment characters—makes an unwilling Duke.

Yvonne Bonnamy gives a full-blown Courtezan; Diana Rigg and Susan Maryott—both as edible as ever—preen and blaze off one another with some gusto, as Adriana and Luciana; while James Booth is cheerfully directed, as Pinch, doing the nearest possible thing to a Shakespearean Tommy Cooper—getting blown up by his own flash-powder, fighting hard to maintain a satanic dignity, and drawing Cabalistic symbols which emerge as a completed game of noughts and crosses.

If this production is the result of leaving a Shakespearean play un-directed for a couple of decades then the best possible way we can celebrate the Bard's impending 400th Anniversary is to put the already suggested, 12 months' ban on all Shakespearean productions. Who knows what we may rediscover?

Originally published by Edmund Gardner, *The Stratford-upon-Avon Herald*, 14 September 1962. Reprinted with the permission of Herald Publishing.

Figure 7. Deguchi production, 1989, Tokyo, Tokyo Globe Theatre. Antipholus of Syracuse and a Dromio. Courtesy of Yoshiko Kawachi. Used with the permission of the Tokyo Globe Theatre.

Shakespeare in Britain:
Williams Production, 1962

Robert Speaight

"The myriad-minded man, our own and all men's Shakespeare."
Coleridge's famous words introduced his half page of commentary
on *The Comedy of Errors*. It was no slight affair but a very solid and
intricate piece of dramatic carpentry that Mr. Clifford Williams so
brilliantly brought to life a year ago. Designed as a stop-gap, this
has become one of the most popular items in the Stratford
repertoire. I saw it both in 1962 and 1963, and the difference
between the two productions—apart from one or two minor
changes in casting—was the difference between a wine which had
been only a year or two in bottle and a wine which had matured.
This particular wine is now perfectly ripe for drinking. The last
legitimate laugh had been squeezed from audiences only too glad
to give them; the "business" had not yet become over-labored; and
the company still gave the impression of enjoying their night out.
The merit of the production lay not only in its unflagging
invention and verve, but in its refusal to allow the deeper
implications of the farce—and nothing is more serious than
farce—to become obscured for those who were ready to receive
them. Aegeon's long recital of his misfortunes became, in Mr.
James Welsh's deeply sincere treatment of it, something much
more than a *récit de Théramène*; we were genuinely concerned that
he should escape the block. The Shakespearian themes of
reconciliation and rediscovered identity announced, already, their
later and more famous repetitions. The Abbess was an authentic
dea ex machina—no mere figure of fun; it was not for nothing that
Ephesus and Syracuse would henceforward exist in amity; and
although the average spectator would hardly have guessed how
much Shakespeare had taken from St. Paul's Epistle to the
Ephesians, he might have been prepared to verify the references
once they had been pointed out to him.

Mr. Williams used the convention of the *commedia dell' arte* to much effect without overdoing it. Mr. John Wyckham had designed a sloping platform set on three levels—a lucid and economical solution which allowed the hilarious charade of improbabilities to flow without let or hindrance. I thought the costumes were rather lacking in color and fantasy, but the incidental music, with its accompanying mime, marked appropriately the progress of the story. The Dromios were so identical that I was often at a loss as to say which was which, but the Antipholi were rightly more distinguishable. Mr. Ian Richardson's Antipholus of Ephesus had grown in definition since I first saw the production and stood out in forceful contrast to Mr. Alec McCowen's Antipholus of Syracuse, whose bewilderment was pointed with every nuance of vocal and facial expression. Miss Diana Rigg's attractive Adriana would have been improved by a steadier diction, but apart from this my only criticism was to question the utility of the introductory parade where the actors presented themselves in black shirts and jeans. I suppose the intention of this was to emphasize the artifice of what we were presently to see, but the effect was merely to remind us that the Royal Shakespeare Company were about to perform a play—a fact of which we were happily aware already. This production was a worthy companion to Komisarjevsky's *charivaria* of thirty years ago. Stratford generally regards *The Comedy of Errors* as beneath its attention, but in neither case was there the slightest condescension in its treatment of the play.

Originally published by Robert Speaight, "Shakespeare in Britain," *Shakespeare Quarterly* 14 (1963): 419–32 (excerpted, 427–8). Reprinted with the permission of *Shakespeare Quarterly*.

Comedy of Errors at Stratford: Williams Production, 1962/1972

Michael Billington

Clifford Williams's famous production of *The Comedy of Errors* is a milestone in post-war theatrical history; for back in 1962 it was the first production to indicate the formation of a genuine Royal Shakespeare Company ensemble style. And it was heartening to see it at Stratford last night, after a slowish start, coming across almost as fresh, buoyant and inventive as a decade ago.

Two things make it remarkable: Mr Williams's recognition of the fact that Shakespeare's intricate farce about double identical twins is rooted in human character and his ability to highlight the weirdness and mystery inherent in the story. Thus, in a brilliant comic performance, John Wood's Antipholus of Syracuse reacts to the whirlwind events around him like someone imprisoned in a Kafkaesque nightmare: a shrill panic invades his voice as [he is] feverishly importuned by women he has never seen before, he frantically wards off a devilish courtesan by making the sign of the cross and, as people flee in terror before his drawn weapon, he concludes with superb deliberation—"I see these witches are afraid of swords." Mr Wood triumphs by following a classic rule of farce: playing the character as if he believed the nightmares around him were real.

But for all this, the production is still a group achievement. Judy Cornwell's Adriana, for instance, makes the crucial Shakespearian point that there is a genuine core of feeling under the women's shrewish exterior. The two Dromios, Geoffrey Hutchings and Chris Harris, are also like opposite sides of the same comic coin: the one reared in music hall, the other in mime. And even a minor character like the Goldsmith gets his due from Gerald James who makes him an epicene Ephesian, in yellow gloves and striped turban. Starting with nothing but a troupe of players in black sweaters and jeans and a triple-tiered stage, Mr.

Williams gradually adds colour and detail like a painter filling out a canvas; but the production's ultimate success lies in its suggestion that behind the mistaken identities and manic confusions of farce there are often genuinely dark and disquieting forces at work.

Originally published by Michael Billington, *The Manchester Guardian*, 21 June 1972, p. 8. Reprinted with the permission of *The Guardian*.

The *Comedy of Errors* in Japan

Peter Milward, S.J.

If I may begin this essay on a personal note, my first encounter with *The Comedy of Errors* in Japan, or indeed anywhere else— apart from a reading of the play for a paper at Oxford—took place on May 2, 1974. The actors were a student group of mine, who called themselves the "Shakespeare Study Circle" (or *Shakespeare Kenkyūkai* in Japanese), and they presented the whole play in Shakespeare's English. It was, I thought, a splendid production that would have done credit to any professional group. I was particularly impressed by the liveliness and similarity of behaviour, if not of facial appearance and stature, of the twin Dromios, Noriko Yoshida and Mayumi Tsuneyasu. To me it showed how much student productions of this kind have contributed to the knowledge and love of Shakespeare in Japan—though this country is one of the "states unborn" and its language one of the "accents yet unknown" envisaged by the dramatist himself in *Julius Caesar*.

On that occasion I contributed a brief account of the play for the programme, under the title of "Error and Forgiveness"; and I hope I may be forgiven for the error of quoting it here and in full:

> "To err is human," said Pope, adding, "To forgive, divine." For Shakespeare, too, the human comedy, on which he lavished so much attention and affection in his early career, is a comedy of errors. He sees human beings wandering about in the world, mistaking appearance for reality. He laughs at them, but he has pity on them. He cannot but remember that he, too, is a man like them, subject to error. If he exposes their folly in his plays, it is not so much to criticize as to forgive.
>
> Appropriately, therefore, Shakespeare set out on his dramatic career with a play entitled *The Comedy of Errors*.

It is not one of his best known plays. It is better known, and more often quoted, for its title than for its contents. Yet already it reveals much of his genius, and much of his characteristic technique. As with most of his plays, he borrows his plot from another source, in this case a play of the old Latin dramatist Plautus. And as with everything he borrows, he transforms his source by the power of his genius into "something rich and strange."

First, there is something strange in the schematic setting of the play. Everything seems to go in pairs, like the animals going into Noah's Ark. There are two places, Ephesus and Syracuse; twin brothers, each named Antipholus; twin slaves, each named Dromio, one to each brother; two sisters, Adriana and Luciana, a predestined match for the twin brothers; and two aged parents long separated from each other, like the brothers and their slaves, Aegeon, a merchant of Syracuse, and Aemilia, an abbess at Ephesus.

A shipwreck off the coast of Ephesus precipitates the confusion of the comedy by bringing all these pairs together. One is mistaken for another; and the confusion becomes so confounded that they all come to feel themselves bewitched in a fairy world. Yet out of this confusion Shakespespeare skillfully brings a harmony and an order, in which all is known and all is forgiven. Thus the play is an apt reflection of human life.

My second encounter with this play took place some six years later, on the somewhat unique date of February 29, 1980. This time the production was a professional one, by the group named En (Japanese for Globe), and sadly in Japanese. The translator and producer was my former student and colleague at Sophia University, Tetsuo Anzai, and so I had received a complimentary ticket. Without any flattery, I may say it was a performance I really enjoyed, all the more as it was presented with the setting (all through) of a stage within the stage, and the typically Shakespearian implication of layer on layer of reality. The theatre was the Kinokuniya Hall in Tokyo, where it ran for two periods in the same year 1980 and a third in 1981, before going on a tour to various provinces of Japan—with great acclaim. Now let me quote Professor Anzai's own account of the production:

> My general intention in the production was *not* to make the play a mere farcical comedy of confusion, but to emphasize its overall structure as a play showing restoration of harmony through the confusion of mistaken identity. It was, in other words, to treat the play as a variation on the romance play; for I produced *The Comedy of Errors* after *Pericles* (in 1976), which is based on the same source as the framework story of *The Comedy*.
>
> More specifically, I tried to emphasize the weird aspect of the comic confusions in the main body of the play. Unlike Plautus, Shakespeare does not treat the confusions drily as mere farcical imbroglios. When the confusions of mistaken identity reach their intensest moments, they approach something really threatening and weird, genuinely nightmarish. Hence the final resolution gives a sense of deep wonder, almost miraculous, strongly suggesting supernatural intervention. Thus the two heterogeneous elements of the play, the romantic framework and the farcical main plot, are effectively fused into a harmonious whole.
>
> In artistic terms, I rather consciously relied upon the style of the Commedia dell'Arte. We built a sham, play-within-a-play stage roofed with a tent upon the real stage of the hall; and all the action was done on this counterfeit stage, but its purpose was not to emphasize the artificiality of the action. Our real intention was to induce a more willing suspension of disbelief by making the audience aware that everything is a play, so that we could pursue the intensity of the action to a greater extremity than possible otherwise. That is, we wanted to be freed from the conventions of a realistic style of presentation. We also used live music played by the players themselves. This was also for the purpose of enhancing the more active involvement of the audience

in what was being presented on the stage. All in all, we tried to make the whole play not a mere spectacle to be looked at objectively or critically, but a lively, active experience positively shared by the audience.

(Incidentally, I might add that, as adviser—together with myself—to the Shakespeare Study Circle at Sophia University, Professor Anzai had already enjoyed some experience in the production of this play in 1974, though then the actual producer had been one of the students, Masami Kawasaki.)

Professor Anzai's production of the play in 1980 was, however, by no means its first production in Japan—though it has never been one of the more frequently produced of Shakespeare's plays in this country. So far as I have been able to ascertain, its first professional production only goes back to 1951, when it was presented by the Shakespeare Repertory Theatre (or *Kindai Gekijō*) at the Okuma Hall of Waseda University under the direction of Chōji Katō, following the translation of the great Shakespeare translator and former Waseda professor, Shōyō Tsubouchi. This première production was revived in the same place by the same company and under the same direction in 1954. Subsequently, in 1969, the actor-director Yoshiya Nemoto revived the production with the same company at the Nōkyō Hall in Tokyo, using the same translation and following the directions of the original performance.

As for these directions, they have been summarized for me by my good friend, the Shakespearian scholar-actor, Professor Yoshio Arai:

> Considering this is the shortest of Shakespeare's comedies, the omission of lines was minimal and all the scenes were presented. The décor and costume were designed by the famous theatre art specialist Dr. Shizuo Toyama, who had planned all décor for Chōji Katō since 1928 (when the Globe Theatre Company had been founded).
>
> The revolving door was effectively used in the scenes showing the house of Antipholus of Ephesus, especially for the encounters of the twin Dromios. The costumes

were oriental, and all the male characters wore turbans, except the Dromios.

The most unique direction was the adding of a short prologue to *The Comedy*, telling the audience about the twin brothers so as to avoid confusion. A puppet manipulator also appeared on the stage and, while the prologue told of the twin brothers and the theme of mistaken identity, he portrayed the plot with the use of his two hands.

The next turning-point in the history of *The Comedy's* production in Japan is part of an impressive collaboration between the director Norio Deguchi and the translator Yūji Odajima, professor at Tokyo University. It was Deguchi who had originated the Shakespeare Theatre in 1975 and proved to be the first to produce all Shakespeare's plays at the popular Jean-Jean Theatre by 1983. It was in the August of 1975 that he turned to *The Comedy of Errors*; and he returned to this production in May 1987. Of this latter production I may quote the description given by Kazuko Matsuoka, under the title borrowed from Antipholus of Syracuse, "I to the world am like a drop of water."

The most striking feature (of this production) was that all the characters were played with masks, suggesting the convention of the Commedia dell'Arte, and emphasizing the symmetrical nature of the play, while enhancing the stylization of the production as a whole. Most impressive was the moment when all the players put off their masks in the dénouement, when all mistakes were resolved and family reunion was achieved. This moment effectively revealed the fact that the comedy was indeed a play of recognition. (*Subete no Kisetsu no Shakespeare / Shakespeare for All Seasons*, Tokyo: Kawade Shobō, 1993)

Finally, mention may be made of a fine series of public readings of Shakespeare's plays instituted by the above-mentioned scholar-actor, Professor Yoshio Arai, as part of a campaign for the raising of funds in Japan to help rebuild the Globe Theatre near its original location on the South Bank, London (under the late Shakespearian actor, Sam Wanamaker). He gave his reading of *The Comedy of Errors* in the original English on April 24, 1988, and in Japanese translation on October 17, 1989, completing the reading of all 38 plays, plus the sonnets and poems, by 1992. The following description of Professor Arai's performance of *The Comedy* is contributed by Mr. Osamu Hirokawa:

Gold coins, beautiful shells and necklaces are symmetrically arranged on the floor of the small space for reading. Shells represent the seashore which Egeon and his family have reached beyond the stormy sea; coins, the thousand marks of Antipholus; and necklaces, the confusion of love. The reciter appears in black. On the wall behind him are two identical portraits of Shakespeare, as it were twins watching the audience. The tone of the duke's voice is set a little high, and that of the old man a little heavy, emphasizing his serious situation. At the end of the first scene, a colourful poncho is worn, creating an atmosphere of Mediterranean brightness, full of sunshine.

To distinguish one twin from another, the reciter puts purple bands on his wrists, red ones on his ankles. He raises his right hand towards the audience when reading Antipholus of Ephesus, his left hand when reading Antipholus of Syracuse. Similarly, he moves one foot forward, then the other, to indicate which of the twin Dromios he is reading.

Now, if I may end as I began, on a more personal note, I would like to mention a certain appeal this comedy has for the Japanese in view of both their history and their tradition. For one thing, the whole setting of the play, in which a foreign merchant by trespassing on the soil of another country may be subject to the death penalty, seems to reflect the actual situation no less of Tokugawa Japan—during the period of what is called *sakoku*, or exclusion of foreigners from the country—than of Elizabethan England, when Catholic priests entering Protestant England (often disguised as merchants) faced such a penalty.

For another, the stylization with deliberate reference to the Italian Commedia dell'Arte observed in the productions of both Professor Anzai and Mr. Deguchi appeals to something in the tradition of Japanese *kyōgen*, a lighter, even comic form of Noh play. Noh is, of course, a highly stylized form of drama, not unlike the old Greek tragedy; but the stylization of *kyōgen* is all the more impressive as it aims at a more realistic effect and at more vigorous action on the part of the players. There is even a feeling of ritual purification, as the story is reduced to its simplest, most basic elements, with a stereotyping of character that is more prominent in Shakespeare's source, the comedy of Plautus.

Yet another point of deep appeal for Japanese audiences is, as Professor Anzai points out in speaking of his production, the weird, supernatural atmosphere which Shakespeare superimposes on his Plautine source—with more than a glance at the Biblical Ephesus, which is described in Acts as a city of witchcraft and superstition devoted to Diana (whose other name is Hecate). Ghosts of various kinds are a staple of Japanese folklore, as retailed for English-speaking readers by Lafcadio Hearn; and they make regular appearances in Japanese theatre, both Noh and Kabuki. In the Japanese countryside, moreover, one may still encounter *miko*, priestesses or witches, who specialize in calling up the spirits of the dead, like the witch of Endor for Saul.

Finally, the development of the play from a melancholy opening to a happy outcome, with a continuing contrast between the good fortune and even merriment of the visitors from Syracuse and the misfortune and fear of diabolic possession among the residents of Ephesus, may be explained in terms of the mediaeval and classical Wheel of Fortune; but such a concept is by no means foreign to the Japanese mind, for whim, the law of fate (or *inga*), is presented in terms of a turning water-mill (or *meguru mizu-guruma*). There is, moreover, something deeply archetypical in the fact that this law is embodied in the character of the aged merchant Aegeon, as well as the complementary fact that his wife who brings about the happy outcome is presented as abbess of Diana (not without echoes, recognizable to Shakespeare's original audiences, of the old Priory of Holywell in whose precincts stood his original Theatre).

For these reasons it may even be claimed that the Japanese, the closer they remain to their own popular and dramatic tradition, the better equipped they are to appreciate the original *Comedy of Errors* as it was presented to its first Elizabethan audience—better even than average modern audiences in England or America.

Trevor Nunn's
Musical Production, 1976

Sally Emerson

Shakespeare raided Plautus to create *The Comedy of Errors* and it in turn has fuelled many an extravaganza and musical. Komisarjevsky's outstanding production at Stratford in 1938 helped to release a stampede of irreverent, entertaining variations on the theme. In multifarious costumes from many ages, the characters embellished the text with their colourful bowler hats, graceful dances and lively songs. The stuffy objected to this production, considering it an insult to Shakespeare, but the public loved it. Next came the American musical *The Boys from Syracuse*, turned into a film in 1940. Other transformations include a Victorian musical comedy set in the North of England, an operetta in Regency costume, an Edwardian extravaganza and a New Orleans waterfront musical. In 1970 the Young Vic presented it complete with motorcycles and bicycles and in 1962, revived in 1965 and 1972, Clifford Williams directed it at Stratford in the Commedia dell' Arte style, adding some exquisite mime scenes.

Stratford's last production, by Trevor Nunn, is more rollicking fun. Songs, music and dance oil the wheels of this cleverly constructed but rather mechanical farce and spirited acting galvanizes the slight characters into life. The text reads drily nowadays: the puns are dated and, as H.B. Charlton has remarked, the plot appears "a mathematical exhibition of the maximum number of erroneous combinations of four people taken in pairs." But there's nothing arid about this version.

Even in the morning, when Aegeon arrives looking for his lost family, Ephesus has the pleasure-loving air of a seaside town. Tourist shops are gaudy with postcards, straw hats and T-shirts emblazoned "Ephesus." Whorish girls lean from balconies in silky dressing gowns, a gloved 30's gangster lurks and a fat poof minces. It's lorded over by a comically vast dictator, Brian Coburn, with equally oversize epaulettes. This disreputable town is very much the domain of the shady Antipholus, played with lean, gum-chewing sleaziness by Mike Gwilym. His cruel confidence makes his confusions all the funnier and more satisfying, as if the Godfather slipped on a banana skin. Although he and his twin look startlingly alike, Roger Rees gives Antipholus of Syracuse the charming innocence of an overgrown schoolboy. When he's mistaken for his brother by nefarious characters—the gangster-merchant, the poof-goldsmith, the courtesan—his bewilderment is magnificent to behold.

The two Dromios are red nosed, red haired clowns with short baggy jeans and braces. Their stocky bodies shift easily into expert acrobatics and footwork but their faces lack the range of their masters. Nickolas Grace has a catchy song, 'My Master Beats Me,' which he delivers with bouncy verve and nimble movements. I only wish they did not look quite so similar: the audience should always know who's who so that they can immediately see the hilarious confusions on stage.

Judi Dench as Adriana, the discontented wife of Antipholus of Ephesus, mixes sourness with passion and creates a character both shrewish and sympathetic. Her studious and myopic sister Luciana (Francesca Annis) is a comic contrast to the sturdy Adriana with a liking for the revealing dress and the bottle. The lightly sketched love of Antipholus of Syracuse for Luciana is here expanded into a delightful duet which Francesca Annis and Roger Rees perform wittily and gracefully.

The RSC's melody maker Guy Woolfenden has composed nine new songs in a variety of styles, from rock to Greek. The zappy choral songs add pace and lift to the production but the delicate solos occasionally slip the play into first gear. Gillian Lynne's choreography is inventive and well-matched by the skills of the actors.

Originally published by Sally Emerson, *Plays and Players*, 24 (December, 1976): 37. Published with the permission of Heathmill Multimedia.

Theory and Practice: Stratford, 1976

Roger Warren

For *The Comedy of Errors*, John Napier transformed the permanent set into a contemporary, cluttered Turkish market; Aegeon was clearly in the rag trade, and garments festooned the balconies; the balcony of Adriana's house overlooked this market; the Porpentine and the Tiger were bars in the market, complete with a group to provide a backing for Guy Woolfenden's interpolated musical numbers. Again and again, a scene would stop for a song based on fragments of the text at that point, or simply on doggerel supplied for the occasion. Adriana and Luciana had a duet, "A man is master of his liberty," Antipholus of Syracuse a solo based on "Am I in earth"; a large-scale ensemble illustrated his

> There's not a man I meet but doth salute me
> As if I were their well-acquainted friend

which turned into a nightmare of illusions; Pinch's exorcisms were built up into an even longer ensemble; both Dromios had extended numbers, one to illustrate the feeble jokes about Time and baldness, the other to elaborate on the beatings he receives. Although these numbers appeared to derive from the text itself, they in fact had the effect of superimposing one medium on another.

Trevor Nunn rightly says that the play works "when it genuinely uplifts us, when it makes us feel better." The RSC's previous celebrated version (1962–72, directed by Clifford Williams) achieved exactly that, but there the "company" feel derived not from generalized routines but from the characters being sharply detailed individuals, reacting to each other and to their situations, out of which the humour arose. Here, the spoken text was again packed with appropriate invention, often very funny, especially the shutting out of Antipholus of Ephesus and the contradictory evidence of the finale, played as a courtroom drama, complete with 'exhibits'; but the sung ensembles tended to merge everyone into puppets, and to blunt personality. These interpolations may have been good for the general morale of the company but they did not seem to me actually to help the performances of its individual members in any way.

Roger Rees's Antipholus of Syracuse, for instance, was potentially excellent, but the director's routines did not help him develop that potential into a complete characterization. Luciana was a bespectacled bookworm, trotting out Renaissance clichés on order and male mastery from her reading, preserved from caricature by Francesca Annis's natural charm and poise. Both she and Judi Dench (Adriana) had suddenly to switch off their performances of the text itself in mid-scene and concentrate on singing; these moments did nothing to support their interpretations; I thought they strained them unnecessarily. Smaller roles stood even less chance of being sustained: the Duke was a Greek military dictator, switching from declarations of the law over a public address system to private sympathy for Aegeon; but he made absolutely nothing of the moment-to-moment bewilderment of the finale, which a succession of very human Dukes in the Williams version made much more of than was allowed to emerge here. Mr. Nunn certainly appeared to "give the audience a really good time," but I thought he did so by imposed routines rather than, as the Williams production did, by emphasizing Shakespeare's distinctive humanizing of his rather inhuman Plautine models.

Originally published by Roger Warren, *Shakespeare Survey* 30 (1978): 169–79 (excerpted, 176–7). © Cambridge University Press, 1978. Reprinted with the permission of Roger Warren and Cambridge University Press.

The Comedy of Errors:
Reflections of an Actor

Roger Rees

This is a really funny play. But as with all really funny jokes, let us say, someone's approach to a banana-skin and our childlike joy in their undignified fall, we are ready to feel a little bit ashamed of ourselves afterwards. It is about the separation of twins and so very reminiscent in some respects of *Twelfth Night*. There are, however, two sets of twins in *The Comedy of Errors*. They are distinguished only by the name of the town from which they come. We have Antipholus of Syracuse and Antipholus of Ephesus. Then there are the twins who act as their servants, Dromio of Syracuse and Dromio of Ephesus.

Antipholus of Syracuse, together with Dromio of Syracuse, arrives in Ephesus. Although they have never been here before, all the inhabitants seem to recognise them. The merchants and their wives greet them as though they were old friends who had lived there all their lives. Ephesus is in fact a very lame footed place. It is full of jealous wives, anxious husbands and avaricious merchants. The Duke of Ephesus has in his power an old man who has been travelling around Greece and Asia for many years in search of one of his sons:

> Five summers have I spent in farthest Greece,
> Roaming clean through the bounds of Asia,
> And, coasting homeward, came to Ephesus;
> Hopeless to find, yet loath to leave unsought
> Or that or any place that harbours men.   1.1.133–7

This old man is given one day, which conveniently enough is the timespan of the play, to raise enough money to pay a fine, which has been imposed because inhabitants of Syracuse were forbidden to set foot in Ephesus. He will be executed at sunset if he does not pay. His life hangs in the balance throughout the play, and his fate frames the whole farcical conundrum of the play, giving it a profound ring. Another serious aspect of the play is linked with his name, which is Egeon. Syracuse and Ephesus are separated by the Aegean Sea. The two words ring with similarity, and the sea holds the play together, in the same way that the name Aegean holds the two sets of twins together. The sea symbolism thus provides an interesting parenthesis around the farcical action. The play finishes with hands being held out across this symbolic ocean:

> We came into the world like brother and brother,
> And now let's go hand in hand, not one before another.
> 5.1.423–4

This clasping together and celebration of being "hand in hand" is all part of a seriousness that envelopes the farcical action. Antipholus of Syracuse is rather like George Formby in one of those early 1930s films. He is the white-faced innocent abroad. He is a very loveable creature, who associates himself with the play's sea symbolism:

> I to the world am like a drop of water
> That in the ocean seeks another drop,
> Who, falling there to find his fellow forth,
> Unseen, inquisitive, confounds himself.   1.2.35–8

It's wonderful, but it's also dopey. He's the "fall-guy," as he's too sympathetic, polite and sad to be anything else. The first of many mix-ups takes place when he sends his servant, Dromio of Syracuse, to go and put some money in the hotel. It is, of course, the other servant, Dromio of Ephesus, who has to explain about the money:

ANTIPHOLUS OF SYRACUSE:
Where have you left the money that I gave you?
DROMIO OF EPHESUS:
O—sixpence that I had a Wednesday last
To pay the saddler for my mistress' crupper?
The saddler had it, Sir; I kept it not.

ANTIPHOLUS OF SYRACUSE:
I am not in a sportive humour now;
Tell me, and dally not, where is the money?
We being strangers here, how dar'st thou trust
So great a charge from thine own custody?
DROMIO OF EPHESUS:
I pray you jest, Sir, as you sit at dinner.
I from my mistress come to you in post;
If I return, I shall be post indeed,
For she will score your fault upon my pate.
Methinks your maw, like mine, should be your clock,
And strike you home without a messenger.
ANTIPHOLUS OF SYRACUSE:
Come, Dromio, come, these jests are out of season;
Reserve them till a merrier hour than this.
Where is the gold I gave in charge of thee?
DROMIO OF EPHESUS:
To me, sir? Why, you gave no gold to me.　　　1.2.54–71

When Dromio of Syracuse finally appears on the scene, he is given a thrashing and told to stop messing about. Master and servant then sit down, perhaps at a café or maybe they are just taking their ease in the market square. They are almost immediately confronted by a woman, who greets Antipholus with a fierce, menacing "where have you been darling?". This is Adriana, wife of Antipholus of Ephesus, and she believes she is talking to her husband:

ADRIANA:
How dearly would it touch thee to the quick,
Shouldst thou but hear I were licentious,
And that this body, consecrate to thee,
By ruffian lust should be contaminate!
Wouldst thou not spit at me and spurn at me,
And hurl the name of husband in my face,
And tear the stain'd skin off my harlot-brow,
And from my false hand cut the wedding-ring,
And break it with a deep-divorcing vow?
I know thou canst, and therefore see thou do it.

I am possess'd with an adulterate blot;
My blood is mingled with the crime of lust;
For if we two be one, and thou play false,
I do digest the poison of thy flesh,
Being strumpeted by thy contagion.
Keep then fair league and truce with thy true bed;
I live dis-stain'd, thou dishonoured.
ANTIPHOLUS OF SYRACUSE:
Plead you to me, fair dame? I know you not.   2.2.129–46

This is a wonderful moment in the theatre. After Adriana has gone on for such a long time, Antipholus just says "who are you?". When I played the part I was lucky enough to have Judi Dench serving it up for me, like Chrissie Evert. Adriana goes crazy when she isn't recognised and keeps on at poor Antipholus so much that he agrees to have dinner with her. She says "we will dine above," which I believe means more than coffee and sandwiches. Then along comes Adriana's real husband, Antipholus of Ephesus, and he is unable to get into his own house. The fact that it is Dromio of Syracuse who tells him to go away adds insult to injury. It is getting very convoluted and we've hardly started. Antipholus of Syracuse is given an expensive gold chain a little later on. It is one which his twin, Antipholus of Ephesus, was having made up for Adriana. As soon as the wrong Antipholus is given the chain, further complications are set in motion. The play is rather like one of those little toys that flip on two little strings: flipping right down and then starting back up again. It is a game of "Consequences."

People often say to actors "I wish you'd done it as Shakespeare had written it." They are really referring to Victorian productions, such as the extraordinary ones of *Henry VIII* with thousands of slaves, millions of courtiers and a budget to match. Today we don't have that sort of money, so our theatre is moving towards presenting Shakespeare in small arenas with few frills. We, not the Victorians, stage more exact reproductions of what actually happened in Shakespeare's day. Plays were performed then in the open air with no artificial lighting. The actors had to shout their heads off even to be heard above the noise of the bear-baiting and of the ferries on the river. It is highly likely that *The Comedy of Errors* was first produced with a considerable emphasis on music, interludes and farcical slapstick areas. The writing itself supports this, as Shakespeare sometimes leaves out rhythmic beats in the pentameter. You know that in a play like *The Comedy of Errors* this is when you have to hit someone round the face to complete the line with a thump: di dum, di dum, di dum, di dum, di smash. Modern productions also add comic routines to complete the action. I remember at one time I had to slide right across the length of the stage, from up in the wings at the top of the house, on a wire dressed to look like a laundry line. I swung right across the stage hanging onto a pair of underpants.

It is good to remember that Antipholus of Syracuse was frightened of Ephesus before he even got there. The place was notorious for being the home of witches, conjurers and mountebanks. St. Paul mentions it as being a town of witchcraft and naughtiness. This is probably why Shakespeare changed the Epidamnum of the original story into Ephesus. When the little "Buster Keaton" figure of Antipholus of Syracuse comes into Ephesus, the seeds of fear have already been sown:

> They say this town is full of cozenage;
> As, nimble jugglers that deceive the eye,
> Dark-working sorcerers that change the mind,
> Soul-killing witches that deform the body,
> Disguised cheaters, prating mountebanks,
> And many such-like liberties of sin.   1.2.97-102

He is genuinely frightened by the time the second act is well underway. Everybody appears to be possessed. They really need that joy and celebration at the end of the play. One of the characters, Dr. Pinch, is described as a conjurer. I imagine him to be rather like Malvolio; bitter, crazy and mad. Pinch is employed by Adriana to exorcise the Devil from Antipholus of Ephesus and his Dromio. He calls the Devil forth from them; and it is very frightening. The thing about farce is that, if it is played with real feeling and truth, it can prove far more revealing than the darkest tragedy.

The Comedy of Errors is very like *The Merry Wives of Windsor* in that it deals with a domestic situation in true time. It is not like *Twelfth Night*, which has a double time sequence, or *Cymbeline*, where great liberties are taken with the chronology so that many years will pass in two or three minutes. *The Comedy of Errors* gives us the more realistic timescale of one day in the life of Ephesus. We know too that it is an early play because at this stage of his career Shakespeare, rather like me, tends to use a great many lines to express one thought. The language is sprawling and beyond the thought, placing the play very early, just coming up to *Romeo and Juliet*. When you come to later plays like *Cymbeline* and *The Winter's Tale*, you can find maybe five characters with two rhythmic beats each in a line sharing a lot of thoughts within that one line.

It is the strength of the comedy which spurs on the play. There is a very famous exchange between Antipholus of Syracuse and his Dromio which is reminiscent of Max Miller, perhaps even more like Dean Martin and Jerry Lewis. Dromio has been chased by a kitchen wench who is a very fat girl. He says that she is so round that she is like a globe and claims to be able to find out countries in her:

ANTIPHOLUS OF SYRACUSE:
In what part of her body stands Ireland?
DROMIO OF SYRACUSE:
Marry, sir, in her buttocks. I found it out by the bogs.
ANTIPHOLUS OF SYRACUSE:
Where Scotland?
DROMIO OF SYRACUSE:
I found it by the barrenness, hard in the palm of her hand.
ANTIPHOLUS OF SYRACUSE:
Where France?
DROMIO OF SYRACUSE:
In her forehead, arm'd and reverted, making war against her heir.
ANTIPHOLUS OF SYRACUSE:
Where England?
DROMIO OF SYRACUSE:
I look'd for the chalky cliffs, but I could find no whiteness in them; but I guess it stood in her chin, by the salt rheum that ran between France and it.

ANTIPHOLUS OF SYRACUSE:
Where Spain?
DROMIO OF SYRACUSE:
Faith, I saw it not, but I felt it hot in her breath.
ANTIPHOLUS OF SYRACUSE:
Where stood Belgia, the Netherlands?
DROMIO OF SYRACUSE:
O, sir, I did not look so low.   3.2.115-37

The strength of the play lies in its verse as well as its comedy.
There are some sensational pieces of verse, if you look for them
and are brave enough not to cut them out. There are some
wonderful descriptions. One of these which really fulfills the
whole play for me is when Aegeon finally sees the first of his
two sons. You'll remember that he has been looking for him for
years and years and years, then he suddenly sees him protesting
his innocence before the Duke in the market place. Aegeon is
handcuffed and ready to be executed. He sees his son, but he is
unable to believe it. The boy ignores him because he has never
seen his father before. Aegeon is at the end of his tether; his
speech about growth and continuity is one of the sad grace-notes
of the play:

Not know my voice! O time's extremity,
Hast thou so crack'd and splitted my poor tongue
In seven short years that here my only son
Knows not my feeble key of untun'd cares?
Though now this grained face of mine be hid
In sap-consuming winter's drizzled snow,
And all the conduits of my blood froze up,
Yet hath my night of life some memory,
My wasting lamps some fading glimmer left,
My dull deaf ears a little use to hear;
All these old witnesses—I cannot err—
Tell me thou art my son Antipholus.   5.1.306–17

This wonderful speech is there in the middle of a farce. Aegeon
brought up Antipholus of Syracuse, although he has not seen
him for seven years. He thinks that he is delivering the speech to

him, but is in fact addressing Antipholus of Ephesus, whom he has not seen since he was a little baby. I find it very moving.

Adriana too is to be pitied, despite being the bossy, almost stereotyped, matriarchal figure in a farce. Her husband goes off with other women because she nags too much. Aemilia, who turns out to be the mother of the Antipholus twins, tells her as much in another of the play's wonderful speeches:

> The venom clamours of a jealous woman
> Poisons more deadly than a mad dog's tooth.
> It seems his sleeps were hind'red by thy railing,
> And thereof comes it that his head is light.
> Thou say'st his meat was sauc'd with thy upbraidings:
> Unquiet meals make ill digestions;
> Thereof the raging fire of fever bred;
> And what's a fever but a fit of madness?
> Thou say'st his sports were hind'red by thy brawls.
> Sweet recreation barr'd, what doth ensue
> But moody and dull melancholy,
> Kinsman to grim and comfortless despair,
> And at her heels a huge infectious troop
> Of pale distemperatures and foes to life?
> In food, in sport, and life-preserving rest,
> To be disturb'd would mad or man or beast.
> The consequence is, then, thy jealous fits
> Hath scar'd thy husband from the use of wits.   5.1.69–86

Kate has a wonderful speech of subservience to her mate Petruchio in the very last scene of *The Taming of the Shrew*. She puts her hand underneath his foot to show how subservient she is, but you don't know whether she is going to trip him up, pull his boot off or what. I think that even in Shakespeare's time that kind of subservience was very tongue-in-cheek. Adriana has a sister called Luciana, who falls in love with Antipholus of Syracuse thinking, of course, that he is her sister's husband. Although she says that men are very intelligent and wise and that women ought to be subservient to them, she really protests too much:

LUCIANA:	A man is master of his liberty;
	Time is their master, and when they see time,
	They'll go or come. If so, be patient, sister.
ADRIANA:	Why should their liberty than ours be more?
LUCIANA:	Because their business still lies out o' door.
ADRIANA:	Look when I serve him so, he takes it ill.
LUCIANA:	O, know he is the bridle of your will.
ADRIANA:	There's none but asses will be bridled so.
LUCIANA:	Why, headstrong liberty is lash'd with woe.
	There's nothing situate under heaven's eye
	But hath his bound, in earth, in sea, in sky.
	The beasts, the fishes, and the winged fowls.
	Are their males' subjects, and at their controls.
	Man, more divine, the master of all these,
	Lord of the wide world and wild wat'ry seas,
	Indue'd with intellectual sense and souls,
	Of more pre-eminence than fish and fowls,
	Are masters to their females, and their lords;
	Then let you will attend on their accords.

[2.1.7–25]

When she finds true love with Antipholus of Syracuse, we suspect that she will not be quite so subservient.

The play could not be funny without the danger that old Egeon *really* will be beheaded, and not be funny without the audience's supposition that, off-stage, Adriana might well have gone to bed with Antipholus of Syracuse. What is more patently serious about the play is the way in which the characters cope in this town of mistaken identity. A kind of rococo theme associated with Antipholus of Syracuse is "who am I without my other half?", which is similar to the themes of *Twelfth Night*. Antipholus thinks that he has finally found himself when he meets Luciana:

Call thyself sister, sweet, for I am thee;
Thee will I love, and with thee lead my life.   3.2.66–7

When he says "I am thee" he says that he is incomplete without her. The play is about people finding each other, and therefore, themselves.

When Adriana thinks that she is speaking to her husband, she declares that it would be easier for her to separate a drop of water from the ocean than it would be to separate out their love. Everybody in the play is looking for the other half of their jigsaw, just like us.

Originally published by Roger Rees, *Shakespeare in Perspective*, ed. Roger Sales, 2 vols. (London: British Broadcasting Corporation, 1982-85), vol. 2: 224–31. Reprinted with the permission of Roger Rees and the British Broadcasting Corporation.

Robert Woodruff's Circus Production, 1983

Joel G. Fink

The Comedy of Errors, Shakespeare's earliest comedy, is the framework within which director Robert Woodruff has devised a showcase for some of America's new vaudeville performers. Featuring the Flying Karamazov Brothers and Avner the Eccentric, Woodruff's production at the Goodman Theatre in Chicago turned the play's setting, the City of Ephesus, into a land of comic jugglers, jokers, and clowns. To a surprising degree, Shakespeare emerged triumphant, if not unscathed.

The director has freely adapted and reshaped the text for this particular cast and incorporated juggling and circus skills, not as a pastiche to the action, but as its essence. In Ephesus, juggling was a necessary language of communication: a game, a sport, a way to make music, and even a way to fight. In a land where *everyone* juggled and joked, the Syracusean Antipholus and Dromio were forced to read books on "How-to-Juggle" and "How-to-Joke" in order to learn how to behave properly in that society. At one point, a circle of jugglers surrounded the foreign pair as chords sounded from the gang-music of *West Side Story*. But nothing in Ephesus was serious for long, and musical strains from *The Wizard of Oz*, *Gone With the Wind*, and even *Evita* also filtered through the vaguely Middle-Eastern air.

Given the setting of an exotic bazaar, David Gropman created a three-sided, white-walled set, reminiscent of Peter Brook's famous *A Midsummer Night's Dream* with the Royal Shakespeare Company. Simple changes were suggested with assorted doors, windows, stage-floor traps, and colorful cloth awnings. The costumes, by Susan Hilferty, caught the varied colors, textures, and shapes needed to blend contemporary variety entertainers with Shakespearean characters. The lighting by Paul Gallo, and the music, composed and directed by Douglas Wieselman, joined the scenographic ensemble to create a bright, fast-paced circus atmosphere.

Even before the show began, the false noses and glasses on the Goodman's decorative statuary gave fair warning of what was to come. Opening the program on the title-page revealed *The Three Sisters* in large print, scratched out, with the correct Shakespearean title scrawled below. Among the useful program notes included for the audience's edification were: "Each company member plays several parts. If you're confused, ask the person next to you"; "The plot has something to do with twins and juggling"; "...it is safe to assume that the play dates sometimes between Plautus' *The Twin Menaechmi* and the first episode of 'The Patty Duke Show'"; and "Understudies never read the play unless a specific announcement is made at the time of the performance." Irreverence was clearly the order of the day. Besides juggling and joking, the production made extensive use of other circus techniques: plate-spinning, unicycling, acrobatics and tumbling, slack-rope walking, stilt-walking, baton and sword twirling, trapeze work, various clown routines, and other assorted skills such as roller-skating and belly-dancing.

However, even in Woodruff's land of pandemonium, greater directorial clarity in staging, pacing, and tempo was needed to clarify the action and to successfully sustain over two hours of manic energy. Although not a text which requires the extensive mastery of language needed to interpret Shakespeare's later works, much of the comedy of *The Comedy of Errors* still lives in the written text. Language, however, was this production's weakest element. Dialogue was constantly up-staged with as much action as possible, as if the director had little confidence in the script or in his actors' ability to interpret it. The two consistent vocal dynamics were *loud* and *fast*, with insufficient attention paid to communicating story line. At one—and only one—point in the performance, someone held up a sign that read "PLOT." At that moment the side-show stopped and the audience was allowed a blessed moment of single focus.

The most successful comic bits added to the script were those that grew out of the text, or from the Shakespeare canon: A peddler's cart labeled "A pound of flesh...and stuff"; a mock death evolving into Mercutio's final speech; and even the Duke of Ephesus' incarnation as Duke Ellington. Least successful of the astronomical number of added jokes and puns were 1) the arbitrary "one-liners," a pizza-delivery boy, Mayor Byrne jokes, or lost Channel swimmers, and 2) the overly labored: One actor (Alex Willows) portrayed two characters at the same time, with hair color and costumes cleanly split down the middle. Although the actor did well with one half (one character), the other half never became clearly defined. The result was more confusing than funny, a conceptual gag that *tells* better than it played. However, against a relentless barrage of shtick the audience was forced to surrender all pretense of critical sense or sensibility.

Four of the Flying Karamazov Brothers were cast as the two sets of twins, the fifth playing Shakespeare. All five, though they are not actually brothers, or Russian, are multi-talented performers, exhibiting along with their physical and musical skills a strong sense of humor about themselves and about their work. Although there was always a full commitment to the play's action, their personal identities were never blurred, and a flubbed line could always be commented on appropriately.

Sophie Schwab, as Adriana, the wife of Antipholus of Syracuse, was somewhat shrill and forced in her first scenes, but her energies and skills came into clear focus as she entered into the physical action of the play. Twirling batons or swords, climbing a living "hill" of people in order to swing precariously from a balcony, or even leading a clown knife-throwing routine, Schwab proved to be a performer with the unusual vitality needed to counterbalance the Flying K's. Gina Leishman, as her sister Luciana, also added a strong physical presence and a much needed element of romance to the production. Laurel Cronin, appearing in a number of roles, emerged as a comic performer who could also deal successfully with Shakespeare's text. Particularly in her second-act work as a courtesan, Cronin displayed expert timing and a real sense of play with the audience.

Through all of the orchestrated chaos wandered Avner Eisenberg. In his stage persona as Avner the Eccentric, he blended all aspects of circus to create clown-comedy more akin to the great Russian performer Popov than to contemporary American circus clowns. Particularly in his role as Dr. Pinch,

Avner brought onto the stage echoes of Commedia, Punch and Judy, and even the Marx Brothers. The production began with Avner, as a tramp-clown janitor sweeping a spot of light onto the stage. His homage to Emmett Kelly developed as a complex comic turn and established the pattern that consistently followed: a "bit" emerged from the action, then stopped the action, while the "bit" was played out to its illogical end. Avner used familiar set business, much like Commedia dell'Arte *lazzi*, to bounce off of the script and return to it with no excuses made.

The rich heritage of popular entertainments, too long relegated to television status, seems to be finding genuine resurrection in the street or theatre variety shows of new vaudeville performers. The Goodman must be credited with bringing together a directing, performing and design ensemble that worked with the cohesiveness of a traditional family troupe.

After a particularly good line of verse, the cast called for the author, and naturally, Shakespeare came on stage to accept roses and applause. This seemed a fitting tribute from this very special and talented group to the writer whom they had revealed as one of the all-time great vaudevillians.

Originally published by Joel G. Fink, *Theatre Journal*, 35 (1983): 415–16. © The Johns Hopkins University Press. Reprinted with the permission of The Johns Hopkins University Press.

Adrian Noble's Stratford Production, 1983

Charles Whitworth

The legacy of two famous and brilliant Stratford productions of *The Comedy of Errors* weighs heavily upon any new attempt. Clifford Williams's 1962 production, still being revived ten years later, was one of the most acclaimed RSC productions ever. Trevor Nunn's musical extravaganza of 1976 (Judi Dench, Michael Williams, Roger Rees, Francesca Annis, *et al.*), also filmed for television, was another great success. And, if one cares to go further back in Stratford annals, there was Komisarjevsky's classic of 1938. As the standing ovation continued on first preview night of the current production, an usherette was heard to express relief on behalf of the company: "They were so worried. They've been living in the shadow of the last [1976] one."

No need to have worried. This production has a distinct identity of its own, is overflowing with ideas and energy, and will live in the memory alongside its illustrious predecessors. It will probably be either loved or loathed, for there are no half-measures about it. It is, unashamedly, a show. One recognizes its debts to past productions, a gesture here, a bit of business there, the now-standard musical setting of Dr. Pinch's incantation number. But Adrian Noble's enchanted Ephesus is a circus world, a child's story-book land. Tweedledum and Tweedledee, Pierrot, Coco the clown, Charlie Chaplin, a bobby on a bike, citizens in blackface and whiteface, bowler hats and moustaches (and grey business suits), a duke in purple-and-ermine robe and crown (over a grey business suit and college tie), a saffron-faced Dr. Pinch in tails and mortarboard—St. Paul's Ephesus, with its exorcists and practitioners of *curious arts*, was a drab seaside village to this.

A bare, white semi-circular shell, three storeys high, is the set. A pit orchestra (plaudits to the percussionist-cum-special effects man) occupies a real *pit*, surrounded by playing area on four sides, and on one occasion, several characters sit with their feet dangling down onto the piano keyboard, producing random chords; on another, in the midst of a chase, Antipholus and Dromio of Syracuse, hemmed in on both sides, leap across the abyss. Music has become, in recent years, an outstanding feature of RSC productions. One recalls, for example, Terry Hands's *As You Like It* and *Much Ado* and Trevor Nunn's *All's Well* in that regard. This *Comedy of Errors* is no exception. The five-piece pit orchestra works overtime (even more so on 15 September when, technical problems having postponed the curtain for more than an hour, they cheerfully entertained the equally cheerful audience). Ragtime, jazz, circus tunes, and schmaltz set the rapidly-changing moods. Before the performance, during the interval—there *is* one, despite the programme's bold-faced declaration to the contrary—a foyer combo plays, and then, in what is becoming a RSC signature, joins the cast onstage for the finale.

The Dromios are clowns, with Emmett Kelly faces including red plastic noses which beep (via the percussionist) when pinched, and which must seriously impede respiration. They wear baggy plaid suits with matching caps, the slightly different colours of the plaids being the only variation. Richard O'Callaghan's Dromio of Syracuse is an immensely energetic, nervous character, obsessed with witches and demons. In his increasing bewilderment and incomprehension at being beaten for doing just what his master tells him to do, he breaks down in tears, moving the entire audience to sympathetic sighs. Henry Goodman, brilliant as the hoofer and would-be comic Harry in *The Time of Your Life* (a role created by Gene Kelly) at The Other Place, plays a more lugubrious Dromio of Ephesus, breaking mechanically into a dance step under the conjuring of Pinch. For both these Dromios, the gratuitously vulgar farting duel through the letter slot in the portable door, in the otherwise extremely funny Act III, scene 1, seems slightly ill-conceived.

The Antipholuses are identified as twins by their bright blue faces, the subject of much speculation in post-performance discussions. Perhaps the clue is Antipholus of Syracuse's line "I to the world am like a drop of water" in I.2, or the dominant sea and water imagery in general. It may be a generic trait: Egeon has a blue nose. With their identical grey suits and white gloves and shoes, it establishes twinship in two actors, Paul Greenwood and Peter McEnery, who bear less natural resemblance than, say, Roger Rees and Mike Gwilym, their predecessors in the 1976 production. These two convey quite clearly the differences in temperament of the twins. Peter McEnery is particularly fine as Antipholus of Ephesus, revealing a comic talent unsuspected perhaps by RST habitués who may have seen him in such roles as Pericles, Suffolk (*Henry VI*), Albie Sachs, or Brutus in this season's *Julius Caesar*.

Luciana (Jane Booker) is pale yellow (golden), wears a pink ruffled clown outfit, and an extraordinary blond hairdo, spiralling up to a point some fifteen inches above her head. Unicorn? Ice cream cone? Or seashell? Adriana (Zoë Wanamaker) wears a rather dowdy suit over shocking pink arms, hands, and legs. Miss Wanamaker, who may have been influenced by Judi Dench's Adriana of 1976, has, like Miss Dench, the ability to vary the timbre of her voice, and she uses it to considerable effect here. The genuine anguish felt by Adriana, admittedly muted by the dominant comic-farcical mood of the inner play, is glimpsed. Ought we to be told and retold so emphatically that something more than a *diner intime* has transpired between Adriana and the wrong Antipholus? Shakespeare certainly does not do so. Emma Watson's Courtezan, who rises from a trap pat upon Antipholus's cue, "Some blessed power deliver us from hence!", is attired in bright red leotard with her face made up to the same hue, black stockings and wig, and a very tight white corset with garters—Mistress Satan in the flesh.

I have dwelt upon costumes at some length because, in the absence of any set to speak of, they carry the sole visual dimension of the production. This is a fantasy world in which both the Roman comic farce of twin masters and servants and the errors that ensue from their all being in the same place, and the mouldy old romance tale of hapless Egeon and his long-lost family, are enacted and eventually converge. The director's and designer's conception is fine. The execution frequently goes joyfully and heedlessly over the top. There is simply too much going on. Gimmickry rules. A lift, the sort used for washing skyscraper windows and in which Adriana and Luciana make their first entrance, broke down, and the actors concerned, deprived of this eye-catching device, had to fall back on old-fashioned acting. Very well, we may say, and a good thing too. But not when they were not prepared for it, when the production was geared to one spectacular moment after another. If any of Shakespeare's plays invite such extravagance (and if in any it is more pardonable than in others), it is those in which farce and slapstick-style humour are inherent to a preponderant degree. *The Comedy of Errors* and *The Taming of the Shrew* (which have more than that in common) are the two chief examples of Shakespeare in the farcical vein, but neither is pure farce throughout. From the beginning of his career, Shakespeare delighted in yoking together (sometimes violently) diverse literary and dramatic kinds, the result, for better or worse, being uniquely his. Adrian Noble's production does attempt to distinguish the scenes of wonder, romance, pathos, and lyricism from the farce. When Antipholus of Syracuse, victim of the first "error," mistaking the local Dromio for his twin, recollects the reputation of Ephesus for sorcery, cozenage, "and many suchlike liberties of sin" (I.2), the white light fades to blue and eerie music is heard. When Adriana mourns her husband's apparent infidelity (II.1), a slow, sad melody, the sort that soap operas employ at such moments, is heard. The wooing of Luciana is accompanied by saccharine mood music, as Antipholus hangs upside down (his world becoming more and more that way) from a window, speaking quatrains to Luciana who stands on a ladder that she has carried on and erected to a toy doll's ballet routine.

At the end, the now statutory RSC all-in dance number concludes with the unrolling of an immense tablecloth from under the Abbess's voluminous blue habit. It is stretched the entire width of the forestage and the company lines up behind it as if for the "gossips' feast." "After so long grief, such nativity"—the rebirth and reunion are celebrated to suitably exuberant music.

But despite the laudable attempt to preserve those variegated strands of wonder, mystery, weirdness, romance, lyricism that make the piece not a novice's servile imitation of Plautus, but an unmistakable Shakespearian comic romance, they are simply overwhelmed by the nonstop barrage of gimmickry, buffoonery, vaudeville gags, and Keystone Cops high jinks. But if in the theatre, as opposed to the Eng. Lit. classroom, sheer theatricality, clarity of speech, boundless energy, and wholehearted commitment from all performers count for anything, this is an unforgettable show.

Originally published by Charles Whitworth, *Cahiers Elisabéthains* 24 (1983): 116–118. Reprinted with the permission of *Cahiers Elisabéthains*.

Figure 8. Nunn production, 1976, Stratford-upon-Avon, RSC Theatre. Antipholus of Ephesus (Mike Gwilym) addressing a sinister Angelo (Paul Brooke). Used with the permission of the Shakespeare Centre Library, Stratford-upon-Avon.

Leif Söderström's Stockholm Production, 1983

Lars Ring; translated by Gunnar Sorelius

Even the old Greeks sat down in their open-air theatres with the same kind of eagerness, expectation, and picnic baskets as the people of Stockholm do when the Parkteatern puts on Shakespeare in Vitabergen Park.

For some reason the title *The Comedy of Errors* has been changed to *Tvillingar* [Twins], something which only causes what [Karl August] Hagberg [author of the classic Swedish translation of Shakespeare, 1847–51] called *Flörvillelser* [Errors]. The play is one of Shakespeare's first efforts, a product of the early 1590s. It was inspired by a comedy of Plautus, one of the great *farceurs* of Antiquity. But of course good old Will used his own head when he reworked the action. Among other things he moved it to the city of Ephesus in Asia Minor.

A Beautiful Set

This move has given the designer Örjan Säll the opportunity to create a set which looks as if it had been taken out of *A Thousand and One Nights*. This is perhaps not quite in character with the play as a whole, but the result is strikingly beautiful. The set consists of three houses—one of which can be converted to a ship—and earth colours, light blue, and white. This artificial-looking décor swarms with people dressed in Berit Söderström's confetti-bright colours—red, purple, and gold—in harem skirts and crakows. You could believe you were in a foreign land, had not the lush greenery of the Vitabergen Park reminded you that this was really Sweden in summer.

In Shakespeare's Ephesus two pairs of brothers, and one father and one mother, are reunited after having been separated in a shipwreck many years earlier. But before this happy reunion occurs, a merry-go-round of misunderstandings is set in motion, caused by the fact that the twins Antipholus and Antipholus and Dromio and Dromio are as like as peas in a pod.

Jonas Bergström plays both Antipholi as almost harmless, golden-locked and handsome characters, just as you expect heroes to be. Pierre Wilkner plays the slaves Dromio, who get all the boxes on the ears, and who turn all the somersaults; as well as a truly magnificent kitchen maid. Although Wilkner slips and tumbles and looks silly in a splendid way, he is also a little too quick in the delivery of his lines. He ought to try to find time to pause occasionally in his rattle to give the audience a chance to enjoy the subtlety of his hairsplitting.

One of the Antipholi is married, and his wife, played by Eva Kristin Tangen, has to put up with a great deal. Sometimes he recognizes her, sometimes he doesn't. Tangen is a very talented comedienne and her speaking of the verse is worthy of imitation. Her ingenious little shrieks of anger and frustration contrast strongly with Lisa Hugeson's affected acting style in the role of the wife's sister.

Fortunately there is also a grand vizier in this bewitched city who under the mask of a theatre villain turns out to have a heart of gold when he finally reunites the family in a happy ending.

Ingenious Details

The director Leif Söderström has concentrated on entertaining. His direction of the bustle and rush of the swarming crowds is impressive. The little details are well worked out, as for example the device of having the female prompter take part in the action, and as when he gives us a two-metre-tall Abbess, and a Dr. Knip [Pinch] who looks like a mixture of the Forty Thieves and an African medicine-man [see Figure 9].

Using technical sophistications in an open-air theatre can be dangerous. At the end of the play when the two pairs of twins have to be confronted with each other, walkers-on and the recorded voices of Bergström and Wilkner are used, a trick which does not quite come off. The freezings used whenever a character wants to directly address the audience becomes a cliché instead of adding to the meaning.

The music and the songs by Göran Fristorp composed especially for the production provide restful rallying-points, with the exception, however, of the contributions of Bergström and Hugoson.

When the play is over, and the lemming migration of spectators finds its way down to Ringvägen, one experiences a slight feeling of disappointment. Shakespeare's play contains so much more than what has been shown on the stage. He shows a city where order has been succeeded by chaos—two frames of reference collide, questions are asked and receive meaningless answers. When language no longer suffices to achieve order, people resort to violence. Do we not daily see these kinds of mechanisms at work in the subway?

But such things do not interest Söderström. Of course it is ambitious of the Parkteatern to put on Shakespeare, but one had expected something more than mere entertainment.

Originally published by Lars Ring, *Stockholms Tidningen*, 7 March 1983, 32. Reprinted with the permission of Lars Ring; translated for this volume by Gunnar Sorelius.

Figure 9. Söderström production, 1983 Vitabergen Park. Dr. Pinch (Gunnar Nielsen) ministers to the bound Antipholus of Ephesus (Jonas Bergström), while his servant (Pierre Wilkner) peeks out from behind the hut, and Adriana (Eva Kristin Tangen, far right) looks on nervously. Used with the permission of the photographer, Gösta Glase, courtesy of Gunnar Sorelius.

The *Comedy of Errors* on Television

H.R. Coursen

Of all the plays in the canon, *The Comedy of Errors* seems the most impervious to television. Although four television versions exist, only one was made originally *for* television—and that only because the BBC had determined to do the canon.

The poverty of the modern medium is demonstrated when we consider that *The Comedy of Errors* reaches back to Plautus for its inspiration but has difficulty reaching forward to be incorporated on television. The convention of identical twins—and here we have two sets!—simply does not translate to the "realistic" premises of television. Although television can incorporate the cartoon, we can readily grasp why *The Comedy of Errors* would not work in that genre. We, and the inhabits of Ephesus, would be observing the same figure. There would be no mistaken identity, no confusion of those misidentified, none of the situational irony and attendant laughter that the stage provides.

Locus—the inherited script—is invariably conservative, says Robert Weimann (1988), but can be challenged by the mechanism and circumstances of production, or *platea*. In the case of *Comedy of Errors*, however, the givens are simply denied by the medium. While it might be argued that television's modernist premises deny *Comedy of Errors* its ability to translate to that medium, we must remember that none of the comedies in which twins are mistaken for each other or in which a woman disguises herself as a man have succeeded on film, either. One of the best such efforts is Christine Edzard's *As You Like It*, in which an androgynous Rosalind (Emma Croft) insists that Orlando move through a homoerotic phase and fall in love with Ganymede before she reveals her real gender. The Gade-Nielsen 1920 *Hamlet*, in which Asta Nielsen plays Hamlet *as* woman, is also an effective film. She is trapped in her disguise, as Viola might have been had Sebastian not also come safely from the sea. A comedy which insists that we suspend our disbelief cannot succeed, it seems, in a medium which does not ask that we agree to that contract.

The effort to make *The Comedy of Errors* work on television, however, is instructive, and, in the instance of the televised stage plays makes clear how quickly the stage can "date itself," rendering what might have seemed fresh and original at the moment of production very much a product of a *Zeitgeist* that seems longer ago than it is.

It has long been noted that *The Comedy of Errors* is much more than a Plautine farce. Shakespeare eliminates some of the harsher edges of Plautus and introduces a "psychological" element to the stock characters. That "psychology" is a function of the characters' response to an apparently mad world. But the world of Ephesus is quite sane, indeed rigid in its rationality. It "is not a place of irrationality and dream [as] the Syracusan twins wrongly perceive it to be" (Holland 1992, 177). Its laws, for example, are the inviolate rules that the comic world can sometimes transcend, as in Theseus's overruling Egeus at the end of *A Midsummer Night's Dream*, but that in Ephesus can be delayed but not otherwise extenuated. This world moves literally by the book and by the clock. Neither it nor its characters can allow for chance or coincidence, but Shakespeare introduces precisely those elements to the Ephesian grid. Ephesus does not know that twins have been disgorged into its defined spaces, nor, of course, do the boys from Syracuse know that they are identical to two chessmen already in play on those spaces. Shakespeare makes sure that the timing of events remains exact, even as the playwright's craftsmanship foments greater and greater confusion in the characters. He poises his control of time against their belief that *they* know what time it is. "Here comes the almanac of my true date," says Antipholus S. as, to what will soon be their mutual bewilderment, Dromio E. approaches. The twins cannot confront each other until the promised end, when "the calendars of their nativity" are reestablished within the flow of a continuity that the characters on stage share at last with us. Until then, some of the characters must construe the events and even other characters as "crazy." Beyond that imputation, however, is their inevitable question—am I mad myself?

Ben Jonson, Drummond tells us, "had one intention to have made a play like Plaut[us'] Amphtrio but left it of, for that he could never find two so like others that he could persuade the spectators they were one" (1925–52, 144). The master of intricate dramaturgy, who could persuade a character to debate a puppet, had little confidence in the ability of his own audience to suspend its disbelief. Nor did he recognize that it is not *we* but the characters on stage who must exhibit "mistaking eyes" and convince us of their inability to tell one Antipholus or Dromio from another. Nor did Jonson glimpse the psychology behind apparent identicalness. Jonson left it to Shakespeare to be the first to recognize some of the psychological implications of the "double story," particularly the "shadow" aspects to be explored with particular energy by the 19th century and early 20th century in "The Double," "William Wilson," "The Picture of Dorian Gray," "Dr. Jekyll and Mr. Hyde," "The Jolly Corner," "The Prussian Officer," and "The Secret Sharer," to name a few examples.

"Which is the natural man,/ And which the spirit?" What happens to the Antipholi is similar to a "dissociative reaction, in which the amnesic half is represented by Antipholus S. while the conflicting half is represented by Antipholus E" (Fabricius 1989, 47). The former experiences a regression—"The hours come back"—to an adolescence which pulls simultaneously towards home and maternity and away from home towards matrimony and a new home. Antipholus S. "pursues his future wife while searching for his mother and the past" (Fabricius, 56), dominated, as Peter Blos suggests of the adolescent, by "two broad affective states: mourning and being in love" (1952, 100). The process represents, according to Freud, in describing psychoanalyis, "a second education of the adult, a correction to his education as a child" (1959, 268). "Love" is to be achieved, of course, once Antipholus S. contacts the energizing archetype of his maternal being: "how much more bearable it is for a son to conceive the son-father problem no longer on the plane of individual guilt—in relation, for example, to his own desire for his own father's death, his aggressions and desires for revenge—but as a problem of deliverance from the father, i.e., from a dominant principle of consciousness that is no longer adequate for the son: a problem that concerns all men, and has been disclosed in the myths and fairy tales as the slaying of the reigning old king and the son's accession to the throne" (von Franz 1959, 20). Antipholus E. denies Egeon at the end, but his denial is almost immediately corrected by Antipholus S.'s recognition of Egeon. Antipholus S.'s "sense of having been estranged from a familiar world and sense of [not] having another to hang on to...lies at the heart of the adolescent's conflict and crisis" (Fabricius, 55–6).

The conflict between and within the Antipholi reflects, of course, the conflict between the two cities, each seen by the other as evil. The play must move its characters to that point advocated by Paul in his letter to the Ephesians: "Now therefore ye are no more strangers & foreners: but citizens with the Saintes, and of the housholde of God" (Ephesians 2:19, Geneva version). Into the coincidence that Shakespeare inflicts upon blind Ephesus must flow the grace of God. Coincidence must transform itself to synchronicity. That is the "comic" pattern, here achieved within a perceived dream, or nightmare, as are the results of *A Midsummer Night's Dream* by the young lovers. *The Comedy of Errors* also provides a first glimpse of the rhythm of romance, from storm, shipwreck, separation, from apparent death to rebirth, and to reconciliations of lovers, relatives, and the generations themselves (see Bevington 1980, 96–98 and Foakes 1962, xxxix–li). These may seem "essentializing" or "totalizing" myths, but they are *there*, awaiting what deconstruction may find in the fissures and interstices of the scripts.

That deconstruction, for dramatic literature, is production. But in the case of *The Comedy of Errors*, modern media prove a barrier, as opposed to the challenge that can be overcome in various ways with a script that can be seen as "psychological," as Olivier saw *Hamlet*, or as "realistic," as Branagh saw *Henry V* (with the psyche of the King part of the reality depicted).

From one point of view, *The Comedy of Errors* should work on television. For all the talk of the supernatural and for all of the emphasis on exorcism, there is no cosmic intersection here. Therefore the focus is on the psychology of the characters, which invents a thesis of insanity or of the outer mystery to explain what we the audience know to be human interaction. Even when a script does contain a ghost or ghosts, or evidence of non-human intervention, television directors attempt to depict a *human* cause. "Such emphasis upon the psychological rather than the otherworldly," says Alan Dessen, "suits prevailing interpretations...and sidesteps effects that may strike television viewers as questionable, even laughable" (1986, 12). In addition, television lacks the depth for "cosmic" representations *and* for special effects. Language on stage can convince us that the characters are in a different world than we are, or, at least, *believe* they are. But such language emerging from our own machine into our domestic space tends to lack that potency. Special effects on a large screen in a darkened auditorium also have a power which television is wise not to attempt. Dessen asks, "If the medium is indeed hostile to the artist's original strategy, what kind of interpretative logic or rationale should inform any representation?" (1986, 12). Jonson, at least, knew that the twins wouldn't work in a "realistic" medium. Shakespeare, glimpsing greater possibilities for his stage and apparently granting greater flexibility to his audience, shows that *The Comedy of Errors*, although in many ways scaled down to the diminished medium of television, is still irredeemably a play for the stage and our expectations as an audience in the living space where we and the actors work together to create a fiction.

Each of the four available versions is a television production—three are tapes of actual stage productions. In the latter instances, response is complicated. It cannot be just an evaluation of a production on magnetic tape transferred to cassette, but must incorporate a sense of the original site of performance—a stage. But as time takes the production back with it, it becomes less a living thing and more of an artifact.

The Flying Karamazov version, televised on PBS in 1987, was originally presented at the Goodman Theater in Chicago in 1983, and later for the Olympia Arts Festival in Los Angeles in 1984. The televised production was taped during the summer of 1987 at the Vivian Beaumont Theater, Lincoln Center, New York. It tells the story clearly enough and has the virtue of being unabashedly a *stage* production. The semi-circular stage is in view as the television production begins, and an occasional upstage camera shows the audience. Indeed, on several occasions the audience is invaded, à la the Olson and Johnson

"Hellzapoppin'" shows that older members of the Beaumont audience might have recalled.

During a back-stage introduction, a Shakespeare look-alike waves off any connection between himself and the play to follow. Indeed, one of the "tensions" introduced during the production is the question of "authorship." A dramaturg, interviewed at the intermission, says that "Francis Bacon would have been delighted" by the production. Alphonse, the juggling master, suggests that Shakespeare's "text has been cut out of the way of the juggling," a wry glance at the agendas that can crowd in upon any hapless script as it lurches through time. J. Todd Fleming, the dramaturg, claims that he did manage to keep Dromio of Ephesus from becoming "Dromio of Poughkeepsie"—although given the separating expanse of the Hudson River, he might have become "Dromio of Hoboken." As Dromio E. launches into a dying speech, which includes, "Tell Laura I love her," "Shakespeare" comes out pointing at the script, then tears it up and strides angrily off. He appears later on the Abbess's "Behold—a man much wronged!" A transvestite Courtezan calls for "a roundel and a fairy song," then quotes from *Hamlet*, *Coriolanus*, and Jackie Gleason. As the author bows, he is seen from behind. "Bringing up the rear," says the announcer, "is William Shakespeare."

The production does not know whether it wants to be drama or circus. The two elements compete against each other. Adriana and Luciana upstage their first discussion (II.1) with tap routines between their responses. These are not dances that complement the "action," like, say, "Night and Day"—which in its original version incorporates conflict between Astaire and Rogers—or "Fit as a Fiddle and Ready for Love," which is predictably a prelude to romance. The end of the scene, without all the sound and movement, is much more effective in its interplay than is its beginning. Luciana's facial responses to Adriana's questions about her own beauty establish the women as confidantes *and* rivals. But that is a rare parenthesis within the general pandemonium. Later (IV, 2), Adriana undercuts her speeches with some high-flying baton work. She does the same thing in V.1 with a scimitar. We admire the skill involved, but we do not hear the words.

"In Syracuse, you wear a tie;/ In Ephesus, you juggle or you die," we hear as the Syracusian Antipholus and Dromio change into costumes identical to those of their Ephesian twins. Otherwise, the characters are constantly juggling. The production even provides some Busby Berkleyian overhead shots showing the objects flying kaleidoscopically across the screen, along with trapeze work, slack-wire-walking, stilt-walking, acrobatics, knife-throwing, uni-cycling, fire-eating, belly-dancing, and jump-roping. June Schlueter accurately says that the actors "adeptly pull off their balancing acts, but the linguistic structure of the play sadly collapses.... Bring back the text, then bring on the jugglers, and the world of Ephesus could resume its magical shape...in this version it is Shakespeare who is doing the disappearing act" (1987, 10–11)—as the production seems to admit. Here is an instance of *locus* being used almost solely at the service of *platea*.

The physical material is seldom integrated into the dramatic, a fact underscored by the "jokes." The text on "How to Tell a Joke" that Antipholus S. and Dromio S. peruse does not help them with all the joking about hair and baldness in II.2—and that is the "joke." A chicken shot through the door of Antipholus E.'s house becomes a "fowl intrusion." Every time a character says "say," the company repeats what he or she has just said. The word "bark" summons a stuffed spaniel from the cellarage who says "arf." "As I am a Christian," says Antipholus S., revealing a pair of Max Baer's trunks featuring the star of David. Egeon, whose own narrative had been cut, keeps changing his sandwich board. At one point he enters asking that $10,000 be placed in his Swiss bank account. The back side of the board tells us that "Ollie says it's okay." When Dromio E. mentions a football, the company shifts into a single wing mode and the band plays the Notre Dame fight song. When Dromio S. says "besides myself," a dummy Dromio is thrust out from behind the arras. As Adriana and Antipholus E. square off, the troupe hums the "Rocky" theme. Luce attempts to shatter a styrofoam cup with her voice, then bites it. Dromio S. asks, "Is it Memorex?" When Adriana launches into "Thou art an elm, my husband..."—lines apparently written for her by Luciana, who has, in turn, borrowed from Psalms—Antipholus S. asks, "Rod McKuen?" Dromio S. shrugs and guesses "Burma Shave?"

A production which pulls the inherited *locus* almost entirely into topicality can enjoy only the most fleeting communication, depending as it does on an audience precisely contemporary with its allusions. An audience may "get" the reference to the Memorex ad, in which Ella Fitzgerald's tape-recorded voice shattered glass, but is the Burma Shave rhyme available even to a 1980s audience? The signs inhabited the sides of two-lane roads in the 1930s, when the speed limit was 35 or 40 mph. They disappeared in the 1960s, with the advent of superhighways and the prohibition of billboards. One of their originators, Allan G. Odell, did not die, however, until 21 January 1994, at 90. His favorite jingle does find a resonance in *Comedy of Errors*:

> Within this vale
> of toil and sin,
> your head grows bald,
> but not your chin.
> Burma Shave.

The topicality of the production traps it in a too-specific time and place. The pizza delivery man wears a Mets cap. Where are they now? The drummer rushes off for "the dinner show at El Morocco." The Abbess's word "drugs" evokes a "Just say no!" from three suddenly appearing talking heads. And so on—the juggling veins of rhyming nitwits.

Some good moments do come through. Karia Burns doubles Luce and the Duke with rotund gusto. Pinch (Avner Eisenberg) is a Punch sans Judy, with a head and four skillful arms, two of which double as feet. This is adroitness at the service of dramatic values, however farcical. Antipholus S. and Luciana (Paul Magid and Sophie Hayden) conduct a good parody balcony scene. The line "What light through yonder window breaks?" had been interpolated earlier. Alec Willows doubles as Angelo and Second Merchant: he "actually bisects himself," as John Simon says (1987, 91), the Goldsmith in gold, including hair, effeminate and ingratiating, the Merchant on the other side of the same body, in black, including hair, with tattoos, leather, and thuggish menace. Willows is superb as he makes the instant transition simply by turning to face his alter ego. Each is the other's shadow, and the "doubling" captures the psychological element of the script that is not really reached for elsewhere in the production.

Robert Brustein offers this telling commentary on the production: "About the only thing I learned...is that even minor Shakespeare must be acted. [The production seems like] another of those well-intentioned civic efforts to prove to school kids that Shakespeare can be painless.... [T]his *Comedy of Errors* is essentially a yuppie phenomenon. It skirts the surface of experience, offering amusement without involvement, laughter without discovery, technique without depth...I found myself longing for even the most conventionalized presentation of this play" (1987, 28). The "in-group" jokes, for example, could be seen as patronizing, but the audience in the televised version seems to accept being patronized in return for the self-congratulatory process of "getting" the jokes.

It may be that "straight" television is trapped in the *Zeitgeist* of its emergence—modernism, with its insistence on artistic unity, thematic consistency, and chronological preciseness. An occasional adventure into the surreal—MTV—may simply prove the rule. The BBC version does seem to be a victim of its medium. Not only did major problems occur during the taping, as Susan Willis chronicles (1991, 260–91), but the "realistic" medium apparently called for the same actors as the Antipholi (Michael Kitchen) and the Dromios (Roger Daltrey). As Willis explains "television is a more intimate, less forgiving medium than the stage; the willing suspension of disbelief is less readily granted" (1991, 267). One might amend—*if* granted at all. Furthermore, if *The Comedy of Errors* "is a less than coherent play...is a mixture of unreconciled opposites" (Lusardi 1985), its contact with the normative tendencies of television may result in some reconciliation of opposites, but also and crucially, in the single instance we have, can erase much of the interest that (possible) incoherencies and oppositions raise.

The issue of the play's genre is resolved by the nature of our laughter. The script exemplifies the Bergsonian criteria whereby an interrupted sequence elicits our laughter. We laugh, for example, when the expectation of a bag of gold is replaced by a rope's end, one of the many examples here of the way the play interferes with the sequences that the characters have set in motion, sequences interrupted by the sudden appearance of the wrong Dromio or Antipholus. If we laugh just at the circumstances—the juxtaposition of gold versus hemp—we are experiencing farce. If our laughter goes beyond that to incorporate the bewilderment of a character, say that of Dromio of Ephesus ("I am in adversity"), then we are responding to comedy. Our laughter can be cruel or sympathetic, and, of course, its nature can vary within the experience of a single production. Whatever its source, it occurs within the conceptual space created by the difference between a character's expectation and what actually happens—when a Dromio, for example, is sent off on a mission and returns to report to the wrong Antipholus. Our amusement at the end of the play can emerge from generic premises: "The fundamental human emotions on which *The Comedy of Errors* can base its claim to be a comedy rather than a farce are the simple and related ones of sorrow at separation and joy in reunion" (Wells 1972, 34). If it is a comedy, we are laughing *with* the characters, who have reenacted our own sorrows and joys.

The BBC production is not funny, except for the business that Charles Gray invents for his Duke. He is called down from his horse by the Abbess's "Renowned Duke!" "Damn! I just climbed up on this thing!" But he has been falling for the Courtezan—"I should get into town more often!"—and is delighted to escort her into the "feast." He thus challenges the rigidity of the class system established in the master (and mistress)/servant structure so firmly in place in the script. His performance is a good example of *platea* challenging *locus*, making use of what Weimann calls "the extra-dramatic 'aside'" (1988, 410). In this case, Gray uses an actor's "authority" to undercut an "authority figure."

But having the same actors in the leads does not allow for "interference of series," as Bergson calls it. We are not amused by the "mistakes" of the townspeople or the twins since they are not *making* mistakes. As Mel Gussow says of the Karamazov Brothers's version, "the Dromios are instantly distinguishable.... One would have to be a fool to confuse them—and that fact should say something about the other characters on stage" (1987, 24). They—including the twins, of course—simply refuse to come to obvious conclusions, and that refusal generates the variations on a theme that are the plot. In the BBC production the twins respond seriously to their dilemmas—it is a problem play, not a situational comedy. The distinction is partly a matter of style, partly a question of having a live audience or a laugh track. Even fourth-wall comedy, like "All in the Family," is often televised before a live audience. Part of the problem is that the genre decided upon—within television's admittedly narrow range—dictates that the actors are "real," their dilemmas are "real," and none of this is funny. Television tends to create psychological problems for its characters, as Dessen argues, but one wonders how Jane Howell would have directed this script. Her metadramatic approach, vividly successful with *II Henry VI* might have allowed for separate Antipholi and Dromios, and thus for the kinds of disjunctions that evoke laughter. She might even have built in some version of laugh track which commented on its own convention—by being silent at moments, for example, and having one of the characters look at the camera as if to ask where the laugh was.

If Egeon's long disquisition at the outset is accompanied by precisely coordinated mime and mixed consort, his speech comes across as having been planned in advance, as opposed to having been rehearsed towards the effect of spontaneity. Cellan-Jones's approach might work on stage, even if it trivializes Egeon's plight. The stage can absorb the commedia dell'arte conventions easily enough, but on television this opening creates the frictions with the medium that he is at pains to avoid elsewhere. The "ultimate effect of the mime was to distract rather than to support" (Warren 1984, 339). Furthermore, as J.C. Trewin suggests, "Such a piece as the *Errors* is all the better for rising from a basically grave situation" (1978[1], 47). Here, Egeon's story was drained of a specific gravity that is to be erased by other serious issues at the end.

If the play is not meant to be funny, then the BBC version is very good. Willis suggests that "Approaching the play as comedy meant taking the situation more seriously than simply laughing at the dilemmas. The issues of identity raised by the confusion of twins seemed frightening and even dangerous in the experience of the characters, not just the stuff that chuckles are made on" (1991, 260). One could argue that such a view takes the play too literally and gives the audience no space for response. One might also ask why the seriousness of Egeon's narrative and his present circumstances is undercut at the outset. But this is a *television* audience, which, instead of completing production, as in Aristotle's final cause, expects the production to be complete in and of itself.

The production occurs in a sunlit town with a map of the eastern Mediterranean on the pavement. We see a real map just before the transition to color, and again at the very end. The cartography cues the *precision* of things in Ephesus. This emphasis is undercut by the frequent references to a fortune teller and her crystal ball, but the latter suggests that Ephesus has not yet learned how to measure the future, and that it is that determination that will occur within the unity of our experience of the drama. A Daliesque perspective, seen through one of the arches of the market place, reinforces Antipholus S.'s belief that he has stepped into his own bad dream. The interior suggests the opulence of upper-class Pompei, but it is not too busy for television's shallow field of depth. Cellan-Jones permits activity *behind* his speaking characters, however, thus upstaging their lines. Willis tells us that some segments had to be retained simply because time did not permit reshooting (1991, 283–90).

Daltrey gives his Dromio of Syracuse "a small edge of dignity" over the "engaging vacuity" of the Ephesian (Roberts 1984, 4). In fact, Daltrey shows that Dromio of Syracuse is by far the more intelligent of the two, and that Dromio of Ephesus may have become retarded because of the continual beatings he receives from his master. Certainly, the servile crouch of the Ephesian Dromio suggests a constant anxiety, in contrast to the confident smile of his Syracusan brother. Kitchen distinguishes between his Antipholi, making the Ephesian harsher and more sexist: "hot tempered and prone to violence, a response the servant anticipates" (Willis 1991, 275). The actors try to avoid the problem that Peter Holland isolates in responding to a recent RSC production, in which Des Barrit and Graham Turner doubled the roles: "One of the great pleasures for the audience watching *Errors* is that we know the answer.... What we do find, though is that the over-weening confidence with which we begin...is shaken in the course of the play...when both Dromios are played by the same actor the audience's ability to be confused, a confusion that, I am suggesting, the play wants us to undergo, is simply evaded, evaded because the audience comes to follow actor, not role, Graham Turner, not Dromio.... The histor[ies] of the actor[s are] replaced by the history of the [single] performance" (1992, 176).

The BBC production, aware of this issue, deals with it in several ways. Cellan-Jones invents "a mirror sequence in the market for the Dromios, so that when Dromio of Syracuse discovers the frame has no mirror in it and that the other self he saw was no reflection, he begins II.2 full of confusion" (Willis 1991, 267). He has seen Dromio E. also trying on a hat, and he wants to explain what he has seen to Antipholus S., but he is not given a chance. Jeanne Roberts notices that "at one moment, Antipholus actually saw 'himself' entering the Porpentine and shrugged his vision off. Such apparitions nicely crystallized the question in the audience's mind—why does Antipholus so resist the very obvious explanation for which he has so long been searching? Openly acknowledging his strange oblivion served to point up the irrational blindness of the psyche in search of itself" (1984, 4). If the subject and the object of the search are the same, one cannot really see the other. And, unintentionally, Antipholus becomes the viewer of television: neither can suspend his disbelief and accept something beyond the givens of a naturalistic medium, whether Ephesus or tube. Antipholus S. closes his eyes and squeezes his nose at this point, attributing his double to a long and confusing day. The production, then, "enhanced...credibility...without the loss of potential for confrontation entailed in stage doubling" (Roberts 1984, 4) and "made...the confusion over identity more realistic" (Pearce 1984, 114). But is credibility the criterion? Or is the need for credibility forced upon the production and its audience by the medium?

In spite of the issues that the production failed to resolve, it achieved some fine moments. The wooing scene, cued by the consort we had heard earlier behind Egeon, is excellent. Luciana's quiet plea for her sister contextualizes Antipholus S.'s awe ("Are you a god? Would you create me new?"), even as she wonders at the lyric voice suddenly coming from her blunt brother-in-law. His thesis of divinity makes some sense of his experience for him, as does a similar attribution by Ferdinand in *The Tempest*. Dromio S. gets the speech about times turning "back an hour" (IV.2)—often cut—and makes a mysterious and mystifying moment of it. Warren notices that Adriana's (Susanne Berish) "scene with Wendy Hiller's formidable battleax of an Abbess made the brilliant point that strife between mother- and daughter-in-law began instinctively, before the two of them were even aware of the relationship" (1984, 340). And it may be that this sober rendition permits comedy, as Wells describes it above—"sorrow at separation, joy in reunion"—to emerge movingly at the end. We have not been allowed to laugh. Perhaps we can smile as what has been clear to us becomes at last clear to the characters who have been so implicated in their dilemmas that we have had to respond to them as, if not serious, at least as not funny.

This version, for Roger Warren, "made for a refreshing change from the extraneous gags and music numbers which usually load down productions of the play" (1984, 340). "The Pinch scene and the finale," he says, "were the least hectic I have seen. Everyone spoke very slowly to Antipholus of Ephesus, as to a child, when they thought him mad" (1984, 339–40). The Pinch is tall and dignified and does not reappear, singed and smoldering, as he does in the RSC version. Antipholus E. is angry, not insane, and the approach here helps underscore the irrelevance of this exorcism and the phoniness of exorcism generally as viewed by the Elizabethan establishment, which did not want freelancers crowding on to the deity-contacting network. "The power to perform an exorcism is the power to control the supernatural" (Neely, 18 March 1994). An exorcism overdone, as in most productions of *Errors*, misses the point, which is that exorcism itself is unnecessary. Here, *locus*, properly understood, is very much at the service of established authority. That it is a punishment of Antipholus E., who is himself a scapegoat for the debts and transgressions of others in the play, is true, but he is not possessed by any literal evil spirit. The "exorcism" is often a metaphor for spiritual change, or "individuation," as in *A Midsummer Night's Dream*, for example, but in Shakespeare it must be seen as fraudulent as a specific practice. Shakespeare's application in *Errors* undercuts any belief that the supernatural is actually interfering with identities or relationships. It takes no exaggeration in performance to make the point that exorcism is an inauthentic ceremony, dangerous from an official standpoint to its practitioners. The example of *Twelfth Night*—the response of Toby and Maria to Malvolio after Olivia sends them to look after him, and the scene between Feste/Sir Tophas—makes the point clearly. No matter what is said, Malvolio is a victim of a plot perpetrated by human beings and of his own narcissism.

The RSC version was taped on a rainy night in Stratford in the spring of 1976 and shown on television on the Arts and Entertainment Channel in 1990. It incorporates the fact of theater, beginning with an audience plunging through puddles towards the Memorial Theatre, shows a "No Cameras" sign (smiling at the television cameras that would be present and at Antipholus S.'s taking a picture of Luciana during the performance), scans the audience many times during the production and follows them at the end out into soggy Warwickshire.

If BBC "over-integrated" through the use of two actors for four roles, the RSC suffers like the Karamazov version from disintegration—in this instance from the imposition of music on drama.

Roger Warren points at a crucial problem in this production, assuming that it tries to "emphasiz[e] Shakespeare's distinctive humanizing of his rather inhuman Plautine models" (1977, 177). The problem is that "the director's routines did not help [Roger Rees's Antipholus of Syracuse] develop...into a complete characterization" (1977, 176). This is particularly true of his solo after falling in love with Luciana: "This can't be me...do I exist?" It is badly sung and it stops the action cold. The same routines force Francesca Annis's Luciana and Judi Dench's Adriana "suddenly to switch off their performances of the text itself and concentrate on singing" (1977, 176), as in their long duet, "A man is master of his liberty." The protracted song-and-dance number based on "hair" and "baldness" (II.2.70–119) erases the wonderful moment when Judi Dench appears on her balcony and peremptorily commands Antipholus S. to her. J.C. Trewin calls "Dench's jealous Adriana, her glance like a lazer beam...the best in recollection" (1978[2], 292)—and that is a lot of recollection!

But things get shallowed-out to the premises of musical comedy, which seldom involves depth of characterization or over-complexity of plot. In musical comedy, what "plot" there is a framework for the songs, as in "Anything Goes," where what everyone knows will be the briefest of incarcerations is a pretext for Cole Porter's plaintive "All Through the Night." "I don't need you or anybody. I got it figured out for myself," says Billy Bigelow before singing "If I Loved You," in "Carousel." While "Oklahoma" does include Jud and his "Lonely Room," the issue explored is: will Laurie go with Curley to the box supper?

Furthermore, the musical depended on singing, not acting, or on great dancing, when the voice (Astaire's or Kelly's, for example) was not itself outstanding. The great age of musicals started earlier on Broadway, of course, than in Hollywood, but was simultaneous from, say 1935 and "The Gay Divorcee" through the 1950s, as Hollywood did its own musicals—its "Broadway Melodies," "Big Broadcasts," "Goldwyn Follies," "Singin' in the Rain" and "American in Paris"—as well as film versions of "Kiss Me, Kate" and "Guys and Dolls." Film musicals have disappeared and stage musicals are rare except for Webberizations, revivals like "No, No, Nannette" and "Carousel" or conflations like "Crazy for You." That was as true in the late 70s as it is today, so that not only are the songs in the RSC *Errors* show stoppers in a negative sense, the genre is already out-of-date by some twenty years.

It follows that the musical format exacerbates the problems inherent in any recorded stage production. It will be at least as trapped in its moment and its conventions as a film or television version, so that it is likely to become at least as much of a record of *Zeitgeist* for us as a production of the script. *Platea* itself, then, detached from *locus*, may become the focal point of our response, as, in several ways, are the musical interventions in the RSC *Errors*. That will happen with recorded versions of past productions, as it must with plays placed exclusively in modern contexts, where we respond to the contextualization but are robbed of any sense of the script's contact with its *locus*. The givens of its inherent "'glass of fashion,'" as Weimann says, "far from showing 'her own' already-given image, c[an] be quite distorted by a whole set of socially, spatially, and verbally encoded forms of theatricality" (1988, 410), like, in the case of the RSC *Errors*, the musical comedy itself. One irony inherent in the RSC version is that "The Boys from Syracuse" had appeared almost 40 years before—in 1938—with songs by Rodgers and Hart like "Falling in Love with Love," "Sing for Your Supper," and "This Can't Be Love." That was probably not as good a score as their "Babes in Arms" the previous year, but the show was done with singers and dancers, and its songs were certainly better than those devised by Trevor Nunn (as he no doubt would agree). One point is that if you want to go to a musical, you go to a musical.

In *Errors* all things lead to situations in which *we* know why the characters are confused—until, as Holland suggests above, we become confused ourselves. The game requires speedy play which the musical interludes deny. Furthermore, although Trevor Nunn's "numbers appeared to derive from the text itself, they in fact had the effect of superimposing one medium on another" (Warren 1977, 176). "These interpolations," Warren says, "may have been good for the general morale of the company but they did not seem to me to help the performance of its individual members in any way" (1977, 176).The four male actors are not "sharply detailed individuals, reacting to each other and to their situations" (1977, 176). What we get is the situation and the blurring of character distinction in the precisely apportioned musical numbers that, for example, each Dromio is given. The songs are "utterly pointless," says J. Fuzier (1978, 75). The one possible exception is the ensemble number in which Antipholus S. sings his puzzlement as he wanders through the myriad greetings he receives (IV.2.1 ff.). Here, the music coincides with the thrust of the action, which deepens into Antipholus S.'s nightmare. The Pinch "Satan come forth" sequence (IV.4), however, just goes on and on. The music is particularly unfortunate for the otherwise excellent Dromios, each a red-headed ragamuffin. Nikolas Grace is a pop-eyed mimic of his Ephesian master. He shows how much his master controls whatever "individuality" he might otherwise have found for himself. Michael Williams (Dromio S.) is a canny operator. The distinction is again a reflection of how each master has dealt with his servant. Mike Gwilym (Antipholus E.) is wonderfully active and inventive in his explanation to the Duke at the end, as is

Dench, who runs through her speech in a mind-boggling but comprehensible double-time. Richard Griffiths as the hapless Officer, handcuffed to a chair and to Antipholus E. as the latter yanks him hither and yon, and Paul Brooke, fat, effeminate, and prone to faint, as the Goldsmith, are also splendid. The performances are not enhanced by the imposition of music on situational comedy and excellent actors.

The 1989 Stratford, Ontario version, directed by Richard Monette, released on cassette in 1995, was part of a "double bill" with *Titus Andronicus*. It is short—about 80 minutes (although the cassette says 138)—and very lightweight. A "mirthful divertissement" perhaps on stage (Gussow 1989, C-18), its television manifestation picks up only the exaggeration of the stage production and turns out to be dull. It employs two actors to play the twins, Keith Dinicol for the Dromios and Geordie Johnson for the Antipholi. The Dromios are so identical that "The wrong twin approaches" is a subtitle for the first appearance of Dromio of Ephesus. He wears glasses, as his twin does not, but little, if any, distinction is made between them otherwise. We lose any sense of which is which immediately, so that much of the situational irony is also lost. Johnson's Antipholus of Syracuse is a silly, giggly fellow. His Ephesian version is a sadistic villain. Neither one—the Sir Andrew nor the Don John—seems worth the effort at reunion and reconciliation that the play depicts. The women, Goldie Semple as Adriana and Lucy Peacock as Luciana, work at full decibel. The potential parenthesis of Antipholus of Syracuse's wooing is obliterated. The production is insecure about the play itself and has to keep telling its audience that this is all very funny. As too often at Stratford, Ontario, the humor is a result of broad gags as opposed to the wit in the lines or the laughter in the situations. The production on television is at once over-loud and coy. C.E. McGee suggests that the gags and special effects might have been ineffective in the theater as well: "Gimcrackery?—I would think not if only I could convince myself that the sense of wonder stirred by these spectacular effects went beyond them to Shakespeare's story, to its happy family reunion" (1990, 115). Admittedly, this was a cut-down version of a short script (under 1800 lines). That does not mean that serious issues cannot be explored as context for more farcical sequences, but the disruption of "the characters' expectations for their status and thus their sense of self-possession" can only be achieved by "the unwitting efforts of two (sets of two) bodies to occupy the same space," as Susan Baker argues (1990, 6–7).

The exception that indicts the rest of the production as *merely* "flourishes, and sparkling surfaces" (McGee 1989, 12) is the late Nicholas Pennell's quiet Egeon. His opening exposition is meant seriously but is then linked without preparation or transition to a slapstick farce. The final moments are also played quietly and soberly and work in spite of what has gone before. Variation of tone throughout the production might have integrated romance and farce, but no one, it seems, pays any attention to the intelligent cue that Pennell gives at the outset. The production delights its main stage audience, but it cannot overcome the initial wrong decision to double the leads and thus rob us immediately of our "superior stance" relative to the bewildered characters on stage. Again, as with the Royal Shakespeare Company production with Barrit and Turner, the Stratford production has to bring out doubles for the last scene. "Monette," says critic Wallace Sterling, "is forced to provide four bodies. This bit of directorial trickery works, but physical and vocal differences between each of the twins signal Monette's faith in the audience's willingness to suspend disbelief" (1989, 19). Not so. We have been "educated" away from doubleness and from consequent mistaken identity, so we don't suspend our disbelief at the end but wonder where those others have come from and what they look like. The introduction of these sudden twins raises extra-dramatic questions that drain the ending of some of its otherwise built-in enjoyment.

"The best way with *Errors*," says J.C. Trewin, "is to play it lightly, not to batter at the clowning, and not to undervalue that sudden lyrical blossoming for Luciana and Antipholus of Syracuse in the third act.... However [*Errors*] is done, it has to be brief" (1978[1], 49, 47). By these criteria, the BBC-TV version is the best of the four we have. As yet, however, this relatively under-performed script retains its latency, awaiting the imagination that can translate it and its stageworthiness to the magnetic medium of television tape. But then, the possibilities inherent in its location might make it a candidate for bright realization in the light-sensitive medium of film as well. This, then, should be considered a prolegomenon rather than a coup de grâce.

PRODUCTION CREDITS

Royal Shakespeare Company, 1976. Stratford-on-Avon, Main Stage. Directed by Trevor Nunn. Designed by John Napier and Dermot Hayes. Lighting by Clive Morris. Music by Guy Woolfenden. Directed for television by Philip Casson.

Francesca Annis (Luciana). Paul Brooke (Angelo). Brian Coburn (Duke). Judi Dench (Adriana). Susan Dury (Luce). Nikolas Grace (Dromio of S.). Richard Griffiths (Officer). Mike Gwilym (Antipholus of S.). Griffith Jones (Egeon). Marie Kean (Emilia). Roger Rees (Antipholus of E.). Barbara Shelley (Courtezan). Norman Tyrrell (Balthazar). Michael Williams (Dromio of E.). Robin Ellis (Pinch).

BBC-TV, 1984. Produced by Shaun Sutton. Directed by James Cellan-Jones. Designed by Don Homfray.

Suzanne Bertish (Adriana). Cyril Cusak (Egeon). Roger Daltrey (Dromios). Charles Gray (Duke). Wendy Hiller (Emilia). Michael Kitchen (Antipholi). Joanne Pearce (Luciana). Ingrid Pill (Courtezan). Geoffrey Rose (Pinch).

The Flying Karamazovs at the Vivian Beaumont Theater, New York, 1987. Directed by Robert Woodruff. Sets by David Gropman. Costumes by Susan Hilferty. Lighting by Paul Gallo. Directed for television by Kirk Browning and Alan Skog.

Karla Burns (Duke and Luce). Ethyl Eichelberger (Emilia and Courtezan). Avner Eisenberg (Janitor and Dr. Pinch). Timothy Furst (Shakespeare). Sophie Hayden (Adriana). Gina Lieshman (Luciana). Paul Magid (Antipholus S.). Daniel Mankin (Egeon). Randy Nelson (Dromio E.). Jay Patterson (Antipholus E.). Raz (First Merchant). Mark Sackett (Balthasar). Sam Williams (Dromio S.). Alex Willows (Angelo and Second Merchant).

Stratford, Ontario, 1989. Main Stage. Directed by Richard Monette. Designed by Patrick Clark. Lighting by Louise Guinand. Directed for television by Norman Campbell.

James Blendick (Duke). Douglas Chamberlain (Angelo). Juan Chioran (Merchant). Keith Dinicol (Dromios). Michael Hanrahan (Officer). Susan Henley (Courtezan). Kate Hennig (Luce). Andrew

Jackson (Balthazar). Geordie Johnson (Antipholi). Lucy Peacock (Luciana). Nicholas Pennell (Egeon). Goldie Semple (Adriana). Joseph Shaw (Pinch). Wenna Shaw (Emilia).

WORKS CITED

Baker, Susan. "Status and Space in *The Comedy of Errors.*" *Shakespeare Bulletin* 8/2 (Spring 1990): 6–7.

Bergson, Henri. *Le Rire*. Paris: Lycee Henry IV, 1900.

Bevington, David. "Introduction to *The Comedy of Errors.*" *Complete Works*. Glenview, Illinois: Scott, Foresman, 1980.

Bible. Geneva: Rovland Hall, 1560.

Blos, Peter. *On Adolescence*. New York: Free Press, 1952.

Brustein, Robert. "Vaudeville and Radio." *The New Republic* (6 July 1987): 28–9.

Dessen, Alan. "The Supernatural on Television." *Shakespeare on Film Newsletter* 11/1 (December 1986): 1, 12.

Fabricius, Johannes. *Shakespeare's Hidden World*. Copenhagen: Munksgaard, 1989.

Foakes, R.A., editor. *The Comedy of Errors*. London: Methuen, 1962.

Freud, Sigmund. *Psychoanalysis. The Complete Works*. Vol. 20. James Strachey, editor. London: Hogarth Press, 1959.

Fuzier, J. "Review." *Cahiers Elisabethains* XII (1978): 74–5.

Gussow, Mel. "Review." *New York Times* (1 June 1987): 24.

———. "Stratford Offers Majesty, Mirth, Farce and Gore." *New York Times* (12 June 1989): C–13 and C–18.

Holland, Peter. "Shakespeare Performances in England." *Shakespeare Survey* 44 (1992): 175–78.

Jonson, Ben. *Works*. Eds. C. Herford and P. and E. Simpson, Oxford: Oxford U.P., 1925–52. Vol. 1.

Lusardi, James. "*The Comedy of Errors.*" *Shakespeare Bulletin* 3/5 (November/December 1985).

Lyons, Richard. "Allan G. Odell, 90; Burma Shave Executive Linked Beards to Bards." *New York Times* (22 January 1994).

McGee, C.E. "The Stratford (Ontario) Festival 1989: A Canadian's Overview." *Shakespeare Bulletin* 7/6 (November/December 1989): 12–14.

———. "Shakespeare in Canada: The Stratford Season, 1989." *Shakespeare Quarterly* 41, no. 1 (1990): 114–120.

Neely, Carol. "Madmen and Strong Women in *Twelfth Night* and *Comedy of Errors.*" Lecture. Clemson University (18 March 1994).

Pearce, G.M. "Review." *Cahiers Elisabethains* 25 (April 1984): 113–15.

Roberts, Jeanne. *"The Comedy of Errors." Shakespeare on Film Newsletter* 9/1 (December 1984): 4.

Schlueter, June. *"The Comedy of Errors." Shakespeare Bulletin* 6/4 (July/August 1987): 10–11.

Simon, John. "Review." *New York Magazine* (15 June 1987): 91.

Sterling, Wallace. *"Titus Andronicus* and *The Comedy of Errors." Shakespeare Bulletin* 7/6 (November/December 1989): 18–19.

Trewin, J.C. *Going to Shakespeare.* London: Allen & Unwin, 1978. [1978[1] in text]

——. "Shakespeare in Britain." *Shakespeare Quarterly* (Spring 1978): 212–22. [1978[2] in text]

von Franz, Marie-Louise. *Complex/Archetype/Symbol in the Psychology of C.G. Jung.* New York: Pantheon, 1959.

Warren, Roger. "Theory and Practice: Stratford, 1976." *Shakespeare Survey* 30 (1977): 169–77.

——. "Shakespeare in England." *Shakespeare Quarterly* 34/3 (Autumn 1984): 334–40.

Weimann, Robert. "Bifold Authority in Shakespeare." *Shakespeare Quarterly* 34/9 (Winter 1988): 401–17.

Wells, Stanley, editor, *The Comedy of Errors.* London: Penguin, 1972.

Willis, Susan. *The BBC Shakespeare Plays.* Chapel Hill: University of North Carolina Press, 1991.

Crinkles in the Carnival: Ideology in South African Productions of *The Comedy of Errors* to 1985

Rohan Quince

Open to a variety of interpretations on the stage, Shakespeare's plays may serve not only as cultural showpieces but also as public arenas for trying out current myths, ideologies, and systems of belief. The continued regularity of Shakespeare productions in South Africa attests not only to the unquestioned genius of the plays, but also to the high cultural prestige conferred on those producing them, itself a reflection of the tenacious, albeit diminishing, hegemony of English culture in South Africa. Even when intended only as a cultural showpiece, a Shakespeare production invariably reveals the ideological assumptions of its producers, whether purposeful or unconscious. Furthermore, the ideology of Shakespeare's plays in South Africa refers not only to their production, but extends also to their evaluation and preservation.[1] Records of township productions by black South Africans, for example, tend to be dependent on word-of-mouth and the fortunes of oral history, whereas productions by and largely for whites are often prevented from being overcome by history or forgetting, continuing as articulations of a white-constructed memory through their preservation in state archives and published memoirs.

From the first production of a Shakespeare play in South Africa in 1799 until the end of World War II, Shakespeare productions were largely the monopoly of English-speaking whites. While local amateur and professional companies gained strength and confidence during this long period, their productions were invariably based on theatrical styles in England. Performances were judged on how closely they managed to imitate what was being done on the stage of London. The highlight for local audiences was inevitably a tour of South Africa by some English company. It comes as no surprise, therefore, that the first production of *The Comedy of Errors* in South Africa was performed by the touring Henry Herbert Company in 1913.

After World War II, other racial and language groups began to produce Shakespeare's plays, reflecting the widespread perception of Shakespeare as a litmus test of civilised culture. The first play performed by so-called "coloureds" was *The Tempest* in 1946; an Afrikaans *Hamlet* was staged in 1947. The first production using black actors took place in 1953, a production of *The Comedy of Errors*. Ian Bernhardt, long active in multiracial cultural activities, was approached by a friend who worked in the Welfare Department of PUTCO (the Public Utility Transport Corporation), eager to organise some instructional activities for the black workers. A number of workers requested a drama group, and thus the Bareti Players was formed—so called after the tribal eulogist who composes songs of praise to a chief. Colin Romoff was invited to direct *The Comedy of Errors*. The cast consisted largely of PUTCO office workers and clerks, but also included a few outsiders, mainly teachers. The play was performed at the University of the Witwatersrand Arts Festival and toured the black townships around Johannesburg in a bus provided by PUTCO, receiving an enthusiastic reception.

"It was a real eye-opener," said Mr. Romoff at the time. "Modern audiences miss a lot of Shakespeare's wit, but the Natives laughed at things whose humour I'd never realised before." He noted that "with their natural exuberance...they probably have a lot more in common with the spirit of Elizabethan comedy than White South Africans." He was equally impressed with the cast. "It took them a little while to get the feel of the play and the convention in which it is written. After that they just bounded forward."[2]

According to Ian Bernhardt, they bounded forward rather further than Romoff's original conception. The comedy was played broadly, and this tendency increased as the run progressed, much to the delight of the audiences. The director, who attended about every third performance, was horrified at all the new "business" which crept in. He would have serious discussions with the cast explaining that they must perform the play the way he had directed it and that they must not be diverted by the audience response. They would all agree, but somehow by the time he returned, the play would have evolved once more into a communal festival.[3]

The gales of laughter from the audiences in the township halls and the elaborate comic improvisations which the actors evolved as a result suggest that a spirit of Bakhtinian "Carnival" prevailed. What Colin Romoff, looking through the lens of 1950s liberalism, saw as "natural exuberance" might now construct itself as a communal refusal to be bound by the rigid strictures of theatrical norms developed by white culture, analogous to the role of popular culture in medieval times. Bakhtin writes:

> A boundless world of humorous forms and manifestations opposed the official and serious tone of medieval ecclesiastical and feudal culture.... They offered a completely different nonofficial, extraecclesiastical and extrapolitical aspect of the world, of man, and of human relations; they built a second world and a second life outside officialdom....[4]

The parallels between the two worlds of medieval official and popular culture and the two worlds of South African official white culture and popular black culture are easy enough to perceive. In each case the carnivalesque aspects of popular culture serve to subvert and interrogate official culture, keeping alive and legitimising an attitude of resistance on the part of the exploited classes.

A vital element of carnival, as Bakhtin notes, is the suspension of hierarchy:

> As opposed to the official feast, one might say that carnival celebrated temporary liberation from the prevailing truth and from the established order, it marked the suspension of all hierarchical rank, privileges, norms, and prohibitions.[5]

This temporary liberation serves to subvert the dominant ideology which asserts all that is "stable, unchanging, perennial:

the existing hierarchy, the existing religious, political and moral values, norms and prohibitions."[6]

A clue to the mutually infectious rapport between actors and audience in this particular production might lie in the way in which *The Comedy of Errors* organises the audience's experience. Although the play initially threatens a tragic mode by presenting the draconian Ephesian law at work, it soon converts into comedy. As Ralph Berry argues, instead of succumbing to the potentially tragic forces of legalised oppression, the play,

> defying the logic of "therefore by law", wills the marvellous, the death-suspended, the comic, and the audience assents to the logic. The "law" will yield to a yet stronger force.[7]

Clearly the issue of mounting legal restrictions, the experience of arrest for being in the wrong place without authorisation, was an increasing reality for black South Africans in the early 1950s, and the audience responded to and evidently approved of the subversion of the law in the play.

In spite of the parallels with contemporary South Africa, however, the production made no attempt to localise the play, or to exploit the master-servant relationships between the Antipholuses and the Dromios in a South African context. The text, though attacked with great verve, was played straight, and the costumes suggested a conventional period setting. Nevertheless, representing the sometimes violent interactions between masters and servants on stage, contained within the framework of comedy, allowed an interrogation, albeit fantastic, of class relations in South African society. As Berry suggests, the comic force which overcomes the law in *The Comedy of Errors*

> manifests itself through fantasy. *The Comedy of Errors* is organized along two lines of psychic advance. One is that of erotic promise, unbelievable good fortune, discovered identity, the fulfillment of all one's desires. The other is that of loss, shattered identity, pain. The first line is stronger, and its triumph never really in doubt. The second is always present often uppermost, at all

times shadowing the experience of cast and audience. Threat and promise make up the fantasies of this play....[8]

By inverting the customary South African order in which threat tends to overwhelm promise, the play allowed the audience to experience the promise of change, subverting the official myth of permanence.

The very fact that these Bareti Players were performing a Shakespeare play, of course, attests to the power of white cultural hegemony. Such a play falls under the rubric of official "high" culture, albeit one which incorporates elements of carnival. In most productions these elements are comfortably contained, forming part of an enjoyable evening for audiences who belong to the official culture. Yet the township audiences, clearly excluded from official culture, seized on the carnivalesque aspects of the play, and through their response, encouraged the cast to disregard the prescriptive norms of official theatrical style. "Carnival" thus operated on two levels in this production—first the carnivalesque elements in the text resonated more powerfully in the ideological context of the townships than is usual in white theatres, and second, the presentation of Shakespeare as official culture was transformed by the cast and audience into a representation which subverted the theatrical norms of the dominant ideology.

In 1968, the Speech and Drama Department at the University College for Indians (now the University of Durban-Westville), presented the first "Indian" Shakespeare production in South Africa. David Horner, the head of the department, directed *The Comedy of Errors* in a *commedia dell'arte* style with all the characters wearing masks and *commedia* costumes, thereby invoking the traditional spirit of carnival. Horner thus began a tradition, which later University of Durban-Westville directors like Devi Bughwan and Robin Singh continued, of presenting unusual, experimental productions of Shakespeare. The ideological assumption underlying these Indian productions suggests that Shakespeare is perceived not as an awesome icon which must be mastered in order to prove one's level of educated sophistication, but rather as the great playwright of another culture, different but not necessarily superior. This eclectic, experimental approach, by drawing attention to changing theatrical styles through history, might serve to remind the mainly Indian audiences of the ancient roots of their own culture, whose Golden Age of Sanskrit drama in the time of Kalidasa predates by more than a millennium Shakespeare and the Elizabethan theatre.

In 1970, the PACT (Performing Arts Council of the Transvaal) Youth Group produced *Kinkels innie Kabel*, an Afrikaans adaptation of *The Comedy of Errors* by André Brink. The title means literally, "twists in the cable," a proverbial saying equivalent to "a fly in the ointment." The play is written in the so-called Cape Coloured dialect of Afrikaans, set in a fishing village called, ironically, Witbaai, and takes place shortly before "Coon Carnival", the annual New Year procession through the streets of Cape Town (later restricted to a sports stadium and only allowed to take to the streets once more in 1988/89). Solinus, Duke of Ephesus, becomes the carnival leader, Sollie, while Egeon, merchant of Syracuse, is now a lollipop seller from Johannesburg called Aikona. The twins Antipholus become Apools-van-die-Kaap and Apools-van-die-Pêrel, while the Dromios are Drommel-van-die-Kaap and Drommel-van-die-Pêrel. Angelo, the goldsmith, becomes Magiel, a hippie.

The production opened in a carnivalesque explosion as the minstrel troupe in their bright satin finery entered with a burst of song from the back of the theatre, winding their way onto the stage which was adorned with fishing baskets, a jetty, and fishing boats. The music included traditional and original songs, and was performed by the cast playing banjo, guitars, and a mouth organ.

The production abounded with satirical references to South African society and topical events, expressed in the language of the street dialect, an integral element in the subversive nature of popular culture, providing "so many sparks of the carnival bonfire which renew the world."[9] The most searing came from Drommel of Paarl, who talked of paying a ten rand find, "one-two, finish; kondem," and later of sitting in "tjoekie" (jail) and getting rice water and hard labour, a reference to the "non-white" experience of the South African justice and prison systems. Jokes were made about the Publications Control Board, the ban on "mixed sport," and even that most sacred of

Afrikaner cows, the Day of the Covenant. Liberal causes were also treated irreverently: the Black Sash, Peter Hain (the anti-apartheid activist in England seen as responsible for South Africa's sporting isolation), and political protests at the English-speaking universities were all the targets of jokes. According to the director, Carel Trichardt, the biggest laugh generally greeted the Paarl Apools' suggestion to spy on the Capies from the inside, "Hertzog-style," referring to Cabinet Minister Albert Hertzog who broke away from the ruling National Party to form the extreme right-wing Herstigte Nasionale Party. Flower children, Christian Barnard's heart transplants at Groote Schuur hospital, and the Miss World competition, to which South Africa sent two contestants, a white Miss South Africa and a "non-white" Miss Africa South, were all satirised.

The satirical nature of *Kinkels innie Kabel* undoubtedly reflected, and perhaps gave an impetus to, the evolving maturity of Afrikaans theatre. Satirising even the "liberal" enemies of apartheid ideology allowed the production a certain license to take swipes at the dominant ideology itself. The problem of determining the political significance of this play is complicated, however, by the fact that the first production in 1970 took place at the height of theatre segregation in terms of both casts and audiences. As one critic pointed out:

> The whole thing is given a final touch of South African absurdity by the fact that we have a stage full of White South Africans leaping around with blacked-up faces and trying to swing like Capies (who wouldn't be allowed into the theatre to see the performance anyway).[10]

It seems that what we have here is an attempt at a "controlled carnival," one that would amuse without actually threatening the established order.

The reception from critics and audiences alike was enthusiastic. Having "whites" play "coloureds" in a play written by a white man would suggest problems of racial stereotyping, but theatre critics in 1970 found little fault on this score. They applauded the young cast for imitating "the peculiar intonation and rich drawls of the Afrikaans of the coloured people and their clipped way of speaking English,"[11] for getting "under the skin of the Cape folk,"[12] for capturing "the quick fire repartee typical of the Cape Coloured."[13] Janice Honeyman was singled out for her portrayal of Adriana, "large and common," with her front teeth missing, her "cumbersome movements and awkward stances."[14] The culture depicted was comfortably categorised as the Other. If any authentic "coloureds" were offended by the stereotypical portrayals, then some conservative Afrikaners were absolutely outraged at the whole production. "Stefan" of Pietersburg wrote to *Die Transvaler*, attacking the production for its vulgar, suggestive actions and gestures, and its shameless mockery of God's Word. He accused PACT of being used by those moral underminers who wished to condition the Afrikaner to the norms of the permissive society. Evidently the carnivalesque elements in the production were threatening to some.

A year later, Robert Mohr directed *Kinkels innie Kabel* at the University of Cape Town's Little Theatre. In this production the cast was made up largely of English-speaking whites with a sprinkling of Afrikaans and "coloured" students performing to racially integrated audiences. In a programme note, Robert Mohr wrote:

> André Brink's delicious improvisation…has an air of festivity and celebration about it that invites more improvisation from the cast and director. We have seized upon this aspect of the play with relish, and absolve Mr. Brink from all blame for our more demented strokes!

As one would expect from Mohr, much of his inventiveness went into exploiting the anomalies in South African society, thus sharpening the socio-political satire. Instead of interpreting all the characters as stereotypical happy-go-lucky, vulgar, servant-class Cape Coloureds, the actors determined to which class they belonged, and modified their dialects accordingly. As a result, the master-servant relationship between the Apools and the Drommels was emphasised with the obvious reverberations for South African society. The servants would accuse each other of "acting like whites" when they behaved "above their station." In addition, there was considerable interplay between the characters and the audience; in the true carnival spirit of suspending hierarchical privileges, the actors were instructed to address all the "whites" in the audience as if they were "coloured," and *vice-versa*. Thus "coloured" patrons were respectfully called "sir" and "madam," while whites were spoken to in the familiar tones of the street dialect. This treatment became a running joke which extended even to the ushers. "Coloured" people arriving at the theatre were politely shown to their specific seats, whereas whites were told to go and sit "over there."[15]

Critics were warm in their approval. One stated, "There is no condescension in the play, incidentally, it is wholly affectionate in tone."[16] Another praised Robert Mohr for showing "just how valuable an outlet is theatre, to allow us to laugh at ourselves—a luxury we don't indulge in enough in this mad and sunny land."[17] An Afrikaans critic commended Mohr for his courage in using a largely English-speaking cast, but hoped to see the play done by experienced Cape Afrikaans actors, or better still, the Eoan Group.[18]

Brink's adaptation has been revived on several occasions, and during the 1970s was, in fact, produced by Eersterus, a "coloured" drama group in the Transvaal. In 1979, William Egan directed *Kinkels innie Kabel* for CAPAB (the Performing Arts Council of the Cape) at the Nico Malan Theatre. But as political realities changed, the concept of a state-sponsored controlled carnival lost its subversive novelty and seemed increasingly appropriated and contained by the dominant ideology. Although many of the topical allusions were updated (with references, for example, to Eschel Rhoodie and the Information scandal, which eventually forced the resignation of President B.J. Vorster), the play nevertheless seemed outdated. One critic complained of Magiel as a hippie, pointing out that the humour was now ten years too late.[19] Another made a more serious charge. By 1979, the ban on theatre integration had been lifted, yet the entire CAPAB cast was white. The critic wondered "whether such a talented cast of white actors so clumsily taking off a set of essentially coloured characters were not really reinforcing stereotypes." He pointed out that most of the cast "come across for what they are: white actors looking like white actors trying to play coloured people." He asked:

Surely the formula for a completely successful performance...would be to use coloured performers? And here we come full circle again. Where are they? What are the problems? Are there any coloured drama students? And—would they want to play characters which white entertainers have turned into such cliches over the years?[20]

PACOFS (the Performing Arts Council of the Orange Free State) produced *Kinkels innie Kabel* in 1977, and again in 1981 as part of the 20th anniversary Republic celebrations, directed by Sandra Kotzé. In this production, five black actors performed as part of the dance troupe, a surprising inclusion in the politically conservative Orange Free State. One critic felt that an English play, translated into Afrikaans, set in a "coloured" milieu, played by Afrikaans actors, with black performers as part of the troupe, was the best choice for the Republic celebration theme of unity and diversity.[21] Her comment suggests the comfortable delusion of a ruling class which interprets its own small concessions as symptomatic of a whole new dispensation for the dispossessed masses, as if five black dancers were the equivalent of a fully integrated cast, as if integrated theatres meant an integrated society.

PACT also mounted the play in 1981 to open the new State Theatre in Pretoria, with Carel Trichardt again directing. Janice Honeyman was asked to repeat her role as Adriana, but she turned down the offer on the grounds that there were excellent coloured actresses to play the part. In a 1985 interview, she told me that what had been fine in 1970 was no longer acceptable in the changed political climate of the eighties. Not only should whites not be playing coloured people, but the very interpretation of coloureds in the play was dated. Honeyman said:

> You can't interpret Coloured people now as those happy-go-lucky Coon Carnival characters because, in a funny way, it is a put down, a "shame, the simple-hearted, good-natured Klopse," and it ignores the whole political side, a conscious side of the Coloured person.[22]

What was wonderful in 1970 was no longer so wonderful in the changed political situation since the rise of Black Consciousness and the 1976 Soweto Uprising. Carel Trichardt, who directed the all white cast in 1981, agreed that in 1985, "You wouldn't think of doing *Kinkels innie Kabel* with whites anymore."[23] The belief that the official culture could sponsor popular carnival was being steadily eroded.

In 1985, Janice Honeyman directed a modern dress production of *The Comedy of Errors* for PACT, set in contemporary Greece. In a programme note, she explained her choice of setting:

> I have deliberately chosen a modern context because I believe that the Shakespearian comedies, in particular, gain from being given modern equivalents. *The Comedy of Errors*...touches on issues that are still prevalent today: summary justice (with echoes of a type of Group Areas Act), chauvinism, sex-role stereotyping, sexual repression/liberation materialism, sectism, morality, violence, and so on. Yet it remains very much a comedy, and, like all Shakespeare's romantic comedies, requires a romantic, exotic milieu.

To underscore the historical applicability of the play, the programme was peppered with quotations, including a report in a local newspaper at the time of the production about twin brothers in South Africa who had been separated at birth and were to meet for the first time in thirty-two years. Ironically, one was brought up speaking English and the other Afrikaans.

The set depicted the village square in front of the "Tiger Tavern" looking onto the jetty. The upper level of the tavern was connected by a walkway to the upper level of Antipholus's house, providing multi-levelled acting areas. Alleys, arches, outside stairs, and television aerials lent an air of higgledy-piggledy authenticity. The costumes added to the atmosphere of colourful, bustling humanity. The square was inhabited by old ladies in black, drunken sailors, pimps and prostitutes. The Duke was resplendent in military uniform: white jacket liberally beribboned, black riding breeches and boots. The Antipholuses wore light blue suits and white panama hats; the Dromios were in yellow peasant smocks and straw hats. Dr. Pinch appeared as a "John Lennon, guru, hippie waistcoated, dagga-smoking, Hare Krishna" conman.[24]

The cast was predominantly white. There were, however, two black actors as policemen, and Honeyman used them effectively to comment on the South African situation. In the opening scene, Egeon wandered into the square and was immediately accosted by the two black policemen who demanded to see his papers. No South African could fail to notice the inversion of the usual hierarchy in which white policemen demand to see a black person's "pass." Bedlam ensued as Egeon tried to escape, and white police reinforcements arrived. Suddenly the stage was filled with running policemen shouting into loudhailers with sirens screaming. All this was performed in a very broad Monty Python, idiot-goon, carnivalesque style. Egeon was then brought back by the black policemen who proceeded to hit him periodically with sjamboks during his interrogation. Even the hilarity of the "banana republic" atmosphere could not quite eradicate the twinge of discomfort felt by the largely white audience in Pretoria's State Theatre; in fact, both the violence and the absurdity of the South African system were illuminated.

A further critique of South African society was made by a nameless worker, also played by a black actor, whose job was to paint an upturned boat while the chaos of the comedy revolved about him. One of the running jokes of the production was having each of the two Dromios periodically get his foot stuck in the worker's paint bucket. Each time Dromio would clatter offstage with his foot in the bucket, only to reappear later with a different coloured shoe and sock. Interesting from the point of view of social commentary was the way in which the painter himself, dressed in overalls like any black South African worker, was ignored by the other (white) characters. No-one ever apologised to him for interrupting his work, spoiling his paint, taking his bucket: his job was to get on with his job, and he did so in silent resignation. Though not in the text, this character certainly belongs in the context of the play's thematic exploration of master-servant relationships. The production did not shrink from depicting the Antipholuses's repeated physical assaults on the Dromios, though the violence was handled in a very stylised, acrobatic manner. As all four actors were white, an interrogation of South African master-servant relationships lurked in the shadows. The only other racial inclusion of note was one of the merchants metamorphosed into an Indian carpet seller, played rather stereotypically by a white actor. While adding exotic colour to the scene, the interpretation seemed out of place in an interrogation of racist ideology.

If the preceding discussion gives the impression that this was a heavily political production, let me hasten to add that any critique of South African society was smoothly integrated into the comic action. The production's emphasis was firmly on bawdy comedy, an essential element of carnival. Critics praised Honeyman for making Shakespeare palatable to modern audiences by recognising "the inherent bawdiness of the humour" and playing it "broadly in order that it can be immediately understood by unsophisticated minds." The programme quotations included a psychoanalytic theory of farce: "Farce enacts a primitive superego punishment for its characters' transgression in the form of a maniacal plot which both arranges libidinal gratification and punishes for it." Also quoted was a comment by a nineteenth century American theatregoer: "Shakespeare, Madam, is obscene, and, thank God, we are sufficiently advanced to have found it out." Thus the audience saw the ladies of ill repute repeatedly dropping panties from their clothesline onto Emilia's head, watched Dromio-of-Syracuse buttoning up his trousers after having his way with his twin brother's wife, and even caught a glimpse of Antipholus's bare bottom—still risque in puritan South Africa. Even gays were included in the bawdiness. Antipholus and Dromio of Syracuse arrived with a boatload of tourists, including a stereotypically gay merchant who was quickly solicited by a very macho stud who lolled against the tavern wall suggestively caressing his silken running shorts. The merchant's speech excusing himself from Antipholus was given a certain urgency by his interest in the young man, with the final line, "My present business calls me from you now," delivered hastily as he raced off in pursuit! Antipholus-of-Syracuse's later comment, "Some offer me commodities to buy," was accompanied by a gesture towards the young stud who was making obscene movements of solicitation.

The offensiveness of the stereotypical portrayal of the gay merchant was perhaps partially compensated for by having such a taboo subject integrated into the carnivalesque bawdiness of humanity. Within the confines of state-sponsored theatre, therefore, the production managed to utilise carnivalesque elements to interrogate and subvert the dominant ideology.

Researching these productions *of The Comedy of Errors* offered interesting insights into the mechanisms of evaluating and preserving theatrical productions in South Africa. The 1953 production, for example, is preserved as oral history and in an isolated newspaper report apparently chronicling the novelty of blacks performing Shakespeare's plays ("Shakespeare Comedy Is Played by Natives" reads the headline). By contrast, the Afrikaans adaptation, *Kinkels innie Kabel*, produced a flurry of articles, reviews, and interviews, all carefully preserved in various state archives around the country. Although lopsided, an examination of *The Comedy of Errors* in South Africa reveals, nevertheless, the adaptability of this play. South Africans have turned it into a spontaneous festival in the township communities; they have presented an academic *commedia dell'arte* production; they have adapted it to a local setting to satirise the society; they have updated it to a modern Greek setting and still offered a critique of South African conditions. The play has been performed by "black," "coloured," "Indian," "white," and "mixed" casts, together offering a mosaic of insights into the workings of this peculiar society.[25] While attesting to the continued privileging of Shakespeare as the pinnacle of high culture, these productions reveal the flexibility of the text, which, by incorporating subversive elements of carnival, allows itself to be used as an instrument for interrogating the dominant ideologies.

Originally published by Rohan Quince, "Crinkles in the Carnival: Ideology in South African Productions of *The Comedy of Errors* to 1985," *Shakespeare in Southern Africa*, 4 (1990–1): 73–81. Reprinted with the permission of *Shakespeare in Southern Africa*.

NOTES

1 Martin Orkin, in *Shakespeare Against Apartheid* (Johannesburg: Ad Donker, 1986), argues this point at length.

2 *Argus*, 14 August 1953.

3 Ian Bernhardt, personal interview, 22 July 1985.

4 Mikhail Bakhtin, *Rabelais and His World*, trans. Helene Iswolsky (Cambridge, MA: MIT Press, 1968), pp. 4, 6.

5 *Ibid.*, p. 10.

6 *Ibid.*, p. 9.

7 Ralph Berry, *Shakespeare and the Awareness of the Audience* (New York: St. Martin's Press, 1985), p. 37.

8 *Ibid.*

9 Bakhtin, *op. cit.*, p. 17.

10 Roy Christie, *Daily News*, November 1970.

11 Kathleen Marquard, *Friend*, 3 December 1970.

12 Colin du Plessis, *Financial Gazette*, 16 October 1970.

13 Lucas Fouché, *Star*, 14 October 1970.

14 *Ibid.*

15 Ian Ferguson, personal interview, 4 July 1985.

16 Owen Williams, *Argus*, 5 April 1971.

17 Terry Herbst, *Cape Times*, 5 April 1971.

18 Victor Holloway, *Burger*, 5 April 1971.

19 Kemeels Breytehbach, *Burger*, 12 April 1979.

20 Derek Wilson, *Argus*, 11 April 1979.

21 Georjane Groenewald, *Volksblad*, 22 May 1981.

22 Janice Honeyman, personal interview, 22 July 1985.

23 Carel Trichardt, personal interview, 10 June 1985.

24 Janice Honeyman, *op. cit.*

25 Editor's note—CAPAB's 1989 revival of Brink's *Kinkels innie Kabel* elicited the following comment by Temple Hauptfleisch:

> Marthinus Basson's...production has gone a stage, further by ignoring (consciously and obviously) the racial element in his casting. It is not an unusual appoach in itself, having been in operation for a number of years in virtually all companies, but what makes it a point of critical importance here, specifically at this time, is the implicit difference between a "coloured" actress satirising a shrew from the "community" and a bourgeois "white" actress doing it. It may appear a petty point, representative of the over-sensitiveness we have all come to display about such things..., yet there was a feeling of awkward patronisation about the entire performance, which made this critic at least, doubt the real suitability of the choice of play.
>
> (*Shakespeare in Southern Africa* 3, 1989, p. 90)

Ian Judge's Stratford Production, 1990

Peter Holland

In *The Conversations with Drummond of Hawthornden*, Ben Jonson talked about his plans for various plays. Drummond records: "he had ane intention to have made a play like Plaut[us'] Amphtrio but left it of, for that he could never find two so like others that he could persuade the spectators they were one" (*Works*, ed. C. Herford and P. and E. Simpson [Oxford, 1925–52] vol. I, p. 144, lines 420–3). Jonson, never one to place small demands on theatre companies, wanted two pairs of identical twins. When Shakespeare had tackled the problem of twins in *Twelfth Night* he had deliberately based the likeness of Viola and Sebastian on an impossibility: you cannot have identical twins of different genders. In production now Viola and Sebastian rarely look convincingly alike nor, I suspect, could Shakespeare's boy-actor have looked so like the adult actor playing Sebastian that Antonio's line "An apple cleft in two is not more twin / Than these two creatures" (5.1.221–2) could have been visibly true. When Orsino describes "One face, one voice, one habit, and two persons" (5.1.213) we can only fully assent to the similarity of costume. The "natural perspective, that is and is not" (5.1.214) which he calls it is true in the play's fiction and untrue in the play's performance. But audiences are often rather troubled by the discrepancy.

Modern technology doesn't really help: when, in a television production some time ago, Joan Plowright doubled Viola and Sebastian, the addition of a small moustache only made her Sebastian look ridiculous and the attempt at a gruff male voice would never have fooled anyone. The difficulty of the gender change was simply insurmountable. The twin Antipholuses and the twin Dromios of *The Comedy of Errors* pose no such problems. The BBC Shakespeare series' production of *Errors* used similar techniques to have each pair of twins played by one actor. This year the RSC did the same. But television is not the stage. Desmond Barrit (both Antipholuses) and Graham Turner (both Dromios), fine actors though they are, lack the paranormal skill of bilocation, necessary without cameras and editing.

Since the idea cannot possibly work in the theatre, I shall be wondering what is lost along in the process. But I also want to wonder whether it would be worth doing even if it could be done. One of the great pleasures for the audience watching *Errors* is that we know the answer. We know, because Egeon has told us, that there are two pairs of twins; we know why Antipholus of Syracuse is recognized by the inhabitants of Ephesus and that the reason has nothing to do with Ephesus' reputation for sorcery nor is it a dream.

What we do find, though, is that the over-weening confidence with which we begin, knowing the answers, is shaken in the course of the play. I find, every time I watch the play, that I end up forgetting which Dromio has been sent on which errand by which Antipholus, which one is locked up with Pinch, which one has ended up in the priory. We know how the play will end, in that moment when the Antipholuses and Dromios will all be on stage together, but along the way we end up nearly as confused as the characters. When both Dromios are played by the same actor the audience's ability to be confused, a confusion that, I am suggesting, the play wants us to undergo, is simply evaded, evaded because the audience comes to follow actor, not rôle, Graham Turner, not Dromio. The two Dromios were differentiated by the colour of their waistcoats but the audience, rather than trying to remember which Dromio wears the green one, abandons its interest in the confusions, comforted by its recognition of the actor, not the rôle. When, finally, the character has to face his doppelgänger onstage for the last scene, we come to see not two Dromios but two actors, one whom we know and another whom we do not. The history of the characters is replaced by the history of the performance.

It is the emotional force of the ending that is especially harmed. For Shakespeare's ending teeters gloriously on the edge of sentimentality. As brother finds brother at last there is an emotional release for the characters and for the audience. When it works—and it usually does—there is something oddly tearful about the reunions, the reconstitution of the family. Even the inevitably funny rediscovery of the missing mother does not prevent our joy, prefiguring something of the force of the families re-formed at the end of the late plays. By doubling the Antipholuses the force is diluted. The audience watches how the doppelgänger still tries to keep his back to them, following the theatrical technique, the actor's skill, not the play's argument. Even more unfortunately, Ian Judge's production misjudges Shakespeare's carefully downbeat ending. As the stage empties the two Dromios are left alone, their tentative awareness of their equality deliberately low-key yet moving: "We came into the world like brother and brother, / And now let's go hand in hand, not one before another" (5.1.429–30). The play denies the full-stage ending and ends up with two servants, beaten and mocked throughout the play, now finding a dignity in what they have in common, their brotherhood. Their exit in Judge's production, into the rays of the setting sun, was pure Hollywood schmaltz; it encouraged the audience to find the moment ludicrous, missing completely its simplicity and innocence.

Once past a sombre prison set for the first scene, the design, by Mark Thompson, was unrelentingly excessive, nine garishly coloured doors surrounding a rectangular playing-area. The games played with surrealism, the echoes of Escher and Magritte and the Beatles' *Yellow Submarine*, became in the playing of Pinch a grotesque parody of Dali turned into a cheap stage-conjuror. Dali, the great modern example of artist as showman, would perhaps have been amused. Such work makes no sense of Dr. Pinch—productions rarely do—but the magic was a perfect example of the production's obsessive busy-ness. As Dromio was sawn in two and Antipholus vanished from a cabinet skewered with swords, Pinch-Dali's aides rushed meaninglessly around the stage in a frenzy of activity not generated by a response to the action.

But the set's bizarre extravagances also transformed Ephesus into the world that the Syracusan twins wrongly perceive it to be. For Ephesus is not a place of irrationality and dream. Antipholus of Syracuse, confronted by the tirade of Adriana, wonders "What, was I married to her in my dream? / Or sleep I now, and think I hear all this?" (2.2.185–6) but he is not asleep. The play charts the passage of a day, the day that threatens Egeon's execution, but, apart from the inhabitants of Ephesus appearing from behind their front doors to take in the morning milk, there was nothing in the production that recognized that fundamental diurnal rhythm in the text. The play's stage suggests a single place, with houses on a street and, all the time, the beckoning possibility of that road to the harbour, the route by which the Syracusans might escape the perils of Ephesus. But this set could do nothing with this. Its only gestures to place, large objects hanging over the stage representing the Centaur, the Phoenix and the other places the text refers to, were empty gestures; indeed, on both the occasions I saw the production, I heard bemused members of the audience wondering what the hedgehog was, unable to connect it with any of the play's five references to the Porcupine. The front door to Antipholus' house was a frame without a building.

Against such a setting the actors were driven to unremitting excess. Estelle Kohler screamed her way through Adriana in a grotesque parody of comic acting. Desmond Barrit's preening, largely undifferentiated Antipholuses were an exercise in high camp, only becoming effective in the quiet wooing of Luciana in 3.2, helped by the calm work of Caroline Loncq, a Luciana easily able to forget her kinship to Antipholus. David Killick seemed embarrassed by the leopard-skin drape jacket, tight black leggings and six-inch platform shoes of Dr. Pinch—as well he might—and sought to hide behind a Spanish lisp. Only David Waller's Egeon, narrating his history with dignity and drawing helpful diagrams of the distribution of his family on the mast, showed that comedy is not hyperactive.

But the most serious problem with the production was that it simply wasn't funny. Let me take one example. Antipholus of Ephesus, locked out of his house, is confronted by a voice down an entryphone. The device is, of course, a fine solution to the problem of having only one Dromio where two are needed, though I wonder why, with the sophistication of modern sound technology, the lines had to be so muffled as to be incomprehensible. The gag was "derived" from an earlier RSC production, the brilliant musical version directed by Trevor Nunn. But watching on video Mike Gwilym in that version, sheltering under an umbrella as defence against the indoor Dromio's assault, tearing the entryphone off the wall only to find that the damn thing still went on answering him back, I found a comic energy, a theatrical inventiveness and dramatic pace that I missed this time. I do not ask the production to be that good—for even the RSC has rarely been better—but it is sad to see a production borrowing jokes and gags and business and not learning how to copy the energy and style.

Originally published by Peter Holland, "Shakespeare Performances in England, 1989-1990," *Shakespeare Survey* 44 (1992): 157–90 (excerpted, 175–8). © copyright Cambridge University Press, 1992. Reprinted with the permission of Peter Holland and Cambridge University Press.

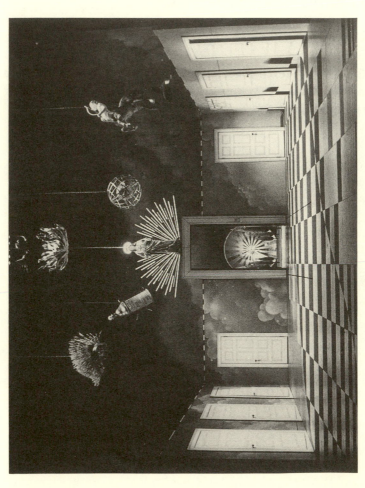

Figure 10. Judge production, 1990, Stratford-upon-Avon, RSC Theatre. Set design by Mark Thompson. Used with the permission of the Shakespeare Centre Library, Stratford-upon-Avon.

Errors: Shakespeare, Rattled & Droll: Shenandoah Shakespeare Express Production, 1992

Pamela Sommers

It's not every day that the performance of a Shakespeare play is preceded by two scruffy young folkies singing Paul Simon's "Kodachrome" and a tune about a guy more in love with his dog than his girlfriend. But then, there is nothing routine about the Shenandoah Shakespeare Express's interpretation of *The Comedy of Errors*.

This young, uninhibited company of 12, based in Dayton, Va., is dedicated to contemporary, pared-down, fast-paced renderings of the Bard's work; not for them the overheated oratory and extravagant production values that many theatergoers have come to associate with the name "Shakespeare."

Truly playing to and with the spectators—the houselights never dim, and the actors think nothing of roaming the aisles or perching in strangers' laps—the Express immediately established a sense of give-and-take Saturday afternoon at the Folger Elizabethan Theatre. The fact that its *Comedy of Errors* unfolds in a relaxed seaside locale certainly helps create a feeling of unhinged, good-natured fun. Players bounded about in baggy shorts, tank tops, caps, shades and high-tech sneakers, tossing beach balls and whipping each other with towels. A collection of portable wooden cubes served as sets, and several pairs of actors even metamorphosed into swinging doors. And many actors filled two or more roles, which made this tale of twins and mistaken identities even more entertaining.

Much of the 85-minute, intermission-less performance struck me as like an extended "Saturday Night Live" sketch circa 1978—and I mean that in a positive way. Because the play is not particularly deep but very clever, an all-stops-out, beautifully timed, ultra-physical approach is just the ticket. Director Steve Cardamone has gotten his cast to engage in 101 bits of business that lend the proceedings a hip, but not overly so, gloss.

Impersonations are big. At the start of the play, water pistols are given to two audience members, who are instructed to shoot the twin servants Dromio of Ephesus and Dromio of Syracuse any time they launch into a W.C. Fields or Arnold Schwarzenegger routine. And a particularly off-the-wall actor named Chidester Harrell plays a merchant as Don Corleone, with a cat puppet curled up in his menacing palm. Grapes, petroleum jelly and other unexpected props are used effectively. And a line such as "I understand thee not" is delivered à la "Wayne's World": "I understand thee. *Not!*"

Though this *Comedy* is very much a team effort, certain performers stand out. Colby Codding makes a lovable Dromio of Syracuse; his fevered speech about the ample, unappealing body geography of Nell the kitchen maid is an absolute hoot. Lauren Kerr portrays the upstanding Luciana as an accident-prone goof to hilarious effect. And Harrell demonstrates his versatility as an unyielding Duke, a sadistic mad doctor of a Pinch, the mafioso merchant and a between-scenes crooner, warbling "Don't Be Cruel" like some B-grade Elvis impersonator.

Having seen only the ensemble's *Comedy*, I find it hard to imagine it performing dramas such as *The Merchant of Venice* or *Macbeth*—which it in fact does, in repertory, this week. But judging from the invention inherent in this lighthearted production, one can assume that the others will offer more of the same.

Originally published by Pamela Sommers, *The Washington Post*, 13 July 1992, B1, B5. Reprinted with the permission of Pamela Sommers and *The Washington Post*.

SHAKESPEARE CRITICISM
PHILIP C. KOLIN, *General Editor*